Nothing But Glory

Pickett's Division at Gettysburg

By
Kathy Georg Harrison
and John W. Busey

THOMAS PUBLICATIONS
Gettysburg PA 17325

Printed in the United States of America

Published by THOMAS PUBLICATIONS
P.O. Box 3031
Gettysburg, PA 17325

ISBN-0-939631-56-3

Front cover illustration "Give Them Cold Steel Boys" by Don Troiani is courtesy of Historical Art Prints, Ltd., P.O. Box 660, Southbury, CT 06488.

Cover design by Ryan C. Stouch

The following publishers have generously given permission to use extended quotations from copyrighted works:

Quotation on page 18 from, *Reminiscences of Big I,* by William N. Wood. Copyright 1987 by Broadfoot Publishing Company, Wilmington, NC. Reprinted by permission of Broadfoot Publishing Company.

Quotations on pages 26 and 46 from, *John Dooley Confederate Soldier, His War Journal,* edited by Joseph T. Durkin. Copyright 1963 by University of Notre Dame Press. Reprinted by permission of University of Notre Dame Press.

Quotation on page 133 from, *The Haskell Memoirs, John Cheves Haskell,* edited by Gilbert E. Govan and James W. Livingwood. Copyright 1960 by G.P. Putnam's Sons. Reprinted by permission of G.P. Putnam's Sons.

Contents

List of Maps

All maps drawn by Kathleen Georg Harrison

List of Illustrations

Sketches of Officers and Flags
by Kathleen Georg Harrison

List of Photographs

List of Abbreviations

AAG	Assistant Adjutant General
AAIG	Assistant Adjutant & Inspector General
ACS	Assistant Commissary of Subsistence
ADC	Aide-de-Camp
Adjt.	Adjutant
AIG	Assistant Inspector General
AQM	Assistant Quartermaster
Art.	Artillery
Asst.	Assistant
AWOL	Absent Without Leave
Bat. (Bty.)	Battery
Bdg. Gen.	Brigadier General
Bn.	Battalion
Bvt.	Brevet
Capt.	Captain
Co. (Cos.)	Company (Companies)
Col.	Colonel or Color
Cpl.	Corporal
CS	Commissary of Subsistence
CV	*Confederate Veteran Magazine*
Dept.	Department
Drum.	Drummer
Enl.	Enlisted
Gen.	General
GNMP	Gettysburg National Military Park
Hosp.	Hospital
Inf.	Infantry
La.	Louisiana
Lt.	Lieutenant
Lt. Col.	Lieutenant Colonel
Maj.	Major
Med.	Medical
Mus.	Musician
NCO	Non-Commissioned Officer
O	Officer
OR	United States War Department: *The War of the Rebellion: A Compilation of the Official Records of the Union and Confederate Armies*
Pvt.	Private
QM	Quartermaster
Sgt.	Sergeant
SHSP	*Southern Historical Society Papers*
Surg.	Surgeon
USAMHI	U.S. Army Military History Institute
Va.	Virginia
VMI	Virginia Military Institute

Acknowledgements

Many institutions provided manuscript material and permission to quote from and use that material, most of which contained the personal experiences of Pickett's veterans. To those institutions I am most grateful, particularly to the University of Virginia, the guardians of that untapped watershed of Virginia history in the John W. Daniel Papers. I am forever indebted to William Matter for bringing this collection to my attention. To Howard Michael Madaus, whose forthcoming book on the regimental flags of the Army of Northern Virginia is eagerly awaited, I owe gratitude for permission to extract information in depicting the known Gettysburg colors and their ultimate fates. To my fellow collaborator, John W. Busey, I owe a debt for his determined and unrelenting persistence in seeing this project through and for allowing us to finally separate each of these individuals heretofore only known as "Pickett's men." To my husband Tom I owe every author's debt for his support and encouragement in allowing me to stack and pile papers and books in seemingly endless and numberless locations. And finally, to my parents who started it all by tolerating and participating in those oh so many trips to historic sites and battlefields years ago, I am obliged for a love of history and our country.

Kathy Georg Harrison
Hanover, Pa.
October 1986

Additional Acknowledgements

A work of this nature could not be initiated, prosecuted, or completed without the support and encouragement of numerous individuals. Foremost, among these are my wife Sandra, my daughters Amy, Barbara, Jill and Lorraine, and my son Travis. Without their continued support, my contribution to this study would not have been possible. Thanks are also due to my daughter Sharon, who, though 3,000 miles away, expressed support and enthusiasm for my work. Specific thanks are owed to Kathy Georg Harrison for her assistance, patience and support during the project, and to Mike Musick and the staff of the Military Reference Branch of the National Archives in Washington, D.C. Their prompt and efficient responses to my numerous requests for original documents was of great help in completing this project. I would also like to thank Arthur J. Costigan for his assistance in researching the names of the burials at Finns Point, N.J., and David Martin for his patience and skill in editing and proofreading the manuscript. Finally, I would like to acknowledge the patience and fortitude of Joe Shea in particular, and Nancy Artherholt, Carol Stobaugh, Sally Dobbins and the remainder of my co-workers at the Food and Nutrition Service of the U.S. Department of Agriculture, who endured countless unsolicited lectures concerning the successes and failures of the project as it unfolded over a period of two-and-one-half years. The kind support and understanding of all these individuals was and is deeply appreciated.

John W. Busey
Centreville, Va.
February 1987

Foreword to the Text

This is the story of Pickett's Virginia Division at Gettysburg, as seen through the eyes of the men in the ranks and by the officers who commanded them. Many histories of the Battle of Gettysburg have based the narrative and theme upon often retold accounts, early post-battle histories, and even later secondary works. Few authors or historians have relied upon the primary sources of the survivors themselves, who left a remarkable record rich in personal insight and experience, as well as descriptive detail. Analyses of military movements and command decisions abound in Gettysburg histories, but there has been little effort to document the experiences of the combat soldier in any of the battle action. To undertake such a retelling of the story for a body of men as famed as Pickett's Division in its unforgettable charge at Gettysburg on the third day of July 1863, has been a challenging but rewarding experience. Each individual recollection of that day's events was a reflection of each singular participation in a massive historical drama. None could describe the entirety of the conflict, but each contributed to the compilation of the story. We can witness in our mind's eye the booming cannon, the screeching shell, the clash of arms, the piteous moans of the wounded and dying, the desperate struggle, the gallant charge, the comrades falling. The words of the participants transport us back to that deadly field south of the town of Gettysburg in a manner any paraphrasing of their thoughts could not.

The essence of the battle of Gettysburg, of the charge by Pickett's Division, of combat at the time of the Civil War was captured in the words of the participants and survivors:

> A soldier who is in battle can tell you about as little about the battle as anyone in the world. It's not what you think. It's all smoke and dust and noise. At first we could see the Confederates moving around and putting up their guns. At that stage there was just occasional firing by the skirmishers and not enough smoke to hide anything. But later when the volleying began you might as well have been blind. The smoke lay over everything so that you were lucky to see the man next to you. Your ears couldn't distinguish shot from shot. It was all one roar, so that the hillside shook. You couldn't hear orders or guess them from seeing the man who gave them. You did just what the man ahead of you did, or the man next to you. When the officers gave orders, they would start one man going the way they wanted him to go, or doing the thing they wanted him to do. The rest would follow as well as they could.
>
> After the first order to fire, everyone fired as often as they could. That part was alright, for you had something to keep your mind on. Load as fast as possible and shoot as often as you could see anything to shoot at.
>
> When I first went into a battle, each battle, I would be scared and rattled and nervous, like all the rest. But after I had been fighting a little while, I would get control of myself again before I knew it. I would realize what was going on and see it and hear the noise. It had all been a kind of dazed feeling before. I could keep pretty calm while I was shooting away, but when I had to stand still and take fire— well, that tries the nerves.
>
> But the battle as a whole leaves just an impression of being hot and sweaty and seeing people fall, and a jumble of smoke and dust and roar and now and then a glimpse of the hot sun, and being too busy to feel tired and feeling tired none the less. And then a bullet and then quiet and the rain, and not much more.[1]

Despite this soldier's kaleidoscopic impressions of the battle, many others were to remember more than just the "jumble" initially remembered and described by so many. Although each soldier cannot tell the whole history of the battle from his own experiences, the piecing together of these individual recollections weaves a fabric which is often bold in color, coarse in texture, but fabulously rich in detail and originality. Pickett's men provided us with scores of documents written in their own words, some within days of the battle and others after decades had passed to dim all but the most vivid of memories. These documents and the thoughts which they express were the threads of that fabric, now woven into a tapestry depicting their fleeting contact with destiny. Because the intent is to see the battle through the eyes of Pickett's men, the "tapestry" is small. Movements and activities of Union and Confederate troops other than Pickett's three brigades and artillery battalion are not woven into this fabric except where those events were part of the memories and directly affected the Virginians.

The foreshortening of the tapestry is the author's deepest source of chagrin, since it leaves whole bodies of men unaccounted for in an event that will forever live in American history. The Confederate columns under Pettigrew and Trimble, whose long march to the enemy's wide-mouthed guns rivalled that of Kemper, are not documented. Indeed, for the majority of the assault their movements would have been hidden from view of Pickett's soldiers by the intervening ridges and undulations in the terrain. The misguided and futile support offered by the brigades of Wilcox and Lang is only briefly touched upon, and cannot convey the sense of despair and hopelessness that these men of the Deep South must have felt as they found themselves fighting and falling on the same ground as the previous day, and to the same result. Neither does the story of Pickett's men include the defiant, desperate, and courageous defense offered by the Union divisions of Gibbon and Doubleday, upon whom the weight of the Virginians would be aimed. Their stories are yet to be told in their own words, as vividly and dramatically as Pickett's ranks described their day of glory.

The intent of the narrative is not only to describe the events of that memorable July day in 1863, but to convey a sense of the battle that is often missing from military histories of the Gettysburg Campaign. In the course of the research, certain new and heretofore unpublicized conclusions were reached about the assault. All were based on primary sources and the terrain of the battlefield itself, which together are an indispensable resource for any Gettysburg historian. The preservation of the battlefield landscape is imperative for the interpretation of these primary accounts, as well as for a full understanding of the odds which Pickett's Division had to overcome in its marathon advance upon Union lines. The elimination of the embankments that paralleled the Emmitsburg Road, for instance, have prevented a full comprehension of that road's importance as an obstacle and a refuge. The thousands of feet of post and rail and Virginia worm fencing that crisscrossed the field of march can now only be seen in photographs and maps, whereas they were most real to the ranks of Pickett's Division that had to crawl over them under fire.

Pickett's Virginians did not secure their goal that day of Longstreet's Assault, but instead were wrecked on the ridges and farm fields of the Keystone State.

Pennsylvania, ironically, had been the keystone in the arch of the Revolutionary Union, and it was on the battlefield of that state that the arch was most severely tested. The keystone was not broken as a result of the battle. Indeed, today we realize that the arch was made stronger by the blood of Virginians and Pennsylvanians, of North Carolinians and New Yorkers, that cemented the arch on fields such as Gettysburg. We commonly share the pride in the Union victory and in the Confederate audacity. Pickett's men did not win laurels, but secured for themselves a place in our hearts and in our history which can be *Nothing but Glory*.

KGH
Hanover, PA
1 October 1986

NOTHING BUT GLORY

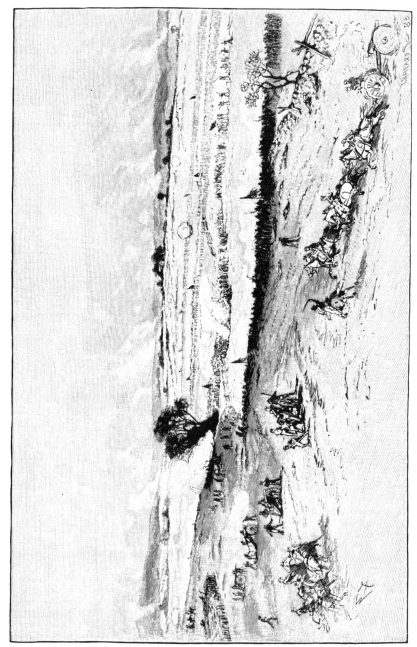

Pickett's Charge As Seen From The Union Lines
(Battles and Leaders of the Civil War)

Chapter

I

"And Away We Go Againe"

S moke curled up from innumerable campfires through the foliage over-head, imparting with it the smell of dry wood, boiling coffee, and frying rations, contrasting sharply with the sulfurous odor of the smoke still hanging in clouds over the fields to the south and east. An occasional boom and intermittent cracks and pops acknowledged that a battle was unwillingly breaking off with the setting of the sun. Pickett's Virginians had missed two days of the battle at Gettysburg, but were now within earshot of these final exchanges as they relaxed in their encampment near Marsh Creek, some three miles west of the little Pennsylvania town whose roads brought the armies against each other. In the woods south of the turnpike connecting Gettysburg and Chambersburg, the footsore soldiers were recuperating from their march of almost 25 miles to rejoin Lee's Army of Northern Virginia, and were fully cognizant that their commander would require their participation in the continuation of the fighting on the morrow.

Those last 25 miles brought the division to the eve of battle, the conclusion of about 500 miles of marching in quest of such a fight. The division had been on detached duty from the army during the last great Confederate victory at Chancellorsville, accompanied by Hood's Division of Longstreet's (their own) Corps in a separate campaign to southern Virginia and northern North Carolina. That campaign to Norfolk and Suffolk had been a success in that Union forces in those localities were kept preoccupied with Longstreet's might, while Confederate foraging parties secured necessary provisions and supplies from the surrounding countryside. But the division had missed the great victory in the woods of Virginia, and its men chafed to rejoin their victorious brothers in arms and seal the ultimate defeat of the Union invaders in another pitched battle.

Indeed, Pickett's Division had not fought as a unit with the Army of Northern Virginia since the summer campaign of 1862. Only one brigade had been required to complete the defeat of the Union army at Fredericksburg in December, and the Suffolk campaigning had been primarily skirmishing and foraging for the division instead of the glories that shower a fighting unit during a pitched battle. The five brigades that entered Petersburg in the first week of May 1863 were, therefore, untried as a single force; before they could pass through Petersburg, it became obvious that they might not get the opportunity to prove their worth as a unit. Jenkin's South Carolina Brigade was detached from the division and pressed into service guarding the approaches to the Confederate capital at Richmond, and was destined never to rejoin Pickett's men.

After resting a few days at Chester Station, the march was resumed towards Richmond, and then on to Taylorsville (located south of Hanover Junction near the junction of the Virginia Central and Richmond, Fredericksburg & Potomac Railroads). The division remained in the Taylorsville area throughout the month of May, where religious camp meetings were held and where several men reaffirmed their loyalty to their country and their God.[1] The march was resumed the beginning of June to Culpeper Court House, where the division bivouacked some eight miles from the town on June 10. Once again, however, the higher command whittled at the strength of the division, and ordered Corse's Virginia Brigade to remain in the vicinity of Taylorsville to guard the roads and bridges leading to Richmond. Numerous entreaties from General George Pickett himself failed to gain the brigade back from this vital duty, necessary while the bulk of the Confederate army in Virginia was leaving the Richmond area for the northern campaign.

Leaving the Culpeper bivouac on June 15, the three remaining brigades of the division, those of James L. Kemper, Richard B. Garnett, and Lewis A. Armistead, headed toward the Blue Ridge Mountains, passing through Snicker's Gap about June 20, and crossing the Shenandoah River at Castleman's Ferry. They remained there and near Berryville for several days within supporting distance of the cavalry which was then engaged with the enemy east of the mountains at the battlefields of Aldie and Upperville. It was not long, however, before the march was again taken up northward through Martinsburg toward the Potomac River. On June 24 the division crossed the river at Williamsport, where the execution of a deserter from the ranks was witnessed by the men, to act as an example and a deterrent.[2]

The deserter was not the first casualty to the division during the campaign. Amongst the first was the brigade commander, General Richard A. Garnett, who was kicked by a high-spirited horse ridden by Major Robert A. Bright of Pickett's staff.[3] The blow from the hoof hit Garnett's lower leg while he himself had been mounted, and became so painful that the general had to quit his own horse and take to an ambulance for the duration of the march. The incident occurred about the time the division was to pass through Snicker's Gap. Garnett wrote on June 21 that he was "partially *hors de combat*" from the kick, having to place Colonel Eppa Hunton of the 8th Virginia Regiment in command of the brigade during the march.[4]

The division continued towards Hagerstown, Maryland, on June 25, but was detained by permitting some of A. P. Hill's brigades to pass in front of it. The following day the division passed through Hagerstown, and before sundown was across the Mason-Dixon line into Pennsylvania, where it spent the night at Greencastle. From this place, General Garnett confided to a friend that his leg was still quite sore, and prevented him from riding horseback. The wound was so uncomfortable that he had to admit that he could not sit up for long periods of time. He feared that it would be a week or even more before he could be mounted, but hoped that he would recover before the Union army made its appearance. As to where that meeting of the armies would take place, Garnett was as ignorant as the ranks of his command; although he knew they were heading in the direction of Chambersburg, he admitted, "Where we will 'bring up,' no one knows, I fancy, except Gen'l L."[5]

The division arrived at Chambersburg, as Garnett had predicted, on June 27. Armistead's Brigade started for that place at 7:00 A.M., and the brigades passed through it —"a large place and nice looking." They proceeded a couple of miles more out the York Road before making a bivouac for the evening.[6] The 38th Virginia, of Armistead's Brigade, was ordered that night to proceed to Scotland (a small town northeast of Chambersburg) to guard commissary stores, and would not rejoin its brigade until June 29.[7] Meanwhile, the rest of the division was assigned the duty of destroying the railroads, and spent the next four days engaged in tearing up the tracks, destroying the turntable, battering down railroad houses, burning railroad cars, and otherwise incapacitating that vital form of logistical transportation. Plying methods later to be made infamous by Sherman's armies in Georgia and South Carolina, the division found that the most effective means of preventing repairs to destroyed track was to pile up the wooden ties, fire them, and lay the rails atop them and then bending them out of shape around the trunks of trees.[8]

On June 30, while the remainder of Lee's army was concentrating east of Chambersburg in the direction of Gettysburg, Pickett's Division was still engaged in this duty. Many men, however, were beginning to find time for other pursuits, as the destruction of the railroads was nearing completion. A member of the 9th Virginia in Armistead's Brigade wrote that, besides tearing up the tracks, the men of the regiment were also "visiting Pensilvanians and find cherries a plenty."[9] The division provost guard, the 56th Virginia of Garnett's Brigade, made its headquarters at the courthouse[10] and would be called upon to enforce General Lee's orders concerning private property as a result of these roaming bands of men. Lee's orders commanded his soldiers to respect the personal property of the civilian population and to pay for any items when they were taken for use of the army. Because many of the men of Pickett's Division marched through their own communities during the northward movement from the Norfolk area into Maryland, they were first-hand witnesses to the kind of destruction and impressment of household and personal items that their farms and homes had endured from the Yankees while they were away. While many were thus eager to exact retribution on those Pennsylvanians, who up until now had been so far removed from the war, General Lee was just as eager to prevent such vengeance. General Garnett noted this civility to the populace, but realized that the order would be "generally disapproved" among his own men. He had to agree with Lee's orders, if not so much from moral grounds at least from the necessity to "preserve the discipline of our army, now so essential to our success, and which would inevitably be destroyed, were indiscriminate plundering allowed."[11]

On June 29 the camps of much of Pickett's Division were moved south of the town from the west side, and on July 1, when the battle between the advance of Hill's Corps and Union cavalry and infantry occurred near Gettysburg, the division was still in the vicinity of Chambersburg, drilling in camp three times a day as a means to keep the men in camp instead of roving about the countryside. Word·came back before nightfall that there had been a fight at Gettysburg between Ewell and the enemy, and orders were relayed to have the division ready to march at midnight.[12]

At 2:00 A.M. on July 2 Pickett's Division was awakened by the beating of the long roll, and was soon passing once again through Chambersburg, this time towards the battlefield of the previous day at Gettysburg.[13] After the lengthy marches of May and June, the brief respite in Chambersburg had been a welcome period for Armistead's, Garnett's, and Kemper's Brigades; but when the division set foot on the turnpike in those morning hours of July 2 one veteran could only record in his diary, "and away we go againe."[14]

These men who marched into the darkness and toward the sunrise along the dusty Pennsylvania road were all Virginians, some 5,800 infantrymen strong, including those on detail as teamsters, drovers, cooks, aids, and ambulance drivers. They hailed from almost every part of Virginia — the 1st Virginia Infantry Regiment was almost exclusively from Richmond; other regiments had companies within their organizations that combined the farmers of northern and western Virginia with the carpenters, mechanics, and laborers of seaports like Portsmouth and Norfolk. They came from places like Walton's Mill, Haymarket, Aldie, Buffalo Springs, Chestnut Fork, Prospect Depot, Cascade, Botetourt Springs, and scores of other small communities, as well as from county seats and larger towns like Lynchburg, Culpeper Court House, Charles City Court House, Charlottesville, and Richmond. The vast majority of the soldiers were farmers by occupation before their enlistment into the army. Those who classified themselves as farmers, and those who claimed the distinction of planter, outnumbered all other occupations combined by a two to one ratio, thereby affirming the agrarian nature of Virginia at the time of the Civil War. Scattered amongst these farmers were clerks, carpenters, and merchants, the most numerous of the other professions. And throughout each regiment in much fewer numbers were lawyers, teachers, students, laborers, millers, wheelwrights, and masons. But there were also tobacconists, sash makers, bakers, plumbers, salesmen, painters, printers, postmen, tanners, well and fence diggers, physicians, overseers, harness makers, barkeepers, auctioneers, butchers, and almost every other occupation common to mid-nineteenth century Virginia. Their average age was between twenty-two and twenty-four, with the majority of the division aged between eighteen and twenty-five. The youngest was perhaps sixteen, and the oldest, forty-six years of age.

As this assimilation of men from over forty Virginia counties marched through that night air, their identities as individuals from all walks of life were merged into the anonymity of the common soldier whose recognition and fame was destined to be forever linked as one with the unit to which he belonged. Sharing that destiny were the four Virginia batteries of Major James Dearing's artillery battalion, attached to the division as part of the reorganization of the artillery arm after the Battle of Chancellorsville. Altogether there were fifteen infantry regiments and four batteries in that column, the entire force now totalling over 6,200 men and eighteen artillery pieces. The composition of the brigades and battalion was organized so that each brigade was made of five infantry regiments.

Kemper's Brigade was commanded by Brigadier General James L. Kemper, who had been a planter and lawyer in the years before the war, had seen service in the Mexican War, and had dabbled in local politics. He had commanded the brigade since June 1862, inheriting an organization commanded by future corps command-ers James Longstreet, Richard S. Ewell, and A. P. Hill. Since the fall of 1862 the brigade was composed of five regiments, among which was the 1st Virginia Infantry Regiment, known as "Williams' Rifles" and the "Old First." The 1st Virginia contained only six companies by the time of the Gettysburg Campaign, the other five original companies having been assigned to other units or disbanded. It was the smallest of the fifteen regiments in Pickett's Division, having only about 220 in the rank and file. During the campaign the regiment was commanded by Colonel Louis B. Williams, Jr. Joining the 1st Virginia was the 3rd Virginia Infantry Regiment, with its standard of ten companies totalling over 350 officers and men, and commanded by Colonel Joseph Mayo, Jr. Colonel Waller Tazewell Patton commanded the 7th Virginia Infantry Regiment during this march across the Potomac River, leading close to 360 men in the column. The regiment was comprised of only nine companies in 1863, one company having been disbanded because its members were citizens of the District of Columbia and not resident Virginians. The 11th Virginia Infantry Regiment, with ten companies, was the second largest in Kemper's Brigade, with over 400 officers and men. Major Kirkwood Otey commanded the regiment, but during this march and while the regiment was at Chambersburg the 11th Virginia was led by Captain James R. Hutter of Company H.[15] The largest regiment under General Kemper's command was that of Colonel William R. "Buck" Terry, with the almost 450 officers and men of the 24th Virginia Infantry Regiment. Together, these five regiments gave Kemper an effective force of almost 1800 officers and men.

Comparable in size to Kemper's Brigade was that brigade commanded by Brigadier General Richard B. Garnett, a career soldier who had resigned his U.S. Army commission to accept service with the Virginia troops in 1861. He had commanded this brigade since November 1862 and had served under Jackson in the Valley before the brigade was assigned to Longstreet's Corps. At this time the brigade had about 1800 officers and men in five regiments, including the 8th Virginia Infantry, which was commanded by Colonel Eppa Hunton. There were so many members of the Berkeley family in field and line command within the regiment that it was often called the "Berkeley Regiment" in deference to its lieutenant colonel, the major, and a company captain. Hard service had depleted the ranks of this regiment, making it the smallest in the brigade, even though it retained its full contingent of ten companies. Including even the men on detailed assign-ments, the regiment could number only a few more than 240, with four of the companies mustering only twenty or fewer members on duty. Outnumbering the 8th Virginia by over 100 muskets was the 18th Virginia Infantry Regiment, with almost 380 officers and men present for duty when the brigade entered Chambersburg. The regiment was commanded by Lieutenant Colonel Henry A. Carrington, who had been acting as colonel of the regiment since the wounding of Colonel R. E. Withers at Gaines' Mill in 1862.[16] Colonel Henry Gantt had the honor of commanding Garnett's largest regiment, the 19th Virginia Infantry Regiment, with 426 officers and men present for duty. Although the 28th Virginia Infantry Regiment was composed of only nine companies it approximated the size of the 18th

Regiment, with almost 380 officers and men in the ranks, and was ably led by Colonel Robert C. Allen. Another large regiment within the brigade was the 56th Virginia Infantry Regiment, with Colonel William D. Stuart leading 430 infantrymen loyal to Virginia's cause.

By far the largest of the three brigades in Pickett's Division was commanded by Brigadier General Lewis A. Armistead, son of an army officer and heir to the military prestige of a family of military men. His uncle had defended Fort McHenry during the War of 1812 and was therefore the guardian of the "Star Spangled Banner." A student of West Point, Armistead had been dismissed before graduation after an altercation with classmate and now fellow Confederate general Jubal Early. One of his regimental officers characterized Armistead as a strict disciplinarian who regarded obedience to duty as the primary qualification of a soldier. If there was an infringement of this sense of duty, such as straggling on the march, the general held the officer in immediate command of the guilty party accountable for the infraction. As expressed by one who had knowledge of Armistead's methods of accountability, "The private must answer to the officer, but the officer to him."[17] Armistead's experience included service in the U.S. Army prior to the war, which he entered as a civilian after his dismissal from the Military Academy. Like Garnett, Armistead resigned his commission and parted with old army friends to offer his services to his native state when Virginia seceded in 1861.

The 9th Virginia Infantry Regiment was the smallest regiment under Armistead's command, comprised of only eight companies and having just over 260 men. Much of this regiment was recruited out of the ports of Norfolk and Portsmouth, as well as from the communities along the James River upstream from those ports. Its commander, Major John C. Owens, was himself a ship's carpenter before the war. The 14th Virginia, commanded by Colonel James G. Hodges, had almost 480 officers and men. It was thus larger than any regiment in either Kemper's or Garnett's commands, though it was not the largest in its own brigade. A similarly large command was led by Colonel Edward C. Edmonds in the 38th Virginia Infantry Regiment, with just over 480 men in the column. The 53rd Virginia had within the ranks of its almost 470 officers and men some descendants of America's famous patriots, including the colonel. Colonel William R. Aylett, great-grandson of Virginia firebrand Patrick Henry, had risen from commanding Company D to the field command of the 53rd Virginia. Within the ranks of Company K and serving in the regimental color guard was Private Robert Tyler Jones, grandson of former President John Tyler. The largest of all regiments in Armistead's Brigade and within Pickett's Division was the 57th Virginia Infantry Regiment. It had over 500 officers and men in ten companies, commanded by Colonel John B. Magruder. Magruder had risen from command of Company H, composed of his neighbors and friends from the Charlottesville area. These five regiments of Armistead's Brigade brought a complement of 2188 officers and men into the Chambersburg area.

Accompanying the division of infantrymen was the 38th Battalion Virginia Volunteer Light Artillery, better known as Dearing's Battalion. Led by Major James Dearing, who formerly commanded one of the batteries within the battalion, the battalion brought with it two 20-pound Parrott rifles, three 10-pound Parrott

Major James Dearing (1840-1865)
38th Battalion Virginia Volunteer Light Artillery

rifles, and twelve 12-pound Napoleon guns. Appraised as "one of the bravest and best of artillery officers"[18] by one of Pickett's regimental commanders, Dearing came from an old military family. His penchant for things military was exhibited at an early age, when as a young boy he was already being called "Little Soldier." He attended the U.S. Military Academy but left that institution at the head of his class when Virginia seceded. He then entered Confederate service, and was assigned temporarily to the Washington Artillery, with whom he was engaged at the Battle of First Manassas. He was later promoted to the captaincy of the Latham Battery of the 38th Battalion before his promotion to battalion command before the Battle of Fredericksburg.[19]

The Fauquier Artillery (Company A of the battalion) was commanded by Captain Robert M. Stribling and was recruited out of Fauquier County. The battery had seen service in almost all of the battles and campaigns in Virginia, and had most recently taken part in the Suffolk Campaign where it had been given a poor and almost unsupported position guarding the channel of the Nansemond River. The battery's five guns were attacked from the rear by an overwhelming force and many of its personnel, including Captain Stribling, fell into enemy hands. The men of the

7

battery were exchanged before the Gettysburg Campaign. The battery was then reorganized and rearmed at Richmond and ready to seek revenge for its losses.[20] This six-gun battery (two 20-pound Parrott rifles and four Napoleons) was the largest in the battalion and had the most officers and men as well with over 120.

The Richmond Fayette Artillery (Company B of the battalion) was commanded by Captain Miles C. Macon and could trace its lineage back to 1824 when it was named in honor of the Marquis de Lafayette. Like Stribling's Battery, the Richmond Fayette Artillery had seen service in almost all of the Virginia battles. It took with it two Napoleons and two 10-pound Parrott rifles into Pennsylvania as well as 100 men.[21]

The Hampden Light Artillery (Company C of the battalion) was also known as Caskie's Battery, as it was commanded by Captain William H. Caskie. Like Macon's Battery, this was a Richmond battery. It was armed during the Gettysburg Campaign with a mixture of guns, including two Napoleons, a 3-inch ordnance rifle, and a 10-pound Parrott rifle. The battery had been with Jackson in the Valley, and with the rest of the army in most of the Virginia battles. This battery had just over 100 men accompanying the guns with Pickett's Division.[22]

The battery of Company D of the battalion was always known in conjunction with the surname of the captain commanding it. Originally it was Latham's Battery, and later was Dearing's Battery, but at the time of the Gettysburg Campaign it was known as Blount's Battery because it was commanded by Captain Joseph G. Blount. The unit was from the Lynchburg area, and had 100 officers and men in the ranks to service its four Napoleon guns. This battery had also seen active field service since First Manassas, and had joined the battalion with the reorganization of the artillery into this 38th Battalion.[23]

The general condition and attitude of these men in the regiments and batteries of the division was perhaps at its peak. General Garnett evaluated the army itself as being in "fine condition" despite "having some rough times in the way of rainy weather." Another member of his brigade characterized its attitude by remembering that he "never knew more spirit and elan among the men. The idea of 'going ahead' was exhilarating." In Kemper's Brigade a member noted that the ranks were being filled up from absentees as the campaign began, as those who had been sick or wounded and those who had been away without leave returned to duty. The "passionate ardor" of the people had reached a crest, and nearly every man fit for service had been brought to the army. It was unlikely that the army would ever have opportunity to fill its ranks again with such eager recruits, and the army Lee was leading was perhaps the largest number of men ever again to be expected in the ranks. Most of them were veteran soldiers, and well prepared to endure hardships and battle, while the cowards and malingerers had been pared from the army by July 1863. In Armistead's Brigade, a field officer described the character of the division:

> The *esprit de corps* could not have been better; the men were in good physical condition, selfreliant and determined. They felt the gravity of the situation, for they knew well the metal of the foe in their front; they were serious and resolute, but not disheartened. None of the usual jokes, common on the eve

of battle, were indulged in, for every man felt his individual responsibility.... I believe the general sentiment of the division was that they would succeed in driving the Federal line from what was their objective point....

There was no straggling, no feigned sickness, no pretence of being overcome by the intense heat; every man felt that it was his duty to make that fight; that he was his own commander, and they would have made the charge without an officer of any description; they only needed to be told what they were expected to do.... Many of them were veteran soldiers, who had followed the little cross of stars from Big Bethel ... they knew their own power, and they knew the temper of their adversary; they had often met before and they knew the meeting before them would be desperate and deadly.[24]

A non-commissioned officer in the ranks of Armistead's Brigade echoed these same sentiments when he wrote that even though he had been "broke down" for almost half a year, he was "always up when dear Mars Bob" wanted him for a fight, even though that might mean being put in "some tight places sometimes."[25]

Therefore, the men of Pickett's Division passed through Fayetteville with resolution and in good condition. Armistead's Brigade went through the village about mid-morning. The men passed the smoking ruins of radical abolitionist Thaddeus Stevens' iron furnace as they approached the mountains overlooking Cashtown, and were subjected to occasional bushwhacking by civilians and hastily organized militia units.[26] As they reached the east side of these mountains, the roar

Major General George E. Pickett (1825-1875)

of the guns from Gettysburg was plainly audible. This "sullen booming" caused a stir among the men, curious about how their comrades were doing. A quartermaster coming from the front met them in the Cashtown area and shouted out the words the division was anxious to hear: "Been fighting for two days — driving the Yankees all the time — got 6,000 prisoners already — hurrah for Lee!" This last command elicited cheers and hurrahs from the ranks as they continued marching under the sound of the guns.[27]

Approaching Gettysburg, General Pickett rode off in advance of the division to report to General Longstreet that the force was within five miles of the battlefield. Pickett dispatched his adjutant and inspector general, Major Walter Harrison, to General Lee to inform the commanding general that the division had had a long march, but a rest of two hours would ready them for use anywhere on the field. Apparently, General Lee believed that the division would be of little use by the time it arrived; a delay to rest the men would only prolong their absence until the sun went down and the battle would break off anyway, while pressing them forward after the long march without rest would only guarantee further tiring the division. The battle was already in progress without their participation, and Longstreet's Corps was driving the Federals from their positions on almost all points of the field just as Harrison was reporting. As a result, Lee advised Major Harrison to tell General Pickett that he was not needed that evening, but to let the men rest; word would be sent later as to when the division would be needed.[28] Major Dearing, however, was not to remain in camp. After seeing about the disposition of his battalion, the major hastened toward the sound of the guns and volunteered his services to Colonel E.

Confederate Artillerymen At Dinner
(Battles and Leaders of the Civil War)

P. Alexander, commanding the artillery reserve for Longstreet's Corps. Dearing was permitted to accompany and command Woolfolk's and Jordan's Batteries as they charged towards the Peach Orchard after the infantry dislodged the enemy there. In this action, Major Dearing was allowed to share in what Alexander described as an "artillerist's heaven," following the routed enemy and throwing shells and canister into their retreating and disorganized ranks, meting out revenge and feeling the exhilaration of victory.[29]

Upon returning to his battalion about dusk, Major Dearing relayed his orders to Captains Stribling, Macon, Caskie, and Blount to remove the battalion from its bivouac near Marsh Creek and move to the battlefield, remaining for the night in the rear of the line of battle of the First Corps. The site selected for the overnight bivouac was most probably on the farm of Samuel Pitzer, just north of the Eiker's Mill or Millerstown Road, and near the field headquarters of General Longstreet.[30] The infantry of Armistead's, Garnett's, and Kemper's Brigades did not move their bivouac, and the men soon scattered about in the woods south of the Chambersburg Pike, some three miles from Gettysburg, gathering wood for their campfires, filling canteens and coffee pots, and spending their last evening before the battle conversing with friends, writing letters and making entries in diaries and journals. Arms had been stacked, and the men were issued rations and ammunition in anticipation of more marching and fighting on the morrow.[31]

Chapter

II

"Quiet Hours of Just Waiting"

W hile Pickett's men snatched some sleep after sundown, General Lee was undoubtedly thinking about the morrow's plans and his proposed use of this Virginia division. Because the divisions of McLaws and Hood, also from Longstreet's Corps, were facing the Union Fifth and Sixth Corps in an almost impregnable position, Lee perceived it as a useless loss of life to pursue any advantage that could be gained on the right of his line by attacking those Union strongholds at the Round Tops and along the southern crest of the enemy's line on Cemetery Ridge. Instead, Lee decided to form a column of attack on that part of the Union line where A. R. Wright's Georgia Brigade had pierced the Union defenses on the evening of July 2, near the left-center of Meade's battle line. Wright's Brigade had attacked, practically unsupported, at the close of the echelon attacks by Longstreet's and Hill's Corps and had managed to break through the Yankee defenses and penetrate some hundred or so feet beyond that line before lack of support compelled it to retire back to its original position. Wright had encountered only the remnants of Hall's and Harrow's Union Brigades after many of the Union defenders had been shifted to other parts of the field to parry blows on the left and right. Lee did not realize that these troops had returned to their defensive positions on the night of July 2, and had been substantially reinforced by brigades from the Third and First Corps in their immediate rear. Therefore, the numbers of Union defenders were much greater in that vicinity than they had been at any time on the previous day, with much of the support protected and out of sight from Seminary Ridge, sheltered by the eastern slopes of Cemetery Ridge.

Lee, however, had prepared in several ways for the contingency that Meade had reinforced his center—by massing a major infantry force to spearhead the attack, by preparing for the attack through use of his artillery, by coordinating coincident action on the enemy's right flank and a demonstration on the enemy's left to prevent Meade from using troops from these parts of his line to bolster his defenses, and by planning for infantry and artillery support of the main attack. So sure was Lee that his plan might actually break the Union line and result in the headlong retreat of the Union army that he ordered his cavalry to get into such a position that they could harass and perhaps cut off any retreat down the Baltimore Pike, the major artery in the rear of Meade's army.[1]

Hood and McLaws were originally envisioned as part of the general attack on July 3, much as they had been on July 2. However, the position of the Union troops on Lee's right was such that not only was the Federal position strong and defensible, it was also a threat to attack Lee's line in reverse if Hood and McLaws were outmaneuvered or did not guard the right flank. Longstreet convinced Lee to make a reconnaissance in that direction, and after examining the situation, the commanding general agreed with Longstreet's appraisal of the threat. As a result, he determined to use troops of A. P. Hill's Third Corps command to accompany Pickett's Division; Heth's Division was to be part of the attacking column, and the column would be supported by parts of Anderson's and Pender's Divisions. However, the delay caused by this juggling of participants and completion of dispositions created a serious setback to the day's plans as envisioned by General Lee. It was now impossible to coordinate the attack with that by General Ewell on the enemy's right, which had begun before sun-up on July 3.[2]

At about the same time that the artillery opened the fighting at Culp's Hill on Ewell's front, Pickett's Division was awakened when reveille was sounded at 3:00 A.M. The men were ordered to prepare to move after breakfast was eaten and roll call had been taken.[3] Captain James R. Hutter, in temporary command of the 11th Virginia in Kemper's Brigade, must have been ruminating over the thoughts conveyed to him just hours before by Colonel A. L. Long of the artillery staff. Colonel Long had assured Captain Hutter that all the division needed to do was to follow up on the previous two days of victory to insure final defeat of the Yankees.[4] Hutter must have been hoping it would be that easy.

The regiments filed into the Chambersburg Pike, heading toward Gettysburg, but only went a short distance in that direction before turning off towards the right side of the road, heading south on what appeared to be a road used merely by local farmers. Private Robert B. Damron of Company D in the 56th Virginia described the march on this road that morning. After going between half a mile and three-quarters of a mile southward, the march turned again, this time to the left and paralleling the turnpike. The division followed this parallel road "until it reached a wheat field to right of road where fourth Alabama regiment had fought over the day before."[5] Damron's description of the march provides us with the best explanation of the route followed by Pickett's Division to the battlefield from their Marsh Creek encampment. The column left the turnpike and turned south on a ridge road called the Knoxlyn Road, and followed it until it turned eastward at its junction with Hereter's Mill Road. After that latter road entered the woods just below the crest of Herr Ridge, the division left it and followed the field road through those woods in a southerly direction, reaching and crossing the Hagerstown Road and following the Willoughby Run Road for a short distance before crossing Willoughby's Run itself.[6] A lieutenant in Garnett's Brigade remembered what a "shady quiet march" this was en route to their battle positions, mainly because of the woodlots scattered along the roads and lanes of their march.[7] From the run another farm road which connected the Emmanuel Pitzer Farm buildings to the run and the Hagerstown Road continued the journey eastward towards the Confederate lines on Seminary Ridge, only thee-quarters of a mile distant. In following the Pitzer lane past the farm buildings, the division indeed passed a wheatfield on their right where Wilcox's Alabama Brigade had clashed with elements of the Union Third Corps the previous day. Although Private Damron did not get the numerical designation of the

Route of March from Marsh Creek

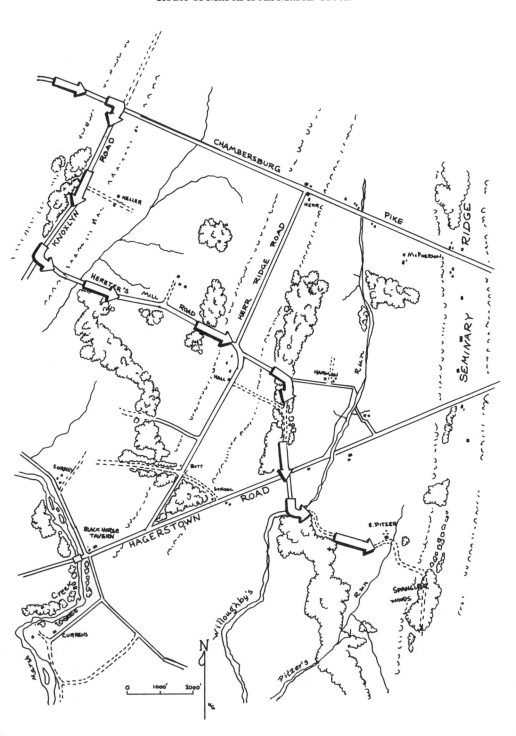

Alabama regiment correct (it was the 10th and 11th Alabama Regiments), his description was detailed enough to help fabricate the march using contemporary topographic maps of the described areas.

Pitzer's farm lane came out at the woodlot of Henry Spangler, and the division was halted at the edge of this woods "for some time." Their march had been partially concealed from the enemy by the ridge, and as they remained in this small valley just west of the ridge and at the fringe of Spangler Woods, the regiments had a final inspection of arms and ammunition.[8] From here at least the men of Garnett's Brigade were able to see through the woods to the field beyond, where artillery was being posted in accordance with Lee's orders for the planned assault. After this pause of perhaps an hour at the most, the division was ordered into line, forming along the western edge of this Spangler Woods. The men were ordered forward, and they advanced to the other edge of the woods where they were halted again. A Virginia worm fence running along the woods-line was ordered to be taken down during this halt, so that it would not "disarrange" the line.[9] It was probably at this time that it was seen that the terrain and the positions of other troops was such that the entire division would not be able to advance in a common front. Garnett's line overlapped a little the front of Heth's Division, which prevented Armistead's Brigade, then on the left, from continuing the line in that direction. Armistead was, of course, anxious to know what he was to do with his brigade—to push out anyway and come up in front of Heth, or hold a position in rear of the rest of the division.

Major Walter Harrison of Pickett's staff was notified of Armistead's dilemma and attempted to find General Pickett to ascertain his wishes for the large brigade. Not being able to find him immediately, Major Harrison espied Generals Longstreet and Lee on the ridge to the east of Spangler Woods and rode up to discuss the matter with Longstreet. Preoccupied with examining the enemy position, General Longstreet curtly replied to Harrison's query that it was General Pickett's responsibility and that he, not Longstreet, would give Armistead the orders. Before Harrison could retreat before this rebuff, General Longstreet realized his curtness, and brushed it off with a "Never mind, Colonel." He also told Harrison to let Armistead remain where he was, in rear of the other two brigades of the division, and to make up the distance when the advance was made.[10]

With these orders conveyed to General Armistead, Kemper's and Garnett's Brigades were given the command to forward their men. The regiments were ordered to keep their colors furled and covered during this advance from the screen of the woods, and those on the left of the line (more visible to the enemy because the intervening ridge dropped off in that direction) were ordered to stoop over to conceal their line from the Federals.[11]

Because James Kemper's Brigade had occupied the lead position in column during the march from Marsh Creek, it would occupy the right brigade position when the column dispersed into battle line on the western edge of Spangler Woods. The 24th Virginia under Colonel William Terry had led off the brigade that morning and thus occupied the extreme right of the brigade line as it advanced from the woods to its new position in rear of the Confederate artillery. To its left was the 11th Virginia, which was just to the right and rear of Dearing's guns as they occupied the

15

ridge near the Emmitsburg Road. Occupying the center of the brigade line was the small but valorous "Old First." The 7th Virginia of Colonel Patton was next in line, and the extreme left was occupied by Colonel Mayo's 3rd Virginia.

The men of these regiments left memories of those morning and early afternoon hours while they awaited the continuation of the struggle and their part in it. Chaplain J.C. Granbery of the 11th Virginia took the opportunity to take a walk in front of the brigade line in order to look around. It turned out that several other officers and men of Pickett's Division used this "waiting" time to roam about their lines, and many would be unpleasantly surprised by the view they had toward the enemy position. Chaplain Granbery was just one of those, and when he returned to his regiment, several company commanders questioned him about what he had seen. After hearing his description of the fields and forces, many shook their heads and remarked that "it would require a very bloody battle to win the day."[12] Captain Hutter was relieved of his responsibility for commanding this 11th Regiment sometime about noon, when all officers and men of the division under arrest were released by orders of General Lee, and Major Kirkwood Otey again assumed command of the regiment.[13] Hutter, again second in command, would direct the activities of the right wing of the 11th through the remainder of the afternoon.

While drawn up in line here, many officers and men looked about for some way to escape the insufferable and oppressive heat and sun. Captain Hutter, returning to the right wing of the regiment, saw a large apple tree of the Spangler Farm just to the rear, and went back to enjoy its shade with Chaplain Granbery. Upon arriving there, Hutter found that General Pickett and General Longstreet were also enjoying the shade of this tree, and was even more surprised when General Lee himself rode up. Hutter's version of what transpired between those commanding officers was recorded decades after the battle, but his account, if true is surprisingly revealing:

> Gen. Lee in passing stopped under this apple tree and conversed with Gen. Longstreet; I remember catching portions of the conversation; Gen. Longstreet saying his command would do what any body of men on earth dared to but no troops could dislodge the enemy from their strong position. Gen. Pickett said he thought his division could drive them from his front. My recollection is that Gen. Lee on pressing Gen. Longstreet said, "ask the men if they can dislodge them." One or two companies from the 11th probably more, and I presume some number from other Regiments were moved up to the crest of the hill, and the men were asked if they would drive the enemy from his works. I walked up with Capt. Thos. Horton when he moved his Co. B. up. I was anxious to hear what the men would say. They would clasp each other by the hand and say "boys many a one of us will bite the dust here today but we will say to Gen. Lee if he wants them driven out we will do it."[14]

While Captain Hutter's imagination may have been the inspiration for the recollection, the reaction of the men in the 11th who studied to enemy position from the crest of the hill at the artillery line seems to ring with the same convictions expressed by other men in other regiments, including that already related by Chaplain Granbery. Nevertheless, it seems illogical that General Lee would be consulting enlisted men in the ranks about his tactical decisions and ignoring advice offered by his corps and division commanders, unless, of course, he was certain that the confidence that he had in the invulnerability of the Army of Northern Virginia was shared by those soldiers and they would help him in convincing his First Corps commander that they were as confident as himself in the task. Nevertheless, it does not seem likely that General Lee would make this kind of effort and thus expose whole bodies of men to unnecessary enemy fire just to reconnoiter and make a point to his lieutenant.

Corporal Charles T. Loehr of the 1st Virginia, in the center of the brigade line, was another of those individual soldiers who struck out from the line in order to get some relief from the "sweltering heat of the sun," where the men were fully exposed and lying in an open field. Corporal Loehr took his canteen in search of water and found a well near one of the batteries along the artillery line in their front. This well was probably on the property of Joseph Sherfy, whose house and outbuildings had been part of the battlefield of the previous day, and which was located on the Emmitsburg Road just to the right and front of Kemper's position. Here, Loehr spoke with some of the artillerists about the Union position visible in the distance on Cemetery Ridge, and upon returning to his company after this foray, he remarked, "I would not give 25 cents for my life if the charge is made."[15]

David Johnston of the 7th Virginia Regiment was a corporal and possibly acting sergeant-major in his regiment when their own line cleared away the fence along the Spangler Woods and moved forward into a field of rye, where they stacked arms. Here Johnston and his comrades received word that they were to lie flat on the ground when they heard the fire from two signal guns. But, this fire was not forthcoming, and he remembered that the heat became "excessively oppressive," with men lacking water and suffering here and there from sunstroke. Like the rest of the brigade, the 7th Virginia was about 200 yards in rear of the batteries, and from their particular place in line the regimental members could see the enemy's signal station on Little Round Top.[16]

Colonel Mayo of the 3rd Virginia on Kemper's extreme left was given his brigade commander's "earnest injunction" to make the men of the regiment aware that General Lee had assigned Pickett's Division the post of honor that day. And, almost to add endorsement to that injunction, General Lee himself was seen passing in front of the regiment, coming from the right, having ridden the length of the brigade line. In their position some 200 yards in rear of the artillery, the men were allowed to rest at will and to stack their arms. Mayo noticed a difference in his men, however, that even the presence of the commanding general did not seem to dissipate:

> ... but one thing was especially noticeable; from being unusually merry and hilarious they on a sudden had become as still and thoughtful as Quakers at a love feast. Walking up the line to where Colonel Patton was standing in front of the Seventh, I said to him, "This news has brought an awful seriousness with our fellows, Taz." "Yes," he replied, "and well may they be serious if they really know what is in store for them. I have been up yonder where Dearing is, and looked across at the Yankees."[17]

With this foreboding warning still ringing in his ears, Colonel Mayo rejoined his own command to spend what seemed a "long, painful interval of suspense" in awaiting the orders for the regiment to do its duty. As the morning wore into afternoon, the command was given for each regiment to assign fifteen men as skirmishers, and these details moved up just behind the artillery line.[18] Corporal Loehr of the 1st Virginia was thus given another opportunity to visit the artillery; he was assigned to this detail of skirmishers from Colonel Williams' regiment, to advance some 200 yards in front of his regiment during the anticipated attack.

Many of these same kinds of events were taking place in Garnett's Brigade, on the left of the 3rd Virginia of Kemper's Brigade, and north of the lane leading to the Spangler Farm buildings. General Garnett was still not on the field with his brigade, and Colonel Eppa Hunton of the 8th Virginia was responsible for directing the men into position after their advance from the woods. His own regiment, then under command of Lieutenant Colonel Norbonne Berkeley, was on the right of the brigade, and was formed along the slope of the Emmitsburg Road ridge behind the Confederate artillery line, out of sight of the enemy.[19] Colonel Hunton estimated that the brigade came into position about 8:00 A.M., but others estimated later times, including one who believed that they came into position as late as noon.[20] Sometime during the late morning or early afternoon Colonel Hunton would be relieved of brigade command by General Garnett and would assume command of his own 8th Regiment.

On the left of the 8th Virginia was the 18th Regiment of Colonel Carrington. Lieutenant Richard Ferguson, acting as its adjutant, remembered moving into this position in support of Dearing's Battalion (the bulk of which was on Garnett's front) "under the eye of Gen. Lee himself."[21] Gantt's 19th Virginia moved into line on the left of the 18th soon thereafter, occupying the center of the brigade battle line. Lieutenant William N. Wood of Company I recalled filling canteens in a "branch" between Spangler Woods and the Pitzer farm buildings, which surely must have been Pitzer's Run. Lieutenant Wood recalled the movement forward from these woods and the events of the morning after establishing position:

> ... as we halted we dressed upon the colors, forming a line of battle. The other regiments of our brigade dressed upon us — ours being the centre regiment. We were ordered to lie down. Our position was, at this time, on the south side of Cemetery Hill and near its eastern end, and more than a hundred yards from the top in our front. For how many hours we sweltered on the side of this hill that hot third day of July, 1863, I know not, but my opinion is about five hours.
>
> The field officers rode about us and held frequent short consultations. Leaving my command I walked up to the top of the hill and took a birds-eye view of the situation, just as Colonel Dearing rode up to see about locating his artillery. I heard him say "that hill must fall" as he rode off to the right. I walked back to the regiment with "that hill must fall" still ringing in my ears. Artillery came, it seemed to me, from every direction, and quickly prepared, on or near the hill top, for action. I never before saw such a display of artillery and felt, "that hill must fall."
>
> An hour or more passed in silence. The sun was making the hillside very uncomfortable.[22]

When the 28th Virginia established its position as the left-center regiment, there were barely 100 yards remaining between the infantry line and the curving line being occupied by the artillery.[23] These guns were occupying positions at the crest of the ridge and were following its diagonal direction which reached from the northeast corner of the Spangler Woods in a southeasterly direction to and across the Emmitsburg Road. There was even less space between the infantry and the cannon as the last regiment of Garnett's Brigade filed into battle line, as indicated by this reminiscence of the lieutenant commanding Company K of the 56th Virginia:

> In my immediate front we were so close to the guns that I had to "break to the rear" my little company to give the men at the limber chest room to handle the ammunition. The Caisson with its horses and drivers was just in my rear... Garnett's five regiments took their usual order from right to left as follows: 18th, 19th, 28th, and 56th. This, you see, threw my regiment on the left of the first line, and my company (K) was second or third from the extreme left of the division. After we got into position we were ordered to lie down and wait for the order to advance after our guns had bombarded the position we were to assault.[24]

These guns of Dearing's Battalion were being placed along this line in conjunction with almost fifty others as part of General Lee's overall plans for the proposed assault. It had been planned that the artillery would open a concentrated fire on the enemy's position, cease firing, and then advance in supporting distance of the infantry to prevent the enemy from throwing out any flanking columns and to assist in silencing batteries and destroying Union positions. Plans for the proposed cannonade were firmed up in the morning hours, when a dispatch was sent from General Longstreet to Colonel Walton, then commanding his corps artillery, requesting that he report to field headquarters immediately. Longstreet was there with Lee and several division commanders discussing the plans of the attack. The discussions concluded with orders to Colonel Walton to have two guns of the Washington Artillery in the vicinity of the Peach Orchard fire a signal which would have the artillery line commence the cannonade.[25] Orders would be sent to Colonel Walton when preparations were completed and when the batteries should open fire.

Captain Stribling was visited by Major Dearing shortly after this meeting between Walton, Longstreet, Lee and others. Walton had briefed Colonel Alexander and other battalion commanders in the artillery line, and Dearing was subsequently briefing his battery officers as to what was expected of them. Stribling was told that the battalion would advance en echelon with the infantry, and would advance by batteries from the right, beginning with Stribling's Fauquier Artillery. Captain Stribling then accompanied Major Dearing in an examination of the ground in front of the battalion line, and found that the conditions were such that they could not cross the Emmitsburg Road on their front because the road had been cut into a hill side, and the steep embankments were such that it would endanger dismounting a gun in passing over them. They would have to move in column to the front of a house on their right (the Sherfy Farmhouse) and pass into the road where there was a farm gate, between the house and barn. Then the battery would have to move by column down (north) the Emmitsburg Road another several hundred yards to where there was another farm gate on the opposite side of the road in order to gain entry to the fields on the east side. (This second gate may have been at the junction of the Emmitsburg Road and the Trostle Farm Lane.)[26]

Major Dearing reiterated these orders to Captain Blount and Lieutenant Joseph Thompson of Company D's Battery, revealing that the Washington Artillery would provide the signal to commence firing, and that the whole line of guns would open fire thereafter. He also told these officers that they were to advance with the infantry and continue firing, and that this would take place about ten or fifteen minutes after the cannonade began.[27] The intention of the command for the early advance was so that the artillery would have sufficient ammunition to support the infantry properly. Colonel Alexander was to inform General Pickett at the close of this period, when he thought the Confederate fire was at its most effective, and his advice would therefore begin the Confederate attack.

As an additional precaution, Colonel Alexander had secured from the Third Corps of A. P. Hill nine howitzers, perfect for mobility and close-range fire, and placed them under the immediate command of Major Charles Richardson of Garnett's Third Corps Artillery Battalion. These nine pieces were intended to advance with and in support of Pickett's Division, and Alexander arranged that they had fresh men and horses as well as full ammunition chests. They would be kept in reserve during the cannonade and not participate in that firing so that they would remain in top condition. Alexander foresaw that the guns which participated in the cannonading would be losing men, horses, and ammunition during the firing and would not be in a position to promptly and effectively support the infantry as these nine fresh guns might. By having the guns sent from the Third Corps front, where they would not have been participating at all, Alexander was freed from reserving any of his own guns of the First Corps from the cannonade, as he had originally planned had he not been able to secure the howitzers. They were sent to a sheltered position in rear of the artillery line, and were ordered to await the commands of Colonel Alexander.[28]

Likewise awaiting the commands of the day were the men of Armistead's Brigade. Also lying in a diagonal line another hundred yards or more behind Garnett's position, the left flank of the line was within Spangler's Woods itself in order to remain behind the artillery line that terminated at its northeast corner there. On the right of the brigade was the 14th Virginia, and in the center was the 53rd Regiment of Colonel Aylett. The two regiments on the left of Armistead's Brigade would enjoy the shade of Spangler's Woods while the rest of the division sweltered in the July sun. The 57th Virginia, occupying the left-center of the brigade, was joined under the boughs of the oaks by the 38th Virginia on the extreme left. Almost 1000 men in the ranks of these two largest of Pickett's regiments nearly filled the northern half of Spangler's woodlot as they prepared for the attack. Of Armistead's Brigade, a field officer in the 53rd Regiment would say of their feelings that morning that "they knew that many, very many, would go down under the storm of shot and shell ... but it never occurred to them that disaster would come after they once placed their tattered banners upon the crest of Seminary Ridge."[29]

As the morning passed without the anticipated orders to advance, there was a grim recognition that the afternoon must undoubtedly bring those orders. Men in Garnett's Brigade characterized the fatalistic determination shared throughout the division, as expressed by Colonel Hunton of the 8th Virginia: "All appreciated the danger and felt it was probably the last charge to most of them. All seemed willing to die to achieve a victory there, which it was believed would be the crowning victory and the end of the war."[30] Some had seen the position they were to assail, almost a mile away over open fields, with what seemed to be dozens of fence lines intervening to impede an orderly advance. Some had even heard about the enemy's position from those who had first-hand experience trying to gain it the day before. General Cadmus Wilcox, whose Alabama Brigade was posted to the front of Kemper's Brigade and to the right, had attacked the ridgeline opposite on the evening of July 2, and spoke of his futile efforts to the officers of Garnett's Brigade. Wilcox compared the position to that held by the Federals at Gaines' Mill in 1862, where Confederate losses had been extraordinarily heavy, and went so far as to pronounce this Cemetery Ridge position as twice as formidable as that at Gaines' Mill. Although Wilcox told them that he had lost between 400 and 500 men within fifteen or twenty minutes attacking the opposite ridge, without making the slightest impression in the enemy's lines, Major Edmund Berkeley believed he "never saw men march more steadily up to their work than our line."[31]

Sergeant Levin Gayle of the 9th Virginia was one such resolute veteran who had witnessed his division chief riding along his front that morning, accompanied by Generals Lee and A. P. Hill. After this inspiring spectacle, his regiment was told that they were expected "to Charge that Hill and take those cannon." By one o'clock Sergeant Gayle and his comrades were "all ready" to do just that. His last entry in his journal during these final moments of reflection and calm mirrored his own equanimity before the imminent advance:

"There is a great deal of Artillery here with us and it does look Beautiful all in an open Field and A clear day and sun shines."[32]

Chaplain Granbery of the 11th Virginia most likely best summarized the feelings in the ranks of the division, however, as the long hot and silent morning hours passed — "Those quiet hours of just waiting were very trying."[33]

Cannonade Positions c. 1:00 - 3:00 P.M

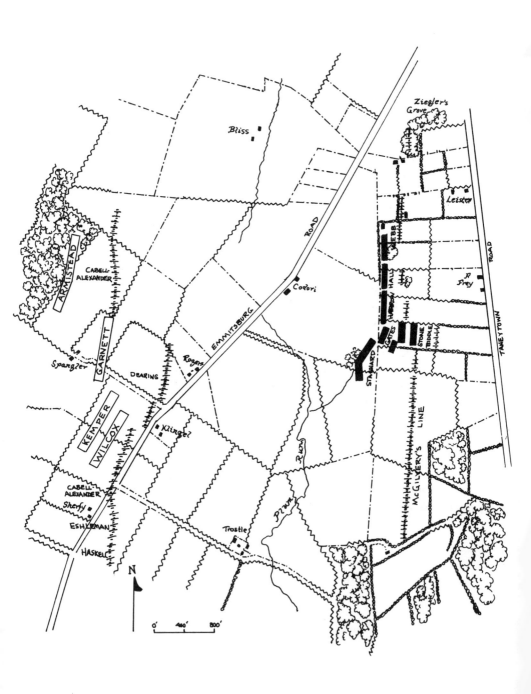

Chapter

III

"There is no safe place here"

S ometime shortly after 1:00 P.M. a courier rode up to Colonel J. B. Walton and handed him a slip of paper torn from a memorandum book by his corps commander, General Longstreet. The long-awaited orders read, "Let the batteries open. Order great care and precision in firing. If the batteries at the peach orchard cannot be used against the point we intend attacking, let them open on the enemy on the rocky hill."[1] The orders came to Walton instead of Colonel Alexander because Walton was in command of all First Corps artillery, and Alexander was subordinate to him as reserve artillery chief. On the other hand, the 28-year old officer had been given unprecedented authority over Walton in directing operations of the 75 or more pieces in the cannonade line on July 3 because of his familiarity with the grounds (he had fought in the vicinity on July 2) and because of General Longstreet's high opinion of Alexander's "promptness, sagacity and intelligence."[2] Although he would be the one who would advise Pickett and Pettigrew when to advance, Alexander was still subservient to Walton in this initial phase of the cannonade. The artillery chief relayed the orders from Longstreet to Colonel Eshleman of the Washington Artillery Battalion, so that the signal guns could be fired. One Napoleon gun of Captain M. B. Miller's Battery was discharged. What were supposed to be practically simultaneous discharges of this first gun and a second Napoleon did not occur, however. A faulty friction primer on the second Napoleon caused the gun's discharge to be delayed a brief moment.[3]

At the sound of the signal the line of artillery burst into flame and smoke and noise. Along Seminary Ridge and the ridge transversing the Emmitsburg Road there were over 120 cannon discharging one round every thirty seconds, sending 240 shells and solid shot each minute toward the Union lines on Cemetery Ridge. The experience was one never to be forgotten for those who had spent the better part of five hours in unexpected silence. Major Walter Harrison spoke for Pickett's staff when he described the effects and vision of this exchange of fire between the Confederate artillery about him and the Union guns on the ridge opposite his position:

> The atmosphere was broken by the rushing solid shot, and shrieking shell; the sky, just now so bright, was at the same moment lurid with flame and murky with smoke. The sun in his noontide ray was obscured by clouds of sulphurous mist, eclipsing his light, and shadowing the earth as with a funeral pall; while through this sable panoply, ever descending and wrapping this field of blood in the darkness of death, shot the fiery fuses, like wild meteors of a heavenly wrath; hurtled the

Lieutenant General James Longstreet (1821-1904)

discordantly screaming shell, bearing mangled death and mutilation in its most horrible form.

The enemy had the exact range of our lines of battle, and just overshooting the artillery opposed to them, as usual, their shot and shell told with effect upon the infantry, exposed as they were without cover of any sort...Many of the men, and several valuable officers were killed or disabled long before a movement was ordered; but the line remained steadily fixed...[4]

On General Kemper's front where Stribling's Battery and the Washington Artillery concentrated their fire on a number of targets, the incoming fire was probably the worst on any part of Pickett's line, if not along the whole of the assault battle line. The brigade was closest to the Union lines because of the curving nature of the artillery and infantry line following the ridgeline, and thus was exposed to the greatest concentration of artillery fire from the opposite ridge and from the Little Round Top sector. Hoping to reduce casualties in some way, General Kemper ordered his men to lie flat on the ground. Despite this meager precaution shots "pelted them and ploughed through them, and sometimes fragments of a dozen mangled men were thrown in and about the trench left by a single missile."[5] Amidst this destruction Kemper was astonished to see General Longstreet riding his horse quite alone along the front of his brigade line, exhibiting to Kemper the "grandest moral spectacle of the war:"

> I expected to see him fall every instant. Still he moved on, slowly and ma-
> jestically, with an inspiriting confidence, composure, self-possession and re-
> pressed power, in every movement and look, that fascinated me. As he neared me,
> I walked up to him, intending to remind him of his peril of which he seemed really
> unconscious, and said "General, this is a terrible place." Said he, "What! is your
> command suffering?" "Yes," I answered, "a man is cut to pieces, here every second
> while we are talking; sometimes a dozen are killed by one shot."[6]

Somewhat surprised at this, Longstreet asked why Kemper had not found a safer position for his men. Knowing that the only safe place in the vicinity was behind the crest of the ridge where his men were lying, Kemper could only plead that he was making the best of a bad situation. Longstreet parted with the reassurance that the charge would be made "presently" and asked that Kemper hold the ground until that movement.

If many men of Kemper's Brigade raised their heads above the crest to share Kemper's view of Longstreet astride his charger, few were awe-struck enough to write about it later. The awe-inspiring scenes and sounds to these men would continue to be the firing of those hundred or more cannon along the Yankee lines, which rained iron hail upon them and gave them no place to find shelter. On the right of the line, Major Joseph Hambrick of the 24th Virginia was in the rear of his regiment, near the orchard of the Spangler Farm when a shell exploded. Part of the shell tore splinters from an apple tree by which he was standing, holding the bridle of his bay horse, and slightly wounded him, while another part of the shell passed through his mount, killing it.[7] Hambrick's memories of the cannonade were likely more about what he and his horse went through than of any display of courage by a general on horseback.

To Hambrick's left was the 11th Virginia, lying in a field of grass so thick and deep that it seemed impossible to get any air. Coupled with the intense heat of the sun, many of the men were suffering as much from this discomfort as they were from the effects of the shelling. Indeed, some members of the regiment were prostrated by sunstroke, while this "terrible and horrible" pounding went on.[8] Most of the casualties, however, could be attributed to the cannonade itself. Captain James R. Hutter of the 11th Virginia described it as such a pouring of shot, shell, grape, and canister from the front and right flank as he had never before witnessed. Captain Hutter concluded that none would ever be able to sort out how many men were lost in this exchange of cannon fire. Yet, he remembered forever the sight of Chaplain J. C. Granbery going to each of the wounded men in the regiment during this outpouring of misery and kneeling by each one, praying with and for the sufferers.[9] Captain John H. Smith's Company G, with 29 men in line during this cannonade, lost about ten in killed and wounded under the fire of the Union artillery, while Company E, on his right, suffered even higher casualties. Captain Smith recalled that William and Thomas Jennings, brothers who had enlisted together when the regiment was at Suffolk in May, were killed in line behind the Confederate artillery pieces, as was Edward Valentine. Of the over half dozen others who were wounded within the company, Charles J. Winston was fortunate enough to escape with only minor injuries. Private Winston was on detail with the ambulance corps when a piece of shell hit his pocket book, which luckily had more than mere Confederate paper money within. The shell "blended together two half-dollar silver pieces,"[10] perhaps saving Winston's life. The men of Company G were treated to a show of heroics from high-ranking officers on their front, defying the rain of shot and shell which created such heavy casualties within their own ranks. Captain Smith remembered seeing no less a personage than General Longstreet himself during the height of this artillery fire, mounted and riding between the batteries and the infantry line from the right of Pickett's line to the left, "as quiet as an old farmer riding over his plantation on a Sunday morning," and looking neither to the left or right at the men as he rode along.[11] Other saw the conspicuous Major James Dearing, riding between the cannons of his battalion and the infantry line, "waving a flag and cheering on his men," while watching the effect of his fire on the enemy's lines.[12]

The amount of casualties in the center regiment of Kemper's Brigade, the "Old First," was similarly heavy, and caused Colonel Williams to order J. R. Polak of Company I to bring up the ambulance corps, as "men were falling right and left and needed attention." Polak went off on Colonel Williams' mare, Nelly, to more speedily execute the orders and bring relief to his wounded comrades.[13] Lieutenant John Dooley of Company C saw the effects of the Union overshots within the ranks of his regiment, where men "lay bleeding and gasping the agonies of death all around, and we unable to help them in the least." Dooley heard that one of the regiments lost 88 men in killed and wounded during this interval, and was not surprised by such a figure, since the brigade was immediately in the rear of Dearing's artillery line and was receiving nearly all the shots intended for those guns. The discomfort caused by the heat of the sun added to Lieutenant Dooley's misery, but could not compare with the sight of some comrade raising his head "disfigured and unrecognizable, streaming with blood, or stretch his full length, his limbs quivering in the pangs of death." The lieutenant and his friends no longer had the opportunity to amuse themselves as they had in the morning hours, resting under Henry Spangler's apple trees and throwing small green apples at one another for entertainment. With death and fearful wounds round about them, Lieutenant Dooley recognized how frivolous those moments now seemed, but could still admire the defiance of Major Dearing who was seen waving the battalion flag and now and again taking the place of a gunner who was struck down. And amongst the crash and explosion of the shells, were the sounds and sights connected with the resupply of ammunition—wagons flying back and forth, the horses' hooves pounding the earth in competition with the solid shot.[14]

Colonel Tazewell Patton's 7th Virginia Regiment occupied the left center of Kemper's Brigade line during this cannonade, and acting Sergeant-Major David Johnston was at the left of his regiment, accommodated by the shade of an apple tree behind the line and near the right of the next regiment on the left (the 3rd Virginia). After the firing of the two signal guns, Colonel Patton and Colonel Joseph Mayo joined each other at this same apple tree and lay down just beneath it, while Johnston placed himself between two soldiers of the 3rd Regiment and Lieutenant James Brown of his own 7th Virginia. While lying there at the feet of the two colonels, the enemy's fire appeared to slacken and Johnston raised his head momentarily to catch a breath of fresh air. A quick reprimand by Lieutenant Brown for exposing himself caused Johnston to argue that it was just as sure a way to die by having a shell take off his head as it was to suffocate. His reply was cut short by a "terrific explosion," which threw Johnston some feet away, causing him to lose his breath and "sensibility." Trying to catch his breath, Johnston soon discovered he was surrounded by brains, blood, and skull bones, and immediately feared that his colonel's head had been shot away. But Colonel Patton was uninjured and was immediately at

Johnston's side inquiring as to his health. Johnston could but tell him of his own wounds—some ribs broken away from the backbone and a bruised lung. Lieutenant Brown was wounded, and the two unfortunates from the 3rd Virginia were killed.[15] These two victims proved to be men of Company D, of Mayo's regiment.

Colonel Mayo himself was able to fill in some of the episode in the years after the war, when he wrote about the details of the cannonade which swallowed up the "long, painful interval of suspense" of the early morning and afternoon hours with "excruciating reality." At the sound of the signal guns, Mayo assumed a place in the immediate rear of his center, and seated himself in front of the regimental flag of the 3rd Virginia on a pile of blankets. Like the men of his command, however, Mayo was soon beat into submission by the heat of the sun and went to the apple tree to seek relief with its shade. Here he found men of the 3rd and 7th Regiments as "thick as herring in a barrel," and he squeezed himself between Colonel Patton and Mayo's second-in-command, Lieutenant Colonel Alexander D. Callcote. Mayo's recollection of the moments under that tree mirrored his concern for himself and for his command, and spoke of a like concern by his friend Colonel Patton:

> The first shot or two flew harmlessly over our heads; but soon they began to get the range, and then came...'pandemonium.' First there was an explosion in the top of our friendly tree, sending a shower of limbs upon us. In a second there was another, followed by a piercing shriek, which caused Patton to spring up and run to see what was the matter. Two killed and three frightfully wounded, he said on his return. Immediately after a like cry came from another apple tree close by in the midst of the Third. Company F has suffered terribly; First Lieutenant A. P. Gomer, legs shattered below the knee; of the Arthur brothers, second and third lieutenants, one killed the other badly hit [Patrick and John C. Arthur; the latter the 3rd lieutenant, died of wounds at the division hospital]; Orderly Sergeant Murray [?] mortally wounded, and of the privates, one killed and three wounded. Then, for more than an hour it went on. Nearly every minute the cry of mortal agony was heard above the roar and rumble of the guns.[16]

Eventually, Colonel Patton suggested that the infantry lines move up closer to the artillery in order to prevent the kinds of losses that were being incurred by the tremendous amount of Union overshot on their sector of the line. Colonel Mayo cautioned against such a move without orders from General Kemper, and pointed out that a recent slackening in Federal fire meant the close of the cannonade. No sooner had he made this reassuring prediction than the bursting of a shell overhead threw a "handful of earth mixed with blood and brains" onto Mayo's shoulder. At first fearing it was his adjutant, Lieutenant John Stewart, who had been struck, it proved to be the two enlisted men of Company D and Davey Johnston of Patton's 7th Regiment.

On Kemper's left, Garnett's Brigade fared almost as badly, particularly his right regiments. These regiments on the right were closer to the artillery line than those on the left because of the lay of the ground which Garnett's Brigade was employing to shelter itself. The 8th Virginia Regiment, on the extreme right of the brigade, lost five killed during this artillery barrage.[17] As the regiment was lying to the rear of Dearing's batteries, the enemy succeeded in getting the range on the guns and the supporting 8th Virginia. Private Randolph Shotwell of Company H witnessed the opening of the cannonade and its subsequent destruction:

> The cannoneers open their ammunition chests; the caison [sic] drivers crouch in shallow trenches they have scooped out for their protection during the row. Suspense for 20 seconds. Boom! err-BANG!! — a thundering explosion on the right of the line! The sound startles us, though we have been expecting it; just as we shrink from the crack of thunder which a previous flash has foretold. Then a crash of unearthly peals!... It is an artillery duello of 250 cannons at short range, throwing 500 shells per minute and each shell bursting into myriad fragments with its own special scream and explosion!... The earth quivered under the incessant concussion. Nor is the sensation of sound alone appalling; the eye takes in a a work of destruction that well may shake the steadiest nerves.
>
> Reclining in front of my company, I was watching the struggles of a wounded artillery horse, when a shell whizzed over my head, and struck behind me. Seeing a peculiar expression upon the countenance of an officer, who was looking back, I also glanced around, and saw a most shocking spectacle. The heavy missile had descended six feet behind me, and ploughed through the bodies of Morris and Jackson of my own company. Poor fellows! they were devoted friends, and lay side by side on their blankets: and side by side were ushered into eternity! While assisting in removing the mangled remains, Lieut. Charles D — left his sword and haversack where he had been lying. A shell burst upon the spot, tearing those articles into shreds — a narrow escape for their owner.
>
> This was within the first ten minutes. Presently the air seemed full of flying lead and iron; and it was not entirely fancy for the fields was covered with fragments of metal after the battle. Fortunately the Federal gunners began to aim higher, supposing the woods in our rear to be full of troops, and sending most of the missiles screaming beyond us.[18]

The incident recalling the deaths of Albert Morris and Benjamin E. Jackson was also recounted by Major Edmund Berkeley, who correctly remembered them as members of his brother Williams' Company D (and not of Shotwell's Company H). Major Berkeley was close enough to the sorrowful event to have the brains of Morris plastered over his hat when his head was taken off by the shell, and noted that this same shell killed the company's file closer, Jackson.[19]

The Lieutenant Charles D — could have been none other than Second Lieutenant Charles Dawson of Company H, whose own close call with death may have affected his decision to leave his post without permission during the retreat back into Virginia and allow himself to be captured by the enemy.[20]

After the Union shelling began to sail further overhead to the rear at Spangler's Woods, there was some time for men in the ranks of the 8th Virginia to think of things other than self-preservation. Major Edmund Berkeley suddenly noticed that he could feel an old deck of playing cards in his pocket, and remembered fondly the many hours of amusement they had afforded himself, his brothers, Colonel Hunton, and General Garnett around the nightly campfires. He could only think with remorse that he would not want these tokens of happier moments falling into the hands of the enemy if found on his dead body. Digging a hole in the ground beside him, Major Berkeley placed the deck in it and covered the hole with a stone, while holding back tears at this little funereal ceremony. It was as if he were burying the memories of friendships that could never be recalled again, and mourning the loss of something which had created an avenue of escape from hours such as these.[21]

This hour was proving to be a hard one for others in Garnett's Brigade. In the 18th Virginia, to the left of Hunton's 8th Regiment, Lieutenant Richard Ferguson was kin to the men in Kemper's and Garnett's Brigade because of his common experiences with the heat of the intense sun, the "roar and whirl and whiz" of cannon shot, and the unwelcome sight of men torn into pieces.[22] Some in the regiment were overcome by the heat, which was recorded in town near the conclusion of the cannonade as 87 degrees Fahrenheit. There seemed little respite among the men from the sun, although this same meteorologist recorded that the skies were almost half filled with cumulus clouds, tossed about very little by the gentle breezes out of the southwest.[23]

In the center of Garnett's line, the men of the 19th Virginia were not excepted from this common suffering. Lieutenant William Wood of Company I, who had been musing about Major Dearing's conviction that "that hill must fall" just moments before, now found himself in the midst of a holocaust where musings were subverted by emotions and sensations. Wood experienced the earth seeming "to leap from its foundation," the atmosphere seeming "to quiver." At once, the heat of the sun was secondary to the need to cling to mother earth "with a soldier's ardour." The clouds of cannon smoke rose like balloon shapes and drifted off to the left of the line, carried by the day's breezes towards the town of Gettysburg, while increasing numbers of the enemy's shells burst behind the line of the 19th Virginia. Most of the damage to the regiment was inflicted by artillery fire coming in from the right flank, from the direction of Little Round Top, where only the six 10-pounder Parrotts of Battery D, 5th U.S. Artillery could be employed against Dearing's line. Lieutenant Wood dreaded those "miserable enfilading solid shots" hailing from Little Round Top because they generally bounced on the ground just at the right of the regiment and then ricochetted along the line creating injury and death in their path. Lieutenant Colonel John T. Ellis, "a good officer, a good man as well as a polished gentleman," was one to fall to this enfilading fire during the cannonade. Lying in a "small wash" on the western side of the ridge during the artillery fire, Ellis received a forewarning from one of his soldiers before one of these ricochetting balls struck. After hearing the cry "Look out," Ellis raised his head just in time to receive the solid shot in the face. Carried to the rear beneath the shade of an apple tree, Lieutenant Colonel Ellis lingered in an unconscious state for several hours before succumbing to death at the division hospital on Marsh Creek. He was later interred in Richmond's Hollywood Cemetery.[24]

The 28th Virginia of Colonel Robert Allen did not suffer as badly, because it was posted even further to the left and so was spared the Union overshot that came mostly from its front. Private William P. Jesse of Company F took this time to look around from his prone position, a luxury that most in Kemper's Brigade and on the right of Garnett's Brigade could not enjoy. Private Jesse glanced off to the right of the line and saw Major Dearing waving the battalion flag along the line of his guns, encouraging his gunners and surveying the effect of his shots. As the cannonade progressed and seemed to be slackening, Jesse saw Generals Lee, Longstreet, and Pickett riding along the lines together.[25] As the generals rode off to the left to the end of Alexander's artillery line they passed in front of the extreme left of Garnett's Brigade, a position held by the 56th Virginia Regiment. With Spangler's Woods in their rear and Alexander's guns in their front, the regiment was sheltered like the rest of the brigade in the open by the small ridge which ran diagonally from the Emmitsburg Road. This ridge prevented the regiment from seeing the position of the enemy, but judging from the return fire of Union guns it was easy to surmise that the Army of the Potomac must have a strong position and quite a few guns. The crouching infantrymen admired the effectiveness and efficiency of Alexander's gunners on their front, and marveled at their ability to stand and serve their pieces under such a fire. For the men of the 56th Regiment, the gunners were the focus of their attention for this hour or so of cannonading. Watching their courage may have inspired the infantrymen and prevented demoralization caused by the losses incurred by the shot and shell that sometimes rained upon them. To Lieutenant George Finley, commanding Company K, it seemed that his men waited almost impatiently for the order to advance, since "anything would be a relief from the strain upon them" from the heat and the shelling.[26]

The soldiers in the rear of the two brigades, initially spared by the artillery concentrating on the Confederate guns, were likewise soon subjected to Union shot and shell. On Armistead's right flank was the 14th Virginia, which was posted in the open and not within Spangler's Woods, where much of the brigade was located. In the hours after coming into position, Private Erasmus Williams of Company H had used a case knife he carried with him to dig a hole, throwing the dirt in front of the hole as a small brestwork. A lieutenant who was standing behind Williams and leaning against a sapling, watched the private's efforts to make a defendable position. "Why Williams, you are a coward," the lieutenant said in good nature. But the enlisted man continued digging, and replied that "You may call me what you please, but when the time comes I will show up all right, and when the artillery begins the hole I am digging will be a good place for me to be in." When Williams was finished, he had "a good little fort for the accommodation of one." He soon overheard Colonel James G. Hodges telling his company commander Captain Richard Logan that the cannonade was to begin soon, and that a signal gun would begin it. Private Williams recounted the episodes that followed:

> So I settled myself in my little fortification and awaited events. The Lieutenant behind me kept guying me and said, "I am going to stand right up here and witness the whole proceeding." Smiling and chatting, he took things as easy and less cautiously than I did. In a little while the signal fired and there came a terrific blast upon us all along our lines from the enemy's guns in reply. In a few minutes I was covered with dirt from the shot and shell striking near me. Presently, indeed almost instantly, the defiant Lieutenant was swept away by a shot or shell, and his blood sprinkled all over me. A shell struck in the ground right by me with the fuse still burning. I had just time to stretch my hand and pull out the fuse, else both I and others might have been killed by its explosion.[27]

The presence of mind as retold by Private Williams seems strikingly overplayed in this autobiographical sketch, written almost forty years after the events. In Private Williams' account, the lieutenant who kept haranguing him was identified as belonging to the 11th Virginia Regiment of Kemper's Brigade, and so was some distance from his post of duty. Williams must have confused the regimental membership of the lieutenant, unless perhaps this lieutenant was skulking so far to the rear of his brigade that he felt safe enough without digging any holes! Notwithstanding a possible misidentification of the lieutenant's unit, the tone of Private Williams' recollection is sufficient to convey the common soldier's urgent desire to find any kind of protection from the expected hail of shot and shell. That Williams dug a hole with his knife to shelter himself seems as reliable a fact as Private Shotwell's vision of Dearing's artillerymen scooping up trenches of earth for their own protection.

The fears incurred by that cannonade were echoed in other regiments of Armistead's Brigade, including the men of the 9th Virginia Infantry on the left of the 14th Regiment. Lieutenant John H. Lewis of Company G remembered that many of the men of the regiment were in the open, and not in Spangler's Woods; only the extreme left of the regiment appears to have been deployed within the confines of the shade. The "hot and oppressive" sun that was overhead of Lieutenant Lewis was soon obscured by the effects of this artillery cannonade. The smoke from the almost 125 guns along the line blackened the sky and blotted out the sun, and seemed to Lewis to be like a thunderstorm. Years later, he attempted to find words to express the sensations:

> Man seldom sees or hears the like of this but once in a lifetime; and those that saw and heard this infernal crash and witnessed the havoc made by the shrieking, howling missiles of death as they plowed the earth and tore the trees will never forget it. It seemed that death was in every foot of space, and safety was only in flight; but none of the men did that. To know the tension of mind under a fire like that, it must be experienced .... For two long hours this pandemonium was kept up, and then, as suddenly as it commenced, it ceased.[28]

The men of Company K were on the left of the regimental line. Here First Sergeant James H. Walker saw round shot whistling through the trees of Spangler's Woods overhead, cutting limbs which came crashing down upon the men of his company. Sergeant Walker noticed that the artillery fire was almost as rapid and regular as musketry fire would be in a battle, and that the enemy was sustaining a fairly accurate range. Men and horses were being struck at almost every burst, and an occasional caisson was seen to blow up along the Confederate line.[29]

The men of the 53rd Virginia, in the center of Armistead's line, were fortunate in incurring few casualties during this shelling. The majority of the Yankee shells passed to their rear, even farther into Spangler's Woods. One of the few shells that fell in their midst, however, was most damaging to the regiment — it wounded Colonel Aylett and incapacitated him from field command. The 53rd Regiment would now be commanded by Lieutenant Colonel Rawley Martin.[30] Captain Benjamin L. Farinholt of Company E ordered his men to lie on the ground at the commencement of the shelling, but many were wounded nevertheless. Soon after the duelling began, the ambulance corps and stretcher bearers had to be doubled in number to accommodate the growing number of casualties in the brigade. Captain Farinholt saw General Cadmus Wilcox visit his brigade commander, General Lewis Armistead, and overheard a conversation between the two during the height of the artillery firing. The tone of the conversation was similar to that held on Garnett's front earlier, when Wilcox declared the Union position stronger than that at Gaines' Mill. Riding up to Armistead, Wilcox saluted and queried what the Virginian thought would follow the unusually heavy cannonade. Armistead supposed that they would charge and carry the enemy's position, and so told Wilcox. Wilcox, as foreboding in his warning to Garnett's officers, continued to spread his gloomy message along Pickett's front, replying that there had already been heavy fighting over the fields in front of them the day previously, and that all that had been gained was given up when they retired. He pointed out that the Union line had almost twenty-four hours in which to strengthen their defenses on that front, and that it would not only be very difficult to dislodge them but would be a great sacrifice of life.[31]

Just as Wilcox was leaving to return to his own line, one of the passing shells struck a small hickory tree near Company E and ricochetted, severely wounding a soldier. This same shell barely missed General Armistead, and caused the company to begin moving to another, perhaps more secure shelter. Armistead, that "gallant, kind and urbane old veteran" reassured the men and halted them from their move with the words that they should "lie still boys, there is no safe place here."[32] To their relief, the shelling began to slow shortly afterwards.

The effects of the cannonade on Armistead's two left regiments appears to have been minimal, since there was scarcely any mention of it afterwards in personal reminiscences of the battle, except for a repetition of the general character of the chaos that befell the division as a whole. These men in the woods owned by Henry Spangler did not share the proximity to danger experienced by the men in Kemper's and Garnett's commands, nor were they privy to the demands and unforeseen shortcomings that would befall the artillery supports.

As previously stated, the cannonade by the Confederate artillery was intended to continue a mere fifteen minutes or so before the infantry advance was to begin, in order to assure that the artillery would have sufficient ammunition to support and advance with the attacking brigades. In preparation for this immediate move, Colonel E. P. Alexander sent for the nine howitzers to move up closer just before the signal guns were fired. This would have assured that they would be in the correct position to render the timely support that was planned for the coordinated artillery-infantry attack. Unfortunately, the guns could not be found, even after several messengers were sent by Colonel Alexander. Thus the cannonade got off to a bad start at the outset. Alexander continued his quest for the guns even after the cannonade opened, but did not discover until after the battle what had happened to them. His own artillery chief, General Pendleton, had ordered four of the guns to return to A. P. Hill's artillery line, and Major Richardson had moved off the other five to a more sheltered position when the shells began landing near them. Neither officer notified Alexander of these movements, and he expended meaningless energies in trying to locate them to provide the infantry advance with the support that had been planned.[33]

In addition, care had been taken to the "convenient posting" of the ordnance trains, particularly on the right of the line, which was the most advanced from Confederate positions and from the main ordnance depot. Pendleton made certain that the battery commanders knew the exact location of the First Corps ammunition depot in its reassigned locale so that they could replenish their ammunition in a timely manner. After about half an hour of the firing, Colonel Alexander concluded that it was apparent neither the Federals nor the Confederates were going to gain a clear advantage in the cannonade. Realizing that continued expenditure of ammunition would render ineffectual his support of the infantry assault, at about 1:30 P.M. Alexander relayed to General Pickett that he should "Hurry up, for God's sake, or the artillery can't help you."[34]

Pendleton, in the mean time, rode over to the Confederate right to see why the cannonade was taking so long, "delayed beyond expectation," and discovered that the batteries of Dearing's command as well as Eshleman's Battalion were low on ammunition. Turning his attention to replenishing their chests, Pendleton forgot to investigate the cause of the delay. He was instead mortified and horrified to find that the First Corps artillery train was not where he had ordered it to be parked. The Union overshots had endangered the train to such an extent that it it had become a necessity to move it farther to the rear. According to Pendleton, this "necessitated longer time for refilling caissons." Upon investigation, it was discovered that the supplies in the ordnance train itself were not what was expected or needed, and the stock of the First Corps was soon exhausted. Pendleton had nowhere to go but to the ordnance trains of the reserve train, which was even further off, thus prolonging the delays in replenishing the ammunition chests of the guns along Alexander's artillery line. The only solution to the predicament was to order a "relaxation of the protracted fire" and to cut back on the number of guns which would be sent in support of the infantry.[35]

Meanwhile, Colonel Alexander was visited by General Longstreet himself and briefed the First Corps commander about the ammunition difficulties. General Longstreet was alarmed enough to send orders to Pickett to have him halt where he was until the ammunition could be replenished. But Alexander reminded his superior that the Union artillery and infantry line would find this time to strengthen their own lines, and the supplies that could be recovered from the ordnance trains could lengthen the cannonade by merely fifteen minutes (about thirty rounds each per gun), and would therefore have little additional impact on the Yankee lines. With these chilling facts before him, General Longstreet was compelled to recall his orders just sent to Pickett to halt, and commanded Alexander to advance whatever artillery he could in aiding the attack.[36]

It appears that a visit to Dearing's Battalion convinced General Longstreet of the necessity of pushing the attack, and instigated his visit to Colonel Alexander. While on Dearing's front, Longstreet had seen that the enemy put fresh batteries in place almost as rapidly as others were driven off by Confederate fire. The commander concluded that, if any results were to be had before evening, the attack must be made almost immediately, after refilling the batteries' ammunition chests. His ride to the left of the artillery line, where Alexander was stationed, revealed to him the plethora of difficulties facing any coordinated effort by the artillery and infantry.[37]

Dearing's gunners knew as well as anybody the limited nature of their ammunition, and thus their power and ability to support effectively. Captain Stribling recognized that any well-sustained fire could not be kept up for much more than an hour because of the limited number of rounds that could be carried in the battery chests. Because Dearing and his officers were under the impression that the cannonade was to last only fifteen minutes, efforts were not made to replenish the supply. The batteries would still have enough for at least forty-five minutes more of firepower. Since they expected the order to advance would be forthcoming any moment, it was no wonder that Major Dearing and the other battery and battalion commanders did not take the time to send back the men and horses to bring up more ammunition. As the chests became emptied, however, it was a necessity to find more ammunition. Unfortunately, it was also at this very time, after almost an hour or a little more of sustained firing by the artillery, that the command for the infantry to advance was given.

It was hard on men such as Major James Dearing to be unable to fulfill the commands given to him. He had made himself conspicuous with his bravery during the cannonade, and had been seen by men in many of Pickett's regiments as he remained in the very front of the action. Colonel Joseph Mayo of the 3rd Virginia Regiment had noticed Major Dearing before the cannonade when the artilleryman rode out to the skirmish line to get a closer look at the Union lines upon which his guns were to concentrate. While there, a courier rode up from no less than General Lee himself with a message for Dearing. The major most likely thought it was a summons to brief the commander after his reconnaissance of the enemy, but was disappointed instead to read a reprimand in the dispatch. General Lee wrote: "Major Dearing, I do not approve of young officers needlessly exposing themselves; your place is with your batteries."[38] Colonels Patton and Mayo had seen the "gallant bearing" of Dearing during the cannonade while he galloped from gun to gun with the battalion flag in hand, presenting an inviting target for Union gunners. Fortunately, none were able to dismount him. He was there while the shelling was continuing to assure Colonel Eppa Hunton of the 8th Virginia that he would be going in with Garnett's Brigade during the charge. He was not foreseeing anything to prevent him from doing so, since he had always gone in with his division.[39]

The losses in men and horses and the expenditure of ammunition would inevitably shatter Dearing's expectations. In Blount's Battery alone five men were killed and 41 of the 48 horses on the line were felled. At one time the battery was the only one firing, probably towards the end of the cannonade, and this concentrated most of the Union fire upon them. Elcanah Campbell had much of his thigh shot away, and cried to his lieutenant, "I'm killed." Lieutenant Thompson was compelled to agree, but said "I can't do anything for you." "Can't you see me off?" he replied, but Thompson's other duties prevented him from doing so, although he assured Campbell that he would go with him. Campbell died, and was carried back to George Arnold's farm along Willoughby Run. Thompson remembered that his gunners and crew could see many of the enemy cannon balls coming at them, many ricochetting and bouncing along the ground. Private Martin Ferguson was not lucky enough to see one which struck him, just as he was ramming a charge home, and he was killed without warning. Lieutenant Thompson had few pleasant memories of that day, but one which would linger for over forty years was an incident involving fellow lieutenant James Dickerson. One of the artillerymen was standing near a battery horse whose head had just been shot off by a cannon ball. The man was struck with pieces of the horse's brains, blood, and head, which were spattered all over him. The man's only thought was that he himself had been hit, and he cried to Lieutenant Dickerson, "Look here, Lieutenant. Oh, I am killed! Lieutenant, look, my brains are all knocked out!"[40] It took some reassuring to convince the man he was unhurt. Dickerson then devoted his full energies to preparing his battery section for its intended and ultimate advance.

Although the right of Dearing's battalion was most likely concentrating its fire on the guns along McGilvery's line (on their flank), the majority of his guns were probably sending missiles towards the aiming point of the attack — the line of the Union Second Corps. Those survivors of this incoming fire would remember its destructiveness. The men of the 19th Massachusetts, just to the rear of the Copse of Trees, attested to the accuracy of the guns serviced by men such as those in Dearing's Battalion:

> The report from the second gun had not died away before another shot came over the ridge, striking among the gun stacks of the Nineteenth Massachusetts, and then every rebel gun on Seminary Ridge opened in one grand salvo, with concentric fire on Gibbon's Division...
>
> The air was full of grass and dirt cast from the soil by the jagged rebel iron... The rain of shot and shell was continuous. Fragments of bursting shell were flying everywhere. There seemed to be no place where thy did not strike and no spot from whence they did not come. Officers and men alike, keeping their alignment, crawled to places of apparent cover. Some got behind the few large boulders, others took advantage of depressions in the ground.
>
> So thick did the missiles fly that in a few moments nearly all of the inverted muskets were knocked down or shot off; pieces of shell were plainly visible as they hissed by; limber boxes and caissons were hit and blew up with stunning reports; the battery horses were nearly all shot down.[41]

In the ranks of the 143d Pennsylvania, to the left and rear of the main defensive line of Gibbon's Division on Cemetery Ridge, the words of a survivor of the cannonade echoed those of Armistead to his men:

> Such a storm of shell and solid shot was never heard before. No place was safe. They passed through the regt. killing and wounding, bursting over us, ploughing through the earth under us. It was our duty to remain where we were. There was no more lounging and not without casualties. We had 4 killed and 21 wounded out of less than 200. We remained quietly and firmly awaited orders.[42]

The sentiments of the men in this Union division which was destined to withstand Pickett's attack were summarized by their commander:

> The larger round shells could be seen plainly as in their nearly completed course they curved in their fall towards the Taneytown road, but the long rifled shells came with a rush and a scream and could only be seen in their rapid flight when they "upset" and went tumbling through the air, creating the uncomfortable impression that, no matter whether you were in front of the gun from which they came or not, you were liable to be hit. Every moment or so one would burst, throwing its fragments about in a most disagreeably promiscuous manner, or, first striking the ground, plough a great furrow in the earth and rocks, throwing these last about in a way quite as dangerous as the pieces of exploding shell.... Over all hung a heavy pall of smoke underneath which could be seen the rapidly moving legs of the men as they rushed to and fro between the pieces and the line of limbers, carrying forward the ammunition.... Of course, it would be absurd to say we were not scared. How is it possible for a sentient being to be in such a place and not experience a sense of alarm? None but fools, I think, can deny that they are afraid in battle....
>
> Getting tired of seeing men and horses torn to pieces and observing that although some of the shells struck and burst among us, most of them went high and bust behind us, the idea occurred to me that a position further to the front would be safer and rising to my feet, I walked forward.... I had made but a few steps when three of Cushing's limber boxes blew up at once, sending the contents in a vast column of dense smoke high in the air, and above the din could be heard the triumphant yells of the enemy as he recognized the result of his fire.[43]

Confederates Waiting For The End Of The Artillery Duel
(Battles and Leaders of the Civil War)

Smoke now covered much of the battlefield, dissipating slowly to the north and east as fewer and fewer guns recoiled with shot. Generals Longstreet and Pendleton, Colonel Alexander, and Major Dearing now recognized the proposed infantry advance was to be made without the artillery support envisioned and planned by General Lee. The men of Pickett's Division were unaware that their task was now a solitary one, and that the supports calculated to protect and strengthen them had been unwittingly taken from them. Impatient to prove their worth as a fighting unit after months of relative inaction, relieved to be free of the incessant Union shelling, Pickett's men prepared to be launched into the annals of military history. They did not know that they were going to prove merely that they day of the unsupported infantry assault was coming to an end.

Position of Pickett's Division Before the Attack

The modern view looks northwestward along the front of Kemper's Brigade during the cannonade and before the attack. The camera position is approximately at the location held by the 24th Virginia on the extreme right. The Spangler Farm buildings appear in the front of Spangler's woods, where the brigade first aid station was located. (Photographed by Kathy Georg Harrison)

Chapter

IV

"The Marching was Beautifully Exact"

W hen Colonel E. P. Alexander sent final word to Generals Pickett and James J. Pettigrew (on Pickett's left) that they must advance then if at all, his reasoning was based on the fact that most of his guns now had a mere five to fifteen rounds each left in their chests.[1] If the assault was delayed any longer, there would be no artillery support whatsoever. Word reached the two generals as the last shots of the cannonade were reverberating against the stony ridges south of Gettysburg. Pickett rode over to his commanding officer, General Longstreet (who was most likely in the area of the Spangler Woods, and nearby to Colonel Alexander), and there received the now-famous tear-choked nod of the head to proceed with the assault.

General George E. Pickett thereupon began the first strides of his horse along his lines to pass on the words of command and to begin the legend that would be known for decades as "Pickett's Charge." The command was most likely given to Armistead first, since he would have been in the greatest proximity to Pickett at the outset, but none in Armistead's Brigade later wrote of seeing such an exchange. Continuing his ride to the right of his line, Pickett next passed the regiments of Garnett's Brigade. Private William P. Jesse remembered seeing Generals Longstreet and Lee with him at the time General Pickett conveyed the orders to advance.[2] This may have been due to the fact that the two higher-ranking officers were in the vicinity of Spangler Woods at the outset of the attack. Another member of the 28th Virginia in Garnett's Brigade recalled seeing Pickett ride in front of the brigade and give the command "Forward!" to which every man responded.[3] Private Robert Damron of Company D, 56th Virginia in Garnett's Brigade heard General Pickett himself give the command to go forward to his part of the line, before the general resumed his gallop toward Kemper's Brigade. As he passed the extreme left of Kemper's line, the colonel of the 3d Virginia heard General Pickett call out for the men to raise to their feet and prepare for the advance, closing with "Remember Old Virginia!"[4] Continuing on to the next regiment, the 7th Virginia, Pickett gave a similar entreaty: "Up, men, and to your posts! Don't forget today that you are from Old Virginia." That General Pickett himself did not appear to have advanced beyond the 7th seems to have been confirmed by no less than General Kemper himself, who would have been with or near the center regiment (the 1st Virginia). Kemper revealed that he received his orders not from Pickett, but through Pickett's volunteer aide Captain Robert A. Bright, who galloped up to the general. As he rose

View From Pickett's Left Before the Attack

This modern view is taken from the position held by the last guns on the left of Alexander's cannonade line, and from in front of the extreme left flank of Garnett's Brigade. The position of the Union line on Cemetery Ridge was visible from Ziegler's Grove on the left to the present Clump of Trees at the right of the photograph. Garnett's line of march would take him in the direction of the intermittent trees on the horizon. (Photograph by Kathy Georg Harrison)

View From Garnett's Position Before the Attack

The modern view from the left of Garnett's Brigade is almost due east towards the Union positions of Stannard's Brigade and McGilvery's artillery line. Those Union positions were not visible from this point because of the rising ridge on the west side of the Emmitsburg Road. The 1883 Codori Barn is visible to the left-center (the house being obscured by non-historic trees). The ground over which Kemper's Brigade would march by the left flank and obliquely covers that ridge from the right of the photograph to the Codori Barn. (Photographed by Kathy Georg Harrison)

41

to meet him, Kemper removed a handkerchief from under his hat, which he had used to cover his face during the cannonade in order to keep the dust and dirt out of his eyes. Bright's only orders to Kemper were, "General Pickett orders you to advance your brigade immediately." A glance to the left showed General Kemper that Garnett and Armistead had already received these orders and that they were executing the movement before him.[5]

Colonel Louis Williams, commanding the 1st Virginia in the center of Kemper's Brigade line, was nearby to Kemper when Captain Bright rode up and rushed forward to tell the staff officer, "Captain Bright, I wish to ride my mare up." Bright protested, reiterating orders which had been conveyed that all officers would go into battle on foot. Williams replied, "But you will let me ride. I am sick to-day, and, besides that, remember Williamsburg." Recalling that Colonel Williams had been wounded in that 1862 battle, Captain Bright relented, and told the regimental commander, "Mount your mare, and I will make an excuse for you."[6]

The orders which had been passed to brigade commanders to prevent field and staff officers from riding into the assault were supposed to aid in saving the lives not only of horses, but also of valuable officers. The terrain over which Pickett's Division was to advance was completely open and devoid of cover, with the exception of an occasional tree or hedgerow. There was no other vegetation to offer cover. Only the intervening crest of the ridgeline which ran obliquely between the Emmitsburg Road and Seminary Ridge could provide any kind of barrier to artillery and infantry fire. For this reason it was already being used to shelter the brigades at this point. The multitudinous rows of rail fencing which checker-boarded the terrain in the fields that intervened between Union and Confederate lines would provide more of an obstacle than a shelter to the advancing lines. The men would have to climb over these fences, go around them, or tear them down under enemy fire before reaching Yankee lines.

The order of battle for Kemper's Brigade, as in the other brigades of Pickett's Division, was the outcome of the order of march to the battlefield from Marsh Creek in the early morning hours of July 3d. As a result, the brigade's battle line as it prepared for the advance placed the 24th Virginia Infantry Regiment on the extreme right of the division and Kemper's Brigade, with the 1st Virginia in the center of the brigade, flanked on the right by the 11th Regiment and on the left by the 7th Regiment. The 3rd Virginia was the left regiment of Kemper's Brigade, and that on which Garnett's Brigade was originally ordered to guide its movements.

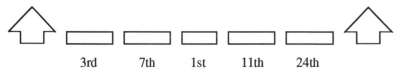

3rd   7th   1st   11th   24th

The report of the 24th Virginia Infantry, never formally submitted and incorporated into the post-war Official Records, described the initial movements of Kemper's Brigade during this advance after orders were relayed by Colonel Terry to prepare to advance. The brigade moved immediately by the left flank for the depth of a regiment (perhaps as much as 250-300 yards if the size of the 24th

Regiment itself was the guide for sizing the "depth of a regiment").[7] This was probably done under orders of General Kemper to rectify what he saw as an increasing and divergent interval in the lines created by the earlier movements of General Garnett and Armistead.[8] That the two brigades on the left were ordered to advance before Kemper seems illogical, merely because Kemper's regiments had the greatest distance to march in order to reach what ultimately became their objective. Whereas Garnett and Armistead both had to cover approximately 1200 yards to reach the Union lines, Kemper's movements required that he cover over 1500 yards. The move by Kemper to the left flank was intended to help direct his advance towards the objective conveyed by Bright — a "red barn" that was a prominent landmark feature along the Emmitsburg Road.[9] This red barn was probably the red brick farmhouse of Nicholas Codori. It was apparently selected as the aiming point because of its high visibility once the initial ridge crest was crossed. The advance of the 24th Virginia, after the movement to the left, was alternately to the front and by the left flank in order to align its movements with those of General Garnett's brigade. As soon as the regiment reached the crest of the Emmitsburg Road, however, it received the musketry fire from the enemy's skirmishers and advanced men of Stannard's Vermont Brigade. Throughout this flanking fire, especially as it executed the movements by the left flank, the regiment received the benefit of strong discipline in not pausing to return the fire.[10]

In the 11th Virginia, on the left of Terry's 24th Regiment, it appeared that many of the men would not be able to join in the advance because of the effects of the oppressive heat. Captain James Hutter appealed to the men of the regiment in the name of Virginia to go if possible. Captain Hutter went from company to company, trying to rally the men to their duty. Haunting the ranks of Company G, Hutter seemed relentless in his efforts to persuade one particular soldier to get up and go with his comrades. Captain John Holmes Smith, commanding Company G, found out what was going on. Resenting Hutter's interference in his command, he curtly defended his man to Hutter, saying, "When he says he is sick, he is sick." With that Hutter returned to his duties as acting lieutenant colonel of the regiment, and soon after found himself in a predicament of his own. The regiment was encountering a white weatherboard farmhouse that formed an obstacle fouling the line. Because of the series of movements by the left flank, this house could have been the Rogers Farmhouse, on the west side of the Emmitsburg Road.[11] Hutter was originally ordered by the regiment's adjutant, Lieutenant Valentine Harris, to maneuver the right wing (then under the direct command of Hutter) around the house. Captain Hutter believed the obstacle too large for such a movement and ordered instead, "by right of company to the front." When even a company front seemed inadequate for the obstacle, Hutter commanded two companies to march by right and left flanks respectively to pass the house and the fencing enclosing its yard. As this movement was occurring, Hutter was informed that Major Kirkwood Otey had been wounded and that he was now in command of the 11th. Hutter tried to find someone to take charge of the right wing, but found after sending successively for Captains Andrew Jones of Company I, David Houston of Company D, and Andrew Houston of Company K that all were wounded or mortally wounded. While engaged with this dilemma of trying to find who was the surviving senior captain on the field, Captain Hutter was confronted with a relentless pressure on his right flank from the 24th Virginia, which was forcing the advance into a left oblique. At this point, Colonel Williams of the 1st Virginia rode up and demanded that Hutter do something with his men, as they were crowding him out of line. With his own companies trying to get realigned while suffering from the heavy musketry and artillery fire coming from the front and right flank, Hutter became understandably angry, and retorted, "If you will go and attend to that damned little squad of yours, and let my Regiment alone we will get along better." His reference to the 1st Virginia as a "little squad" was in response to the small numbers of Williams' regiment, the smallest in the division, and must have caused Hutter to immediately regret his words, for he hastily added that he was having his own difficulties by being pressed on his own right by the 24th.[12]

Company D, which would have the smallest casualty rate in the regiment that day, was on skirmish detail. Its captain, David Houston, had been assisting Major Otey in command of the regiment while the skirmishers were under command of Lieutenant John Thomas James. Lieutenant James was responsible for clearing the regimental front of Union sharpshooters and skirmishers along and beyond the Emmitsburg Road. His duties would have thrown the company as far as 300 yards in front of his brigade. But, instead of being exposed in its forward position, Company D found itself the most fortunate unit in the regiment. According to Lieutenant James, it appeared that the Union lines continually fired over the heads of his skirmish line, "seeming to prefer the larger mass" of the division behind them, and thus the company was spared the casualties which were to be inflicted on the other companies of the 11th Regiment.[13] James, obviously busy with events in his own front, did not have the opportunity to glance over his shoulder at the movements of the brigade as often as he would have liked. To his chagrin, he discovered that while he and his company had been advancing to the front, the regiment had been obliquing to the left and not following them. Trying to rectify his movements with those of the regiment, Lieutenant James attempted to get his men to move to the left and rejoin the brigade, but the noise and confusion was so great and his line of skirmishers spread out in so long a line that his efforts were a failure. Most of the skirmishers were fighting their own foray on a front far to the right of Pickett's Division, and would soon only be able to watch while the "death rate increased" as Kemper's Brigade neared the enemy's position without them.[14]

The casualties being inflicted on the 11th Virginia Regiment as it paralleled the Emmitsburg Road and moved obliquely to the left towards the Codori Farm buildings did much to dampen the ardor first expressed at the close of the cannonade. At that time, when the command came to advance, Private Charles Jones of Company C was among the first to his feet, calling out to the men of all ranks in the regiment, "Come on, boys, let's go and drive away those infernal Yankees." Charles Jones would not be returning to his farm after this advance, for one of those infernal Yankees killed this enthusiastic farmer during the attack. Company C lost others of its members, including Private Dabney Tweedy, another young farmer. He was wounded in the knee and carried to the rear on a stretcher with his lifeblood fast

44

"Part of Ground of Pickett's Charge, July 3rd, 1863"
This view was taken by Gettysburg photographer William H. Tipton in the early 1870's. It starkly shows the formidable nature of the post and rail fencing which enclosed the Emmitsburg Road, and the sunken nature of that road, especially in front of the Codori Farmhouse. The wartime appearance of that brick dwelling is visible on the horizon to the left of the road. The outbuildings on the right side of the photograph were not standing at the time of the attack. (Gettysburg NMP)

flowing, singing a hymn which he and his messmates had shared on many an occasion. Robert W. Morgan, in the army barely a year, was wounded in both feet. While going forward he was struck on the instep of his right foot with a minie ball and halted to ascertain whether or not he was hurt enough to go to the rear. While examining his foot, another ball struck his left foot at the base of his toes and tore its way through the length of the foot, stopping at the heel. No longer a question as to whether or not he could go on with the advance, Private Morgan picked up his musket and another lying nearby. Using them as crutches, he hobbled to the rear, where he was met and taken care of by the family's faithful Negro servant, Horace.[15]

Captain John Homes Smith, who had been so perturbed by Captain Hutter's "worrying" of his men before the advance, had only about nineteen men in the ranks after the casualties of the cannonade. As skirmishers of the regiment under Lieutenant James were thrown forward at the command "Attention," the remainder of the body of the regiment was ordered not to fire until commanded to do so. During the advance, Smith was surprised that the Union skirmishers were not giving ground, and that they had seemed to have brought the division's skirmish line to a halt. Indeed, when the 11th Regiment had come up within one hundred yards of their own skirmish line, some Confederate skirmishers began to fall back, firing as they went, and soon rejoined the brigade line. The Union skirmishers, on the other hand, continued firing and did not fall back to their lines. They were soon caught between the fire of Pickett's Division and their comrades, causing many to throw down their muskets and come into the line of the 11th Virginia for refuge from this crossfire.[16]

The "Old First" was to hold the center of the brigade line during the advance. Colonel Williams mounted his mare, Nelly, in time for the advance. Nelly had been brought from the rear by Jacob Polak just as the command to advance was given. After turning the mare over to his colonel, Polak returned to his place in the ranks while Colonel Williams mounted and wheeled in front of the regiment.[17] Whereas men in the ranks felt relief just to be rid of the long strain of waiting,[18] and finally to be able to rise and advance, there were others who had opposing sensations. Lieutenant John Dooley of Company C of the 1st Virginia Infantry eloquently spoke for this other segment of the brigade:

> ... when you rise to your feet as we did today, I tell you the enthusiasm of ardent breasts in many cases ain't there, and instead of burning to avenge the insults of our country, families and altars and firesides, the thought is most frequently, Oh, if I could just come out of this charge safely how thankful would I be!
>
> We rise to our feet, but not all. There is a line of men still on the ground with their faces turned, men affected in 4 different ways. There are the gallant dead who will never charge again; the helpless wounded, many of whom desire to share the fortunes of this charge; the men who have charged on many a battlefield but who are now helpless from the heat of the sun; and the men in whom there is not sufficient courage to enable them to rise....
>
> Some are actually fainting from the heat and dread. They have fallen to the ground overpowered by the suffocating heat and the terrors of that hour.[19]

Colonel Louis B. Williams (1833-1863)
1st Virginia Infantry
(killed during the advance)

Nevertheless, the small Richmond regiment presented about 200 men to their colonel before Company D was dispatched to the front as skirmishers. When the order was given to start forward, the color bearer and guard of the 1st Virginia stepped four paces to the front of the regimental line, where they would maintain that distance until one after another they were to be shot down in the advance and attack. Color Sergeant William M. Lawson of Company H would carry the regimental colors as he had done since May 1862 when he joined the color guard. He was accompanied by his guard: Pat Woods, Private Theodore R. Martin (also of Company H), Corporal John Q. Figg of Company B, and Private Willie Mitchel of Company D. Mitchel, son of an exiled Irish patriot, was wounded sometime before the regiment reached the Codori Farm buildings, but insisted on staying with the colors. About one hundred yards further and he would be struck down again and killed,[20] the first of the color guard to be lost to the regiment. Another one of the regiment to fall wounded during this advance was Private Samuel Sloan of Company C. His namesake owned the farm on which he fell some sixty years previously; a Samuel Sloan was the original settler on the battlefield's Codori Farm.

Colonel Williams, spurring his mount back to his command after his confrontation with Captain Hutter of the 11th Virginia, was soon knocked out of the saddle by a ball in his shoulder near the Codori Farmhouse. In falling from Nelly, Colonel Williams reputedly fell on his own drawn sword and was killed. Had he not been mounted he would not have presented such a visible target. The ball which struck him in the shoulder would have surely passed over his head.[21] Williams' insistence that he be permitted to ride his mare into the battle may have written his epitaph. Not yet thirty years of age, Colonel Williams had left a distinguished career as a lawyer and a professor at the Virginia Military Institute to serve his native state only to be killed before even reaching the enemy's lines. Nelly, however, continued on without her rider, keeping up with the men in the charge. Colonel Mayo of the 3d Virginia could envision her in later years limping and sadly crippled coming back down from Cemetery Ridge after the attack.[22]

In the ranks of the 7th Virginia Infantry Regiment, to the left of the center regiment, Color Sergeant G. W. Watson of Company F stepped to the front to bear the regimental colors. David Johnston, struck in the back by the exploding shell during the cannonade, was not to be among those to fall in behind the flag. He was one of Lieutenant Dooley's "helpless wounded" propped in the shade of the same tree under which he had been sheltered from the sun in the morning and early afternoon hours. He watched his comrades as they marched over the crest of the little ridge in his front to the Emmitsburg Road and out of sight, but within ten minutes the wounded men came streaming back over that ridge. A wounded lieutenant, passing Johnston, picked up a fallen limb of the apple tree and covered the headless bodies of Albert Morris and Benjamin Jackson of the 8th Virginia, which still lay at the feet of Johnston. Grateful for the lieutenant's attempt to spare Johnston's sensitivity, the non-commissioned officer nevertheless concentrated his attention on the seemingly endless stream of wounded and "malingerers" leaving Pickett's column and flowing to the rear past him.[23]

The men of the 3rd Virginia Regiment had fallen into ranks under the eye of General Pickett himself, with his admonition to "Remember Old Virginia" ringing in their ears. As the men prepared to advance, Colonel Joseph Mayo passed along the ranks giving no further commands than those conveyed by Pickett. Mayo was affected by the sight of Joshua Murden, the color-bearer who had left his life as a mechanic at Portsmouth two years ago, "as fine a type of true soldiership as ever stepped beneath the folds of the spotless stars and bars, now lying there stark and stiff, a hideous hole sheer through his stalwart body." Murden was killed during the cannonade, fulfilling his duty to his flag to the end. His right hand was closed in a death grip around its staff, the color-bearer clinging to his death to the new flag which had been unfurled for the first time that day. Murden was the first to die guarding this regimental color which would "for the first and last time" brave the breeze and the battle.[24]

Soon after going through and clearing Dearing's guns, Colonel Mayo found that he would have to change direction to the left again. While Mayo was executing this movement under the fire from Cemetery Ridge and from Little Round Top's battery, General Pickett cautioned him to maintain the proper interval between Kemper's Brigade and Garnett's Brigade. As the left of Kemper's Brigade approached the Emmitsburg Road, Kemper rode up and commanded that Mayo keep control of matters on the left flank of the brigade, while he rode back to see what troops were coming up in the rear. Looking back, Colonel Mayo saw a line "compact and solid as a wedge," marching rapidly at a left oblique, which turned out to be Armistead's Brigade. Mayo could hear the rousing cheer of Armistead's men as they greeted Kemper, cantering up to their front on his "mettlesome sorrel." Looking back to his front and the left again, Mayo could see General Pickett and some of his staff officers, including Lieutenant Stuart Symington and Captain "Ned" Baird, trying to stop a disorderly crowd of men heading for the rear. On his own front, Mayo observed one of his captains looking "lazy and lackadaisacal" to the point of looking bored. Pleading with his company, "Don't crowd, boys; don't crowd," the captain rested his sword point on his shoulder as Colonel Mayo approached him. "Pretty hot, Captain," Mayo commented, referring to the Yankee musketry and artillery that was pouring into them as they approached the Codori buildings. "It's redicklous, Colonel; perfectly redicklous," replied the captain, which, according to Mayo meant "as bad as bad could be."[25]

Kemper's Brigade was having somewhat of a hot time indeed during its advance to the red building on the Emmitsburg Road. It was subjected to the firepower of over forty cannon stretching from Meade's left center towards Little Round Top, as well as to the heavy skirmish line of Stannard's Brigade and Gibbon's Division. On its left Garnett's Brigade did not have to execute the kinds of left-flank maneuvers which exposed Kemper's flank to the enemy, but it was nonetheless exposed to the artillery fire from the front and from Little Round Top.

Garnett's Brigade was destined to cross the crest of the ridge where it obliqued from the road. It then had to march across open fields for several hundred yards without the protection of the ridge, before reaching the sunken Emmitsburg Road and its row of parallel post and rail fencing. As in Kemper's Brigade, the regiments went into the battle line as a result of the formation they had adopted en route to the battlefield in the morning hours, with the leading regiment taking position on the right of the line of the brigade.

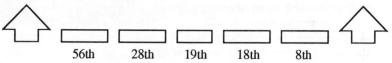

56th   28th   19th   18th   8th

Thus, the 8th Virginia Regiment was stationed on the right of the brigade, with 200 muskets and twenty officers reporting for duty at the close of the cannonade.[26] Colonel Eppa Hunton was relieved of commanding Garnett's Brigade just before the order to charge was given, when General Richard Garnett rode up on horseback to resume command of his brigade. Colonel Hunton could see that he was still in pain from the leg injury and so was unfit for active service, but Garnett's desire to be with his brigade on this day "could not be restrained."[27] Mounted on his big bay thoroughbred, Red Eye, Garnett was wearing a "fine, new gray uniform" purchased in Richmond when the Brigade passed through there in June.[28] Private James W. Clay of the 18th Virginia noted that the uniform coat had a general's star and a wreath on the collar, and covered trousers which were tucked into top boots. Garnett was wearing a black felt hat with a silver cord, which he took off now and again to cheer on the brigade.[29]

The officers of the 8th Virginia were near enough to General Garnett to hear a brief conversation transpire between himself and General Pickett as the command was given to begin the assault. Lieutenant Colonel Norbonne Berkeley and his brother William overheard Pickett say, "Dick, old fellow, I have no orders to give you, but I advise you to get across those fields as quick as you can, for in my opinion you are going to catch hell."[30]

Colonel Hunton sent Company H out as skirmishers for the regiment, with the orders that they drive in Union sharpshooters and tear down obstructing fences, in hopes that they could in some small way help the 8th Virginia to cross those fields as quickly as possible and to catch less hell. Private Randolph Shotwell, with Company H, was therefore one of the first in Garnett's Brigade to get a glimpse of the enemy they were expected to assail and the grounds over which they would pass. Crowning the crest of Cemetery Ridge were scores of flags, waving above stone brestworks and masses of blue-coated soldiers. The only major obstruction in the line of march of the 8th Virginia appeared to be the Codori Farm buildings.[31] In their rear they heard the command given to "Forward! Guide on the right. March!" and Shotwell looked back to see General Pickett on the crest among the artillery pieces, sending forward his brother Charles to command the skirmishers to maintain an interval of about 120 yards in front of the division. Shotwell's view of the division was much closer but similar to that presented to the Federals on Cemetery Ridge:

> Now we hear the murmur and jingle of a large corps in motion. Colonels on horseback ride slowly over the brow of the ridge; followed by a glittering forest of bright bayonets. The whole column is now within sight, coming down the slope with steady step and superb alignment. The rustle of thousands of feet amid the stubble stirs a cloud of dust, like the dash of spray at the prow of a vessel. The flags flutter and snap — the sunlight flashes from the officer's swords — low words of command are heard—and thus in perfect order, this gallant array of gallant men marches straight down into the valley of Death! Two armies, for a moment, look on, apparently spell-bound; then the spell is broken by the crash of one hundred guns trained upon the advancing troops. Shot, shell, spherical case, shrapnel and canister — thousands of deadly missiles racing through the air to thin our ranks![32]

Soon after he saw the brigades of Garnett and Kemper surmount the small ridge crest beyond the Emmitsburg Road, Shotwell would have seen Kemper's Brigade make another of his movements towards the left. The circumstances of that movement were related by an officer on Garnett's right flank, who saw a mounted officer gallop up to General Garnett. Word was soon sent to Garnett's regimental commanders to "dress to the left on Pettigrew." Since the original order of the day was that Garnett's Brigade was to have dressed to the right on Kemper, Kemper's Brigade being the battalion of direction, word would have to be sent to Kemper as well. George Hummer, serving as orderly to Colonel Hunton stated that he did not see any orders being sent to General Kemper, and asked his colonel if he could go over and inform the general. Hunton agreed, and sent Hummer on his way. Since Hunton was on horseback due to old illnesses and war wounds, his orderly was probably mounted as well in order to keep up with him. Hummer proceeded as rapidly as possible to General Kemper and relayed the orders which had been given to Garnett. Kemper replied that he had not received such orders himself, but would obey them even though he had received them in such an unofficial fashion.[33]

Kemper then ordered his own brigade to dress to the left on Garnett, executing a movement which may have been misinterpreted as a "half wheel" by observers on the Union line. Major Berkeley believed that this change of dress from right to left by the two lead brigades in Pickett's Division was indeed seen by the Federals as the more difficult "half wheel" movement, an action that would have been quite complicated for a line a half mile long under artillery and musketry fire. The enfilading fire from Little Round Top continued to be very destructive; one shot passing over the 8th Virginia was seen to kill three or four men in the 18th Virginia Regiment.[34]

Among those to fall during the advance of the 18th Virginia were two of the color bearers. The regimental colors were eventually carried by Lieutenant Colonel Henry A. Carrington, who bore them to the enemy's works.[35] Adjutant Richard Ferguson admired the way the regiment continued moving forward steadily and promptly despite this destructive fire, while he was even more impressed with the handsome maneuvers of his skirmish line (Company G).[36] Captain Henry T. Owen of Company C believed that the enemy's skirmishers were more impressive. From their prostrate positions in the tall grass, they had fired at the column since it had come into their view. When within fifty yards of the Union skirmishers, the 18th Virginia could see the enemy rise up from their concealments as a unit and fire a volley into their front. From that point these Federal skirmishers trotted to the rear, keeping ahead of Garnett's brigade, reloading and firing as quickly as possible as they went.

Approaching the Emmitsburg Road, the column received the orders to "left oblique" (probably those given to Garnett to dress on Pettigrew) and the direction of march was changed forty-five degrees from the front towards the left. As the regiment neared the sunken roadway, a line of Union infantry was detected "stationed behind a stone fence" there,[37] pouring a heavy fire of musketry into the Confederate ranks. Unable to restrain themselves any longer, individual members of the 18th Virginia, as well as those in adjoining regiments, responded with a sporadic fire. This brought almost immediate reaction from General Garnett, who rode along the front of his line commanding the men to "Cease firing." Those who had been firing reloaded their guns and, shouldering them again, continued on with the brigade at the quickstep. The very strength of the brigade front overpowered the Union skirmish line at the Emmitsburg Road, which was "swept away before the division like trash before the broom." Initial resistance on their front seemed amazingly light, but the men began to realize that although two-thirds of the distance had been crossed they were not hearing any response from the cannon in their rear to those "hotly worked guns" on their front.[38]

In Garnett's center regiment, the 19th Virginia Infantry, Lieutenant William N. Wood (Company A) shared these mutual concerns. His earliest thoughts during the advance had turned to the "singular excitement" that electrified the regiment at the very first command, "Attention!" He was appalled by the numbers of men who fell from apparent sunstroke, "with dreadful contortions of the body, foaming at the mouth, and almost lifeless." These unfortunate men were carried to the shade and order had to be restored to the ranks before the command "advance" could be given.

The initial movement brought them to the crest of the ridge with their artillery, where a brief halt was made and opportunity was afforded Lieutenant Wood to look up and down the magnificent line. Kemper's line was moving forward on the right and Armistead seemed to be marching more quickly in their left and rear to close the distance between them. Seeing Armistead's long line of battle moving together in unison, Wood recalled once again Dearing's words and began to believe them: "That hill must fall." As they resumed the advance at common marching time, the excitement had waned in the men of the 19th Virginia. Orders were relayed to guide their actions and emotions: "Steady, boys," "Don't fire," "Close up," and "Never mind the skirmish line." Up to this point, the brigade had not incurred many casualties. But as it clambered over the fencing between the ridge and the Emmitsburg Road, its men could see more artillery being brought up on the enemy's lines. The artillery fire reopened upon them with a vengeance, and soon was joined by musketry. Lieutenant Wood noticed how thin the ranks were getting.[39]

At the left-center of the brigade, the 28th Virginia was commanded by Colonel Robert C. Allen. Major Nathaniel C. Wilson, who was acting as lieutenant colonel of the regiment, quickly jotted an entry in his daily journal before the 19th began its forward movements. Taking a place in front of the left wing when the advance began, Major Wilson called out to his men, "Now, boys, put your trust in God, and follow me!" Before one-third of the distance was covered, the major was pierced by a grape shot while leading the advance of the regiment, and was carried back to the division hospital at Bream's Mill. His condition was such that nothing could be done to save him, and he died within fifteen or twenty minutes after his arrival there. His last words, which were spoken to the regimental chaplain, Reverend Peter Tinsley, reflected his calm acceptance of his faith: "Tell my mother I died a true soldier, and I hope a good Christian." Upon his death, Chaplain Tinsley looked about for a coffin for this officer of his regiment. However, he was unable to procure one and so was compelled to wrap Major Wilson in his military overcoat and use his army blanket as a coffin and a shroud. Tinsley could reassure his comrades and friends that their Nathaniel Wilson died calmly: "His features were not distorted, but as placid and natural as if quietly sleeping in bivouac, with his comrades around him." His diary entry, the last thoughts penned before the chaos of war again invaded his senses, echoed his first command to his troops and his last words to his chaplain:

> July 3. In line of battle, expecting to move forward every minute. With our trust in God, we fear not an earthly enemy. God be with us![40]

Thus died the "true soldier" and the "true Christian," his last thought and words reflecting sentiments common to soldiers in both armies — thoughts of mother and home, thoughts of his soldierly bearing, and thoughts of his faith.

Major Wilson was not the only loss in the 28th Virginia during this advance and perhaps not even the most conspicuous. The story of a loss in Captain Michael P. Spessards's Company C would be widespread after the battle. Colonel Eppa Hunton of the 8th Virginia noticed Captain Spessard seated on the ground with the head of a young man cradled in his lap. As Hunton approached, Spessard looked up and implored, "Look at my poor boy, Colonel." Leaving his canteen of water with his son, Captain Spessard kissed him tenderly and laid his head on the ground to resume command of his company. Rising to his feet, the captain put his sword to his shoulder and ordered "Forward, boys!" to his command. The pathetic and touching scene must have reminded eyewitnesses of the words to a song popular during the war:

> Father, I have done my duty in the camp and 'mid the strife;
> Soon I'll seal my deep devotion to my country with my life.
> But it soothes my dying moments when I know that you are by
> Put your loving arms around me; kiss me father, ere I die.[41]

After the mortal wounding of his son Hezekiah, Captain Spessard seemed instilled with a vibrant fervor to get the attack over with as quickly as possible — to exact retribution on his enemies and return to his son. A private in Company F noted that Captain Spessard seemed inclined to press forward in advance of the other companies in the regiment during the latter part of this advance. Colonel Allen had to order him to keep in line with the regimental colors in order to hold him back from single-handedly dealing with the Federals.[42]

The duties of the 56th Virginia Regiment during the advance initially were to dress to the right, with the remainder of the brigade dressing to the left on their movements in order to close any gaps in the line as men were killed or wounded. From the ranks of Company D Private Robert Damron could see General Pickett following them for a short while during the advance, with his headquarters flag flapping in the breeze. Lieutenant George W. Finley of Company K had seen Pickett dash out of Spangler's Woods at the conclusion of the cannonade and speak to the brigade in words he could not hear about what was expected of them. Lieutenant Finley remembered seeing the division commander ride off to the right after giving the orders of advance, and never saw him again during the attack.[43]

Although Company D was ordered to advance at trail arms and quick step, Lieutenant Finley recalled that the orders were to advance slowly and with arms "at will." Other orders included no cheering or firing, no breaking from common step to quickstep until told to do so, and to dress on the center of the regiment. After passing through the guns of Alexander's line and crossing the crest of the little protecting ridgeline, the men got their first view of the Union position. Finley and his comrades noted a kind of restlessness in the Yankees which they hoped meant there would be no stubborn resistance, but they also noticed the number of "thickly planted" artillery pieces in rear of the first infantry line. The fencing immediately began to pose a challenge to the advance, and a worm fence was scaled by the regiment. The line had to be reformed after that, and then continued over the open fields again under increasing artillery fire. The regiment was particularly hurt by the enfilading fire from Little Round Top. A shell exploding from there in front of Company D knocked down five men, killing two and wounding three. Another shot felled sixteen men in Company C, to the right of the color company. Lieutenant Finley may have noted the latter shot when he reported seeing a company a little to his right being swept almost to a man from the line by a single shell from Little Round Top.[44]

Colonel William D. Stuart fell mortally wounded not far beyond the guns of Alexander's line, a victim of either the Union skirmishers or the death-dealing artillery on the Union Second Corps front. With no other field officer present with the regiment, the command devolved upon the senior captain as the regiment moved steadily on and the fire from the Union lines increased in intensity and accuracy. Because of the oblique angle at which the attack met the Union lines, the men on the left of Garnett's Brigade could see Kemper's Brigade becoming engaged with the enemy before they themselves did. Kemper was hotly engaged before Garnett's left was even within musket range. And, when the 56th approached that range at about the Emmitsburg Road, Lieutenant Finley was relieved that the enemy seemed to be overshooting them because they were higher on the ridge than the advancing Confederates.[45] Even the mounted General Garnett was unscathed by this musketry fire as the brigade reached the post and rail fencing enclosing the Emmitsburg Road.

Because Armistead's Brigade was behind the other two brigades of Pickett's Division during the advance, its men were not exposed to the brunt of fire that was poured into the fronts of Garnett and Kemper as soon as the latter two crossed the oblique ridge. Nevertheless, the Union artillery played upon this large target as long as it could before devoting its energies to other segments of the assaulting column. The front presented by Armistead's Brigade was larger than that of either Garnett or Kemper because its strength was at least twenty percent greater than either of its fellows.

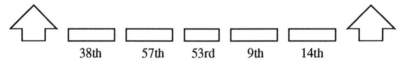

38th   57th   53rd   9th   14th

With their front covered by the other two brigades during the initial part of the advance, the first casualties incurred by Armistead's regiments can be attributed to the Union artillery. On the right end of Armistead's line, the 14th Virginia, under command of Colonel James G. Hodges, was no exception. A single shell killed Captain Richard Logan of Company H, and felled nine others in the company, accounting for one-third of their total casualties for the day.[46] Sergeant William B. Robertson of Company I was game to follow the orders given the regiment after the cannonade, "Now Boys, try them with your bayonet!" but when about halfway across the fields Robertson's enthusiasm was dampened. A shell fragment cut his waist belt, tore his jacket, and "frazzled" the skin of his hip, momentarily impeding his progress and shaking him up. Resuming his place with the column he was almost immediately bowled over by another shell burst which laid him low. After recovering his senses, Sergeant Robertson staggered to his feet and returned to the rear,[47] having seen enough of the action to realize that the 14th Virginia was in it "hot and heavy." Even from his position he could measure the heat of the battle. He proclaimed to a loved one at home in later correspondence: "You may judge of how severe the fire was between the contending armies when I say that the green grass burned swiftly — being set on fire by the guns."[48]

The men of Major John Owen's 9th Virginia, on the left of the 14th, were able to see General Lewis Armistead before the advance began. Second Lieutenant John

H. Lewis of Company G had such a clear recollection of the events that followed the cannonade that it remained with him through the decades after the war:

> If I should live for a hundred years I shall never forget that moment or the command as given by General Louis A. Armistead on that day. He was an old army officer, and was possessed of a very loud voice, which could be heard by the whole brigade, being near my regiment. He gave the command, in words, as follows: "Attention, second battalion! battalion of direction forward; guides center; march!" ... He turned, placed himself about twenty paces in front of his brigade, and took the lead. His place was in the rear, properly. After moving he placed his hat on the point of his sword, and held it above his head, in front of him.[49]

Advancing from the cover of Spangler's Woods, the 9th Virginia marched at common time and got its first glimpse of the Union position. When the regiment started out, there was no sound coming from the Yankee lines. But, after the regiment crossed about two hundred yards the artillery started pounding Armistead's line. First Sergeant James H. Walker of Company K correctly assumed that General Lee's intention for the cannonade was to drive out the Union artillery and infantry at the center of Meade's line and, and when that failed, the Confederate infantry would be called upon to dislodge it. When word came down the line to prepare to charge, Walker knew that the enemy's position must still be intact and strong. The men of the 9th Virginia were on their feet in an instant, and fell into ranks with scarcely a word. At the command "Forward" the regiment left the cover of the woods and passed through the artillery line in their immediate front. The gunners raised their hats and gave them a cheer as the regiment passed the artillery pieces, momentarily raising the spirits of the infantrymen. But once the artillery on Cemetery Ridge and Seminary Ridge discovered their movements, the silence was stunningly broken again.[50] As the regiment advanced, its adjutant, Lieutenant James Crocker, noted that Garnett's Brigade became so reduced by this artillery fire as to appear as a skirmish line.[51]

The ranks of the 9th Virginia were also being reduced by this fire. Sergeant Levin C. Gayle of Company G must have jotted some quick notes in his daily journal as the regiment initiated its advance: "Beautiful and we are moveing under a storme of shot and shell and many of our brave boys hav fallen.[52]

For the men of the 53rd Virginia Infantry, the center regiment of Armistead's Brigade, the cacophony and mere brutishness of these moments contrasted sharply with the drama that had presented itself to them just before the brigade began the assault. At that time, General Armistead had called attention and every man was on his feet. Because the 53rd was the battalion of direction, the colors of the regiment would be paramount as a guide to the brigade. For this reason, Armistead approached the color guard with some last words especially for them. Addressing Color Sergeant Leander Blackburn, the general pointed towards the enemy's lines and asked him if he could plant the colors of the regiment on their works. Blackburn grimly replied, "Yes, sir, if God is willing."[53] Then the general took out a small flask and offered a portion of its contents to Sergeant Blackburn, who gratefully accepted it. Armistead then exhorted the men of the regiment to follow their colors and remember the brave vow of their color bearer. He closed with, "Men, remember your wives, your mothers, your sisters and your sweethearts," a last command that Armistead invariably gave at the approach of a battle.[54]

With the orders, "Right shoulder, shift arms. Forward march," General Armistead occupied a place at the head of the 53rd Virginia in front of the colors. The regiment broke almost immediately into quick time in order to cover the distance between themselves and the front line of the division. All impediments to their hasty progress, including knapsacks, blankets, and unnecessary accoutrements, had been piled in company heaps in the rear of their position before the 53rd Regiment stepped off with their loaded muskets and fixed bayonets.[55] At a distance of about 1000 yards from the enemy's lines the regiment first began receiving the fire from the Union artillery. This fire continued as the distance closed between Armistead's line and that of Garnett and Kemper. While the other two brigades of the division were exchanging fire with the enemy, at and beyond the Emmitsburg Road, men of Armistead's Brigade were still advancing with their guns on their right shoulders not firing a shot. Casualties, however, were being incurred. Lieutenant Colonel Martin saw every man of Company F thrown flat to the ground by the explosion of a single shell fired from Little Round Top. He was relieved to see all those not killed or desperately wounded spring to their feet, collect themselves, and hurry forward to close the gap thus made in the regimental front.[56]

Captain James E. Poindexter of Company I in the 38th Virginia, the left-center regiment, marveled at the "splendid" scene depicted to the men of the brigade as they too crossed the oblique ridge and saw the grounds to their front. The brigades of Garnett and Kemper were clearly visible ahead of them, "moving on like waves of the sea," with battle flags whipping and bayonets and guns reflecting the bright sunlight. The men of the 38th Virginia were determined to follow where Garnett and Kemper led, and followed their General Armistead with deliberate and disciplined tread to keep closing the distance between the two lines.[57]

When a mere few hundred yards or less separated the Union and Confederate lines, General Kemper rode rapidly back toward Armistead's line, reining his horse beside the dismounted brigade commander. Excitedly, Kemper blurted out, "Armistead, hurry up, my men can stand no more. I am going to charge those heights and carry them, and I want you to support me."[58] All the while some of the "heaviest artillery fire" the world has ever seen was falling fast about them all, according to Lieutenant J. Wyatt Whitehead of Company I, 53rd Virginia. The brigade continued to march under it at the quickstep, never faltering. Armistead replied, "I'll do it!" He calmly turned to Colonel Rawley Martin and said, "Colonel, double quick."[59] Then, as Kemper turned and started riding back to his own brigade, Armistead called after him, pointing to his own brigade, "Did you ever see a more perfect line than that on dress parade?" Once again raising his hat on the tip of his sword, Armistead resumed his place about fifteen or twenty paces in front of the brigade, cheering on his men and urging them to follow him.[60] The doublequick would soon bring them, too, to the fencing enclosing the Emmitsburg Road, where they would also have to share the effects of the combined musketry and artillery fire from the ridge in their immediate front, only two hundred yards distant.

56

View Shared by Kemper's Brigade During The Assault – To The Angle

This modern view was taken from the position where Kemper's Brigade was marching by the left flank in a northerly direction toward the Codori Farm buildings (whose later barn is in the center of the photo). Cemetery Ridge is designated by the mass of trees of Ziegler's Grove and the horizion line; the Angle by the Clump of Trees beneath the observation tower. (Photograph by Kathy Georg Harrison)

That Armistead's Brigade could muster a double-quick pace so distant from their objective and maintain it was creditable to the men in the ranks. General Kemper's Brigade moved most of the distance at quick time, and Kemper himself thought that was the limit of his soldiers. Even if it were necessary to quicken the pace, Kemper did not think it possible, so drained and exhausted were his men by the sweltering heat and effect of the artillery cannonade to which they had been exposed for such a sustained period of time. Kemper, like Armistead and Garnett, could be well pleased with the advance up to this point. The infantry fire, particularly against Kemper's flank, had been terrible for a long time. The Virginia regiments were unable to reply in kind. But the men closed up the gaps and restored alignment as quickly as their comrades were cut down. Kemper summarized his estimation of their performance that day:

> I never saw the behavior of men in battle equal to that shown by my command in this advance. The danger to be met was plainly visible. It was as well calculated to terrify as any mortal eye ever saw.... At the most critical moment, our line was a dress-parade line and the marching was beautifully exact."[61]

The perspective from the Union lines was one of awe, which quickly subsided as retaliation took its place. Because the men in Doubleday's Division primarily supported the front lines, they had a better opportunity to scrutinize the advance more calmly. John Nesbit, in the 149th Pennsylvania Volunteers, remembered the "splendid spectacle" presented by the first movements of Pickett's Division. Reinforcements of Union infantry and artillery were soon called forward, and Nesbit recollected the time when

> Berdan's men began to use their rifles, picking off their officers. This seemed to me to be simply murder, but it was part of the game.
> As their lines came closer, our infantry opened fire with musketry, and the batteries changed to canister, both with murderous effect....
> When their front reached the Emmitsburg Road, the smoke was so dense that we could see nothing clearly.[62]

In Cowan's Battery of New Yorkers, which had just taken position, it was observed by the gunners that their own

> infantry at the wall had very slight protection, because it was very low in the angle, certainly not over two feet high. Three or four rails, stake and rider fashion, had previously made it high enough to turn cattle. There was not enough soil there to strengthen the wall and raise it higher. Back of the line held by the batteries the soil was too thin to raise any sort of defenses....
> I could only see from our position that part of the enemy's line was advancing to the Emmitsburg road in our front and to our left, their left being [hidden] from us by the clump of trees. That proved to be Pickett's division of Virginians, numbering about five thousand.
> They came on in perfect order, closing on their left as the shot and shell ploughed gaps through their ranks, and keeping their regular formation until they had to cross the fences at the Emmitsburg road. It was a wonderful sight.[63]

View Shared By Kemper's Brigade During The Assault – Stannard's Brigade

This view northeastward from the position of Kemper's Brigade as it marched by the left flank after crossing the Emmitsburg Road is toward the position on Cemetery Ridge held by Doubleday's Division and Stannard's Brigade. The Vermonters advanced partially forward to fire into the flank of the brigade as it passed and then moved out into the fields to the extreme left of the photograph. When Wilcox beheld this view in the closing moments of the attack, almost the entire expanse of Cemetery Ridge within the limits of this photograph was devoid of Union infantrymen, since the Federals who had been posted here had moved off to the north (left of the photo) to the Angle or to flank Kemper. (Photograph by Kathy Georg Harrison)

At least one veteran in Doubleday's Division had afterthoughts about the reception that his comrades prepared for the Virginians who advanced across the Emmitsburg Road ridge. Sergeant Patrick DeLacy of the 143rd Pennsylvania Volunteers remembered fifty years after the event how Pickett's men seemed unafraid as they advanced on his position:

> We have been hearing about their valor and their courage. Now we are going to see them put to the iron test. We are firing as fast as we can and fairly riddling one of the detachments of that magnificent line. We keep up pelting at this force. I can see no end to the right nor left to the line that is coming. Skilled troops on parade could not hold an alignment of line better. It is a picture that makes man wonder at men being able to hold together in form amidst such terrible havoc in their ranks. There is praise for those men, from the boys in blue. One says "great" and "fine" without even a thought of pity for the deaths that are coming to those brave men as they advance by order of their commanders. Men are being mowed down with every step. And men are stepping into their places. There is no dismay, no discouragement, no wavering. It grows in magnificence as death's sting waxes stronger. Now they are in double quick stride. And we answer their spurt with more shot and shell.[64]

It was totally frustrating for the men of Dearing's Battalion to watch in mute awe as Pickett's Division advanced without them. Knowing well that the success of General Lee's plans depended on the artillery being able to advance and protect the flank of Kemper's line, Major Dearing and Colonel Alexander could do little but scramble frantically for ammunition to serve at least a few pieces. Dearing himself accompanied his caissons as they passed headlong to the rear just as the infantry advance was beginning. Passing Colonel Eppa Hunton of the 8th Virginia in Garnett's Brigade, Dearing cried out, "For God's sake wait till I get some ammunition and I will drive every Yankee from the heights."[65] It was obviously too late, however; the column was already in motion and Dearing would have quite a distance to travel before reaching the ordnance train. It was too late for Major Dearing to fulfill his vision of causing the "fall" of "that hill." It was too late for Colonel Hunton and Pickett's Division, forced to march against replenished and fresh Union batteries, as well as massed infantry, without artillery support. It seemed impossible, but the planning and coordination of the artillery and infantry branches for Longstreet's Assault was a replica of the events that transpired on Ewell's front the day before. The artillery was engaged too early and too long, using valuable ammunition and lives, and was unable to provide any support to the subsequent infantry charge. Hays' and Avery's Brigades had discovered how bad that could be when they launched their attack on Cemetery Hill on July 2, 1863, only to be mown down by Yankee batteries and regiments that were unintimidated by any opposing firepower. If Dearing accompanied his caissons all the way to the ammunition trains he would have been spared the view that Colonel Alexander had. The latter watched helplessly as Pickett's Division put on a show with its parade-line advance, knowing that he was powerless either to silence the enemy artillery that ripped giant holes in Pickett's lines or to discourage the flanking movements made by Union troops.

As it turned out, only five guns were able to move forward at all from the over seventy pieces that Alexander had in his line. Only the guns on the right of the artillery line could find any means to support the advance. Major Eshleman ordered Captain M. B. Miller to advance with his own Third Company and Lieutenant H. A. Battles' Fourth Company of the Washington Artillery in support of Pickett's brigades. Captain Miller's battery had suffered considerable casualties in men and horses, but his three guns still moved forward. Lieutenant Battles was just as badly off, and could move only one of the two Napoleons with which he had begun the cannonade. Major John C. Haskell, commanding half of Henry's Battalion of Artillery on the right, near the Peach Orchard, could offer only one more gun, making a grand total of five lonely pieces to advance and oppose the fire of as many as eight Union batteries. The small consolidated battery was put under the command of Major Haskell, who pushed the guns forward from 400 to 500 yards, a distance that was about midway towards the Union lines from the guns' original position on Emmitsburg Road near the Peach Orchard. All hopes of striking the death blow to the Union lines through the use of the artillery were now past, and Haskell received no orders except to help where he could on Pickett's right flank.[66]

Haskell's five guns were all that was left of General Lee's original grand design and justification for this infantry assault. Lee, like Pickett's men, did not learn this fact until it was too late. When the Union batteries opened fire against the advancing column, Lee found his own artillery was not replying or rendering the "necessary support." Lee discovered all too late that the reason for this silence from his own lines was that his own batteries had "nearly exhausted their ammunition in the protracted cannonade that preceded the advance of the infantry." Lee consequently could do nothing to halt the enemy from sending flanking parties against his infantry. The commanding general made a point in his report of the battle to acknowledge that it was owing to the fact that the artillery did not fulfill his expectations that the enemy was able to flank and enfilade the assaulting column. He also pleaded that the failure to procure sufficient ammunition for the guns was unknown to himself at the time the assault took place. The conclusion might be that, had he been aware of that fact, Lee's plans may have changed drastically and that the frontal assault would not have occurred. Neither General Longstreet nor General Pendleton apprised Lee of the artillery situation until after the attack was finished.[67] The outcome of the battle, therefore, no longer rested on the genius or skill of Robert E. Lee, but was wrested from his control by such small occurrences as misplaced howitzers and relocated ordnance trains. The men in the attacking columns, including those of Pickett's Division, had the weight of the outcome shifted solely to their shoulders as soon as they stepped their first stride at the command "Forward." Color-Sergeant Blackburn's words hauntingly echo from the past: "If God is willing ... If mortal men can do it."

**"Showing Part of Ground Occupied by Hancock
at Time of Longstreet's Charge"**

This William H. Tipton stereo view, taken in the early 1870s shows the Angle and
the Clump of Trees from the Emmitsburg Road. The apex of the Angle is seen just
at the vegetative growth on the center horizon. The Clump of Trees, sparse and few
in number, juts into the horizon to the right of the Angle apex. The view extends
over the open fields crossed by the left of Garnett's Brigade. (Gettysburg NMP)

View Along Cemetery Ridge From Little Round Top (1863)

This is the earliest known photograph showing the fields over which Pickett's Division concluded its attack, taken from a point over a mile distant from the High Water Mark. Mathew Brady captured the appearance of Ziegler's Grove (on the horizon just above the "point" of the boulder) and the fields east of the Emmitsburg Road where disaster struck the Virginians (above the length of the standing boulder). (Library of Congress)

The Attack

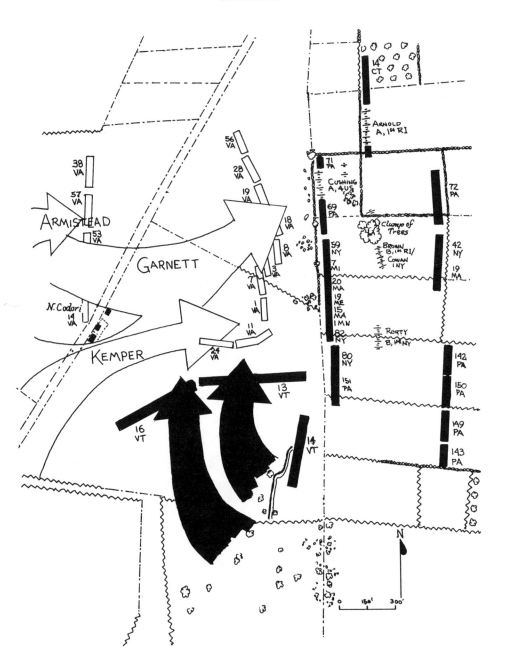

Chapter

V

"Faster, men, faster!"

That part of the assault which brought Pickett's column from its original positions west of the Emmitsburg Road to a convergent point at the road itself has been considered as the advance. It was, in essence, an orderly march at common or quick time with the three brigades devoting their energies to closing ranks and dressing in one direction or another in order to reach an initial objective point (the Codori Farm buildings), while maintaining some large degree of their entities. As the brigades neared these structures, the character of the assault changed abruptly. As we have seen, common time yielded to quick time, and that in turn to double-quick time. Columns would soon lose their order, so well maintained over two-thirds of the advance route. From this point, as one survivor described it, every man was his own general. This, then, was the attack.

General Kemper, still leading his right brigade from atop his bay, later admitted that from the beginning to the end of the assault he never saw any commands or other units than those in Pickett's Division, primarily due to his own concerns and to the pattern of ridges that obscured the extreme left of the assault column from the right.[1] Kemper seemed to be pre-eminently concerned with his own front, and seemed unaware of any threat to his right flank by the absence of any supporting artillery or infantry. It was for this reason that, in hurrying up Armistead's Brigade, he did not specify that it go in on his right flank (perhaps thinking that the artillery or part of Anderson's Division was covering that end of his line), but that it merely come up to support his men and join with them in charging the heights. Shortly after rejoining his brigade, General Kemper must have been shot down, as his influence on the remainder of the battle was curtailed. Captain Hercules Scott of Company G, in Kemper's right regiment (the 24th Virginia Infantry), reported that his general was shot and felled from his horse at or near the brick Codori Farmhouse, falling into the arms of one of his staff,[2] but this seems to contradict Kemper's own recollection of his wounding. General Kemper recalled vividly being close enough to the enemy's line to distinguish individual features and expressions on the faces of the Union defenders, even so far as to think he saw the very man who fired the gun that shot him.[3] While the remainder of his staff was down with wounds, killed or absent on other matter, Kemper was unhorsed by a minie ball that entered his groin and ranged upward into his body. He immediately fell into the arms of his mounted

Brigadier General James L. Kemper (1823-1895)
(wounded near the stone wall and captured)

orderly, Private George T. Walker.[4] From the first, Kemper's wound was "excruciatingly painful," obliterating almost all sensations but the pain. He admitted that he could not tell what his own brigade did afterwards except from hearsay because of his preoccupation with his wound.[5] That he was close to the Federal lines is confirmed once again by Kemper himself, who wrote that while lying on the ground wounded, several Yankees accompanied by an officer loaded him onto a blanket and started carrying him off to their own rear. Some of Kemper's men noticed the abduction and came to his rescue. By "firing over" his body, they chased away the Union party and recovered their general. They then proceeded to carry him some distance rearward to a position where he would be safe from another such close call, but still be near enough to direct brigade movements if he could, before being relocated to the field hospital.[6]

Colonel Mayo of the 3rd Virginia, who would succeed to the command of the brigade after the fall of Kemper, also remembered that General Kemper was still giving commands when within one hundred yards of the Union line. At that distance the brigade fired "one well-directed volley" towards the enemy works, before rushing with a cheer at the command of General Kemper.[7] The volley fired by Kemper's Brigade was their first shots fired as a unit since beginning the advance, after having covered nearly 1000 yards under enemy guns.

Kemper's Brigade was certainly receiving its share of volleys and random shots from the Union line. It had become the special target of Stannard's Vermont Brigade since almost the initiation of the advance. This Second Vermont Brigade, unlike most other Union brigades on Cemetery Ridge that day, was comparable in size to any of Pickett's, having about 1900 officers and men in the ranks. But Stannard's Brigade consisted of only three regiments, averaging over 600 men in each regiment![8] When Kemper's Brigade first came into view at the crest of the Emmitsburg Road near the Klingel Farm buildings, the 14th Vermont Regiment had been given orders to hold its fire until the Confederates were closer, then fire a volley, and ultimately give them the bayonet. But, before the order could be fully executed, Kemper's line had made its movement by the left flank. Then, at about 300 yards' distance, the 14th Vermont opened fire as Kemper made his way across the regimental front. The fire was continued "with very great effect, and a long line of Confederate dead soon marked the route of their march across the front of the Vermont Brigade."[9] It was almost immediately after passing the front of Stannard's Brigade that Kemper's Brigade once again resumed its frontal advance.

As soon as Kemper's resumption of his forward movement was apparent, General George J. Stannard ordered the 13th and 14th Vermont Regiments to continue pouring an oblique fire into the Virginians. He then ordered the 13th Vermont to change front forward on the first company, which placed the 13th Regiment at right angles to the rest of the Union line, but firing directly into the right flank of Kemper's line as he proceeded toward the Union Second Corps. He also ordered the 16th Vermont to do the same, but to form on the left of the 13th, thereby extending this perpendicular line almost as far westward as the Codori Farm buildings. Although this effectively left a considerable gap in the Union lines, General Stannard was not concerned since he saw neither artillery nor infantry coming up from the Confederate side to threaten that gap when the flanking movement was made.[10]

The kind of firepower faced by Kemper's Brigade during the advance from Stannard's front was best described by a survivor of the 13th Vermont Infantry:

> [We] took deliberate aim and with a simultaneous flash and roar fired into the compact ranks of the desperate foe and again and again in quick succession until a dozen or more volleys had been discharged with deadly effect. We saw at every volley the gray uniforms fall quick and fast and the front line hesitated, moved slowly and melted away, could not advance against such a furious and steady storm of bullets in their faces and the raking fire of McGilvery's batteries against their flank and midst this, unexpected fusillade of bullets, grape and canister they halted and quickly in good order massed in columns to our right uncovering the immediate front of Stannard's brigade and with an awful menacing yell dashed forward with the evident purpose of carrying the crest of Cemetery Ridge at our right and rear.

Pickett's massing of columns and verging to his left and our right opened a
clear field in front of Stannard's brigade, furnishing a golden opportunity for a
flank advance attack against General Pickett's advancing battle lines.[11]

The effects of the volleys on Kemper's line were most evident after the brigade
passed to the left towards the Codori Farm buildings, when "the long line of dead
and wounded" covered the ground over which they had passed.[12] After such a loss,
Kemper's Brigade would have to sustain increasing casualties, incurred by short-
range musketry and artillery fire from their front on Cemetery Ridge and from
musketry and bayonet from their right flank by the 13th and 16th Vermont's change
of front.

Major Walter Harrison, inspector general for the division, mistakenly asserted
in his post-war history of "Pickett's Men" that had not the division obliqued to the
left, but continued in its frontal assault, it would have penetrated Meade's line at its
weakest point. On the contrary, had Kemper and Garnett continued their original
direction of march they would have struck perhaps the strongest portion of Meade's
line. There, the brigades would have confronted Stannard's massive brigade,
backed up in reserve by almost the entirety of the Union First and Third Corps,
assisted on the right and left by the Second Corps, and in easy range of reinforcements
from the Sixth Corps. At least a dozen Union batteries were massed there, whereas
only about half that number would face the division at its ultimate object of
advance.[13]

Harrison did note, however, that the division headed for the highest and center-
most point in the enemy's line. This movement did not occur until after "getting in
full view of the enemy's position," when that point was "naturally" selected.[14] It can
be interpreted from this that the division had no point of direction at the outset for
its attack except the Codori Farm buildings. They would be the guide during the
advance, and the point of direction for the attack would only be selected after getting
a better view of Meade's line. According to Major Harrison, a small clump of trees
on the heights was made the prominent feature for the direction of the division after
the advance had commenced and proceeded perhaps as far as half its distance. This
seems to be confirmed by General Kemper's actions and statements, in that he
acknowledged receiving no additional orders than those conveyed by Captain
Bright preceding the charge. His hasty conversation with General Armistead
likewise indicated that the decision to attack Cemetery Ridge at a certain point was
made on the field and not at the rear.[15]

Therefore, when Kemper decided to continue his movements towards the left,
dressing on Garnett's right, he unwittingly opened the opportunity for the flanking
attack by the Vermonters by exposing his right flank. He also created a gap in the
planned column of assault on this right side. Had Kemper not dressed to the left,
Armistead's Brigade would have had a gap between the two Virginia brigades in
which to throw a portion of his line. Kemper's hurried words to Armistead only
directed the latter to support Kemper while he threw his brigade against the heights.

The brigades of David Lang's Florida and Cadmus Wilcox's Alabama troops,
originally intended to support Pickett on his right flank, did not receive their orders
to advance from General Pickett until after fifteen or twenty minutes had elapsed

from the time Kemper had started out. These orders were conveyed simultaneously by Pickett's staff officers Captains Edward Baird, Stuart Symington, and Robert Bright. Sent one after another by Pickett under a heavy fire, the general probably thought that no more than one would get to Wilcox safely. When the last of the three arrived at Wilcox's position, the general had already received the orders from the other two, and, when Captain Bright reined up in front of him, Wilcox could only mildly protest with upraised hands, saying, "I know, I know."[16] Immediately the two brigades arose and moved forward "with their usual courage and alacrity." Like Kemper, near whose position they had also lain during the cannonade, Wilcox's Brigade had been protected by the intervening ridge of the Emmitsburg Road. When they rose to the crest of that ridge, they became the targets of the batteries (particularly on McGilvery's front) that had laid low so many of Pickett's men. Wilcox did not see Pickett's Division, particularly Kemper's Brigade, on which he would have to dress and support. This was because Kemper was not where Wilcox expected him to be. Wilcox apparently was unaware that Kemper had made so drastic a move to the left, and expected him to be on his front somewhere. When he saw no Confederate troops in his immediate front, Wilcox logically assumed that Pickett's Division had not only taken the enemy's works in his front, but had passed beyond.[17] Therefore, he headed his brigade and that of Colonel Lang straight ahead, over much the same ground they had fought the day previously. Because no one told Wilcox otherwise he thought he was following Kemper to glory, when in reality he was marching headlong into the strongest part of the Union line with both flanks exposed and no supports in sight. Although the battle smoke may have been heavy enough to obscure any view of the Union line by this time, Wilcox could have seen a large gap in the Union line where Kemper should have penetrated. This was created by the movement of the 13th and 16th Vermont regiments into the Codori fields, (to Wilcox's front and left). Other units along the Union line, adjacent to Stannard's Brigade were, by this time moving northward to the actual point of penetration by Pickett's Division, creating a widening gap in the line. It would therefore have been easy for General Wilcox to conclude that Pickett had indeed breached the Union line in his front and had driven Stannard and the others beyond the ridge. But Wilcox was wrong. His advance was doomed from the outset, and helped seal the fate of Kemper's Brigade because he was not there to support it and protect its right flank in absence of Alexander's and Dearing's artillery batteries. At the moment Wilcox was making his misguided and late advance, Pickett's Division was engaged with the enemy on two fronts.

The losses in Pickett's Division became even heavier from the Emmitsburg Road onward, when the full might of Union musketry was brought to bear against them in conjunction with short-range artillery. Whereas numbers and statistics are not fully broken down for the different periods of the assault, the increasing number of examples cited by veterans of individuals who fell during the attack support the fact that this was the deadliest part of the assault. In Kemper's Brigade, General Kemper stayed primarily with the left wing of his line and entrusted his adjutant and inspector general, Captain Thomas Gordon Pollock, to oversee the movements of the right wing. Pollock's words to those within earshot at the advance were, "Boys,

I trust you will all behave like Southern soldiers." He was felled from his horse while riding along the lines of Company D in the 7th Virginia, and in the confusion no one knew whether he was killed or not. His body servant, Richard, had accompanied the brigade during the assault and wanted to stay with Captain Pollock, but he was ordered to the rear by an officer under his protestation that he was determined at any and all risks to know the fate of the captain. Richard fell back under the hailstorm of bullets, leading his master's wounded horse to brigade headquarters. He would be noticed during the return march to Virginia often in tears as he rode his master's unwounded horse and led the wounded one, reassured only that Captain Pollock's remains had been interred near the division's hospital with others of Kemper's men.[18]

With Kemper down himself with wounds, the command devolved upon Colonel Mayo of the 3rd Virginia, who wrote later that the brigade had been pared down to a mere line of skirmishers by the time it reached the enemy's lines. Mayo attributed Colonel William Richard Terry of the 24th Virginia and Colonel William T. Fry of Kemper's staff with having saved the brigade from a complete rout. Terry and Fry were responsible for promptly throwing back a portion of the 11th and 24th Virginia Regiments at right angles to the line, in order to exchange fire and in some way protect the brigade from the enfilading fire of the Vermonters. Their action, according to Colonel Mayo, prevented the enemy from completely surrounding the brigade and penetrating Kemper's rear.[19] That the attackers should have come to such a predicament must have been due to the belief of all officers from General Kemper down to his line officers that they were supported on the right by Wilcox, Lang and the artillery. For this reason they believed they had to worry only about their front, not their flank. This interpretation is reinforced by an account related after the war by a veteran of the attack who stated that "I told the Captain that the Yankees were on our flank, but he said we had nothing to do with that. Those in the rear would attend to them. All we had to do was to go forward." It was not until men such as the above felt the muzzle of a revolver at their heads, and heard one of the Vermonters say, "Wall now, I guess you won't go any further in that direction," that the threat to the right flank became a reality from which no brigade of Wilcox or Lang could extricate them.[20]

The 24th Virginia was just "a few paces" from the enemy's lines when Colonel Terry tried to rally his men and force back some companies to the right and rearward to protect the brigade. The site of this point of advance must have been at the area identified as "the slashing," to the southwest and within 150 yards of the clump of trees which had become the secondary objective point of the brigade. The slashing and the rise of ground on which this small cut brush occurred "afforded some cover and protection" to the men of the 24th Virginia who had made it this far.[21] After reaching this slashing, Colonel Terry was compelled to throw back those survivors of the regiment who could be rallied, along with the portions of the 11th Virginia, in order to meet the increasing Union force on his right. The right of Kemper's Brigade would expend its energies attempting to parry the flanking movement by Stannard's two Vermont regiments, and would not share with the others of the division in scaling and penetrating the enemy's defenses.

Colonel William R. Terry (1824-1888)
24th Virginia Infantry

Most of the 11th Virginia, however, did not seem to be a part of the force used by Colonel Terry to defend the brigade against this flanking fire. The attack by the regiment after crossing the Emmitsburg Road was by the left oblique, during which the captain of Company G was shot in the leg. Turning over the command to James Kent, the only non-commissioned officer near him who was still on his feet, Captain Smith was immediately informed that Kent was likewise incapacitated by a leg wound. Tying up his own leg, Captain Smith decided to press on with the company, which was still receiving artillery fire from Cemetery Ridge. Private William H. Winston of Captain Smith's company was knocked down by the explosion of a shell just as the company reached the enemy's works, and was rendered unconscious as the regiment reached its goal.[22] During this attack down the slope from the Emmitsburg Road the 11th Virginia heard the command to "close and dress to the left." During this movement from the road eastward down the gentle ridge and into the depression between the road and Cemetery Ridge, musketry fire from the enemy's ranks swept the line of the 11th Regiment. The colors were knocked down several times. Captain Smith twice saw the color-bearer stagger with wounds and the next man seize the staff and continue ahead. The third time, the bearer fell and, with him, the colors struck the ground as the regiment was still charging down the slope from the road. The artillery had opened on them with canister, and it was with great effort that the regimental adjutant, H. Valentine Harris, could rush forward, seize the colors under fire and carry them ahead once again. Captain Smith could see a

71

substantial line of Union soldiers firing upon the regiment as it neared the works, but was surprised to see more and more of these Northern infantrymen fleeing rearward as the Confederate line approached. When the 11th Virginia reached the enemy's works, "which were a hasty trench and embankment, and not a stone wall at the point...struck" by the regiment there was no organization left in the regimental line. It was described by Captain Smith, instead, as a "mass or ball, all mixed together, without company organization." Even men of the 3rd and 24th Virginia Regiments appeared to be intermingled with Otey's regiment.[23] Nonetheless, Captain Smith's original perceptions of the new position were optimistic. As can be seen in the following recollection by this line officer, his optimism soon turned to despair:

> Not a man could I see in the enemy's works, but on account of the small timber and the lay of the ground, I could not see very far along the line, either right or left, or the position we occupied.
> There were, as I thought at the time I viewed the situation, about three hundred men in the party with me, or maybe less. Adjutant H. V. Harris, of the regimental staff was there dismounted. [Smith also saw AAG Captain William T. Fry of Kemper's staff on foot with a courier, George "Big Foot" Walker, and Captain R. W. Douthat of Company F.] We thought our work was done...for the last enemy in sight we had seen disappear over the hill in front; and I expected to see General Lee's army marching up to take possession of the field. As I looked over the work of our advance with this expectation, I could see nothing but dead and wounded men and horses in the field beyond us, and my heart never in my life sank as it did then....[24]

Captain Smith's recollection placed Private Walker at the enemy's works, but did not recount the means by which he arrived there. As the attacking column approached the Union battle line, Walker dashed up to a bleeding General Kemper and informed him that the ranks were becoming so thin that, unless reinforced, the brigade could advance but little further. General Kemper ordered his courier Walker to ride to General Longstreet and urge him to push forward the supports. After delivering his message, Private Walker returned to the advance line. Finding everybody around the colors of the 11th Virginia shot down and the colors themselves fallen to the ground, he sprang from his mount and snatched up the flag, remounted, and drove forward to the enemy's line. Before reaching the works, his horse was killed beneath him. Nevertheless, young Walker was undeterred in his mission and arrived at the works with the colors of the 11th Virginia, which were planted thereon, despite the passage of a number of Yankee balls through his clothing.[25]

Meanwhile, the men of the 1st Virginia Regiment in the center of Kemper's brigade, were experiencing many of the same casualties incurred by those in Pickett's Division during this headlong attack from the Emmitsburg Road to the Union lines, some 200-300 yards in expanse. The skirmish line of the regiment, comprised of the men of Company D, began to share the sentiments of Captain Smith even before reaching the enemy's lines. M. J. "Monk" Wingfield had turned to Corporal Charles T. Loehr when about half way across the field of advance and asked, "Where are our reinforcements?" Since Corporal Loehr could see nobody but Armistead's Brigade in their rear, he could only reply that he did not see any. Private Wingfield thereupon realized the true state of affairs and predicted to Loehr, "We are going to be whipped, see if we don't." Wingfield himself would not live to see the culmination of his own prediction, as moments later he was struck down and killed.[26]

As in the 11th Virginia, the color guard of the 1st Virginia suffered remarkably from the enemy's accurate fire. Pat Woods, Theodore R. Martin, and Corporal John Q. Figg went down one after another as the line neared the stone wall. Color-bearer William Lawson of Company H was severely wounded in the right arm, a wound from which he would lose his arm near the shoulder. This caused the colors to fall from his hand among the dead and dying. Jacob R. Polak rushed from the ranks of Company I to secure the colors and raise them once again through the battle smoke. He would carry them as far as they were advanced that July day, before he also fell with wounds.[27]

The officers of the regiment suffered casualties in proportion to the color guard. After the dramatic mortal wounding of Colonel Williams, the command had been transferred to Major Frank H. Langley, but he too was soon disabled. Senior Captain George F. Norton thereupon took command but was also brought down by enemy fire, before Captain Thomas Davis of Company B jumped in front of the line to lead the remnant of the small regiment. Almost immediately, Captain Davis was bowled over by a shot, and the regiment continued its forward surge to the enemy's wall without any apparent commanding officer. Some of the enemy left their places and either ran rearward or into the lines of the 1st Virginia for safety. The Union line had been penetrated and won, and the survivors of the 1st Virginia anxiously awaited the reinforcements to secure the position. Already, however, there was concern within the depleted ranks as the men began noting the "massing of the Yankees" on their front, something which Corporal Loehr pointed out to Lieutenant Paul Cabell of Company H.[28]

On the left of the 1st Regiment, the 7th Virginia, under Colonel Tazewell Patton was sharing in both the destruction and the glory of the hour. The colors of the regiment, like those of the "Old First," attracted the fire of the Union lines. Color Sergeant G. W. Watson was the first to be wounded; his duties as color-bearer were assumed by Corporal Jesse B. Young of Company D, who carried the regimental flag to within a few feet of the enemy's line. But Corporal Young was struck down by a shell fragment hitting him, and he and the flag fell just on the Confederate side of the Union works. While down, a Federal officer from behind the stone wall stood up and, with pistol in hand, took careful aim at Young's head. In order to save himself, Corporal Young instinctively threw up his arm to shield his face, and the pistol ball entered his right elbow instead. Since he was incapacitated, another of the regiment would have to resume the advance of the colors. John N. Tolbert of Company B then seized the flag and took it to the stone wall. There, at the very moment of victory, Tolbert was grazed by a minie ball through the scalp, and fell with the colors across the wall. With no one of the regiment close enough to recover

Colonel Waller Tazewell Patton (1835-1863)
7th Virginia Infantry
(wounded during the attack, captured, then died)

the colors quickly, they were snatched by a Union soldier who gathered them up and fled rearward with his trophy. The 7th Virginia was, therefore, probably the first of the regiments in Pickett's Division to lose its colors, having them stolen by a retreating enemy while the Virginia regiment still held the field.[29]

One of the hardest losses to the regiment, aside from its flag, was that of its colonel, Waller Tazewell Patton. According to a survivor, Patton expected to be shot during the attack, since he never escaped getting wounded in any battle in which the regiment was engaged. Standing with his side to the enemy and directing the movements of his regiment, Colonel Patton was struck by a musket ball which passed through his lower jaw and carried it almost entirely away.[30] On his right, Corporal Loehr of the 1st Virginia saw Colonel Patton when he was hit, and rushed to his side to ask how badly he was hurt. Patton tried to answer, but the blood streamed out of his mouth and made it impossible to speak; his tongue was torn and this prevented him from talking.[31]

Colonel Joseph Mayo, Jr. on the left of the brigade with the 3rd Virginia Regiment, felt with his men the effects of the double-shotted artillery which faced the brigade after it left the Emmitsburg Road. The orchard to the right (south) of the Codori Farmhouse was literally riddled with this sheet of artillery and musketry fire as the 3rd Virginia passed amongst the trees. After clearing this obstruction, Colonel Mayo was endeavoring to get his line reformed again, when he was momentarily shaken by a ball which whizzed by his nose. This caused him to duck his head, much to the amusement of his orderly, John W. "Waddy" Forward of Company A. Within moments, the amusement vanished as the colonel was knocked down by an explosion of a shell nearby, which covered his uniform with the "splinters of bone and lumps of flesh" from some victim of his command.[32]

Colonel Mayo's memories of the last portion of the advance, the attack, were the most vivid of his recollections, although they had the characteristics of a "kaleidoscopic whirl":

> [I remember] the impetuous Kemper, as rising in his stirrups and pointing to the left with his sword, he shouted, "There are the guns, boys, go for them." It was an injudicious order; but they obeyed with a will, and mingled with Garnett's people pushed rapidly up the heights.
>
> Within a few steps of the stone fence, while in the act of shaking hands with General Garnett and congratulating him on being able to be with his men... I heard someone calling to me, and turning my head, saw that it was Captain [William T.] Fry [of Kemper's staff]. He was mounted, and blood was streaming from his horse's neck. Colonel Terry had sent him to stop the rush to the left. The enemy in force (Stannard's Vermonters) had penetrated to our rear. He told me that Kemper had been struck down, it was feared mortally. With the help of Colonel Carrington, of the Eighteenth, and Major Bentley, of the Twenty-fourth, I hastily gathered a small band together and faced them to meet the new danger. After that everything was a wild kaleidoscopic whirl. A man near me seemed to be keeping a tally of the dead for my especial benefit. First it was Patton, then Collcotte, then Phillips, and I know not how many more.... Seeing the men as they fired, throw down their guns and pick up others from the ground, I followed suit, shooting into a flock of blue coats that were pouring down from the right, I noticed how close their flags were together. Probably they were the same people whom Hood and McLaws had handled so roughly the day before....
>
> Then I remembered seeing the lank Tell [1st Lieutenant William T. Taliaferro], adjutant of the Twenty-fourth, jumping like a kangaroo and rubbing his crazy bone and blessing the Yankees in a way that did credit to old Jube Early's law partner, and handsome Ocey [Osceola] White, the boy lieutenant of Company A, taking off his hat to show me where a ball had raised a whelt on his scalp and carried away one of his pretty flaxen curls....[33]

Colonel Mayo's recollection of the great number of Union flags clumped so closely together was also noted by Union General Alexander S. Webb, on whose front the 3rd Virginia was attacking. He wrote later that Colonel Norman Hall sent him "few men but a good many colors. It looked like strong reinforcements."[34] Indeed, the men of Hall's Brigade had been subjected to losses on the previous day, which had thinned their ranks, but their losses had been inflicted by others than McLaws and Hood.

Whereas General Kemper was taken out of the attack before his command reached the enemy's line, Colonel Mayo affirmed the fact that General Garnett was still mounted and with his own brigade within a few paces of the stone wall of the famed Angle where General Webb's Brigade and Cushing's Regular Army Battery awaited the fury of their initial attack. Captain Henry T. Owen of Company C, 18th Virginia Regiment remembered that, although Kemper had gone down "terribly mangled," General Garnett was still seen by his brigade towering above it, unhurt. Riding up and down the line of his brigade, Garnett commanded in a strong but calm voice, "Faster, men! faster! Close up and step out faster, but don't double quick!" And, as the brigade advanced, Garnett continued his galloping and commanding: "Faster, men! faster!" Breaking into a double quick, the brigade lunged forward only to be rebuked by Garnett, who called out, "Steady, men! steady! Don't double quick. Save your wind and your ammunition for the final charge!"[35]

On the extreme right of the brigade, the 8th Virginia encountered momentary confusion as it reached the Codori Farm buildings, which squarely blocked the route of its advance at the Emmitsburg Road. The left wing, under the charge of Major Edmund Berkeley, passed to the left, or north, of the farmhouse, while the rest of the 8th, with Berkeley's three brothers, passed to the right of the buildings. Upon reaching the other side of the buildings, Major Berkeley attempted to reunite the two wings. There he found that Colonel Hunton had been shot through the right leg, just below the knee, which was bleeding profusely.[36] Hunton's mount was likewise wounded by the same shot, and it was with the greatest difficulty that he was able to get to the rear on the horse, which collapsed just within Confederate lines. Before retiring, Colonel Hunton passed Will Adams, of Company D, "a gallant soldier" who was wounded. Private Adams looked at Hunton and cried out, "Colonel, I'm hit." Hunton called to a soldier to take Adams from the field, knowing that the look in the private's eye expressed a confidence that his commanding officer would see that the enlisted man was properly cared for and his wound would be dressed.[37]

Garnett's Brigade, being still somewhat in advance of the brigade on its right, struck the Union stone wall before that of General Kemper. Major Edmund Berkeley of the 8th Virginia was shot down very near to the wall itself by a rifleman who got "a nearly horizontal shot" on him, with the minie ball striking him above the knee and running along the bone for a distance of almost twenty inches before stopping. Major Berkeley was assisted back to the shelter of the brick walls of the Codori Farmhouse, where he was laid down on its west side. While there, General Kemper rode by and reined in his horse to inquire whether the major was badly wounded. Berkeley feared that he was and warned the general that it appeared they would all be soon captured anyway. When Kemper asked why Major Berkeley thought such a thing, the officer replied, "Don't you see those flanking columns the enemy are throwing out of our right to sweep the field?" Kemper assured the wounded major that the column was their own men, but Major Berkeley cried after Kemper as he rode away, "You will soon see your mistake."[38] This incident reveals again the utter disbelief in General Kemper's mind that Stannard's flanking Vermonters could be anything but the planned supporting force of Wilcox and Lang.

At the time that Lieutenants T. Benton Hutchison, the regimental adjutant, and John S. Jones, Garnett's aide-de-camp, were making arrangements to get Major Berkeley transported safely to the rear and out of danger of capture or another wound, Berkeley's brother William was lying wounded within the cellar of the

Colonel Eppa Hunton (1822-1908)
8th Virginia Infantry
(wounded during the attack)

Codori Farmhouse. Major Berkeley had seen his brother struck by a shell fragment while leading his Company D down the slope from the Codori Farm buildings, and had seen him disappear around the end of the farmhouse before he himself was wounded. From seeing the blood spurting from his thigh and noticing his painful hobble toward the Codori Farmhouse, he knew William was badly enough wounded that he should not have been able to get off the field unassisted. But William was not to be seen when Major Berkeley was himself taken to the shelter of the brick walls of the dwelling, nor did he think that anyone would have gone inside the house, where they would be invisible to parties taking wounded to the rear. Indeed, a half dozen or more wounded Virginians had taken refuge in the Codori cellar and were surprised to see about an equal number of Union soldiers, probably skirmishers, in the cellar as well. An uneasy truce existed between the groups while the fighting surged around them.[39]

Although Major Berkeley was concerned about the safety of his brothers, particularly William, he was dismayed to hear from Lieutenant Jones the shocking news that his general, Richard Garnett, was among the fallen. Garnett's position must have been near the lines of the 18th Virginia Regiment, the right center regiment of the brigade, as several of its members were the last to see their commander alive. Major Berkeley mentioned in later years that General Garnett was mounted on his bay thoroughbred "Red Eye," wrapped in an old Union overcoat. However, this recollection is disputed by others of the brigade, apparently including General Garnett himself through his pre-battle letters. As already mentioned, General Garnett was not ill, as Major Berkeley asserted as the reason for the general donning the overcoat, but was "not the least sick" on the day of the attack. And "the old blue coat or overcoat, which he always wore in cold or rainy weather, was not worn that third day of July 1863, when the weather was hot enough to scorch a feather."[40] Captain Owen remembered that General Garnett was wearing the new uniform purchased in Richmond during the march to rejoin the army in June. Private James Clay of Company G likewise remembered his last glimpse of the brigade commander, who was wearing a uniform coat, "almost new," with general's stars and a wreath on the collar, with top boots and spurs into which his trousers were tucked.[41] Although Union soldiers told one survivor of the brigade that Garnett had been killed by grapeshot through his body at the waist,[42] his aide, Captain John S. Jones was with him at the time and said he was killed instantly by a musket ball through his brain.[43]

Private Clay's recollections of those last moments of Garnett's life were similar to the "kaleidoscopic whirl" experienced by Colonel Mayo:

> Gen. Garnett was killed while leading his brigade in Pickett's charge across the field and up the slope between the two contending battle lines. Immediately after the great artillery duel, during which many of the enemy's guns were silenced, orders came for the general advance of Pickett's Division, but it was not until we had covered nearly the entire distance between the two lines that General Garnett received his death wound.
>
> I was struck down by a fragment of shell about one hundred yards from the clump of trees near the farthest point reached by our brigade—now indicated by a bronze tablet. [Reference to High Water Mark of the Rebellion Monument.] Semiconscious, my blood almost blinding me, I stumbled and fell among some rocks, severely injuring my knee. The last I saw of Gen. Garnett he was astride his large black horse in the forefront of the charge and near the stone wall, just beyond which is marked the farthest point reached by the Southern troops. The few that were left of our brigade advanced to this point.[44]

The men of the 18th Virginia, mingled with other regiments of Garnett's Brigade, provided General Garnett with that last comradeship and fleeting moment of glory when the Yankee defenses were reached at the Angle wall. Here, according to local newspaper reports of the battle, General Garnett was killed in front of Cushing's Battery.[45] His body appears to have been recovered after the battle by Union survivors. Colonel Norman Hall, whose brigade assisted that of Union General Webb in beating the Confederate attack at the Angle near the guns of Cushing's Battery, reported that Generals Armistead and Garnett were picked up near the point of the Confederate breakthrough at the stone wall, along with colonels

Brigadier General Richard B. Garnett (1817-1863)
(killed near the stone wall)

and officers of lesser rank.[46] Colonel Hall's statement was made within two weeks after the attack, when there would be little reason to question his memory of the facts. The place of interment of General Garnett, however, has remained a mystery; his name does not appear on even the earliest record of Confederate graves on the battlefield. Major Walter Harrison, of Pickett's staff, probably came closest to surmising the ultimate fate of General Garnett's remains when he asserted that the general was "doubtless buried in the trenches near the spot where he fell" with the many dead of the division. Even old army friend and chief of Union artillery Henry Hunt could not find or identify the body of General Garnett after making a "diligent search in person" on the day after the battle.[47] It would seem that the destiny of General Garnett and his division were intertwined on that July day, when he, with so many others of his brigade, fell to be collectively united in glory and anonymity.

At the same time that the brigade was engaging the enemy at the stone wall, Private James Clay and Acting Captain Archer Campbell of Company G, 18th Virginia, were both wounded and seeking refuge at the rock outcropping to the southwest of the Angle wall. Momentarily, a pair of Union prisoners who had thrown down their rifles and come into Confederate lines passed to the rear and came upon the wounded Virginians. Since they were heading for the Confederate rear to get out of the line of fire, they asked if they could assist Clay and Campbell towards Seminary Ridge. Their offer was gratefully accepted, and it was during their rearward trek that the Federals told of the death of General Garnett by a grape shot.

This confirmed the fears of the two "Nottoway Grays," who had watched as Garnett's terror-stricken horse came galloping toward them with a huge gash in its shoulder, while they were still at the clump of rocks. The horse had jumped over the two of them in its mad flight and death throes, and headed back whence it had come.[48]

Lieutenant-Colonel Henry Carrington was then still leading the regiment and carrying its colors. During the final charge of about 400 yards a dreadful sight arose on the right of the 18th Virginia. Captain Owen described this fearful spectacle, perhaps a half mile to his right in an open field, as

> a line of men at right angles with our own, a long, dark mass, dressed in blue, and coming down at a "double quick" upon the unprotected right flank of Pickett's men, with their muskets "upon the right shoulder shift," their battle flags dancing and fluttering in the breeze, created by their own rapid motion and their burnished bayonets glistening above their heads like forest twigs covered with sheets of sparkling ice when shaken by a blast.[49]

And, as if the sight of Stannard's two Vermont regiments bearing down on their right was not unnerving enough, the men of the 18th Virginia could see the enemy strengthening its position in their front, with reinforcements heading in that direction from the right and left. By the time that the men in the ranks could see and distinguish the difference in uniforms of the Union officers and privates, they also heard from behind them "that heavy thud of a muffled tread of armed men" and that "roar and rush of trampling feet of Armistead's column from the rear" as it closed up on Garnett's and Kemper's Brigades. With General Garnett down, General Armistead stepped in front of the lines, now four ranks deep, and took command. With his hat uplifted on the point of his sword, Armistead urged the men forward these last few yards to the Union works, crossing "rapidly and grandly ... the valley of death, covered with clover as soft as a Turkish carpet." Captain Henry Owen would never forget the experience of those last yards of advance:

> There it was again! and again! A sound filling the air above, below, around us, like the blast through the top of a dry cedar or the flock of quail. It was grape and canister, and the column broke forward into a double quick and rushed forward toward the stone wall where forty cannon were belching forth grape and canister twice and thrice a minute. A hundred yards from the stone wall the flanking party on the right, coming down on a heavy run, halted suddenly within fifty yards and poured a deadly storm of musket balls into Pickett's men, double-quicking across their front, and, under this terrible cross fire the men reeled and staggered between falling comrades and the right came pressing down upon the centre, crowding the companies in confusion. But all knew the purpose to carry the heights in front, and the mingled mass, from fifteen to thirty feet deep, rushed toward the stone wall, while a few hundred men, without orders, faced to the right and fought the flanking party there, although fifty to one, and for a time held them at bay. Muskets were seen crossed as some men fired to the right and others to the front and the fighting was terrific — far beyond all other experience even of Pickett's men, who for once raised no cheer, while the welkin rang around them with the "Union triple huzza." The old veterans saw the fearful odds against them and other hosts gathering deeper and deeper still.[50]

Stannard's Brigade Opening on Pickett's Division

John B. Bachelder, the Gettysburg historian, was responsible for the research and was the delineator of this engraving which shows the long line of Stannard's Vermont Brigade firing obliquely into the advancing ranks of Pickett's Division, particularly Kemper's Brigade. Bachelder relied on eyewitness testimony and his own knowledge of the battlefield terrain to interpret the closing sequences of the attack. (G.G. Benedict, *Vermont at Gettysburg*)

Flank Attack of Stannard's Brigade

A companion to the previous engraving, this Bachelder print was likewise commissioned for G.G. Benedict's book, Vermont at Gettysburg. It portrays in the right distance the long line of the 16th and 13th Vermont Regiments in their new position, perpendicular to their own lines, firing into the right flank of Kemper (extreme right). The view is from the former position of the brigade on Cemetery Ridge. (G.G. Benedict, *Vermont at Gettysburg*)

The confusion and deadly nature of the predicament in which the brigades had found themselves was clearly reflected in the post-war writing of Captain Owen. His recollection that there was no "Rebel Yell" during this last phase of the attack was borne out by other observers. Garnett's Brigade gave its battle yell fully 800 yards from the Union lines, during the advance and not during the attack.[51] This seemed remarkable to a participant/observer in the 7th Tennessee Infantry Regiment, comprising part of Pettigrew's force on Pickett's left. He noted that the yell was "started much further from the enemy than usual," and may have been a factor in limiting the success of Pickett's attack. It had almost always been a certainty that the speed of a column was increased when the yell was started, but the speed could not be increased by Pickett's column because it was so far from the enemy's lines when it was raised.[52] The yell was not again taken up by Garnett's Brigade, as verified by Captain Owen, and it was only the Union "huzza" that could be heard on Garnett's front at the Angle. In the cellar of the Codori Farmhouse, Captain William Berkeley heard the cheers and informed the Yankees in that place that they were now his prisoners. But they, recognizing clearly the difference between the high-pierced Rebel Yell and the Yankee's deep- throated "huzza," replied, "Not at all, you are ours."[53]

As the regiment reached within seventy or eighty feet of the stone wall, Captain Edmund Cocke of Company E looked towards his brother William, a second lieutenant in his command, to marvel at his "calm, quiet [and] collected" demeanor under these trying circumstances. Within moments the captain was grazed by a ball in the head and fell. Before staggering again to his feet he lost sight of his brother, who fell amongst the dead of the brigade. No man of the 18th Virginia could tell Captain Cocke of his fate.[54] He, like his general, would fall victim to the loss of life and identity by enemy fire.

Garnett's center regiment, the 19th Virginia of Colonel Henry Gantt, began the attack with the same enthusiasm as the remainder of the brigade. But the overwhelming firepower from the Union lines, coupled with the realization that there were no supports, soon drove the faint-hearted from the ranks. Lieutenant William N. Wood of Company A had been longing for the words of Major Dearing to come true, that the hill would fall, but his dreams were shattered by the harsh reality of musketry and artillery that unfailingly crippled and killed comrades within his regiment. Lieutenant Wood remembered that the depression between the Emmitsburg Road and the Cemetery Ridge battle line of the Federals was speedily reached, but that the advance from the bottom-land to the slopes of the enemy was fraught with grape and canister scouring the ground. Suddenly, there was no fire on their front, and the survivors took renewed courage and rushed forward to the rock wall. When within twenty yards of the works, Lieutenant Wood was struck in the leg by a blow, from which he was compelled to halt to ascertain the extent of the wound. Seeing it to be only a bruise, he rejoined the small remnant of the regiment as it reached the stone fence, only to be surprised by the few numbers of the division who were with him. Looking to his left and right he saw but few Virginians, and momentarily thought the division had disgraced itself, but remembered that he had seen no cowardice but many casualties during the gauntlet which had been run to reach this point. More disturbingly, Lieutenant Wood saw that the enemy was forming a line of battle a few hundred yards away, on the Confederate side of the wall. He, too, realized that this movement by Stannard's regiments was the worst thing that could have happened to the column, as he watched the Vermonters' left wing rapidly extend into the field in the rear of the brigade. As the Vermont line began its forward movement toward the flank and rear of the division, Lieutenant Wood felt he had but one choice—to stay was life in prison, to flee could mean death in crossing the open fields, but possible safety within Confederate lines. Turning his back to the fence and his comrades, Lieutenant Wood started back across that same stretch of countryside over which the regiment had so recently come.[55]

Another survivor of the 19th Virginia Regiment made his painful way to the rear, meeting the assistant surgeon William Taylor at the eastern fringe of Spangler's Woods. Inside those woods the medical staff of Garnett's Brigade had been stationed to care for the immediate needs of the wounded, and although many were driven out by the shelling during the cannonade, Doctor Taylor had remained because of a slight wound he himself suffered during the height of the shelling. Recovering from the initial shock of a wound in his buttocks, Taylor limped forward to see if he could assist any of the men now streaming rearward with their own wounds. He was surprised to see his own commander, Colonel Henry Gantt, making his way toward the woods with "nearly all his teeth neatly and effectively extracted by a bullet received in his mouth." Although his ordeal must have been excruciating, Colonel Gantt's concern for the safety of his men, including the assistant surgeon, was overriding. He made the effort to "speak sufficiently plainly" enough to warn Doctor Taylor that he could not go forward without being killed, and, when he gave the orders to go back, Taylor "understood him very well."[56]

On the left of the 19th Virginia, Colonel Robert C. Allen's 28th Regiment pressed ahead, apparently in advance of the remainder of the brigade. Whether or not this was due to the hasty marching by Captain Spessard is unclear, but the 28th Virginia had even been slowed by a rail fence, where it seemed to one survivor they would all be killed by the enemy's shells. As they forged on to the rock wall, several of the color bearers were killed and wounded in leading the regiment. Colonel Allen seized the colors and carried them himself, just as Lieutenant Colonel Carrington was carrying them in the 18th Regiment. Drawing attention to himself in this manner, Colonel Allen became a target for the Union lines, and fell mortally wounded near the wall with the regimental flag still in his grasp. The enemy fell back some twenty-five to thirty yards from the wall on the front of the 28th Virginia, and the remnants of the regiment took possession of the works, where they halted for a few minutes to get organized. Private William Jesse of Company F saw Captain Waller Boyd of the 19th Virginia cross the wall to the right, urging his men to follow him, and many of that regiment crossed the wall there. Jesse himself scaled the wall before he was wounded in the thigh. This prompted him to fall back to his own lines on Seminary Ridge,[57] so joining that increasing stream of wounded and those assisting the wounded that surged rearward across the Emmitsburg Road.

Lieutenant John A. Lee of Company C was not only the first man of the 28th Virginia, but of the division, to cross the wall and enter the Union lines. Carrying the colors of the regiment after the fall of Colonel Allen, Lieutenant Lee jumped atop the wall and over it, waving the flag to hearten the men. A shot from the Union lines struck the flagstaff and caused the flag to topple backwards over the wall, but Lee retrieved it.[58] Others in the regiment would later verify his claim as the first of Pickett's Virginians to cross the stone fence.

Before reaching the enemy's line at the Angle, the 56th Virginia would lose its colonel, who fell wounded sometime during the advance or attack. This regiment on the extreme left of Garnett's line was next commanded by Captain James C. Wyant of Company H, who was given those orders by the regimental adjutant, Lieutenant Richard Wharton. Although he had enlisted in May 1862, this was apparently Captain Wyant's first fight and it would be his last. Wounded in the face, he was taken to Chester Hospital after the battle and died on July 31. Wyant's company command devolved on Lieutenant Henry C. Michie, who received a slight wound but continued with his company as it went over the stone fence. The colors of the 56th Virginia were placed at the stone wall to the right of Lieutenant Michie's position. Michie's Company H was immediately to the left of the regimental color guard, and the colors remained there as long as the survivors held the stone wall.[59] Corporal Alexander L. P. Williams of Company I was the last to be entrusted with the colors of the 56th and held them defiantly near the angle in the stone wall.[60]

Thus, with the possible exception of the 8th Virginia Regiment on the extreme right of the brigade line, the colors of each of Garnett's regiments were planted on or over the stone wall of the enemy's line at the close of the attack. The cost in getting them there, however, had been enormous and included the loss of many irreplaceable officers and men. In the 56th Virginia, much loss was incurred at and just beyond the Emmitsburg Road, where the fencing slowed the attack and men fell all around, the victims of cannon and muskets. According to Lieutenant G. K. Finley of Company K, there was no sound from the regiment as it ascended this last slope towards the enemy's line on Cemetery Ridge except for an occasional "clamor" from the men to be allowed to return the enemy's fire. It was not until within 75 or 100 yards of the stone wall, when the enemy began to break and flee to the rear, that a volley or two was fired from the 56th Regiment. These few volleys were followed by a great rush upon the stone fence, where several Union soldiers were captured crying "Don't shoot! We surrender!" and "Where shall we go?" Instructed to go to their rear, these few Union prisoners went unescorted, and were probably those encountered by men such as Private Clay and Acting Captain Campbell in the fields between the Emmitsburg Road and the Union lines.[61]

The field momentarily belonged to the men of Garnett's Brigade. The survivors held the wall and drove back the few Union infantry and gunners that had held that section of the Angle wall (the men of Battery A, 4th U.S. Artillery, and portions of the 69th and 71st Pennsylvania Regiments). Lieutenant Finley was undeniably impressed with the gunners of Cushing's Battery. He would later remember how manfully they stood to their pieces, and remarked that he had never before seen such gallant bearing in any men as in those of Cushing's Battery. Finley could be envious of their bravery, but was fortunate not to have felt the full effects of the battery. He wrote that they fired their last shots directly into the faces of the

56th Regiment, and so close that he could distinctly feel the flame of discharge. It was not until its infantry supports were crushed and driven out that the gunners abandoned their rifled pieces.

Eager and anxious for supports to help press the victory home, Lieutenant Finley was one in Garnett's Brigade who could not contain himself when portions of Archer's Tennessee Brigade under Pettigrew's command joined him at the wall to his left. He could not help but notice that they were also but a remnant, having suffered two-fold in this battle — once on the 1st of July and again on this day. He, nevertheless, was cheered by the prospect of some of the Tennesseans joining him at the wall and holding it until proper supports arrived.

What transpired in the moments thereafter is best related by Lieutenant Finley himself, who was sticking it out with the remainder of his 56th Virginia:

> For several minutes there were no troops in our immediate front. But to our left the Federal line was still unbroken. This fact is impressed upon my mind by my taking a musket from one of my men who said he could not discharge it and firing it at that line to my left and obliquely in front, and further by seeing our brave Brigadier-General Garnett, who, though almost disabled from a kick from a horse while on the march from Virginia, would lead us in action that day, riding to our left, just in my rear, with his eyes fastened upon the unbroken line behind the stone fence, and with the evident intention to make such disposition of his men as would dislodge it. At that instant, suddenly a terrific fire burst upon us from our front, and looking around I saw close to us, just on the crest of the ridge, a fresh line of Federals attempting to drive us from the stone fence, but after exchanging a few rounds with us they fell back behind the crest, leaving us still in possession of the stone wall. Under this fire, as I immediately learned, Gen. Garnett had fallen dead.[62]

The troops that Finley saw deployed behind the stone wall to his left and front were the men of Hays' Division of the Union Second Corps, who never would be driven from their defenses on this day. But, the Federal element that most damaged the front of the 56th Virginia was those men of the enemy who emerged from behind the crest of Cemetery Ridge as the supports of Webb's Brigade — the 72nd Pennsylvania Infantry Regiment. According to Lieutenant Finley, it was the volleys fired by the 72nd Pennsylvania that felled General Garnett with the ball through his head. Indeed, if he were still alive and mounted at the time that the brigade held the stone wall, it was most likely that it was the fire from one of these volleys that laid him low. Because General Webb was unable to get the 72nd to advance under the fire from the Confederate-held stone wall, the regiment fell back behind the crest once again to reorganize.

The position where Lieutenant Finley reckoned the fatal ball struck his brigade commander was staked and mapped over thirty years after the battle by the U.S. War Department (see map, p. 96). This location for the site of Garnett's death may go a long ways toward explaining why his remains were never properly recovered or identified. If the general fell as closely to the wall as indicated by Lieutenant Finley,

Union soldiers would have had free access to the body and its contents after the fighting was over and they had recovered their original position. They would have been free to cross over the wall after the battle and take whatever trophies they could—swords, personal papers, collar insignia, spurs, etc. Garnett would have thus appeared very much like every fallen enemy infantryman on the Union front in one of the trench graves that would then hold their remains. Once so gallant and singular in life, Garnett would merely become a reminder of the fact that death is indeed the great leveller as he joined the ranks who fell to unknown graves.

Lieutenant Finley's account also reveals that Garnett's Brigade was awaiting some support to drive the victory home. The stone wall recently used as a defense by the Union forces became a shelter from the flying shot and shell by the weary men of Garnett's Brigade, all initiative to continue the assault drained from them. It would be the impetus of Armistead's Brigade coming up almost simultaneously into their midst from the rear that would encourage these men of Garnett's regiments to resume their advance from the Angle wall. It would be the regiments of Armistead's Brigade, intermingled with those survivors of Kemper's left and Garnett's line, who would finish the attack by Pickett's Division.

Armistead's Brigade came up primarily in the rear of Garnett's Brigade. His right lapped on Kemper's confused masses near the slashing and eventually forced his two right regiments to become engaged in the fighting on two flanks created by the flanking movement on that end of Pickett's line.[63] This last brigade to reach the Emmitsburg Road and surmount the fencing there was to experience the same terrors which befell the brigades of Garnett and Kemper. Survivors would long remember the moments of "anxious suspense and the length of time it seemed to climb up to the top of the fence," tumble over it, and fall flat into the bed of the road. All the while, the bullets continued to bury themselves into the bodies of victims and the sturdy chestnut rails. Some regiments of Pettigrew's column seemed compelled to stay within the shelter provided by the road bed and trade volleys with the Union line opposite, their positions at the Emmitsburg Road being even closer to the enemy's works and subject to an even more accurate and deadly fire, which mowed down the bravest who tried to cross the fencing. Armistead's Brigade remained within the roadbed but a few seconds before leaping again atop the five-rail fences that enclosed the roadway, leaving behind scores of dead and wounded comrades in the dust of the road. Another withering fire from the Union lines staggered the column after crossing the second line of fencing. The brigade returned the fire as best it could before rushing forward with a shout.[64] There were others in the brigade who had crowded in large numbers at small openings and gaps in the fencing, which had been torn down the previous day, in order to find an easier way to avoid the fencing obstacles. These crowding and confused groups provided excellent targets for the infantry and artillery on Cemetery Ridge. Even more casualties were incurred by those trying not to provide themselves as single targets atop a fence-rail.[65]

While the men of Kemper's Brigade huddled behind the protection afforded by the slashing and the small knoll in front of the Angle, they poured a continuous fire into the lines at their front, occasionally picking off gunners and mounted artillerymen of Cowan's 1st New York Battery. The six guns of this battery, however, continued to return the fire — first shell, and then canister — into the approaching ranks of Armistead's Brigade, adding to the destruction caused by the musketry from Hays' and Gibbon's Union Divisions.

The 14th Virginia Regiment of Colonel James G. Hodges, occupying the right of Armistead's Brigade, was sharing the same disbelief and surprise as Kemper's right regiment in finding there were no supports or any other body of troops on their right. Sergeant Drewry B. Easley, acting as a file closer for the regiment this day, was eager to rejoin his company in the fighting now that the advance was nearly completed. As the regiment approached the stone wall on Cemetery Ridge, he took the first opportunity he could find to rush through an opening between his regimental line and that of the 9th Virginia on the left. Wanting only to turn around to glance up and down the line to find his place with his Company H, Sergeant Easley instead ran smack into a bunch of blue-coated Union soldiers. Instinctively, the sergeant brought down his bayonet but soon saw that these Yankees had their hands up in the air. These were some of the men from the 69th and 71st Pennsylvania Regiments that Garnett's line had captured and sent rearward. Easley again put up his gun and pushed through these defenseless Federals. From that point the stone wall was just paces ahead. Sergeant Easley rushed toward it, mounted it, and then glanced to his right and left to take in Garnett's brigade "dug in" there. General Armistead reached the wall just to Easley's left with only one of Cushing's guns, which had been run up to the wall, between the general and the sergeant.[66]

The remainder of the regiment was to the right of Easley's position when he rushed around the left flank between the 14th and 9th Regiments. Colonel Hodges was to be a singular and noteworthy casualty of the brigade, falling during the latter stages of the attack before reaching the enemy's works. Colonel Theodore Gates, commanding the Union 20th New York State Militia in its movement to the right in conjunction with those of Hall's and Harrow's Brigades, recalled that Colonel Hodges was killed within a hundred feet of his position and that "he led his regiment up almost to the muzzles of the muskets of my men, through a fire that thinned his ranks at every step."[67] Another survivor of the 20th New York stated that Hodges fell in front of the stone wall within 150 feet of the Union lines, his sword and scabbard destroyed by a shot; yet another member of the New York regiment stated that Hodges was killed as close as four feet from the stone wall.[68] Although Colonel Hodges was clearly identified by these and other Federal survivors, his body, like that of General Garnett, eventually was interred without identification. Lieutenant James F. Crocker, adjutant of the 9th Virginia, attempted to assist the Colonel's widow and family in locating the remains of Colonel Hodges after the war since the widow was his sister. Their efforts were in vain, and it was surmised that he was interred in one of the many trench graves that held the remains of Pickett's dead. During a post-war visit to the battlefield, Crocker addressed a group of Union veterans and revealed that he had come to Gettysburg bearing a request from Mrs. Hodges and the fatherless sons to pray over the spot where the colonel was killed. Since they had been unable to find his remains, the family wished to in some way identify the site of his death. General Henry Hunt was among the Union veterans present, and volunteered to take Crocker to "the very spot where he fell." General Hunt had been looking for the body of General Garnett after the close of the battle, and

> when he came to the stone wall a long line of Confederate dead and wounded, lying along the wall, met his view, but his attention was arrested by the manly and handsome form of an officer lying dead on his back across other dead. He thought he had seen the face before, and on inquiry was told that it was Col. Hodges of the Fourteenth Virginia, whom he remembered to have seen in social circles before the war. The spot where Col. Hodges fell was identified by General Hunt and others, and is at the stone wall near the monument of the 69th Pennsylvania.[69]

Because General Hunt and others were specific about the body of Colonel Hodges near the position of the 69th Pennsylvania monument at the stone wall, it is apparent that the colonel of the 14th Virginia indeed fell within four feet of the enemy's works.

Among those to fall near or at the side of their colonel were Major Robert H. Poore and his adjutant, Lieutenant John Summerfield Jenkins. Crocker concluded that these two officers were probably among those men whose bodies fell beneath that of Colonel Hodges, "and whose limbs were interlocked in death as their lives had been united in friendship and comradeship in the camp." Captain Richard Logan, commanding Sergeant Easley's Company H, fell while facing the enemy, pierced by a ball near his heart, without uttering a word. Crocker's eulogy for his intimate friend Lieutenant Jenkins, could very well be applied to all those young men of Pickett's Division who went down into the valley of death on July 3rd 1863:

> He fell among the bravest, sealed his devotion to his country by his warm young blood, in the flush of early vigorous manhood when his life was full of hope and promise. He gave up home which was particularly dear and sweet to him, when he knew that hereafter his only home would be under the flag of his regiment, where it might lead, whether on the march, in the camp or on the battlefield. His life was beautiful and manly — his death was heroic and glorious, and his name is of the imperishable ones of Pickett's charge.[70]

A member of the 9th Virginia, which was fighting at the left side of the 14th Virginia, watched his brigade commander (Armistead) rush forward after the brigade scaled the Emmitsburg Road fencing. When within a hundred or so yards of the stone wall he was met by a mounted officer, whom the regimental adjutant believed was General Garnett. After the exchange of a few words, the horseman and Armistead parted company.[71] General Armistead fell back to a position behind the brigade to allow it to deliver its fire into the Union lines. Then, dashing forward once again to the front of his five regiments, Armistead led the brigade in its last rush toward the stone wall and the determined survivors of Garnett's and Kemper's Brigades in their front.[72]

Perhaps one of the most lamented to fall that day within the ranks of the 9th Virginia was its colonel, John C. Owens. Admired as intelligent, quiet, gentle, kind and considerate, Colonel Owens fell while gallantly leading his men before the regiment reached the enemy's lines. Carried to the rear, Colonel Owens died at the division field hospital at Bream's Mill before the day was spent, and was buried there by his comrades.[73] Meanwhile, in the ranks of Company I of the 9th Regiment, 21-year-old Lieutenant John C. Niemeyer impressed his company with his conspicuous bravery. After the regiment cleared the obstruction of the Emmitsburg Road and the line was once again dressed, Niemeyer turned to his friend and fellow lieutenant, John Vermillion, with a bright smile, saying "John, what a beautiful line!" Within minutes, Lieutenant Neimeyer's pride had vanished. He had fallen dead, pierced through the head by a Yankee bullet. His body was never recovered by his friends, and his remains were interred by the enemy in one of the many "unknown" graves that would soon furrow the slopes of Cemetery Ridge.[74]

The center regiment of the brigade, the 53rd Virginia, continued in the immediate rear of General Armistead, being the regiment of direction and guarding the guiding colors. Lieutenant-Colonel Rawley W. Martin, commanding the regiment in place of the wounded Colonel Aylett, maintained his place near the side of General Armistead, until the color-bearer of the 53rd was struck down by a shell. Calling for someone to take the flag, the bearer (probably Sergeant Blackburn) yielded it to Colonel Martin, who had appeared instantly at his side. With words of encouragement, Martin called for his men to follow, and carried the flag until relieved of that duty by another member of the color guard.[75]

The 53rd Virginia was being decimated at every step from the Emmitsburg Road. Lieutenant J. Irving Sale of Company H recalled that a solid shot from the direction of the Round Tops struck the right of the company line and dropped a dozen men, cutting one of the victims completely in two. Soon after passing through this menace, the regiment was subjected to canister fire. Lieutenant Sale remembered trying to crawl through a fence and heard the ping of the shot and balls striking the fence rails all around him. His head got caught between two rails in the midst of this, and the horror crossed his mind that he could be killed in that position and left there hanging so unceremoniously. Extracting his head, he gave up the notion of trying to crawl between the rails, and leaped over the fence instead. Relieved of his own predicament, Sale was soon keenly aware of the numbers of his comrades falling in the fields between the road and the stone wall, and lamented that it was "awful the way the men dropped."[76] Lieutenant Wyatt Whitehead of Company I recollected that the firing became even worse when he was within forty yards or so of the Union lines. At that time the Federals rose from behind the walls and poured such a murderous fire into their ranks "as no human tongue can describe."[77] Lieutenant James A. Harwood of Company K agreed that the fire of shot and shell to which the brigade was subjected was the "most terrific...that mortals ever encountered," whittling down the effectives to almost one-third of the force that had left the Marsh Creek encampment about twelve hours earlier.[78]

Corporal James Carter of Company I, 53rd Virginia, had been near to General Armistead during the entire advance as part of the color guard. He observed that the point of the saber on which the general had placed his hat as a guide had soon cut through his hat, which slipped down to the hilt. Armistead continued to wave it in this state, however, seemingly oblivious of it for most of the advance, as he urged his men forward to the enemy's heights. Corporal Carter himself soon had other matters to preoccupy his attention, after Sergeant Blackburn was shot down. He seized the colors from the color-sergeant, but they were snatched from his grasp by Corporal John B. Scott of Company G, another member of the guard. Scott ran about fifteen feet beyond the brigade front and waved them to cheer on the men. He was instantly shot and killed by the sheet of musketry that was staggering the advance from the Emmitsburg Road. Corporal Carter was struck by this same continuous withering fire. When he fell wounded, Private Robert Tyler Jones of Company K ran forward and picked up the fallen colors. Almost immediately after raising them again, Jones was shot in the arm, but maintained his place and continued the attack bearing his regimental banner. When he reached the stone wall of the Angle, Jones leaped on top of the loose rocks and triumphantly waved the flag of the 53rd Virginia back and forth. His actions could do nothing but attract the fire of the Federals. Thus the grandson of President Tyler at once toppled forward over the wall severely wounded with another gunshot wound.[79]

Lieutenant Sale was near General Armistead when the regiment approached within a few feet from the stone wall. There, like Garnett's Brigade, the regiment was brought to a standstill by the fire from the Yankees in their front. After a minute or two of exchanging fire, men like Sale realized that they could not stay in that position long and survive. Armistead turned to Colonel Martin and remarked, "Martin, we can't stay here; we must go over that wall." Replying, "Then we'll go forward!" Colonel Martin mounted the wall and cried, "Forward the colors!" Armistead again placed his hat atop the point of his sword, so that his men and those of the other brigades could see it through the smoke of battle. Then he scaled the wall while waving the makeshift guide and cried, "Boys, give them the cold steel! Who will follow me?"[80]

On his left, Colonel John Bowie Magruder, commanding the 57th Virginia Regiment, became another casualty of the attack. When he fell mortally wounded within twenty steps of Cushing's guns, his last words to his regiment expressed the pride of a hard-won fight. "They are ours!" He was struck almost simultaneously by two shots. One hit him in the left breast and the other struck him under his right arm, passing through his body and crossing the first wound. Since no one was able to get him to the rear in his condition, Colonel Magruder would eventually fall into the hands of the enemy. He would later be taken to the Twelfth Corps hospital, where he languished until he died on July 5 at the age of 23 years.[81] Since they were compelled to leave him on the site of their momentary victory and in the hands of the Federals, there could be little consolation to the survivors of the regiment that he was one of the few field commanders to reach such an advanced position.

The large 38th Virginia, on the extreme left of Armistead's column, must have shared similar experiences with the regiments to their right, but there were few inclined to leave a record of those moments of the attack. Captain George Griggs of Company K revealed only that the regiment moved steadfastly even when forced to climb over the two high fences along the Emmitsburg Road, under the concentrated fire of Union artillery. They participated in driving the enemy from the Angle wall, and helped capture the four pieces of Cushing's Regular Battery which had been pushed up to the fence.[82] But they also lost their regimental commander when Colonel Edmonds was killed. Edmonds was one of seven comrades at VMI who fell that day as colonels, but it was not until six weeks after the battle that the regiment finally entered him as killed on the field of battle. Up to that time the men of the 38th Virginia believed that Edmonds had been merely wounded or captured and were trying to make contact with anyone knowing of his prison or hospital whereabouts. It was for them, as it was for the men of the 9th Virginia, a bitter and sorrowful realization.[83]

These forty-odd acres of once peaceful pasture and farmed fields over which Pickett's Division launched its final attack could rightly be signified as that place where the Union commands of "Webb, and Hall, and Harrow fought and dug Secession's grave."[84] Surely, the losses sustained by the division filled many a grave as they fell before the storm of lead pouring into their ever-thinning ranks. The slashing, the grounds in front of the stone wall of the Angle, and the fields of Garnett's and Armistead's attacks, were described later by the Union survivors of those attacks. A veteran of the 13th Vermont, which had so effectively cut at the flanks of Kemper and Armistead, gave his appraisal of this small portion of the battlefield of Gettysburg:

> If there was any spot on that great field of battle that approximated more nearly than any other the maelstrom of destruction, this was the place. They lay one upon the other clutched in death, side by side. The dead, dying and horribly wounded, some had on the blue, but nearly all wore the gray.... This was indeed the great slaughter pen on the field of Gettysburg, and in it lay hundreds of the brave heroes who an hour before buoyed up with hope and ambition were being led by the brave and intrepid Pickett....[85]

To see that this veteran knew first hand what he was talking about, we have to merely look at the burial map of the battlefield laid out sometime after August 1863 (see map, p.135). Two massive trenches held the bodies of 552 and 175 Confederates who were killed outright in these fields. These demarcations and figures probably do not include scores of other burials that were overlooked by this early map maker. The numbers and rows of lines bear sad witness to the effectiveness of the Federal fire as Pickett's column passed the Emmitsburg Road en route to the enemy works. The farm fields of Nicholas Codori and Pius Small were transformed within twenty-four hours' time from meadows and pastures to battlefields, and within another forty-eight hours from battlefields to cemeteries. Yet, even this field of slaughter could not deter the survivors of Pickett's Division who reached the Union defenses on Cemetery Ridge. For many the attack was over, but for men from each of the fifteen regiments the fighting was not yet completed.

View From Union Lines to Clump of Trees and Field of Kemper's Attack

This April 1882 Tipton photograph was taken from a platform along the route of the proposed Hancock Avenue, and looks southwestward to the Clump of Trees (the larger mass of trees to the left), the line of the 69th Pennsylvania Regiment (from the Clump of Trees to the large solitary tree at the right), and beyond into the fields east of the Emmitsburg Road. The rocky outcropping used by a portion of Kemper's men to shield themselves near the conclusion of the attack is just visible between the Clump of Trees and the tree to which the guide is pointing. (Gettysburg NMP)

The Angle, the Stone Wall, and the Fields Over Which Pickett's Division Advanced

The gentleman astride the wall with arm upraised approximates the position where General Armistead crossed. Above him are the Codori Farm buildings as they appeared in 1882 (only the barn and the front portion of the house were standing in 1863), and in the distance to the right of the Codori buildings can be seen the rooftops of the Spangler Farm buildings. The Klingel buildings are on the horizon at the extreme left, and the tree line on the distant horizion represents Seminary Ridge. (Gettysburg NMP)

Apex of Angle Wall and Seminary Ridge

The third in the series of panorama photographs by William H. Tipton in 1882 shows the northern salient of the Angle wall and the woods of Seminary Ridge in the background. Most of the terrain over which Armistead's Brigade crossed is visible from the woods to the stone wall in the foreground. The point of woods where General Lee met the division after its retreat is visible directly above the meeting point of the two Union stone walls. The roofs of the Pitzer Farm buildings show that point where General Pickett's men first rallied before being sent back to camp, beyond the woods of Seminary Ridge. (Gettysburg NMP)

A Map Showing the Scene of Longstreet's Final Assault

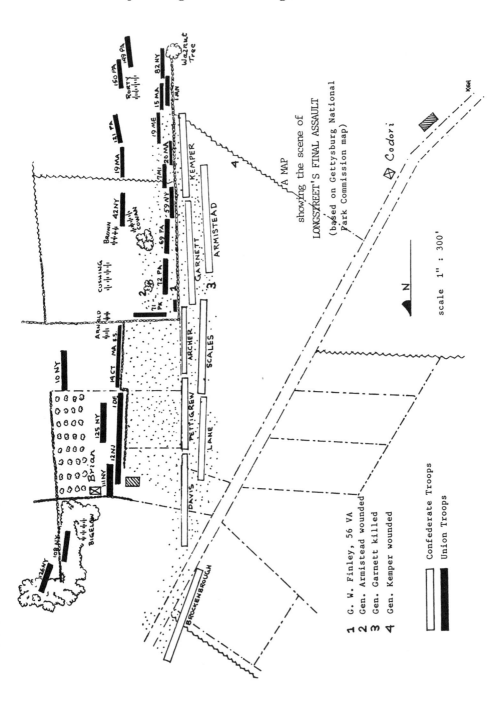

A MAP
showing the scene of
LONGSTREET'S FINAL ASSAULT
(based on Gettysburg National
Park Commission map)

scale 1" : 300'

N

1 G. W. Finley, 56 VA
2 Gen. Armistead wounded
3 Gen. Garnett killed
4 Gen. Kemper wounded

☐ Confederate Troops
■ Union Troops

Chapter

VI

"The Earth Seemed to be on Fire"

There was a sense of momentary victory for those few hundreds of Pickett's soldiers who advanced as far as the stone wall and the slopes immediately adjacent. The enemy's line had abandoned its position. The guns of Cushing's Battery were silent and unmanned, out of ammunition and short of gunners. In their rear, however, there were few left to support and strengthen the Virginian's successful attack. The five guns under Major John Cheves Haskell were firing even their last shots now. McGilvery's artillery on the south end of Cemetery Ridge had inflicted disastrous casualties on the gunners and horses of Miller's and Battle's Louisiana commands. Lieutenant Battles' section was completely disabled by the concentrated fire from these Yankee batteries, which dismounted one piece by breaking its axle. The other gun was struck by a shot on its face and bent out of shape so much that it could not be loaded again. The loss in horses was so great that it became imperative to remove the guns shortly or they would not be able to be maneuvered with ease if necessary. At last, with his small amount of ammunition completely exhausted, Major Haskell ordered the men to abandon the position.[1] Major Eshleman then ordered all the guns that were still fit and with ammunition to occupy a new, and less exposed position, to the left. They reoccupied the place held during the cannonade by Dearing's Virginia Battalion, which had limbered to the rear when there was no further ammunition forthcoming to replenish depleted supplies. From here, only five guns of the battalion (including two howitzers) were in condition to continue to assist the attacking column. These appear to be the only guns on the right of Alexander's line that were still firing by the time the remnants of Pickett's Division reached the stone wall.

From this place the rifled gun recently added to Captain J. B. Richardson's Battery (captured the previous day) was serving its new masters with accuracy. Shots from it, or the two Napoleons in Richardson's command, were responsible for firing at least two very accurate and deadly shots into the Union line. Richardson saw the men of Harrow's Federal Brigade as they left their place in the division line on Cemetery Ridge and moved to the portion of wall attained by Pickett's men. The Confederate gunners fired first one solid shot and then another that "tore a horrible passage through the dense crowd of men in blue ... and fairly cut a road through the mass."[2] The captured rifle, after firing all its ammunition, was disabled when its axle was broken before it could be withdrawn. The artillery support so vital to the success of General Lee's plan of attack had now vanished completely just as Pickett's infantrymen reached the point from which they most desperately needed it to press their momentary advantage.

General Kemper's command, now under the direction of Colonel Joseph Mayo of the 3rd Virginia, would be the first to feel the overwhelming effects of the Northern movements that surged to the right in mass, regiment after regiment, upon the Confederate invaders. Harrow's Union Brigade was ordered to the support of the Union line where Webb's Brigade and Cushing's Battery had been overrun by Garnett and Armistead. In the process of moving toward the Clump of Trees in that vicinity, they became the targets not only of Eshleman's remaining guns but also of Kemper's infantrymen. Brigade organization was now almost completely lost because of the flanking fire from Stannard's Vermonters on their right and from frontal fire of Hall's and Harrow's Brigades, with Rorty's New York and Weir's Regular Batteries adding their fury. For this reason, Kemper's Brigade had been seeking whatever shelter was available. Many hundreds had stopped at the rock outcropping and knoll just northwest of this slashing. From these two points they continued to lay down a continuous fire on these men from Kemper's Brigade, the fire from whom was becoming annoying and deadly. While riding through Cowan's guns, General Henry J. Hunt had his mount shot from under him by the fire from these sheltered Confederates.[3] Hunt was temporarily trapped beneath his fallen horse until he could be freed. For about five minutes the men of the 15th Massachusetts exchanged fire with these men of Kemper's Brigade, as well as those of Armistead's Brigade at the stone wall in front of the Clump of Trees. Because the Union shots affected the protected Virginians very little, one of the Yankee privates was prompted to cry out, "For God's sake, let us charge, they'll kill us all if we stand here."[4] The Massachusetts regiment thereupon continued its movement beyond the small Clump of Trees toward the stone wall.

In the 11th Virginia Regiment, Major Kirkwood Otey was wounded and no longer capable of command, so Captain Hutter found himself once again in temporary command of the regiment. He, however, also pulled up wounded near the stone wall. He did not necessarily think it serious until Lieutenant H. Valentine Harris, the regimental adjutant, came up and putting his finger on Hutter's back indicated that the ball entered at that point. Looking down to see the blood on the front of his uniform, apparently where the ball had exited, Hutter could but exclaim, "I am a dead man." An exploding shell overhead (perhaps from their own artillery) sent Harris and Hutter sprawling, and Harris sprang to his feet to see about his duties elsewhere. Captain John Ward of Company E was momentarily at Captain Hutter's side offering him a drink of water or whiskey from his "double barreled" flask. Gratefully accepting some drink, Hutter listened while Captain Ward joyfully pointed out how they were whipping the Yankees, indicating Union prisoners streaming to the rear. On closer examination, they were chagrined to see that these prisoners had guns on their shoulders, and were escorting captured men of Kemper's Brigade to the Union lines. Believing himself to be dangerously wounded, Hutter asked the sergeant in charge of the prisoner guard detail to send a Union officer to accept his surrender. As soon as the blue clad soldiers left, Captains Ward and Hutter closely examined the wound to find that Hutter had been merely grazed by a ball across his chest. Before the Union sergeant could return, the two captains retreated as rapidly as possible and hastened back to a position near where they began the charge at the Emmitsburg Road.[5]

Line and staff officers of the brigade and the 11th Virginia held a hasty conference near or at the slashing and sent "Big Foot" George Walker, Kemper's courier, to the rear to bring up reinforcements. They then took the precaution to send another courier immediately after him in case Walker did not make it. So worried and anxious were these officers to hold the position so recently gained at such a cost that they stood and watched as the two couriers disappeared one after the other over the ridge of the Emmitsburg Road.[6] Walker had expressed these same concerns only moments before being sent to the rear to Colonel Mayo. While Mayo was giving a hurried glance over the field that the brigade had crossed, he heard Private Walker at his side voice the words which had already formed in his own mind: "Oh! Colonel, why don't they support us?" Colonel Mayo could not answer the question, but could only send Walker to the rear to urge forward those much needed supports.[7]

The men of the 11th Virginia held on a few minutes longer. Since they were faced with an ever stronger enemy on the right and front, and since no reinforcements were forthcoming, the men were instructed to scatter as they retired. This would give the Union artillery fewer massed targets at which to aim. So, the men began to fall back singly and in small groups. As the rest of the regiment retired, Captain John Smith remained at the works in order to dress a slight bleeding wound on his right leg. Captain Robert Douthat of Company F remained with him, picking up a musket and firing several shots into the Union lines. While Smith wrapped his leg in a towel from his haversack, Douthat wordlessly continued his regular fire. Finally looking up, Smith was shocked to see a large column of Yankees only about 75 yards off at their right front, and was surprised that Douthat had gone calmly about the business of firing into this huge mass by himself, not wanting to alarm Smith as he set about the duties of nursing his thigh. Coming immediately to his senses, Captain Smith jumped up and said at once "Douthat, what are you doing?" Douthat dropped the empty musket, and in classic understatement said, "It's time to get away from here." The duo ran as fast as they could toward the Emmitsburg Road, covering almost 150 yards before drawing enemy fire.[8]

They left behind the many incapacitated men of the regiment who were unable to join them in their flight to safety. One of these men, Private William H. Winston, had been knocked unconscious by an exploding shell near the works during the attack. By the time he recovered his senses, Winston found none but Union troops around him, gathering up the wounded. He was sent to the rear as a prisoner.[9] Lieutenant Green B. Long of Company F and Lieutenant James W. Wray of Company E met when they were each falling back and happened to stop for shelter behind the same boulder. As Lieutenant Wray got up to leave he heard the thud of a bullet striking nearby, and realized as he fled rearward that the lieutenant was not with him any longer. Lieutenant Long had been hit in the shoulder and was to be captured before reaching Confederate lines.[10]

First Lieutenant John T. James of Company D, 11th Virginia, summarized feelings about the long advance and eventual repulse of the Virginians in a letter written within a week of the battle. Here he echoed the disappointment felt throughout the division:

After terrible loss to the regiment, brigade and division, we reached and actually captured the breastworks. Some of the men had taken possession of the cannon, when we saw the enemy advancing heavy reinforcements. We looked back for ours, but in vain; we were compelled to fall back and had again to run as targets to their balls. Oh, it was hard, too hard to be compelled to give way for the want of men, after having fought as hard as we had that day. The unwounded...soon got back to the place where we started from. We gained nothing but glory and lost our bravest men.[11]

In the ranks of what used to be the center of the brigade line, the men were initially ecstatic to see the enemy surrender and pass to their rear without a guard. Lieutenant Edward P. Reeve of Company D found himself in command of the "Old First" Virginia there, after the loss of Colonel Williams, Major Langley, and all company commanders. Kemper's adjutant, Captain William Fry, brought the regiment the order to move by the right flank along their position at the stone wall. Giving the order for his men to "fall in" in preparation for executing the order, Lieutenant Reeve watched as about a dozen of the regiment, all that could be found, took position. Many were shot as soon as they took their places by the terrible fire still coming in on their right and front, and Reeve turned to Captain Fry to say that it was too late for such a movement, since there was no 1st Virginia left to execute the order. Reeve was shortly thereafter also wounded, while the regiment tried to inch its way forward. Seeing one of the color bearers of the division out in front of its remnants, Lieutenant Reeve noted that the flag bearer turned to see what following he had. Obviously disappointed at the sparseness and inadequacy of the force, the color bearer kept his face to the rear, and marched from the field with his colors.[12] The colors of the 1st Virginia could not be carried rearward; they remained where they fell near the stone wall when Jacob Polak had been wounded, since the color guard was all killed or wounded. Color Sergeant William Lawson of Company H had done all that any member of a guard could accomplish that day he lost his right arm near the shoulder while carrying forward the colors of the 1st Regiment. His gallant conduct at Gettysburg would be rewarded with a promotion and commission after his release from the prison hospital.[13]

For Corporal Charles T. Loehr, who had come across the fields with the skirmishers of the regiment, there seemed little else to do but retreat when no reinforcements came. With the enemy advancing to recapture their works, Loehr decided it was time that the regiment "got," and that is what he did. Slightly wounded in the face and arm, Corporal Loehr found it to be even more difficult to scale the fencing along the Emmitsburg Road than during the advance. The fencing appeared to him at this point to be ten rails high, twice their actual height, but he managed to pass the obstructions unscathed and paused to catch his breath when about a quarter of a mile from the battle action. From here he saw General Lee riding unattended, observing the activities on his front for a few minutes. Loehr saw him ride to the rear and then return shortly thereafter with General Longstreet in tow, establishing a point on which the returning men could rally.[14]

Colonel Mayo, commanding the brigade, realized it was time to yield the ground when, in looking back, he saw Colonel William R. "Old Buck" Terry standing with "a peculiarly sad smile on his face" between the colors of the 11th and 24th Regiments, pointing rearward with his sword. From Mayo's position near the wall he could not hear Terry's words, since he was more than midway between the Emmitsburg Road and the stone wall, but he knew the meaning of the gesture. Colonel Terry realized it would be suicidal for his men to hold on much longer with ever dwindling forces against the mounting pressure on the right. Mayo acknowledged this same reality, and ordered the group around him to spread themselves out and follow him in the opposite direction toward Seminary Ridge.[15] In his own 3rd Virginia the casualties had been staggering. In Company F, on the extreme right of the regiment, Lieutenant Azra P. Gomer would relate that of the twenty five men reporting for duty that morning, twenty four had been casualties. Gomer himself had been severely wounded in the left leg upon reaching the stone wall and was lucky enough to be assisted from the field to his own lines.[16] Not so fortunate was Lieutenant Fenton Eley Wrenn of Company I, the only line officer remaining in this unit. When ordered by Mayo to fall back, Lieutenant Wrenn expressed the conviction that it was against his better judgment to retreat back over those hostile fields with nothing but their exposed backs between the enemy and the safety of the Confederate lines. Although he was able to find only four of his men who were willing to follow him, he nevertheless led them back into the open fields. Lieutenant Wrenn never made it back to his own lines, and his remains were never identified; his men only knew that he was never seen again after the retreat from the stone wall began.[17]

General Kemper's staff suffered another heavy loss with the mortal wounding of aide de camp Lieutenant George Geiger. After his horse was shot out from under him during the charge, Lieutenant Geiger kept with the brigade on foot. He reached the lines with the men safely, but was shot during the retreat ordered by Mayo. It would take two weeks of suffering as a prisoner in a Gettysburg hospital before the 37-year-old officer died.[18]

In Kemper's Brigade, the cost in high ranking officers was reflected in the severe wounding of Kemper himself. Among his regimental commanders Colonel Williams was killed and Major Langley wounded in the 1st Virginia; every company commander had been taken out of action in the "Old First" as well, and its casualties were the highest percentage total in the brigade with sixty two percent. Although Colonel Mayo of the 3rd Virginia had exposed himself gallantly at the head of his regiment, and then assumed brigade command up to the enemy works, he was the only regimental commander not wounded. Lieutenant Colonel Alexander D. Callcote, however, was killed and buried on the field of battle. Colonel Patton of the 7th Virginia was mortally wounded in the face. Major Kirkwood Otey, so recently under confinement for earlier infractions, had been wounded while commanding his 11th Virginia Regiment, and so perhaps atoned for past mistakes. Whereas the high command of the 24th survived the battle, the casualties within the regiment mirrored the action of this outflanked right regiment. Many men were captured outright, and the occasional mention of gunshot wounds in the back and sides among the enlisted men confirms the surprise with which many of them were felled by Stannard's Vermont regiments. But there were also those amongst the

24th Virginia who advanced beyond the enemy's works. Private Nathaniel Law of Company D was burned by a shell burst, and perhaps by the discharge of the guns in Rorty's or Cowan's Battery.

The fierceness with which Kemper's command attempted to take the guns in their own front contrasted with the experiences on Garnett's front. Whereas Cushing's guns had been silenced by the time Garnett's command reached the stone wall, the guns of Rorty's and Cowan's New York Batteries continued to pour their destructive canister into the ranks of Kemper's command, as well as into the right regiments of Armistead's Brigade as it came up to assist Kemper's stalled advance. When the soldiers of Hall's and Harrow's Brigades crowded to their right in the direction of the Clump of Trees, the front of the two New York batteries was uncovered. This permitted them to fire canister at the most depressed angles for full efficiency, without worrying about striking their own men in front. Kemper's men were quick to take advantage of the unsupported battery when they saw the infantry leave their front, but they were unprepared for the welcome that the New Yorkers had awaiting. One of Rorty's guns was loaded with a triple charge of canister as the Virginians left the shelter of the slashing and knoll in their rush on the guns. The force of the discharge from this powerful load was such that the gun was overturned. But the death and destruction which poured fourth from its muzzle was like a "khamsin wind," blowing the enemy from its front. Double canister was fired from the remaining pieces of Rorty's Battery, opening great gaps in Kemper's and Armistead's masses. For the first and last time in the history of the battery, however, Confederate hands were laid upon the guns as the Virginians swept over the battery. Rorty's men resorted to handspikes, rammers, pistols, and whatever weapons were handy as close combat for possession of the guns transpired. An unidentified captain, carrying one of the regimental flags, advanced to the fourth gun of the battery and planted the colors thereon, with the cry "Those guns are ours!" Having emptied his revolver into the oncoming foe, the gun's commander, Sergeant Louis Darveau, picked up a handspike, replied, "Not by a damned sight," and smashed him across the forehead, killing this bold Confederate officer instantly. Although Darveau was almost simultaneously riddled with bullets for his actions, the spirited defense of the artillery men lasted long enough to save them from becoming Kemper's prisoners. The Union lines closed fast around those who had stayed near the guns too long, so preventing their escape with those who followed Colonel Mayo and Lieutenant Reeve to the rear. In this way, hundreds of wounded and prisoners fell into Yankee hands.[19]

To the left, Garnett's Brigade, which had first gained the enemy's position, endured an even longer interval between the time the wall was secured at the Angle and the time that the Union counterattack occurred. During that interval, the brigade reflected the defensiveness exhibited on their right by Kemper's Brigade. When the 8th Virginia survivors attained the Union works they stopped on the west side of the wall and continued to fire individually into the enemy's ranks at and near the Clump of Trees. Lieutenant Charles Berkeley, commanding Company D after his brother William had been shot near the Codori Farmhouse, reached the wall with three men of his command. A large rock had been displaced from the wall at their position and formed a sort of porthole through which they could see the enemy on the other side without exposing themselves to Union gunfire. Private James D. Lunceford of Company F was at the wall there with Lieutenant Berkeley and kept up a rapid fire through this opening while the other men loaded the guns and passed them to him. It was said by those around them that Lunceford killed more men than any other man in the battle during this marathon of sharpshooting, and Berkeley was inclined to confirm it. The enlisted man was quite resistant to the ideas of surrendering when the Union forces began to fill the Angle. When Lieutenant Berkeley handed him his handkerchief with instructions to tie it to his ramrod and wave it in token of surrender, Lunceford protested, "Hold on a while, Lieutenant. I am getting two at a crack."[20]

Because of the confusion created by having to pass the Codori farmhouse and outbuildings during the advance and attack, the 8th Virginia appears to have been disunited in its efforts. Some of the men from the regiment may have been intermingled with those of the 11th and 24th Virginia Regiments of Kemper's Brigade in parrying the flanking movement by Stannard's 13th and 16th Vermont Regiments. In any event, the 8th Virginia lost its battle flag to the 16th Vermont sometime during the repulse of the attack.

It was one of five flags lost in Garnett's Brigade this July afternoon, as each regiment lost its stand of colors in the confusion and death that swirled about the men trying to take and hold Cemetery Ridge.[21]

Major Edmund Berkeley, wounded and incapacitated by his leg wound, was unable to return to the position he held before the cannonade, where he had buried his beloved pack of playing cards. Major Berkeley was not able to return to the battlefield until at least fifteen years had elapsed. He then endeavored to find these tokens of comradeship shared with his brothers, General Garnett, and Colonel Hunton. Since he was not able to locate them on the field of battle, Berkeley visited the stores of relic collectors in Gettysburg. He finally discovered from one of the store keepers that a boy had brought in a pack of cards which he had found under a stone. Since they were but a mass of pulp after so long exposure to the elements and the wet soil, the collector (probably Joel Danner) paid the boy a nickel for them. The collector then took them to the Chicago Exposition and sold them as a genuine relic of the battle for 200 times what he paid for them. To Major Berkeley, this tangible relic of the war years was worth very much more, but it was forever afterward out of his reach.[22]

The right center regiment, the 18th Virginia, continued to follow Lieutenant Colonel Henry A. Carrington to the Union defenses after leaving the Emmitsburg Road. After reaching the stone wall, Private James Clay, although wounded, saw the men engaged with the butts of their rifles in their struggle at the Angle for almost fifteen minutes.[23] Adjutant Richard Ferguson watched regimental Sergeant Major James C. Gill fall close by with a fatal wound in his side. When Corporal Jordan C. Webb of his old Company G tried to aid the Sergeant Major, he too fell at his side, wounded by a gunshot below the eye. A momentary cessation in the firing caused a number of the 18th Virginia Regiment to take advantage of the safety and try to scatter and save themselves from capture. Lieutenant Ferguson saw his old company mates, Charles Atkinson, already wounded, and William Ovid Williams running back during this respite. For the pair it did not matter. Private Atkinson would be captured anyway, and Ovid Williams was never seen again and probably was killed during the retreat. As soon as the fresh Union troops entered the Angle in his front and opened fire immediately into the fleeing backs of those who had begun the initial retreat, Adjutant Ferguson realized it was sheer folly to attempt escape across the open fields. Throwing himself to the ground, Ferguson began firing, and continued doing so until he realized that further resistance was useless.[24] Lieutenant Ferguson's indecision whether or not to retreat and face death or remain and face death was made over and over again along Pickett's line as the attack withered and the repulse ripened. Kemper's men were already experiencing the harvests of those decisions, and now the men in Garnett's fading line would feel the same fears. Ferguson was one of the stalwart who made a determined stand in hopes of some miraculous support or victory, until he was himself overwhelmed, taken prisoner, and sent to prison.

Captain Henry T. Owen of Company C, 18th Virginia, would write later of the incredible firepower still felt from the Union survivors in the Angle, and of the repulse and defeat caused by the reinforcement of the Federals from their right:

> Pickett's men were within a few feet of the stone wall when the artillery delivered their last fire from guns shotted to the muzzle—a blaze fifty feet long went through the charging, surging host with a gaping rent to the rear, but the survivors mounted the wall, then over and onward, rushed up the hill close after the gunners who waved their rammers in the face of Pickett's men and sent up cheer after cheer as they felt admiration for the gallant charge. On swept the column over ground covered with dead and dying men, where the earth seemed to be on fire, the smoke dense and suffocating, the sun shut out, flames blazing on every side, friend could hardly be distinguished from foe, but the division, in the shape of an inverted V, with the point flattened, pushed forward, fighting, falling and melting away, till half way up the hill they were met by a powerful body of fresh troops, charging down upon them, and this remnant of about a thousand men was hurled back out into the clover field.[25]

Once back out in this cloverfield west of the Angle wall, the men of Garnett's Brigade "showed a disposition to return for another charge,"[26] so unwilling were they to retreat unprotected across the open fields again.

The Danville Grays of Captain Robert McCulloch suffered its last casualties in this struggle at the Angle and during the retreat to Seminary Ridge, and McCulloch reported that his Company B had no more to give. His recollection was that every member of the company had been hit by a bullet, although some were only slightly wounded. McCulloch received two wounds, his last coming within the Angle itself. He remembered seeing the soldier who fired the shot that finally felled him, less than twenty feet distant. Toppling near one of the gun carriages of Cushing's Battery, the captain would later be placed atop it as a makeshift ambulance when the guns were taken from the field.[27]

Lieutenant Colonel Henry A. Carrington, carrying the colors of the 18th Virginia up to the stone wall, fell wounded. The colors themselves, however, may have escaped capture by the enemy, as reported by Captain Andrew Cowan of the 1st New York Battery. That Union officer reported that when the Confederates in his front fell back, a couple of men from his battery ran across the wall and brought back at least two battle flags and a flagstaff which they had picked up from the ground in front of the wall. With no other officers to assist him in the dispositions of his battery, Captain Cowan was too busy to attend immediately to the flags and they were momentarily forgotten by him. He soon learned that a staff officer had demanded the flags from his men and carried them off with him, leaving behind the flagstaff. According to Captain Cowan, he discovered that the flagstaff belonged to the 18th Virginia Regiment, the name being stencilled on a strip of canvas next to the staff. Fragments of the flag were still attached to this shred of canvas heading, and Cowan surmised that one of Carrington's men tore the flag from the staff and escaped with it.[28]

With Colonel Gantt and Lieutenant Colonel Ellis wounded, the one-armed Major Charles S. Peyton became the ranking officer in the 19th Virginia. At the end of the attack, he was the only field officer in all of Garnett's Brigade left unscathed. Peyton's forces were not apt to give up without resistance at the wall, and the attitude of the color bearer reflected that grim determination neither to let hold of their hard won victory nor relinquish the pride of the regiment. As Private Benjamin Falls of the 19th Massachusetts Regiment approached the wall in front of the Clump of Trees he made for a Confederate battle flag flying above it. Supposing it to have been left there because he saw no one beside it, he reached for the flag but was surprised that he could not move it. Peering over the wall he saw one of the 19th Virginia boys lying on the ground, still grasping the base of the staff. Private Falls raised his bayonetted musket like a spear over the Confederate's head, saying, "Hut, Tut! Let alone of that or I'll run ye through." With little option but to surrender, the man and the battle flag were thus captured by Falls, who would later win a Medal of Honor for the deed.[29] When brigade commander Hall received the colors from the 19th Massachusetts, it could only be assumed that this was the battle flag of the 19th Virginia, because the number of the regiment had been torn out.[30] There was no record as to whether one of the regimental survivors of the 19th Virginia tore out the numerical designation to prevent confirmation that the battle flag had been lost, or one of the veterans of the 19th Massachusetts Volunteers tore out the numbers as a souvenir, or it was torn out by artillery fire. There is also now no record of the identity of this last defender of his regiment's flag, who could not bring himself to abandon the colors at the wall and fall back with many of his comrades.

One of those who had fallen back without the colors was Lieutenant William Wood of Company A, who had made his escape when he saw the vast numbers of Union troops coming in on his right while he was at the stone wall. Limping from the bruise on his right leg, Lieutenant Wood stumbled as best he could to the Emmitsburg Road, where, tired, hot, and thirsty he wanted little more than to take refuge behind a pile of rails there near the Codori Farmhouse. They looked all the more inviting as the enemy began to open fire on the retreating survivors just as

Wood reached that point. Wood, who had felt such high hopes that the "hill must fall," had felt momentary disgrace when he and his comrades were compelled to retire. But upon seeing the numbers of dead and wounded in the field between the stone wall and the Emmitsburg Road during his retreat, he realized why there were so few numbers at the stone wall with the battle flags. As Wood reached his lines he was sorrowfully welcomed by General Pickett himself, who extended his hand to the lieutenant and then turned aside to almost sob out the words, "My brave men! My brave men!" The sights of his fallen comrades and the lamentable words of praise from his division commander were of some comfort to Wood, who could write, "I felt that after all we were not disgraced."[31]

In the 28th Virginia, the left center regiment of Garnett's Brigade, the wounding of Colonel Robert C. Allen had ultimately placed the colors of that regiment in the hands of Lieutenant John A. J. Lee of Company C, who had claimed to have been the first of the division to cross the stone wall. When Lee was toppled with a slight wound and saw the enemy closing in fast around him, he grasped the broken flagstaff and attempted to break his sword to keep it from falling into Yankee hands. A Union solder described as a "big, burly German" demanded the surrender of Lieutenant Lee while brandishing his own sword as an incentive to follow his command. Seeing his predicament, a member of the regiment came to Lee's aid and "dispatched the German with his bayonet."[32] But, with the flag apparently coming to rest against one of Cushing's guns, it was ultimately captured by Private Marshall Sherman of the 1st Minnesota. The men of the 1st Minnesota experienced the kind of close fighting that characterized the final fighting between the forces in the Angle area, and their own color guard was decimated there. With the lines so close to each other, the fire was deadly, and the same shot which tore through the color bearer's hand also broke the flagstaff of the 1st Minnesota in two. As the men of both sides rushed to save their own colors from capture, the lines of the 1st Minnesota and the 28th Virginia became intertwined. Here the bayonet was used for a few minutes and rocks were hurled over the heads of comrades from those in the rear of the mass. It would be the flag of the 28th Virginia which would ultimately fall into the hands of the enemy, and its own broken staff would be used to splice that of the 1st Minnesota into one piece.[33]

Although Private James R. McPherson was wounded some hundred or more yards from the stone wall, he was to hear of the exploits of Captain Michael Spessard and the Craig Mountain Boys as they clashed with the Union masses at the Angle. While his men fell about him Captain Spessard fought the enemy with his drawn sword, probably stirred by the anger and anxiety of a father worrying about his wounded son back at the Spangler Farm. It took three Yankees to overpower Captain Spessard and tear his sword from his grip, as they ordered him to surrender. But Spessard was undaunted in his quest to deliver vengeance upon those who struck down his son and company mates, and, instead of surrendering, took the offensive. Picking up rocks and stones lying about him, he drove the three from the field by pelting them with these primitive missiles, venting his aggression in literal hand to hand combat. Captain Spessard was one of those fortunate enough to have done his duty to his utmost and lived to escape back to Seminary Ridge, where he saw to it that his son Hezekiah was properly cared for in the field hospital. His personal bravery and conduct were particularly cited in the report of Major Charles Peyton for Garnett's Brigade, and he was soon thereafter promoted because of his gallantry on the field of Gettysburg.[34]

On the extreme left of Garnett's Brigade, Colonel William Stuart had been mortally wounded while commanding the 56th Virginia Regiment, and company commanders shared in succession as acting colonel of the regiment until they likewise became casualties. Private Robert B. Damron would after report that all twenty three men that comprised Company D in the charge fell killed or wounded; he himself was wounded after approaching one of the abandoned pieces of Cushing's Regular Artillery. He managed to escape capture at the Angle when some of his company carried him back from the enemy's works to their own lines. However, he would not accompany the retreat back to Virginia with the brigade.[35]

It so happened that the 56th Virginia had halted at the wall at the point where General Armistead would lead his own brigade over it, encouraging them also with the words to "Follow me." Lieutenant Henry C. Michie of Company H was actually hit on the right elbow by Armistead when the general clambered over the wall immediately beside him. Michie later remembered that the general crossed the wall just at the colors of the 56th Virginia, because Company H was the left color company and the flag was at Michie's right while they held the stone wall. After ordering them forward, Armistead cleared the wall with his "hat on his hand with [his] sword sticking through & held aloft," and rapidly strode forward another thirty or forty paces before Michie saw him fall at one of Cushing's rear guns. Michie and others near him were not disposed to bare themselves to a similar fate, and continued to remain at the stone wall, where they could fire into the increasingly powerful enemy ranks from behind the shelter of the fence. Never receiving any orders to fall back or retreat, Michie and his companions, Captain John W. Jones of Company B, Lieutenant Andrew C. Rudasill of Company D, Captain Joseph Frazer of Company E, Lieutenant Francis Barnes of Company G, and Lieutenant George W. Finley of Company K, would be captured at the wall and would join each other in prison. Michie was bitter about not getting the proper support once they attained the enemy's lines, and "always blamed General Pickett for not getting us the order to fall back" when it was obvious that the charge was a failure.[36]

Lieutenant Finley of Company K survived the advance, attack, and the eventual repulse of Pickett's Division, and provided one of the most detailed and vivid descriptions of the fifteen minutes of struggle by Garnett's remnants at the Angle. Because of its immediacy and strength, the recollection of Finley should be relayed in his own words:

> ... Gen. Armistead, on foot, strode over the stone fence, his hat on his sword and calling upon his men to charge. A few of us followed him until, just as he put his hand upon one of the abandoned guns, he was shot down. Seeing that most of the men still remained at the stone fence I returned, and was one of the very few who got back unhurt.

Again there was comparative quiet for a while in our immediate front, but bullets came flying from the unbroken line to our line. During one of these pauses I took a rapid but careful look at the ground over which we had advanced and was surprised to see comparatively so few men lying dead or wounded on the field. Doubtless many of the wounded had gotten back before I looked.... But we were not left long at leisure to survey the field. We were in plain view of the Federal officers and they saw that we were but few in numbers and well nigh exhausted by what we had already accomplished.... While we were lying there and the Federals were completing their disposition of forces to repulse and capture us, someone ran rapidly along our line calling out to the men, "Gen. Lee says fall back from here." Many of the men attempted to obey, but a few of us not recognizing the order as authentic, held our men in line and encouraged them to look for support. Just then the Federals advanced in heavy force. The bullets seemed to come from front and both flanks, and I saw we could not hold the fence any longer. I again looked back over the field to see the chances of withdrawing. The men who had begun to fall back seemed to be dropping as they ran, like leaves, and in a very few moments the number on the ground was four or five times as great, apparently, as when I had looked before. It seemed foolhardy to attempt to get back. The Federal line pressed on until our men fired almost into their faces. Seeing that it was a useless waste of life to struggle longer I ordered the few men around me to "cease firing" and surrendered. Others to the right and left did the same, and soon the sharp quick huzza! of the Federals told of our defeat and their triumph. As we walked to the rear I went up to Gen. Armistead as he was lying close to the wheels of the gun on which he had put his hand, and stooping looked into his face, and I thought from his appearance and position that he was then dead.... As soon as the Federal cheer announced our repulse our batteries opened a brisk fire upon the hill, on friend and foe alike, to check any advance that might be contemplated....[37]

From Finley's account, it is apparent that indeed someone was coming along giving orders in General Lee's name to quit the field, as denied by Lieutenant Henry Michie. But Finley, and most likely Michie, agreed that this was merely a ruse by some unauthorized individual trying to save his own neck, and deliberately ignored him. It may have been to the benefit of Finley and Michie had they believed the orders and allowed themselves and their companies to retire, thereby saving many from entering prison camps. It also seemed ludicrous for the few hundreds of remaining men at the wall to be looking for supports to come to their aid. If there were none to be seen on the field by the time Armistead had been shot, it was obvious that Pickett's remnants could not hold out against the massing forces of the Union First, Second, and Third Corps long enough to await them. But Finley, like others in Garnett's Brigade, realized that falling back without supports across so wide an open expanse would be an invitation to certain suicide for many. Lieutenant Finley's one regret of this day, however, was that he did not take Armistead off of the field and back to the stone wall after he was shot down at Cushing's rear guns. Lieutenant Finely once had served on the general's staff. For this reason, he knew and respected Lewis Armistead, and would not have wanted him to fall into the Union hands as a prisoner. Finley declared that he would have made every effort to save the officer and see that he was carried to Seminary Ridge, if he had known that the general had been merely wounded and not killed.[38]

108

Brigadier General Lewis A. Armistead (1817-1863)
(wounded in the angle, captured, then died)

According to Finley, the stone wall at this Angle averaged about three feet in height, but on the left, where the officers of the 56th Virginia seemed so eager to cling to its defensive strength, the wall was between four and five feet in height on the Confederate side. It was no wonder that Armistead was not able to get many men from this regiment of Garnett's Brigade to accompany him after leaping the wall; it had served them quite well up to that point as a screen against enemy balls and was not freely given up in exchange for exposure to such dreadful fire. Despite that, Finley calculated that the loss in the 56th Virginia was greatest in the three combats at the stone wall: where they first broke the line of the 69th and 71st Pennsylvania Volunteers that held it; in repulsing the first attempt to retake the fence; and ultimately in the resistance to the final effort by the combined forces of Webb's, Hall's, Harrow's, Stannard's and Gates' regiments to overwhelm them.[39]

The flag of the 56th Virginia fell into the hands of the Federals when Corporal Alexander L. P. Williams was captured inside the stone wall with the colors. The colors were not specifically credited to any unit, but they may have been taken by the 71st Pennsylvania Regiment during the counterattack by Webb's Brigade. There were also units in Harrow's and Hall's Brigades, as well as those reported by Cowan's Battery, that had colors taken from them by other units before they could be officially turned in for credit.

Because General Armistead was the only one of the three brigade generals to pierce the enemy's line, those of his brigade who survived associated these final moments of the attack with their last visions of their commander. Their own

109

predicament seemed lesser because of the eventual fall of Armistead, and their reminiscences were overshadowed by this great loss during the very peak of the brigade's triumph. On the right, the men of the 14th Virginia who had made it this far responded promptly when Armistead ordered them over the wall. Private Erasmus Williams of Company H heard his brigade commander call out to the men who accompanied him over the wall to "Turn the guns!" Williams was one who leaped to respond, and he helped turn one of Cushing's guns that had been left at the stone wall. In the process, he got his hand caught while turning one of the cannon and his left forefinger was torn as if by a knife cutting it almost in two. With Armistead only steps away, and Colonel Rawley Martin of the 53rd close by, Williams took this opportunity to survey the field to their rear. Like the men of Kemper's and Garnett's Brigades, he was chagrined to see no reinforcements coming to meet the foe, who was closing in on front, left, and right at the same time. Williams called to Martin, "Look, the Yankees are flanking us, we must get out from here." But Colonel Martin tried to calm Private Williams' fears by replying, "No, hold on me, rally, rally, right here." Within a few moments, Armistead fell near one of the guns, and Private Williams could see that the Union soldiers were pressing them increasingly now on their front and flanks. Deciding it was time to quit, Williams and others began now to "commence to recede" to the wall, still keeping their faces to the enemy and discharging their guns. Williams again cried out to Colonel Martin, the only field officer remaining in the Angle, "We must get away from here!" According to Williams, Martin was about to return to the wall himself when he fell near the prone body of General Armistead. With little left to do but get away as best he could, Private Williams struck out into the fields over which they had advanced with such precision. He had proceeded scarcely thirty yards from the wall when he was wounded in the left wrist. Knowing it was either death or prison to remain, Williams continued along as rapidly as possible and did not stop until reaching the place from which they had begun the advance. Finding the hole he had dug to protect himself from the cannonade, he retrieved his knife and knapsack, and continued further rearward to find the hospital and aid for his wound.[40]

Sergeant Easley, file closer for the 14th Regiment, found himself at the left of the regiment when he crossed the wall with Armistead. After glancing to his right and left from atop the wall, he noted that two of Cushing's guns were to his right and two to the left. He then saw Armistead crossing just to his left, with one of the guns between them. No longer thinking about looking for his place with his company, Drewry Easley stepped off the fence in unison with General Armistead and started toward Cushing's second line of artillery. Just before reaching the guns, Easley could see a squad of dozens of Yankees around a stand of colors to the left who fired a volley at them. Armistead fell forward, his sword and hat almost striking one of these rifled guns.[41]

When Armistead fell to the left of the gun, Easley came to a halt at the right of the artillery piece, and glanced over his shoulder to see some of the line crossing the wall behind him. But upon seeing Armistead fall, to a man they went back to the wall, and Easley found himself popping off shots at the squad that felled Armistead all by himself, his gun resting on the tube of the artillery piece as a support.

I fired several shots and then they paid their respects to me pouring back a volley similar to the one that killed Armistead. I was behind the gun between it and the wheels but something seemed to strike me all over. They must have fired too low and knocked gravels against me. I felt of myself and when I found I was not hurt I grabbed for my ramrod to return their compliment and found it was shot off just where it enters the stock. I did not see that I could do much without a ramrod and so bore to the left in order to avoid them and went back to the stone wall, looking for a gun. One of our men gave me his gun saying "He was wounded." I rammed a ball about halfway down when it hung, and I began driving the rammer against the stone fence when he turned over and said "Don't load it; it's loaded." I went off the handle and said "Where are you wounded anyhow; I don't see anything the matter with you." He turned over and groaned and made no answer. I clubbed the musket and started to burst his head with it, but happened to think and raised it as high as I could and dropped it on the back of his head. From the way he groaned he thought a shell struck him. I grabbed another gun with the bayonet twisted like a cork screw, and blew through it. I expected if I had fired it the bullet would have hit the bayonet, but just as I got it loaded three bayonets came against me and they hauled me in....I forgot to say that Armistead did not groan or move while I fired several shots near him, and I thought him dead, but he was an old man 63 and was probably exhausted....[42]

Easley's recollections reflected not only his persistence in trying to inflict damage on the enemy after coming so far across the "valley of death," but his exasperation at those who did not do their utmost against the Yankees as he was doing. Like Lieutenant Finley, Sergeant Easley believed that General Armistead had been killed by the volley that felled him, or that he was completely exhausted because of the the appearance of his advanced age. (He was actually only 46 years old.) Easley may have been correct in his appraisal of Armistead's aged appearance during this final assault. The surgeon who attended the general after the battle, concluded from Armistead's physical and mental condition that the general had been suffering from "over exertion" during the campaign.[43]

Colonel Hodges' body fell near the front of the 69th Pennsylvania Infantry, in front of the men of his regiment and some of Kemper's Brigade who had halted at the rocky knoll some rods in front of the Angle. As Confederate resistance waned, men from the 20th New York State Militia called across the wounded, writhing, and dead in their front for the Southerners to come in, reassuring them they would not be harmed. At those words, hundreds rose up and came into the Union lines, dropping their arms and trying their best to avoid being hit by the same Confederate artillery noted by Lieutenant Finley of the 56th Virginia in Garnett's Brigade. From the slashing came a signal of a white flag, where another dozen or more men came dashing into Union lines. As the fire died away on their front, the men of the 20th New York took the opportunity to look about the battlefield. The ground was nearly covered with dead and wounded on their advanced front (where the 7th Michigan and 59th New York had originally lain). The remains of Colonel James Hodges would later be identified under the body of another officer. They were only two of about four or five Confederate officers lying together within twenty yards of the advanced line of Gates' New Yorkers. They noted that the one lying across the body of Colonel Hodges was still gasping, but they did not go near until they were sure he had died. Perhaps they didn't wish to personalize the death and dying, killing and maiming in which they had participated.[44]

The men of the 19th Massachusetts later acknowledged that at least three Confederate battle flags, including that of the 14th Virginia, were planted at one of Cushing's guns. According to that regiment's history, a color bearer had rushed forward with his colors and planted his flag at one of Cushing's 3-inch rifles before falling dead. Another ran out to retrieve the flag before it was lost, but he also was slain. A rush by a few more men ended with the same result, and the flag still waved from the cannon, to be joined shortly by two other flags. Corporal Joseph DeCastro of the 19th Massachusetts, who had become separated from his command and was fighting with the 72nd Pennsylvania Volunteers of General Webb's Philadelphia Brigade, was credited with capturing the flag of the 14th Virginia at this cannon. Apparently he knocked down one of the other color guard of the 14th Virginia to secure it.[45]

Major Owens' 9th Virginia was also with Armistead at the stone wall. When Armistead cried "Follow me," some of that command accompanied the general another fifty paces within the Federal lines until Armistead was shot down. Those not killed or wounded fell back to the wall again, as did the remnants from other commands, and the fight continued for another fifteen to twenty minutes. Corporal John H. Lewis of Company G watched men falling in heaps while the fighting persisted, noting that there were few officers present anymore to give leadership while the men looked to the rear for assistance. With fire coming into the regiment from the front and both flanks, the 9th Virginia held on as long as possible. Eventually they realized that the intensity of the struggle there could not last. With no help at hand, almost all the officers down, wounded or dead, and many starting for the rear amidst shot and musket ball, Corporal Lewis found himself surrounded and captured.[46] Those who fell back took their commander, Major John C. Owens, with them from the spot where he had fallen wounded before the regiment reached the stone wall. Recently appointed to the command of the 9th Virginia from the captaincy of Company G, Owens had won the respect of his men for his intelligence, kindness, and gentleness. He would die before the morning's light at the division hospital, to be interred in the shade of the woods along Marsh Creek.[47]

Sergeant Levin C. Gayle of Company G wrote in his journal that after taking the enemy's works, the 9th Virginia held the stone wall for twenty minutes. But, before Sergeant Gayle could react, he found himself "hemmed up" and carried to the rear with other prisoners.[48] Also carried to the rear by the Yankees was the battle flag of the regiment, credited to Private John Clopp of the 71st Pennsylvania Volunteers as being captured from the remnant of the 9th Virginia at the Angle.[49] It was the second of the five regimental flags in Armistead's Brigade which would fall into the hands of the enemy on this day.

Martin's 53rd regiment, the center guide of the brigade, had accompanied General Armistead from the front of Spangler's Woods these 1300 yards. Its colors were held aloft by the last of the color company, who had dared each other to keep the flag in pace with their striding commander. Although wounded in the arm,

Robert Tyler Jones had carried the colors to the wall and waved them triumphantly from it before falling with a more severe wound. Thereupon, Lieutenant Hutchings Carter of the Chatham Grays seized the colors and raced among the enemy's abandoned artillery with it, following Armistead as he advanced to Cushing's rear section. Planting the flag at the guns as a signal that the 53rd Virginia had captured the piece, the colors of the regiment were among three that were carried to the farthest point in the Union lines that day.[50] Of the ten guards who started the advance with the duty of protecting the flag, eight had been killed and two wounded.[51]

Armistead, leading between 150 and 300 survivors beyond the stone wall, reached for one of the captured guns of Cushing's Battery and called out to those around him, "The day is ours men, come turn this artillery upon them." Captain B. L. Farinholt joined General Armistead at these guns, and attempted to follow his commander's direction to use the captured cannon on the enemy, but was soon shot through the thigh at a time when "pandemonium reigned complete." This was the time when Union reinforcements from Hall's Brigade were crowding into and through the Clump of Trees to Armistead's right and into their front. At the same time, "many shots were fired at such close range as afterward to burn the clothes or flesh of the victims with powder."[52] Although Captain Farinholt and Erasmus Williams (14th Virginia) both separately testified to the attempt to turn Cushing's guns, neither claimed that any shots were fired from them. It would have been unlikely that the gunners would have left the necessary implements, let alone ammunition, to allow the enemy to do such a thing. However, after the war Second Lieutenant James A. Harwood wrote that General Armistead had turned to him and said, "Lieutenant, we must use their own guns on them." Armistead then directed the lieutenant and his sergeants to take charge of one of the guns while the general himself took command of another. Purportedly, the two officers managed to fire three rounds into the face of the enemy before the overwhelming Union forces swept in at double quick and felled them with its first fire. Despite the fact that many Union and Confederate observers claimed that Armistead fell at one of the guns of Cushing's Battery, Harwood was the only one to relate that Armistead fell while actually working one of these pieces.[53] Aside from the fact that no other account from survivors of the Angle fight report such an incident, which would surely have been impressed on their memories, there is the possibility that Harwood himself was not even at the Battle of Gettysburg. His service record indicates that he was captured at Chambersburg on July 5th with some infirmity (not a wound). Because the retreat route of the Confederate army did not take it through Chambersburg, Lieutenant Harwood may have been left at the hospital on July 1st when the division marched to Gettysburg.[54]

Lieutenant Colonel Rawley Martin fell within the Angle with those of his regiment who scaled the wall. His thigh was shattered near the hip and he was left crippled for the remainder of his life. His friend, Sergeant Thomas Tredway of Company I, ran to his assistance but was shot and fell across Martin's body.[55] Nearby, Robert Tyler Jones reflected the defiance and determination of the regiment. Bleeding profusely from his two wounds, he was waving a pistol and threatening to shoot the very first man who offered to surrender. Lieutenant Carter,

Lieutenant Colonel Rawley W. Martin (1835-1921)
53rd Virginia Infantry
(wounded in the angle and captured)

with seventeen bullet holes in his clothes, remained unscathed but was surrounded by Yankees and had to surrender, despite Jones' threats. In doing so, Carter was compelled to leave behind the flag of the 53rd Virginia leaning against Cushing's gun, the third of Armistead's flags which was to be lost.[56]

Also left at the guns was Armistead himself, who was lying where Sergeant Easley had watched him fall seemingly lifeless. At his side was Captain Thomas C. Holland of the 28th Virginia (Garnett's Brigade), who had crossed the wall to the left of the general and fallen practically unconscious with wounds to his face and neck. Holland was with Armistead when he and other officers were removed from the Angle to a temporary hospital in the rear later that afternoon. They rode in the same ambulance, which was stopped once by someone directing the ambulance to its ultimate objective.[57] Doctor D. G. Brinton, in charge of the Second Division, 11th Corps Union Hospital at the George Spangler Farm was given the responsibility of being the attending surgeon to Armistead after his arrival about 4:00 P.M. He and another doctor examined and dressed Armistead's two wounds, neither of which was considered to be serious. One was in the fleshy part of the arm and the other a little below the knee on the other side. Both were caused by rifle balls, but the general was fortunate in that neither bone, artery, or nerve was injured by either. In conversing with Armistead, Surgeon Brinton discovered that the Virginian had "suffered much from over exertion, want of sleep, and mental anxiety within the last few days." While lying on a cot or stretcher on the ground after being taken to the hospital, Armistead was within earshot of Captain Holland when he said, "Please don't step so close to me," to doctors and nurses treating the wounded beside him. When Armistead died about 9:00 A.M. on July 5th, after intense suffering, Doctor Brinton was astonished to learn of it. He felt Armistead's prospects of recovery were good, but deduced that the death was not caused directly by the wounds but by secondary fever and prostration.[58] Lieutenant James Crocker of the 9th Virginia visited the Union corps hospital to see General Armistead, but was disappointed on arriving to be shown the freshly made grave instead. He was then told that Armistead's wounds were not mortal, but that "his proud spirit chafed under his imprisonment and his restlessness aggravated his wound."[59] A. J. Rider, a member of the 107th Ohio Volunteers, had been directed by Dr. James Armstrong to bury Armistead's body on this George Spangler Farm, where it remained undisturbed for about four weeks. After that time, a Dr. Chamberlain of Philadelphia had the body disinterred from the rough box in which it lay and embalmed it, thinking that the general's friends would pay handsomely for his body. The remains were eventually sent to Baltimore and placed in the Hughes Armistead vault of St. Paul's Cemetery.[60]

Color Sergeant Benjamin Jellison of the 19th Massachusetts would have the honor of capturing the flag of the 57th Virginia. Already carrying both regimental colors of the 19th Massachusetts, Jellison spied the flag of the 57th at Cushing's gun with the two others and made a grab for it as well. This flag-laden soldier would win another Medal of Honor for Gibbon's Union Division for the activities performed against Pickett's men on this day.

The losses were also considerable in the ranks of the 38th Virginia on the extreme left. According to Captain George K. Griggs, who was wounded during the assault, the loss to the regiment was irreparable. The "noble and beloved Colonel E. C. Edmonds [was] killed; Lieutenant Colonel [Powhatan] Whittle, who had lost an arm at Malvern Hill, was seriously wounded in the thigh; Captain Townes killed; and all the other company officers more or less seriously wounded." The flag of the 38th Virginia, which was saved from capture at the Angle where the other four colors of the brigade were lost, was carried back towards Seminary Ridge by the survivors. But the soldier bearing the colors was cut off by the flanking surge of the 8th Ohio Volunteers, which had swept the Confederate left during the advance and continued after the repulse to encircle those attempting to escape. Thus the flag of the 38th Virginia was captured by Sergeant Daniel Miller of the 8th Ohio Regiment, who like almost all other recognized captors of flags was presented with a Medal of Honor.[61]

The struggle along and beyond the stone wall was particularly severe and savage, as recorded by Confederate survivors. But those who wore the blue also remembered the events of Pickett's attack and repulse. The reminiscences of Captain Andrew Cowan, who commanded the battery which, with that of Rorty, inflicted the most damaging artillery casualties on the brigades after they cleared the Emmitsburg Road, were characteristic and give an indication of the kind of firepower that met Kemper, Garnett, and Armistead. Firing canister as low as possible during the attack, Cowan finally ordered his five cannon to be loaded with double canister. With no more canister left in the chests and the enemy closing on the stone wall, Cowan realized this would be his last shot and hurriedly instructed his men what to do after the last discharge of the guns. Cushing's guns were then in the possession of Armistead's group and Garnett's survivors at the wall, and Cowan's front was abandoned by his infantry supports. With the five guns double shotted, the muzzles run to their lowest point, Cowan could see a young officer (thought by him to be a major) waving his sword and leap the wall. Hearing him shout, "Take the gun," Cowan ordered "Fire!" At ten yards distance, this final surge in his front felt the full fury of 220 chunks of lead. Without looking to see the effect of his fire, Cowan drew his guns back to the crest of the ridge by hand, to continue firing percussion shell from there at retreating groups and enemy artillery. He had a young Confederate captive set up on one of the horses of the teams from which a driver had been shot down, and kept him there a while as a deterrent to sharpshooting by his Confederate comrades. When Pickett's men began retreating, Cowan again ran his guns below the crest toward the wall. His purpose was to fire at Pickett's men during their retreat and at those of Alexander's few guns that were trying to cover them. To Cowan it was a certainty that no one would ever forget the sight after the repulse. In his front, he could not exaggerate when he said the dead lay in heaps. Union soldiers covered the ground between his guns and the wall, while beyond the wall he could see the terrible execution of his canister. A few Confederates fell between the wall and Cowan's guns, including the young officer who Cowan had seen trying to take his gun. Killed by that last blast of canister, the officer was buried with honors by Cowan at the side of the graves of his own men and that of Captain Rorty. Despite his efforts, Cowan was never able to learn the identity of this young man, who left behind only his sword as a physical reminder of his anonymous heroism.[62]

Cowan's canister was rivaled in front of the Clump of Trees by the close range firepower of the 69th Pennsylvania Volunteers. They were firing the infantry's brand of canister, manufactured by themselves on the eve of this day's battle. While collecting the wounded of Wright's Georgia Brigade on the night of July 2nd, the regiment brought in what Confederate small arms and ammunition that could be gathered up as well. Selecting the best of the lot they reloaded them, and leaned them up against the stone wall beside them. Finding the ammunition to be three buckshot and a ball, the regiment abstracted the buckshot from the ammunition and reloaded the spare guns with twelve buckshot to a load, almost every man having from two to five guns loaded in this manner. One veteran remembered that the ammunition had a label that noted that it had been made in Birmingham, England, and remarked that it inflicted more harm upon the Confederates of Pickett's Division than it was capable of rendering unto the Federals.[63]

Another Union recollection could apply just as well to Pickett's Division as it did to those they faced after gaining the enemy's works:

> One thing struck me very much. It was the intelligence of the men. For a good part of the time, and in the heaviest of the fight, the ranks were lost, and there was no organization. The officers were in our midst everywhere; but still we kept together, and seemed to understand, without orders, what to do, and to feel that the quicker we fired the sooner the thing would be over. As to standing in line and blazing away regularly, why we never thought of it...[64]

This same memory of the confusion of those last fifteen minutes after Armistead led the charge over the wall, was reflected by Medal of Honor winner Major Edmund Rice of the 19th Massachusetts the same regiment that captured three of the five colors in Armistead's column:

> This was one of those periods in action which are measurable by seconds. The men near seemed to fire very slowly. Those in rear, though coming up at a run, seemed to drag their feet. Many were firing through the intervals of those in front, in their eagerness to injure the enemy. This manner of firing, although efficacious, sometimes tells on friend instead of foe.... All the time the crush towards the enemy in the copse was becoming greater. The men in gray were doing all that was possible to keep off the mixed bodies of men who were moving upon them swiftly and without hesitation, keeping up so close and continuous a fire that at last its effects became terrible. I could feel the touch of the men to my right and left, as we neared the edge of the copse. The grove was fairly jammed with Pickett's men, in all positions, lying and kneeling. Back from the edge were many standing and firing over those in front....Every foot of ground was occupied by men engaged in mortal combat, who were in every possible position which can be taken while under arms, or lying wounded or dead.[65]

For the men of Pickett's Division, however, no amount of effort on their part could hold the position they had won against the envelopment that the Union forces were able to employ. The objective point had been reached, but the battle had been lost for them. The Union army just closed in on those who remained at the enemy's works, and was not forced off the ridge. General Lee's grand scheme to break the Federal line in two with a combined strong infantry and artillery column had been reduced to a shambles. It was not the Union soldiers, but the Virginia soldiers, who had to yield the ground, their freedom, and their lives. Lieutenant James of the 11th Virginia expressed the resounding disappointment and sorrow in Pickett's Division when he wrote, "We gained nothing but glory and lost our bravest men."

Chapter

VII

"Oh, my country, my country!"

As Pickett's survivors melted away toward and across the Emmitsburg Road, a feeble attempt was made to cover their retreat with one battery which had been run up to the road and unlimbered. After exchanging a few shots with Cowan's New York Battery, in which the Confederates had one of their limber chests exploded, more Union batteries concentrated their fire on this sole Southern battery. With little choice but to admit it was outgunned, the battery limbered and retired from view, letting the surviving Virginians to get away as best they could.[1] The Union defenders, encouraged and enlivened by their victory, were determined to inflict continuing injury to the division. Men of the 19th Massachusetts jumped the wall at the Angle and followed after Pickett's men, firing as they went. The momentary shelling by the Confederate battery on the Emmitsburg Road drove them to seek the sparse shelter in the field between the road and their lines on Cemetery Ridge, but they kept up a fire at the retreating Virginians as long as they were in view and within range.[2]

The scene in front of and behind the Angle wall bore testimony to the intensity and fierceness of the conflict that July afternoon. Here Pickett's Division had struck Gibbon's defenses, and here the force of its attack had been blunted against the stones of the wall and the iron of the Pennsylvanians, New Yorkers, Vermonters and Bay State Soldiers. Lieutenant J. Irving Sale of the 53rd Virginia remarked that he had never seen as many dead men in his life as there were in the Angle. They were not solely of Pickett's Division, but were primarily of Gibbon's Division "the blue coats were lying all over so thick that you could scarcely help stepping on them."[3] The Yankee survivors would speak to each other in the highest praise of the Confederate advance and attack in the days following the battle. But, with the heat of the battle still upon them, there were few who were weighing the merits of the Virginia soldiery. In the ranks of the 13th Vermont, which had initiated the flanking movement that dissipated the strength of Kemper's attack, there was at least one gunshot fired after the Virginians had surrendered or retreated from their front. When one of Pickett's veterans refused to give up his gun after being captured and surrounded, a soldier from Company D of the 13th Vermont convinced him of his defeat by shooting him in the head.[4]

General Meade, in the meantime, had hastened to the Union battle front, followed by the depleted ranks of the Third Corps. Unable to believe that this unsupported infantry attack on his center was to be Lee's sole thrust on his front, Meade made preparations for yet another decisive attack on his line. Ranks were reformed and reinforced. Two brigades from another corps also took their place here to bolster the line. When no forthcoming attack was imminent, the wounded Confederates in and in front of the Angle were sent to the rear. Captain B. L. Farinholt of the 53rd Virginia was taken to the rear with other prisoners, and had, for the first time, the opportunity to see the extent of the harvest which they themselves had reaped. He noticed in his rearward passage down the eastern slopes of Cemetery Ridge toward the Taneytown Road, that "every nook in the fence, every barn and shed, every yard and shade tree were literally burdened with their dead, wounded, and dying."[5] This was small consolation to a survivor of Armistead's Brigade, who had seen almost one half of its numbers reduced to the grave, the hospital, or the prison camp in the span of one afternoon. Uppermost in his thoughts was the goal of trying to obtain a surgeon's care and an ambulance from the Union victors for the more severely wounded Colonel Martin and Lieutenant William H. Bray, who had been left behind in the Angle while he himself was marched to the rear with his lacerated thigh.[6]

For the men in Gibbon's Division the fighting was not over even after the retreat of Pickett's men. For decades the regiments would be engaged in verbal conflicts over who was most responsible for striking the decisive blow in defeating Pickett's Division. The capture of the Virginia battle flags prompted much heated protest from units such as the 69th Pennsylvania Volunteers. That regiment had been posted in the Angle at the left of Cushing's guns and never fell back beyond the Clump of Trees in its often hand to hand struggle with the men of Garnett's and Armistead's Brigades. Yet they, like Cowan's Battery, were never given credit for the capture of a single battleflag from those Confederate units. Having inflicted tremendous casualties on Garnett's front with their buckshot loaded guns, the 69th Pennsylvania was too busy trying to reform its line and take care of its own casualties to secure the battle trophies on its front. One veteran attested that at least ten flags were picked up along the stone wall in front of the 69th Regiment, all gathered by men from other regiments who had wandered over their lines out of curiosity after the fighting had ceased.[7] In fact, the veterans of the 69th protested that many of Pickett's flags "were not captured in the sense that any honor could attach to it. It was just like picking up muskets that had been thrown down."[8] As has been related by the surviving witnesses of Pickett's Division, many of the Division's flags were lost in this way after the color guard had been felled by shots from Union lines.

General Lee's thoughts were not possessed of the loss of the colors as much as they were of the loss of life and opportunity, both of which had been shattered across the plains on Cemetery Ridge. General Lee watched the attack and repulse of the division from a point near Spangler's Woods near where the Virginia Monument was erected nearly fifty years later. Here he was joined by Colonel James Thompson Brown (chief of Ewell's artillery) just as Stannard's Vermonters were executing the movement against Pickett's right flank. As the successive movements by Hall's, Harrow's and Gates' Union brigades toward the Angle broke Pickett's Division, Lee and Brown could hear the Federals cheering. This sound of the Union "Huzzah" aroused General Lee from a position he had taken at that point of observation. During the whole of the charge, the commanding general had been seated on a large

General Robert E. Lee (1807-1870)

oak stump with his oil cloth spread on the stump beneath him. Holding the reins of Traveler in his left hand, he had placed his right elbow on his right leg, supporting his bowed head in his right hand. Colonel Brown surmised that the General was praying.[9] We may also surmise that General Lee had realized the necessary artillery support was not to be forthcoming, and that the charge was doomed without it. He may not have been able to bring himself to witness the annihilation of so many men because of unconsummated plans, or he may have indeed been praying for a miracle to deliver Pickett, Pettigrew, and Trimble from the jaws of death which were closing upon them. He may have also been composing himself for the task of meeting the survivors of the repulse and rallying them, offering them words of encouragement.

Major Edmund Berkeley of the 8th Virginia, who was being carried rearward by some of his men, remembered seeing General Lee near or in Spangler Woods. Here he could see Lee directing the formation of a line of slightly wounded men in preparation for a possible counterattack. Berkeley overheard Lee comforting some survivors of Pickett's Division with, "My men it was not your fault."[10] Most of Pickett's men, however, fell back behind, or west of, Seminary Ridge, near where they had formed in the morning before moving to the support of the artillery. There, many were bleeding and bathing their wounds in Pitzer's Run, "making its clear water run red," while others were trying to quench their burning thirsts. Corporal Charles Loehr of the 1st Virginia estimated that between 300 and 400 men were gathered in a group around the creek, including General George Pickett, who rode among the men talking to small groups here and there. Corporal Charles Belcher of the 24th Virginia was waving one of the two regimental battle flags of Kemper's Brigade which escaped capture, and cried out as Pickett approached him, "General, let us go at them again!" Attention, however, was focused on General Kemper, who had been compelled to halt because of the crowding there. General Lee himself momentarily rode up, and the men gathered around him in anticipation of hearing some orders or words of encouragement. Instead, they saw General Pickett burst into tears as Lee met him, and the two generals shook hands. Corporal Loehr could see that General Lee was affected by the sight of these survivors of the repulse and slaughter of the division, and heard him speak in a slow and distinct manner to Pickett, saying, "General Pickett, your men have done all that men could do; the fault is entirely my own." Turning next to the gravely wounded General James Kemper, Lee queried if he could do anything for him. Kemper looked up and replied, "General Lee, you can do nothing for me; I am mortally wounded, but see to it that full justice is done my men who made this charge." General Lee assured him that he would, before riding off.[11]

Pickett thereupon turned to the mass of men here behind Spangler's Woods and told them, "You can go back to the wagons and rest until you are wanted." Following his recommendations, the survivors made for the rear and the division trains, with little or no organization. As they neared the crossing of Willoughby's Run by the same route they had taken with such anticipation in the morning hours, Pickett's Division became a dispirited and disorganized mob. The terrain was such that a bottleneck was created, backing up those trying desperately to get away from the horrors of the battlefield which had decimated their ranks. The continuing overshots from Union batteries, which were determined to wreak as much destruction as possible upon the retreating Confederates, did not alleviate the situation. Captain H. T. Owen of the 18th Virginia was a witness to this scene near the Samuel Dixon Farm, just south of the Hagerstown Road:

> At this point there is a bluff on one side and a slight swamp on the other, creating a narrow pass, through which the fugitives, without distinction of rank, officers and privates side by side, pushed, poured and rushed in a continuous stream, throwing away guns, blankets and haversacks as they hurried on in confusion toward the rear. Here another effort was made to rally the broken troops and all sorts of appeals and threats made to officers and men who turned a deaf ear and hurried on, some of the officers even jerking loose with an oath from the hand laid on their shoulders to attract attention. At last a few privates hearkening to the appeals halted and formed a nucleus around which about thirty others soon rallied and with these a picket was formed across the road as a barrier to further retreat and the stream of stragglers dammed up several hundred strong.[12]

Having already received General Pickett's permission to retire as far as the division wagon trains out the Chambersburg Pike, it is understandable that many men resented the interference of the picket guard trying to stop their rearward progress. Indeed, General Pickett himself momentarily intervened to enlighten the picket line. Riding down the slopes of the Pitzer Farm to Willoughby's Run, Pickett arrived and was seen to be weeping openly and bitterly. Reprimanding the officer in charge of the picket guard, the general said, "Don't stop any of my men. Tell them to come to the camp we occupied last night." With that, Pickett rode rearward himself, unaccompanied by staff or friends.[13] Some, overcome with exhaustion from their ordeal, did not make it back to the camp or to the wagon trains that night. Men like Charles Loehr and some of his comrades halted and slept in buildings en route, such as the mills along Marsh Creek, and rejoined their brigade on the morning of July 4th. The roll call of many of the regiments on that morning brought home the sense of loss. For example, in the 1st Virginia, now commanded by Captain B. F. Howard, only about thirty men stood in the ranks to be counted.[14]

For the wounded, the ordeal was even greater. Those who were captured at or near the Angle wall would be treated in Union field hospitals before being sent to prisons and prison hospitals elsewhere. For those who were carried to the rear by comrades or managed to struggle to Seminary Ridge under their own power, the division hospital at Francis Bream's Mill and at the John Currens Farm along Marsh Creek became their refuge. General Kemper was taken to the more spacious home of Francis Bream at Black Horse Tavern, where he could benefit from some of the comforts provided by a private home. His vocal agonies that night were such that the wounded men in the yard and adjoining outbuildings could hear them. His ordeal on the battlefield was perhaps accentuated and aggravated by his ordeal in getting to that hospital. Private Erasmus Williams of the 14th Virginia Infantry encountered an ambulance coming down Pitzer's Lane while he himself was heading rearward with the belongings he had retrieved from his knife dug shelter at Spangler's Woods. The top of the ambulance was suddenly smashed up by a Union shell, which toppled the ambulance and threw its passenger to the ground. The driver was unhurt, and called out to Private Williams to come over and help carry off the wounded man. Williams protested on account of his own wound in the wrist, but the driver insisted in such a manner that Williams eventually agreed to help with his good arm. Looking at the wounded man, Williams still tried to escape the duty by saying, "I believe he is already dead, it is not worth while carrying him anywhere." But the driver was loyal to his patient and was not to be swayed from his mission, replying, "No, you must help me." Struggling to the rear with their burden in a blanket between them, they finally reached the field hospital, and Williams was glad to be relieved to attend to his own wound. Before leaving, he asked the driver the identity of this man for who they had endangered their lives and was informed that it was no less than General Kemper himself.[15] Kemper would stay at the Black Horse Tavern for almost three weeks before being moved to the Seminary hospital and then as a prisoner to Baltimore. Exchanged because of the gravity of his wound (for Union Brigadier General Charles K. Graham, also a Gettysburg casualty), Kemper returned to the command of Virginia reserves in May 1864. However, he never again would resume the active field service that he had begun with his 7th Virginia Regiment in 1861.

Those wounded of Pickett's Division who could be transported joined the wagon trains commanded by General John Imboden, who left Gettysburg on July

4th. Among these was Colonel Eppa Hunton of the 8th Virginia, who managed to secure a buggy to which he hitched his horse "Morgan." Accompanied by Major Berkeley, the two wounded officers thus returned to Virginia.[16] Many were not so fortunate. Literally hundreds of Pickett's men remained in the Union and Confederate hospitals surrounding Gettysburg until they either succumbed to their wounds or recovered sufficiently to be sent to prison.[17]

Those who had fallen prisoners into Union hands with either slight or no wounds found themselves taken soon after midnight to Westminster, Maryland, under guard. After resting in Westminster for over twenty four hours they boarded trains to Baltimore in the afternoon of July 5th. Initially they were taken to Fort McHenry, where those with slight wounds were separated from those without. Those with wounds were cared for by Union surgeons and stayed a few days longer at Fort McHenry, while those without wounds were sent on July 6th to "that Hell on Earth called Fort Delaware." Seeing Fort Delaware, one of Pickett's veterans could only write, "Oh What a place."[18]

Having seen first hand the condition of Pickett's survivors, General Lee knew of their depleted ranks, which had been reduced by almost one half.[19] With General Imboden's command burdened with the duty of safely transporting the army's wounded across the Potomac, Lee had no reserve force to act as Provost Guard for the thousands of Union prisoners captured during the three day battle. He had little choice but to assign some of his weaker brigades to the detested task of escorting the prisoners toward Staunton. Pickett's division was ordered to this task on July 4th, and about 3400 Union prisoners were put under their charge. Pickett apparently protested almost immediately, since this duty would take them from the ranks of the rest of the army again. The division felt it was being reduced to guard duty instead of being elevated to a post of honor for its valor and losses in the charge of July 3rd. As the division neared the Potomac, where it would be permitted to relieve itself of the prisoners, General Pickett formally protested this apparent indignity to his Virginians. General Lee, anxious to assuage Pickett's indignation, wrote a letter to Pickett, which was published for the reading of the entirety of the division. In it, Lee referred often to the gallantry of Pickett's men, in such terms as to convey his respect and concern for the division:

> It was with reluctance that I imposed upon your gallant division the duty of conveying prisoners to Staunton. I regretted to assign them to such service, as well as to separate them from the army, though temporarily, with which they have been so long and efficiently associated. Though small in numbers, their worth is not diminished, and I had supposed that the division itself would be loth to part from its comrades at a time when the presence of every man is so essential.... I regret that [the assignment of escorting prisoners] has occasioned you and your officers any disappointment.... I still have the greatest confidence in your division, and feel assured that with you at its head, it will be able to accomplish any service upon which it may be placed.... No one grieves more than I do at the loss suffered by your noble division in the recent conflict, or honors it more for its bravery and gallantry.[20]

Confederate Prisoners on the Baltimore Pike
(Battles and Leaders of the Civil War)

On July 9, 1863, Pickett was relieved of the prisoners by General Imboden's command after the latter had safely escorted the wounded to Winchester. The division commenced crossing the Potomac River itself the following day. Pickett's men then began the slow process of healing their wounds and recruiting and refilling their much depleted ranks.

General Pickett, still distraught from the losses incurred by his division in what seemed such a forlorn attack, submitted his report of the campaign to General Lee. Perhaps the report was not in accordance with the commanding general's own assessment of the loss, since Lee ordered that General Pickett destroy both the copy and the original of the report. Since General Lee was prepared to accept all responsibility for the loss, and General Pickett was apparently placing that responsibility on other heads, the report probably was not consistent with Lee's assessment of the failures of July 3rd. General Lee could only counsel the division commander by asking that he submit a report that merely confined itself to a listing of the casualties. Once again Lee reiterated his gratitude for the sacrifices of the Virginia Division. Lee wrote, "you and your men have crowned yourselves with glory," and then proceeded to caution Pickett, "but we have the enemy to fight, and must carefully, at this critical moment, guard against dissensions which the reflections in your report would create." General Pickett obeyed these orders of his commander, as he had willingly obeyed the orders to send his division across the open fields to Cemetery Ridge and their "crowning glory," and submitted no formal report of the Battle of Gettysburg.[21]

Whereas General Pickett was lamenting the losses in his division, which was once again broken up and disassociated from the Army of Northern Virginia after its return to the Richmond area in September, one of the wounded survivors of Armistead's final surge at the Angle had come to fully understand the scope of the division's defeat on those fields of farmers Codori, Frey, Small, and Spangler. Lieutenant Colonel Rawley Martin, who advanced at the side of Lewis Armistead while leading the remnants of his 53rd Virginia Infantry over the three foot high stone wall of the Angle, had fallen with a shattered thigh as the Confederate wave was about to ebb. Lying close to death for three days afterwards, he was still slowly recuperating at the general hospital at Gettysburg (Camp Letterman) on September 10th. In a letter to his father, describing his expectations of momentarily being sent to prison, Martin closed with a dirge for the Southern Confederacy:

> I expect to be with them at Sandusky or Johnson's Island in a short time. I am not able to walk yet on account of the tenderness of the left leg where it was shot. I guess I shall see them again soon. My love to all at home, and tell them to pray for me and for the success of the Confederate cause, which is so near to the hearts of us all.... Oh, my country, my country.[22]

Cemetery Ridge After Pickett's Charge
(Battles and Leaders of the Civil War)

Marker Where General Armistead Fell, Bloody Angle

Taken about twenty-five years after the battle, this Tipton photograph shows most of the land over which Garnett's and Kemper's Brigades advanced from the Angle. Monumentation includes the obelisk of the 69th Pennsylvania Volunteers, accompanied by its ten company position markers. In the foreground is the sole marker to Pickett's Division on the field of attack – the marker designating the point where General Armistead fell wounded – erected by the survivors of Webb's Brigade and Cushing's Battery in 1887. (Gettysburg NMP)

Where Colonel Hodges Fell

This photograph looks across the front of Cowan's New York Battery, to the stone wall defended by the 69th Pennsylvania Volunteers and attacked by the disorganized masses of Pickett's center and right. The body of Colonel James Gregory Hodges of the 14th Virginia was found in the vicinity of the small growth of trees along the wall, and marked that spot where Confederate losses were so high. The trees on the distant ridgeline designate the original position of A. P. Hill's assualting columns. (Photograph by Kathy Georg Harrison)

Where Were General Pickett and His Staff?

The incredible losses sustained by high ranking officers in Pickett's Division, particularly those who went into the attack mounted on horseback, were such that there were very few officers of field grade left unwounded when Pickett's column was repulsed from the wall. However, neither General Pickett nor a man of his staff was hurt or unhorsed during this attack. Although accounts and histories written after the battle by his staff officers and admirers depicted a General Pickett bravely leading his brigades to the very guns of the Union line on Cemetery Ridge, others disputed such participation by the division commander. Even Pickett himself could understand how the circumstances of his survival on July 3rd, 1863 would raise questions in the minds of his comrades and his critics as well. Captain William W. Wood of Company G, 14th Virginia Infantry, wrote in an early summary of the attack of this controversy which later embroiled division veterans:

> Strange to say, that although throughout the artillery combat and the subsequent charge General Pickett most recklessly exposed himself, yet neither he nor any member of his staff was struck. The General afterward said to me that on the day after the battle he felt that he would have no right to resent the insult if someone should accuse him of cowardice, because he was not among the killed, wounded or captured....[1]

Captain Robert A. Bright of Pickett's staff affirmed the leadership and direction of General Pickett during the advance and attack, being an eyewitness to his movements that day. Captain Bright, accompanied by Major Charles Pickett, Captain E. R. Baird, and Lieutenant W. Stuart Symington, were the only members of the staff to join Pickett in the advance from the Spangler Farm. Captain Bright's memories of that day were etched with details that seem to color his recollections with logical and factual sequence:

> I have nothing to guide me as to the farthest point General Pickett reached in person. We started in where Armistead's right was ... and at the Emmitsburg road General Pickett sent me to General Longstreet to tell him that he would take the enemy's position, but could not hold it without help; when I returned to General Pickett with General Longstreet's answer, I found General Pickett between the Emmitsburg Road and Cemetery Heights. Then three of us, one directly after the other, were sent to urge General Wilcox to bring his brigade to our assistance. On my return I found him near the descent of the last hill, facing the Federal works. Then I called his attention to a column of the enemy which was moving by head of column around our left flank, which was much too short. He sent me at once to Dearing's artillery battalion to order them to open on the column, and in this way protect his flank. Lieutenant [William] Marshall was on left of battalion, and I

came to him first. He said his battery had only three rounds of shot. He opened at once with them, after which I rode to General Pickett, who ordered our men back, so as to get out before being inclosed. At this time he was near the last valley in front of Cemetery Ridge.[2]

Captain Bright's memoir verifies that Pickett, like General Lee, was unaware of the critical lack of ammunition in the artillery chests of those batteries whose support was imperative to the success of the attack. Indeed, Pickett's orders to have the battalion open fire on a flanking threat had been anticipated by General Lee, who had planned the lengthy advanced artillery line to provide the support and protection for the grand assault. After Stribling's Battery had fired its last three shots at a flanking movement by the 8th Ohio and 111th New York Regiments, Pickett was informed that there would be no more help from that quarter. It was then that the general realized that the only recourse was to escape and retreat before the advanced remnants of the division would be encircled by the two Union flanking parties from the left and right. According to Captain Bright, Pickett's advance appears to have been as far as the rocky knoll in front of the Angle where a number of Kemper's and Garnett's men had taken cover. Nevertheless, his orders to retreat were apparently not heard by those fighting at the stone wall and in the Angle, who were unanimous in their conviction that no orders to fall back had reached them.

Lieutenant Symington also remembered that General Pickett had taken a position between the lines of Armistead and Garnett during the initial movements of the division. Symington could not be positive as to how far the general advanced with the division, but knew that he was within musketry range "and much closer than was prudent or necessary for a Major General commanding an assault."[3] Pickett's staff was not with him during the charge since they were apparently sent in different directions to deliver orders and coordinate the attack.[4] However, Thomas Friend, who remained with General Pickett throughout the assault, said they were "a few feet in the rear of the advancing column during the fight." Friend remembered that Pickett gave the last command in person on the field of battle "Forward, double quick! Boys, give them a cheer!" Thereafter, the general rode some distance along the line and dismounted, moving in a left oblique direction, before mounting again and following the men.[5] Friend did not mention hearing any commands by Pickett to fall back, but contradicted that notion in stating that Pickett's last orders on the battlefield were still urging the men to the attack.

To others, General Pickett's presence was not noticed during the advance or attack. Two of Longstreet's staff officers were sent off to warn Pickett of flanking movements from the right and left, but neither encountered the general. Major Moxley Sorrel rode among the lines of Armistead and Garnett and found both those officers, but, strangely, did not find Pickett, whose own staff attested to his presence between the two lines. These two mounted officers likewise were unhorsed when their mounts were killed beneath them in this mission undertaken for General Longstreet along Pickett's front.[6]

Major Kirkwood Otey, wounded in the shoulder while commanding his 11th Virginia Regiment of Kemper's Brigade, wrote that he "never heard a positive statement as to where General Pickett was in that charge; never heard him located or placed," except in general terms by staff officers. He continued that in "no account of the third day's fight at Gettysburg does the writer remember ever to have seen General Pickett's name mentioned, except as in command of his division; no incident, circumstance, or event connected therewith...identify or locate him." Major Otey was certain that Pickett was "there, on the field, commanding his division" but he could never recall seeing or hearing of any specific order, act, or incident to indicate his location during the critical moments. Indeed, Otey surmised that Pickett's place must have been some distance from the battle. When helped to the rear to a field hospital, he witnessed two officers of Pickett's staff helping themselves to a ration of whiskey from a surgeon's wagon, and assumed that if the pair were behind the lines that General Pickett must also be somewhere in the neighborhood.[7]

Most acerbate of those who testified that Pickett was nowhere to be seen during the advance and attack was the commanding officer of the 8th Virginia Regiment in Garnett's Brigade. Colonel Eppa Hunton wrote in his autobiography that "No man who was in that charge has ever been found, within my knowledge, who saw Pickett during the charge." Colonel Hunton used the obvious lack of casualties in men or horses among Pickett and staff as support for his argument. It seemed improbable that they would have all escaped without wounds or without their horses having been killed or wounded, when "every man who was known to have gone into that charge, on horse back, was killed or wounded, or had his horse killed." It seemed most likely to Hunton that Pickett did not advance with the division on the field of battle. He found support for his argument from eyewitnesses to Pickett's location, including a man from his command who had been detailed to carry water to the general and his staff. This man told Hunton that the officers were "behind a lime stone ledge of rocks, about 100 yards in the rear of the position we held just before the charge."[8] To Hunton this place 100 yards in the rear of the cannonade position of the brigade may as well have been 100 miles from the battlefield, for the protection it offered the division's officers.

Although various speculations have been advanced over the years to the identity and location of this "limestone ledge of rocks," no one has positively identified the site. The Gettysburg National Park Commissioners had to admit during the turn of the century that the limestone ledge had never been found or located. Subsequent authors and historians have speculated that the ledge of rocks must have been the foundation walls or bridge leading to that bank of the Codori Barn. This was fortified by the apparent depiction of General Pickett and his staff at the Codori Barn in the Cyclorama painting of "Pickett's Charge" by Paul Philippoteaux, who painted them there on information from Mrs. Pickett. However, the Codori Barn did not have a significant foundation nor a bridge during the battle in 1863, but was a small one story barn, probably log with siding. The present large bank barn was constructed almost twenty years after the Battle of Gettysburg. Limestone itself is not a native stone to the Gettysburg Battlefield, especially in that portion traversed by Pickett's Division.

But Colonel Hunton provided another clue to the location of this ledge of rocks when he asserted that "a Confederate surgeon says that he had his field hospital

130

behind [it], and that Pickett was there during the charge of his division."[9] Any temporary field hospital or aid station would have to have been to the rear of Pickett's Division, but the identity of the surgeon making the statement has always been clouded in mystery. At last, the source of the legend has been unearthed, and gives more credence to the story because of its very lack of publicity at the time it was originally related. That recollection was shared by Dr. Clayton G. Coleman to Senator John W. Daniel in 1904, when the latter was collecting data for a history of Virginia's participation at the Battle of Gettysburg. Doctor Coleman, who had been recently assigned to Kemper's Brigade as a surgeon at his own request, in order to use his skills as a doctor instead of service as an officer in Steuart's 23rd Virginia Infantry, wrote of his participation in the battle:

> Before the commencement of the fight, which was opened by the artillery, Gen. Kemper suggested to me a point about 300 yards in rear of the line as a suitable point to which the wounded should be taken, and I directed the first men wounded, before the charge of the infantry, to be taken by the ambulance corps to that point.
> I remained with the line until the infantry charge commenced, when I went back to the point which had been selected (which was under a large maple tree), and arriving there, found only two men, both wounded and without an attendant. While preparing a bandage for one of these men, they were both killed by a shot or shell which ricocheted at that point; and so concentrated was the artillery fire the maple tree was entirely destroyed. As it was impracticable for the litter bearers to do anything under this terrible fire, no other wounded were brought to that place, and as I was alone and could do nothing, I went to the woods, about 200 yards distant and waited for some abatement of the artillery fire.[10]

This artillery fire was no doubt created by the overshots by Union guns on Cemetery Ridge as they poured their fire against the ranks of Pickett's Division as it approached the Emmitsburg Road. Dr. Coleman, abruptly relieved of his patients by the shell that destroyed the maple tree, made for the shelter of the Spangler Woods:

> Upon arriving at the edge of the woods, I saw Gen. Pickett standing behind a large oak tree, holding his horse by the bridle, while his chief of staff, Maj. Harrison was similarly situated a few steps distant. Just then a shell exploded in the tree behind which Maj. Harrison was standing, a few feet above his head, when both and he and Gen. Pickett mounted their horses and rode rapidly to the rear.[11]

Although Dr. Coleman never referred to a ledge of rocks in his description, it is most possible that anyone seeking shelter from the fire in Spangler Woods would have used the natural entrenchment caused by a wash or drain that flowed in a north south direction through Spangler Woods and eventually flowed into Willoughby's Run. This wash is characteristically dry during the summer months, only holding water during spring thaws, winter snows and rains, and during sustained storms. It could have been described in retrospect as a ledge of rocks by someone who only momentarily took note of the incident.

The strongest endorsement of Dr. Coleman's narrative was his closing editorial comments to Senator Daniel:

> I have very rarely made any reference to Genl Pickett in connection with that sad and memorable occasion; never except to those who were participants; and I trust you will give no publicity to what I have written to you. Let us cover the deficiencies with the mantle of charity, and let our tears blot them from the tablet of our memory forever.[12]

Apparently John W. Daniel never did make public the letter written by Dr. Coleman, and the reference in Hunton's autobiography has heretofore been the only hearsay evidence of such an encounter between a surgeon and General Pickett.

Major Edmund Berkeley, also of the 8th Virginia Regiment, was not as vehement in his denials of Pickett's personal participation in the attack as his commander, but supported the contents of the arguments, nevertheless. Major Berkeley had an "uninterrupted view of the whole field going and also while being brought back and it would have been impossible for him (Pickett) and his staff" to have escaped his notice had they been there. He also repeated Hunton's assertion that it would have been extremely unlikely for the officers or their mounts to have escaped being wounded or killed had they advanced with the column. The most interesting and worthy of Berkeley's comments was qualified with his own assessment of the prescribed position of a division commander "I have been often asked if Pickett was in the charge. I have always replied that he was not and in my opinion, if he had been would have been out of his proper place."[13]

The "proper place" for a division commander charged with coordinating the attack of his division with the movements of other participating Confederate brigades and of the countermovements by the enemy, should have been in a location which provided an overview of the developing attack. That position would have been to the rear of the advancing Virginians, and was apparently selected (at least at the outset) by General Pickett. But the same ridges that concealed his division from the Union lines during the morning hours and cannonade also obscured their movements from his view after they crossed them and entered the valleys beyond. Pickett may have ridden to the right, along the artillery line, in search of a better vantage point to assess the progress of the attack. At least two separate written records substantiated each other in reporting the presence of General Pickett and members of his staff on the right of the artillery line during the conclusion of the advance. Colonel David Aiken wrote soon after the battle that he, as well as some of the men in his 7th South Carolina Infantry (Kershaw's Brigade), saw Pickett during the charge. The 7th South Carolina was posted in the vicinity of the Peach Orchard, near the junction of the Emmitsburg and Wheatfield Roads on 3 July 1863, and was therefore on the extreme right of the artillery line established by Alexander and Walton.[14]

Major John Cheves Haskell, who was assigned to the command of the two batteries of Henry's Battalion which participated in the cannonade, and later commanded the five guns eventually run forward into the fields between the

Emmitsburg Road and Cemetery Ridge, also asserted that he saw General Pickett and his staff at this same place as Colonel Aiken. When Haskell was unhorsed and partly disabled by the concentrated fire of McGilvery's Battalion on his advance position, he returned in the direction of the Wentz Farm buildings at the junction of the above mentioned roads:

> When I got there I found General Pickett and his staff, his division by this time having got back, except for those who were killed or captured, in great confusion. I have had the statement very severely questioned by General Pickett's admirers as reflecting on him and denying him the credit which history has generally given him. But I repeat it positively and solemnly as a fact, which justice to the brave men he commanded but did not lead demands.
>
> If any proof is needed, look at the reports. While not a single general and scarcely a field officer came out of the charge unhurt, neither Pickett nor any of his staff and he had a large and gallant one was touched. I left him at the barn when I went in, and I found him at the barn unscathed, when near all of the officers outside of him and his staff were killed and wounded when I came out.[15]

While Major Haskell's narrative seems to be strident in its condemnation of General Pickett and his staff in not being with the division, it is noteworthy in its description of the location of the apparent whereabouts of General Pickett during the latter part of the advance and attack. Haskell was specific in placing the general in a barn to the left of the original position of his battery, which was in the immediate vicinity of the Wheatfield Road and the mature Sherfy Peach Orchard. From that point, Pickett had one of the best views of the attack itself, since the post was elevated on the Emmitsburg Road ridge and overlooked the entire valley and Cemetery Ridge. From this vantage point General Pickett would have been instantly informed of the developments along his own line, as well as those along the lines of Wilcox and the enemy, and would have been in a position to send staff officers with orders or requests of aid to threatened points along the line. His presence at this point, where he could do the most good for the division, may have accounted for the lack of observations of the general and his staff once the column passed the Emmitsburg Road.

Although his staff and his courier, as well as some enlisted men, recorded seeing General Pickett during the attack between the Emmitsburg Road and the Union lines, the overwhelming majority of officers and men who advanced, fought, and retired over that same point did not confirm these observations. The hurried consultations between Kemper, Garnett, and Armistead while on the field of battle seemed to belie that the division commander was present or anywhere near their midst. The corroborating testimonies by Aiken and Haskell place Pickett on the right of the entire attacking column, where he would be posted in such a manner to perform the duties incumbent to a division commander in such an attack. It seems reasonable that General Pickett would have been maintaining a place in the rear of the line, or at a point where his field of observation would have been such as to encompass the extent of the battlefield on the front of his division. His observations of the separate flanking attacks, the failing of parts of Pettigrew's line, and his subsequent actions to deal with those events indicate that Pickett was in a position where he could not only see, but could act to meet, those threats. Kemper was totally unaware of the threat to his right flank, yet Pickett apparently saw it as well as the flanking movement by Hays' Union Division on the left. Had Pickett been with the column his effectiveness as a division commander would have been as impaired and short sighted as the narrow view seen by each of his brigade commanders. Through no fault of his own, Pickett was doomed to witness the decimation of his division, to send for reinforcements in Wilcox's and Lang's brigades (which marched in a direction that took them from the field of support and into the muzzles of a waiting foe), and to order the support of that artillery which had been unwittingly stripped of its power to assist him and his men in their dire need for the designed support. It was no wonder that Pickett was weeping bitterly after the repulse and writing reports of the battle that asked questions as to who was to blame for the decimation of his division. He had done what a division commander was supposed to do when his men are committed to such a movement, but they had been washed away in their own blood and he had escaped untouched. His situation was worsened by the wounding of Generals Pettigrew and Trimble, who had accompanied their forces to the guns of the enemy, and had not remained behind as division commanders were supposed to do. Therefore, his only statements after the battle, to those like Captain Wood, indicated his expectation of being condemned for not falling with his men, as Pettigrew and Trimble had done.

Perhaps then we would have an answer to the exact location of General Pickett during the attack, if he had fallen to the enemy's fire. We, like Pickett's men, are left to speculate how far, and where, and when, the general accompanied them toward the foe, and decide in our own minds (as did his comrades and veterans) the extent of his participation on those Gettysburg fields.

Elliott's Burial Map of the Battlefield of Gettysburg

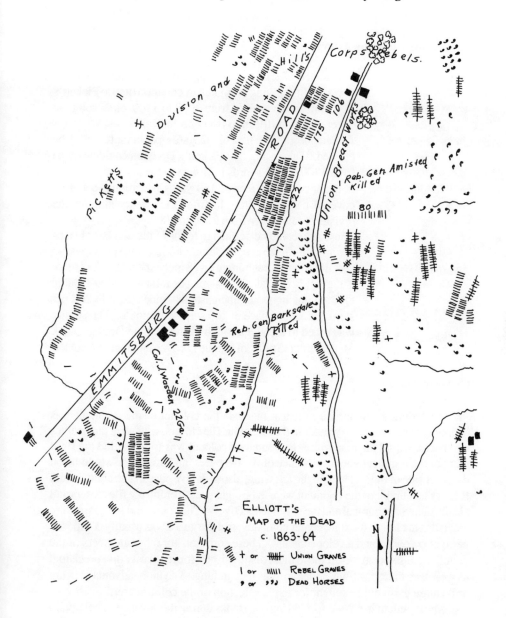

Hill's Corps Rebels.

Pickett's Division and

ROAD

175 106

522

Union Breast works

Reb. Gen. Amisted Killed

80

Reb. Gen. Barksdale Killed

EMMITSBURG

Col. J. Wasden 22 Ga.

ELLIOTT'S
MAP OF THE DEAD
c. 1863-64

+ or ✚✚✚ UNION GRAVES
I or |||| REBEL GRAVES
9 or 99 DEAD HORSES

N

Appendix B
Tactics and Terms

The Advance and the Attack

Common Time: A distance of 210 feet or 70 yards per minute could be covered. In applying the march at common time to Pickett's Division, an advance of from 1050 to 1400 yards could be covered within fifteen to twenty minutes.

Quick Time: A distance of 256 feet or 82 yards per minute could be crossed. This meant that Pickett's Division could advance from 1200 to 1600 yards in fifteen to twenty minutes.

Double-Quick Time: A distance of 454 feet or 150 yards per minute could be covered using this step. In fifteen to twenty minutes the division could cover from 2200 to 3000 yards.

These also could be defined in terms of the number of steps per minute. In the case of Common Time, the soldier was to take ninety steps per minute (at 28 inches per step); for Quick Time he should take 110 steps per minute; and at Double Quick Time he would increase his stride (to 33 inches per step) and keep a pace of 165 steps per minute. The soldier was urged to breathe through his nose at the Double Quick Step in order to prevent fatigue in covering longer distances.

Order of March

According to the infantry tactical manuals the colonel of the regiment was supposed to be about thirty paces in the rear of his file closers, who were themselves two paces behind the rear rank. The lieutenant colonel was to be behind the right wing of the regiment about a distance of twelve paces, and the major would be on the other side of the line behind the left wing, also at twelve paces. The adjutant and the sergeant major of the regiment were to be eight paces behind the file closers and aid the lieutenant colonel and the major respectively. The colors and the guard were located at the left of the right center company, and the guard was usually composed of eight corporals and a color sergeant. These corporals (or other members of the guard) were selected "from those most distinguished for regularity and precision, as well as in their positions under arms as in marching. The latter advantage ... are to be more particularly sought for in the selection of the color-bearer."

The regiment itself was formed into two ranks during the advance. The captain of each company marched on the right of his company, and the covering first sergeant (also known as the right guide) was located directly behind his captain.

Appendix C

Mounted Officers and Men in Pickett's Division During the Attack

1. Major General George E. Pickett
2. Major Charles Pickett, Adjutant General of Division
3. Captain Edward R. Baird, aide-de-camp to General Pickett
4. Captain Robert A. Bright, aide-de-camp to General Pickett
5. Lieutenant W. Stuart Symington, aide-de-camp to General Pickett
6. Private Thomas R. Friend, courier for General Pickett
7. Brigadier General James L. Kemper (wounded and captured)
8. Captain T. G. Pollock, Inspector General of Kemper's Brigade (killed)
9. Lieutenant George E. Geiger, aide-de-camp to General Kemper (wounded and captured, later died)
10. Captain William T. Fry, Adjutant General of Kemper's Brigade
11. Private George Walker, orderly to General Kemper
12. Colonel Lewis B. Williams, 1st Virginia Infantry Regiment (killed)
13. Brigadier General Richard B. Garnett (killed)
14. Lieutenant John Simkins Jones, aide-de-camp to General Garnett (wounded)
15. Private Robert Irvine, courier for General Garnett (horse killed)
16. Colonel Eppa Hunton, 8th Virginia Infantry Regiment (wounded)

Appendix D

The Casualties — Hospitals and Cemeteries

Over 2600 casualties, about 42% of Pickett's force, did not return to Virginia. The wounded and the prisoners would be transported to other locations where their battle of survival still continued. For those killed during the advance, attack, and retreat, there were hastily dug graves after General Lee's army surrendered the battlefield to the Union forces. There at least 225 remains[1] from Pickett's Division were interred in common trench and individual graves by Union burial details after the battle. No individual graves were identified during this early post-battle effort, and those killed outright on the field of battle would join the great leveller of death in promoting the conformity of anonymity. Each soldier who was killed on Gibbon's battle-front became kin in sharing only one identity — one of Pickett's men. Officers and enlisted men rested side by side in the fields of the Codori and Small farms, between the Emmitsburg Road and the Angle. During the duration of the war, the remains were unattended to, and many were forgotten to veterans and farmers alike before being disinterred and transported to Richmond's Hollywood Cemetery on June 13, 1872. These unidentified men of Pickett's Division were given the single honor of being among those first removed to Richmond. They were reinterred in 26 boxes in rows 4 and 5 of Section 2 of the Gettysburg lot of that cemetery. Among those forgotten graves was one unearthed by Gettysburg farmer D. A. Riley on June 5, 1886, when he was plowing the fields of the Codori Farm. Near that point where Colonel Mayo saw Colonel Terry pointing rearward with his sword (site of the present marker erected by the survivors o the 15th Massachusetts to designate the site where their own Colonel Ward fell on 2 July 1863), the plow turned up a piece of skull and a thigh bone, each with bullets embedded in it. Once the very sinew of Pickett's strong and willing band, this forgotten member of the division became the mere object of local curiosity.

Those dead of the division who were buried by friend or foe at the hospitals where they died were often fortunate enough to have their identities preserved by way of crude headboards made of disassembled wooden boxes, fences, flooring, or siding. Perhaps a handful were recovered by friends and relatives before the war's end, and another dozen or so were brought back to Virginia in the first years after the war. But the vast majority of Pickett's mortally wounded remained in their hospital graves until, like those killed while following their generals on the field of battle, they were disinterred to Richmond. In the decade that passed after the battle, many of the marks of those hospital graves were obliterated by the climate and weather, as well as by some persistent farmers who erected fencing or plowed over the graves. The South was fortunate that at least one local resident remembered that

138

these too were human beings and once fellow countrymen. Doctor John W. C. O'Neal traveled over the battlefield and its hospitals, recording in his "day books" and a ledger the locations of Confederate graves along with notations about them. O'Neal became the contact for all later reinterment efforts, whether they were by relatives or friends or by Ladies' Memorial Associations. Altogether, he recorded the identifications of over 1100 Confederate burial sites before the rains eradicated the legends on the headboards. Although it was impossible for O'Neal to identify the dead who rested in Codori's fields, he preserved the identities of those Virginians who died at Pickett's Division hospital and at those Union hospitals where the mortally wounded were taken as prisoners. Most of these dead came from the three largest hospitals that served the wounded of Pickett's Division.

The division hospital itself was located along Marsh Creek, south of the Hagerstown Road at Bream's Mill and the two houses of Jeff Myers and John Currens that adjoined the mill. About ten years before the battle, a local advertisement described the mill as being almost brand new and the houses as being somewhat older. One house (Myers') was a two-story log dwelling with a stone back building attached, while the other (Currens') was also a two-story log farmhouse. The three-story high grist mill was also joined by a saw mill, cooper shop, and a blacksmith shop, and there was plenty of stabling and other sheds scattered about. This location was attractive for hospital use because of the large and commodious buildings at Bream's Mill, the abundance of shade from the trees that lined the banks of nearby Marsh Creek, and the mineral springs on the site. A large orchard of peach, pear, plum, and apricot trees would handily provide needed fruits for the wounded either from the trees themselves or from the preserves that the family must have had stored away.[2]

It was here at Bream's Mill and the Currens farm of 67 acres that the wounded of the cannonade and assault like Colonel Eppa Hunton and Lieutenant Colonel John T. Ellis were treated or given their last comforts from comrades. Here, too, were those who were killed but carried back by friends to be interred in marked graves beside those who meant so much to them when living, like Captain Thomas Pollock and Major Nathaniel C. Wilson. Today, Bream's Mill is but a memory and a faded photograph, its dam and water wheels long gone. The Currens Farmhouse, around which at least 34 of Pickett's men were originally laid to rest still remains on the hill overlooking Marsh Creek. Included among those Virginians who mouldered in the soil of orchard and wood and garden was the young farmer George Dabney Tweedy of Company C, 11th Virginia. His three older brothers, Fayette, Edmund, and Smith buried him on the banks of Marsh Creek near the dam, to be sheltered in his final sleep by the overhanging boughs of swamp oaks. The scene of those moments where Pickett's surviving wounded clasped hands in farewell with their retreating comrades has succumbed to alterations of its pastoral nature. Suburban development on neighboring lands began in the 1970s, and continues in earnest today, encroaching on and altering the landscape of those fields which became the hospital ward and cemetery for many of the division. Regimental comrades of those treated and buried here went to great lengths to prevent their friends from falling into Yankee hands, but they could not halt the imprisonment of their memories in the twentieth century by studded walls and two-car garages, as development subverts the significance and poignancy of Pickett's Division Hospital.

The vast majority of Pickett's wounded, however, were treated in Federal hospitals, first at Gettysburg and then in Harrisburg, Philadelphia, and Baltimore. Since many of the wounded were originally not able to move from where they fell, they were captured by the forces which opposed them — the men from the Union Second Corps and First Corps. The Union Second Corps hospital, established on the Widow Schwartz Farm, southeast of Gettysburg and off of the Baltimore Pike, became the gathering point for most of Pickett's captured wounded. Nestled between Rock Creek and White Run, the Schwartz Farm consisted of 156 acres of open land and woodlot, and had a small orchard near the farm buildings. Its location near the Union supply and communication line (Baltimore Pike) placed it on the route leading to rail transport, and the combination of the two creeks and two wells of water near the buildings made it attractive for bathing wounds and securing water for drinking, cooking, and cleaning. The farm had a two-story brick house and a brick bank barn which served as the primary hospital and recovery wards. These two main structures were surrounded by a wagon shed, corn crib, carriage house, and smoke house. North of these buildings were those of the Aaron Sheely Farm. A high ridge forever known to those who had friends buried there as Red Hill connected the two farms north of the Schwartz buildings. Almost fifty of Pickett's veterans were laid in identified graves on the Schwartz estate, behind the barn, in a cornfield, and in a field west of the buildings near Rock Creek (known as Yard B). Another 34 unidentified Confederate graves joined the 100 additional identified Southern graves on this farm. Pickett's dead were reinterred to Richmond's Hollywood Cemetery during the first shipment of remains in June 1872, and were interred in rows one and two of Section 2 of the Gettysburg plot.[3]

A description of the conditions at the Schwartz Farm was given by a member of the Christian Commission, who was serving as the chief nurse in the Schwartz barn:

> The old farmhouse was only one of half a dozen occupied by the men of Hancock's corps, but it was a type of them all. Its every room was a chamber of death and the boards of the shambling porch that girdled it were stained with the blood of the men for whom there was no room inside. The shade of a vine-clad trellis gave these poor fellows partial shelter from the scorching heat. West of the farmhouse, and only a stone's throw from the vine-clad porch with its freight of human misery, stood the old barn. This was devoted exclusively to the wounded of the Confederate army, and while the soldiers of the North were dying for lack of care it was not strange that these poor strangers were left in even worse condition....
>
> The smaller of the barn doors had been unhinged to serve as surgeon's tables, and there on the threshing-floor and haylofts of peaceful husbandry war had garnered its awful harvest of death and agony .... Every available inch of space was occupied. The men lay close to each other, side by side in long rows, as compactly as when a few days before ... they marched shoulder to shoulder across the

Emmitsburg Road, ... as compactly as we laid their mangled bodies a few days later, shoulder to shoulder in the long trenches of the stubblefield. The cattle pens, too, still reeking with the litter of the barnyard, were as densely packed with victims as the threshing floor above, and I noticed with horror, as I assisted the dressing of a bleeding wound, that the blood of the patient filtered through the cracks and knot-holes of the floor and dripped upon the suffers below.

As night came on darkness threw a kindly mantle over such repulsive sights, but the horror of the situation was hardly less acute. The only illumination of the place came from the sickly yellow glow of an army lantern. A square box-like contrivance hung from a joist, with an oil lamp in the middle and four cracked panes of glass, so soiled that the dull yellow rays barely struggled through them. The men — restless, suffering, and unable to sleep — tossed and moaned and raved in wild delirium. The weather-beaten barn resounded with a horrid chorus of curses, imprecations and groans that sounded doubly awful at dead of night, and the old army lantern's glimmering light wrought weird, fantastic shadows among the cobwebbed rafters of the roof.[4]

Although the Schwartz Farm was a Union hospital, the vast numbers of Pickett's Division who were cared for there in its buildings and buried in its fields near the Baltimore Pike gave it as much significance to the division as the hospital at Bream's Mill. Here were treated those Virginians who fell at the very muzzles of the Northern guns, who had experienced the exhilaration of momentary victory and the despair of capture. Its position southeast of the town of Gettysburg and slightly detached from any major road frontage managed to protect the Schwartz Farm from alterations and development through the hundred and twenty years after the battle. The recent construction of a wastewater treatment plant and access roads to and from that plant, have begun the process of undermining the historical integrity of the site. With the presence of sewage and water facilities within yards of the buildings and with road construction sweeping through the fields of the Aaron Sheely and Schwartz Farms, it is only a matter of time before that place where Pickett's men lay "shoulder to shoulder" becomes a subdivision like its neighboring farms. It is currently advertised as "prime" for industrial, commercial, or residential development in this unzoned community.

The other major Gettysburg hospital to treat Pickett's wounded was established about three weeks after the end of the battle at the woods of the George Wolf Farm, about a mile east of Gettysburg along the York Pike. Known as the General Hospital, it soon was called Camp Letterman in honor of the chief medical officer of the Union Army of the Potomac. Here it was intended to concentrate all the Union and Confederate wounded into a general field hospital, and so disband the scores of small farm hospitals throughout the countryside. This would facilitate the disbursement of medical supplies, foodstuffs, and clothing to the wounded, and make treatment and transport of the wounded a more systematic effort. By mid-August, those Confederate wounded who were not well enough to be transported to prisons or major hospitals in the North were brought to the General Hospital to be nursed by Union and Confederate surgeons. An estimated 1600 wounded were housed in tents at the Wolf Woods, and the addition of surgeons, nurses, attendants, and guards swelled the population of the camp to at least 2000.[5] Over thirty of Pickett's veterans died at this site along the York Pike in the four months during which it was active. They were buried in the trench graves of Camp Letterman's cemetery on the ridge back (southeast) of the woods. The entirety of the "Hospital Woods" was included for acquisition in the law creating Gettysburg National Military Park in 1895, but the site was never acquired because of lack of funding or change in attitudes. In 1932, a civilian eyewitness to the days following the Battle of Gettysburg wrote of his surprise that "the government, when it was acquiring the historic fields upon which the battle was fought and other sections now included in the reservation, did not buy this woods, one of the most historic and sacred spots on the field."[6] Now this site, like the Bream's Mill and Schwartz Farm hospitals, is threatened by the spread of suburban development. The woods are located near a major highway interchange, and have become an attractive parcel because of their road frontage and the recent construction activities of a shopping center adjacent to it on the east. The War Department refused to pay a little over $100 an acre for it at the turn of the century, citing that it was too much to pay to preserve the woods. Now the price has risen to astronomical levels because of adjacent development. Its true historical value has been subverted to mere economical value. Thus, the largest of Gettysburg's hospital sites faces imminent destruction because our nation has forgotten the significance of the George Wolf Woods and has elevated the significance of a convenient shopping mall.

Thus we see that of the three major hospitals that cured or buried Pickett's wounded, none are preserved or protected as national historic sites, and all three face a precarious and short-lived future unless some major intervention is implemented by a national politic that remembers the significance of its own past. The field of Pickett's assault is preserved as part of the National Park Service, but those places where hundreds of the division's wounded continued their struggle for survival are still outside the scope of any preservation activities. We must hope that those who remember and care will not feel the emptiness and despair that Pickett's men faced when they turned to see no supports coming to secure the victory. It would be the ultimate defeat of Pickett's Virginians, to be forgotten in their deaths and agonies for the sake of housing and shopping centers that could be constructed elsewhere.

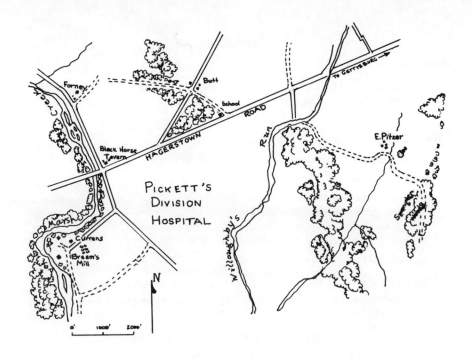

Hospitals at Gettysburg

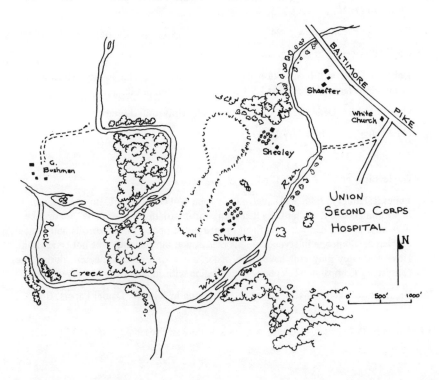

143

Notes

Foreword

1. Account of Bernard Matthews, Company A, 108th New York in "Leg Taken Off by Gettysburg Shell," *The Louisville Evening Post* (3 July 1913), in Gettysburg Newspaper Clippings, Vol. 6, p. 102.

Chapter One

1. David Johnston, *Four Years a Soldier* (Princeton, WV: n.p., 1887), p. 234.

2. Ibid., p. 240. This man was probably Private John Riley, Company E, 18th Virginia Infantry, who enlisted as a substitute 6 December 1862 and was AWOL within a fortnight. Apprehended and arrested almost immediately, Riley remained under arrest through his court martial on June 14th, when he was sentenced to be shot. Telephone conversation with John W. Busey, 23 January 1986.

3. H. T. Owen, Letter, *CV* 12 (January 1904), p. 7.

4. Richard B. Garnett to Mrs. Dandridge, 21 June 1863 in Bedinger-Dandridge Family Correspondence, Duke University Library; Eppa Hunton, *Autobiography of Eppa Hunton* (Richmond: William Byrd Press, 1933), p. 86.

5. Garnett to Mrs. Dandridge, 25 June 1863, Duke University Library.

6. Sergeant Levin C. Gayle, 27 June 1863 diary entry. Typescript copy in Gettysburg National Military Park Library files.

7. Colonel George K. Griggs, "Memorandum of the Thirty-eighth Virginia Infantry," *SHSP*, 14 (1886), pp. 252-253.

8. Hunton, p. 87; Johnston, p. 243.

9. Gayle, diary entry of 30 June 1863.

10. Robert B. Damron, "Recollections of some of the incidents of the Battle of Gettysburg," in John W. Daniel Papers, Box 23, University of Virginia Library.

11. Garnett to Mrs. Dandridge, 25 June 1863, Duke University Library.

12. Gayle, diary entry of 1 July 1863.

13. Johnston, p. 243.

14. Gayle, diary entry of 2 July 1863.

15. James R. Hutter to John W. Daniel, n.d., in John W. Daniel Papers, Box 23, University of Virginia Library. Major Otey had been court-martialled in April 1863 for drunkenness on duty and had been confined to quarters, dropped from the rolls and almost cashiered. Someone intervened on his behalf, and the sentence was not carried out. However, Otey may still have been under some kind of confinement during the Gettysburg Campaign. Telephone conversation with John Busey, 23 January 1986.

16. Biographical sketch of Col. Henry A. Carrington in John W. Daniel Papers, Box 23, University of Virginia Library.

17. James E. Poindexter, "General Armistead's Portrait Presented," *SHSP* 37 (1909), p. 145.

18. Eppa Hunton to John W. Daniel, 15 July 1904, in John W. Daniel Papers, Box 1849-1904, Duke University Library.

19. Biographical sketch of James Dearing in John W. Daniel Papers, Box 22, University of Virginia Library.

20. Walter Harrison, *Pickett's Men: A Fragment of War History* (New York: D. Van Nostrand, 1870), pp. 166-170.

21. Ibid., pp. 160-161.

22. Ibid., pp. 163-164.

23. Statistical data, battery composition, occupational information, and age within the units was ascertained through use of the material gleaned from company muster rolls and incorporated as part of the appendix of this book by John W. Busey.

24. Garnett to Mrs. Dandridge, 25 June 1863, Duke University Library; Randolph Shotwell, "Virginia and North Carolina in the Battle of Gettysburg," *Our Living and Our Dead*, IV (1876), p. 87; Johnston, p. 237; Rawley W. Martin and John H. Smith, "The Battle of Gettysburg, and the Charge of Pickett's Division," *SHSP* 32 (1904), pp. 184-185.

25. William B. Robertson to Mattie _____, 28 July 1863, in John W. Daniel Papers, Box 23, University of Virginia Library.

26. Sergeant Gayle, diary entry of 2 July 1863; Johnston, p. 243; Griggs, p. 253.

27. Johnston, p. 244; Shotwell, p. 87.

28. Harrison, p. 88.

29. *OR*, Series I, Vol. 27, Part 2, p. 430; E. P. Alexander, "The Great Charge and Artillery Fighting at Gettysburg," *Battles and Leaders of the Civil War*, Vol. 3 (New York: Thomas Yoseloff, 1956), p. 360.

30. *OR*, Series I, Vol. 27, Part 2, p. 388.

31. Erasmus Williams, "A Private's Experience in the 14th Virginia Infantry at Gettysburg," in the John W. Daniel Papers, Box 23, University of Virginia Library.

Chapter Two

1. *OR*, Series 1, Vol. 27, Part 2, p. 697; Martin W. Hazelwood, "Gettysburg Charge. Paper as to Pickett's Men," *SHSP* 23 (1895), p. 229.

2. *OR*, Series 1, Vol. 27, Part 2, pp. 320, 259.

3. Damron, "Recollections," Daniel Papers, University of Virginia Library; Sergeant Gayle, 3 July 1863 diary entry; Johnston, p. 246.

4. Hutter to Daniel, n.d., Daniel Papers, University of Virginia Library.

5. Damron, "Recollections," Daniel Papers, University of Virginia Library.

6. Johnston, p. 246.

7. Lt. William Nathaniel Wood, *Reminiscences of Big I*, ed. Bell I. Wiley (Jackson, Tenn.: McCowat-Mercer Press, 1956), p. 43.

8. Johnston, p. 246; Harrison, p. 90.

9. Damron, "Recollections," Daniel Papers, University of Virginia Library.

10. Harrison, pp. 91-92.

11. Damron, "Recollections," Daniel Papers, University of Virginia Library.

12. J. C. Granbery to John W. Daniel, 25 March 1905, John W. Daniel Papers, Box 23, University of Virginia Library.

13. Hutter to Daniel, n.d., Daniel Papers, University of Virginia Library.

14. Ibid.

15. Charles T. Loehr, "The 'Old First' at Gettysburg," *SHSP* 32 (1904), pp. 33, 40.

16. Johnston, p. 250.

17. Joseph Mayo, "Pickett's Charge at Gettysburg," *SHSP* 34 (1906), pp. 328-329.

18. Loehr, pp. 33-34.

19. Shotwell, p. 88.

20. Hunton, p. 89; George W. Finley, "Bloody Angle," *Buffalo Evening News* (29 May 1894), in Gettysburg Newspaper Clippings, Vol. 4, p. 43.

21. Richard Irby, *Historical Sketch of the Nottoway Grays, afterwards Company G, Eighteenth Virginia Regiment, Army of Northern Virginia* (Richmond: J. W. Ferguson & Son, 1878), p. 27.

22. Wood, pp. 43-44.

23. J. R. McPherson, "A Private's Account of Gettysburg," *CV* 6 (1898), p. 148.

24. Finley, p. 43.

25. William M. Owen, "Pickett's Charge," *Gettysburg Star and Sentinel* (6 July 1886).

26. Robert Stribling to John W. Daniel, 7 March 1904, in the John W. Daniel Papers, Box 23, University of Virginia Library.

27. Account of Joseph L. Thompson, n.d., in the John W. Daniel Papers, Box 23, University of Virginia Library.

28. "Colonel E. P. Alexander's Report of the Battle of Gettysburg," *SHSP* 4 (1877), p. 327.

29. Martin and Smith, pp. 184-185.

30. Hunton to Daniel, 15 July 1904, in the John W. Daniel Papers, University of Virginia Library.

31. Edmund Berkeley to John W. Daniel, 26 September _____, in the John W. Daniel Papers, Box 23, University of Virginia Library.

32. Gayle diary entry of 3 July 1863.

33. Granbery to Daniel, 25 March 1905, in the John W. Daniel Papers, University of Virginia Library.

Chapter Three

1. William Owen, "Pickett's Charge."

2. James A. Longstreet to Col. J. B. Walton, 6 November 1877, in the Historic New Orleans Collection, Tulane University.

3. William Owen, "Pickett's Charge."

4. Harrison, pp. 96-97.

5. James L. Kemper to E. P. Alexander, 20 September 1869 in the Dearborn Collection of Confederate Civil War Papers, Houghton Library, Harvard University.

6. Ibid.

7. Charles D. Walker, *Memorial, Virginia Military Institute. Biographical Sketches of the Graduates and Eleves of the Virginia Military Institute who Fell During the War Between the States* (Philadelphia: J. B. Lippincott & Co., 1875), p. 262.

8. Account of John T. James, July 9, 1863, in Thomas D. Huston, "Storming Cemetery Hill," *The Philadelphia Times* (21 October 1882).

9. James R. Hutter to John W. Daniel, n.d., in the J.W. Daniel Papers, Box 23, University of Virginia Library.

10. Smith, *SHSP*, p. 190; William H. H. Winston account in the J.W. Daniel Papers, Box 23, University of Virginia Library.

11. Smith, p. 190.

12. Winston account, J.W. Daniel Papers, Box 23, University of Virginia Library.

13. Loehr, "The 'Old First' at Gettysburg," p. 36.

14. Joseph T. Durkin, ed., *John Dooley: Confederate Soldier—His War Journal.* (South Bend, Ind.: University of Notre Dame Press, 1963), pp. 102-104.

15. Johnston, pp. 271-272.

16. Mayo, "Pickett's Charge at Gettysburg," pp. 329-330.

17. Hunton, p. 99.

18. Shotwell, "Virginia and North Carolina at the Battle of Gettysburg," pp. 89-90.

19. Berkeley to Daniel, 26 September _____, J.W. Daniel Papers, University of Virginia Library.

20. See roster of the 8th Virginia in the Appendix.

21. Berkeley to Daniel, 26 September _____, J.W. Daniel Papers, University of Virginia Library.

22. Irby, p. 27.

23. Rev. Dr. [Henry] Jacobs, "Meteorology of the Battle," Gettysburg Newspaper Clippings—Relating to the Battle, Gettysburg National Military Park Library, p. 35.

24. Wood, p. 44; Walker, Memorial, Virginia Military Institute, p. 192.

25. Account of William P. Jesse, in the J.W. Daniel Papers, Box 23, University of Virginia Library.

26. Finley, "Bloody Angle," p. 43.

27. Williams, "A Private's Experience in the 14th Virginia," J.W. Daniel Papers, University of Virginia Library.

28. John H. Lewis, *Recollections from 1860 to 1865* (Portsmouth, VA: 1893), p. 78.

29. James H. Walker, "The Charge of Pickett's Division," *The Blue and the Gray*, Vol. 1 (1893), pp. 222-223.

30. Maude Carter Clement, ed., *The History of Pittsylvania County, Va.* (Lynchburg: 1929), p. 248.

31. B. L. Farinholt to John W. Daniel, 15 April 1904, in the J.W. Daniel Papers, Box 23, University of Virginia Library.

32. Ibid.

33. "Colonel E. P. Alexander's Report of the Battle of Gettysburg," *SHSP*, IV (1877), p. 237.

34. *OR*, Series 1, Vol. 27, Part 2, p. 352; "Colonel Alexander's Report," *SHSP*, p. 238.

35. *OR*, Series 1, Vol. 27, Part 2, p. 352.

36. "Colonel Alexander's Report," *SHSP*, p. 238.

37. *OR*, Series 1, Vol. 27, Part 2, p. 360.

38. Mayo, "Pickett's Charge at Gettysburg," *SHSP*, pp. 329, 331.

39. Hunton to Daniel, 15 July 1904, J.W. Daniel Papers, University of Virginia Library.

40. Ibid.

41. Ernest Linden Waitt, *History of the Nineteenth Regiment Massachusetts Volunteer Infantry 1861-1865* (Salem, MA: The Salem Press Co., 1906), pp. 235-237.

42. John D. Musser, 15 September 1863 letter, in the John D. Musser Papers, Ronald Boyer Collection, Military History Institute.

43. John Gibbon, *Personal Recollections of the Civil War* (Dayton: Morningside Books, 1978 reprint), pp. 146-159.

Chapter Four

1. Colonel E. Porter Alexander to Adam L. Alexander, 17 July 1863, in the Alexander-Hillhouse Papers, University of North Carolina.

2. Jesse account in the J.W. Daniel Papers, University of Virginia Library.

3. McPherson, "A Private's Account of Gettysburg," p. 149.

4. Mayo, "Pickett's Charge at Gettysburg," *SHSP*, p. 331; Johnston, p. 255.

5. R. A. Bright, "Pickett's Charge at Gettysburg," *CV* Vol. 37 (July 1930), p. 264; James L. Kemper to John B. Bachelder, 4 February 1886, in Bachelder Correspondence, New

Hampshire Historical Society. Microfilm Reel 1, p. 285; Kemper to Alexander, 20 September 1869, Harvard University.

6. Bright, p. 264.

7. Report of _____ for the 24th Virginia Infantry, 9 July 1863, in George Pickett Papers, Duke University Library.

8. Kemper to Bachelder, 4 February 1886, in Bachelder Correspondence, New Hampshire Historical Society.

9. J. H. Stine, *History of the Army of the Potomac* (Washington: Gibson Brothers, 1893), p. 539.

10. Report of the 24th Virginia Regiment, in the George Pickett Papers, Duke University.

11. The Klingel Farmhouse, the only other dwelling between Kemper's original position and the Codori buildings, was apparently an exposed log house at the time of the advance.

12. Hutter to Daniel, n.d., in J.W. Daniel Papers, University of Virginia Library.

13. Huston, "Storming Cemetery Hill," p. 22.

14. Ibid.

15. William H. Morgan, *Personal Reminiscences of the War of 1861-65* (Lynchburg: J. P. Bell Co., Inc., 1911), pp. 166-167. According to his brother, "Horace, by taking Robert on his back, when no other means of conveyance was at hand, and by getting him in an ambulance or wagon when possible, brought him safely out of the enemy's country, across the Potomac, on down the Valley to Staunton, and in due time landed him safely at home...."

16. Martin and Smith, "The Battle of Gettysburg and the Charge of Pickett's Division," *SHSP*, pp. 190-191.

17. Loehr, "The 'Old First' at Gettysburg," *SHSP*, p. 35.

18. W. H. H. Winston account in the J.W. Daniel Papers, University of Virginia Library.

19. Durkin, pp. 104-105.

20. Loehr, "The 'Old First' at Gettysburg," *SHSP*, p. 36. Mitchel's body was recovered the day after the battle by a Charles Joice and three others when they were in search of wounded soldiers between the lines. His remains were found near a "little brick house" that was probably the Codori Farmhouse, wrapped in a blanket that was pinned with three pins, the center one being larger and with a black head, whereas the two others were "common pins." Joice found that Private Mitchel's face had been washed and that a slip of paper had been pinned to the blanket with the words "W. J. Mitchel" thereon. With the assistance of a black man they dug a grave "on the banks of a small cabin so close that no plow would ever disturb it" and laid Mitchel in it. They took a cracked board and fastened the slip of paper to it at the head of the grave. It was not until May of the following year that Mr. Joice was able to locate Private Mitchel's mother and describe to her the location of the grave. Rebecca O'Connor-Moulder to Superintendent, Gettysburg National Cemetery, 18 May 1864 enclosure, Gettysburg National Military Park files.

21. Lieutenant John E. Dooley of the 1st Virginia, however, gives differing circumstances for Colonel Williams' death. Dooley fell at the Emmitsburg road, shot through both thighs, and was carried about ten yards from the road on the morning of July 4th, to be laid down near the mortally wounded Williams. Dooley reported that the Colonel's spine had been cut in two at the neck joint, and he was suffering "continual and intense agony" in trying to find a comfortable position for his head. By mid-day Colonel Williams was carried to the Union rear, where Dooley heard he died after four or five days of subsequent suffering. Durkin, ed., pp. 108-109.

22. Mayo again saw Williams' bay mare at Williamsport during the retreat, in the care of the colonel's faithful servant Harry, who asked Colonel Mayo what he thought "old master would say when she was all belonging to Mars Lewis he had to take home." Mayo, "Pickett's Charge at Gettysburg," *SHSP*, p. 333.

23. Johnston, p. 273.

24. Mayo, p. 331.

25. Ibid., p. 332.

26. Hunton, p. 99; Edmund Berkeley to Daniel, 26 September _____, J.W. Daniel Papers, University of Virginia Library.

27. Hunton, p. 90.

28. Edmund Berkeley to Daniel, 26 September _____, J.W. Daniel Papers, University of Virginia Library; Owen, Letter in CV, p. 7.

29. Winfield Peters, "The Lost Sword of Gen. Richard B. Garnett, Who Fell at Gettysburg," *SHSP*, Vol. 33 (1905), p. 29.

30. Edmund Berkeley, "Rode with Pickett," *CV*, Vol. 38 (May 1930), p. 175.

31. Shotwell, "Virginia and North Carolina in the Battle of Gettysburg," p. 91.

32. Ibid., pp. 91-92.

33. Berkeley to Daniel, 26 September _____, J.W. Daniel Papers, University of Virginia Library. This last episode raises questions concerning the effectiveness of General Pickett and his staff during the advance. Although the latter were seen trying to stem the flow of retreating soldiers on the left, no one seemed to be paying much attention to the right of the line, even to the point of neglecting to pass important orders to Kemper's Brigade. Indeed, Kemper's orders from the beginning seemed quite sparse.

34. Hunton to Daniel, 15 July 1904, J.W. Daniel Papers, University of Virginia Library.

35. Biographical sketch of Colonel Carrington, Daniel Papers, Box 23, University of Virginia Library.

36. Irby, p. 27.

37. Although there was no recorded stone wall along the Emmitsburg Road at the point where Pickett's Division would have crossed it, there is the possibility that stones had been piled by the farmers beneath the lower-most rails of a post and rail fence to the height of two feet or so, as was common in other parts of the battlefield. The posts and rails were probably destroyed in the previous day's action, and only the stone wall and loose rails remained.

38. Captain H. T. Owen, in Jacob Hoke, *The Great Invasion* (New York: Thomas Yoseloff, 1959), pp. 385-386.

39. Wood, pp. 44-46.

40. Walker, *Memorial*, VMI, pp. 538-539.

41. Hunton, p. 100; *OR*, Series 1, Vol. 27, Part 2, p. 387; Willard A. and Porter W. Heaps, *The Singing Sixties. The Spirit of Civil War Days Drawn from the Music of the Times* (Norman, OK: University of Oklahoma Press, 1963), p. 191.

42. Jesse account, in the J.W. Daniel Papers, University of Virginia Library.

43. Damron, "Recollections of the incidents of the Battle of Gettysburg, July 3, 1863," in the J.W. Daniel Papers, University of Virginia Library; Finley, "Bloody Angle," p. 43.

44. Ibid.; Henry C. Michie to John W. Daniel, 27 January 1904, in the J.W. Daniel Papers, University of Virginia Library.

45. Finley, "Bloody Angle," p. 43.

46. Williams, "A Private's Experience in the 14th Virginia Infantry at Gettysburg," in the J.W. Daniel Papers, University of Virginia Library.

47. Robertson to Mattie, 28 July 1863, in the J.W. Daniel Papers, University of Virginia Library.

48. Ibid.

49. Lewis, p. 78.

50. Walker, "The Charge of Pickett's Division," pp. 221-223.

51. Stine, p. 540.

52. Gayle, diary entry for 3 July 1863, Gettysburg National Military Park Library.

53. Also reported as, "Yes, General, if mortal man can do it," Rawley H. Martin, "Armistead at the Battle of Gettysburg," *SHSP*, Vol. 39 (1914), p. 186.

54. James T. Carter, "Flag of the Fifty-third Va. Regiment," *CV*, Vol. 10 (June 1902), p. 263; Martin and Smith, "The Battle of Gettysburg and Charge of Pickett's Division," *SHSP*, p. 188; Martin, "Armistead at the Battle of Gettysburg," *SHSP*, Vol. 39 (1914), p. 186.

55. B. L. Farinholt to Daniel, 15 April 1904, in the J.W. Daniel Papers, University of Virginia Library.

56. Martin and Smith, "The Battle of Gettysburg and Charge of Pickett's Division," *SHSP*, p. 188.

57. Rev. James E. Poindexter, "Address on the Life and Services of Gen. Lewis A. Armistead, delivered...before R. E. Lee Camp, No. 1, Confederate Veterans," (Richmond: January 29, 1909), p. 3.

58. Clement, p. 248; Poindexter, p. 5; Martin, "Armistead at the Battle of Gettysburg," *SHSP*, p. 186.

59. Clement, p. 248; Martin, p. 186.

60. Martin and Smith, "The Battle of Gettysburg and the Charge of Pickett's Division," *SHSP*, p. 188; Clement, p. 249.

61. Kemper to Alexander, 20 September 1869, Harvard University.

62. John W. Nesbit, "Recollections of Pickett's Charge," *The National Tribune* (29 January 1914).

63. Cowan, "When Cowan's Battery Withstood Pickett's Splendid Charge," *New York Herald* (2 July 1911).

64. "Terrific Fight of Third Day," *The Scranton Truth* (3 July 1913).

65. Hunton to Daniel, 15 July 1904, in the J.W. Daniel Papers, University of Virginia Library.

66. *OR*, Series 1, Vol. 27, Part 2, p. 435; Gilbert E. Govan and James W. Livingood, eds., *The Haskell Memoirs: John Cheves Haskell* (New York: G. P. Putnam's Sons, 1960), pp. 50-51.

67. *OR*, Series 1, Vol. 27, Part 2, p. 321.

Chapter Five

1. Kemper to Bachelder, 4 February 1886, John B. Bachelder Papers, New Hampshire Historical Society; A member of the 26th North Carolina Regiment admitted these same sentiments. The 26th North Carolina was on the right of Pettigrew's (Heth's) Division, and therefore to the immediate left of Pickett's Division. Major John T. Jones said from his position on Pettigrew's right he "could see nothing of the rest" of his own division, they being too far to the left and out of his field of vision. His whole attention had been directed to his own front and to Pickett's Division, on which he had been ordered to dress. John T. Jones, "Pettigrew's Brigade at Gettysburg," in Walter Clark, ed., *Histories of the Several Regiments and Battalions from North Carolina in the Great War 1861-65*, Vol. 5 (Goldsboro, NC, 1901), p. 133.

2. Johnston, p. 258.

3. Kemper to Bachelder, 4 February 1886, in John B. Bachelder papers, New Hampshire Historical Society.

4. Walker was detailed as courier to Kemper from Company C, 11th Virginia Infantry. He was affectionately known to his comrades as "Big Foot" because of his long legs and big feet.

5. Kemper to Bachelder, 4 February 1886, in John B. Bachelder Papers, New Hampshire Historical Society, p. 286; Kemper to Alexander, 20 September 1869, Harvard University.

6. Johnston, p. 259.

7. Report of Colonel Joseph Mayo, 25 July 1863, in George Pickett Papers, Duke University.

8. John W. Busey and David G. Martin, *Regimental Strengths and Losses at Gettysburg* (Hightstown, NJ: Longstreet House, 1986), p. 29.

9. George Grenville Benedict, *A Short History of the 14th Vermont Regt.* (Bennington, VT: Press of C. A. Pierce, 1887), pp. 11-12.

10. Stine, pp. 527-528.

11. Ralph Orson Sturtevant, *Pictorial History Thirteenth Regiment Vermont Volunteers War of 1861-65* (Burlington: Regimental Association, 1910), p. 301.

12. Ibid., pp. 804-805.

13. Harrison, p. 183. The batteries on the left-center of Meade's line included those under Freeman McGilvery's Artillery Reserve command (the guns of Daniels' 9th Michigan; Parson's 1st New Jersey; Thomas' C, 4th U.S.; Hart's 15th New York; Sterling's 2nd Connecticut; Copper's B, 1st Pennsylvania; Dow's 6th Maine; Ames' G, 1st New York; Thompson's C and F, 1st Pennsylvania), and Smith's 4th New York, Cowan's 1st Independent New York, and Fitzhugh's K, 1st New York Batteries. The batteries confronting Pickett's Division at the point where they ultimately struck included Rorty's B, 1st New York; Brown's B, 1st Rhode Island; Cushing's A, 4th U.S.; Arnold's A, 1st Rhode Island. Cowan's and Fitzhugh's Batteries eventually moved from the left to relieve or support the four batteries that received Pickett's attack.

14. Ibid.

15. Martin, "Armistead at Gettysburg," *SHSP*, p. 186.

16. Bright, "Pickett's Charge at Gettysburg," p. 264.

17. Cadmus M. Wilcox, "Report" for his brigade to Major Thomas A. Mills, July 1863, in Virginia Historical Society.

18. Rev. John Lipscomb Johnson, *The University Memorial Biographical Sketches of Alumni of the University of Virginia who fell in the Confederate War* (Baltimore: Turnbull Brothers, 1871), p. 444. Pollock must have been carried rearward to the dwelling of Jeff Myers, just above Bream's Mill, where he was buried.

19. Colonel Joseph Mayo, "Report" for Kemper's Brigade, 25 July 1863, in George E. Pickett Papers, Duke University Library.

20. Benedict, p. 37.

21. Report of _____ for 24th Virginia Regiment, 9 July 1863, in Pickett Papers, University of Virginia Library.

22. W. H. H. Winston account in J.W. Daniel Papers, University of Virginia Library.

23. Martin and Smith, "The Battle of Gettysburg, and the Charge of Pickett's Division," *SHSP*, pp. 191-192. The point where the 11th Virginia struck the Union line, as described by Captain Smith, must have been to the left, or north, of the slashing, where there was a break in the stone wall and where a gate once provided access between one farm and another. This break in the wall was used by the Union forces on the previous day as a means to move artillery in and out of their lines to and from forward positions. Lieutenant James W. Wray of Company E seems to indicate that members of the 11th Regiment were intermingled with regiments even further to the left, stating that he himself saw General Armistead penetrate the stone wall, slap a Yankee gun and say "This is mine" before he was shot down. James W. Wray account in the J.W. Daniel Papers, Box 23, University of Virginia Library.

24. Martin and Smith, p. 192.

25. Johnston, pp. 257-258.

26. Loehr, "The 'Old First' at Gettysburg," *SHSP*, p. 40.

27. Ibid., p. 36.

28. Ibid.

29. Johnston, p. 263. Hugh Carey, Company E, 82nd New York received a Medal of Honor for the capture of the colors of the 7th Virginia; see John F. Kane, *The Medal of Honor* (Washington: G.P.O., 1948), p. 138.

30. Ibid., pp. 232, 262.

31. Loehr, *SHSP*, p. 36; James J. Hurt to John W. Daniel, 28 October 1904, in the J.W. Daniel Papers, Box 23, University of Virginia Library. Colonel Patton had recently, at the age of 28, been elected to the Virginia Assembly. He died on 21 July at Chester Hospital as a result of his wound. During that time, the officer could communicate with others around him only by writing on a slate, until his weakness prevented even that. In a letter to his mother, written a few days before his death, Colonel Patton recalled the suffering and hardship of the two weeks in the field hospital, where his Bible and faith were his only solace. He asked that his mother be told that he was about to die in a foreign land but that he cherished the same intense affection for her as always. Shaking the hands of those who were with him at the end, and expressing gratitude for every little favor rendered him, Colonel Patton met death "as became a soldier and a Christian," surrounded by the tears of those at his bedside, including some Union officers. Walker, *Memorial*, VMI, pp. 426-427. One of his boys remembered him as always "patriotic, gentle as a child, a polished gentleman." Johnston, p. 262.

32. Mayo, "Pickett's Charge at Gettysburg," *SHSP*, pp. 332-333.

33. Ibid, pp. 333-335.

34. Alexander S. Webb to his father, 17 July 1863, in Webb Papers, Yale University. Copy in Gettysburg National Military Park files.

35.. Captain H. T. Owen, "Pickett's Charge," *Gettysburg Compiler* (6 April 1881), p. 1.

36. Hunton to Daniel, 15 July 1904, in the J.W. Daniel Papers, Box 1849-1904, University of Virginia Library.

37. Hunton, pp. 99-100.

38. Berkeley to Daniel, 26 September _____, in the J.W. Daniel Papers, Box 23, University of Virginia Library.

39. Ibid.

40. Owen, *CV*, p. 7.

41. Peters, "The Lost Sword of Gen. Richard B. Garnett, who Fell at Gettysburg," *SHSP*, p. 29.

42. "About the Death of General Garnett," *CV* 14 (February 1906), p. 81.

43. Berkeley to Daniel, 26 September _____, in the J.W. Daniel Papers, Box 23, University of Virginia Library.

44. "About the Death of General Garnett," *CV*, p. 81.

45. *Pennsylvania Daily Telegraph* (Harrisburg) 7 July 1863. An official dispatch to the Associated Press from the battlefield at 10 P.M. on July 3rd, reported that the "Rebel Generals Garnett and Kemper fell in front of the 69th and 71st Pennsylvania Volunteers." *Reply of the Philadelphia Brigade Association to the Foolish and Absurd Narrative of Lieutenant Frank A. Haskell...* (Philadelphia: Bowers Printing Co., 1910), p. 40.

46. *OR*, Series 1, Vol. 27, Part 1, p. 440.

47. Harrison, pp. 184-185.

48. "About the Death of General Garnett," *CV*, p. 81.

49. Owen, "Pickett's Charge," *Gettysburg Compiler*.

50. Ibid.

51. Lewis, p. 82.

52. J. H. Moore, "Longstreet's Assault," *The Philadelphia Weekly Times* (4 November 1882) in Gettysburg Newspaper Clippings Relating to the Battle, p. 30.

53. Berkeley to Daniel, 26 September _____, in the J.W. Daniel Papers, Box 23, University of Virginia Library.

54. Johnson, p. 455.

55. Wood, pp. 46-47.

56. William H. Taylor, "Some Experiences of a Confederate Assistant Surgeon," *Transactions of the College of Physicians of Philadelphia*, Vol. 28, p. 118.

57. Jesse account in the J.W. Daniel Papers, Box 23, University of Virginia Library. Color Sergeant John H. Eakin of Company B had been wounded and yielded the colors to a man supposedly named "Grayson" (probably Color Corporal Lindsey Creasey or Corporal Madison Graybill), who was shot almost immediately. Colonel Allen then picked up the colors at this point. Ida Lee Johnson, "Over the Stone Wall at Gettysburg," *CV* 31 (July 1923), p. 249.

58. Ida Lee Johnson, pp. 248-249.

59. Henry C. Michie to Vincent Tapscott, 21 February 1904, in the Daniel Papers, Box 23, University of Virginia Library.

60. Address query in *CV*, 5 (April 1897), p. 162.

61. Finley, "Bloody Angle," p. 43.

62. Ibid., pp. 43-44.

63. William Ralton Balch, "Pickett's Charge," *Gettysburg Compiler* (11 August 1887), p. 1.

64. W. H. Swallow, "The Third Day at Gettysburg," *The Southern Bivouac*, 4 (February 1886), p. 568.

65. Martin and Smith, "The Battle of Gettysburg, and the Charge of Pickett's Division," *SHSP*, p. 188.

66. D. B. Easley, "With Armistead When he was Killed," *CV*, 20 (August 1912), p. 379; D. B. Easley to Howard Townsend, 24 July 1913, in D. B. Easley Papers, USAMHI.

67. Theodore B. Gates, *The "Ulster Guard" and the War of Rebellion* (New York: B. H. Tyrell, 1879), p. 415.

68. James F. Crocker, "Colonel James Gregory Hodges," *SHSP* 37 (1909), pp. 195-196; M. J. C. Woodworth to T. B. Gates, 13 October 1888, in Seward Osborne, Jr. collection (copy in GNMP files). After the battle a Union soldier would detach the sword belt and give it to Captain John Cook of the 20th N.Y.S.M. as a "treasured relic of the battle."

69. Crocker, p. 195. Colonel Gates revealed he had taken the diary of Colonel Hodges from his body as a souvenir, thus helping to confound the identification of the remains. Theodore Gates to P. F. Rothermel, 28 April 1868 in Peter F. Rothermel Papers, Pennsylvania Historical and Museum Commission.

70. Crocker, *SHSP*, 33 (1905) pp. 133-134.

71. Stine, p. 541.

72. Lewis, p. 82.

73. Crocker, *SHSP*, pp. 132-133.

74. Walker, p. 407.

75. "Col. and Dr. R. W. Martin, of Virginia," *CV*, 5 (1897), p. 70.

76. "Pickett's Charge," *The Philadelphia Weekly Press* (4 July 1887), p. 1. The fence that Lieutenant Sale recollected with such visions of terror is still part of the battlefield landscape, and runs in a generally oblique east-west line from the Emmitsburg Road to the Angle wall and through the slashing. This post and rail/Virginia worm fence would have been the only fence crossed by Armistead's attack, and would have been in the full line of Union fire.

77. Clement, p. 249.

78. J. Howard Wert, *A Complete Hand-Book of the Monuments and Indications and Guide to the Positions on the Gettysburg Battlefield* (Harrisburg: 1886), p. 55.

79. Carter, "Flag of the Fifty-third Virginia Regiment," p. 263.

80. "Pickett's Charge," *Philadelphia Weekly Press*; Carter "Flag of the Fifty-third Virginia Regiment," p. 263; "Col. and Dr. R. W. Martin, of Virginia," p. 70; Martin and Smith, "The Battle of Gettysburg, and the Charge of Pickett's Division," *SHSP*, pp. 186-187; John B. Bachelder, "The Third Day's Battle," *The Philadelphia Weekly Times* (15 December 1877).

81. William H. Stewart, "Col. John Bowie M'Gruder," *CV* 8 (1900), p. 329. Since he was a member of Epsilon Alpha Fraternity, Colonel Magruder's remains were encased in a metallic coffin with all his personal effects by a fraternity brother. This was sent by flag of truce to Richmond in October 1863.

82. Griggs, "Memorandum of the Thirty-eighth Virginia Regiment," *SHSP*, p. 253.

83. Walker, pp. 186-187.

84. J. Howard Wert, *Poems of Camp and Hearth.* (Harrisburg: Harrisburg Publishing Co., 1887), p. 123.

85. Sturtevant, pp. 385-389 passim.

Chapter Six

1. *OR*, Series 1, Vol. 27, Part 2, p. 435; Govan and Livingood, pp. 51-52.

2. Edmund Rice, "Repelling Lee's Last Blow at Gettysburg," *Battles and Leaders of the Civil War,* III (New York: Thomas Yoseloff, 1956), p. 389; *OR*, Series 1, Vol. 27, Part 2, pp. 434-435.

3. New York Monuments Commission, *In Memoriam Alexander Stewart Webb 1835-1911* (Albany: J. B. Lyon Company, 1916), p. 66.

4. A. C. Plaisted to John B. Bachelder, 11 June 1870, in John B. Bachelder Correspondence, New Hampshire Historical Society, Microfilm Reel 1, pp. 97-98.

5. Hutter to Daniel, n.d., in the J.W. Daniel Papers, Box 23, University of Virginia Library. Ward and Hutter were captured late that evening by Union skirmishers who came upon them in that position, still recuperating from their ordeal.

6. Martin and Smith, "The Battle of Gettysburg, and the Charge of Pickett's Division," *SHSP*, p. 192.

7. Mayo, "Pickett's Charge at Gettysburg," *SHSP*, p. 335.

8. Martin and Smith, p. 193.

9. W. H. H. Winston account in the J.W. Daniel Papers, Box 23, University of Virginia Library.

10. James W. Wray account in the J.W. Daniel Papers, Box 23, University of Virginia Library.

11. Thomas D. Huston, "Storming Cemetery Hill."

12. E. P. Reeve, "Casualties in the Old First at Gettysburg," *SHSP* 17 (1889), P. 408. These colors going to the rear could have been the flags of either the 11th or 24th Virginia Regiments (neither apparently was captured) or those of the 8th Virginia (apparently captured during the advance or retreat by Stannard's men.)

13. Loehr, *SHSP*, p. 36. The flag of the 1st Virginia was picked up along with the colors of the 7th Virginia and captured by someone in the 82nd New York Volunteers of Harrow's Brigade. *OR*, Series 1, Vol. 27, Part 1, p. 426.

14. Ibid.

15. Mayo, "Pickett's Charge at Gettysburg,"p. 335.

16. Gomer's leg was amputated at the hip by regimental Surgeon Thomas P. Mayo immediately after arriving at the field hospital. Unable to be moved, he fell into Union hands on July 5th at the hospital. According to Gomer, Company F had eight killed or mortally wounded, nine wounded, and seven captured or missing. A. P. Gomer, "Service of Third Virginia Infantry," *CV*, 18 (1910), p. 228.

17. Johnson, *The University Memorial Biographical Sketches*, p. 484.

18. Ibid., p. 437.

19. William F. Fox, ed. *New York at Gettysburg*, III (Albany: J. B. Lyon Company, 1900), pp. 1325, 1183-1184; Elbert Corbin, "Petit's Battery at Gettysburg," *The National Tribune* (3 February 1910).

20. Berkeley to Daniel, 26 September _____, in the J.W. Daniel Papers, Box 23, University of Virginia Library.

21. *OR*, Series 1, Vol. 27, Part 1, p. 1041; Frank Moore, ed. *The Rebellion Record: A Diary of American Events, with Documents, Narrative, Illustrative Incidents, Poetry, etc.*, 7 (New York: D. Van Nostrand, 1864), pp. 340-341.

22. Berkeley to Daniel, 26 September _____, in the J.W. Daniel Papers, Box 23, University of Virginia Library.

23. "About the Death of General Garnett," *Confederate Veteran*, p. 81.

24. Irby, p. 28.

25. Owen, "Pickett's Charge," p. 1.

26. Hoke, p. 390.

27. [Captain Robert McCulloch] "St. Louisians Among Gettysburg Heroes," *St. Louis Globe-Democrat* (9 March 1913), p. 15.

28. Andrew Cowan to John P. Nicholson, 27 July 1913, tipped in Gettysburg Newspaper Clippings Relating to the Battle, GNMP library, p. 188. Lieutenant C. E. Hunt of the 59th New York Volunteers, however, was credited with capturing the colors of the 18th Virginia in his brigade commander's postscript report. OR, Series 1, Vol. 27, Part 1, p. 441. Physical investigation of the colors of the 57th Virginia reveals that the flag is missing its heading and was certainly torn from its staff. It may have been this flag (and not that of the 18th Regiment) that Cowan remembered. H. Michael Madaus to Kathleen Georg, 13 June 1986.

29. Ernest Linden Waitt, *History of the Nineteenth Massachusetts Volunteer Infantry 1861-1865* (Salem, MA: The Salem Press Co., 1906), p. 246.

30. Ibid., p. 247.

31. Wiley, p. 47.

32. Johnson, "Over the Stone Wall at Gettysburg," p. 249.

33. H. D. O'Brien to John B. Bachelder, 23 March 1883 in J. B. Bachelder Correspondence, New Hampshire Historical Society, p. 511; *OR*, Series 1, Vol. 27, Part 1, p. 425; C. C. Andrews, ed., *Minnesota in the Civil and Indian Wars 1861-1865*, 2nd ed. (St. Paul: Pioneer Press Co., 1891), p. 373.

34. *OR*, Series 1, Vol. 27, Part 2, p. 387; McPherson, "A Private's Account of Gettysburg," p. 149. Hezekiah Spessard died on July 19th.

35. Damron, "Recollections," in the J.W. Daniel Papers, Box 23, University of Virginia Library.

36. Michie to Tapscott, 21 February 1904, in the J.W. Daniel Papers, Box 23, University of Virginia Library. Lieutenant Michie closed his caustic remarks about Pickett's failure

to relieve them with the rejoinder that the men at the stone wall "had as good a right to run as he had."

37. Finley, pp. 43-44.

38. Michie to Tapscott, 21 February 1904, in the J.W. Daniel Papers, Box 23, University of Virginia Library.

39. Finley, p. 44.

40. Williams, "A Private's Experience," in the J.W. Daniel Papers, Box 23, University of Virginia Library.

41. Easley, p. 379.

42. Easley to Townsend, 24 July 1913, Military History Institute.

43. D. G. Brinton to John B. Bachelder, 22 March 1869, Bachelder Correspondence, New Hampshire Historical Society.

44. Captain John S. D. Cook, "Personal Reminiscences of Gettysburg," Read before the Kansas Commandery of the Military Order of the Loyal Legion of the United States, 12 December 1903, War Paper No. 24, p. 18.

45. Waitt, p. 241; Col. A. F. Devereux to John B. Bachelder, 22 July 1889, in John B. Bachelder Correspondence, New Hampshire Historical Society, Microfilm Reel 5. DeCastro similarly received a Medal of Honor for capturing the colors of the 14th Virginia.

46. Lewis, pp. 82-83.

47. Crocker, *SHSP*, pp. 132-133.

48. Sergeant Gayle, diary entry, 3 July 1863, GNMP typescript.

49. *OR*, Series 1, Vol. 27, Part 1, p. 432n.

50. Apparently the colors of the 53rd were joined by those of the 14th and 57th Regiments at one of the guns in Cushing's original line beyond the stone wall. These were all captured by men of the 19th Massachusetts. Waitt, p. 241.

51. Carter, "Flag of the Fifty-third Virginia," p. 263.

52. Farinholt to Daniel, 15 April 1904, in the J.W. Daniel Papers, Box 23, University of Virginia Library; Colonel B. L. Farinholt, "Battle of Gettysburg—Johnson's Island," *CV*, 5 (September 1897), p. 469.

53. Wert, *A Complete Hand-Book of the Monuments*, p. 55.

54. However, four or five Confederate wagons with wounded entered Chambersburg on July 5th and were unloaded at hospitals there; there is the possibility that Lieutenant Harwood was among this small number of Gettysburg wounded and sick that did not make the correct turn at Greenwood and continued straight into Chambersburg. Hoke, p. 405.

55. Carter, p. 263; R.W. Martin to sister, 6 September 1863. Southern Historical Collection, University of North Carolina.

56. Ibid., Farinholt, p. 469. Isaac Tibbins of the 71st Pennsylvania was also credited with capturing the flag of the 53rd Virginia. Col. R. Penn Smith, "The Battle—the Part Taken

by the Philadelphia Brigade in the Battle." *Gettysburg, Compiler* (7 June 1887).

57. Captain T. C. Holland, "With Armistead at Gettysburg," *CV*, 29 (February 1921), p. 62.

58. Ibid; D. G. Brinton to John B. Bachelder, 22 March 1869, in Bachelder Correspondence, New Hampshire Historical Society.

59. J.F. Crocker, *Gettysburg—Pickett's Charge and Other War Addresses* (Portsmouth, VA: W. A. Fiske, 1915), p. 54.

60. A. J. Rider to John B. Bachelder, 2 October 1885, in Bachelder Correspondence, New Hampshire Historical Society; Mrs. Lewis A. Armistead to Frederick J. Tilberg, 20 January 1939 (?), in GNMP files.

61. Griggs, "Memoranda of Thirty-eighth Virginia Infantry," *SHSP*, p. 253; OR, Series 1, Vol. 27. Part 1, p. 462.

62. In Memoriam Alexander Stewart Webb, p. 67; Andrew Cowan, "Remarks," in Alexander S. Webb Papers, Yale University; Andrew Cowan, "When Cowan's Battery Withstood Pickett's Splendid Charge," *New York Herald* (2 July 1911).

63. John Buckley to John B. Bachelder, n.d., in Bachelder Correspondence, New Hampshire Historical Society.

64. R. Steuart Latrobe, "The Pinch of the Fight. Gettysburg, July 3, '63," *Gettysburg Compiler* (7 December 1877).

65. Rice, "Repelling Lee's Last Blow at Gettysburg," pp. 388-389.

Chapter Seven

1. Cowan, "When Cowan's Battery Withstood Pickett's Splendid Charge." The identity of this Confederate battery is not known.

2. Waitt, p. 244.

3. "Pickett's Charge," *Philadelphia Weekly Press*.

4. Sturtevant, p. 528.

5. B.L. Farinholt, "Battle of Gettysburg—Johnson's Island," *CV* (1897), p. 469.

6. Farinholt to Daniel, 15 April 1905, in the J.W. Daniel Papers, Box 23, University of Virginia Library.

7. Anthony McDermott to Bachelder, 2 June 1886, in John B. Bachelder Correspondence, New Hampshire Historical Society.

8. John Reed, Sylvester Byrne, Frederick Middleton, et al., representing the survivors of the Seventy-second Regiment of Pennsylvania Volunteers, Plaintiffs vs. Gettysburg Battlefield Memorial Association, and John P. Taylor, J. P. S. Gobin, John P. Nicholson, and R. B. Ricketts, Commissioners appointed by the Governor of the State of Pennsylvania, Defendants. Testimony in the Court of Common Pleas of Adams Co. In equity, No. 1, January Term, 1889, p. 235.

9. "Lee Statue Site," *Industrial School News* (Scotland, PA), n.d., in Virginia Monument Correspondence, GNMP archives.

10. Berkeley to Daniel, 26 September _____, in the J.W. Daniel Papers, Box 23, University of Virginia Library.

11. Loehr, "The 'Old First' at Gettysburg," *SHSP*, pp. 36-37.

12. Hoke, *The Great Invasion*, pp. 426-427.

13. Ibid., p. 427.

14. Loehr, *SHSP*, p. 37.

15. Williams wrote that he met General Kemper in Richmond after the war and related the details of the incident to the general, who replied, "Well, that is a true tale." Williams, "A Private's Experience in the 14th Virginia Infantry at Gettysburg," in the J.W. Daniel Papers, Box 23, University of Virginia Library.

16. Hunton, p. 101.

17. See Appendix D for summaries of hospitalization and burials.

18. Levin Gayle, diary entry of 3 July 1863, GNMP typescript.

19. Lieutenant Nathaniel Wood reported that only 1100 men reported present on July 5th. A study of the regimental records reveals at least 2655 of the 6262 men engaged were killed, wounded, or captured. The disorganized retreat beyond Seminary Ridge which Lee witnessed, and the dispersal of survivors to farmsteads and shelters in all directions, may have accounted for Wood's low figure on the morning of July 5th. Wood, "Pickett's Charge at Gettysburg," p. 1.

20. *OR*, Series 1, Vol. 27, Part 3, pp. 986-987.

21. Ibid, p. 1075. One can only surmise what "reflections" Pickett was reporting, but a post-war account left no doubt as to where General Pickett was to eventually place the blame. In relating his memories of that July afternoon, Pickett said:

> When orders were given to form the column of attack I formed the column and then rode through the ranks to see if everything was right. As I finished this inspection I rode to the rear to report to General Longstreet and to receive orders to move. I found Longstreet sitting on the top rail of a fence whittling a stick. Saluting the General, I said, "General, my column is ready to charge. Shall I charge?" Receiving no answer from the General, and waiting a reasonable time, I returned to my command and again rode through the ranks.
>
> A second time I reported to the General, with the same result. A third time I reported. The General was still sitting on the fence. As I received no answer I remarked: "General, if I am to make the charge, it must be made now or it will be too late. Shall I make the charge?" Without saying a word he simply bowed his head. I immediately rode off and made the charge, and you know the result.

Pickett concluded his remarks with a vituperative indictment of Longstreet's "criminal indifference to results and to the lives of his men." This article, however, originated in the New Orleans Picayune, a city that had no love for General Longstreet because of his post-war activities there. Quoted in the *Gettysburg Compiler* (23 September 1902), p. 4.

22. Clement, p. 251. Colonel Martin was eventually sent to the prison at Point Lookout, Maryland, where he was held for ten months. After his exchange, he returned to Virginia but then accepted duty guarding prisoners in Charleston, South Carolina. "Col. & Dr. R. W. Martin," *CV*, V (1897), p. 70.

Appendix A

1. Colonel William W. Wood, "Pickett's Charge at Gettysburg," *Gettysburg Compiler* (22 August 1877), p. 1.

2. Stine, pp. 538-539.

3. Kirkwood Otey, "Some War History," *Richmond Times* (7 November 1894), p. 4.

4. Lieutenant Symington noted that he was ordered by Pickett to rally some of Pettigrew's line when it began to waver. Captains Bright and Baird likewise were later sent to hasten forward the brigades under Wilcox.

5. Thomas R. Friend, "Pickett's Position," *Richmond Times-Dispatch* (24 November 1903), p. 4.

6. G. Moxley Sorrel, *Recollections of a Confederate Staff Officer* (New York: Neale Publishing Co., 1905), p. 173.

7. Otey, "Some War History," p. 4.

8. Hunton, pp. 98-99.

9. Ibid.

10. Clayton Coleman to Daniel, 1 July 1904, in the J.W. Daniel Papers, Box 23, University of Virginia Library.

11. Ibid.

12. Ibid.

13. Berkeley to Daniel, 26 September _____, in the J.W. Daniel Papers, Box 23, University of Virginia Library.

14. David Aiken to unidentified captain, n.d. [1863], South Carolina Library, University of South Carolina. Aiken's 1863 letter offered the surprising observation that although his division fought well, Pickett himself was drunk, and was seen in such a condition by Colonel Aiken and members of the 7th South Carolina, who thought he should be cashiered. Aiken's comments were contained in the body of a letter intended for private consumption, and appear not to be malicious in nature.

15. Govan and Livingood, pp. 51-52.

Appendix D

1. Also listed on reinterment records as 325 remains.

2. *Gettysburg Compiler* (7 June 1852).

3. Ibid., (9 July 1855); records of reinterments to Hollywood Cemetery in collections of Confederate Museum.

4. Ibid., (15 March 1887).

5. *Adams Sentinel* (11 August, 18 August 1863).

6. Daniel Alexander Skelly, *A Boy's Experiences During the Battle of Gettysburg* (Gettysburg: Daniel Alexander Skelly, 1932), pp. 24-25.

A DESCRIPTIVE ROSTER
OF PICKETT'S DIVISION AT GETTYSBURG

Introduction to the Roster

They came from places like Fancy Grove, Kentuck, Roaring Run, Yellow Branch, and Mount Gilead. They were destined for places like the Emmitsburg Road, the Codori farm, the Slashing, the Stone Wall, and the Copse of Trees. They were young farmers, mostly. In their early 20s, they had earned their livelihoods with the sweat of their brows and the strength of their hands. Their company units bore the proud, boastful names given during the early days of the war, when young, naive, patriotic fervor ran rampant in the land. Here stood the "Black Eagle Rifles" of the 18th Virginia, the "Southern Rights Guard" of the 19th Virginia, the "Mecklenburg Spartans" of the 56th Virginia and the "Franklin Fire Eaters" of the 57th Virginia. Here stood, also, the individual men forming these and the remaining units of Pickett's Division. Men like 5th Sergeant Calvin P. Hansford, a 26 year old Richmond dentist of the 1st Virginia; 1st Corporal Joseph R. Edwards of Southampton County's "Southampton Greys" of the 3rd Virginia; John and Levi Pennington of Company "B," 8th Virginia; and Private Thomas W. Dunn of the "White Hall Guards" of the 56th Virginia. Each of these men, making the supreme sacrifice for the cause in which he believed, was killed during the division's assault. Yet their names, together with those of the other 923 Virginians of this division who died on the field of battle, in hospitals, or in squalid Union prison camps as a result of this attack, have long since been forgotten and ignored by historians of the battle. Such historians generally think in terms of the assault of "Pickett's Division," "Armistead's Brigade," the "57th Virginia" or other units. Except for the well-known names of Colonels and Generals, the true makeup of these units—the individual soldiers—has been too long neglected. This study seeks in a small way to remedy this oversight.

As the reader scans the pages of this roster, try, if you will, to return with the mind's eye to the smoking fields of Gettysburg on that oppressively hot 3rd of July 1863. There they stand, some 6,000 men in their double ranked battle lines of sweat-soaked gray, crowned with burnished steel and the blood red battle flags which are the proud symbols of their cause. As your eye touches each name, feel the discomfort of the moment—the heat of the day, the smell of gunsmoke in the air, the gut-wrenching fear of men preparing to offer their bodies and lives to a cause in which they fervently believe. Feel, also, the precious, calming thoughts of home most of these soldiers must have had as they followed those blood red banners into the gray mists of history. Though their cause was lost, their valor and devotion to duty remain a symbol of perseverance and fortitude which will serve as an example for generations of Americans to come. These were Pickett's men.

The Methodology

The individual unit rosters which follow were compiled from contemporary Confederate company muster rolls on file in the National Archives, in Washington, DC. The rolls used were primarily those of the April/June 1863 muster period which was conducted by the division on 30 June at and near Chambersburg, Pennsylvania.

In a small number of instances, unit July/August 1863 muster rolls were used when 30 June rolls could not be located. In rare instances—such as with the 38th Virginia of Armistead's Brigade—when muster rolls were not available, either for the pre- or post-battle period, the author conducted a complete review of all individual compiled service records of soldiers who served with the unit during the entire course of the war. Every effort was made in reviewing these records to determine if each soldier was or could have been at the battle. Those who could definitely be determined to have been absent from the engagement were deleted and the residue were included in the roster. While this may at first seem to be a relatively inaccurate way of determining those present for such units, it is, given the current condition of Confederate records, virtually the only way a roster for the units could be compiled. All unit rosters were correlated against the personal recollections of participants in the assault which are contained in the narrative portion of this book. Only in rare instances did the roster fail to match the recollections of survivors. While it is virtually certain that some men listed in this roster were not at Gettysburg, and that some who were in the assault may not in fact be listed, the author is confident that it is as complete and accurate as is currently possible, given the passage of 129 years and the current condition of Southern war records.

Contemporary Civil War records, though they are as close as we can currently come to the actual situation as it existed at that time, can only be considered a "Pandora's Box" for researchers, such as the author, who can only be satisfied with absolute accuracy of information. Record keepers of that era were prone to infuriating lapses of memory, duplications, only minimal entries of vital information, and a plethora of other frustrating habits which often leave the current scholar in fits of incredulity and dismay. Records are frequently difficult to decipher, conflicting, and often so incomplete as to be virtually useless. This is particularly true of Confederate records, so many of which were lost or destroyed following the surrender of the Southern armies, that documentation of many units is practically nonexistent. Nevertheless, these documents are all the current researcher is left with to attempt to establish exactly "how things were" at the time of the Battle of Gettysburg.

Southern hospital records are perhaps in the worst disarray at this time. Not only are they few in number, but many are also incomplete and do not record brief stays of slightly wounded soldiers. For this reason, it is likely that perhaps as many as 300 of Pickett's slightly wounded Virginians are not listed as such in this roster. This is regrettable, but unavoidable, considering the documentation available.

Burial locations for some of Pickett's men were provided by a Dr. John W. C. O'Neal of Gettysburg who, sympathizing with the plight of Southerners attempting to locate the final resting places of friends and loved ones on the battlefield, listed names, inscribed on headboards, which he found during his various tours of the field following the battle. A man named Rufus B. Weaver, also of Gettysburg, contracted to identify and remove the remains of Southern soldiers, still buried on the field in 1872 and 1873, to Richmond's Hollywood Cemetery. He left an extensive listing of the grave sites of many both named and unidentified Confederate soldiers which has been used in the compilation of this roster. Most headboards were located at the various Southern divisional hospitals scattered behind the battlefield. The men serving Pickett's hospital at Bream's Mill had a chance to learn the identity of some of their dying patients and provide a decent burial complete with headboard. Those killed on the field, however, were buried by enemy hands in long, hastily dug trenches in the fields where they died. No time was taken toward attempting the identification of the men. Rather, they were thrown into the trenches and covered with earth as rapidly as possible as Union efforts to clear the battlefield proceeded. They lay in these undignified resting places until 1872 and 1873 when, together with some of the fallen of Wright's Georgia Brigade, who fell in this same locality on July 2nd, they were removed in large boxes, containing ten or more bodies each, to Richmond's Hollywood Cemetery where they remain, unidentified, to this day. A sad fate, indeed, for such gallant and courageous soldiers.

As previously stated, the primary source for identifying the soldiers present during the assault were the individual company muster rolls for the various units comprising Pickett's Division at the battle. The 30 June 1863 muster rolls for 6 regimental field and staff units and 108 companies were located listing the names of 356 officers and 3,834 enlisted men as present for duty on that date in these organizations. This "present for duty" category did not include those men absent on detached service, with leave, without leave, sick and in arrest or confinement, present on extra or daily duty, sick, or in arrest or confinement. Some of those present on extra or daily duty, and in arrest are included in this roster or in the unengaged appendix of this book. Others are not. The author's primary purpose, however, was to present those who actually took part in the assault and he feels that this objective has been obtained as completely and accurately as is currently possible. Company muster rolls were, however, discovered to be incomplete in certain rare instances. The author found that a very small number of men, not listed as present on the 30 June rolls, did in fact show up in time to participate in the attack. These instances numbered less than half-a-dozen and so have little if any effect on the divisional roster as a whole.

The majority of the roster is taken from the compiled service records of the individual soldiers themselves. These records are maintained on microfilm in the National Archives and contain information derived from muster rolls, Union and Confederate hospital records, Union prisoner of war records, casualty reports, pay vouchers, detachment muster rolls, clothing receipts, company muster-in rolls, and so forth. Ages, occupations, dates and places of enlistment, and the like were all obtained from this source. The records contained in these individual compiled service records, like most records of the Civil War period for both sides, are fraught with contradictions, inconsistencies, and errors. Again, however, they represent the most complete and accurate information which is currently available relating to the Southern soldiers who participated in the Civil War.

The Format

Each unit roster begins with a brief organizational history of the unit through the reorganization of the army of May 1862, followed by a description of the source from which the roster was obtained, and, where available, a description of the condition of the unit on the date of the muster. Conditional status of the unit was obtained from the individual company muster rolls, but was not provided in all instances. The company rosters are arranged in order of rank, as was the accepted practice on all muster rolls of that era. Where the ranks are the same (as with Privates), the listing is provided in alphabetical order.

Entries for individual soldiers are given in the order of surname, given name, rank, age (in parentheses), occupation, battle fate, and prisoner of war exchange date, original burial location on the field, disinterment information, and other information where available.

Name spellings were taken from information provided in the individual compiled service records and represent the generally accepted spelling as derived from data contained therein. They may not always be accurate, however. Individuals making out the rolls often spelled the names phonetically when they were uncertain as to the proper spelling. Often, the same soldier's name would be spelled differently at each muster as individuals responsible for filling out the rolls changed from one muster period to another. The spellings provided in this roster are those accepted as correct by the United States War Department, which compiled the individual service records, and are taken, primarily, from company muster-in and descriptive rolls.

Ranks are given as of the company's muster date (30 June 1863 in most cases). Some individuals were elevated to higher ranks immediately following the July 3rd assault to replace casualties sustained in that attack. The ranks shown in the roster, however, are intended to reflect those held by Pickett's men when they entered the battle area on 3 July.

Ages, occupations, and enlistment dates and locations were primarily derived from company muster-in rolls, data from which are contained in the soldiers' individual service records. Ages and occupations are given as of the date of enlistment. A year or two will have to be added to obtain the soldier's battle age. This procedure was adopted in an effort to provide as much accuracy as possible in this area. A few entries state an age for a given year (such as "24 in 1864") for the same reason, when enlistment information was not provided in the service records.

Dates and locations of enlistment are provided only for those soldiers whose enlistment was different from that specified for the companies of which they were a member. Therefore, where no enlistment information is provided for an individual soldier, it can be assumed that this date is exactly the same for that soldier as that provided for the company as a whole. Owing to the inconsistencies in many Confederate service records, it is likely that the enlistment data of some men may actually reflect 1862 re-enlistments rather than original enlistments. Extant records, however, do not clearly reflect this fact.

Deaths, wounds, and captures are intended to reflect casualties which were sustained during the assault of July 3rd. These losses are indicated by italicizing the type of casualty. Other losses, which occurred subsequent to the attack, are not italicized. This segregation of losses was attempted in an effort to establish actual combat losses during the cannonade and attack which are reflected in the strength/

loss tables included as an appendix to this work. In some instances, a casualty will be noted as having been incurred during the "cannonade," "advance," "attack," "repulse," or "retreat." These five segments of the division's July 3rd assault are the same as those used in the narrative portion of this work and are intended to represent the unit's losses incurred during the pre-attack artillery bombardment ("cannonade"), its advance to the Emmitsburg Road ("advance"), the assault from the Emmitsburg Road to the Union positions behind the Stone Wall ("attack"), the fighting which occurred after the division reached the Union positions ("repulse"), and the withdrawal of the division to the Confederate lines on Seminary Ridge ("retreat"). Contemporary records are far from specific enough to isolate casualties into a particular battle time period. Therefore, all such notations in the roster were derived from personal reminiscences of survivors which are contained in the narrative section of this book. While few in number, they do provide a weak representation of casualties sustained by the division during various periods of the assault. Information concerning wounds and hospital deaths was primarily derived from Union hospital records, excerpts of which are found in Confederate individual service records. These records are also replete with errors, contradictions, and inconsistencies. For example, there appears to be no end to discrepancies as to exactly which leg or arm was wounded on individual soldiers. You would think that the doctors would have had the ability to determine right from left and hold some consistency, but alas, this was not the case in all situations. Many wounded and sick Virginians were exchanged from Union hospitals and prisons during the months following the battle to relieve pressure on overburdened Union facilities. Exchange dates for these soldiers are provided, and reflect the actual time of transference to Confederate authorities. The locations from which the soldiers were exchanged are also shown in most instances.

Original burial sites for some of Pickett's men were obtained from the previously mentioned listing of Dr. John W. C. O'Neal and Mr. Rufus B. Weaver. The terminology used for the various burial locations was taken directly from the listings and reflect property ownership at the time the listings were prepared. They cannot in all instances be directly correlated to information presented on the well-known 1876 Warren/Bachelder map of the battlefield. Disinterment information, such as date, location and box number are provided primarily to satisfy the author's penchant for detail, and to render as complete an accounting of Pickett's men as is possible. This data may also be of use in identifying some of Pickett's soldiers who currently lie, unidentified, in Richmond's hollywood Cemetery.

Finally, unless stated otherwise, all dates where no year is mentioned in the roster are meant to indicate 1863, and all localities, unless otherwise indicated, refer to locations in Virginia. Additionally, where no specific rank is provided for a soldier, it is to be presumed that the man held the rank of Private.

Strengths and Losses

This issue has been a source of debate since the smoke of battle dissipated over 129 years ago. Most pro-Virginia veterans of the Army of Northern Virginia, in an effort to glorify the division's exploits while concurrently denigrating those of Pettigrew's and Trimble's men whom they blamed for the defeat, insisted after the war that the division was small in number and suffered horrendously high combat losses. Some placed these losses as high as 60 to 70 percent of the force engaged. This study places the assault strength of the division on July 3rd at 504 commissioned officers, 1,006 non-commissioned officers, and 4,750 privates for a total of 6,260. Casualties are set as 498 killed in action, 1,476 wounded (833 of whom were captured), and 681 unwounded and captured for a total of 2,655 officers and enlisted men or 42.4 percent of the attacking force. These figures include the 430 officers and enlisted men of Dearing's 38th Virginia Artillery Battalion. Considering that most historians accept a smaller assaulting force suffering a higher rate of casualties, the author feels that some explanation and justification of his findings is warranted.

Apparently Major Walter Harrison, Assistant Adjutant and Inspector General of Pickett's Division at Gettysburg, is the primary source for the establishment of the unit's strength at below 5,000 officers and enlisted men. Major Harrison stated after the war that the division had 4,481 officers and men present for duty on that fateful July day in 1863. Although he does not explain the source of these figures in detail, it is probable he was referring to infantry strength, only, for artillery battalions attached to the various divisions were often excluded from division totals when compiling reports. It is difficult to explain this figure of 4,481 men, considering the fact that June 30, 1863 company muster rolls for 6 regimental field and staff units, 1 artillery battery, and 107 infantry companies establish a total present for duty strength of 356 officers and 3,834 enlisted men (a total of 4,190) for these units four days before the July 3rd engagement. It is highly unlikely that the remaining 9 regimental field and staff units, 3 batteries, and 34 infantry companies aggregated only 291 officers and enlisted men at that time. If only infantry strength is considered, 30 June strength for the 107 infantry companies and 6 regimental staff units aggregated 352 officers and 3,736 men (a total of 4,088). This would mean that the remaining 34 infantry companies and 9 field and staff units would would total no more than 393 men between them. Again, this is highly unlikely as each company would average only about 11 men each.

Another consideration is the 21 September 1863 muster conducted by the division which showed 232 officers and 2,814 enlisted men (a total of 3,046) as present for duty at that time in the division's three infantry brigades. Review of compiled service records for some of Pickett's units establishes that few new recruits or other reinforcements joined the division between the time of the battle and the 21 September muster. These few additions were more than offset by the large number of deserters who left the unit during the retreat to Virginia after the battle. A figure of 5,987 infantry is obtained if one adds the officially reported 2,946 casualties sustained during the battle to the 3,046 officers and men present for duty on 21 September. Additional figures of 5,921 or 5,686 are obtained if the results of

Robert K. Krick's study of Confederate battle casualties in the Gettysburg Death Roster, The Confederate Dead at Gettysburg or of this study, respectively, are added to the 21 September figure of 3,046. It is likely that the lower figure of 5,686 would be more appropriate as many of those included in the higher casualty figures were only slightly wounded, stayed with their commands, and were probably included in the 21 September muster. Adding the 430 officers and men of the 38th Virginia Artillery Battalion (not included in the 21 September muster) to these infantry figures would result in a total strength for the division of 6,417; 6,351; or 6,116 depending upon which set of casualty statistics are accepted. This study's total of 6,262 officers and enlisted men, therefore, seems very close to the actual strength of the division prior to the cannonade and assault. Brigade totals using this method also are very compatible with the results of this study. Armistead's Brigade would total 2,324; 2,325; or 2,159; Garnett's Brigade: 1,793; 1,795; or 1,797; and Kemper's Brigade: 1,875; 1,777; or 1,770. Study results list these strengths as Armistead: 2,188; Garnett: 1,851; and Kemper: 1,781.

It seems apparent, then, that the division must have had more men at Gettysburg than the generally accepted strength of 4,481 offered by Major Harrison, although the author is at a loss to explain why the division's AA&IG would arrive at such a low figure considering the evidence. It is possible that Major Harrison was referring to the number of enlisted infantrymen or privates in the unit and not to the division's strength as a whole. The results of this study show that there were 954 non-commissioned officers and 4,392 privates in the infantry force of the division (a total of 5,346), and 4,750 privates in both the infantry and artillery elements of the division. The latter figure is fairly close to that specified by Major Harrison, and the infantry private figure of 4,392 is only a 89 man difference from his cited strength. This might also account for the officially reported figure of 1,287 men for Garnett's Brigade. This study shows 1,378 privates as present for duty with that unit, a difference of only 91 men. The overall strength of the attacking force, as determined by this study (5,830 infantry prior to the cannonade), would also account for the division's success in temporarily breaking the Union line. After sustaining brutal casualties during the cannonade, advance, and attack, the division still maintained sufficient strength at the point of assault to force a portion of the sheltered Federal line to relinquish its positions. Whatever the differences, the author believes that the results of this study reflect the actual strength of the division as it came upon the field on July 3, 1863.

Data for divisional casualties has been set forth in the official report of Dr. Guild, Medical Director of the Army of Northern Virginia (see the OR, Series I, Volume 27, Part 2, pp. 329-337), a study by Mr. Robert K. Krick (The Gettysburg Death Roster), and this study as follows:

	Killed	Wounded	C or M	Total
Guild	237	1,235	1,499	2,971
Krick	599	1,223	1,082	2,904
This Study	498	1,476	681	2,655

Mr. Krick's study includes the mortally wounded with the killed and continues to count an undetermined number of men as missing, while this study includes the mortally wounded with the wounded and accounts for all those reported as missing or for whom no further record is found in the service records. This study shows 498 killed on the field and 233 who subsequently died of their wounds (a total of 731 combat related deaths as opposed to the 599 specified by Mr. Krick). The study also shows 681 unwounded captures from the division, while Mr. Krick lists 1,082 as captured or missing. This latter figure, however, continues to list men as missing and does not account for the ultimate fate of many of these soldiers. The main difference in the two studies, however, pertains to the number of wounded men, and this author readily admits that perhaps as many as 300 slightly wounded men may not have been accounted for in this study. This is confirmed by the fact that a number of men were mentioned as having been hit, but not incapacitated, in personal reminiscences of survivors, no record of which could be discovered in individual service records. The Southern army was in the habit of reporting such wounds as casualties although individual soldiers never left the ranks for treatment or received only cursory treatment at field hospitals. None of these wounds were reported by such hospitals as they were generally too occupied with the severely hurt to take time to record them, and their record keeping was far from comprehensive to begin with. These slightly wounded soldiers would, therefore, account for the difference in the Guild report and the Krick study, both of which place total divisional casualties at approximately 2,900 men as opposed to this study's figure of 2,655. However, the author believes that the results of this study more accurately reflect the actual losses of the division, as only those soldiers who were taken out of action for an extended period of time are accounted for while those who returned to the ranks within hours or days are not.

The 42.4 casualty percentage for the division, while high, does not seem to reflect the recollections of utter devastation which many survivors had of the state of the division by the time it reached the Union positions. A number of factors probably account for this. 1) An undetermined number of men were killed or badly wounded during the cannonade preceding the attack. 2) Reminiscences document that an unknown number of soldiers, suffering from sunstroke or lack of courage, did not join the attacking column when it formed for the advance. 3) Reminiscences also support the fact that many slightly wounded men, together with "malingerers" and "play outs" left the ranks during the advance. 4) A number of men remained in the slight shelter of the sunken Emmitsburg Road, behind the Codori buildings, or in other sheltered positions, while the residue of the division advanced to attack the Union positions. 5) Large numbers of men probably took whatever shelter was available, where they found it, to seek some escape from the torrent of Union fire which decimated their ranks at every step. Considering all these depletions from the original column, it is logical to assume that brigades would resemble "a skirmish line," or "small knots of men," rather than a cohesive force, as survivors pressed forward toward the Union positions. The author, therefore, believes that the results of this study do correlate well with the recollections, and perceptions of survivors and that the strength of the division was, indeed, in the area of 6,300 officers and enlisted men when it entered the battle area on July 3rd. The fact that large numbers of men in the terror of the moment, while not retreating from the field, sought personal safety rather than continuing to face what must have seemed impossible odds, in no way detracts from the courage and devotion to duty of the division as a whole. Descendants of these men can share a common pride in the strength and steadfastness of their forebearers.

Owners of the author's previous work concerning this subject (*Regimental Strengths and Losses at Gettysburg*, Baltimore: Gateway Press, 1986, co-authored with Dr. David G. Martin) will note a number of inconsistencies between the results of that study and those of this effort. The 1986 study specifies that 564 officers and 5,379 enlisted men (a total of 5,943) were present with the division as of 30 June 1863 and that 549 officers and 4,924 enlisted men (a total of 5,473) of that unit were engaged in the battle. The current study shows a total of 504 officers and 5,756 enlisted men (a total of 6,260) as having been engaged in the cannonade and assault of July 3rd. Some explanation of these variances is, therefore, required. Initially, it should be pointed out that the 1986 study projected 30 June strengths based upon a number of different methodologies. This was particularly true of the 19th and 56th Virginia of Garnett's Brigade and the 38th Virginia of Armistead's Brigade for which 30 June data is nonexistent. The total strengths of the 19th and 56th Virginia, and 80% of the strength of the 38th were projected in this manner. The 1986 study projected the 30 June strength of these units as 111 officers and 980 enlisted men (a total of 1,091). A complete review of the service records of all men who served with these units during the war established results for this study of 102 officers and 1,236 enlisted men (a total of 1,338). This difference of 247 officers and men accounts for the majority of the 319 officer and men 30 June variance noted between this study and that of 1986. Also, while approximately half of the 30 June figures cited for companies in the two studies agree precisely, the remaining units often show a variance of from one to as many as fourteen men. This is due to the fact that the 30 June muster roll figures used in the 1986 study are precise only for the exact time of the muster. Men were constantly joining or leaving units for one reason or the other, becoming ill and unfit for duty and so forth. A company's present for duty figures, therefore, rarely remained constant from one hour or day to the next. These fluctuations undoubtedly account for the remaining gain of 95 officers and men (over and above the 250 accounted for in the 19th, 38th, and 56th Virginia) noted for 30 June in this study as opposed to the 1986 study. It is also possible that two or three companies may have reported 30 June strengths in August 1863 without specifying losses incurred between 30 June and the actual muster date. This would account for the relatively large variances (12 to 14 men) noted for these units between the 1986 study and this one. Finally the 5,473 officer and enlisted men "engaged" figure cited for the division in the 1986 study is probably too low. That study projected a 7.1% loss rate between the 30 June muster and the division's arrival on the field on 3 July. Given the fact that the unit remained at Chambersburg for the majority of the battle and advanced by relatively short marches to reach the battlefield, it is very likely that few if any men left the ranks during this time. This is confirmed by the fact that less that 10 men were noted as having deserted at

Gettysburg following the 30 June muster and that some of these men may have in fact left the ranks following the assault and repulse of the division, not before. Considering all of these factors, the author is confident that the results of this study more accurately reflect that actual strength of the division on 3 July 1863 than those previously presented in the 1986 effort, although the results of that work were based on the best evidence available at that particular time.

Conclusion

They came from places like Fancy Grove, Kentuck, Roaring Run, Yellow Branch, and Mount Gilead. They died in the smoking fields of Nicholas Codori's farm, in the shallow bed of the Emmitsburg Road, or behind the stone wall of "The Angle," stained red by the blood of their sacrifice. They died in agony on the blood soaked operating tables of field hospitals or in the pestilence of Union prisons. Many would forever carry the horrors of this day on bodies lacking feet, hands, arms, and legs. Many others, known but to God, would lie buried in anonymity for eternity. Let the reader remember them for their courage and tenacity in battle, but, more importantly, for their humanity whose common chord ties us, today, to the realities of 130 years ago. These were Pickett's men!

The author hopes that in some small way the results of his efforts will assist future scholars in their attempts to further clarify the circumstances and events of "Pickett's Charge." He also apologizes in advance to descendants of Pickett's men who are excluded from, or incorrectly listed in this roster. No slight was intended. Rather, in a massive work of this nature, and considering currently available documentation, errors are regrettably unpreventable. The author will be happy to accept any documented additions, deletions, or corrections to the roster which may further enhance the accuracy of the work. Questions, comments, and suggestions are welcome.

Pickett's Division

This division consisted of Pickett's, Armistead's, Kemper's, and Jenkins' Brigades commanded by Major General George E. Pickett. On 26 November 1862, a new brigade was organized for General Corse, who had succeeded General Pickett in command of his brigade, and Brigadier General Garnett was assigned to Pickett's Brigade. On 5 March 1863, Jenkins' Brigade was transferred to the Department of North Carolina. Armistead's, Kemper's, Garnett's, and Corse's Brigades constituted the division's organization, with several command changes, until the end of the war.

General and Staff

Pickett, George Edward. (Major General): Born 28 January 1825 at Richmond, Va.; lawyer; graduated West Point 1846; brevetted Lt. and Capt. for service at Vera Cruz and advance on Mexico City during Mexican War; served in Texas, Virginia and Washington Territory until 25 June 1861 when he resigned his infantry captaincy to enter Confederate Army; originally entered the service as a Col. in the Provisional Army of the Confederate States and was assigned to temporary command of the Lower Rappahannock 23 September through 22 October 1861 and the Aquia District, Army of Northern Virginia 22 October 1861 through 28 February 1862; promoted to Brigadier Gen. 13 February 1862 to rank from 14 January 1862; commanding Cocke's (old) Brigade, Longstreet's (2nd) Division 28 February 1862 through 27 June 1862; wounded in the shoulder at Gaines' Mill 27 June 1862; commanding division 1st Corps, Army of Northern Va. late September 1862 through 25 February 1863; promoted Maj. Gen. 11 October 1862 to rank from 10 October 1862; assigned to the command of his own division 6 November 1862; commanding division in Department of Va. and North Carolina 25 February to 1 April 1863; commanding division in Department of Southern Va. 1 April through May 1863; commanding division, 1st Corps, Army of Northern Va. May through September 1863.

Baird, Edward R. (Capt., ADC): Appointed 1st Lt. and ADC on Pickett's staff 10 July 1862; promoted to Captain between October 1862 and 2 June 1863.

Bright, Robert A. (Volunteer ADC): Enl. 31 August 1861 at Upper Grafton as a 3rd Lt. in Cosnahan's Company Virginia Artillery; resigned due to ill health as a 1st Lt. of Artillery 4 August 1862; announced as Captain and ADC on Pickett's staff 24 September 1863.

Fairfax, Raymond (Capt., Chief of the Division Pioneer Corps): Enl. 17 April 1861 as a private in Company "A," 17th Virginia Infantry; (31), engineer; elected captain 26 April 1862; reported by his company as commander of the Division Pioneer Corps 6 November 1862 through 9 August 1864 muster rolls.

Gossett, John R. (2nd Lt., Provost Marshal): Enl. 24 October 1861 at Pickinsville, South Carolina as a 3rd Lt. of Company "E," 2nd South Carolina Rifles; (30 in 1861); his company reported him as a 2nd Lt. and Pickett's Provost Marshal on its May 1863 muster roll.

Harrison, Walter (Major AA&IG): VMI class of 1845; volunteer ADC to General Pickett May 1862; appointed Major and AA&IG on Pickett's staff 14 November 1862.

Jones, Horace W. (Major, Commissary of Subsistence): Enl. 8 May 1861 as a private in Company "B," 19th Virginia Infantry; (28), farmer; appointed Captain and Quartermaster 19th Virginia 22 October 1861; appointed Major and Commissary of Subsistence on Pickett's staff 14 November 1862; the Confederate Senate failed to confirm this appointment, however, so Jones was considered "assigned"to this post rather than "appointed"; announced as Chief Commissary of Subsistence on Pickett's staff 24 September 1863.

Leitch, Samuel G. (1st Lt. Acting Chief Ordnance Officer): Enl. 25 May 1861 as a 1st Lt. in Company "F," 19th Virginia Infantry; (21), student; Acting Chief of Ordnance on Pickett's staff 12 March 1863; announced as Captain and Chief of Ordnance on Pickett's staff 24 September 1863.

Lewis, Magnus M. (Chief Surgeon): Enl. 17 May 1861 at Alexandria in the 17th Virginia Infantry; surgeon; appointed Surgeon of 17th Virginia 1 July 1861; promoted to Division Surgeon sometime between 30 April and 30 June 1863.

Pickett, Charles (Major, AAG): Appointed 1st Lt. and ADC on Pickett's staff 18 March 1862; promoted Capt. and AAG on Pickett's staff 10 July 1862; promoted to Major and AAG on Pickett's staff 14 November 1862.

Scott, R. Taylor (Major, Quartermaster): Originally Captain Co. "K," 8th Virginia Infantry; appointed to Major and Quartermaster on Pickett's staff 31 October 1862.

Symington, W. Stuart (1st Lt., ADC): Enl. 23 May 1861 at Richmond as a 2nd Lt. in Company "B," 21st Virginia Infantry; appointed 1st Lt. and ADC on Pickett's staff 14 November 1862.

Williams, Andrew W. (Captain, Division Paymaster): Appointed Captain and AQM 2nd Infantry Battalion, Hilliard's Alabama Legion 19 July 1862; appointed Captain and AQM 11th Virginia and transferred to Pickett's staff and appointed Division Paymaster 1 June 1863.

Division Postmaster

Jacheri, Pompeo: Detailed from Company "B," 19th Virginia; enl. 8 May 1861 at Charlottesville; (25), janitor.

Division Blacksmith

Beedle, Andrew P.: Detailed from Company "E," 8th Virginia; enl. 29 May 1861 at Philomont; AWOL 15 July 1863.

Division Commissary

Seargeant, Nathaniel R.: Detailed from Company "A," 19th Virginia; enl. 16 April 1861 at Charlottesville; (22).

Sneed, Henry H. (3rd Sgt.): Detailed from Company "G," 38th Virginia; enl. 18 May 1861 at Boydton.

Wingfield, Thomas F., Jr.: Detailed from Company "A," 19th Virginia; enl. 16 April 1861 at Charlottesville; (22).

Division Commissary Train

Owen, John D.: Detached from Company "D," 57th Virginia; enl. 12 March 1862 at Pittsylvania Court House.

Rorer, Charles H.: Detached from Company "D," 57th Virginia; enl. 12 March 1862 at Pittsylvania Court House.

Division Headquarters Guard

Daniel, Joseph: Detailed from Company "E," 14th Virginia; enl. 12 May 1861 at Clarksville; (28); farmer.

Payne, William A. (3rd Sgt.): Detailed from Company "C," 57th Virginia; enl. 21 July 1861 at Pig River.

Walker, John F.: Detached from Company "K," 57th Virginia; enl. 1 August 1861 in Craig County.

Division Ordnance Train Guard

Clay, Thomas J.: Detailed from Company "F," 38th Virginia; enl. 14 March 1862 at Republican Grove.

Stump, Elijah: Detailed from Company "C," 57th Virginia; enl. 15 July 1861 at Pig River.

Division Pioneer Corps

Kent, William H.: Detailed from Company "G," 11th Virginia; enl. at Lynchburg; enrolled for service 12 June 1861 at Manassas Junction; (31), farmer.

Stone, George W.: Detached from Company "K," 57th Virginia; enl. 17 April 1862 at Ford Dillard, North Carolina.

Division Provost Guard

Addison, John W.: Detailed from Company "F," 9th Virginia; enl. 14 April 1862 at Cedar Point.

Daniel, J. Thomas: Detailed from Company "G," 14th Virginia; enl. 6 March 1862 at Cascade.

Earles, Hyram: Detailed from Company "I," 57th Virginia; enl. 1 May 1861 at Cascade.

Goode, Henry F.: Detailed from Company "B," 57th Virginia; enl. 15 June 1861 at Young's Store.

Goode, William H.: Detailed from Company "B," 57th Virginia; enl. 24 June 1861 at Young's Store.

Hodges, Habron: Detached from Company "G," 57th Virginia; enl. 13 July 1861 at Sydnorsville.

Millner, Cornelius W. (Jr. 2nd Lt.): Detached from Company "I," 57th Virginia; enl. 1 March 1862 at Bachelor's Hall.

Payne, William T. (3rd Sgt.): Detailed from Company "D," 57th Virginia; enl. 23 July 1861 at Galveston.

Ramsey, William H.: Detailed from Company "B," 57th Virginia; enl. 4 July 1861 at Young's Store.

Self, George R.: Detached from Company "C," 1st Virginia; enl. 26 January 1863 in Cumberland County.

Wagoner, Frederick: Detailed from Company "F," 9th Virginia; enl. 22 May 1861 at Chuckatuck.

Couriers

Campbell, Martin V.: Detailed from Company "G," 19th Virginia; enl. 10 June 1861 at Culpeper Court House; (20); farmer.

Friend, Thomas R.: Detached from Company "C," 9th Virginia; enl. 29 August 1861 at Craney Island.

Hempston, Robert T.: Detailed from Company "H," 8th Virginia; enl. 13 July 1861 at Leesburg.

Watkins, John L.: Detailed from Company "K," 18th Virginia; enl. 24 April 1861 at Charlotte Court House; (18); farmer.

Clerks

Avery, Richard W.: Detailed from Company "A,", 17th Virginia; enl. 17 April 1861 at Alexandria; clerk.

Hough, Harry: Detailed from Company "H," 17th Virginia; enl. 17 April 1861 at Alexandria; (19), clerk.

Teamsters

Legwin, Charles H.: Detached from Company "G," 57th Virginia; enl. 28 October 1862 in Franklin County.

Powell, William B.: Detailed from Company "E," 53rd Virginia; enl. 16 May 1861 at Cumed.

Riggins, Charles A.: Detailed from Company "E," 14th Virginia; enl. 12 May 1861 at Clarksville; (24); mason.

Unknown Assignment

Ryals, James D.: Detailed from Company "E," 18th Virginia; enl. 10 August 1861 in camp.

Stultz, George W.: Detached from Company "H," 24th Virginia; enl. 5 June 1861 at Lynchburg.

Kemper's Brigade

On 25 July 1861, the organization of Brigadier General Longstreet's Brigade was announced as the 1st, 7th, 11th, and 17th Virginia. Of these regiments the 1st, 11th, and 17th were in Longstreet's Brigade and the 7th Virginia was in Early's Brigade during the Battle of 1st Manassas on 21 July 1861. Brigadier General Longstreet, having been promoted to Major General, was succeeded in command of the brigade by Brigadier General R. S. Ewell, who was assigned 8 November 1861. On 26 March 1862, Brigadier General A. P. Hill assumed command vice Ewell promoted to Major General. On 4 June 1862, Brigadier General James L. Kemper was assigned to command, vice Hill promoted to Major General. The 24th Virginia, previously in Early's Brigade, joined before the Seven Days' Battles. At the time of the formation of the First Corps, 6 November 1862, the brigade was composed of the 1st, 7th, 11th, 17th, and 24th Virginia. On 10 November 1862, the 3rd Virginia joined from Pryor's Brigade, and on 26 November 1862, the 17th Virginia was transferred to Corse's Brigade. Thereafter, the brigade retained its organization until Appomattox.

General and Staff

Kemper, James Lawson (Brigadier General): Born in Madison County, Va. 11 June 1823; served on the VMI Board of Visitors from 1856-1858 and was president 1857-1858; graduated from Washington College 1842; read for the law; Capt. and regimental QM and AQM of Virginia volunteers during Mexican War; member of Va. House of Delegates; appointed Col. of the 7th Virginia Infantry 2 May 1861; commanding A.P. Hill's (old) Brigade, Longstreet's Division 27 May through July 1862; promoted Brig. Gen. 3 June 1862; commanding division, 1st Corps, Army of Northern Va. August through September 1862; commanding brigade Jones Division, 1st Corps, Army of Northern Va. September through October 1862; commanding brigade Pickett's Division, 1st Corps, Army of Northern Va. October 1862 through 25 February 1863; in Dept. of Va. and North Carolina 25 February through 1 April 1863; in Dept. of Southern Va. 1 April through May 1863; commanding brigade Pickett's Div., 1st Corps, Army of Northern Va. May through 3 July 1863; *wounded* in the groin (the bullet ranging up into his body) when within 100 yards of the stone wall during the attack; *captured*; exchanged September 1863.

Beckham, Abner Camp (Volunteer ADC): VMI class of 1863; never officially appointed ADC; with Kemper from the beginning of the war.

Crisler, Nelson W. (Major, Quartermaster): Enl. 25 April 1861 at Madison Court House as a 2nd Lt. in Company "A," 7th Virginia Infantry; appointed Major and Quartermaster on Kemper's staff 13 June 1862.

Fry, William T. (Captain, AAG): VMI class of 1862; Appointed 1st Lt. and Adjutant of the 1st Virginia Infantry 27 April 1862; appointed Captain and AAG on Kemper's staff 14 June 1862.

Geiger, George E. (1st Lt., ADC): (37 in 1863); appointed 1st Lt. and ADC on Kemper's staff 5 November 1862; *wounded* during the repulse and *captured*; died two weeks later.

Green, James W. (Major, ACS): Enl. 30 April 1861 at Culpeper Court House as 1st Lt. in Company "C," 7th Virginia Infantry; (37 in 1861); appointed Major and ACS on Kemper's staff 13 June 1862.

Nelson, Kinloch (1st Lt., Ordnance Officer): Assigned duty as a 1st Lt. of Ordnance 11 April 1863; on duty as Ordnance Officer on Kemper's staff 15 June through 24 July 1863.

Pollock, Thomas Gordon (Captain, AA&IG): Originally Captain of Company "F," 60th Virginia; appointed 1st Lt. and Adjutant 60th Virginia 1 May 1862; appointed Captain and AAG on Kemper's staff 7 June 1863; *killed* during the attack and carried back to Pickett's Hospital; buried near Jeff Myers' house.

Courier

Walker, George T. ("Big Foot"): Enl. 29 July 1861 at Centreville; detailed from Company "C," 11th Virginia.

Kemper's Clerk

Barnes, Edward C.: Detailed from Company "G," 11th Virginia; enl. 10 March 1862 at Lynchburg.

Major Crisler's Clerk

Holland, William P.: Detailed from Company "G," 11th Virginia; enl. 25 April 1861 at Lynchburg; (24); merchant.

Artisan

Moyers, J.M.: Detached from Company "F," 7th Virginia; enl. 27 April 1861 at Stannardsville.

Teamsters and Wagoners

Fariss, Reuben W.: Detailed from Company "C," 11th Virginia; enl. 18 March 1862 at Lynchburg.

Lindsay, Joshua Mc.: Detailed from Company "B," 11th Virginia; enl. 23 April 1861 at Yellow Branch; (30).

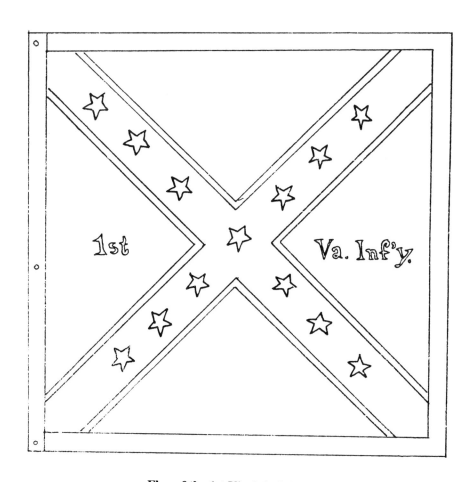

**Flag of the 1st Virginia Infantry,
captured near the stone wall
by the 82nd New York Infantry**

1st Virginia Volunteer Infantry Regiment
"Williams' Rifles"

Organized at Richmond 1 May 1851, this regiment was originally composed of nine volunteer militia companies which had been attached to local residents of the line. Composed of ten companies in 1856 and seven companies in 1858, this regiment was organized with eleven companies on 21 April 1861 and was mustered into Confederate service on 1 July 1861 for the war. It was reorganized with six companies on 27 April 1862. Company "A" was assigned to the 12th Virginia Infantry as Company "G" soon after 31 August 1861; Company "F" was taken from the regiment in September 1861 and mustered as (1st) Company "C," 1st Regiment Virginia Artillery; Companies "E" and "K" were disbanded about 27 April 1862; and Captain Chambers' company was assigned to the 2nd Regiment Virginia Infantry prior to 30 June 1861.

Field and Staff

The following listing was obtained from the company's April/June 1863 muster roll captioned 30 June 1863 at Chambersburg, Pennsylvania. Only those listed as "present" are provided.

The unit reported the condition of its clothing as "bad" but its military appearance, arms, accouterments, discipline, and instruction, as "good."

Williams, Lewis Burwell, Jr. (Colonel): Born 13 September 1833; graduated VMI 1855; lawyer and professor at VMI; unmarried; Capt. Co. "A," 13th Virginia 17 April 1861; Lt. Col. 7th Virginia 15 May 1861; Col. 1st Virginia 27 April 1862; wounded in the shoulder during the advance, fell on his own sword and *killed*; removed from Greenmount Cemetery, Baltimore, Md. and reburied in Hollywood Cemetery, Richmond, Va. 16 February 1896.

Langley, Francis H. (Major): Born in Maryland; enl. 21 April 1861 in Henrico County as a Sergeant in Company "G"; (31); carpenter; *wounded* during the attack.

Stockton, John N.C. (1st Lt.) (Adjutant): VMI class of 1857; Appointed to the regiment 18 August 1862.

Allan, William G. (Capt., AQM): Enl. 7 June 1861 at Richmond as a Jr. 2nd Lt. in Company "H"; (27); farmer; appointed Captain and AQM 23 September 1861.

Harney, Henry (Capt., ACS): Enl. 21 April 1861 at Richmond as a 2nd Lt. in Company "D"; (26); clerk; appointed Captain and ACS 11 October 1861; transferred to a post commissary of subsistence in August 1863.

Grigsby, Alexander (Surgeon): Assigned to the regiment 6 October 1862; left in charge of the wounded at Gettysburg and captured 5 July; exchanged 21 November 1863.

Butler, Marcus A. (Asst. Surgeon): Appointed Assistant Surgeon 4 December 1862; assigned to this regiment in March 1863.

Jones, Robert McC. (Sgt. Major): Enl. 21 April 1861 in Richmond in Company "D"; (22); clerk.

Hudgins, Elias P. (Ordnance Sgt.): Enl. 21 April 1861 in Henrico County in Company "G"; (25); clerk.

Dean, William H. (Quartermaster Sgt.): Enl. 21 April 1861 in Richmond in Company "B"; (20); tobacconist.

Color Guard

Woods, Patrick (3rd Sgt.): Detailed from Company "C"; enl. 21 April 1861 at Richmond; (25); laborer; *wounded* during the attack and *captured*; exchanged from Point Lookout 20 March 1864; returned to his company in April 1864.

Figg, John Q. (4th Sgt.): Detailed from Company "B"; enl. 21 April 1861 at Richmond; (21): wood turner; *wounded* during the attack.

Lawson, William M. (4th Sgt.): On extra duty from Company "H"; enl. 4 May 1861 at Richmond; (23); clerk; with color guard since 20 May 1862; *wounded* in the right arm (amputated at the shoulder) and *captured*; exchanged from DeCamp Hospital 16 September 1863.

Martin, Theodore R.: Detailed from Company "H"; enl. 4 May 1861 at Richmond; (18); clerk; *wounded* during the attack.

Mitchel, William L.: Detailed from Company "D"; enl. 3 November 1862 at Culpeper Court House; (16 or 19 in 1863); *killed* while carrying the flag during the advance; buried at the Codori house.

Company "B" ("Riflemen"; also "Richmond City Guard")

This company enlisted 21 April 1861 in Richmond for one year and was reorganized 27 April 1862.

The following listing was obtained from the company's April/June 1863 muster roll captioned 30 June 1863 at Chambersburg, Pennsylvania. The company noted that it was not mustered on 30 June being on picket near Chambersburg. There are no entries subsequent to 30 June on the roll, and only those listed as "present" are provided below. The company reported its clothing as "bad" and its military appearance, arms, accouterments, discipline, and instruction as "good."

Davis, Thomas Herbert (Captain): (25); school teacher; *wounded* during the attack and *captured*; escaped from Johnson's Island, Ohio 1 January 1864.

Robins, Logan S. (1st Lt.): (20); sash maker.

Payne, Jesse Armistead (2nd Lt.): (19); grocer; *wounded*.

Littlepage, John L. (1st Sgt.): (26); farmer.

Crow, Benjamin M. (2nd Sgt.): (19); bookkeeper.

Ogden, Lewis W. (3rd Sgt.): Enl. 8 July 1861 at Manassas.

Carter, William Irvin (1st Cpl.): (21); tobacconist; *wounded* and *captured*; exchanged 30 April 1864.

Stoaber, William A. (3rd Cpl.): (18); salesman.

Acre, Thomas (Drummer): Enl. 23 May 1863 at Richmond.

Buchannan, Mungo P.: (21); plumber.

Crigger, W.H.: Enl. 2 April 1862 at Wytheville, (19 in 1861).

Daniels, Joseph R.: Enl. 27 January 1863 at Charlotte, Virginia; (20 in 1865); mail carrier; born in Charlotte, *wounded*.

Franklin, Fendall: (21); carpenter; the company initially lists him as having been captured. He is subsequently listed as having died of wounds received at Gettysburg. Federal records do not mention him, however. He was probably *killed* at Gettysburg.

Garrett, John R.: Enl. 30 January 1863 at Charlotte, Virginia.

Gotze, Ernst Augst: (20); baker; *captured*; discharged from Ft. Delaware 26 October 1863. The company lists him as having deserted to the enemy.

Heath, George R.: (18); carpenter; *shot* in the right side and *captured*; exchanged from Chester Hospital 20 August 1863.

Jacobs, John, Jr.: (44); coach maker.

Lumpkin, William J., Jr.: (26); merchant; AWOL 1 August. Present by 24 November 1863.

Mallory, William J.: (19); iron maker; *wounded* and *captured*; exchanged 1 August 1863.

Otey, Edward T.: (21); saddler.

Overstreet, John P.: Enl. 9 February 1863 in Bedford County; received flesh *wounds* from gunshots in the shoulder and thigh and *captured*; exchanged from DeCamp Hospital 28 August 1863.

Spickard, H.L.: Enl. 10 February 1863; *wounded*.

Stagg, James: (31); tobacconist; *wounded*; captured while serving as a nurse, probably at Pickett's Division Hospital; exchanged 20 March 1864.

Street, Richard H.: Enl. 2 May 1861 near Richmond; (21); carpenter; *wounded* and *captured*; exchanged 20 or 21 February 1865.

Sullings, G.L.: Enl. 19 September 1862 in King William County.

Tilghman, George M.: Enl. 31 January 1863 in Fluvanna County; *captured*; exchanged 20 or 21 February 1865.

Toomey, Jerry: (29); carpenter.

Vermillera, Philip J.: (23); blacksmith; *wounded*.

Company "C" ("The Montgomery Guard")

This company enlisted 21 April 1861 at Richmond for one year, and was reorganized 27 April 1862.

The following listing was obtained from the company's April/June 1863 muster roll captioned 8 August 1863 at Mountain Run, Virginia. The caption indicates that the company was not mustered on 30 June, being on picket duty near Chambersburg, Pennsylvania. There are no entries subsequent to 30 June on the roll, however, indicating that it was compiled to reflect the company's status as of 30 June. Only those listed as "present" on this roll are listed below.

The company reported the condition of its clothing as "bad" and its military appearance, arms, accouterments, discipline, and instruction as "good."

Hallinan, James (Captain): (21); laborer; *killed*.

Dooley, John E. (1st Lt.): Enl. 11 August 1862; *shot* in both thighs and *captured*; paroled for exchange 24 February 1865.

Byrnes, Edward (2nd Sgt.): (38); mechanic; the company lists him as having been wounded and captured but there are no Federal records concerning him. He was probably *killed*.

Kean, Charles (4th Sgt.): (34); saddler; the company lists him as having been wounded and captured; a relative, filing a claim for back pay due Sgt. Kean, reported that he died at Gettysburg. There are no Federal Records concerning him, however, and he was, therefore, probably *killed* in action.

Moriarty, John (5th Sgt.): (28); laborer; *wounded* in the back and *captured*; exchanged from Chester Hospital 20 August 1863.

Costello, Timothy (2nd Cpl.): Enl. 12 November 1862; deserted 3 or 4 July and captured 5 July. No further records concerning him. He may have joined U.S. service.

Clarke, James D.: Enl. 22 August 1862; received a scalp *wound* and *captured*; died in Ft. Delaware 22 July 1863; buried at Finns Point, N.J.

Collins, Hillery, W.: Enl. 15 September 1862; *wounded* and *captured*; exchanged from Chester Hospital 23 September 1863.

Consadine, Michael: (21); laborer; deserted 3 or 4 July and captured 5 July; joined U.S. 1st Connecticut Cavalry.

Crenshaw, William H.: Enl. 27 January 1863 at Charlotte, Virginia; the company lists him as having been wounded and captured but Federal records do not mention him. He was probably *killed*.

Davis, Eli M.: Enl. 11 January 1863 in Henry County; *wounded* in the right side and arm and *captured*; exchanged from DeCamp Hospital 16 September 1863.

Edwards, James: Enl. 26 January 1863 in Cumberland County.

Giles, Richard E.: Enl. 10 February 1863 in Bedford County; *wounded* in the shoulder and left chest and *captured*; died at DeCamp Hospital 21 August 1863 and buried in Grave #815, Cypress Hill Cemetery, Long Island, New York.

Gillespie, Samuel H.: Enl. 27 October 1862.

Johnson, John N.: Enl. 9 February 1863 in Bedford County; received a gunshot *wound* which fractured his left leg and *captured*; exchanged from West's Buildings Hospital 27 September 1863.

Maiden, E.R.: Enl. 1 February 1863 in Lunenburg County.

McCary, Benjamin J.: Enl. 28 February 1863 in Fluvanna County; *shot* in the thigh and *captured*; exchanged from DeCamp Hospital 16 September 1863.

McCrossen, James: (24); laborer.

Nobles, Benjamin R.: Enl. 3 September 1862.

Powell, Alex E.: Enl. 9 February 1863 in Bedford County; shot in the head and *captured*; exchanged from Chester Hospital 20 August 1863.

Schammel, John H.: Enl. 26 January 1863 in Surry County; shot in the thigh and *captured*; there is no further mention of this soldier in Federal records subsequent to Gettysburg. May have died in an undetermined U.S. hospital.

Sloan, Samuel H.: Enl. 23 October 1862; *wounded* during the advance and subsequently *captured*. Federal records show that he died 29 November 1863 but also indicate that an S.H. Sloan was released from Ft. Delaware on 26 June 1865. Probably died in Federal prison.

Thomas, James: Enl. 9 February 1863 in Bedford County; widow was Mrs. Irabella R. Thomas; the company lists him as having been wounded and captured but Federal records do not mention him. He was probably *killed*.

Thorpe, James A.: Enl. 27 January 1863 at Charlotte, Virginia.

Tompkins, John: Enl. 22 August 1861; the company lists him as having been wounded and captured but there are no Federal records mentioning him. He was probably *killed.*

Trueman, Jackson: Enl. 9 February 1863 in Bedford County.

Youell, Robert: Enl. 16 October 1862; *killed.*

Company "D" ("Old Dominion Guard")

This company enlisted 21 April 1861 at Richmond for one year and was reorganized 27 April 1862.

The following listing was obtained from the company's April/June 1863 muster roll captioned 12 August 1863 at Mountain Run, Virginia. The caption indicates that the company was not mustered on 30 June, being on picket duty near Chambersburg, Pennsylvania. There are no entries subsequent to 30 June on the roll, however, indicating that it was compiled to reflect the company's status as of 30 June. Only those listed as "present" on this roll are provided below.

The company reported the condition of its clothing as "bad" and its military appearance, arms, accouterments, discipline, and instruction as "good."

Regimental skirmish company during the attack.

Norton, George F. (Captain): (21); VMI class of 1860; *wounded* during the attack.

Reeve, Edward P. (1st Lt.): (28); clerk; *wounded.*

Keiningham, William H. (Sr. 2nd Lt.): (19); clerk; *wounded* and *captured*; released from Ft. Delaware 12 June 1865.

Blair, Adolphus (Jr. 2nd Lt.): (18); clerk; born at Petersburg, Virginia; *wounded.*

Keplar, John Hanson (1st Sgt.): (22), clerk; captured; exchanged 14 or 15 February 1865.

Blanton, Lee M. (2nd Sgt.): (19); clerk.

Simpson, Andrew J. (3rd Sgt.): (26); clerk.

Finn, James M. (4th Sgt.): Enl. 21 July 1861; *wounded* and *captured*; exchanged 20 or 21 February 1865.

Jennings, John C. (5th Sgt.): (19); clerk.

Perrin, J.P. (1st Cpl.): Enl. 15 July 1861; AWOL 25 July through 14 August 1863.

Meanly, George L. (2nd Cpl.): Enl. 25 August 1861.

Craig, George E. (3rd Cpl.): clerk; *wounded.*

Loehr, Charles T. (4th Cpl.): (18); clerk; slightly *wounded* in the face and arm.

Doyle, Benjamin H. (Drummer): Enl. 1 May 1863.

Angle, James B.: (19); clerk; *wounded.*

Armstrong, William J.: (20); clerk; *wounded* in the hip.

Bowe, N.W.: Enl. 23 July 1861; captured while serving as a hospital nurse at Gettysburg; exchanged 14 or 15 February 1865.

Draper, Jackson: Enl. 18 May 1863 near Taylorsville, Virginia.

Edwards, David S.: (22); clerk; mother was Mary S. Edwards; received a *wound* which fractured his right arm and *captured*. Died at Camp Letterman Hospital 11 September 1863 and buried in Section 7, Grave #28 of that hospital's cemetery; disinterred to Richmond 13 June 1872 in Box #76.

Farmer, John T.: Enl. 26 August 1862 in Chesterfield County.

Freeman, J.W.: Date and place of enlistment not shown; the company lists him initially as missing in action and subsequently as "supposed *killed.*"

Fuqua, Peter P.: Enl. 9 February 1863 in Bedford County.

Furcron, Henry W.: (22); clerk.

Govan, Archy: Enl. 27 April 1862.

Jarvis, David A.: Enl. 16 September 1861.

Johnson, George W.: (22); clerk; received a gunshot *wound* to his right elbow resulting in a fracture of the joint and *captured*; exchanged from West's Buildings Hospital 17 November 1863.

Keiningham, John C.: Enl. 15 January 1863; *shot* in the neck and mouth and *captured*; exchanged from DeCamp Hospital 8 September 1863.

Mahane, W.P.: Enl. 18 September 1862 in Goochland County.

McMinn, Delaware: (18); clerk; *wounded.*

Mitchell, George W.: (20); carpenter.

Morton, Tazewell, S.: (17); clerk; received *wounds* which fractured his lower jaw and injured his left arm and *captured*; exchanged from Chester Hospital 20 August 1863.

Moss, Alexander C.: Enl. 27 April 1862.

Priddy, E.: Enl. 15 July 1861; *wounded.*

Steger, A.G., Jr.: Enl. 30 June 1861.

Sublett, Chasteen M.: Enl. 9 February 1863 in Bedford County; *wounded.*

Turner, William W.: Enl. 23 July 1861.

Van Riper, John: (23); carpenter.

Walthall, Howard M.: (30); clerk.

Westmoreland, William A.: Enl. 27 January 1863 in Amelia County.

Wheat, N.F.: Enl. 2 August 1861; AWOL 25 July through 14 August 1863.

Wheeley, John F.: (27); laborer; *wounded.*

Wingfield, L.R.: Enl. 15 July 1861; *wounded* in the chest and *captured*; exchanged from DeCamp Hospital 8 September 1863.

Wingfield, M.J. ("Monk"): Enl. 16 August 1861; *killed* during the advance.

Wingfield, S.L.: Enl. 23 July 1861; *wounded.*

Company "G"

This company was organized before the war and was enrolled for service 21 April 1861 in Henrico County for one year. It was reorganized 27 April 1862.

The following listing was obtained from the company's April/June 1863 muster roll captioned 30 June 1863 at Chambersburg, Pennsylvania. The caption indicates that the company was not mustered on 30 June, being on picket duty near Chambersburg. There are no entries subsequent to 30 June on the roll, however, indicating that it was compiled to reflect the company's status as of 30 June. Only those listed as "present" on this roll are provided below.

The company reported the condition of its clothing as "bad" and its military appearance, arms, accouterments, discipline, and instruction as "good."

Morris, Eldridge (Captain): (29); machinist; *wounded.*

Woody, William T. (1st Lt.): (23); carpenter; *wounded.*

Ball, George W. (1st Sgt.): Enl. in Richmond; (25); painter; *captured*; exchanged 21 January 1865.

Deane, William H. (2nd Sgt.): (31); tailor; *wounded.*

Wright, Elijah (3rd Sgt.): (22); blacksmith.

Durham, Thomas H. (5th Sgt.): (25); clerk; *shot* in the right eye resulting in its loss.

Miller, William T. (1st Cpl.): (22); leather worker; *wounded* in the leg resulting in its amputation. Tetanus developed and he died in an unspecified Gettysburg hospital.

Spraggins, William S. (2nd Cpl.): (19); box maker.

Allen, John (3rd Cpl.): (22); bricklayer; *wounded.*

O'Keeffe, James (Musician): Enl. 1 May 1863 in Richmond.

Ashby, Benjamin F.: (23); carpenter; *captured*; exchanged 13 February 1865.

Atkinson, James Rosser: (18); shoemaker.

Chapman, Gustavus A.: (22); carpenter; *wounded* and *captured*; exchanged from Chester Hospital 20 August 1863.

Doss, Gehu: Enl. 15 January 1863 at Richmond; *killed.*

Epps, James Ryland: (18); carpenter; captured while serving as a nurse at Gettysburg; exchanged 20 March 1864.

Farrar, James: (23); plumber; *wounded.*

Fergusson, Henry C.: (24); painter; *wounded* in the left humerus requiring amputation at the primary joint and *captured*; exchanged from West's Buildings Hospital 17 November 1863.

Fergusson, William J.: (28); carpenter.

Fuller, James R.: Enl. 15 January 1863 in Richmond; *captured*; died at Ft. Delaware 9 October 1863; buried at Finns Point, N.J.

Gary, Hezekiah B.: (30); cooper.

Gentry, Charles W.: (17); student; *wounded.*

Harvey, Thomas P.: Enl. 15 January 1863 in Richmond.

Haskins, Augustus L.: (24); bricklayer; *captured*; exchanged 14 or 15 February 1865.

Hay, Thomas W.: (27); cabinet maker; *wounded* and *captured*; exchanged 20 or 21 February 1865.

Hord, Benjamin H.: (22); fence digger; *shot* in the right lung and *captured*; exchanged from DeCamp Hospital 28 August 1863.

Hord, William F.: (18); farmer; *wounded* and *captured*; exchanged from DeCamp Hospital 28 August 1863.

Jackson, John D.: (19); machinist.

Kendrick, William F.: (20); blacksmith; *wounded.*

Layard, William Samuel: (19); painter; *wounded* and *captured*; exchanged from Chester Hospital 20 August 1863.

Lord, John R.: (32); carpenter; deserted in Pennsylvania 3 July "supposed to the enemy." There are no Federal records concerning this soldier. Probably deserted on the march to the field and made his escape.

Martin, William H.: Enl. 20 February 1863 in Richmond; *wounded* and *captured*; released from Ft. Delaware 7 June 1865.

Miles, Thomas W.: (18); student.

Patterson, William: (23); bricklayer; deserted 4 July and captured 5 July; joined U.S. 3rd Maryland Cavalry 22 September 1863.

Payne, Pleasant H.: Enl. 20 February 1863 at Richmond.

Prease, Charles W.: Enl. 9 February 1863 at Richmond.

Redford, Cornelius A.: (24); carpenter; *wounded.*

Rogers, Thomas S.: (22); carpenter; *wounded.*

Royster, James A.: (21); clerk.

Royster, Norborne L.: (19); clerk; *wounded.*

Vaughan, Alfred J.: Enl. 15 July 1861 at Bull Run; *wounded.*

Via, James T.: (22); printer.

Walker, Alexander: (21), carpenter.

Walker, Daniel M.: Enl. 9 February 1863 in Albemarle County.

Walthall, Robert R.: (18); machinist; *wounded* in the right arm.

Walthus, George: Enl. 17 September 1862, born in Germany; *captured*; joined U.S. 3rd Maryland Cavalry 5 September 1863.

Wilkinson, John K.: (24); carpenter.

Wood, William A.: Enl. 1 November 1862 at Fredericksburg, Virginia.

Company "H" ("Richmond Grays Number 2")

This company enlisted 4 May 1861 at Richmond for one year and was reorganized 27 April 1862.

The following listing was obtained from the company's April/June 1863 muster roll captioned 12 August 1863 in camp near Orange Court House. The caption indicates that the company was not mustered on 30 June, being on picket duty near Chambersburg, Pennsylvania. There are no entries subsequent to 30 June on the roll, however, indicating that it was compiled to reflect the company's status as of 30 June. Only those listed as "present" on this roll are provided below.

The company reported the condition of its clothing as "bad" and its military appearance, arms, accouterments, discipline, and instruction as "good."

Watkins, Abner J. (Captain): (33); coach maker; *wounded.*

Martin, Ellison W. (1st Lt.): Enl. 15 May 1861, coach maker; *wounded.*

Cabell, Paul Carrington (2nd Lt.): Enl. 8 August 1861 at Fairfax Court House; (28 in 1862); lawyer; born in Amherst County; *wounded.*

Norvell, Ryland H. (3rd Sgt.): (24), merchant.

Hansford, Calvin P. (5th Sgt.): (24); dentist; *killed.*

Kilby, Walter R. (2nd Cpl.): Enl. 22 May 1861, (18); printer; received a gunshot *wound* which partially fractured his right tibia and *captured*; exchanged from Point Lookout Hospital 30 April 1865.

Chadick, Richard (3rd Cpl.): (27); merchant; *shot* in the thigh and *captured*; died 13 July 1863.

Anderson, William N.: Enl. 15 May 1861 at Richmond; (18); farmer; *wounded* and *captured*; exchanged from Chester Hospital 20 August 1863.

188

Banks, Solomon: Enl. 3 February 1863 in Mathews County; *wounded* and *captured*; exchanged 22 September 1864.

Bresnaham, Mathew: Enl. 21 April 1861 in Richmond; discharged 8 December 1862; re-enlisted 3 February 1863 at Richmond; (22); laborer, native of County Kerry, Ireland and not a U.S. citizen; *shot* in the right thigh and *captured*. Died at Camp Letterman Hospital following amputation of his right leg 1 August 1863. Buried in Section 2, Grave #10 of that hospital's cemetery. Disinterred to Richmond in Box #50 13 June 1872.

Camp, James W.: Enl. 25 August 1861 at Fairfax Court House.

Clayton, Allen O.: (20); shoemaker; *wounded*.

Daniel, John H.: Enl. 29 August 1861 at Fairfax Court House; received a *gunshot* fracture of his right foot and *captured*; exchanged from West's Buildings Hospital 27 September 1863.

Davidson, E.F.: Enl. 9 March 1863 in Bedford County.

Dignum, Robert E.: Enl. 30 May 1861; (19); coach trimmer; *shot* in the head and *captured*; at 2nd Division, II Corps Hospital 3 July; exchanged.

Duerson, William H.: Enl. 13 November 1862 in Spotsylvania County; *wounded* and *captured*; exchanged 22 September 1864.

Dunn, Robert N.: (21); clerk; *wounded*.

Farson, Stephen: Enl. 15 January 1863 in Pittsylvania County; (36 in 1863); widow was Mrs. Lucy A. Farson; *wounded* in the left arm and leg and *captured*; pyemia developed following amputation of the arm 3 July and he died 29 August 1863 at the Seminary Hospital near Gettysburg. He was buried in the southwest corner of Seminary Woods and was disinterred to Richmond with five others in Box "U" on 17 May 1873.

Fiser, E.C.: Enl. 9 March 1863 in Bedford County; *wounded*.

Flowers, David: Enl. 4 March 1863 at Petersburg, Virginia; *captured*; exchanged 6 March 1864.

Hite, H.C.: Enl. 23 January 1863 in Halifax County; *wounded* and *captured*; exchanged 22 September 1864.

Joseph, Wilson B.

Mosby, William B.: Enl. 11 June 1862; *shot* in the right hip and *captured*; exchanged from West's Buildings Hospital 17 November 1863.

Mouring, Thomas: Enl. 1 May 1861; (18); carpenter; *wounded* in the leg and *captured*; exchanged from Chester Hosptial 20 August 1863.

Nolting, George A.: (25); clerk.

Nuckols, Edward G.: Enl. 8 January 1863 in Hanover County; received a flesh *wound* in the lower third of his forearm and *captured*; exchanged from DeCamp Hospital 16 September 1863.

Payne, James William: Enl. 20 December 1862 in Orange County; *shot* in the shoulder and *captured*; exchanged from Chester Hospital 20 August 1863.

Sinnott, John J.: (21); cabinet maker; *hit* by a spent ball in his right hip and *captured*; exchanged 20 or 21 February 1865.

St. Clair, B.S.: Enl. 19 February 1863 in Bedford County; *killed*.

Toler, H.H.: Enl. 15 January 1863 in Pittsylvania County.

Vaughan, Nicholas L.: Enl. 23 January 1863 in Halifax County; *shot* in the right side of his chest and *captured*; exchanged from Chester Hospital 23 September 1863.

Waddell, William D.: Enl. 23 January 1863 in Halifax County; *wounded* in the right ankle and *captured*; amputated 8 August; died of nervous exhaustion at Chester Hospital 12 August 1863 and buried in Grave #146 of that hospital's cemetery.

Womack, R.E.: Enl. 23 January 1863 in Halifax County.

<u>Company "I"</u>

This company was organized 18 June 1860 and was enrolled for active service at Richmond on 21 April 1861 for one year. It was reorganized 27 April 1862.

The following listing was obtained from the company's April/June 1863 muster roll captioned 30 June 1863, Chambersburg, Pennsylvania. The caption indicates that the company was not mustered on 30 June being on picket duty near Chambersburg. There are no entries subsequent to 30 June on the roll, however, indicating that it was compiled to reflect the company's status as of 30 June. Only those listed as "present" on this roll are provided below.

The company reported the condition of its clothing as "bad," and its military appearance, arms, accouterments, discipline, and instruction as "good."

Howard, Benjamin F. (Captain): (25); stonecutter.

Ballow, Henry C. (1st Lt.): (25); carpenter.

Caho, William A. (2nd Lt.): Enl. 27 April 1861, (25); stonecutter; *shot* in the thigh requiring amputation of the leg and *captured*; died at Chester Hospital 31 July 1863 and buried in Grave #92 of that hospital's cemetery.

Crew, John T. (2nd Sgt.): (23); carpenter; *captured*; exchanged 8 May 1864.

White, William T. (3rd Sgt.): (31); carpenter; *captured*; exchanged 15 November 1864.

Goodson, Edwin C. (4th Sgt.): (19); agricultural machinist; *captured*; exchanged 15 November 1864.

Terry, William F. (1st Cpl.): (22); carpenter; *wounded.*

Ellett, Lemuel O. (2nd Cpl.): *Shot* in the head and *captured*; died 12 July 1863 and buried in Yard "D" of the U.S. II Corps Hospital cemetery in Jacob Schwartz's cornfield on Rock Creek; disinterred to Richmond 13 June 1872 with 110 others in ten large boxes marked "S."

Parker, Calvin L. (3rd Cpl.): Enl. 29 April 1861; (24); carpenter; suffered a gunshot *wound* which fractured his left leg and required amputation; *captured*; exchanged from West's Buildings Hospital 17 November 1863.

Ayres, John T. (4th Cpl.): (20); machinist; received a shell *wound* to his left ankle and arm and *captured*; exchanged from West's Buildings Hospital 27 September 1863.

Traylor, Thomas E. (5th Cpl.): (19); machinist; *wounded* in left leg and left knee.

Pleasants, John (Drummer): Enl. 18 May 1863; deserted July or August 1863.

Wildt, Lewis (Drummer): Enl. 18 May 1863, (16 in 1865); harness maker; deserted in July or August 1863 and went to Richmond. Found there by the Federals on 26 April 1865 serving in the local reserves.

Boler, George W.: Enl. 1 August 1862 at Orange, Virginia.

Chappell, C.H.: Enl. 23 Jaunary 1863 in Halifax County; *wounded.*

Clark, Samuel: Enl. 22 August 1862; re-enlisted 23 January 1863 in Halifax County; suffered a scalp *wound* and *captured*; exchanged 20 or 21 February 1865.

Duke, Henry T.: Enl. 17 June 1862.

Eubank, George W.: (30); carpenter; "deserted in the face of the enemy at Gettysburg." Federal records do not mention him, however; probably deserted during the march to the field on 3 July and made his escape.

Fignor, Alphonzo A.: (19); painter.

Griffin, E.J.: Enl. 10 February 1863; *shot* in the arm and knee and *captured*; died of tetanus 18 July 1863.

Ish, Milton A.: Enl. 11 June 1861 at Fairfax, Virginia.

Joy, George: Enl. 27 February 1863; *wounded.*

Lester, Thomas P.: Enl. 20 February 1863 in Halifax County.

Loving, Edwin B.: (23); clerk.

McLaughlan, Hugh: Enl. 15 May 1863; *wounded* and *captured*; died of his wounds.

McLear, James M.: Enl. 31 January 1863 in Fluvanna County.

Meredith, Richard O.: (28); carpenter; *wounded* and *captured*; exchanged from DeCamp Hospital 27 September 1863.

Minor, Andrew T.: (19); carpenter; AWOL 27 July through 14 August 1863.

Neal, S.S.: Enl. 23 January 1863 in Halifax County; (30 in 1863); *shot* in the left portion of the abdomen and *captured*; exchanged from West's Buildings Hospital 27 September 1863.

Polak, Jacob: (23); clerk; *wounded* during the attack.

Robinson, James E.: (18); machinist; *captured*; released from Point Lookout 17 June 1865.

Shoemaker, George W.: (19); *shot* in the right elbow.

Smith, William P.: (23); carpenter.

Taliaferro, Edwin: Enl. 29 April 1861 in Henrico County; (18); the company reported him missing in action; there are no further records concerning him; probably *killed.*

Taliaferro, William C., Jr.: (21); bricklayer; captured; exchanged 20 or 21 February 1865.

Wills, Charles A.: Enl. 9 February 1863 at Liberty, Bedford County; *wounded.*

Wingo, William W.: Enl. 25 May 1861 in Henrico County; (46); plasterer.

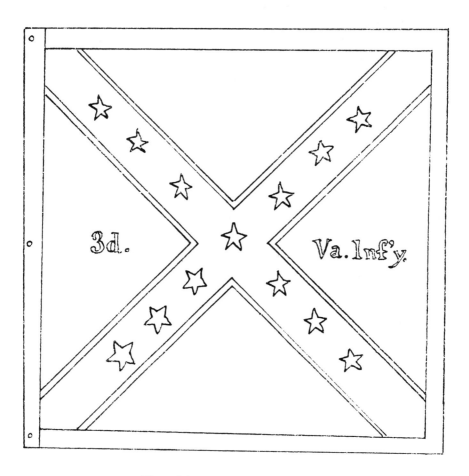

Flag of the 3rd Virginia Infantry,
captured on 3 July 1863
time and captor not known

3rd Virginia Volunteer Infantry Regiment

Organized at Portsmouth 1856-1857 from the volunteer companies attached to the 7th Rgt. (Norfolk County) Va. Militia. Contained seven companies before April 1861. Ordered into service by the Governor 20 April 1861. Consisted of ten companies by mid-June 1861 but six of these were removed and new ones added so by the end of 1861 the regiment again numbered ten companies. The regiment was organized 3 May 1861, accepted into Confederate service 2 July 1861, and reorganized 27 April 1862.

The following roster was obtained from April/June 1863 company muster rolls captioned 30 June 1863, Chambersburg, Pennsylvania. The April/June muster roll of Company G failed to provide both the date and station of its muster but it is undoubtedly the same as the other nine companies of the regiment.

All companies reported the status of their clothing, military appearance, arms, accouterments, discipline, and instruction as "good."

Field and Staff

Mayo, Joseph, Jr. (Colonel): Born 5 February 1834; lawyer; married Mary Armistead Tyler; graduated VMI 1852; appointed Lt. Col. 6 November 1861; appointed Colonel 27 April 1862.

Callcote, Alexander Daniel (Lt. Col.): Born Isle of Wight County, Va. June 1830; graduated VMI 1851; teacher and farmer; married Mrs. Harriet Hancock Land; enl. 23 June 1861 at Smithfield as Captain of 1st Company "K"; *killed.*

Pryor, William Hamlin (Major): Born 25 September 1827; graduated VMI 1848; married to Margaret H. Pryor; enl. 13 November 1861 at Camp Pemberton as a 2nd Lt. in Company "C."

Stewart, John R. (1st Lt., Adjutant): Enl. 20 April 1861 at Portsmouth; (25); sheriff; *wounded* through the buttocks.

Tabb, Thomas (Capt., AQM): Enl. 13 May 1861 at Hampton as a 2nd Lt. in Captain Charles L. Smith's company of artillery ("Washington Artillery") Virginia Volunteers which became 1st Company "K," 32nd Virginia Infantry; appointed Captain and AQM 23 June 1862 to report to 3rd Virginia Infantry.

White, John R. (Capt., ACS): Enl. 20 April 1861 at Portsmouth; (34); lumber getter; appointed regimental ACS 19 November 1862.

Jones, Isaac N. (1st Lt., AACS): Detailed from Company "I"; enl. 23 June 1861 at Smithfield; resided at Smithfield; (24 in 1865).

Mayo, Thomas P. (Surgeon): Appointed Surgeon 18 November 1862; captured 4 July; exchanged from Fort McHenry 21 November 1863.

Sykes, Joseph H.M. (Asst. Surgeon): Enl. 11 May 1861 at Jerusalem; (26); physician; appointed Assistant Surgeon 18 November 1862.

Hume, Thomas, Jr. (Chaplain): Appointed Chaplain 11 July 1861.

Blackwell, Robert G. (Commissary Sgt.): Detailed from Company "I"; enl. 23 June 1861 at Smithfield; (19); clerk.

Forward, John W. ("Waddy") (Orderly for Col. Mayo): Detailed from Company "A"; enl. 26 May 1861 at Portsmouth; (19); student.

Ghent, Emmet M. (3rd Cpl.) (Medical Department): Detailed from Company "C"; enl. 23 May 1861 at Dinwiddie Court House; (18); student; captured while serving as a nurse at Gettysburg; died at Point Lookout 18 September 1863.

Crocker, Joel (QM's Department): Detailed from Company "I"; enl. 25 February 1862 at Isle of Wight Court House.

Color Guard

Murden, Joshua (Color Bearer): Detailed from Company "B"; enl. 14 June 1861 at Portsmouth; (25); mechanic, *killed* during the cannonade.

Company "A" ("Dismal Swamp Rangers")

This company enlisted 20 April 1861 at Portsmouth for one year, was mustered into state service at the Naval Hospital, Portsmouth 30 June 1861, re-enlisted 22 March or 20 April 1862 for two years, and re-enlisted 1 March 1864 for the war.

Hodges, Thomas M. (Captain): (26); farmer; *shot* in the thigh.

Gary, Samuel W. (Sr. 2nd Lt.): (19); clerk; *captured*; exchanged 21 October 1864.

White, Osceola T. (Jr. 2nd Lt.): Enl. 26 May 1861; (17); student; received a slight *contusion* of the scalp during the attack.

Hodges, Nathan H. (1st Sgt.): (32); carpenter; *captured*; died at Point Lookout 18 January 1864.

Miller, Patrick H. (2nd Sgt.): (26); laborer; received a gunshot fracture of his left shoulder, the ball lodging in the *wound*, and *captured*; exchanged from West's Buildings Hospital 17 November 1863.

Cherry, John H. (3rd Sgt.): (35); overseer.

Barter, Thomas B. (5th Sgt.): (33); farmer.

Herring, Gideon L. (1st Cpl.): Enl. 26 May 1861; (18); farmer.

Hodges, Patrick H. (2nd Cpl.): (22); laborer.

Cherry, James E. (3rd Cpl.): (23); farmer.

Kilgore, Mallory (4th Cpl.): (20); farmer; *wounded.*

Barnes, Edward: (22), farmer.

Benton, Joseph J.: Enl. 26 May 1861; (26); overseer.

Bright, Thomas J.: Enl. 30 June 1861 at Camp Huger; *captured*; released on oath from Point Lookout 23 February 1864.

Creekmore, Malachi: Enl. 1 June 1861; (19); blacksmith.

Culpepper, Miles: (30); laborer.

Duke, Gideon: (22); farmer.

Fentress, Batson: (22); farmer.

Freidlin, John: Enl. 7 May 1861; (26); laborer.

Gallop, John, Jr.: (21); laborer.

Godfrey, Mark: Enl. 7 May 1861; (19); farmer.

Hodges, Josiah: Enl. 26 May 1861; (22); farmer.

Jolliff, John W.: (27); farmer.

Liverman, Hardy A.: (23); laborer; *shot* in the right knee and *captured*; exchanged from DeCamp Hospital 16 September 1863.

Nash, William H.: (32); farmer.
Taylor, John: (33); laborer.
White, Edward P.: (26); clerk.

Company "B" ("Virginia Rifles")

This company enlisted 20 April 1861 at Portsmouth and was reorganized 26 April 1862.

Hutchins, George W. (Captain): (23); mechanic.
Gleason, Thomas H. (2nd Lt.): (25); mechanic; *captured*; exchanged 22 March 1865.
Guy, Robert F. (3rd Lt.): (21); mechanic; *wounded* (right shoulder torn off); died 4 July and buried at Pickett's Hospital at Bream's Mill on the hill; disinterred to Richmond 3 August 1872 with 33 others in three large boxes labeled "P Curns."
Brownley, Daniel T. (1st Sgt.): (20); mechanic.
Hutchins, Robert A. (2nd Sgt.): (19); mechanic; *captured*; released on oath from Point Lookout 22 January 1864.
Lumber, William H. (4th Sgt.): (20); mechanic; *captured*; released on oath from Point Lookout 14 March 1864.
Leggett, Walter M. (5th Sgt.): (24); mechanic.
Broughton, Joseph E. (Cpl.): (18); mechanic.
Morrissett, Peter B. (Cpl.): (22); mechanic.
Mouring, William H. (Cpl.): (22); mechanic; *captured*; released on oath from Point Lookout 22 January 1864.
Archer, James H. (Musician): (20); mechanic.
Anderson, Charles E.: (20); mechanic, *wounded* and *captured*; released on oath from Point Lookout 28 March 1864.
Bowen, Hine: (24); mechanic.
Butler, Hezekiah: Enl. 24 April 1863 in Nansemond County.
Butler, John: (21); mechanic.
Cutherell, Arthur: Enl. 24 May 1861 at Gosport Navy Yard; (23); butcher; received a flesh *wound* in the right shoulder.
Fiske, William A.: Enl. 17 September 1861.
Herbert, William E.: Enl. 26 May 1861; (23); carpenter; *captured*; exchanged from Point Lookout 20 or 21 February 1865.
Host, George: Enl. 29 May 1861 at Gosport Navy Yard; (24); brick mason; deserted near Gettysburg 3 July, probably while on the march to the battlefield.
Morrisett, William: (20); mechanic.
Powell, Benjamin F.: Enl. 20 June 1861; (24); mechanic.
White, Charles: Enl. 16 September 1861.
Wilkins, William: (21); mechanic.

Company "C" ("Dinwiddie Grays")

This company was organized in April 1861 and enlisted 23 May 1861 at Dinwiddie Court House, Dinwiddie County. It was reorganized 27 April 1862.

Scott, Thomas B. (1st Lt.): (21); farmer.
Brown, James E. (Sr. 2nd Lt.): (20); farmer; *wounded*.
Jackson, Thomas B. (Jr. 2nd Lt.): Enl. 18 March 1862 at Camp Pemberton; *shot* in both thighs and *captured*; exchanged 22 March 1865.
Gray, William G. (1st Sgt.): (28); farmer; *wounded* (fractured right hip) and *captured*; died at Camp Letterman Hospital 6 October 1863 and buried in Section 9, Grave #5 of that hospital's cemetery; disinterred to Richmond 13 June 1872 in Box #77.
Haddon, Joseph F. (2nd Sgt.): (20); farmer.
Jones, William F. (1st Cpl.): (18); student.
Keys, Edmond T. (2nd Cpl.): (22); farmer; *wounded*.
Brooks, Ira W.: (34); farmer.
Crowder, William M.: (18); farmer; *captured*; exchanged from Point Lookout 20 or 21 February 1865.
Cummings, Caleb H.: (25); farmer.
Franklin, Benfamin E.: (21); clerk.
Jackson, George T.: Enl. 9 August 1962 at Richmond; *shot* in the lung and thigh and *captured*; exchanged from DeCamp Hospital 27 September 1863.
Keys, Alexander: (18); farmer.
Meredith, Lucas L.: (19); farmer.
Mitchell, Daniel B.: (29); farmer; *wounded* in the heel and *captured*; exchanged from DeCamp Hospital 8 September 1863.
Mitchell, Robert F.: (18); farmer.
Puryear, Mathew J.: Enl. 1 July 1861 at Camp Cook; *wounded*.
Scott, Walter or William F.A.: Enl. 18 March 1862 at Camp Pemberton; *captured*; died at Point Lookout of chronic diarrhea 23 January 1864.
Vaughan, Alexander: Enl. 1 April 1863 at Kinston, North Carolina as a substitute; deserted 4 July; captured at Gettysburg 5 July; exchanged from Point Lookout 28 December 1863.
Wells, William J.: (25); mechanic.
Westmoreland, David P.: Enl. 10 November 1861 at Camp Pemberton.
Williams, Richard H.: (21); farmer.
Williamson, Williams S.: (28); farmer.

Company "D" ("Southhampton Greys")

This company enlisted 3 May 1861 at Jerusalem (now Courtland), Southampton County, Virginia; was mustered into state service 3 June 1861 at Berlin; and was reorganized 17 April 1862.

Gay, Littleton A. (1st Lt.): (21).
White, William W. (Sr. 2nd Lt.): Enl. 1 August 1861 at Camp Cook; *captured*; released from Fort Delaware 12 June 1865.

Drewry, Samuel T. (Jr. 2nd Lt.): (21); *captured*; exchanged from Johnson's Island, Ohio 24 February 1865.

Applewhite, Benjamin F. (2nd Sgt.): (34).

Clayton, Julian T. (3rd Sgt.): (18); *killed.*

Everett, Richard B.L. (4th Sgt.): (24); *killed.*

Holmes, John W. (5th Sgt.): (23).

Edwards, Joseph R. (1st Cpl.): Enl. 16 September 1861 at Camp Cook; *killed.*

Darden, John Wilson (2nd Cpl.): (19).

Stephenson, John B. (3rd Cpl.): (21).

Joyner, Robert T. (4th Cpl.): (24).

Applewhite, George A.: Enl. 6 April 1862 at Camp Pemberton.

Arnold, Richard W.: (18).

Bailey, George H.: (26); *killed.*

Barden, William D.: (22).

Barham, George A.: Enl. 1 April 1862 at Camp Pemberton.

Barrett, John H.: (19); *wounded.*

Branch, John H.: (24); *killed.*

Branch, Patrick B.: (26).

Clary, Thomas L.: (20).

Clayton, James K.P.: (18).

Clayton, John A.: (20); *captured*; exchanged 18 February 1865.

Cogsdale, James: Enl. 25 May 1862 at Camp Pemberton.

Crichton, Robert H.: Enl. 3 March 1862 at Camp Pemberton.

Derby, Alonzo T.: (21).

Derby, Junius N.: (18).

Drewry, Joseph H.: (22).

Drewry, Robert A.: (19); *captured*; exchanged 15 November 1864.

Edwards, William E.: Enl. 26 September 1861 at Camp Cook.

Felts, Benjamin F.: (25).

Flythe, Thomas J.: (24).

Gardner, Charles S.: (18); *captured*; died at Point Lookout 23 December 1863.

Gardner, Ezra J.: (24).

Gardner, William J.: Enl. 26 March 1862 at Camp Pemberton; *killed.*

Harcum, George C.: (27).

Hundley, Benjamin F.: (19).

Jelks, James K.: (25); *killed.*

Joyner, John H.: (23); *captured*; exchanged 15 November 1864.

Joyner Matthew: (24).

Laine, James C.: (26).

Pittman, William H.: (18).

Rawls, George T.: (22).

Rowe, Jason E.: (18).

Simmons, Benjamin O.: Enl. 1 April 1862 at Camp Pemberton.

Spivey, James F.: (30).

Spivey, Jeremiah J.: (22).

Stewart, George W.: (32).

Taylor, John R.: (32).

Turner, John W.: Enl. 26 September 1861 at Camp Cook.

Vick, William R.: (26).

Wells, Thomas R.: (21).

White, James T.: (21); *captured*; exchanged 20 or 21 February 1865.

Williams, George W.: (19).

Williams, Henry K.: (21).

Williams, John L.: Enl. 26 March 1862 at Camp Pemberton.

Williams, Robert N.: (28).

Company "E" ("Cockade Rifles")

This company enlisted 20 April 1861 at Petersburg, Virginia; was mustered into state service 4 May 1861 at Petersburg; and was reorganized in April 1862.

Bond, Antrobus (Captain): (30).

Birdsong, Solomon T. (1st Lt.): (23); *wounded.*

Fraetas, Canazio (2nd Lt.): (30).

Livesay, Turner T. (1st Sgt.): (22).

Nowlan, Thomas B. (3rd Sgt.): (25).

Blankenship, Joseph R. (4th Sgt.): (24).

Sheppard, William A. (1st Cpl.): (30).

Fields, George M. (2nd Cpl.): (18); *captured*; exchanged 20 or 21 February 1865.

Bryant, Samuel H. (4th Cpl.): (23).

Booth, Richard H.: (30).

Buck, William M.: Enl. 9 May 1861 at Fort Powhatan; (23).

Burcher, Robert E.: (25).

Burke, Michael: (28).

Caughlan, William T.: (16); printer; deserted and captured 5 July; joined U.S. 3rd Maryland Cavalry 5 September 1863.

Charles, Edward H.: (39).

Cox, Evelton M.: (19).

Crowder, Stephen L.: (18); probably *wounded*; *captured*; exchanged 1 August 1863.

Fuqua, George H.: (35).

Fuqua, James W.: (27).

Jones, John F.: Enl. 14 March 1862 at Camp Pemberton.

Lamb, Theoderick L.: (22).

Minetree, William D.: (23); *captured*; exchanged 20 or 21 February 1865.

Parsons, William H.: (19).

Reaney, John P.: (22).

Wells, Charles E.: (22).

Wells, Edward T.: Enl. 9 May 1861 at Fort Powhatan; (19).

Winfree, George A.: (26).

Wynne, Irwin J.: (32).

Young, Alexander J.: (27).

Company "F" ("Nansemond Rangers")

This company enlisted 21 April 1861 at Hargrove's Tavern, Nansemond County. The unit was mustered into state service 22 May 1861 and was temporarily attached to the 1st Regiment Louisiana Infantry 1 June 1861 from which it was subsequently assigned to the 3rd Virginia Infantry.

Extreme right company of the regiment during the attack.

Phillips, C. Crawley (Captain): (26); professor; *killed.*

Gomer, Azra P. (1st Lt.): Enl. 22 June 1861 at Godwin's Point; (25); clerk; *wounded* in the left thigh during the attack at the stone wall (leg amputated about 5 July at the upper third of the thigh); captured in Pickett's Division Hospital 5 July; exchanged from Point Lookout 6 March 1864.

Arthur, Patrick H. (2nd Lt.): (21); farmer; *killed* during the cannonade.

Arthur, John C. (3rd lt.): (23); farmer; badly *wounded* during the cannonade; died 3 July probably at Pickett's Division Hospital; mother was Mrs. Charlotte Arthur; Lt. Arthur had no wife, child or father at the time of his death.

Taylor, James D. (1st Sgt.): (24); farmer.

Emmerson, James M. (2nd Sgt.): (20); clerk.

Higginbotham, Alexander (1st Cpl.): (41); farmer.

Lancaster, William Thomas (2nd Cpl.): (22); farmer; *shot* in the left hand (little and index fingers amputated) and right side of the head (temporal parietal spheroid, and frontal bones fractured); captured; died 11 August 1863 at West's Buildings Hospital.

Ames, Benjamin Franklin (3rd Cpl.): (28); farmer; *wounded* in the abdomen; died at Pickett's Division Hospital 3 July; disinterred to Richmond 3 August 1872 with 33 others in three large boxes marked "P Curns."

Richardson, John W. (Musician): (21); farmer; captured while serving as a hospital nurse at Gettysburg; exchanged from Point Lookout 20 or 21 February 1865.

Batten, Junius: Enl. 18 June 1861 at Godwin's Point; (18); farmer.

Cross, Alfred B.: (22); farmer.

DeGaribody, John: (28); farmer; *captured*; exchanged from Point Lookout 20 or 21 February 1865.

Dunford, Robert J.: (18); farmer; *killed.*

Eason, George F.: (25); mechanic.

Holland, Matthew: Enl. 18 June 1861 at Godwin's Point; (18); farmer; captured while serving as a nurse at Gettysburg; died of chronic diarrhea at Point Lookout 2 February 1865.

Holland, Richard Thomas: (21); farmer; *wounded* and *captured*; exchanged from Point Lookout 20 or 21 February 1865.

James, Cornelius E.: (18); farmer; *shot* in the left arm and *captured*; exchanged from Chester Hospital 17 August 1863.

Jordan, John Chappel: (19); student; *hit* by a round shot in the thigh; died of erysipelas 12 July 1863 at Pickett's Division Hospital and buried at Bream's

Mill above Myers' house at the side of a fence; disinterred to Richmond 3 August 1872 with 33 others in three large boxes marked "P Curns."

Lancaster, Joseph O.: (18); clerk.

Lawrence, Albert: (21); farmer.

Murray, Elisha: (28); farmer; suffered a *contusion* of the shoulder; died of tetanus 21 July 1863 probably at Pickett's Division Hospital.

Phelps, William A.: (20); farmer; *captured*; exchanged from Point Lookout 20 or 21 February 1865.

Riddick, Robert E.: Enl. 22 June 1861 at Godwin's Point; (18); farmer.

Company "G" ("Rough and Ready Guards")

This company enlisted 11 May 1861 at Jerusalem (now Courtland), Southampton County, Virginia. The unit was mustered into state service 19 June 1861 and was reorganized 27 April 1862.

Francis, Nathaniel T. (1st Lt.): Enl. 3 May 1861; (27); farmer.

Gilliam, Joseph S. (Sr. 2nd Lt.): (19); student; VMI class of 1863.

McLemore, Benjamin F. (1st Sgt.): (20); clerk, *captured*; exchanged from Point Lookout 30 April 1864.

Pond, Everett M. (2nd Sgt.): Enl. 15 May 1861; (20); laborer.

Reed, David C. (3rd Sgt.): (21); apprentice carpenter.

Harrison, Benjamin F. (4th Sgt.): Enl. 15 May 1862 at Chickahominy, Virginia.

Chitty, William L. (1st Cpl.): laborer.

Pope, Joseph W. (2nd Cpl.): Enl. 3 June 1861; (23); farmer; *wounded* in the shoulder and back; died at Pickett's Division Hospital 11 July 1863 and buried at Bream's Mill above Myers' house at the side of a fence; disinterred to Richmond 3 August 1872 with 33 others in three large boxes marked "P Curns."

Marks, Lewis (3rd Cpl.): (27).

Fuller, John J.W. (4th Cpl.): Enl. 21 May 1861; (18); clerk; *captured*; exchanged 20 or 21 February 1865.

Conley, James T.: Enl. 21 May 1861; (23); overseer.

Cornelius, Thomas R.: Enl. 21 May 1861; (21); laborer.

Ellis, Richard P.: Enl. 21 May 1861; (29); overseer.

Felts, Richard A.: (20); farmer; *killed.*

Ferguson, Benjamin: Enl. 22 May 1861; (18); laborer.

Ferguson, Colin J.: Enl. 15 March 1862 at Camp Cook.

Gray, Benjamin J.: Enl. 10 June 1861 ; (30); blacksmith.

Gray, Joseph H.: Enl. 1 June 1861.

Gray, Mills R.: Enl. 6 May 1862 at Camp Pemberton.

Gray, Thomas H.: Enl. 15 March 1862 at Camp Pemberton.

Harris, Claiborne A.: (19); apprentice carpenter.

Harrison, Andrew J.: Enl. 7 January 1863 at Fredericksburg.

Hill, Sion: (25); laborer.

Holland, George W.: (19); laborer.

Ivey, Benjamin B.: Enl. 15 March 1862.

Johnson, Jesse: (28); farmer.

Jones, James R.: Enl. 15 March 1862.

Kirkland, Joseph J.: Enl. 15 March 1862.

Knight, Charles: Enl. 3 May 1861; (24); overseer.

Myrick, Henry L.: (24); laborer.

Myrick, Nathaniel T.: Enl. 15 March 1862.

Norsworthy, John S.: Enl. 20 July 1861 at Vellines Farm; received a flesh *wound* in his right leg and *captured*; exchanged from Point Lookout 6 March 1864.

Peete, Thomas E.: Enl. 21 May 1861; (18); overseer.

Pope, Herod: Enl. 20 February 1862 at Camp Pemberton.

Pulley, Benjamin: Enl. 15 March 1862.

Simmons, George H.: (30); laborer.

Simmons, Peter: (18); laborer; *captured*; died of asthma at Fort Delaware 7 September 1863; buried at Finns Point, N.J.

Sturdivant, George W.: (20); overseer.

Turner, George W.: (30); farmer.

Turner, John F.: Enl. 15 May 1861; (21); laborer.

Turner, Joseph: (18); laborer.

Vick, Davis: (27); laborer.

West, Henry G.: (24); laborer; received a shell *wound* in the lung and subsequently captured; died 16 July 1863 probably at Pickett's Division Hospital.

Company "H" ("Portsmouth National Greys")

This company enlisted 20 April 1861 at Portsmouth and was reorganized 27 April 1862.

Whitehead, John Dudley (Captain): (26); auctioneer; *captured*; released at Fortress Monroe 3 February 1865.

Mitchell, George William (1st Lt.): (25); block maker; *killed.*

Fulford, John C. (1st Sgt.): Enl. 18 June 1861 at Gosport Navy Yard; carpenter.

Smith, James (2nd Sgt.): Enl. 1 July 1861 at Gosport Navy Yard.

Tynan, Francis T. (3rd Sgt.): Enl. 20 May 1861 at Gosport Navy Yard; (22); stonemason.

Mahone, Daniel H. (Cpl.): Enl. 30 April 1861 at Gosport Navy Yard; (20); bricklayer.

Mahone, Willmore W. (Cpl.): Enl. 30 April 1861 at Gosport Havy Yard; (19); bricklayer.

O'Donnell, Patrick C. (Cpl.): (22); sparmaker.

Tee, John C. (Cpl.): (20); carpenter; *captured*; exchanged from Point Lookout 14 or 15 February 1865.

Foiles, Henry P. (Musician): Enl. 16 May 1861 at Gosport Navy Yard; painter.

Ashton, Edgar E.: (21); clerk.

Barrett, George W.: Enl. 8 May 1861 at Gosport Navy Yard; (25); carpenter.

Barrett, Solomon H.: Enl. 8 May 1861 at Gosport Navy Yard; (20); carpenter.

Beeks, William H.: Enl. 21 May 1861 at Gosport Navy Yard; (19); tailor.

Blackwell, Joseph D.: Enl. 25 May 1863 at Dublin Depot.

Culpepper, David: Enl. 17 June 1861 at Gosport Navy Yard; (35); oysterman.

Etheridge, John E.: (35); cabinet maker.

Goodson, Calvin: Enl. 30 April 1861 at Gosport Navy Yard; (26); ship carpenter; *shot* in the knee and *captured*; exchanged from West's Buildings Hospital 27 September 1863.

Hanrahan, George T.: Enl. 4 May 1861 at Gosport Navy Yard; (18); brick mason.

Hickman, Josiah T.: Enl. 24 June 1861 at Gosport Navy Yard; (18); clerk.

Hofler, Elias: Enl. 30 May 1861 at Gosport Navy Yard; (29); carpenter.

Howard, James T.B.: Enl. 18 June 1861 at Gosport Navy Yard; (19); car builder; *captured*; exchanged from Point Lookout 20 or 21 February 1865.

Jenkins, Miles: (28); cigar maker.

Keeling, William H.: (22); laborer; *wounded* in the left thigh and *captured*; exchanged from West's Buildings Hospital 24 August 1863.

Kirby, Johnson: (32); laborer.

Lash, James K.P.: Enl. 8 July 1861 at Gosport Navy Yard.

Loomis, James M.: Enl. 30 April 1861 at Gosport Navy Yard; (18); laborer.

Mahoney, William H.: (22); sailmaker.

McFarland, William P.: (28); ship carpenter.

Monserrate, Michael D.: (23); barber.

Stell, Clark E.: Enl. 1 April 1863 at Richmond.

Stokes, Edward S.: Enl. 30 April 1861 at Gosport Navy Yard; (18); no trade.

West, William E.: Enl. 30 April 1861 at Gosport Navy Yard; (27); tailor.

<u>Second Company "I" ("James River Artillery")</u>

Formerly First Company "K" prior to the 1862 reorganization, this company enlisted and was mustered 23 June 1861 at Smithfield, Isle of Wight County, Virginia. Detached 5 August 1861 to serve the guns at Fort Boykin, Burwell's Bay, Isle of Wight County. Detached and ordered to Barrett's Point Battery, Nansemond County in November 1861.

Delk, Owighton G. (Captain): (23); merchant.

Wrenn, Fenton Eley (Sr. 2nd Lt.): Enl. 8 July 1861; (21); student; *killed* during the repulse.

Jones, Jacob (Jr. 2nd Lt.): (19); clerk.

Chapman, Robert J. (1st Sgt.): Enl. 29 June 1861; (19); clerk; *captured*; died at Point Lookout 31 July 1864.

Stringfield, Chapman J. (4th Sgt.): (19); student.

Dews, Edwin (5th Sgt.): (20); tailor; *captured*; died at Point Lookout 7 September 1864.

Goodson, Thomas N. (1st Cpl.): Enl. 8 April 1862 at Barrett's Point.

Hall, John (3rd Cpl.): Enl. 22 July 1861 at Fort Boykin; (25); farmer; *captured*; died at Point Lookout 25 February 1864.

Jones, Abraham (4th Cpl.): (22); carpenter; received a flesh *wound* in the left thigh and *captured*; exchanged from West's Buildings Hospital 27 September 1863.

Adams, George W.: (21); student.

Atkins, James H.: Enl. 8 March 1863 at Petersburg.

Atkins, Moses: Enl. 12 August 1861 at Fort Boykin; (27); farmer; died of disease at Winchester, Virginia 14 July 1863.

Batten, Archer J.: Enl. 2 August 1861 at Fort Boykin; (21); farmer; *killed.*

Batten, Edmond: (18); oysterman.

Burns, William: (21); oysterman.

Corran, Edgar: Enl. 10 March 1862 at Barrett's Point; *captured*; died of remittent fever at Point Lookout 15 July 1864.

Coulter, George: Enl. 25 February 1862 at Isle of Wight Court House; *killed.*

Coulter, James: Enl. 25 February 1862 at Isle of Wight Court House.

Coulter, John: Enl. 2 February 1863 at Chesterfield; *wounded.*

Delk, Sidney E.: (18); farmer.

Edwards, Benjamin F.: (22); farmer.

Edwards, Benjamin K.: (22); overseer.

Edwards, Charles: (22); overseer.

Edwards, James: (21 in 1865); enl. 25 February 1862 at Isle of Wight Court House; *captured*; died of chronic diarrhea at Point Lookout 19 February 1865.

Edwards, Miles: Enl. 23 June 1861; (22); farmer.

Edwards, Patrick H.: Enl. 23 June 1861; (23); farmer; *shot* in the chest and *captured*; exchanged from DeCamp Hospital 28 August 1863.

Eley, James M: Enl. 25 February 1862 at Isle of Wight Court House.

Eley, John M.: Enl. 25 February 1862 at Isle of Wight Court House.

Flake, Joseph D.: (19); farmer.

Fulgham, Mills L.: Enl. 25 February 1862 at Isle of Wight Court House.

Gale, William H.: Enl. 25 February 1862 at Isle of Wight Court House.

Gray, James L.: Enl. 8 July 1861; (23); clerk.

Gray, Lubertus: (19); farmer; *captured*; joined U.S. service at Point Lookout 2 February 1864.

Gwaltney, Benjamin L.W.: (19); gunsmith; *shot* in the right little finger and *captured*; died of chronic diarrhea and scurvy at Point Lookout 6 March 1865.

Gwaltney, John T.: Enl. 1 August 1861 at Fort Boykin; (22); hireling.

Holland, Malory M.: Enl. 25 February 1862 at Isle of Wight Court House.

Jones, James M.: Enl. 6 August 1861 at Fort Boykin; (18); farmer.

Jones, Junius W.: Enl. 1 April 1863 at Kinston, North Carolina.

Little, Adoniram J.: Enl. 6 August 1861 at Fort Boykin; (18); farmer.

Moore, James G.: Enl. 22 July 1861 at Fort Boykin; (33); waterman.

Parkerson, George W.: Enl. 18 July 1861 at Fort Boykin; (28); farmer; *captured*; died at Point Lookout 20 August 1864.

Parkerson, Mills D.: Enl. 11 July 1861 at Fort Boykin; (25); farmer; *killed.*

Schofield, Addison H.: (20); farmer.

Thomas, William H.J.: Enl. 25 February 1862 at Isle of Wight Court House.

Turner, Benjamin F.: Enl. 8 July 1861.

Vellines, John A.: (21); farmer; *wounded* in the left groin and face (fractured inferior maxilla); died 26 July 1863 probably at Pickett's Division Hospital.

Wiley, John W.: (19); farmer.

Williford, Richard H.: Enl. 5 September 1861 at Fort Boykin.

Williford, Samuel: Enl. 5 August 1861 at Fort Boykin; (19); factory hand; *captured*; exchanged from Point Lookout 14 or 15 February 1865.

Wrenn, Virginius: (19); student; *wounded* in the left shoulder and head and *captured*; exchanged from Chester Hospital 20 August 1863.

Second Company "K" ("Halifax Rifles"; also "High Hill Rifles")

Formerly Company "L" prior to the reorganization of the regiment in 1862, this company was organized in August 1861 and enlisted 28 October 1861 at Halifax Court House, Halifax County, Virginia. The unit was mustered 11 November 1861, attached to the 3rd Virginia Infantry 5 December 1861, and reorganized in 1862.

Tuck, Richard H. (Captain): *Wounded.*

Cage, Fielding (1st Lt.): (29 in 1865); *captured*; exchanged 20 March 1864.

Tuck, William M. (2nd Lt.): *Captured*; released from Fort Delaware 12 June 1865.

Tuck, Paul P. (1st Sgt.): *Wounded* in the shoulder and *captured*; exchanged from Chester Hospital 20 August 1863.

Tuck, Phaltile W.S. (2nd Sgt.):

Throckmorton, Branch S. (3rd Sgt.):

Allen, John A. (4th Sgt.): *Wounded* in the left shoulder and right knee and *captured*; serving as a nurse at Camp Letterman Hospital 10 August 1863; escaped from Camp Letterman during the night of 16 September 1863; recaptured in the moutains 36 hours later; exchanged from Point Lookout 14 or 15 February 1865.

Murray, William H. (5th Sgt.): Enl. 6 February 1862; *shot* in the shoulder and *captured*; exchanged from Point Lookout 20 or 21 February 1865.

West, Napoleon B. (1st Cpl.): *Captured*; died of chronic diarrhea at Point Lookout 2 March 1864.

Cage, Thomas W. (2nd Cpl.):

Tuck, Detrien P. (3rd Cpl.):

Throckmorton, Andrew J. (4th Cpl.): Enl. 6 February 1862.

Boyd, Charles F.: Farmer; deserted at Chester Gap, Virginia 21 July 1863.

Bray, Richard:

Bray, William J.:

Chaiffin, James E.: Enl. 6 February 1862.

Conner, Benjamin E.:

Conner, James R.: Enl. 6 February 1862.

Davenport, John W.: *Captured*; exchanged from Point Lookout 20 or 21 February 1865.

DeJarnette, Albert: Enl. 15 January 1862.

Elliott, Richard T.: Enl. 6 February 1862.

Glasscock, Ransome B.: Enl. 6 February 1862; probably *wounded*; *captured*; exchanged from Fort Delaware 31 July 1863.

Guthrey, Charles:

Hall, Howson M.: Enl. 15 January 1862; *captured*; died of chronic diarrhea and buried at sea 9 November 1864 enroute to exchange at Savannah, Georgia.

James, Robert R.: Enl. 7 April 1862.

King, Emanuel:

Long, Henry C.: Enl. 15 January 1862.

McCann, Joseph J.: Enl. 1 March 1863 at Petersburg.

McKinney, George W.: Enl. 6 February 1862; *died of wounds* 3 July probably at Pickett's Division Hospital.

Mealler, William L.: *Captured*; died of chronic diarrhea at Point Lookout 26 November 1863.

Merrell, John:

Morriss, Zachariah T.: Enl. 6 February 1862.

Pool, William A.:

Rickman, Ethelbert T.: Enl. 6 February 1862.

Thomas, John William: *Wounded*; died of wounds 3 July 1863 probably at Pickett's Division Hospital.

Tuck, Phaltile R.T.: Enl. 6 February 1862.

Vaughan, Richard:

Wier, John A.: Received a flesh *wound* in the knee inflicted by a shell burst; erysipelas developed and the lower third of his left femur was amputated; tetanus subsequently developed and he died at Pickett's Division Hospital 8 July 1863; buried at Bream's Mill above Myers' house at the side of a fence; disinterred to Richmond 3 August 1872 with 33 others in three large boxes marked "P Curns."

Wilbourn, John P.:

Wilkerson, Richard F.:

Wilkerson, Robert C.: Enl. 6 February 1862; *captured*; exchanged from Point Lookout 20 or 21 February 1865.

Williard, Humbleton C.: Enl. 6 February 1862.

Wilson, William W.:

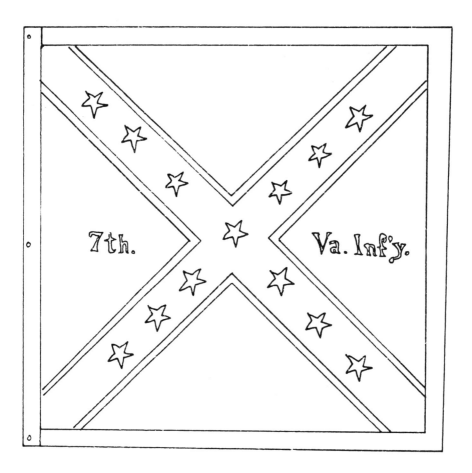

**Flag of the 7th Virginia Infantry
captured near the stone wall
by the 82nd New York Infantry**

7th Virginia Volunteer Infantry Regiment

Organized in May 1861, this regiment was accepted into Confederate Service 1 July 1861 for twelve months and was reorganized 26 April 1862. Company "E," 1st Virginia Infantry, was transferred to become Company "H" of this regiment 22 April 1862. Company "E," 1st Virginia, was disbanded about 27 April 1862, and Company "H," 7th Virginia ("Washington Volunteers"), being citizens of the District of Columbia, was disbanded as non-residents of the state about 16 May 1862. The regiment had only nine companies at Gettysburg.

The following roster was obtained from company April/June 1863 muster rolls captioned 30 June 1863 near Chambersburg, Pennsylvania. Rolls for Companies "A" and "F" were captioned 12 and 13 August 1863, respectively, "near the Rapidan River." These two rolls did not contain post-30 June 1863 information, indicating that they were intended to reflect the companies status as of that date.

All companies reported the condition of their clothing, military appearance, arms, accouterments, discipline and instruction as "good."

Field and Staff

Patton, Waller Tazewell (Colonel): Born 15 July 1835 at Fredericksburg, Va.; graduated VMI 1855; lawyer at Culpeper, Va.; never married; Capt. Co. "B," 13th Va. Inf. 17 April 1861; Major 7th Va. 1 July 1861; Col. 7th Va. 3 or 24 June 1862; *wounded* in both jaws and in the lungs during the attack and *captured*; died 21 July 1863 at the Pennsylvania College Hospital; eventually buried in the Stonewall Cemetery, Winchester, Va.

Flowerree, Charles Conway (Lt. Col.): Born Fauquier County, Va. 26 October 1842; attended VMI; Acting Adjt. 7th Va. summer 1861; appointed Lt. Col. 7th Va. 3 or 24 June 1862; resided at Warrenton, Va.

Parr, John H. (Adjutant): Enl. 5 June 1861 at Lynchburg in Company "C"; (25); clerk; born in Caroline County; appointed Adjutant 1 June 1863; *wounded.*

Graves, Richard M. (Capt., AQM): Appointed AQM 16 June 1862.

Lightfoot, John (Capt., ACS): Enl. 25 April 1861 at Madison Court House in Company "A"; (25); farmer; appointed ACS 16 June 1862.

Morton, Charles B. (Surgeon): Appointed Asst. Surgeon 1 July 1861 and Surgeon 5 February 1862; Brigade Surgeon in August 1864.

Oliver, James W. (Asst. Surgeon): Appointed Asst. Surgeon 5 August 1862; assigned to regiment 25 November 1862.

Worthington, Robert H. (Asst. Surgeon): Joined regiment 20 April 1863.

McCarthy, Florence (Chaplain): Appointed Chaplain 14 January 1862; transferred to 9th La. Infantry 11 September 1863; resigned 1 November 1863.

Tansill, George S. (Sgt. Major): Enl. 22 April 1861 at Alexandria; (49); soldier.

Gibson, Robert B. (Ordnance Sgt.): Enl. 30 April 1861 at Culpeper Court House in Company "C"; (28); farmer.

Berkley, R.C. (Quartermaster Sgt.): Enl. 26 June 1861 at Manassas.

Shotwell, William J. (Hospital Steward): Detailed from Company "C"; enl. 30 April 1861 at Culpeper Court House; (18); clerk; captured while serving as a nurse at Gettysburg 5 July; exchanged 14 or 15 February 1865.

Morton, Jeremiah, Jr. (Quartermaster's Dept.): On extra-duty from Company "C"; enl. 30 April 1861 at Culpeper Court House; (29); farmer.

Somerville, Robert B. (Adjutant's Clerk): On extra-duty from Company "C"; enl. 30 April 1861 at Culpeper Court House; (20); farmer; the company reports that he died but Federal and Confederate records do not confirm this; probably mortally *wounded*, dying in an unspecified Federal hospital (see William H. Hill, of Company "C").

Clarke, Thomas C. (Colonel's Orderly): Detailed from Company "I"; enl. 18 March 1862 at White Hall; Colonel's Orderly since 1 October 1862.

Collins, Van Buren (Commissary Dept.): On extra-duty from Company "C"; enl. 30 April 1861 at Culpeper Court House; (24); farmer.

Color Guard

Watson, G.W. (Color Sgt.): Detailed from Company "F"; enl. 27 April 1861 at Stanardsville; *wounded* during the attack.

Johnston, David E. (Color Cpl.): Detailed from Company "D"; enl. 13 May 1861 at Giles Court House; *wounded* in the back during the cannonade and subsequently captured; exchanged from Chester Hospital 17 August 1863.

Young, Jesse B. (Color Cpl.): Detailed from Company "D"; enl. 13 May 1861 at Giles Court House; *shot* in the right elbow or wounded by a shell fragment at the enemy's line during the attack and *captured*; exchanged from Chester Hospital 17 August 1863.

Band

Hughes, Richard (Chief Msuician): Enl. 16 April 1861 at Charlottesville.

Aylor, Robert H. (Musician): Enl. 25 April 1861 at Madison Court House in Company "A"; (20); clerk.

Brown, William H. (Musician): Enl. 30 April 1861 at Culpeper Court House in Company "C"; (21); farmer.

Burrows, Francis M. (Musician): Enl. 18 July 1862 at Richmond.

Carder, Joshua W. (Musician): Enl. 30 April 1861 at Culpeper Court House in Company "C"; (22); carpenter.

Gaar, William H. (Musician): Enl. 25 April 1861 at Madison Court House in Company "A"; (18); student.

Heaton, John M. (Musician): Enl. 30 April 1861 at Culpeper Court House in Company "C"; (25); clerk.

Hunton, John (Musician): Enl. 25 April 1861 at Madison Court House in Company "A"; (22); farmer.

Jones, William A. (Musician): Enl. 25 April 1861 at Madison Court House in Company "A"; (20); clerk.

Lacy, David W. (Musician): Enl. 25 April 1861 at Madison Court House in Company "A"; (22); mechanic.

Melton, James F. (Musician): Enl. 30 April 1861 at Culpeper Court House in Company "C"; (19); farmer.

Nichol, Thaddeus W. (Musician): Enl. 25 April 1861 at Madison Court House in Company "A"; (23); clerk.

Wayland, James E. (Musician): Enl. 25 April 1861 at Madison Court House in Company "A"; (22); student.

Company "A" ("Richardson Guards")

Organized 9 August 1859, this company enlisted 25 April 1861 for twelve months at Madison Court House, Madison County, Virginia, and was reorganized 28 April 1862.

Fry, William O. (Captain): (26); lawyer.

Fry, Thomas V. (1st Lt.): (24): farmer.

Harrison, William F. (2nd Lt.): (20); clerk.

Carpenter, William B. (1st Sgt.): Enl. 13 May 1861 at Culpeper Court House; (23); farmer.

Gulley, John W. (4th Sgt.): (18); student.

Conway, Catlett (5th Sgt.): (21); student; received a slight *wound* in the side penetrating the top of the ileum and lodging in the abdomen; exchanged from West's Buildings Hospital 27 September 1863.

Bradford, Osmond (1st Cpl.): (28); farmer.

Conway, Charles C. (3rd Cpl.): (18); student; *shot* through the bottom of the right foot and *captured*; exchanged from West's Buildings Hospital 27 September 1863.

Thomas, Robert A. (4th Cpl.): (23); farmer.

Whitlock, John (Musician): Probably *wounded*; captured 4 or 5 July; exchanged from DeCamp Hospital 16 September 1863.

Aylor, John W.: (19); farmer.

Blankenbeker, Elias F.: (23); farmer; *wounded.*

Blankenbeker, George M.: (27); farmer.

Bohannon, Thomas A.: (21); doctor; captured 4 July; exchanged 1 August 1863 suffering from intermittent fever.

Booton, Sinclair: (18); student.

Bowler, Napoleon B.: (19); mechanic; captured while serving as a nurse at Gettysburg 5 July; attendant to General Kemper in September 1863.

Carpenter, Albert W.: (27); mechanic.

Carpenter, Cumberland G.: (28); farmer.

Carpenter, James H.: (19); farmer.

Carpenter, John A.: (21); farmer.

Carpenter, Robert F.: Enl. 13 May 1861 at Culpeper Court House; (23); farmer.

Clore, Robert W.: Enl. 28 October 1862 at Winchester.

Darnold, Richard Z.: (26); mechanic; probably *wounded*; captured 4 July; exchanged 1 August 1863.

Davis, John W.: (23); mechanic; probably *wounded*; captured 3 July; exchanged from DeCamp Hospital 8 September 1863.

Evans, T.L.: Enl. 2 March 1863 at Petersburg; *killed.*

Ford, William N.: (20); mechanic.

Fray, William H.: (18); student.

Gallehugh, George W.: (23); farmer.

Harrison, George R.: Enl. 6 March 1863 at Petersburg.

Hawkins, John W.: (18); mechanic; received a severe gunshot *wound* in the hip and *captured*; exchanged from DeCamp Hospital 27 September 1863.

Hume, William S.: (23); farmer; captured while serving as a nurse at Gettysburg 4 July; exchanged 20 March 1864.

Jackson, John H.: (21); farmer.

Keyseear, John: Enl. 1 March 1862; *captured*; exchanged 15 October 1864.

Layton, John L.: Enl. 1 March 1862.

McClary, James G.: (18); farmer.

Thomas, Reuben S.: (19); farmer.

Tyson, John W.: Enl. 6 October 1862; *captured*; joined U.S. service at Point Lookout 23 January 1864.

Weaver, Benjamin F.: (25); stage contractor.

Weaver, Elijah F.: Enl. 25 June 1861 at Camp Wigfall; (19); farmer.

Yager, Champ C.: (26); student.

Company "B" ("Washington Grays")

This company enlisted 20 April 1861 in Rappahannock County for one year and was reorganized 26 April 1862.

Popham, Thomas G. (Captain): (20).

Porter, Henry T. (Jr. 2nd Lt.): (22).

Rudasill, Andrew C. (3rd Sgt.): (23).

Compton, Edward H. (4th Sgt): (20).

Martin, Johnson B. (5th Sgt.): (20).

Brown, William H. (1st Cpl.): Enl. 4 May 1861; (23).

Hartley, George H. (2nd Cpl.): (23).

Manuel, Willis A. (3rd Cpl.): (20).

Kendall, Richard A. (4th Cpl.): (21).

Bayliss, James W.: (21).

Bowen, Henry E.: Enl. 4 May 1861; (21); wounded.

Bowen, John: Enl. 18 December 1862; married; (36 in 1863); shot in the knee and severely *wounded* in the middle third of the left thigh and *captured*; leg amputated at upper third; died at Letterman Hospital 15 August 1863 and buried in Section 1, Grave #35 of that hospital's cemetery.

Brown, James M.: Enl. 29 April 1861; *wounded.*

Burke, John W.: Enl. 4 May 1861; (21); deserted 24 July 1863.

Clarke, James W.: (22); probably *wounded*; captured 5 July; exchanged from DeCamp Hospital 8 September 1863.

Cooper, John B.: (23).

Cornwell, Hezekiah: (19).

Dodson, Reuben: (21).

Elliotte, James O.: (19); the company lists this man as having been wounded and captured, dying about 1 August 1863 from his wound. Federal records do not confirm this, however. Probably *killed.*

Elliotte, William: (22); *shot* in the thigh and *captured*; exchanged from DeCamp Hospital 16 September 1863.

Fincham, Green S.: (23).

Fincham, Jonas: (24); AWOL 24 July 1863, returned to his company 26 September 1863.

Grubbs, John W.: (29); captured while serving as a nurse at Gettysburg; exchanged 20 arch 1864.

Heiffling, John R.: (27).

Jenkins, John A.: Enl. 10 March 1862.

Johnson, John M.: Enl. 4 March 1862.

Johnson, John W.: (18); father was Henry Johnson; captured either 3 July at Gettysburg or 7 July 1863 at Boonsboro, Maryland; died of disease at Point Lookout 21 January 1864.

Kendall, William B.: (31).

Kilby, Henry Clay: Enl. 1 August 1861 at Fairfax.

Menefee, Henry L.: Enl. 22 July 1861.

Noakes, James N.: (23); deserted 24 July 1863.

Oden, James C.: *Captured*; exchanged 30 April 1864.

Partlow, Elisha S.: Enl. 4 March 1862.

Ritenour, Ambrose B.: Enl. 1 March 1863; *wounded* and *captured*; exchanged 1 August 1863.

Sandbower, John D.: Enl. 18 December 1862; *killed.*

Settle, Jackson: (26).

Smoot, John E.: Enl. 13 March 1862.

Tolbert, John N.: (21); *shot* in the scalp at the enemy line during the attack; *captured*; exchanged from DeCamp Hospital 28 August 1863.

Woodard, James G.: (25).

Yancy, Francis G.: (22).

Company "C"

This company enlisted 30 April 1861 at Culpeper Court House, Culpeper County, Virginia for one year and was known as Company "E" on the 30 April-30 June 1861 muster rolls. The unit was reorganized 26 April 1862.

Almond, James W. (Captain): (22); farmer.

Moore, Charles W. (1st Lt.): (24); carpenter; VMI class of 1864; *wounded* and *captured*; exchanged 22 March 1865.

Bartley, Nathan T. (2nd Lt.): (20); farmer; *wounded* and *captured*; released from Fort Delaware 12 June 1865.

Smith, George (2nd Lt.): (30); tailor; *captured*; exchanged 22 March 1865.

Eliason, George P. (1st Sgt.): (19); farmer.

Apperson, Cincinnatus (Sgt.): (20); farmer.

Rhoades, Richard B. (Sgt.): (26); farmer.

Willis, Joseph G. (Sgt.): (23); farmer.

Yowell, Thomas O. (Sgt.): (19);

 Jenkins, Fountain (1st Cpl.): (21); farmer.

Foushee, David M. (Cpl.): (20); farmer; *killed.*

Hill, William H. (Cpl.): (19); carpenter; his company lists him simply as having died; the same notation also appears to have applied to personnel of this unit who died in Federal hospitals; probably mortally *wounded* and *captured* at Gettysburg.

Jones, James H. (Cpl.): (18); farmer; *wounded.*

Bashaw, John W.: Enl. 10 March 1862.

Biscoe, William E.: (18); carpenter.

Byram, Edward: Enl. 10 March 1862 in Orange County.

Childress, William A.: Enl. 10 March 1862 in Orange County.

Coleman, Joseph A.: Enl. 10 March 1862 in Orange County; *shot* in the neck and *captured*; exchanged from DeCamp Hospital 8 September 1863.

Coleman, Thomas P.: Enl. 10 March 1862 in Orange County; slightly *wounded* in the leg and *captured*; exchanged from DeCamp Hospital 8 September 1863.

Crutchfield, Peter: (30); farmer.

Davis, Thomas: Enl. 1 April 1862 in Orange County; the company lists this man as absent wounded, sick in enemy hands or missing through August 1864; Federal records do not confirm this, however; he was probably *killed* at Gettysburg.

Davis, William A.: Enl. 10 March 1862 in Orange County.

Dempsey, Coleman H.: Enl. 10 March 1862 in Orange County.

Dempsey, Levi J.: Enl. 10 March 1862 in Orange County; *captured*; died at Fort Delaware 3 October 1863; buried at Finns Point, N.J.

England, Robert M.: Enl. 13 September 1862 at Orange.

Finks, Henry L.: (21); farmer.

Fox, Thomas: (19); blacksmith.

Gaines, John L.: Enl. 10 January 1863 at Fredericksburg.

Hackley, Andrew J.: farmer.

Hall, Henry J.: Enl. 13 September 1862 at Orange; (21 in 1863); *shot* in the right thigh and *captured*; exchanged from DeCamp Hospital 28 August 1863.

Hull, John E.: (20); farmer; *shot* in the side and *captured*; exchanged from DeCamp Hospital 16 September 1863.

Hume, Francis: Enl. 10 March 1862 in Orange County.

Jenkins, Lewis: (18); farmer.

Johnson, James S.: Enl. 10 March 1862 in Orange County.

Kilby, William A.: (20); farmer.

Lewis, William W.: Enl. 10 March 1862 at Culpeper Court House.

Matthews, Joseph O.: (19); farmer; *wounded* in the right knee and *captured*; exchanged from West's Buildings Hospital 24 August 1863.

Moore, Daniel J.: Enl. 25 May 1861 at Stevensburg; (21); carpenter.

Morris, Thomas: Enl. 10 March 1862 in Orange County.

Oden, Alexander: (45); farmer; captured while serving as a nurse at Gettysburg (apparently sick with "debility"); exchanged 15 November 1864.

Reed, Richard S.: (19); farmer.

Shadrack, Abraham W.: (22); farmer; *wounded*; the company reports that he died of wounds 30 August 1863, apparently in a Confederate hospital.

Simms, Edmund B.: (18); farmer.

Sisson, Newton H.: Enl. 10 March 1862 in Orange County.

Smith, Nathaniel: Enl. 10 March 1862 in Orange County; *shot* in the left foot and *captured*; exchanged from West's Buildings Hospital 27 September 1863.

Smith, Richard A.: (21); farmer; shot in the thigh and captured; exchanged from DeCamp Hospital 8 September 1863.

Tinsley, James W.: (24); carpenter.

Turner, Benjamin F.: Enl. 3 March 1862.

Webb, John W.: Enl. 10 March 1862 in Orange County.

Webb, Richard O.: Enl. 10 March 1862 in Orange County.

Winston, Arthur W.: (28); farmer; *wounded*.

Wolfrey, Jerry: Enl. 10 March 1862 in Orange County.

Company "D" ("Giles Volunteers")

This company enlisted 13 May 1861 at Giles Court House, Giles County, Virginia, for twelve months and was reorganized 26 April 1862.

Bane, Robert H. (Captain):

Mullins, John W. (1st Lt.):

Stone, Elisha M. (2nd Lt.): *Captured*; exchanged 22 March 1865.

Walker, Elijah R. (2nd Lt.): *Wounded.*

Taylor, Thomas S.L. (1st Sgt.):

Fry, Allen L. (Sgt.):

Snidow, William H.H. (Sgt.):

Thompson, Andrew J. (1st Cpl.):

Bish, Daniel (Cpl.): The company reports him as missing in action but there are no Federal records concerning him; *killed.*

Mullins, George C. (Cpl.): Enl. 15 July 1861.

Shannon, Joseph C. (Cpl.):

Akers, David C.: Enl. 10 March 1862; (27); farmer; born in Floyd County, widow was Mrs. Elmira J. Akers; *killed.*

Barrett, Jesse: The company reports him as missing in action but there are no Federal records concerning this man; *killed.*

Bolton, Alexander H.:

Crawford, John R.:

Darr, Tim P.: Enl. 15 July 1861.

Dudley, John S.:

Fortner, James H.: Enl. 15 February 1863; *shot* in the thigh and *captured*; exchanged from Chester Hospital 23 September 1863.

Fortner, William C.: Enl. 15 July 1861; *captured*; exchanged from Point Lookout 20 or 21 February 1865.

Gordin, Francis M.: Enl. 15 July 1861.

Hale, Charles A.:

Hight, John W.: *Captured*; joined U.S. 3rd Maryland Cavalry at Fort Delaware 22 September 1863.

Hurt, James J.: *Wounded* in the left arm above the elbow and *captured*; exchanged from Chester Hospital 17 August 1863.

Jones, John F.: Received a gunshot *wound* which fractured his left ankle joint (leg amputated) and *captured*; exchanged from West's Buildings Hospital 17 November 1863.

Lewey, Joseph:

Meadows, Anderson: Enl. 15 July 1861.

Meadows, John: Enl. 10 March 1862.

Muncey, Wiley Winton: Enl. 15 July 1861; *wounded*.

Sarver, Demarcus: Enl. 15 July 1861; *wounded*.

Sublett, John P.: The company lists him as missing in action but there are no Federal records concerning him; *killed*.

Thompson, Adam: Enl. 10 March 1862.

Yager, Edward Z.:

Company "E" ("Hazelwood Volunteers")

This company enlisted 25 May 1861 at Stevensburg, Culpeper County, Virginia; was mustered into state service 6 June 1861 at Culpeper Court House; and was reorganized 26 April 1862.

Tansill, James G. (1st Lt.): Enl. 22 April 1861 at Alexandria; (20); soldier.

Antrim, Edward M. (Sgt.): Enl. 30 April 1861 at Culpeper Court House; (18); clerk.

Doggett, Basil M. (Sgt.): (21); workman.

Jones, James E. (Cpl.): (19); farmer; *wounded*, suffering a compound fracture of his cheek and upper jaw and *captured*; exchanged from Point Lookout 20 March 1864.

Pitts, Benjamin F. (Cpl.): Enl. 12 June 1861 at Culpeper Court House; (34); shoemaker.

Brown, Beverly W.: Enl. 4 June 1861 at Culpeper Court House; (27); farmer.

Brown, Daniel T.: (32); farmer.

Brown, George P.: Enl. 4 June 1861 at Culpeper Court House; (19); farmer.

Brown, Lemuel F.: (27); workman.

Brown, Thornton S.: (25); workman; captured 4 July; exchanged 3 March 1864.

Burrows, Henry C.: Enl. 20 June 1861 at Culpeper Court House; (18); clerk; captured 4 July; exchanged 14 or 15 February 1865.

Byram, James N.: Enl. 19 July 1861 at Culpeper Court House.

Canaday, John D.: (27); carpenter; *killed*.

Carpenter, Jeremiah A.: Enl. 20 February 1863 at Madison Court House.

Dennis, Jasper: Enl. 20 February 1863 in Rappahannock County.

Embrey, Sandford E.: Enl. 1 October 1862 at Richmond; *captured*; joined U.S. service at Point Lookout 25 January 1864.

Glass, James M.: Enl. 12 June 1861 at Culpeper Court House; clerk; *captured*; exchanged 14 or 15 February 1865.

Gough, John J.: Enl. 1 October 1862 at Richmond.

Grimsley, Reuben B.: (18); farmer.

Jones, George H.: (20); workman.

Legg, Alexander F.: Enl. 10 July 1861 at Occoquan; *killed.*

Legg, John T.: Enl. 1 July 1861 at Culpeper Court House.

Smith, James K.P.: (18); farmer.

Souter, James R.: Enl. 19 July 1861 at Culpeper Court House.

Suddith, Benjamin B.: Enl. 20 February 1863 at Madison Court House.

Tanner, Robert K.: Enl. 10 March 1862 at Culpeper Court House.

Welsh, Willis W.: Enl. 14 February 1863 in Fauquier County; *killed.*

Company "F"

This company enlisted 27 April 1861 at Stanardsville, Greene County, Virginia for twelve months and was reorganized 26 April 1862.

McMullen, J.N. (1st Lt.): *Wounded.*

Dulaney, William E. (Sgt.): Born in Greene County; *captured* 4 July; died of typhoid fever at Chester Hospital 12 August 1863 and buried in Grave #145 of that hospital's cemetery.

Piper, R.R. (Sgt.): Captured; exchanged 20 or 21 February 1865.

Haney, Bazel (Cpl.):

Walker, John B. (Cpl.): *Killed.*

Bell, L.L.: Enl. 1 April 1862 at Winchester; the compnay reports him as missing in action but there are no Federal records concerning him; *killed.*

Clatterbuck, William J.:

Cox, William Henry: Enl. 29 March 1862 at Camp Taylor.

Desmond, Michael: Enl. 29 March 1862 at Camp Taylor.

Dickenson, Edward D.:

Durrow, William: Enl. 29 March 1862 at Camp Taylor.

Garton, W.A.: Enl. 11 March 1863 at Petersburg; *wounded* and *captured*; exchanged from DeCamp Hospital 28 August 1863.

Gilbert, A.J.: Enl. 29 March 1862 at Camp Taylor.

Haney, R.A.:

Harris, W.T.: Enl. 1 September 1862 at Winchester, born in Greene County; *wounded*; died at Pickett's Division Hospital and buried in the corner of "Curn's" garden west of the house; disinterred to Richmond 3 August 1872 in Box #250.

Huckstep, Benjamin J.: Enl. 29 March 1862 at Camp Taylor.

Huckstep, J.P.:

Jarrell, J.E., Jr.: Enl. 29 March 1862 at Camp Taylor; the company reports him as missing in action at Gettysburg, but Federal records list him, probably incorrectly, as having been captured at Boonsboro, Maryland 7 July; probably *captured* at Gettysburg; died of chronic diarrhea at Fort Delaware 21 September 1863; buried at Finns Point, N.J.

Long, James T.:

Marshall, J.S.: Enl. 25 May 1863 at Taylorsville or Orange Court House.

Mitchell, R.O.: Enl. 4 December 1862 at Fredericksburg; *captured*; died at Fort Delaware 3 October 1863; buried at Finns Point, N.J.

Mooney, E.: Enl. 29 March 1862 at Camp Taylor.

Page, Zebulon K.:

Sheler, W.J.:

Southards, James: Enl. 15 May 1863 at Taylorsville or Orange Court House; *wounded* in the right arm and left hand (radius fractured in two places) and *captured*; exchanged from West's Buildings Hospital 27 September 1863.

Vernon, Alexander: Enl. 29 March 1862 at Camp Taylor or Orange Court House; the company reports him as missing in action but there are no Federal records concerning him; *killed*.

Watson, N.T.: Enl. 15 March 1863 at Petersburg.

Company "G" ("Rappahannock Guards")

This company enlisted 1 May 1861 at Woodville, Rappahannock County, Virginia for one year; was mustered 25 June 1861; and was reorganized 26 April 1862.

Hill, Alvin T. (Captain): (19); carpenter.

Rivercomb, Richard H. (1st Lt.): (25); farmer.

Brown, James W. (Sr. 2nd Lt.): (23); carpenter; *wounded* during the cannonade.

Story, Columbus (Jr. 2nd Lt.): (18); farmer; *killed*.

Henshaw, Robert S. (4th Sgt.): (18); farmer.

Story, James R. (5th Sgt.): (23); distiller.

Sparks, Champ C. (1st Cpl.): (24); blacksmith; *shot* in the head and *captured*; died at Fort Delaware 3 October 1863; buried at Finns Point, N.J.

Romine, Joseph B. (2nd Cpl.): (21); farmer; *captured*; exchanged 15 November 1864.

Hudson, John W. (3rd Cpl.): (18); farmer.

Hawkins, Charles W. (4th Cpl.): (24); carpenter.

Aylor, William J.: Enl. 6 March 1862.

Berry, James F.: (20); farmer.

Brown, J.V.: Enl. 9 March 1862 in Madison County; captured 5 July while serving as a nurse at Gettysburg; deserted from the hospital 16 July 1863 and joined U.S. service 17 October 1864.

Brown, Paul C.: (18); carpenter.

Brown, W.T.: Enl. 1 August 1862 at Gordonsville; *wounded*.

Burke, Arthur W.: (22); carpenter; *captured*; exchanged 20 or 21 February 1865.

Burke, John R.: (19); farmer.

Butler, Napoleon: (20); farmer; *wounded*.

Butler, Robert: (31); carpenter.

Campbell, Richard: (22); farmer; deserted 24 July 1863.

Carder, Silas B.: (21); farmer.

Deal, Charles T.: Enl. 1 October 1862 in Rappahannock County; *wounded.*

Dodson, Albert: Enl. 10 November 1862 at Culpeper; *killed.*

Graham, J.S.: Enl. 23 June 1862 at Richmond.

Hawkins, Augustus: Enl. 6 March 1862 in Madison County; *wounded.*

Henshaw, A.L.: Enl. 1 October 1862 in Madison County.

Hitt, Martin L.: (18); blacksmith.

Hitt, Paskill A.: Enl. 8 March 1862 at Culpeper; *shot* in the right leg and *captured*; died of gangrene at Chester Hospital 27 July 1863 and buried in Grave #70 of that hospital's cemetery.

Hudson, Samuel: Enl. 30 March 1862 at Orange Court House.

Jenkins, J.W.: Enl. 12 March 1862 at Chickahominy.

Jenkins, James M.: (19); farmer; *wounded* and *captured*; exchanged from DeCamp Hospital 8 September 1863.

Jenkins, Walker: (19); farmer.

Kilby, Andrew J.: (25); farmer; *wounded.*

Kilby, Joseph M.: Enl. 1 October 1862 at Culpeper Court House.

Kilby, Thomas M.: (21); farmer.

Leek, Presley: Enl. 10 November 1862 at Culpeper Court House; *wounded.*

Mitchell, Thomas J.: (18); farmer; *wounded.*

Rosson, George W.: (21); shoemaker.

Streets, Willliam M.: (23); farmer; *captured*; exchanged 20 or 21 February 1865.

Thornhill, Armstead: (24); farmer.

Thornhill, Champ C.: (22); farmer.

Thornhill, Charles E.: (25); farmer.

Williamson, W.J.: Enl. 10 March 1862 at Chickahominy; *captured*; exchanged 15 November 1864.

Woodward, William W.: (19); carpenter; *wounded*; died of wounds 15 July 1863 at Winchester, Virginia.

Company "I" ("Holcombe Guards")

Organized at White Hall, Albemarle County, Va. in May 1861, this company enlisted 3 June 1861 at that location, was mustered 11 June 1861, and was reorganized 26 April 1862.

Brown, Bezaliel G. (Captain): (24); farmer; *wounded* in the leg and *captured*; released from Fort Delaware 30 May 1865.

Wyant, John E. (1st Lt.): (22); postmaster.

Brown, Charles B. (2nd Lt.): (25); farmer.

Good, Albert H. (2nd Lt.): (18); farmer; *wounded* in the left leg (amputated) and *captured*; died at DeCamp Hospital 29 August 1863 and buried in Brady's Receiving Tomb, 2nd Avenue, New York City.

Wiserman, John F. (1st Sgt.): (30); farmer.

Parrott, William N. (2nd Sgt.): (19); farmer.

Fulcher, Thomas J. (3rd Sgt.): (20); farmer; *captured*; joined U.S. service 15 February 1864.

Bailey, James T. (4th Sgt.): (21); farmer; *captured*; exchanged 14 or 15 February 1865.

Clarke, George P. (5th Sgt.): (20); farmer; *wounded* and *captured*; exchanged from DeCamp Hospital 8 September 1863.

Keyton, William L. (1st Cpl.): (26); farmer; *wounded*.

Brown, Bezaliel G., Jr. (2nd Cpl.): (26); farmer.

Ward, Equin H. (3rd Cpl.): (20); farmer; *wounded*.

Fielding, Eppa (4th Cpl.): (25); farmer.

Ambroselle, John J.: (24); mechanic; the company reports him as missing in action but there are no Federal records concerning him; *killed*.

Belew, John T.: (20); mechanic.

Blackwell, Henry Clay: (19); farmer.

Brown, Robert C.: (23); farmer.

Brown, William H.H.: (20); farmer; *wounded*.

Clarke, J.L.: Enl. 15 February 1863.

Clarke, William N.: Enl. 3 June 1861; (21); farmer.

Clements, Mathew J.: (23); farmer; *killed*.

Clements, Miles E.: (22); farmer.

Cox, J.E.N.: Enl. 1 March 1863 at Chester Station.

Davis, Henry T.: (23); farmer; *wounded* and *captured*; exchanged 15 November 1864.

Davis, Peter L.: (19); farmer.

Fielding, William B.: (21); farmer; *shot* in the thigh and *captured*; exchanged from West's Buildings Hospital 24 August 1863.

Fisher, George R.: (18); farmer.

Herndon, William G.: Enl. 1 March 1863 at Chester Station.

Herring, N.B.: Enl. 1 March 1863; *wounded* in the left leg (amputated) and *captured*; died 27 July at U.S. II Corps Hospital and buried in Grave #6 in back of Schwartz's barn; his widow was Mrs. V. Herring.

Jarman, William D.: (31); farmer.

Kidd, J. Luther: (19); farmer.

McQuary, William H.: (21); farmer.

Racer, Charles: Enl. 1 March 1863 at Chester Station; *wounded*.

Rea, R.B.: Enl. 18 March 1862; *wounded* in the forearm and head and *captured*; exchanged from Chester Hospital 20 August 1863.

Riley, A.: Enl. 1 March 1863 at Chester Station.

Sandridge, W.O.: Enl. 18 March 1862; *wounded* and *captured*; joined U.S. service 24 January 1864.

Sandridge, William R.: Enl. 28 September 1862.

Sandridge, Zachariah: (19); farmer.

Slater, John R.: Enl. 18 March 1862.

Thurston, Andrew J.: (22); farmer.

Thurston, John N.: Enl. 18 March 1862; *wounded* in the lower third of the left tibia and *captured*; exchanged from Fort Wood, New York Harbor 7 January 1864.

Thurston, John T.: Enl. 25 November 1862.

218

Toombs, R.A.: Enl. 18 March 1862.

Via, Robert C.: (20); farmer.

Via, Thomas D.: (19); farmer; *captured*; joined U.S. service at Point Lookout 1 February 1864.

Ward, John:

Wolfe, Ezra M.: (19); farmer; captured while serving as a nurse at Gettysburg; exchanged 20 March 1864.

Wood, Aelick F.: (19); farmer.

Wood, William T.: (23); farmer; *killed*.

Company "K" ("Madison Grays")

This company enlisted 23 April 1861 at Madison Court House, Madison County, Virginia; was mustered 19 May 1861; and was reorganized 26 April 1862.

Jones, Alphonso N. (Captain): (22); farmer.

Wayland, Robert B. (Sr. 2nd Lt.): (27); farmer.

Rosser, James M. (Jr. 2nd Lt.): (19); farmer; *wounded*.

Racer, James O.B. (1st Sgt.): (20); farmer; *wounded* and *captured*; died 15 July 1863 at U.S. II Corps Hospital and buried in Yard D, Row 3 of that hospital's cemetery in Schwartz's cornfield on Rock Creek; disinterred to Richmond 13 June 1872 with 110 others in ten large boxes marked "S."

Weaver, Robert H. (2nd Sgt.): (18); farmer; *wounded*.

Levell, Joseph W. (3rd Sgt.): (26); farmer.

Estis, Cornelius W. (4th Sgt.): Enl. 25 April 1861; (19); student.

Dawson, James F. (5th Sgt.): Enl. 25 April 1861; (23); farmer; *captured*; died of chronic diarrhea at Fort Delaware 30 August 1863; buried at Finns Point, N.J.

Hunton, George H. (1st Cpl.): (19); farmer.

Harlow, John W. (2nd Cpl.): (30); farmer; *captured*; exchanged 14 or 15 February 1865.

Kirtley, John A. (3rd Cpl.): (20); farmer; *wounded*.

Austin, James W.: (32); mechanic.

Cheek, Richard: (25); farmer; *wounded*.

Clayton, John W.: Enl. 25 May 1861; (20); farmer.

Clore, Charles L.: Enl. 25 May 1861; (30); farmer.

Coppage, Robert: (18); farmer.

Davis, William: Enl. 25 July 1861 at Centreville; *wounded* in the right arm (amputated) and *captured*; exchanged from DeCamp Hospital 8 September 1863.

Delph, W.S.: Enl. 25 July 1861 at Centreville.

Dixson, W.H.: Enl. 25 July 1861 at Centreville.

Finchman, William T.: (23); farmer.

Grayson, Robert W.: Enl. 25 July 1861 at Centreville.

Groom, John F.: Enl. 25 July 1861 at Centreville.

Hicks, Herndon F.: (21); farmer; deserted 15 July 1863.

Hoffman, J.W.: Enl. 18 March 1863 at Petersburg.

Hoffman, Moses A.: (24); wheelwright.

Hurt, H.W.: Enl. 10 June 1863 at Culpeper.
Jackson, William H.: (20); farmer.
Jenkins, John W.: Enl. 25 May 1861; (25); farmer.
Jenkins, Powel S.: Enl. 25 May 1861; (24); farmer.
Kennedy, James F.: (25); mechanic.
Kirtley, W.B.: Enl. 23 July 1861 at Centreville.
Long, Edward J.: (23); farmer.
Racer, George H.: (18); farmer.
Roberts, Benjamin D.: (22); farmer.
Rosson, Emanuel Barnette: (17); mechanic.
Skinner, Robert: (20); carpenter; enl. 25 May 1861.
Smith, Joseph B.: (32); mill wright.
Taylor, Thomas J.: Enl. 25 April 1861; (18); farmer.
Thomas, John: (25); farmer.
Wayland, Thomas M.: (20); farmer.

11th Virginia Volunteer Infantry Regiment

This regiment was organized for state service in May 1861; accepted into Confederate service 1 July 1861; and reorganized 26 April 1862.

The exact form of the flag of this regiment is not known. It was probably not captured at the battle.

Field and Staff

The following listing was obtained from a listing of regimental field and staff officers on duty with the unit during the entire service of the regiment. Service records of these men were reviewed to determine those who were not at Gettysburg. The residue are provided below.

Otey, Kirkwood (Major): Born 19 October 1829 at Lynchburg, Virginia; graduated VMI 1849; officer of Lynchburg Home Guard before and after the war; enl. 23 April 1861 at Lynchburg as a 1st Lt. in Company "G"; banker; promoted Major 23 May 1862; promoted Lt. Col. 24 September 1863; *wounded* during the advance.

Harris, H. Valentine (Lt., Adjutant): Enl. 23 April 1861 at Lynchburg as a Private in Company "G"; (22); banker; appointed Adjutant 1 April 1863.

Payne, William M. (Quartermaster): Appointed Regimental Quartermaster 7 March 1862; appointed Major and Brigade Quartermaster June 1864.

Meade, David (Capt. Asst. Quartermaster): Enl. 18 April 1861 at Millwood as a Private in Company "C," 2nd Virginia Infantry; appointed AQM 17 June 1862 and to regiment January 1863; on temporary duty with I Corps ordnance train 15 June 1863; on duty with Pickett's divisional supply train 10 August 1863; transferred to division staff in January 1864.

Franklin, James, Jr. (3rd Lt., Acting Quartermaster): Detailed from Company "G"; enl. 23 April 1861 at Lynchburg; (22); merchant.

Lucado, Leo F. (Capt., ACS): Appointed ACS 10 July 1861.

Ward, John R. (Surgeon): Enrolled for service 8 June 1861 at Manassas Junction having enlisted earlier at Lynchburg; (21); doctor; Asst. Surgeon 28 February 1863; promoted to Surgeon 1 March 1863; appointed regimental surgeon 25 June 1863.

Harrow, John W. (Asst. Surgeon): Appointed Asst. Surgeon 8 March 1863.

Granbery, John C. (Chaplain): Appointed Chaplain 4 July 1861; resigned 23 July 1863.

Toot, William A. (Sgt. Major): Enl. 23 April 1861 at Lynchburg as a Private in Company "G"; (28); corn merchant.

Hobson, Eppie M. (Ordnance Sgt.): Enl. 16 May 1861 at Mount Zion as a Corporal in Company "C"; (24); merchant.

Walkut, William M. (Quartermaster Sgt.): Enl. 10 May 1862 at Jackson, Mississippi.

Clark, Micajah G. (Hospital Orderly): Enl. 23 April 1861 at Yellow Branch in Company "B"; (27); farmer.

Withers, Walter L. (Hospital Steward): Detailed from Company "C"; enl. 18 March 1862 at Lynchburg; captured while serving as a nurse at Gettysburg; paroled until exchanged 4 August 1863.

Hay, James R. (Wagon Master): Detailed from Company "B"; enl. 23 April 1861 at Yellow Branch; (40); surveyor.

Hillsman, William H. (Teamster): Detailed from Company "B"; enl. 23 April 1861 at Yellow Branch; (23).

Barber, William D. (Ambulance Driver): Detailed from Company "D"; enl. 23 April 1861 at Fincastle; (27); driver.

Winston, Charles J. (Ambulance Corps): Enl. at Lynchburg; enrolled for service 25 May 1861 at Manassas Junction; farmer; slightly *wounded* during the cannonade.

Color Guard

Hickok, Martin V.B. (5th Sgt., Color Bearer): Detailed from Company "D"; enl. 23 April 1861 at Fincastle; (24); clerk; *wounded.*

Simpson, Charles W. (5th Cpl., Color Cpl.): Detailed from Company "E"; enl. 5 June 1861 at Lynchburg; (19); no occupation; *wounded.*

Company "A" ("Lynchburg Rifle Grays")

Organized in January 1860, this company enlisted 22 April 1861 at Lynchburg, Campbell County, Virginia for one year, and was reorganized 26 April 1862.

The following listing was obtained from the company's April/June 1863 muster roll captioned 12 August 1863 at Orange Court House, Virginia. The company reported the status of its clothing as "tolerable," and its military appearance, arms, accouterments, discipline, and instruction as "good."

Mitchell, Robert M., Jr., (Captain): (18); student; *wounded.*

Kennedy, Joseph A. (1st Lt.): (18); student; Acting Adjutant 11th Virginia in August 1863.

Akers, Peter B. (2nd Lt.): (20); merchant.

Rainey, Charles W. (2nd Lt.): (22); railroad bag master.

Thurman, James O. (1st Sgt.): (23); saddler.

Rector, Thomas S. (1st Cpl.): (20); salesman; received a gunshot *wound* which fractured his left humerus (shoulder joint resected) and *captured*; exchanged from West's Buildings Hospital 17 November 1863.

Hunt, William R. (2nd Cpl.): (24); cabinet maker.

Akers, William L.: (22); clerk.

Allman, William H.: (28); carpenter.

Atkins, John W.: Enl. 12 August 1862; *wounded.*

Bailey, James H.: (16); student.

Beckwith, Henry Clay: (18); clerk; *wounded.*

Brown, Leslie C.: (20); bricklayer.

Cheatham, Thomas F.: (21); harness maker.

Dinguid, Edward S.: (17); cabinet maker; *shot* in the left side of the chest and *captured*; paroled from Point Lookout 22 August 1863 and exchanged.

Duval, Edmund: Enl. 13 April 1863; born in Paris, France; *captured*; joined U.S. 3rd Maryland Cavalry 22 September 1863 at Fort Delaware.

Feazle, Frank H.: (21); tinner.

Fulkes, James W.: (22); farmer.

Harvey, Charles C: (20); clerk.

Hollins, James E.: (20); miller.

Mitchell, John Rice: (21); druggist; *wounded.*

Mitchell, Thomas H.: (17); salesman.

Parrish, Booker S.: (22); clerk; captured while serving as a nurse at Gettysburg; exchanged 20 March 1864.

Peters, John J.: (27); canal boat captain.

Pugh, Charles E.: (23); carpenter; *wounded.*

Rogers, James B.: (19); overseer in a tobacco factory; *wounded.*

Scurry, John G.: Enl. 8 July 1861 at Lynchburg; *wounded* and *captured*; exchanged from DeCamp Hospital 28 August 1863.

Slagle, David H.: (26); printer.

Stephens, Elias R.: Enl. 16 July 1861.

Stewart, Philip H.: Cigar maker; *killed.*

Thornhill, Jesse T.: Enl. 27 June 1861; (18); farmer.

Turner, John H.: (22); printer.

Tyree, Charles D.: Enl. 16 October 1861.

Warfield, Thomas D.: (31); barber.

Wilmer, T.P.: Enl. 13 April 1863; *wounded.*

Company "B" ("Southern Guards")

This company enlisted 23 April 1861 at Yellow Branch, Campbell County, Virginia for one year, and was reorganized 26 April 1862.

The following listing was obtained from the company's April/June 1863 muster roll captioned 1 July 1863 at Chambersburg, Pennsylvania.

Horton, Thomas B. (Captain): (25); farmer; *wounded.*

Haden, Clarence V. (1st Lt.): (21); farmer; *wounded.*

Lazenby, George W. (2nd Lt.): (34); farmer.

Elliott, Washington A. (3rd Lt.): (30); carpenter; *wounded.*

Clement, William T. (1st Sgt.): (22); farmer.

Phillips, John E. (2nd Sgt.): (21); farmer; received a severe *wound* to the forehead and *captured*; exchanged from West's Buildings Hospital 24 August 1863.

Phillips, William M. (3rd Sgt.): (19); farmer.

Johnson, Jeremiah M. (4th Sgt.): (20); carpenter; *wounded.*

Sandifer, William A. (5th Sgt.): (24); farmer.

Dinwiddie, John W. (3rd Cpl.): Enl. 18 June 1861 at Camp Pickens; (21); farmer.

Farmer, William (Cpl.): (21); farmer.

Scott, William W. (Cpl.): (29); plasterer.

Bondurant, Jacob W.: (33); farmer.

Brooks, Cicero W.: (20); farmer.

Burruss, Thomas G.: (20); farmer.

Callahan, Ezekiel W.: Enl. 11 August 1862 at Campbell Court House.

Dews, Demarquis P.: Enl. 18 June 1861 at Camp Pickens; (30); farmer; sick since 3 July 1863; died at home in Lynchburg 21 August 1864; probably did not participate in the 3 July assault.

Dudley, John A.: (18); farmer.

Dudley, William H.: Enl. 1 February 1862 at Lynchburg; received a *contusion* of the abdomen and *captured*; exchanged 20 or 21 February 1865.

Farmer, Arthur: Enl. 11 August 1862 at Campbell Court House.

Farmer, Edward: (24); farmer.

Farmer, William H.: Enl. 11 August 1862 at Campbell Court House.

Farthing, William F.: (23); farmer; *wounded*.

Finch, Charles H.: Enl. 15 March 1862; wife was Mrs. Sarah J. Finch; *killed*.

Finch, James M.: (19); farmer.

Franklin, Robert H.: Enl. 25 April 1861 at Lynchburg; (25); clerk.

Gill, Jesse H.: (26); farmer; *captured*; exchanged 15 November 1864.

Hendrick, William D.: Enl. 25 April 1861 at Lynchburg, (18).

Hillsman, John C.: (19); *wounded* in the right leg and *captured*; paroled for exchange from West's Buildings Hospital 23 August 1863.

Horton, Edwin R.: Enl. 25 April 1861 at Lynchburg; (23); captured while serving as a nurse at Gettysburg; exchanged from DeCamp Hospital 16 September 1863; probably slightly *wounded*.

Hughes, Barnet W.: (21); farmer.

Little, James T.: (23); received a flesh *wound* to the knee and *captured*; exchanged from West's Buildings Hospital 24 August 1863.

McAllister, John B.: (22); farmer; wounded.

McNamee, James: Enl. 15 March 1862.

Moorman, Samuel E.: (26); *shot* in the abdomen and *captured*; died 17 July 1863.

Morris, James A.: Enl. 15 March 1862; shot in the right thigh and captured; exchanged from DeCamp Hospital date unknown.

Phillips, John N.: Enl. 10 March 1863 at Campbell Court House; the company reports him as missing in action but there are no Federal records concerning him; *killed*.

Sandifer, Robert T.: Enl. 15 March 1862.

Simmons, William S.: Enl. 25 April 1861.

Thurmond, Pleasant L.: (27); *wounded* in the leg and *captured*; exchanged 22 September 1864.

Thurmond, Walker G.: *Wounded*.

Webber, Marcus D.L.: (28); farmer; *wounded*.

Williamson, William H.: (23); farmer; *wounded*; AWOL sometime during July or August 1863.

This company enlisted 16 May 1861 at Mount Zion, Campbell County, Virginia for one year. Formerly 1st Company "E," 28th Virginia Infantry, this unit was transferred to the 11th Virginia in June 1861, and was reorganized 26 April 1862.

The following listing was obtained from the company's April/June 1863 muster roll captioned 30 June 1863 at Chambersburg, Pennsylvania.

The company reported the condition of its clothing and accouterments as "tolerable," and that of its military appearance, arms, discipline, and instruction as "good."

Connelly, James D. (Sr. 2nd Lt.): (25); farmer; *killed.*

Rosser, Jabez R. (Jr. 2nd Lt.): (21); farmer.

Clement, Charles B.J. (2nd Sgt.): Enl. 18 March 1862 at Lynchburg.

Gilliam, Edward G. (3rd Sgt.): (20); farmer, *wounded.*

Cock, Robert M. (4th Sgt.): (24); farmer.

Brown, Watkins L. (5th Sgt.): (22); farmer; *wounded.*

Murrell, Charles H. (1st Cpl.): (19); farmer; *wounded.*

LeGrand, Peter A. (3rd Cpl.): (35); farmer; *killed.*

Creasey, Gustavus A. (4th Cpl.): (19); farmer.

Allen, Charles R.: Enl. 18 March 1862 at Lynchburg.

Blankenship, Charles T.: (18); farmer; *captured*; exchanged from Chester Hospital (apparently sick) 23 September 1863.

Blankenship, Leslie C: Enl. 18 March 1862 at Lynchburg; *captured*; exchanged sometime after August 1864.

Brown, James A.: Enl. 18 March 1862 at Lynchburg; sick since 16 June 1863 but listed as present 30 June.

Caldwell, Daniel R.: (21); farmer.

Callaham, Charles M.: Enl. 24 July 1861 at Manassas.

Cary, Peter: (20); farmer.

Cock, James B.: (18): farmer.

Creasey, Thomas C.: Enl. 18 March 1862 at Lynchburg.

Dunivant, Leroy W.: Enl. 3 October 1861 at Fairfax Court House; received a *wound* which fractured his right tibia 2 1/2" above the lower extremity and *captured*; exchanged from DeCamp Hospital 28 October 1863.

Franklin, Samuel T.: (21); farmer.

Hall, Stephen C.: Enl. 18 March 1862 at Lynchburg.

Holcombe, Ellis H.: (18); farmer.

Jennings, James M.: Enl. 18 March 1862 at Lynchburg.

Jones, Charles W.: (25); farmer; *killed* during the advance.

Jones, James C.: Enl. 18 March 1862 at Lynchburg; (28); *wounded* in the left elbow (arm amputated) and right side and *captured*; exchanged from West's Buildings Hospital 24 August 1863.

Jones, James T.: (19); farmer.

Jones, John Wesley: Enl. 18 March 1862 at Lynchburg.

Jones, Lineous: (24); farmer; *shot* in the throat and lungs; died at Pickett's Division Hospital 8 July 1863 and buried at Bream's Mill above Myers' house by the side of a fence; disinterred to Richmond 3 August 1872 with 33 others in three large boxes marked "P Curns."

Jones, Robert H.: Enl. 11 July 1861 at Lynchburg.

Jones, Robert W.S.: Enl. 18 March 1862 at Lynchburg; *wounded.*

Jones, Walker W.: (20); farmer; *killed.*

Kabler, Frederick: (24); teacher.

Kabler, William S.: (21); farmer.

Martin, James S.: Enl. 24 July 1861 at Manassas.

Mason, Morris W.: Enl. 18 March 1862 at Lynchburg; *killed.*

Monroe, John T.: (20); farmer.

Monroe, William J.: (22); farmer.

Morgan, Robert W.: Enl. 12 August 1862 at Campbell City; *shot* in both feet during the advance.

Murrell, Robert A.: Enl. 18 March 1862 at Lynchburg.

Pillow, Daniel A.: (23); farmer; initially listed by the company as missing in action and subsequently as *killed*; there are no Federal records concerning this man.

Pugh, John J.: Enl. 3 August 1861 at Centreville.

Rice, William A.: Enl. 3 July 1861 at Manassas.

Roberts, Pleasant A.: (18); wagoner.

Rosser, Walter C.: Enl. 18 March 1862 at Lynchburg.

Tweedy, Edmund A.: (20); farmer.

Tweedy, Fayette B.: (25); farmer.

Tweedy, George Dabney (19); farmer; *wounded* in the knee during the advance; died at Pickett's Division Hospital 3 July 1863 and buried by one of his brothers northeast of "Curn's" house in the corner of a field in the edge of the woods and on the south bank of Bream's Mill Dam; disinterred to Richmond 3 August 1872 in Box #248.

Tweedy, Smith P., Jr.: (20); farmer.

Walthall, Isaac G.: (32); tanner.

Wilkerson, William A.J.: Enl. 18 March 1862 at Lynchburg.

Wingfield, William H.: Enl. 18 March 1862 at Lynchburg.

Womack, Benjamin L.: Enl. 18 March 1862 at Lynchburg.

Company "D" ("Fincastle Rifles")

This unit was in existence in December 1859. The company enlisted 23 April 1861 at Fincastle, Botetourt County, Virginia for one year, and was reorganized 26 April 1862.

The following listing was obtained from the company's April/June 1863 muster roll uncaptioned as to date and station of the unit.

The company reported the condition of its clothing and discipline as "tolerable" and that of its military appearance, arms, accouterments, and instruction as "good."

Regimental skirmish company during the attack.

Houston, David Gardiner, Jr. (Captain): (23); lawyer; *shot* in the abdomen during the advance; died at Pickett's Division Hospital 4 July 1863 and buried at Bream's Mill on the hill.

James, John Thomas (1st Lt.): VMI class of 1863; enl. 20 July 1861 at Bull Run.

Camper, John H. (2nd Lt.): (22); clerk.

Frier, Jacob B. (3rd Lt.): (21); printer.

Nofsinger, Lewis (1st Sgt.): (31); tinner.

St. Clair, William H. (2nd Sgt.): (20).

Murry, Oliver H. (4th Sgt.): Enl. 1 March 1862.

Ammen, John N. (1st Cpl.): (18); *wounded* and *captured*; exchanged from DeCamp Hospital 8 September 1863.

McNeal, Robert F. (2nd Cpl.): (32).

Carper, Wyndham R. (3rd Cpl.): (20); *wounded* in the head.

Craig, John G. (4th Cpl.): (23).

Brown, Alfred N. (Drummer): Enl. 1 March 1862.

Anderson, Charles T.: (26); saddler.

Bosserman, William B.: (18); painter.

Camper, Newton L.: (19); mason.

Chafin, John H.: Enl. 1 March 1862.

Davis, Volney: (18).

Dillen, John Edward: (19); carpenter.

Fleig, Joseph A.: Tailor; captured at Greencastle, Pennsylvania 7 July 1863; released from Point Lookout 19 March 1864. Many of those captured at Greencastle were wounded men in Lee's wagon train on the way back to Virginia; probably *wounded*.

Fluke, Abraham W.: Enl. 1 March 1862; *shot* in the shoulder and *captured*; exchanged from DeCamp Hospital 8 September 1863.

Garman, George W.: (37); farmer.

Graybill, William L.: Enl. 1 August 1862.

Hamilton, George W.: (22).

Hazlewood, Charles T.: (21); driver.

Hickok, John F.:

Jennings, John W.: Enl. 13 February 1863.

Johnson George S.: Enl. 1 March 1862.

Jones, William D.: Enl. 1 March 1862.

Keefauver, Edward: (30); laborer.

Kelly, John: (21); farmer; *wounded*.

Kessler, James H.: (20).

Lantz, Lang R.: (27); farmer.

Lemmon, John McL.: Enl. 1 March 1862.

Lemmon, Nathan E.: (21).

Lemmon, Robert N.: (19).

Lowman, Cyrus W.: (25).

Murry, Barney: Enl. 1 March 1862.

Murry, Jacob P.: Enl. 1 March 1862.

Murry, John A.: Enl. 1 March 1862.

Pritchard, James I.: Enl. 1 March 1862.

Rader, Oliver Perry: (20).

Simmons, William: (21); *captured*; exchanged 20 or 21 February 1865.

Simpson, John C.: Enl. 1 March 1862.

Smith, Henry B.: Enl. 1 March 1862.

Smith, Jacob Bailey: (26).

Smith, James E.: Enl. 31 July 1861 at Centreville.

Spickard, John G.: Enl. 1 March 1862.

Company "E" ("Lynchburg Rifles")

This company enlisted 19 April 1861 at Lynchburg, Campbell County, Virginia for one year; was mustered 3 June 1861; and was reorganized 26 April 1862.

The following listing was obtained from the company's April/June 1863 muster roll captioned 1 July 1863 in camp near Chambersburg, Pennsylvania. It did not report its status.

Ward, John C. (Captain): (29); teacher; VMI class of 1853; *captured*; exchanged 15 October 1864 sick with phthisis.

Norvell, George P. (2nd Lt.): (24); carpenter.

Wray, James W. (2nd Lt.): Enl. 5 June 1861; (20); tobacconist.

Marion, John L. (3rd Sgt.): Enl. 6 June 1861.

Seay, William M. (4th Sgt.): (18).

Kelly, John (1st Cpl.): (20); *shot* in the leg and *captured*; released from Point Lookout 13 May 1865.

Whitlow, William P. (2nd Cpl.): Enl. 10 June 1861; (18); farmer; *wounded*.

Davies, Arthur B. (Cpl.): (18); farmer; *killed*.

Atkinson, John: (33); mechanic.

Bailey, Samuel D.: Enl. 10 June 1861; (23); *wounded*.

Bailey, Thomas L.: Enl. 12 May 1862.

Brown, Hillary B.: (24).

Burks, Solomon C.: Enl. 3 June 1861.

Clark, Chastain B.: Enl. 26 July 1861.

Clark, Christopher C.: Enl 26 July 1861.

Coffee, William H.: (24); carpenter; the company lists him as missing in action but there are no Federal records concerning him; *killed*.

Colvin, Henry H.: (23).

Colvin, William O.: (21); *wounded*.

Day, Thomas E.: (23).

Elder, Hiram: Enl. 10 March 1862 at Lynchburg.

Fortune, William: Enl. 5 June 1861 at Lynchburg; (26).

Gilbert, George W.: (26); probably *wounded*; *captured*; exchanged 1 August 1863.

Gilbert, William P.: Enl. 10 March 1862.

Grant, Bluford: Enl. 5 June 1861; (21); farmer.

Gregory, Nathaniel H.: Enl. 10 June 1861; (22).

Haynes, Robert L.: (29); the company lists him as captured at Gettysburg but there are no Federal records concerning him; *killed.*

Hendrick, James D.: Enl. 10 March 1862; probably *wounded; captured;* exchanged 1 August 1863.

Holt, John R.: Enl. 10 June 1861; (30); farmer; *wounded.*

Hurt, William S.: Enl. 3 June 1861.

Jenkins, John S.: Enl. 6 June 1861; (23).

Keaton, James P.: (25); received a gunshot *wound* of his left leg which fractured the bone below his knee; leg amputated at the upper third of humerus; *captured;* treated at U.S. XII Corps Hospital at Gettysburg; exchanged from West's Buildings Hospital 17 November 1863.

Lipscomb, Charles P.: Enl. 6 June 1861; (19); *wounded.*

Maier, John: Enl. 4 August 1862; born in England; *killed.*

Marshal, Charles H.: Enl. 10 March 1862; *shot* in the leg fracturing the femur (amputated) and *captured;* treated at the U.S. 2nd Division, II Corps Hospital; exchanged from West's Buildings Hospital 17 November 1863.

Neville, Louis C.: Enl. 17 July 1861; *wounded.*

Noel, James H.: Enl. 6 June 1861; (21); carpenter.

Padgett, John J.: Enl. 10 June 1861; (22); farmer.

Parris, Thomas H.: (18); well digger.

Pettus, John E.: (28); merchant; *captured;* joined U.S. service 18 October 1864.

Searson, Thomas: Enl. 5 June 1861; (24).

Smith, John G.: (23).

Smith, Robert: (21).

Smith, Thomas J.: Enl. 3 June 1861; (29).

Stewart, William H.: Enl. 5 June 1861; (23).

Sullivan, Michael: Enl. 8 June 1861; (22); *captured;* exchanged 20 or 21 February 1865.

Turski, Francis: Enl. 4 April 1863.

Ward, James S.: (22).

Company "F" ("Preston Guards" also "Montgomery Guards")

This company enlisted 29 May 1861 at Christiansburg, Montgomery County, Virginia for one year, and was reorganized 26 April 1862.

The following listing was obtained from the company's April/June 1863 muster roll captioned 30 June 1863 in camp near Chambersburg, Pennsylvania. The company did not report its status on 30 June.

Douthat, Robert W. (Captain): (21); student.

Ragan, James H. (1st Lt.): (22); carpenter; *wounded.*

Long, Green B. (Jr. 2nd Lt.): (22); carpenter; received a gunshot *wound* which fractured his right humerus during the repulse (shoulder joint resected) and *captured;* exchanged 13 December 1864.

Doud, Sylvester J. (2nd Sgt.): (21); miner; *wounded.*

Cromer, Samuel W. (3rd Sgt.): (18); clerk.

Turner, John R. (4th Sgt.): (23); farmer.

Hanes, James C. (5th Sgt.): (20); carpenter.

Kyle, Robert G. (1st Cpl.): (19); clerk; *shot* in the thigh and *captured*; exchanged from DeCamp Hospital 8 September 1863.

Thompson, Ennis S. (2nd Cpl.): (28); farmer; *wounded.*

Price, Henry C. (3rd Cpl.): (18); tanner.

Burton, Robert W. (4th Cpl.): (25); carpenter.

Akers, John W. (5th Cpl.): Enl. 28 July 1861 at Centreville.

Akers, Amos G.: Enl. 28 July 1861 at Centreville; *wounded* and suffering from chronic rheumatism; deserted from hospital 30 July 1863.

Akers, Dexter: (23); farmer.

Alley, D.S.: Enl. 15 March 1862 at Richmond; *wounded* and *captured*; died at Letterman Hospital 29 July 1863; disinterred to Richmond 13 June 1872 from Section 1, Grave #3, Camp Letterman Hospital cemetery in Box #54.

Bain, Waddy C.: (20); farmer.

Barnett, William H.: Enl. 15 March 1862; (18).

Bishop, Obediah: Enl. 15 March 1862; (37).

Bones, Joseph E.: Enl. 15 March 1862; (19); *captured*; exchanged 15 November 1864.

Borden, George W.: (23); farmer.

Burk, John R.: Enl. 28 July 1861 at Centreville.

Cox, Daniel: (29); laborer; (in arrest 30 June in regimental guardhouse).

Craig, James T.F.: (18); saddler.

Dooley, William H.: Enl. 10 March 1862; (21).

Eakin, Jotham W.: (21); farmer; *killed.*

East, Richard J.: Enl. 2 August 1861 at Centreville; severely *wounded.*

Einstein, Harvey: Enl. 15 March 1862; the company reports him as missing in action but there are no Federal records concerning him; *killed.*

Haley, Charles W.: (19); farmer.

Harman, Joseph H.: Enl. 2 August 1861 at Centreville.

Haymaker, Philip: (20); farmer; AWOL 4 July 1863.

Hite, John T.: (23); farmer.

Hughs, Aaron: (24); farmer.

Long, W.F.: Enl. 15 March 1862; (19).

Lucas, George P.: Enl. 15 March 1862; (20).

Lucas, John B.: (19); farmer.

Lucas, Rice M.: Enl. 15 March 1862; (18); farmer.

Martin, John H.: (34); laborer.

Miles, Thomas W.: (25); farmer; *captured*; exchanged 20 or 21 February 1865.

Myers, Joseph S.: Enl. 15 March 1862; (22); the company reports him as missing in action but there are no Federal records concerning him; *killed.*

Phares, Eli P.: Enl. 15 March 1862; (16).

Rader, George W.: (26); brickmaker.

Rader, William: (22); brickmaker; *wounded* in the right heel.

Roop, Fleming S.: Enl. 28 July 1861 at Centreville.

Roop, H.R.: Enl. 15 March 1862; (35); *shot* in the leg and *captured*; exchanged from DeCamp Hospital 8 September 1863.

Shelton, Samuel C.: Enl. 15 March 1862; (27).

Smith, W.W.: Enl. 15 March 1862; (25).

St. Clair, W.P.: Enl. 15 March 1862; (26); received a gunshot *wound* which fractured his left leg and *captured*; exchanged from West's Buildings Hospital 27 September 1863.

Taylor, John Wade: Enl. 15 March 1862; (18); *captured*; died of acute dysentery at Fort Delaware 28 September 1863; buried at Finns Point, N.J.

Trent, John E.: Enl. 15 March 1862; (19).

Trent, William J.: (21); farmer.

Turner, Chester B.: (22); farmer.

Whitworth, Isaac: Enl. 15 March 1862; (35).

Williamson, James: Enl. 28 July 1861 at Centreville, (23 in 1863); *wounded*; died at Pickett's Division Hospital 4 July 1863 and buried at Bream's Mill on the hill; disinterred to Richmond 3 August 1872 with 33 others in three large boxes marked "P Curns."

Company "G" ("Lynchburg Home Guard")

Organized 8 November 1859, this company enlisted 23 April 1861 at Lynchburg, Campbell County, Virginia for one year; was mustered into service at Richmond 24 April 1861; and was reorganized 26 April 1862.

The following listing was obtained from the company's April/June 1863 muster roll captioned 30 June 1863 near Chambersburg. The company did not report its status as of 30 June.

Smith, John Holmes (Captain): (22); merchant; *shot* in the right thigh during the attack.

Jennings, Tipton D., Jr. (1st Sgt.): (20); merchant.

Guy, Dewitt C. (2nd Sgt.): (19); merchant; *wounded* during the cannonade and sent to the rear.

Franklin, Philip H. (2nd Cpl.): (20); clerk; *wounded*.

Pierce, Roberson C. (3rd Cpl.): (26); merchant.

Kent, James R. (4th Cpl.): (23); farmer; received a flesh *wound* in the upper third of his left leg during the attack and *captured*; exchanged from Chester Hospital 20 August 1863.

Lydick, James H. (Musician): (22).

Agnew, William H.: Enl. at Lynchburg, enrolled for service 25 May 1861 at Manassas Junction; (30); teacher; received a *wound* which fractured both the superior and inferior maxilla (jaw); no further records concerning this soldier; may have died in an unspecified Gettysburg hospital.

Conley, John H.: (29); clerk.

Elliott, Samuel H.: Enl. at Lynchburg; enrolled for service 28 May 1861 at Manassas Junction; (19); trader; *shot* in the foot and/or right knee and *captured*;

treated at U.S. 2nd Division, II Corps Hospital; exchanged from DeCamp Hospital 8 September 1863.

Ivey, O.L.: Enl. at Lynchburg; enrolled for service 12 July 1861 at Manassas Junction; *shot* in the left hip and *captured*; treated at U.S. 2nd Division, II Corps Hospital; exchanged from Chester Hospital 17 August 1863.

Jennings, James H.: (22); merchant.

Jennings, Thomas: Enl. 1 May 1863 at Suffolk; *killed* during the cannonade by the same shell that killed his brother.

Jennings, William: Enl. 1 May 1863 at Suffolk; *killed* during the cannonade by the same shell that killed his brother.

Kent, Robert A.: Enl. 15 March 1862; (17); *wounded.*

Litchford, Edward L.: Enl. 15 March 1862; (27); AWOL in July or August 1863.

Litton, James E.P.: Enl. 15 March 1862; (16).

Moore, James M: Enl. 1 November 1861 at Centreville; thigh fractured and *captured*; *died* at U.S. II Corps Hospital 19 July 1863 and buried in back of Schwartz's barn.

Nelson, William S.: (24); merchant.

Old, John J.: Enl. at Lynchburg; enrolled for service 31 May 1861 at Manassas Junction; (23); student.

Overstreet, Alexander: Enl. 1 October 1862 at Winchester; the company initially reports him as wounded and subsequently as missing in action but there are no Federal records concerning him; *killed.*

Percival, C. Dabney: (25); carpenter; possibly *wounded*; captured while serving as a nurse at Gettysburg; exchanged from West's Buildings Hospital 17 November 1863.

Peters, Richard T.: (19); merchant.

Poindexter, William D.: Enl. 15 March 1862; (18).

Sale, James P.: Enl. 15 March 1862; (17).

Shaver, William H.: (20); student.

Smith, John: Enl. 1 October 1862 at Winchester; *wounded.*

Taylor, James R.: Enl. 15 March 1862; (30).

Turner, G.M.: Enl. 15 March 1862; (19); *captured*; exchanged 21 January 1865.

Valentine, Edward W.: Enl. 15 March 1862; (18); *killed* during the cannonade.

Valentine, Joseph A.: (27); merchant.

Williams, J.M.: Enl. 15 March 1862; (16); at Lynchburg General Hospital 31 August 1863; probably *wounded.*

Winston, William H.H.: Enl. at Lynchburg; enrolled for service 26 May 1861 at Manassas Junction; (21); farmer; knocked unconscious by the explosion of a shell at the enemy's works during the attack; *captured*; exchanged 14 or 15 February 1865.

Company "H" ("Jeff Davis Guard" also "Jefferson Davis Riflemen")

This company enlisted and was mustered into service 15 May 1861 at Lynchburg, Campbell County, Virginia for one year, and was reorganized 26 April 1862.

The following listing was obtained from the company's April/June 1863 muster roll captioned 30 June 1863 near Chambersburg, Pennsylvania.

The company reports the condition of its clothing as "fair," its arms as "Springfield muskets," its accouterments as "complete," and its military appearance, discipline and instruction as "good."

Hutter, James Risque (Captain): (19); VMI class of 1860; U.S. Postal Department; received a gunshot *wound* across the chest near the stone wall during the attack; *captured*; paroled for exchanged 2 February 1865.

Floyd, Nathan D. (1st Sgt.): (19); carpenter; *wounded.*

Hurt, John H. (3rd Sgt.): (23); farmer.

Myers, Samuel W. (4th Sgt.):

Doyle, Henry (5th Sgt.): (24); reporter.

Daniel, John P. (1st Cpl.): (24); day laborer; *wounded* in both ankles (secondary amputation of both legs) and suffering from irritative fever; died at Pickett's Division Hospital 28 or 30 July 1863 and buried at Bream's Mill above Myers' house at the side of a fence; disinterred to Richmond 3 August 1872 with 33 others in three large boxes marked "P Curns."

Burford, William H. (2nd Cpl.): (20); farmer.

Boland, John: Enl. 23 June 1861 at Manassas Junction; (20); driver; *wounded.*

Brown, John C.:

Daprato, John: Enl. 10 March 1862; *wounded* in the left ankle (secondary amputation of leg) and *captured*; exchanged from West's Buildings Hospital 17 November 1863.

Davenport, Joseph: Enl. 26 August 1862.

Davis, John R.: (21); day laborer.

Farrer, Robert H.: Enl. 15 June 1861 at Manassas Junction; (22); farmer; *captured*; released from Point Lookout 25 January 1864 and joined U.S. service.

Fitzgerald, Cyrus: (22); farmer.

Floyd, Alexander: (28); carpenter.

Fox, Edward M.: (19); farmer; *wounded.*

Fulks, Robert:

Rogers, George W.: (32); day laborer.

Seay, Richard B.: Enl. 3 July 1861 at Manassas.

Turner, Charles H.: Enl. 15 June 1861 at Manassas; (21); farmer; *captured*; died of chronic diarrhea at Fort Delaware 10 January 1865.

Whitten, James W.: (22); farmer.

Company "I" ("Rough and Ready Rifles")

This company enlisted 25 May 1861 at Morrisville, Fauquier County, Virginia and was mustered into service 4 June 1861 for one year. The unit was reorganized 26 April 1862.

The following listing was obtained from the company's April/June 1863 muster roll captioned 1 July 1863 near Chambersburg, Pennsylvania.

The company reports the condition of its clothing as "tolerable," its arms as "Springfield muskets," its accouterments as "complete," and its military appearance, discipline and instruction as "good."

Jones, Andrew J. (Captain): (30); farmer; recieved a gunshot flesh *wound* of the right foot during the advance and subsequently *captured*; treated with a simple dressing at the U.S. 1st Division, II Corps Hospital; exchanged 22 March 1865.

Stringfellow, Bruce W. (1st Lt.): (23); farmer.

Embrey, Judson J. (2nd Lt.): (24); teacher.

Embrey, Norman D. (2nd Sgt.): (20); farmer.

Porter, William S. (5th Sgt.): Enl. 6 June 1861 at Manassas; (20); mechanic; the company reports him as missing in action but there are no Federal records concerning him; *killed*.

Bennett, Oscar A. (4th Cpl.): (27); farmer.

Brown, James W.: (19); farmer; the company reports this man as AWOL in July or August 1863; he was actually captured at Kelly's Ford 6 August 1863 and exchanged 15 November 1864.

Brown, Jesse: Enl. 1 October 1862; probably *wounded*; *captured*; exchanged from Chester Hospital 23 September 1863.

Childs, Zachariah S.: (21); farmer; *wounded*.

Claxton, Henry: (21); farmer; *captured*; exchanged sick from Point Lookout 6 March 1864.

Claxton, Robert P.: (23); farmer; AWOL July 1863; captured in Fauquier County 6 August 1863 and exchanged 15 November 1864; probably captured at Kelly's Ford with James W. Brown above.

Coppage, Lewis J.: (26); laborer; *captured*; released from Fort Delaware 19 June 1865.

Courtney, Bazil: (22); shoemaker; *captured*; died of chronic diarrhea at Point Lookout 1 February 1864.

Courtney, Calvin: Enl. 19 July 1961 at Manassas.

Courtney, James E.: Enl. 1 October 1862.

Edwards, Henry: Enl. 19 March 1862 at Warrenton Junction; *captured*; exchanged 20 or 21 February 1865.

Edwards, Inman R.: Enl. 1 October 1862.

Embrey, Charles O.: Enl. 17 June 1861 at Manassas; (23); clerk.

Embrey, James T.: Enl. 12 April 1862 at Louisa Court House; received a gunshot *wound* which fractured the upper third of his right femur (leg amputated) and *captured*; died at Point Lookout 14 April 1864.

Embrey, Jesse C.: Enl. 12 April 1862 at Louisa Court House.

Embrey, Robert E.: (24); laborer; *shot* in the neck and *captured*; exchanged from Chester Hospital 17 August 1863.

Embrey, Thomas R.: (19); farmer; *wounded*.

Evans, John R.: (28); laborer; deserted near Bunker Hill, West Virginia 17 July 1863.

Freeman, Allen: (21); laborer; AWOL July 1863.

Freeman, Samuel: (21); laborer.

Glassell, James S.: Enl. 6 June 1861 at Manassas; (34); clerk; received a *wound* which fractured the base of his cranium and *captured*; died at U.S. II Corps Hospital 5 July 1863 and buried there.

Guthridge, William E.: (28); laborer; AWOL July or August 1863.

Hansbrough, Elijah T.: (19); farmer; *wounded*; no further record; probably died in an unspecified Gettysburg hospital.

Huffman, Thomas: (26); laborer; the company reports him as missing in action but there are no Federal records concerning him; *killed.*

Jacobs, Welford C.: (19); laborer; AWOL July or August 1863.

James, Benjamin D.: (29); laborer; company muster rolls report him as *wounded* through August 1864; captured by Federal cavalry 13 November 1863 at Elk Run, Fauquier County, Virginia apparently while home on wounded furlough; released from Point Lookout 12, 13, or 14 May 1865.

James, Charles H.: (18); laborer; *wounded.*

James, John B.: (26); farmer; the company reports him as absent *wounded* through August 1864; Federal records show him captured at Kelly's Ford near Culpeper, Virginia by the U.S. XI Corps (no date provided); died at Elmira, New York as a prisoner 10 February 1865.

Jones, John O.: Enl. 1 October 1862; received a gunshot flesh *wound* of his left knee and right femur and *captured*; treated with a simple dressing at U.S. 1st Division, II Corps Hospital; died there 15 July 1863 and buried in Yard "D" of the hospital's cemetery in Jacob Schwartz's cornfield on Rock Creek; disinterred to Richmond 13 June 1872 with 110 others in ten large boxes marked "S."

Jones, Thomas E.: Enl. 1 October 1862; deserted 6 September 1863 near Mountain Run Dam near Ellis Ford, Culpeper, Virginia; captured by U.S. 2nd Division, XII Corps 8 September 1863.

Kemper, James G.: (18); farmer; AWOL July or August 1863.

McConchie, John: Enl. 6 June 1861 at Manassas; (22); laborer; *wounded.*

McConchie, William: Enl. 6 June 1861 at Manassas; (24); laborer; the company reports him as missing in action but there are no Federal records concerning him; *killed.*

McConchie, William A.: Enl. 6 June 1861 at Manassas; (29); carpenter.

Stephens, William A.: (30); laborer; deserted at Bunker Hill, West Virginia 17 July 1863; captured by Federal cavalry in Fauquier County 26 August 1863; took the oath of allegiance to the U.S. and sent to Philadelphia, Pennsylvania 28 September 1863.

Stribling, Robert H.: Enl. 1 October 1862; *captured*; died of chronic dysentery at Point Lookout 31 October 1863.

Tulloss, William H.: AWOL in July or August 1863.

Company "K" ("Valley Regulators")

This company enlisted 25 May 1861 at Roaring Run, Botetourt County, Virginia for one year, and was reorganized 26 April 1862.

The following listing was obtained from the company's April/June 1863 muster roll captioned 5 August 1863 near Raccoon Ford, Virginia. There are no entries subsequent to 30 June 1863 on this roll indicating that it was intended to reflect the status of the company as of 30 June.

The company does not report its conditions on this roll.

Houston, Andrew M. (Captain): (20); medical student; received a gunshot *wound* of his left ulna, fracturing same, during the advance and subsequently *captured*; exchanged 29 January 1864.

Houston, Thomas D. (1st Lt.): Received a gunshot flesh *wound* of his right buttock and *captured*; exchanged 22 March 1865.

Hardy, James T.: (2nd Sgt.): (20); farmer.

Bowyer, David W. (2nd Sgt.): (19); farmer; *wounded.*

Hardy, William H.: (3rd Sgt.): (23); farmer; the company reports him as having been wounded and captured but there are no Federals records concerning him; *killed.*

Schindel, Samuel P. (4th Sgt.): (21); farmer; admitted to Fairview Hospital, Lexington, Virginia 10 July 1863 but wound or sickness not recorded; probably *wounded* at Gettysburg.

Sale, George W. (5th Sgt.): (18); farmer.

Parks, Charles P. (1st Cpl.): Enl. 24 July 1861 at Manassas; the company reports him as having been captured but there are no Federal records concerning him; *killed.*

Powers, John (2nd Cpl.): Enl. 24 July 1861 at Manassas.

Agner, George W.: (23); cooper.

Austin, Joseph: Enl. 24 July 1861 at Manassas.

Brafford, Marcellus: (21); student; *captured*; released from Fort Delaware 19 June 1865.

Campbell, Samuel L.: Enl. 24 July 1861 at Manassas; recieved a gunshot flesh *wound* of his right shoulder and *captured*; joined U.S. service at Point Lookout 24 January 1864.

Dooly, Andrew A.: (20); farmer.

Dooly, James P.: (24); farmer; received a flesh *wound* in his left leg (amputated) and *captured*; exchanged from West's Buildings Hospital 27 September 1863.

Furgason, James: Enl. 24 July 1861 at Manassas; *wounded* and *captured*; paroled from West's Buildings Hospital 23 August 1863.

Furgusson, Eldridge: Enl. 26 May 1863 at Hanover Junction; *captured*; died of anemia at Fort Delaware 26 September 1863.

Houston, Edward M.: Enl. 20 April 1863 at Suffolk.

Hunt, B.B.: Enl. 10 March 1862 in Rockbridge County; the company reports him as having been wounded and captured but there are no Federal records concerning him; *killed.*

Isaacs, John R.: Enl. 24 July 1861 at Manassas.

Johnson, James D.: (22); farmer; *captured*; died of chronic dysentery at Fort Delaware 23 October 1863; buried at Finns Point, N.J.

Keyton, Washington J.: Enl. 21 May 1861; (25); teacher.

Markham, William T.: Enl. 15 May 1861 at Buchanan.

McClelland, Joseph E.: Enl. 28 May 1862 at Richmond.

Morton, William A.: (18); farmer.

Reid, James H.: (29); farmer.

Reid, William H.A.: (25); farmer.

Schindle, John H.: Enl. 24 July 1861 at Manassas.

Shorter, William H.: (18); farmer.

Silvey, Alfred: (24); boatman.

Unrue, Henry: Enl. 10 March 1862 in Rockbridge County.

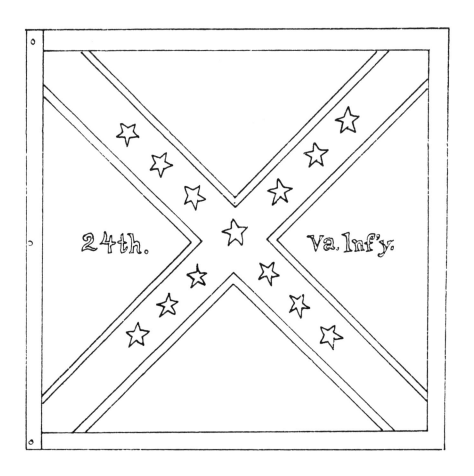

Flag of the 24th Virginia Infantry

24th Virginia Volunteer Infantry Regiment

This regiment was organized in May or June 1861; accepted into Confederate service, 1 July 1861; and reorganized 10 May 1862.

The following listing was obtained from company April/June 1863 muster rolls captioned 30 June 1863 near Chambersburg, Pennsylvania. Company "A" did not provide a date or location for its muster but these are undoubtedly the same as those of the other companies of the regiment.

All companies (excepting "F" and "K" which did not report their condition), reported the status of their shoes as "indifferent," and that of their military appearance, arms accouterments, discipline and instruction as "good."

Field and Staff

Terry, William Richard (Colonel): Born in Bedford County in 1827; merchant in 1861; graduate of VMI class of 1850; commissioned Colonel 21 September 1861; appointed Brigadier General 31 May 1864.

Hambrick, Joseph Adam (Major): Born in Franklin County, Virginia 17 April 1833; graduated VMI in 1857; University of Virginia graduate; lawyer; enl. 23 May 1861 at Lynchburg as Captain of Company "B"; promoted to Major 9 April 1863; slightly *wounded* during the cannonade; his horse (a bay) was killed at Gettysburg and appraised at $550 for which Major Hambrick was reimbursed after the battle.

Taliaferro, William T. (1st Lt., Adjutant): VMI class of 1845; enl. 23 May 1861 at Lynchburg as 1st Lt. in Company "B"; appointed regimental adjutant 14 May 1862; resigned 27 June 1864; received a slight *contusion* of the elbow during the attack.

Woods, Robert C. (Capt., AQM): Enl. 23 May 1861 at Lynchburg as a Private in Company "B"; born in Franklin County, Virginia; appointed AQM 29 June 1861.

Dennis, George E. (Capt., ACS): Enl. 23 May 1861 at Lynchburg as a Sergeant in Company "B"; appointed ACS 29 June 1861.

Harrison, George T. (Surgeon): Appointed Asst. Surgeon 11 October 1861; appointed Surgeon 12 June 1863; born in Albemarle County, Virginia.

Coleman, Clayton G., Jr. (Asst. Surgeon): Enl. 24 April 1861 at Frederick Hall as Captain of Company "G," 23rd Virginia; (21); doctor; appointed Asst. Surgeon 18 November 1862 and assigned to the 24th Virginia.

Wells, George M. (Commissary Sgt.): Detailed from Company "A"; enl. 14 May 1861 at Floyd Court House; (24); physician.

Waller, George E. (Hospital Steward): Detailed from Company "H"; enl. 17 March 1862 at Henry Court House; (23).

Belcher, George P. (Ambulance Corps): Detailed from Company "G"; enl. 4 May 1861 at Lynchburg.

Allen, Obadiah M, (Ambulance Corps): Detailed from Company "H"; enl. 5 June 1861 at Henry Court House.

Dyer, Thomas G. (Hospital Nurse): Detailed from Company "H"; enl. 5 June 1861 at Henry Court House.

Bussey, James O. (Regimental Drummer): Detailed from Company "G"; enl. 16 March 1863 at Petersburg; deserted 18 July 1863.

Cook, Samuel (Teamster): Detailed from Company "F"; enl. 26 December 1859 in Giles County.

Color Guard

Taylor, Henry: Detailed from Company "A"; enl. 14 May 1861 at Floyd Court House; (18); saddler.

Company "A" ("Floyd Riflemen")

This company was organized in Floyd County 28 April 1860; was enrolled for service at Floyd Court House, Floyd County, Virginia 14 May 1861; was mustered into service 16 May 1861 for one year; and was reorganized 10 May 1862.

Headen, John W. (1st Lt.): (19); medical student; *wounded.*

Kitterman, George W. (3rd Lt.): (20); farmer; *shot* in the lower back portion of the right abdomen partially fracturing this spine and causing paralysis of one leg; *captured*; exchanged 20 March 1864.

Bower, Robert H. (2nd Sgt.): (19).

Helms, John W. (3rd Sgt.): (19); barkeeper; *wounded.*

Payne, Francis M. (4th Sgt.): (22); carpenter; *wounded*; no further record; may have died of his wounds in an unspecified Confederate Hospital.

Simmons, Thomas H. (5th Sgt.): (21); farmer; *wounded.*

Lawson, Wilson T. (1st Cpl.): (21); student.

Dobyns, Frazier O. (2nd Cpl.): (18); student; *captured*; exchanged 14 or 15 February 1865.

Martin, Preston H. (4th Cpl.): (26); carpenter.

Atkins, Levi G. : Enl. 12 March 1862; *captured*; exchanged 15 November 1864.

Daniel, Champion T.: (34); laborer.

De Hart, Henry: Enl. 18 March 1862.

De Hart, Jesse H.: Enl. 18 March 1862; the company initially reports him as wounded and captured and subsequently as missing in action but there are no Federal records concerning him; *killed.*

Earls, Gordon C.: Enl. 14 March 1862; (35).

Fergerson, William: (30); farmer.

Goodykoontz, George W.: (21); student.

Goodykoontz, William M.: Enl. 31 August 1861 at Mason's Hill; *wounded.*

Graham, Tazewell T.: (28); blacksmith.

Griffith, Daniel A.: Enl. 31 August 1861 at Mason's Hill; resided in Franklin County; *captured*; released from Fort Delaware 20 June 1865.

Griffith, Elkanah B.: (26); farmer; born in Floyd County; *wounded*; died of gangrene at the General Hospital at Montgomery White Sulphur Springs, Virginia 10 August 1863.

Howell, Dillard C.: (20).

Howell, Thomas: Enl. 7 March 1862; (26).

Huff, Ferdinand A.: (27); farmer.

Hylton, John H.: (26); carpenter.

Hylton, Mathias F.: (24); farmer.

Hylton, Sparrel. L.: Enl. 31 October 1861 in the camp of the 24th Virginia.

Keith, Asa: Enl. 31 August 1861 at Mason's Hill.

Lawrence, Gideon L.: Enl. 13 March 1862; (18).

Lester, George W.: (23); shoemaker.

Mabrey, Joseph J., Jr.: (21); farmer.

Martin, Isaac N.: Enl. 31 August 1861 at Mason's Hill.

Palmer, Isaac: (28); *captured*; died of fever at Fort Delaware 23 May 1864.

Palmer, Samuel: Enl. 31 August 1861 at Mason's Hill.

Pugh, Clark W.: Enl. 14 March 1862; (32).

Simpkins, Richard L.: Enl. 18 March 1862; (23).

Smith, Jacob: Enl. 5 March 1862; (24).

Smith, John: Enl. 18 March 1862; (29).

Sowers, Caleb: (21); farmer.

Switzer, George M.: Enl. 31 October 1861 in the camp of the 24th Virginia.

Underwood, John T.: Enl. 31 August 1861 at Mason's Hill; deserted near Rapidan Station 3 August 1863.

Underwood, William A.: (20); farmer.

Underwood, William L.: (20); farmer.

Weddle, Ahab: (26); farmer; *captured*; died at Point Lookout 7 March 1864.

Weeks, Charles C.: (30); farmer; resided at Jacksonville, Floyd County; *captured*; exchanged 1 August 1863 sick with typhoid fever and chronic diarrhea.

Young, George W.: Enl. 12 March 1862; (23).

Company "B"

This company was orgaized at Gogginsville and Rocky Mount, Franklin County, Virginia 25 April 1861; was mustered into service for one year at Lynchburg 23 May 1861; and was reorganized 10 May 1862.

Bernard, John A. (Captain): AWOL 4 July 1863; reported at home sick on company's July/August 1863 muster roll.

Smith, George A. (1st Lt.): *Captured*; exchanged 22 March 1865.

Webb, Theodore S. (2nd 2nd Lt.): (21 in 1864); resided in Franklin County; *shot* in the left side in back of the chest, the ball lodging in the wound, and *captured*; released 12 June 1865.

Angell, Joshua H. (1st Sgt.):

Crumpecker, William H. (2nd Sgt.):

Harper, Charles C. (3rd Sgt.): Resided in Franklin County; slightly *wounded* in the thigh and *captured*; exchanged from DeCamp Hospital 8 September 1863.

Mansfield, James D. (4th Sgt.): The company initially reports him as missing in action and subsequently as "supposed killed" but there are no Federal records concerning him; *killed*.

Turner, William B. (1st Cpl.):

Creasey, John W. (2nd Cpl.):

James, Isaac L. (3rd Cpl.): Enl. 3 March 1862 at Rocky Mount.

Sink, John H. (4th Cpl.): Father was Mr. Otey Sink; the company initially reports him as missing in action and subsequently as "supposed killed" but there are no Federal records concerning him; *killed.*

Abshire, Esom:

Abshire, Robert T.: *Captured;* died at Point Lookout 12 or 27 February 1864.

Abshire, Tazwell:

Adams, James L.: Enl. 1 October 1862 at Winchester; *captured;* paroled for exchange 27 February 1865.

Beach, Richard R.:

Blankinship, Thomas:

Boitnott, John H.:

Bousman, Josiah: *Wounded* and *captured;* exchanged from DeCamp Hospital 8 September 1863.

Brown, James E.: Enl. 6 March 1862 at Gogginsville; (present in arrest for desertion).

Byrd, William H.: Deserted 14 July 1863 at Martinsburg, West Virgina.

Craddock, William T.:

Creasey, Thomas H.: Enl. 6 March 1862 at Gogginsville.

Crumpecker, Granville:

Davis, Joel:

Dillon, William F.: Enl. 3 March 1862 at Rocky Mount.

Eddy, John C.:

Elliott, Joshua L.:

Finch, Thomas R.: Enl. 27 February 1862 at Gogginsville.

Gearhart, William R.:

Gibson, James: *Captured;* exchanged sick 22 September 1864; died of acute dysentery 25 September 1864.

Guthery, William H.: Enl. 6 March 1862 at Gogginsville.

Hall, James P.:

Hensley, Charles C.:

Hoy, James M.: Enl. 10 March 1862 at Gogginsville; mother was Ruth Hoy; the company reports him as missing in action but there are no Federal records concerning him; *killed.*

Inge, Lawson E.:

Lynch, Christopher: Enl. 3 March 1862 at Rocky Mount; *captured;* died at Fort Delaware 20 December 1863.

Lynch, John L.: Enl. 10 March 1862 at Gogginsville; *wounded* in the right chest and *captured;* exchanged from DeCamp Hospital 27 September 1863.

Lyon, John P.:

Meadors, William C.: The company reports him as missing in action but there are no Federal records concerning him; *killed.*

Merryman, James B.: (present in arrest for desertion).

Metts, Henry A.:

Mills, Major G.: Enl. 3 March 1862 at Rocky Mount; slightly *wounded* in the leg and *captured*; exchanged from DeCamp Hospital 8 September 1863.

Mountcastle, William D.:

Sink, Jesse: Enl. 10 March 1862 at Gogginsville.

Sink, William: Enl. 3 March 1862 at Rocky Mount.

Smith, John P.: Deserted 3 July 1863, probably while on the march to the battlefield.

Starkey, Nathaniel:

Teel, Josiah W.: The company initially reports him as missing in action and subsequently as "supposed killed" but there are no Federal records concerning him; *killed.*

Thompson, William P., Jr.:

Trent, John: Enl. 21 February 1862 at Big Lick; *captured*; died of smallpox at Fort Delaware 4 December 1863.

Trent, William: Enl. 17 March 1862 at Gogginsville; *wounded* in forefinger (amputated); sick in hospital on company's July/August 1863 muster roll.

Wade, John R.: Enl. 10 March 1862 at Gogginsville.

Walker, James R.: Enl. 10 March 1862 at Gogginsville.

Walker, Samuel H.:

Webb, Moses G.: Enl. 17 March 1862 at Gogginsville.

Wells, John C.C.:

Wray, Fields J.: Resided in Franklin County; slightly *wounded* in the right knee and *captured*; exchanged from West's Buildings Hospital 24 August 1863.

Young, Giles H.: Enl. 1 October 1862 at Winchester.

Company "C" ("Carroll Boys")

This company was organized 28 April 1861 at Hillsville, Carroll County, Virginia; was mustered into service for one year at Lynchburg 24 May 1861; and was reorganized 10 May 1862.

Shockley, Martin V.B. (Captain):

Sutherland, William H. (1st Lt.):

Walker, George H. (2nd Lt.): Born in Wythe County, Virginia; *killed.*

Hale, Ellis (2nd 2nd Lt.): Severely *wounded.*

Williams, Early L. (1st Sgt.): (27 in 1865).

Dalton, Isaac, Sr. (4th Sgt.): Enl. 31 August 1861 at Mason's Hill.

Crockett, John G. (1st Cpl.):

Kenney, Nicholas J. (2nd Cpl.): The company initially reports him as missing in action and subsequently as "supposed killed" but there are no Federal records concerning him; *killed.*

Worrell, Seberd W. (3rd Cpl.): Enl. 31 August 1861 at Mason's Hill.

Crawford, Thomas E. (4th Cpl.):

Anderson, Rush F.:

Ashworth, William O.: Enl. 31 August 1861 at Mason's Hill; *captured*; died of acute bronchitis at Point Lookout 10 February 1864.

Bedsaul, Friel: Enl. 23 March 1862 at Hillsville.

Bell, James W.: Captured while serving as a nurse at Gettysburg; exchanged 20 March 1864.

Briggs, Henry L.: Enl. 3 March 1862 at Hillsville: the company reports him as missing in action but there are no Federal records concerning him; *killed*.

Brown, Douglas B.: Slightly *wounded*.

Chappell, George W.: Slightly *wounded*.

Childress, Joshua M.: Enl. 17 March 1862 at Hillsville; possibly *wounded*; sent to hospital 4 July 1863 apparently sick but there are no Confederate hospital records concerning him; present with his company by 31 October 1863.

Dalton, Andrew J.: Enl. 21 February 1863 in Carroll County.

Dalton, Francis M.:

Dawson, Leroy T.: *Wounded* and *captured*; treated at U.S. 3rd Division, II Corps Hospital; died 21 July 1863 at U.S. II Corps Hospital and buried in Yard B, Row 2 of that hospital's cemetery on the hill between Schwartz's and Bushman's under a walnut tree; disinterred to Richmond 13 June 1872 in Box #10.

Dehaven, Wesley: Slightly *wounded*.

Dickens, Franklin C.: Deserted 5 July 1863; captured 6 July; released from Fort Delaware 11 May 1865.

Duncan, James F.:

Early, John W.: Enl. 31 August 1861 at Mason's Hill; *captured*; died of chronic dysentery at Point Lookout 4 February 1864.

Edwards, Creed H.:

Edwards, Richard M.: *Wounded*.

Farmer, Isaac L.: Enl. 21 February 1863 in Carroll County.

Goad, Henderson: (released from arrest 30 June 1863); *captured*; joined U.S. service at Fort Delaware 25 January 1864.

Hall, William T.: *Shot* in the right thigh.

Harrold, Daniel B.: *Shot* in the side, arm, and right temple (fractured perital) and captured; died of head wound at Point Lookout 7 January 1864.

Hicks, Jeremiah: Enl. 8 March 1862 at Hillsville; born in Carroll County; *shot* in the right leg 3 inches below the knee joint and *captured*; died, unconscious, at 11 P.M. 23 July 1863 at the Chestnut Street General Hospital, Harrisburg, Pennsylvania while recovering from his wound.

Hicks, Martin: Enl. 14 March 1862 at Hillsville.

Hicks, William R.: Discharged 20 July 1861; re-enlisted 4 March 1862 at Hillsville.

Irola, Emanuel: Enl. 31 August 1861 at Mason's Hill.

Jennings, Riley: Enl. 21 February 1863 in Carroll County.

Kenney, George H.: Enl. 16 March 1862 at Hillsville.

Kenney, William H.: Enl. 13 March 1862 at Hillsville; slightly *wounded* in the chest and *captured*; exchanged from DeCamp Hospital 28 August 1863.

Kirkbride, John: *Wounded*.

Leslie, Samuel: Enl. 31 August 1861 at Mason's Hill.

Lyon, Stephen B.:

Marshall, Ballard: The company reports him as missing in action but there are no Federal records concerning him; *killed.*

McHone, James: Enl. 21 February 1863 in Carroll County.

McHone, Micajah: Enl. 13 April 1863 near Suffolk; born in North Carolina; received a compound *fracture* of his right arm and *captured*; died at U.S. VI Corps Hospital and buried 40 feet east of a grave in the northeast corner of J. Trostle's field on the south bank of Rock Creek four miles southeast of Gettysburg; disinterred to Richmond 3 August 1872 in Box #251.

Melton, James M.: Enl. 16 March 1862 at Hillsville.

Mooney, Sidney C.: Enl. 3 March 1862 at Hillsville.

Philips, Thomas: Enl. 8 March 1862 at Hillsville.

Pickett, Oliver: Enl. 21 February 1863 in Carroll County.

Pool, John H.: Enl. 30 May 1861 in Company "K."

Rigney, Jehu H.:

Semones, James S.: Enl. 21 February 1863 in Carroll County; *captured*; died at Fort Delaware 6 October 1863.

Semones, Wilson F.:

Shelton, William B.:

Shockley, Richard: Enl. 21 February 1863 in Carroll County; severely *wounded* in the left ankle and *captured*; exchanged from DeCamp Hospital 27 September 1863.

Shockley, William: *Shot* in the neck and *captured*; exchanged from DeCamp hospital 8 September 1863; died from his wound in Carroll County 19 November 1863.

Stephens, William O.: Born in Carroll County; *killed.*

Sutphin, Floyd:

Taylor, John M.: Enl. 31 August 1861 at Mason's Hill; *wounded.*

Utt, William L.: Enl. 31 August 1861 at Mason's Hill.

Vaughan, William K.: Severely *wounded.*

Warf, William: Enl. 31 October 1861 at Union Mills; (18 in 1862); miner; severely *wounded.*

White, Ira: Enl. 4 March 1862 at Hillsville; (23 in 1863); received a gunshot *wound* which fractured his left humerus and *captured*; paroled for exchanged from West's Buildings Hospital 12 Novmeber 1863.

Williams, Absalom B.: Enl. 14 March 1862 at Hillsville.

Wood, Elias:

Wood, George:

Worrell, Josiah: Enl. 21 February 1863 in Carroll County; *wounded.*

Company "D"

This company was organized 13 May 1861 at Rocky Mount, Franklin County, Virginia; was mustered into service 11 June 1861 at Lynchburg for one year; and was reorganized 10 May 1862.

Saunders, Fleming (Captain):

Booth, Peter B. (1st Lt.): *Wounded*; AWOL 1 August 1863; present with his company by 31 October 1863.

Cooper, Giles H. (2nd Lt.): *Wounded*; leg amputated at lower third of left thigh, and *captured*; died 27 July 1863 at U.S. II Corps Hospital and buried in Yard B of that hospital's cemetery on the hill between Schwartz's and Bushman's under a walnut tree; disinterred to Richmond 13 June 1872 in Box #202.

Greer, James E. (2nd 2nd Lt.): Enl. 23 May 1861 at Lynchburg.

Law, John C. (1st Sgt.):

Cooper, George W. (2nd Sgt.): *Wounded.*

Ashworth, William L. (3rd Sgt.): *Captured*; exchanged 20 or 21 February 1865.

Worsham, John B. (4th Sgt.): Resided at Museville; single; (26 in 1863); received a severe flesh *wound* of the right hip and *captured*; exchanged from West's Buildings Hospital 27 September 1863.

Hodges, George R. (1st Cpl.): The company reports him as missing in action but there are no Federal records concerning him; *killed.*

Williamson, William F. (2nd Cpl.):

Belcher, Charles P. (3rd Cpl.): *Wounded.*

Campbell, Alexander J. (4th Cpl.): *Wounded* and *captured*; exchanged prior to 31 October 1863.

Amos, Charles D.: The company reports him as missing in action but there are no Federal records concerning him; *killed.*

Ashworth, John W.:

Barrow, John A.:

Belcher, William J.:

Bird, Daniel M.: Enl. 6 December 1862 at Fredericksburg.

Brewer, Alexander B.:

Burke, John W.: Recieved a flesh *wound* in the right thigh and *captured*; joined U.S. service 24 January 1864.

Cooper, Charles H.:

Cooper, Haley A.: Enl. 6 March 1862 at Rocky Mount.

Cooper, Josiah:

Cooper, Lowry M.:

Cooper, Taswell, T.: Enl. 6 March 1862 at Rocky Mount; the company reports him as missing in action but there are no Federal records concerning him; *killed.*

Cooper, William S.: *Wounded*; died at Lynchburg General Hospital 18 July 1863.

Cooper, William W.:

Crumb, Andrew J.:

Cundiff, Albert A.: Born in Franklin County, Virginia; *killed.*

Cundiff, Samuel C.: Born in Franklin County, Virginia; *killed.*

English, George W.S.:

English, William W.:

Hash, James H.:

Hodges, Josiah: Enl. 6 March 1862 at Rocky Mount.

Huston, William M.: Slightly *wounded* in the hip and *captured*; exchanged from DeCamp Hospital 27 September 1863.

Jarratt, Tazwell T.:

Law, John B.:

Law, Milton B.: Enl. 6 March 1862 at Rocky Mount.

Law, Nathaniel C.: Enl. 13 October 1862 at Winchester; mother was Mrs. Sally Law; face *burned* by a shell burst and *captured*; died of intermittent fever at Fort Delaware 18 September 1863.

Law, William D.:

Martin, James W.:

Mathews, George T.:

McGuffin, John T.: Enl. 6 March 1862 at Rocky Mount; recieved a *contusion* of the back and *captured*; exchanged from DeCamp Hospital 28 August 1863.

Metts, Lewis R.:

Muse, John C.: Slightly *wounded* in the knee and *captured*; exchanged from DeCamp Hospital 8 September 1863.

Ramsey, Jesse H.: Enl. 15 March 1863 in Franklin County; *captured*; died of chronic diarrhea at Fort Delaware 17 January 1864.

Rucker, William T.:

Semones, William G.: Born in Franklin County; *killed.*

Tench, Edwin J.: Slightly *wounded* in the leg and *captured*; exchanged from DeCamp Hospital 18 September 1863.

Thomasson, James H.:

Trail, Daniel M.: Enl. 1 October 1862 at Winchester; AWOL 15 August 1863.

Walker, John N.: Enl. 6 March 1862 at Rocky Mount; *wounded* in the foot (toes amputated) and *captured*; exchanged from DeCamp Hospital 27 September 1863.

White, James O.: Born in Franklin County, Virginia; *killed.*

Wingfield, Lewis F.: Enl. 1 October 1862 at Winchester.

Young, John P.: Enl. 6 March 1862 at Rocky Mount; *wounded.*

Zeigler, Thomas F.: *Shot* in the thigh; died of tetanus at Pickett's Division Hospital 16 July 1863 and buried at Bream's Mill above Myers' house at the side of a fence; disinterred to Richmond 3 August 1872 with 33 others in three large boxes marked "P Curns."

Zeigler, William G.: The company reports him as missing in action but there are no Federal records concerning him; *killed.*

Company "E"

This company was organized 1 May 1861 at Newbern, Pulaski County, Virginia; was mustered into service 27 May 1861 at Lynchburg for one year; and was reorganized 10 May 1862.

Bentley, William W. (Captain): VMI class of 1860.

Gunn, Birdine (1st Lt.): (30 in 1865); resided at Dublin, Virginia; *shot* in the left groin, the ball coming out the buttock.

Saunders, Frederick C. (2nd Lt.):

Harman, John W. (2nd Sgt.):

Hoge, Edward T. (3rd Sgt.):

King, Charles H. (4th Sgt.): *Captured*; exchanged 14 or 15 February 1865.

Hudson, John R. (1st Cpl.):

Mathews, Andrew W. (2nd Cpl.): *Captured*; released on oath from Fort Delaware 26 February 1864.

Clark, Henry C. (3rd Cpl.): Enl. 14 March 1862 at Newbern.

Carper, John C. (4th Cpl.):

Canada, Marshall: Enl. 27 February 1862 at Newbern; recieved a severe gunshot *wound* in the left ankle and *captured*; exchanged from DeCamp Hospital 27 September 1863.

Carper, John T.:

Clark, Josiah F.:

Hudson, George R.: Enl. 30 June 1861 at Camp Pryor.

Hudson, James R.: Enl. 24 May 1862 in the camp of the 24th Virginia.

Kelly, Julius C.:

King, William H.:

Lorton, George:

McDaniel, William:

Reese, William S.:

Runyon, Alexander C.:

Runyon, William B.: *Wounded.*

Smith, Samuel:

Southern, Leander: Enl. 14 March 1862 at Newbern; *wounded.*

Tipton, William R.: Enl. 14 March 1862 at Newbern.

Warden, Johnston:

Whitt, Burgess: Enl. 1 March 1862 at Newbern.

Wood, Solomon: Enl. 14 March 1862 at Newbern; *wounded.*

Company "F" ("New River White Rifles")

This company was organized at New River White, Giles County, Virginia 26 December 1859; was mustered in at Lynchburg 30 May 1861 for one year; and was reorganized 10 May 1862.

Hines, Brainard W. (Captain): *Wounded.*

Snidow, James P. (1st Lt.): Recevied a gunshot *wound* which fractured his left ankle joint (leg amputated below the knee) and *captured*; exchanged 30 September 1864.

Haden, James W. (2nd Lt.):

Bane, William H.L. (Jr. 2nd Lt.): Resided in Giles County; *wounded.*

Porterfield, David H. (1st Sgt.): The company reports him as missing in action but there are no Federal records concerning him; *killed.*

Albert, Jacob A. (2nd Sgt.): Resided in Giles County; recieved a gunshot flesh *wound* to the upper third of his right thigh (hip) and *captured*; exchanged from DeCamp Hospital 28 August 1863.

Hutcheson, John F. (3rd Sgt.): Born in Giles County; *killed.*

Diamond, Thomas J. (4th Sgt.):

Snidow, George L. (1st Cpl.): Resided in Giles County.

248

Hyden, Joseph L. (2nd Cpl.): Mother was Mrs. Hannah W. Hyden; *killed.*

Albert, George A. (3rd Cpl.): Received a *contusion* of the left shoulder and *captured*; exchanged from West's Buildings Hospital 17 November 1863.

Price, George H. (4th Cpl.): The company initially reports him as wounded and captured and subsequently as missing in action but there are no Federal records concerning him; *killed.*

Adams, Jesse G.: *Wounded.*

Adams, Thomas T.:

Atkins, John J.:

Barger, James W.:

Blunt, James R.:

Dowdy, Albert G.: Enl. 30 August 1861 at Camp Ellis; resided in Giles County; wounded.

Echols, Jeremiah G.:

Epling, Floyd: Enl. 31 August 1861 at Camp Ellis; *captured*; exchanged 15 November 1864.

Epling, William A.:

Harless, Russell H.: Enl. 30 August 1861 at Camp Ellis; *wounded.*

Kissinger, Henry H.:

Link, Christian H.:

Lucas, Josephus:

Lucas, Samuel M.: Resided in Giles County; *wounded.*

Martin, Andrew S.: Enl. 30 August 1861 at Camp Ellis.

Martin, George S.: Enl. 30 August 1861 at Camp Ellis; probably *wounded*; *captured*; exchanged 20 or 21 February 1865.

Martin, Michael C.: Enl. 30 August 1861 at Camp Ellis.

McCroskey, John Miles: Enl. 30 August 1861 at Camp Ellis.

Meredith, Chapman J.:

Peck, John H.: Resided in Giles County; *wounded* in the scalp and *captured*; exchanged from Chester Hospital 23 September 1863.

Porterfield, Albert G.: Enl. 20 May 1863 at Taylorsville.

Porterfield, George W.:

Price, James A.:

Rutledge, Granville H.: Enl. 30 August 1861 at Camp Ellis.

Saunders, Gustavus:

Saunders, James H.:

Stanley, William H.:

Webb, William F.:

White, Charles R.T.: Enl. 31 August 1861 at Camp Ellis; *wounded.*

Williams, Floyd S.: *Captured*; exchanged 25 or 28 February or 3 March 1865; an unidentified soldier assumed his name and was exchanged 3 May 1864.

Williams, James M.:

Wingo, John K.:

Company "G"

This company was organized 4 May 1861 in Mercer County (now West Virginia); mustered in at Lynchburg 2 June 1861 for one year; and reorganized 10 May 1862.

Scott, Hercules (Captain): *Wounded.*

Grigsby, Benjamin P. (1st Lt.): VMI class of 1862.

Heptinstall, Leslie H. (2nd Lt.):

White, Harvey G. (1st Sgt.):

Alvis, David M. (2nd Sgt.): Slightly *wounded* in the knee and *captured*; exchanged from DeCamp Hospital 8 September 1863.

Peck, Benjamin W. (3rd Sgt.): The company reports him initially as missing in action and subsequently as *killed* but there are no Federal records concerning him; killed.

Rowland, Rufus F. (4th Sgt.): Severely *wounded* in the left leg and *captured*; exchanged from West's Buildings Hospital 24 August 1863.

Smiley, George W. (5th Sgt.):

Fellers, Zachariah (3rd Cpl.):

Burress, Charles W. (4th Cpl.): *Shot* in the upper third of the left femur and *captured*; died at Camp Letterman Hospital 3 August 1863 and buried in Section 3, Grave #24 of that hospital's cemetery; disinterred to Richmond 13 June 1872 in Box #97.

Austin, Raleigh T.:

Belcher, William McH.:

Bird, Bluford W.:

Calfee, Henderson F.: *Wounded*; died 7 July 1863 probably at Pickett's Division Hospital.

Coburn, John D.:

Cooper, Andrew L.:

East, Samuel A.: *Wounded.*

George, Robert A.: *Wounded*; AWOL from hospital; no subsequent record.

Harris, George A.:

Holstine, Andrew J.: Resided in Mercer County, West Virginia; *wounded.*

Johnson, James H.:

Kinney, James: Born in Ireland; *killed.*

Snead, James: (38 in 1865); *Wounded.*

Stovall, Joseph G.:

Thomas, John P.: *Captured*; died at Point Lookout 12 September 1864.

Vermillion, Levi H.: Born in Pulaski County; father was Mr. James R. Vermillion; *shot* in the brain; died at Pickett's Division Hospital 9 July 1863 and buried at Bream's Mill above Myers' house, at the side of a fence; disinterred to Richmond 3 August 1872 with 33 others in three large boxes marked "P Curns."

White, Henry M.:

Whittaker, William B.:

Company "H" ("Henry Guards")

This company was organized at Henry Court House, Henry County, and was mustered in at Lynchburg 5 June 1861 for one year. It was reorganized 10 May 1862.

Barrow, Orren W. (Captain):
Davis, Peter P., Jr. (1st Lt.):
Fontaine, Samuel C. (2nd Lt.):
Redd, William S. (2nd 2nd Lt.):
Powell, Benjamin F. (1st Sgt.):
Mason, John L. (2nd Sgt.): (21 in 18963); farmer; born in Franklin County; *wounded* in the thigh.
Dyer, William C. (3rd Sgt.): Enl. 17 March 1862 at Henry Court House; (24).
Draper, Jesse H. (1st Cpl.): *Captured*; exchanged 20 or 21 February 1865.
Lamkin, Joseph (3rd Cpl.):
Waller, Samuel G. (4th Cpl.): (23 in 1863); lawyer; *wounded* in the right ankle and *captured*; exchanged 20 March 1864; died at Chimborazo Hospital #9 at Richmond 6 April 1864.
Armstrong, James A.:
Austin, Charles F.: *Wounded*.
Barrow, William W.:
Bocock, Thomas M.: Enl. 17 March 1862 at Henry Court House; (22).
Booker, Thomas L.:
Bousman, George W.:
Coleman, James M.: Enl. 11 January 1863 in Henry County; born in Henry County; *killed*.
Compton, William G.:
Davis, Charles W.:
Davis, Labon J.: Enl. 11 January 1863 in Henry County.
Dodson, Alexander S.:
Draper, Elkanah B.: Enl. 11 January 1863 in Henry County.
Dyer, Hardin H.: Enl. 31 August 1861 at Mason's Hill.
Eggleton, George W.:
Eggleton, Henry H.: Enl. 17 March 1862 at Henry Court House; (34).
Eggleton, Thomas J.:
France, James P.:
Gravely, Joseph S.:
Griffin, Samuel J.: Enl. 1 May 1863 near Suffolk.
Gunnell, William A.: Enl. 30 September 1862 near Winchester; the company reports him initially as missing in action and subsequently as "supposed killed" but there are no Federal records concerning him; *killed*.
Hereford, Hardin H.:
Hodnett, Phillip: Born in Henry County; wife was Mrs. E.N. Hodnett; *killed*.
Jamerson, George W.:
Jamerson, Thomas: Enl. 11 January 1863 in Henry County.

Lawrence, William R.:

Martin, Thomas B.: Residedat Oak Level, Henry County; received a severe gunshot *wound* in the left ankle (lower third of leg amputated) and *captured*; exchanged from DeCamp Hospital 28 October 1863.

Metts, Henry A.: Enl. 17 March 1862 at Henry Court House; (42); *shot* in the arm and *captured*; exchanged from Chester Hospital 23 September 1863.

Nunn, Josiah W.: Enl. 17 March 1862 at Henry Court House; (34).

Peay, Robert P.: *Shot* in the back and *captured*; exchanged from West's Buildings Hospital 24 August 1863.

Pedigo, Elisha F.: Born in Henry County; *killed.*

Pedigo, Leonard A.:

Philpott, Edward, Jr.:

Purdy, George E.:

Reay, Jerman F.: Enl. 17 March 1862 at Henry Court House; (23).

Reay, Joseph O.:

Shelton, Samuel C.:

Stanley, Crockett J.:

Stunz, Charles W.: *Killed.*

Thomas, William H.: Enl. 17 March 1862 at Henry Court House; (18).

Thomasson, James R.: Enl. 11 January 1863 in Henry County.

Thomasson, Stephen G.: Enl. 17 March 1862 at Henry Court House; (34).

Thomasson, Wilson O.: Enl. 17 March 1862 at Henry Court House; (19).

Turner, Josiah: Enl. 17 March 1862 at Henry Court House, (19).

Wells, Franklin M.: Enl. 11 January 1863 in Henry County; porbably *wounded*; *captured*; sick in hospital at Point Lookout and returned to confinement; no further record; the company says he took the oath of allegiance to the U.S. and went north but the records do not support this statement; may have died, unreported, in prison.

Wells, Robert J.:

Wells, Roland B.: Enl. 11 January 1863 in Henry County.

Wells, William T.:

Wilmoth, Pleasant: Enl. 28 February 1863 in Chesterfield County.

Company "I"

This company was organized at Patrick Court House, Patrick County, Virginia 25 April 1861; mustered in at Lynchburg 31 May 1861 for one year; and reorganized 10 May 1862.

Hatcher, Daniel G. (1st Lt.): Received a gunshot flesh *wound* in the upper third of his left thigh and *captured*; treated in U.S. 2nd Division, II Corps Hospital; exchanged 22 March 1865.

Aistrop, Henry C. (2nd Lt.):

Plaster, William Conrad (1st Sgt.): *Wounded.*

Bennett, Charles Henry (3rd Sgt.): Born in Patrick County, Virginia; mother was Mrs. Mary B. Bennett; *killed.*

Wigginton, Thomas S.H. (4th Sgt.):

Shockley, William H. (1st Cpl.): Resided in Patrick County; *shot* in the thigh and *captured*; exchanged from DeCamp Hospital 27 September 1863.

Frashure, Albert R. (2nd Cpl.):

Boswell, Whitmel T.: (reduced to ranks from 1st Sgt. 14 May 1863).

Bryant, William C.:

Clifton, William J.:

Coleman, William:

Conaway, Benjamin D.:

Dalton, Willis:

Edwards, Joseph W.: Enl. 10 March 1862 at Patrick Court House; *shot* in the chest and *captured*; exchanged from DeCamp Hospital 16 September 1863.

Feagans, George W.:

Gilbert, Lorenzo D.: Enl. 10 March 1862 at Patrick Court House; *wounded* in the arm and *captured*; exchanged from DeCamp Hospital 16 September 1863.

Gilbert, Samuel S.: Enl. 10 March 1862 at Patrick Court House; the company reports him as having been captured but there are no Federal records concerning him; *killed*.

Gunter, Joseph H.:

Haley, Samuel H.: *Shot* in the right leg and *captured*; exchanged from West's Buildings Hospital 24 August 1863.

Headen, William D.: Enl. 10 March 1862 at Patrick Court House.

Keister, Andrew M.:

Lawless, George W.: *Wounded*.

Lawless, McNealey A.: Enl. 10 March 1862 at Patrick Court House; sick 4 July 1863 and sent to hospital.

Lawless, Thomas J.: Deserted 3 July 1863, probably while on the march to the battlefield.

Lawson, Henry H.: Enl. 8 April 1863 at Franklin Station; *captured*; joined U.S. service 22 January 1864.

Leak, Thomas J.: Enl. 19 January 1863 at Guinea Station.

Lovins, Arthur J.: Enl. 10 March 1862 at Patrick Court House; born in North Carolina; wife was Mind (spelled her name Loveing): *wounded*; died of erysipelas at General Hospital #2 at Lynchburg 7 August 1863.

Nunn, Edmund:

Plaster, Mark:

Ross, Lewis T.:

Taylor, James L.:

Vipperman, Nicholas T.: Enl. 10 March 1862 at Patrick Court House; *captured*; died at Fort Delaware 7 October 1863.

Waller, James C.: Father was Mr. James A. Waller.

Waller, William P.:

Wigginton, Andrew Jackson: Enl. 10 March 1862 at Patrick Court House; *wounded*.

Wigginton, C.M.: Enl. 10 March 1862 at Patrick Court House; *wounded*.

Wigginton, William J.: Enl. 10 March 1862 at Patrick Court House.
Williams, Francis M.: Enl. 10 March 1862 at Patrick Court House.
Williams, John D.: *Wounded*.

<u>Company "K"</u>

This company was organized 14 May 1861; mustered in at Lynchburg 30 May 1861 for one year; and reorganized 10 May 1862.

Le Tellier, John Henry (Captain):
Whitt, Joseph B. (1st Lt.):
Barnett, Charles T.S. (1st Sgt.):
Haymaker, Robert D. (1st Cpl.):
Mays, George W. (2nd Cpl.): *Shot* in both thighs and *captured*; exchanged from West's Buildings Hospital 24 August 1863.
Craig, Chester: The company initially reports him as missing in action and subsequently as killed but there are no Federal records concerning him; *killed*.
Cromer, Charles D.: Deserted 27 July 1863.
Faulkner, Jacob B.: Received a slight flesh *wound* in the right calf and *captured*; exchanged from DeCamp Hospital 28 August 1863.
Fizer, Peter M.:
Haley, Malcolm L.: Deserted 27 July 1863.
Kirk, James M.: Enl. 27 May 1861.
McDaniel, David E.: Enl. 27 May 1861; *shot* in the right foot and *captured*; died at DeCamp Hospital 31 July 1863 and buried in Grave #707 Cypress Hill Cemetery, Long Island, New York.
Miles, Asa:
Moore, Benjamin: Enl. 31 August 1861 at Mason's Hill; resided in Montgomery County; deserted 27 July 1863; present with his company by 30 December 1863.
Pickering, Thomas B.:
Short, George W.:
Turner, Thomas A.: Deserted 3 July 1863, probably while on the march to the battlefield; captured 5 July 1863; joined U.S. 3rd Maryland Cavalry 22 September 1863.
Winfree, Isaac H.:

Garnett's Brigade

In the organization of the army as announced 23 July 1862, Brigadier General George E. Pickett was in command of a brigade consisting of the 8th, 18th, 19th, 28th, and 56th Virginia. Of these regiments, the 8th, 18th, 19th, and 28th were at the Battle of 1st Manassas, 21 July 1861, in Colonel P. St. George Cocke's Brigade. In the organization of 21 July 1861, the 8th Virginia was detached and in the separate command of Colonel Eppa Hunton at Leesburg, Virginia, but in January 1862, it was again with the brigade. On 28 February 1862, Brigadier General George E. Pickett was assigned to duty with Longstreet's Division, and on 30 April 1862, was in command of the brigade then styled "Pickett's Brigade." The 56th Virginia joined the brigade and served with it through the Seven Days Battles; this regiment had previously served in the Army of the Kanawha, and from the time it was detached from that army until it joined this brigade served about Richmond unattached. With the exception of a few temporary changes during the time the brigade was in southeast Virginia and North Carolina, from September 1863 to May 1864, there was no change in the organization until the surrender at Appomattox 9 April 1865.

General Garnett assumed command of the brigade a few days before the Battle of South Mountain, Maryland 14 September 1862 and retained command until his death at Gettysburg.

General and Staff

Garnett, Richard Brooke (Brigadier General): Born at "Rose Hill," Essex County, Va. 21 November 1817; graduated West Point in 1841; served in Seminole War and Utah Campaign; resigned U.S. Army as Capt. 6th Infantry 17 May 1861 to join Confederate service; Major artillery May 1861; commanding "Stonewall Brigade," Valley District, Dept. of Northern Virginia November 1861 through 1 April 1862; promoted Bgd. Gen. 14 November 1861; commanding Pickett's Bgd., Jones' Div., 1st Corps, Army of Northern Va.; 5 September through late September 1862; commanding brigade Pickett's Division September 1862 through 25 February 1863; commanding brigade Pickett's Division, Dept. of Virginia and North Carolina 25 February through 1 April 1863; in Dept. of Southern Va. 1 April through May 1863; commanding a brigade in Pickett's Division, 1st Corps, Army of Northern Virginia May through 3 July 1863; shot in the head and *killed* near the stone wall during the attack; General Garnett brought two horses to Gettysburg—a dark bay mare, valued at $550, was killed while serving as a mount for 1st Lt. John S. Jones, ADC on Garnett's staff, and a bay gelding, valued at $675, was mortally wounded while serving as General Garnett's mount at the time of his death.

Danforth, Henry D. (1st Lt., Ordnance Officer serving temporarily as Inspector General).

Harrison, Thomas R. (Acting 1st Lt., ADC): Enl. 3 October 1862 at Winchester as a Private in Company "F," 18th Virginia Infantry; company muster rolls reported him as detailed at Garnett's Headquarters as a courier 4 October 1862 through at least 31 December 1864; (23 in 1865); student; *captured*; exchanged 22 March 1865 as a 1st Lt.

Johnston, James A.: (Major, Commissary of Subsistence): Enl. 15 May 1861 in Botetourt County as a Private in Company "A," 28th Virginia Infantry; (25); physician; appointed Captain and ACS 4 October 1861; appointed Major and Commissary of Subsistence on Garnett's staff 10 January 1862; resigned 31 October 1863.

Jones, George T. (Major, Quartermaster): Enl. 8 May 1861 at Charlottesville as Captain of Company "B," 19th Virginia Infantry; (36); merchant; appointed Captain and Quartermaster 19th Virginia 19 July 1861; appointed Major and Quartermaster on Garnett's staff 11 April 1863.

Jones, John S. (Acting 1st Lt., ADC): Enl. 9 May 1861 at Craney Island as a Private in Company "D," 8th Virginia Infantry; company muster rolls reported him as a clerk for General Garnett on all muster rolls from November 1862 through 31 August 1863; appointed as 1st Lt. and ADC on Garnett's staff 11 September 1863; *wounded* by a shell fragment within 100 yards of the clump of trees during the attack.

Linthicum, Charles F. (Capt., AAG): Appointed Chaplain of the 8th Virginia Infantry 31 October 1861; resigned as Chaplain 4 December 1862; appointed Captain and AAG on Garnett's staff 12 December 1862.

McConkey, Samuel A. (Senior Surgeon): Appointed Surgeon of the 28th Virginia Infantry 1 July 1861; transferred from this regiment 10 June 1863, possibly to serve temporarily on the brigade staff; present with the regimental staff on the 28th's field and staff muster roll for July/August 1863; permanently transferred to the brigade staff prior to 11 December 1863.

Miller, James B. (1st Lt., Provost Marshal): Detached from Company "A," 18th Virginia; enl. 23 April 1861 at Danville; (25), merchant; *wounded* and *captured*; died of traumatic erysipelas at Chester Hospital 5 August 1863 and buried in Grave #119 of that hospital's cemetery.

Brigade Forage Master

Moore, Alexander B. (2nd Sgt.): Detailed from Company "D," 8th Virginia; enl. 28 April 1861 at Orlean.

Brigade Postmaster

Wallace, John L.: Detailed from Company "B," 19th Virginia; enl. 8 May 1861 at Charlottesville; (22); clerk.

Couriers

Gulick, David P.: Detailed from Company "D," 8th Virginia; enl. 13 May 1861 at Aldie.

Irvine, Robert H.: Detailed from Company "I," 19th Virginia; enl. 29 April 1861 at Buffalo Springs; (21); student; horse valued at $500 killed at Gettysburg.

Brigade Teamsters

Etcher, James C.: Detailed from Company "I," 8th Virginia; enl. 13 July 1861 at Mount Gilead.

Wells, John T.: Detailed in the Quartermaster's Department from Company "B," 11th Virginia; enl. 23 April 1861 at Yellow Branch; (28); farmer.

Brigade Provost Guard

Hatcher, Thomas A.: Detailed from Company "F," 8th Virginia; enl. 15 July 1861 at Leesburg; *wounded* in the right knee; died at home in Loudon County of disease 18 December 1863.

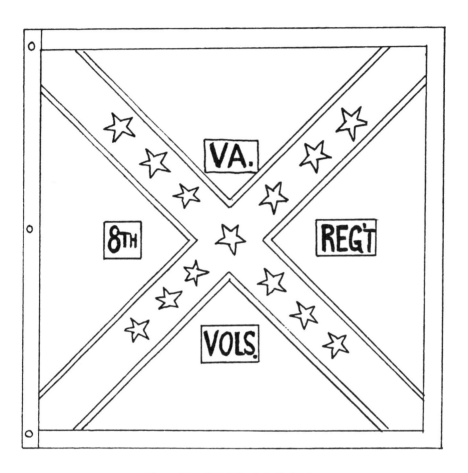

**Flag of the 8th Virginia Infantry
captured by the 16th Vermont Infantry
during the attack or repulse**

8th Virginia Volunteer Infantry Regiment
("Old Bloody Eighth")

This regiment was organized in state service at Leesburg, Virginia 8 May 1861, was accepted into Confederate service July 1861 with ten companies, and was reorganized 26 April 1862.

The following listing was obtained from company April/June 1863 muster rolls captioned 30 June 1863 near Chambersburg, Pennsylvania. Company "E" dated its roll 28 June 1863.

All companies reported the status of their clothing as "some needed," their arms as "long range," their accouterments as "nearly complete," and their military appearance, discipline, and instruction as "good."

Field and Staff

Hunton, Eppa (Colonel): Born 1822 or 1823; attorney and militia brigadier before the war; elected Colonel to rank from 8 May 1861; re-elected 16 April 1862; commanding Pickett's Brigade, Longstreet's Division, Army of Northern Virginia 27 through 30 June 1862; commanding Pickett's Brigade, Kemper's Division, 1st Corps, Army of Northern Virginia August through 5 September 1862; promoted Brigadier General 9 August 1863; *shot* in the right leg below the knee during the attack.

Berkeley, Norborne (Lt. Col.): Born 31 March 1828; graduated VMI in 1848; married Lavinia Hart Berkeley (a cousin); Major in April 1861; elected Lt. Col. 27 April 1862; received a *gunshot* fracture of the left foot and *captured*; exchanged 20 March 1864.

Berkeley, Edmund (Major): Born 7 February 1824; VMI class of 1867; married Mary Lawson Williams; enl. 8 May 1861 at Haymarket as Captain of Company "C"; promoted to Major 3 June 1862; *shot* above the knee, the ball running 20 inches beneath the skin before stopping; wounded near the stone wall during the attack.

Hutchison, Thomas Benton (1st Lt. Adjutant): Appointed Adjutant 15 February 1862; appointed Brigade Commissary of Subsistence 3 December 1863.

Smith, Thomas Towson (Capt., AQM): Enl. 20 July 1861 at Warrenton in Company "K"; appointed AQM 2 December 1862.

Hutchison, John R. (1st Lt., ACS): Enl. 13 May 1861 at Aldie as 2nd Lt. in Company "D"; appointed ACS 24 October 1862.

Burwell, Blair (Surgeon): Appointed Surgeon 2 August 1862.

Estes, James D. (Asst. Surgeon): Appointed Asst. Surgeon 4 March 1862.

Harris, George William (Chaplain): Appointed 9 February 1863; from Upperville, Virginia.

Stephenson, James A. (Commissary Sgt.): Detailed from Company "C"; enl. 15 July 1861 at Leesburg.

Tyler, George Bailey (QM Sgt.): Detailed from Company "C"; enl. 8 May 1861 at Haymarket.

Hummer, George W.F. (Courier for Colonel Hunton): Detailed from Company "H"; enl. 13 July 1861 at Leesburg.

259

Hixon, Abner H. (Hospital Nurse): Detailed from Company "D"; enl. 10 October 1862 at Winchester.

Color Guard

Thomas, William O. (1st Cpl., Color Sgt.): Detailed from Company "D"; enl. 13 May 1861 at Aldie.

Ambulance Corps

Dougherty, John: Detailed from Company "H"; enl. 13 July 1861 at Leesburg; deserted; captured near Greencastle, Pennsylvania 7 July; took the oath of allegiance at Fort Delaware and released, May 1865.

Sinclair, Wallace W.: Detailed from Company "C"; enl. 8 May 1861 at Haymarket.

Skillman, John W. (Driver): Detailed from Company "I"; enl. 13 July 1861 at Mount Gilead.

Spence, James: Detailed from Company "G"; enl. 10 November 1861 at Camp Burt; AWOL 18 July through 18 August 1863.

Wagoners

Able, Robert L. (QM Dept.): Detailed from Company "K"; enl. 30 July 1861 at Warrenton.

Bitzer, George W. (Teamster): Detailed from Company "A"; enl. 31 August 1862 at Gordonsville.

McIntosh, George: Detailed from Company "G"; enl. 16 July 1861 at Centreville.

McIntosh, John: Detailed from Company "G"; enl. 16 July 1861 at Centreville; deserted near Culpeper Court House in July or August 1863.

McIntosh, Robert W.: Detailed from Company "F"; enl. 19 June 1861 at Bloomfield.

Company "A" ("Hillsboro Border Guards")

This company was organized prior to 1 December 1859; was accepted into state service 19 April 1861; and was reorganized 26 April 1862.

Bissell, William Rombough (Captain): Enl. 19 April 1861 at Hillsboro; elected Captain 26 April 1862; *shot* in the head and shaft of upper arm (amputated at the shoulder by C.S. Wood of 66th New York) and *captured*; treated at U.S. 2nd Division, II Corps Hospital; died 16 July; buried in Presbyterian Graveyard, Gettysburg.

Leslie, Samuel D. (1st Lt.): Date and place of enlistment not shown; *captured*; released from Fort Delaware 12 June 1865.

Gibson, Edward C. (2nd Lt.): Date and place of enlistment not shown; *captured*; exchanged 22 March 1865.

Osburn, Decatur (1st Sgt.): Enl. 17 June 1861 at Leesburg; *captured*; released from Fort Delaware 15 June 1865.

Hill, Joseph R. (3rd Sgt.): Enl. 15 June 1861 at Leesburg; reduced to ranks for one month on 30 June 1863 muster roll; AWOL in July or August 1863; joined 6th Virginia Cavalry.

James, Thomas B. (1st Cpl.): Enl. 23 April 1861 at Hillsboro; AWOL July or August 1863 through at least 31 December 1863.

Arnett, Samuel M.: Enl. 13 July 1861 at Leesburg; *captured*; died at Point Lookout 6 January 1864.

Atwell, John J.: Enl. 6 May 1861 at Hillsboro; (20); *wounded* in the right leg and left foot (amputated), and *captured*; exchanged from West's Buildings Hospital 17 November 1863.

Beans, Oscar M.: *Captured*; exchanged from Point Lookout 14-15 February 1865.

Bell, Theophilus:

Bowen, Henry L.: Enl. 24 August 1862 at Keysville; *shot* in the right foot and *captured*; exchanged from West's Buildings Hospital 24 August 1863.

Flowers, James R.: Enl. 24 August 1862 at Keysville.

Furry, Andrew J.: Enl. 18 March 1863 at Staunton; *captured*; released on oath from Point Lookout 30 January 1864.

James, Townsend A.: Enl. 27 April 1861 at Hillsboro; *killed*.

Jenkins, Samuel: Enl. 13 August 1861 at Camp Berkeley; deserted July or August 1863 and said to have joined U.S. service; Federal records do not confirm this, however.

Leslie, William A.: Enl. 1 October 1862 at Winchester; *killed*.

Pamplin, David L.A.: Enl. 24 August 1862 at Keysville; *captured*; exchanged 20 March 1864.

Raber, Henry L.: Enl. 1 May 1861 at Hillsboro; *wounded* in the right arm and right side of the chest and *captured*; died at West's Buildings Hospital 14 August 1863.

Rollins, Alfred F.: Enl. 9 June 1861 at Leesburg; *killed*.

Russell, James W.: Enl. 16 July 1861 at Leesburg; *captured*; exchanged 15 November 1864.

Shrigley, Jacob R.: Enl. 22 April 1861 at Hillsboro; *killed*.

Taylor, Eben: Enl. 20 April 1861 at Hillsboro.

Company "B" ("Piedmont Rifles")

This company enlisted 17 May 1861 at Rectortown, Fauquier County, Virginia for one year, and was reorganized 26 April 1862.

Ashby, John Turner (1st Lt.):

Payne, Fielding F. (2nd Lt.): *Shot* in the head and *captured*; treated at the U.S. 2nd Division, II Corps Hospital; died at U.S. II Corps Hospital 13 July 1863 and buried in Yard "D" of that hospital's cemetery in Jacob Schwartz's cornfield on Rock Creek; disinterred to Richmond with 110 others in ten large boxes marked "S," 13 June 1872.

Reid, William P. (1st Sgt.): *Captured*; exchanged 20 or 21 February 1865.

McArtor, John R. (3rd Sgt.): *Killed*.

Glasscock, Nimrod (1st Cpl.): *Wounded*.

Newlon, James M. (4th Cpl.): Enl. 14 June 1861 at Leesburg; *killed*.

Ashby, James S.: Enl. 15 March 1862 at Hazel River; (present sick); the company lists him as missing in action but there are no Federal records concerning him; *killed*.

Ballard, Albert: *Wounded* by a shell in the right hip and *captured*; exchanged from Point Lookout 20 March 1864.

Balthrope, James F.: (on daily duty since 15 June 1863); *wounded*.

Brummett, Jonathan M.: Enl. 26 February 1863; (conscript from Tennessee).

Carter, Albert: *Wounded*; AWOL from hospital.

Iden, John R.: *Shot* in the shoulder and *captured*; exchanged from West's Buildings Hospital 24 August 1863.

Jewell, Henry L.: Enl. 24 February 1863 at Chester Station; AWOL 19 July through 7 September 1864.

Kerfoot, William F.: Enl. 8 March 1862 at Centreville; (19); recieved a *gunshot* fracture of the right elbow joint (arm amputated), and *captured*; treated at U.S. XII Corps Hospital; exchanged from West's Buildings Hospital 27 September 1863.

Kidwell, Newton J.: Enl. 14 February 1863 at Fredericksburg; *captured*; exchanged 28 December 1863.

Lanham, Thomas L.: *Wounded*.

Milton, Charles A.: Received a severe gunshot flesh *wound* to the upper third of the right thigh, and *captured*; exchanged from Point Lookout 17 March 1864.

Pennington, John: Enl. 26 September 1862 in camp eight miles north of Winchester; *killed*.

Pennington, Levi: Enl. 26 September 1862 in camp eight miles north of Winchester; *killed*.

Rawlings, James W.: (29 in 1865); *shot* in the thigh and *captured*; treated in U.S. 2nd Division, II Corps Hospital which also reported him as having been wounded in the right shoulder; paroled from West's Buildings Hospital 22 August 1863.

Royston, Zachariah V.: Enl. 16 March 1862 at Hazel River; (on extra-duty by order of General Garnett); *wounded*.

Skinner, Charles E.: Enl. 12 July 1861 at Leesburg.

Company "C" ("Evergreen Guards" first known as "Bull Run Rangers")

This company enlisted 8 May 1861 at Haymarket, Prince William County, Virginia for one year, and was reorganized 26 April 1862.

McNealea, John R. (2nd Lt.): Enl. 25 May 1861 at Leesburg; *captured*; exchanged 22 March 1865.

Compton, Alexander H. (1st Sgt.): *Captured*; wounded in the shoulder and hip by a Confederate shell following capture; exchanged 20 or 21 February 1865.

Flesher, Andrew (2nd Sgt.): *Wounded* in the right hip, and *captured*; paroled from West's Buildings Hospital 23 August 1863.

Hurst, Benjamin F. (4th Sgt.):

Dawson, William F. (5th Sgt.): *Wounded*.

Lunceford, Benjamin R. (1st Cpl.): Enl. 13 July 1861 at Leesburg; *captured*; exchanged 20 or 21 Febaruary 1865.

Carter, Thomas J. (3rd Cpl.): *Captured*; released from Fort Delaware 19 June 1865.

Holliday, William L. (4th Cpl.): Enl. 25 May 1861 at Leesburg; AWOL 10 July through 6 August 1863.

Melton, James T. (Musician):

Carter, Landon E.: Enl. 1 September 1861 at Camp Johnson, Loudon County, Virginia; *shot* in left groin and *captured*; exchanged 6 March 1864.

Carter, Robert O.: Enl. 15 June 1861 at Leesburg; *captured*; died of chronic diarrhea at Fort Delaware 21 September 1863; buried at Finns Point, N.J.

Donohoe, Lewis J.: *Captured*; died of chronic diarrhea at Fort Delaware 27 October 1863.

Downs, Cicero: Deserted 9 July 1863.

Downs, William H.: Deserted 12 July 1863.

Dugger, C.C.: Enl. 10 September 1862 in Virginia; the company reports him as missing in action but there are no Federal records concerning him; *killed*.

Fair, William H.: *Killed*.

Fox, Newton T.:

Fry, Joseph: Enl. 1 October 1862 at Leesburg; *captured*; released from Fort Delaware 20 June 1865.

Loving, Cleophas A.: *Wounded* in the abdomen and *captured*; died 7 July 1863.

Lunceford, Evans O.: Enl. 13 August 1861 at Leesburg; AWOL 10 July through 6 August 1863.

Lynn, Robert: Enl. 8 March 1862 at Deseret, Haymarket, or Centreville.

Mattocks, Richard T.: *Shot* in the left foot and *captured*; treated at U.S. 2nd Division, II Corps Hospital; exchanged 20 March 1864.

McNealea, William: Enl. 1 October 1862 at Leesburg; deserted 9 July 1863.

Polend, Charles J.: Enl. 8 July 1861 at Leesburg; AWOL 9 July through 24 November 1863.

Roach, George W.: *Captured*; joined U.S. 1st Connecticut Cavalry in October 1863.

Saunders, George: Enl. 7 March 1863 at Petersburg; *shot* in the left leg and *captured*; exchanged from West's Buildings Hospital 27 September 1863.

Suddith, Oscar F.: Enl. 8 March 1862; the company reports him as missing in action but there are no Federal records concerning him; *killed*.

Swain, James T.: Enl. 8 March 1862; *captured*; released on oath from Fort Delaware 21 June 1865.

Swartz, John B.: Enl. 15 July 1861 at Leesburg; *captured*; exchanged 16 March 1865.

Williams, Charles H.: Enl. 15 October 1862 in Frederick County; AWOL 12 July 1863.

Company "D" ("Champe Rifles")

This company enlisted 13 may 1861 at Aldie, Loudoun County, Virginia for one year, and was reorganized 26 April 1862.

Berkeley, William Noland (Captain): *Wounded* by a shell fragment in the thigh during the attack and *captured*; exchanged 6 March 1864.

Berkeley, Charles Fenton (1st Lt.): *Captured*; exchanged 20 March 1864.

Adams, Edwin Thomas (2nd Lt.): Received a *fractured* left leg and *captured*; treated at U.S. 2nd Divison, II Corps Hospital; died at U.S. II Corps Hospital 18 July 1863 and buried in Row 1, Rad "D" of that hospital's cemetery in Schwartz's cornfield on Rock Creek; disinterred to Richmond 13 June 1872 with 110 others in ten large boxes marked "S."

Hutchison, Benjamin H. (2nd Lt.): *Captured*; exchanged 15 December 1864; (28 in 1864).

Adams, Joel O. (1st Sgt.): Received a gunshot flesh *wound* in the left thigh above the knee and *captured*; paroled from West's Buildings Hospital 25 September and exchanged 27 September 1863.

Gulick, W. French (3rd Sgt.): *Captured*; released on oath 20 June 1865.

Boryer, Frederick A. (5th Sgt.): *Shot* in the upper right humerus and *captured*; treated at U.S. 1st Division, I Corps Hospital; exchanged from West's Buildings Hospital 17 November 1863.

George, John (4th Cpl.): Enl. 12 September 1861 at Camp Johnston (Leesburg).

Adams, William H.: *Wounded* during the attack.

Bailey, Edwin S.: The company reports him as having been wounded and captured but there are no Federal records concerning him; *killed.*

Bailey, John L.: Received a gunshot flesh *wound* in the lower third of the left thigh and *captured*; exchanged from West's Buildings Hospital 27 September 1863.

Bell, Thomas: *Captured*; died of chronic diarrhea at Point Lookout 10 February 1864.

Brawner, James F.:

Campbell, John: Enl. 10 September 1862 in Virginia; captured 4 July 1863; joined Capt. Ahl's U.S. Battery 27 July 1863.

Campbell, Z.C.: Enl. 10 September 1862 in Virginia; captured 4 July 1863; joined Capt. Ahl's U.S. Battery 27 July 1863.

Chinn, Francis W.: (27 in 1863); farmer; *shot* in the right leg and scapula and neck and *captured*; exchanged from West's Buildings Hospital 17 November 1863.

Chinn, John L.:

Cox, Charles L.: The company reports that he was captured 3 July 1863 and subsequently died of wounds but there are no Federal records concerning him; *killed.*

Cox, Samuel L.: (23 in 1865); *captured*; paroled 25 April 1865.

Davis, John L.: *Wounded* in the left ankle and *captured*; exchanged from West's Buildings Hospital 27 September 1863.

Doyle, John: *Captured*; exchanged 14 or 15 February 1865.

Francis, Thomas J.: *Shot* in the right chest and *captured*; exchanged from DeCamp Hospital 28 August 1863.

Gaines, R. Brawner: *Captured*; exchanged 14 or 15 February 1865.

Gant, Richard H.: Deserted July or August 1863.

Griffin, Charles R.: Deserted Jul or August 1863.

Gulick, Hamilton R.:

Jackson, Benjamin E.: Enl. 11 July 1861 at Leesburg; *killed* during the cannonade.

Kelly, George F.: Received a gunshot flesh *wound* in the right thigh and *captured*; treated in the U.S. 1st Division, II Corps Hospital; exchanged from Chester Hospital 23 September 1863.

Morris, Albert J.: *Killed* during the cannonade.

Newman, William R.: *Killed.*

Rogers, Cuthbert B.: Enl. 6 March 1862 at Centreville; (35 in 1865); probably *wounded*; *captured*; exchanged from DeCamp Hospital 8 September 1863.

Rogers, S. Aden

Thompson, John L.: Enl. 11 July 1861 at Leesburg; *wounded* in the shoulder and *captured*; deserted hospital at Gettysburg 13 October 1863.

Tyler, Edmund A.: Warren, John M.: Enl. 12 September 1862 in Virginia; *captured*; exchanged 20 or 21 February 1865.

Warren, John M.: Enl. 12 September 1862 in Virginia; *captured*; exchanged 20 or 21 February 1865.

Williams, Ludwell: Deserted 31 July 1863.

Company "E"

This company enlisted 29 May 1861 at Philomont, Loudoun County, Virginia for one year and was reorganized 26 April 1862.

Tavenner, Joseph A. (1st Lt.): *Wounded.*

Coe, Robert (2nd Lt.):

Milhollen, E.A. (Bvt. 2nd Lt.): *Wounded.*

Wynkoop, James W. (1st Cpl.): (25 in 1865); *captured*; exchanged 20 or 21 February 1865.

Tavenner, A.O. (3rd Cpl.): Enl. 17 July 1861 at Camp Carolina; *captured*; exchanged 20 or 21 February 1865.

Barr, E.M.: Slightly *wounded*; went home to recuperate and deserted.

Cornell, John T.: AWOL 9 July 1863.

Davis, Benjamin: Enl. 25 April 1862 at Yorktown; *wounded.*

Davis, Joseph: Suffered a *fractured* right tibia (leg amputated) and *captured*; treated at U.S. 2nd Division, II Corps Hospital; died at U.S. II Corps Hospital 11 July 1863 and buried in Row 2, Yard "D" of that hospital's cemetery in Jacob Schwartz's cornfield on Rock Creek; disinterred to Richmond 13 June 1872 with 110 others in ten large boxes marked "S."

Davis, William: AWOL 20 July 1863.

Franks, C.F.: *Captured*; exchanged 14 or 15 February 1865.

Hann, William H.: Deserted 9 July 1863.

McCarty, William F.: The company reports him as captured, subsequently taking the oath of allegiance, but there are no Federal records concerning him; *killed.*

Rogers, Robert W.: *Wounded.*

Silcott, James B.: *Captured*; exchanged 14 or 15 February 1865.

Spinks, E.F.: (21 in 1863); AWOL 9 July 1863; arrested by the Federals in Loudoun County 24 October 1863; died at Rock Island Illinois prison 15 April 1864.

Vansickler, James C.: AWOL 10 July 1863 while on the march from Winchester to Front Royal, Virginia.

Vansickler, John B.: Enl. 25 April 1862 at Yorktown.

Wynkoop, S.T.: Deserted 10 July 1863.

<u>Company "F" ("Blue Mountain Boys")</u>

This company enlisted 19 June 1861 at Bloomfield, Virginia for one year and was reorganized 26 April 1862.

Grayson, Alexander (Captain): *Killed.*

Ayre, William Thomas (2nd Lt.): *Shot* in the abdomen and *captured*; died at Chester Hospital 25 July 1863 and buried in Grave #49 of that hospital's cemetery; father was Mr. G.G. Ayre.

Tinsman, Francis M. (2nd Sgt.): *Captured*; exchanged 14 or 15 February 1865.

Furr, Thompson (3rd Sgt.):

James, John T. (4th Sgt.): Enl. 27 April 1861 at Hillsboro in Company "A"; AWOL in the cavalry 14 July through 21 August 1863.

Vanhorn, Craven O. (2nd Cpl.): Received a flesh *wound* in the hip.

Furr, Henry C. (3rd Cpl.): *Killed.*

Kidwell, Thompson (4th Cpl.): *Captured*; released from Point Lookout 14 June 1865.

Bishop, Elijah E.: Received a severe cut over his right eye in destroying public works at Chambersburg; went home 12 July 1863.

Chappell, James W.: *Captured*; exchanged 20 or 21 February 1865.

Kendall, Henry C.: (Present under sentence of a court martial for desertion); *captured*; joined U.S. 1st Connecticut Cavalry in October 1863.

Kercheval, John W.: *Killed.*

Lunceford, James D.: *Captured*; died of an inflammation of the lungs at Fort Delaware 11 or 12 March 1864; supposedly killed more men than any other during the assault; buried at Finns Point, N.J.

McCauley, John O.: Slightly *wounded*; discharged as being over age 28 August 1863.

Miley, Caldwell G.: *Captured*; released from Fort Delaware 20 June 1865.

Owens, Thomas E.: *Killed.*

Tavenner, Thomas E.:

Tinsman, John M.: (23 in 1865); *captured*; exchanged 14 or 15 February 1865.

Warner, Gabriel V.: Enl. 15 July 1861 at Leesburg; (sick in camp); *wounded* in both shoulders and *captured*; exchanged from Fort Delaware 1 August 1863; deserted from Farmville Hospital 1 September 1863.

<u>Company "G"</u>

This company enlisted 22 June 1861 at Dranesville, Fairfax County, Virginia for one year, was mustered into service at Centreville 16 July 1861, and was reorganized 26 April 1862.

Berry, James Owens (Captain):

Bicksler, Henry B. (1st Lt.):

Swink, George W. (2nd Lt.): *Shot* in the right side and *captured*; died at Johnson's

266

Island, Ohio prison 13 February 1864.

Cooper, Joseph (Bvt. 2nd Lt.): Enl. 18 July 1861 at Manassas; (40 in 1865); *wounded*.

Reed, Charles W. (1st Sgt.): *Wounded* in the arm (amputated) and *captured*; died at U.S. II Corps Hospital 17 July 1863 and buried in Grave #14 in back of Schwartz's barn in that hospital's cemetery.

Holden, Thomas W. (Sgt.): Enl. 16 July 1861 at Centreville; *shot* in the left thigh and *captured*; exchanged from West's Buildings Hospital 27 September 1863.

Lynn, Joseph F. (Sgt.): Enl. 16 July 1861 at Centreville; *killed*.

Money, E. Frank (Sgt.): *Killed* (leg shot off).

Coalter, A.M. (Cpl.): *Wounded* slightly and *captured*; exchanged 1 August 1863.

Cummins, George W. (Cpl.): (26 in 1863); farmer; suffered a compound *fracture* of the upper third of his left thigh; captured at Williamsport, Maryland; exchanged 6 March 1864.

Robey, C. Ozias (Cpl.): Enl. 6 April 1862 at Camp Taylor; received slight *wounds* in the arm, shoulder, and left leg (flesh) and *captured*; released on oath from West's Buildings Hospital 23 November 1863.

Butler, John W.: Enl. 3 September 1861 at Camp Johnson.

Davis, George: Enl. 22 March 1862 at Camp Taylor; *shot* in the right side of the back (flesh wound), tongue and mouth and *captured*; exchanged from West's Buildings Hospital 17 November 1863.

Dickey, James H.: *Wounded* in the ankle.

Dyer, Charles C.: Enl. 16 July 1861 at Centreville; *wounded* in the side.

Gheen, George: Enl. 22 February 1862 at Camp Taylor; *captured*; released on oath from Fort Delaware 20 June 1865.

Gunnell, W.H.: Enl. 18 July 1861 at Centreville; slightly *wounded* in the shoulder.

Harrison, Asbury: Enl. 10 March 1862 at Warrenton; *killed*.

Horseman, Samuel E.: Slightly *wounded*.

Hutchison, J.L.: Enl. 16 July 1861 at Centreville; (30 in 1865); AWOL near Piedmont, Virginia 17 June 1863; listed as absent on the company's 30 June 1863 muster roll; *captured*; died of chronic diarrhea at Point Lookout 31 March 1865.

Kidwell, James W.; AWOL 18 July through 25 August 1863.

Lambert, John S.: Enl. 24 August 1862 in Lunenburg County; *wounded* (leg amputated) and *captured*; exchanged from DeCamp Hospital 18 September 1863.

Robey, Lewis H.: *Wounded* in the foot.

Robey, William J.: Deserted near Winchester in July or August 1863.

Scott, R.N.:

Steel, O. Frank: Enl. 10 March 1862 at Warrenton; the company reports him as having been wounded and captured but there are no Federal records concerning him; *killed*.

Swink, Joseph C.: *Wounded* in the shoulder.

Taylor, Peterson G.: Enl. 24 August 1862 in Lunenburg County; *wounded* and *captured*; exchanged from DeCamp Hospital 16 September 1863.

Thompson, Armistead: *Captured*; died of typhoid fever at Point Lookout 23 November 1864.

Company "H" ("Potomac Greys" also "Solomon Grays")

This company enlisted 13 July 1861 at Leesburg, Loudoun County, Virginia for one year and was reorganized 26 April 1862.

Regimental skirmish company during the assault.

Matthews, Albert E. (Captain): Date and place of enlistment not shown; *wounded* in the left thigh (flesh wound) with developing gangrene.

Gray, John (1st Lt.): Date and place of enlistment not shown.

Dawson, Charles G. (2nd Lt.): (28 in 1865); AWOL 15 July 1863; captured at Point of Rocks, Maryland 26 July 1863; released 11 June 1865.

Taylor, Kirkbride (1st Sgt.): *Wounded.*

Fadeley, Charles W. (2nd Sgt.): *Captured*; exchanged 20 or 21 February 1865.

Burch, John L. (3rd Sgt.):

Follin, William R. (4th Sgt.): *Captured*; died of remittent fever at Fort Delaware 27 October 1863; buried at Finns Point, N.J.

Poulton, William F. (Cpl.): *Captured*; exchanged 20 or 21 February 1865.

Smith, Edgar Lovett (Cpl.):

Boss, James P.: Received a gunshot *fracture* of the femur and *captured*; treated at U.S. 1st Division, II Corps Hospital; died.

Dorrell, Archibald P.: *Wounded* and *captured*; exchanged 1 August 1863.

Harper, John T.: Enl. 13 October 1861; *killed.*

Havener, Joseph F.:

Laycock, John F.: Enl. 25 March 1862 at Orange Court House; deserted 13 July 1863.

Loveless, George T.: *Wounded*; deserted September 1863.

Reeves, John F.: *Captured*; exchanged 20 or 21 February 1865.

Saunders, Armistead W.: Enl. 25 March 1862 at Orange Court House.

Saunders, Benjamin F.: Enl. 25 March 1862 at Orange Court House; deserted 11 July 1863.

Saunders, Hector A.: Enl. 25 March 1862 at Orange Court House.

Shotwell, Randolph A.: Enl. 16 August 1861.

Tillett, Samuel R.: (present awaiting sentence of court martial for desertion); *wounded.*

Walters, Columbus:

Company "I"

This company enlisted 13 July 1861 at Mount Gilead, Loudoun County, Virginia for one year and was reorganized 26 April 1862.

Green, John Thomas (Captain): Enl. 7 November 1861 at Leesburg; *killed.*

Presgraves, John R. (2nd Lt.): Received a gunshot *fracture* of his left leg and *captured*; treated at U.S. 2nd Division, II Corps Hospital; leg amputated 13 July by C.S. Wood of the 66th New York; died of tetanus 15 July 1863 at U.S. II

Corps Hospital and buried west of Schwartz's house near Yard "C" in the woods on the red hill above the creek; cared for by one of his brothers who procured a pine coffin for him and buried him; his body was removed sometime prior to the general disinterrment of Confederates to the South in the 1870s.

Etcher, Charles L. (1st Sgt.): *Captured*; exchanged 20 or 21 February 1865.

Dear, Thomas A. (1st Cpl.): The company reports him as missing in action but there are no Federal records concerning him; *killed.*

Presgraves, James R. (3rd Cpl.): *Captured*; exchanged 15 November 1864; paroled at Conrad's Ferry, Maryland 25 May 1865.

Campbell, Carter: Enl. 29 September 1862 near Winchester; (in Division Guard House for desertion); deserted and captured near Gettysburg 5 July 1863; joined U.S. service at Fort Delaware 30 August 1863.

Childers, Lafayette: Enl. 10 March 1863 at Richmond.

Cochran, Robert T.: AWOL 4 July through 14 November 1863.

Cross, Nimrod: (present in arrest for being AWOL); *shot* in the left groin and *captured*; treated at U.S. 2nd Division, II Corps Hospital; joined U.S. service 9 February 1864.

Flinn, George W.: The company reports him as missing in action and subsequently as captured but there are no Federal records concerning him; *killed.*

Kitterman, J.A.: Enl. 10 March 1863 at Richmond; the company reports him as missing in action and subsequently as captured but there are no Federal records concerning him; *killed.*

Presgraves, George W.: *Captured*; released from Fort Delaware 20 June 1865.

Presgraves, William T.: *Captured*; exchanged 15 November 1864; paroled at Conrad's Ferry, Maryland 25 May 1865.

Shipman, John M.: *Captured*; exchanged 16 March 1865.

Webster, Richard H.: Enl. 10 March 1862 at Culpeper Court House; *wounded* in the left leg below the knee and *captured*; paroled from West's Buildings Hospital 22 August 1863.

<u>Company "K"</u>

This company enlisted 30 July 1861 at Warrenton, Fauquier County, and Salem for one year and was reorganized 26 April 1862.

Carter, Edward (Captain): Enl. 21 July 1861 at Salem; VMI class of 1864; *shot* in both legs and *captured*; treated at U.S. 2nd Division, II Corps Hospital; paroled 15 December 1864.

Lake, John L. (1st Lt.):

Herrington, Elias M. (2nd Lt.): Enl. at Salem; suffered a *fractured* left tibia.

Gaskins, William H. (1st Sgt.): (20 in 1863); single; nearest relative was Mrs. Mary Sulliver; received a severe *gunshot* fracture of the right foot (amputated), and suffering from obstinate diarrhea, and *captured*; died at Camp Letterman Hospital 5 November 1863 and buried in Section 9, Grave #14 of that hospital's cemetery.

Athey, Samuel M. (3rd Sgt.): Enl. at Salem; *captured*; exchanged 14 or 15 February 1865.

Fewell, Charles H. (4th Sgt.): Enl. at Salem.

Yates, William W. (5th Sgt.):

Lawrence, Lewis M. (1st Cpl.): Enl. 8 March 1862 at Salem; *wounded.*

McClanahan, James T. (4th Cpl.): Captured at Brandy Station 1 August 1863; died of chronic diarrhea at Point Lookout 15 February 1864.

Anderson, French:

Bagget, Richard: *Wounded* in the left chest and *captured*; paroled from West's Buildings Hospital 23 August 1863 and exchanged.

Bayne, George W.: Enl. at Salem; (26 in 1864); farmer; *shot* in the right leg (flesh wound) and *captured*; treated at U.S. 2nd Division, II Corps Hospital; exchanged 6 March 1864.

Burchett, James M.: Enl. 10 September 1862 in Tennessee; his uncle was Andrew Johnson, Governor of Tennessee; disliked by some of his comrades for professing strong Union sentiments; *wounded* in the lower third of the left leg (amputated) and shoulder dislocated and *captured*; exchanged from West's Buildings Hospital 17 November 1863.

Burchett, William H.: Enl. 10 September 1862 in Tennessee.

Fields, Charles W.: Enl. 22 February 1862 at Salem; *wounded.*

Harris, James E.: AWOL 13 July through 18 August 1863.

Hinson, George: Enl. at Salem; *killed.*

Kirkpatrick, Joseph: Enl. at Salem; *wounded.*

Leach, Peter T.: Enl. at Salem; received a *gunshot* compound fracture of the right arm and wounded in the shoulder; *captured*; treated at U.S. 2nd Division, II Corps Hospital; at Point Lookout 4 October 1863; no further record.

Legg, William: Enl. 8 March 1862 at Salem; AWOL 13 July 1863 through 12 February 1864.

Milton, William L.: (detailed to guard commissary stores); returned to company prior to assault; the company reports him as missing in action but there are no Federal records concerning him; *killed.*

O'Brien, Bat: Not on company rolls following 30 June 1863; no further record; probably *killed.*

Pence, Frank K.: Enl. 18 March 1863 in Rockingham County; *wounded.*

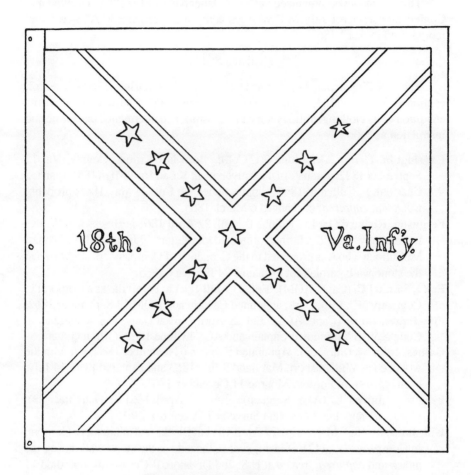

Flag of the 18th Virginia Infantry
probably captured at the stone wall

18th Virginia Volunteer Infanty Regiment

This regiment was organized during the latter part of May 1861; accepted into Confederate service 1 July 1861 with ten companies designated "A" - "K"; and reorganized in April 1862.

Field and Staff

The following listing was obtained from the unit's April/June 1863 muster roll captioned 30 June 1863, Chambersburg, Pennsylvania. The unit reported the condition of its clothing, military appearance, arms, accouterments, discipline and instruction as "good."

Carrington, Henry Alexander (Lt. Col.): Born in Charlotte County, Va. 13 September 1832; graduate of the University of Va. and of VMI in 1851; married Charlotte E. Cullen in 1856; commissioned Lt. Col. 25 May 1861; probably *wounded*; *captured*; exchanged 6 March 1864.

Ferguson, Richard (1st Lt., Adjutant): Enl. 22 April 1861 at Blacks and Whites in Company "G"; (22); farmer; promoted to Adjutant 29 June 1863 vice Robert McCulloch who was promoted to the Captaincy of Company "B"; *captured* at the stone wall; paroled for exchange 24 February 1865.

Price, Samuel C. (Capt., AQM): Enl. 23 April 1861 at Farmville as a Corporal in Company "F"; (30); clerk; appointed Captain and AQM 13 September 1862.

Fitz-James, James (Capt., ACS): Enl. 23 April 1861 at Danville as a Sergeant in Company "B"; promoted Captain and ACS 13 June 1862; (30); merchant.

Gaines, John M. (Surgeon): Appointed Surgeon 6 November 1862; left with the wounded at Williamsport, Maryland 8 July 1863 and captured there 14 July; exchanged from Fortress Monroe 11 December 1863.

Ferguson, James E. (Asst. Surgeon): Enl. 23 April 1861 at Danville; (23); physician; appointed Assistant Surgeon 7 December 1861.

Gill, James C. (Sgt. Maj.): Enl. 22 April 1861 at Blacks and Whites as a Corporal in Company "G"; (17); student; *shot* in the side at the stone wall during the attack and *captured*; treated at U.S. 2nd Division, II Corps Hospital; died 11 July 1863 and buried in Row 2, Yard "D" of the II Corps Hospital cemetery in Jacob Schwartz's cornfield on Rock Creek; disinterred to Richmond 13 June 1872 with 110 others in ten large boxes marked "S."

Pendleton, Elisha H. (Ordnance Sgt.): Enl. 23 April 1861 at Walton's Mill in Company "E"; (27); clerk.

Dougherty, Charles E. (5th Sgt., Commissary Sgt.): On daily duty from Company "B"; enl. 23 April 1861 at Danville; dentist.

Jones, Peter R. (Hospital Steward): Enl. 1 March 1862 at Danville in Company "B"; left with the wounded at Williamsport, Maryland 8 July 1863 and captured there 11 July; exchanged 14 or 15 February 1865.

Dix, Austin (Drummer): A black man; enl. 23 April 1861 at Danville; dischared prior to 31 August 1863.

Clay, Charles T. (QM Dept.): On daily duty from Company "B"; enl. 23 April 1861 at Danville; laborer.

Mottley, John T. (Teamster): Detailed from Company "C"; enl. 23 April 1861 at Burkeville; (35); farmer.

Company "A" ("Danville Blues")

Organized in February 1841, this company enlisted 23 April 1861 at Danville, Pittsylvania County, Virginia for one year; was mustered into service 24 April 1861; and was reorganized 23 April 1862.

The following listing was obtained from the company's April/June 1863 muster roll captioned 30 June 1863 near Chambersburg, Pennsylvania.

The company reported the condition of its clothing as "fair" and that of its military appearance, arms, accouterments, discipline, and instruction as "good."

Holland, James A. (Captain): (29); tobacconist; *wounded* in the neck and *captured*; exchanged 22 March 1865.

Jones, Robert S. (2nd Lt.): (26); merchant.

Paxton, Cyrus H. (2nd Lt.): (27); mechanic; AWOL 3-21 August 1863.

Baugh, William A. (1st Sgt.): (27); mechanic; *wounded* in the left arm (amputated) and *captured*; exchanged from West's Buildings Hospital 24 August 1863.

Walters, Archer E. (2nd Sgt.): Enl. 17 May 1862 at Laurel Church; *wounded*.

Watkins, Thomas D. (Sgt.): (33); constable.

Giles, Joseph, Jr. (Cpl.): (20); mechanic.

Hughes, Henry C. (Cpl.): (22); clerk; *captured*; exchanged 20 or 21 February 1865.

Moore, Samuel T. (Cpl.): (22); laborer; *wounded* and *captured*; paroled for exchange at West's Buildings Hospital 22 August 1863.

Bailiss, William R.: Enl. 12 March 1862; the company initially reports him as missing in action, then as captured, and finally as killed; there are no Federal records concerning him; *killed*.

Barksdale, John J.: Enl. 12 March 1862.

Billings, Charles H.: Enl. 9 October 1861 at Fairfax Court House; *captured*; exchanged 22 September 1864.

Brazzlia, Lewis: Enl. 15 March 1862 at Richmond; *wounded*.

Brown, William H.C.: (18); clerk; *shot* in the left leg and right foot and also received a shell wound of the scalp and *captured*; exchanged from West's Buildings Hospital 27 September 1863.

Bullington, Jasper: Enl. 12 March 1862.

Burch, James R.: Enl. 9 March 1863 at Petersburg; the company initially reports him as missing in action and subsequently as killed; there are no Federal records concerning him; *killed*.

Coleman, Stephen M.: Enl. 12 March 1862.

Coleman, William: Enl. 14 August 1862 at Richmond; *shot* in the left hand, chest and fingers and *captured*; exchanged from DeCamp Hospital 27 September 1863.

Compton, John R.: Enl. 12 March 1862.

Dalton, John A.: Enl. 12 March 1862; born in Pittsylvania County; the company initially reports him as missing in action and subsequently as killed; there are no Federal records concerning him; *killed.*

Dalton, Samuel: Enl. 12 March 1862; *wounded.*

Edwards, Benjamin: (19); painter; *wounded*; captured at Greencastle, Pennsylvania; released 17 May 1865.

Harris, Thomas F.: Enl. 12 March 1862; mother was Mrs. Louisa G. Harris; *captured*; died at Point Lookout 11 March 1864.

Hubbard, James M.: (22); laborer.

Kean, Christopher C.: Enl. 12 March 1862; *captured*; died of chronic diarrhea at Fort Delaware 21 November 1863; buried at Finns Point, N.J.

Lafargue, Henry: Enl. 14 August 1862 at Richmond; *wounded* in the face and *captured*; wanted to take the oath of allegiance to the U.S. but upon hearing that he was to be removed from DeCamp Hospital, he escaped 24 October 1863 for fear of being exchanged.

Lewis, Robert M.: Enl. 12 March 1862; *wounded.*

Loyd, Calvin L.: (23); laborer.

Marshall, Thomas H.: Enl. 12 March 1862; AWOL 10 July 1863 through 4 February 1864.

Midkiff, Levi T.: Enl. 20 August 1862 at Richmond; *killed.*

Payne, John F.: The company initially reports him as missing in action and subsequently as killed but there are no Federal records concerning him; *killed.*

Robertson, William H.K.: Enl. 12 March 1862.

Shields, David T.: Enl. 12 March 1862; *wounded*; sick 16 July 1863.

Shields, John H.: Enl. 12 March 1862.

Smith, Alexander E.: Enl. 12 March 1862; *killed.*

Smith, William H.: Enl. 12 March 1862; *wounded.*

Spencer, William G.: Enl. 26 April 1861; (24); farmer; probably *wounded*; *captured*; joined U.S. service at Point Lookout 23 January 1864.

Trotter, George I.: (28); tobacconist.

Tucker, William H.: Enl. 12 March 1862; *wounded.*

Worrell, James M.: Enl. 12 March 1862.

Company "B" ("Danville Greys")

Organized in December 1859, this company enlisted 23 April 1861 at Danville, Pittsylvania County, Virginia for one year; was mustered into service 24 April 1861; and was reorganized 26 April 1862.

The following listing was obtained from the company's April/June 1863 muster roll captioned 30 June 1863, Chambersburg, Pennsylvania.

The company reported the condition of its clothing as "fair," its arms as "Enfield Muskets," and its military appearance, accouterments, discipline, and instruction as "good."

McCulloch, Robert (Captain): VMI class of 1864; enl. 22 July 1861 at Manassas as a Private in Company "B"; promoted Captain 19 June 1863; *wounded* twice at the Angle during the attack and *captured*; exchanged 22 March 1865.

Murrie, James M. (1st Lt.): (25); clerk.

Vaughn, Lewis L. (2nd Lt.): (24); clerk; probably *wounded*; *captured*; paroled for exchange 21 March 1865.

Wade, Robert D. (Jr. 2nd Lt.): Enl. 24 April 1861; (24); lawyer; *wounded.*

Bagby, Albert L. (2nd Sgt.): (23); mechanic; *wounded.*

Edwards, John E. (3rd Sgt.): (21); mechanic.

Keesee, Robert H. (4th Sgt.): (22); clerk; *wounded.*

Pace, Edmund M. (Cpl.): (18); clerk; *wounded.*

Adkins, Wilson J.: *Captured*; died at Fort Delaware 15 October 1863.

Bagby, George K.: (25); dentist; *wounded.*

Burke, John L.: Enl. at Burkeville in Company "C"; (25); farmer; resided in Prince Edward County; *wounded.*

Collins, Franklin C.: Enl. 14 August 1862 at Richmond; *wounded.*

Compton, Marshall: (23); mechanic.

Crenshaw, James M.: (18); laborer.

Davis, James E.: Enl. 10 February 1863 in Lunenburg County; sick 9 July 1863.

Davis, John J.: (17); laborer; AWOL 13 July through 19 August 1863.

Flippen, Lucian M.: (21); clerk; *shot* in the left arm and *captured*; treated at U.S. XII Corps Hospital; exchanged from Fort Delaware 1 August 1863.

Guill, James H.: (20); laborer.

Haden, Doctor B.: Enl. 10 May 1861 at Richmond; (24); farmer.

Johnson, William H.: Enl. 1 August 1861 at Suspension Bridge; AWOL 3 July through 19 August 1863.

Jordan, Clement H.: Enl. 24 April 1861; (19); clerk; *wounded.*

Moore, Henry P.: (25); stabler; *wounded.*

Moore, William J.: Enl. at Clarksville in 14th Virginia Infantry; *shot* in the left groin and *captured*; exchanged from West's Buildings Hospital 24 August 1863.

Payne, William F.: Enl. 24 April 1861; (25); tobacconist.

Townsend, John T.: Enl. 24 April 1861; (18); mechanic.

Wootten, Henry E.: Enl. 2 May 1861 at Richmond; (18); clerk.

Company "C" ("Nottoway Rifle Guards")

This company enlisted 23 April 1861 at Burkeville, Nottoway County, Virginia for one year; was mustered into service 24 April 1861; and was reorganized 26 April 1862.

The following listing was obtained from the company's April/June 1863 muster roll captioned 30 June 1863, also near Chambersburg, Pennsylvania.

The company reported the condition of its arms and clothing as "fair," and that of its military appearance, accouterments, discipline, and instruction as "good."

Owen, Henry Thweat (Captain): (30); railroad agent.

Watkins, Aurelius A. (Bvt. 2nd Lt.): (21); farmer; father was Mr. George W. Fitchett; *killed.*

Dalton, Francis W. (Sgt.): (21); farmer; *shot* in the left leg and right thigh (flesh wound) and *captured*; exchanged from West's Buildings Hospital 24 August 1863.

Morton, Samuel H. (Sgt.): Enl. 10 March 1862 at Orange Court House; *captured*; exchanged 14 or 15 February 1865.

Temple, William P. (Sgt.): Enl. 11 May 1861 at Richmond; (29); blacksmith; *shot* in the thigh and *captured*; treated at U.S. 2nd Division, II Corps Hospital; exchanged from DeCamp Hospital 8 September 1863.

Verser, Cicero A. (Sgt.): Enl. at Farmville in Company "F"; (23); clerk; father was Mr. William Verser; probably *wounded*; *captured*; died at Point Lookout 27 March 1864.

Borum, Joseph Z. (Cpl.): (21); overseer; severely *wounded* in the right bicep involving injury to the elbow.

Foster, Samuel B. (Cpl.): Enl. at Farmville in Company "F"; (30); merchant.

Robertson, Robert A. (Cpl.): (23); farmer; born in Nottoway County; *wounded* in the arm and leg and *captured*; died at U.S. II Corps Hospital 24 July 1863 and buried in Grave #9 of that hospital's cemetery in back of Schwartz's barn.

Anderson, George L.: (32); carpenter.

Baldwin, Caleb T.: Enl. 26 February 1863 in Prince Edward County.

Borum, Samuel T.: Enl. 10 March 1862 at Orange Court House; received a shell *wound* to the left eye.

Burke, Edwin J.: (21); farmer; *wounded* and *captured*; exchanged from Chester Hospital 23 September 1863.

Burke, William A.: (23); farmer.

Burns, John W.: Enl. 21 February 1863 in Lunenburg County; *wounded* and *captured*; exchanged 1 August 1863; died near Keysville, Virginia 19 August 1863.

Elliott, Willis: Enl. 19 June 1861 at Manassas Junction; (29); farmer.

Fowlkes, Andrew J.: (16); farmer; the company initially reports him as missing in action and subsequently as "supposed killed"; there are no Federal records concerning him; *killed*.

Fowlkes, Hiram O.: Enl. 10 March 1862 at Orange Court House; wife was Mrs. Lucy J. Fowlkes; deserted and captured near Monterey Springs, Pennsylvania 5 July 1863; died of typhoid fever at Fort Delaware 7 September 1863; buried at Finns Point, N.J.

Fowlkes, James T.: Enl. 26 February 1863 in Prince Edward County; born in Price Edward County; *captured*; died at Fort Delaware 6 October 1863; buried at Finns Point, N.J.

Gibbs, William T.: (22); carpenter.

Holloway, Robert G.: Enl. at Richmond; (45); merchant.

Holt, William J.: Enl. at Rice's Depot; *captured*; died of remittent fever at Fort Delaware 4 September 1863; buried at Finns Point, N.J.

Hudgins, Ransom: (23); wheelwright.

Leath, Branch O.: Enl. 10 March 1862 at Orange Court House; *wounded*; captured with wagon train 6 July 1863; exchanged sometime after 31 December 1864.

Leath, James R.: (28); farmer.

Leath, Joseph E.: Enl. 10 March 1862 at Orange Court House.

Leneve, Samuel A.: (19); farmer.

Lipscomb, Junius L.: (19); farmer; *wounded* in the right hand (arm amputated) and *captured*; exchanged from West's Buildings Hospital 24 August 1863.

Newcomb, James R.: Enl. 21 February 1863 in Lunenburg County; *wounded*.

Perkinson, Rowlett: (27); farmer.

Phaup, Joseph H.: Enl. at Richmond; (23); farmer; *wounded* and *captured*; exchanged from DeCamp Hospital 28 August 1863.

Robertson, Abner: Enl. 10 March 1862 at Orange Court House; *wounded* and *captured*; exchanged 20 or 21 February 1865.

Company "D" ("Prospect Rifle Grays" also "Prospect Rifle Guards")

This company enlisted 24 April 1861 at Prospect Depot, Prince Edward County, Virginia for one year; was mustered into service 25 April 1861; and was reorganized 26 April 1862.

The following listing was obtained from the company's April/June 1863 muster roll captioned 30 June 1863, also at Chambersburg, Pennsylvania.

The company reported the condition of its clothing as "tolerable," that of its arms as "mixed calibre .54 in good order," and its military appearance, accouterments, discipline, and instruction as "good."

Glenn, James Peyton. (1st Lt.): (22); planter; *wounded* and *captured*; exchanged 22 March 1865.

Walthall, James A. (2nd Lt.): (22); farmer; VMI class of 1862; severely *wounded* by a gunshot to the left leg (tibia).

Brightwell, Thomas H. (1st Sgt.): (21); farmer.

Glenn, Isaac S. (2nd Sgt.): (19); farmer; the company initially reports him as missing in action and subsequently as "supposed killed," but there are no Federal records concerning him; *killed*.

Glenn, Josiah B. (3rd Sgt.): (20); farmer; *shot* in the left arm (humerus) (amputated at the shoulder) and *captured*; exchanged from West's Buildings Hospital 24 August 1863.

Hunt, Booker F. (4th Sgt.): *Wounded*; captured at Waterloo or Williamsport, Maryland; released 20 June 1865.

Osborne, John E. (5th Sgt.): (24); farmer.

Cunningham, John C. (1st Cpl.): farmer.

Wilkerson, Robert N. (2nd Cpl.): (20); farmer; *shot* in the right arm near the elbow and *captured*; treated at the U.S. 1st Division, I Corps Hospital; exchanged from DeCamp Hospital 8 September 1863.

Gilliam, Rice A. (3rd Cpl.): Enl. 7 May 1861 at Pamplin's Depot in Company "H"; (25); farmer; *shot* in the upper third of the left thigh and *captured*; exchanged from Chester Hospital 23 September 1863.

Sheppard, Josiah (4th Cpl.): (24); gentleman; the company initially reports him as missing in action and subsequently as killed, but there are no Federal records concerning him; *killed*.

Bersch, Benjamin H.: Re-enlisted 6 March 1863 at Pamplin's Depot; *wounded*.

Binford, Joseph T.: Enl. 7 May 1861 at Pamplin's Depot in Company "H"; (19);

farmer; *wounded*; captured at Greencastle, Pennsylvania 5 July 1863; exchanged 1 August 1863.

Calhoun, John L.: Enl. 25 February 1863 at Camp Lee; the company initially reports him as wounded and captured and subsequently as killed, then captured dying 30 April 1864; but there are no Federal records concerning him; *killed*.

Chick, Eugene A.: Enl. 27 September 1861 at Fairfax Court House; *wounded* in the left hip and *captured*; exchanged 20 or 21 February 1865.

Elliott, Henry E.: (26); farmer.

Gallaher, James T.: (36); farmer; *shot* in the middle third of the right thigh and *captured*; exchanged from DeCamp Hospital 8 September 1863.

Glenn, Charles E.: (21); farmer; *wounded* in the right arm.

Harris, John S.: Enl. 7 May 1861 at Pamplin's Depot in Company "H"; (18).

Harris, William H.: Enl. 7 May 1861 at Pamplin's Depot in Company "H"; (21); farmer.

Harvey, Stephen R.: (29); carpenter; *wounded* and *captured*; died of a fractured left thigh at Camp Letterman Hospital 28 July 1863 and buried in Section 1, Grave #10 of that hospital's cemetery; disinterred to Richmond 13 June 1872 in Box #63.

Hubbard, William A.: (21); farmer; *captured*; died of acute diarrhea at Point Lookout 27 December 1864.

Hunt, William N.: farmer.

Johnson, Robert M.: (25); farmer; *captured*; exchaned sick with "debility" 8 May 1864.

Jones, Nathaniel G.: Enl. 25 February 1863 at Camp Lee; resided in Prince Edward County; *wounded* in the abdomen and left shoulder and also suffering from rheumatism and *captured*; treated at the U.S. XII Corps Hospital; exchanged from DeCamp Hospital 28 August 1863.

Laffoon, Jesse G.: Enl. 14 February 1863 at Camp Lee; *captured*; exchanged 14 or 15 February 1865.

Laffoon, John G.: Enl. 14 February 1863 at Camp Lee; *wounded* and *captured*; exchanged 14 or 15 February 1865.

Martin, Peter H.: (20); ditcher.

Martin, Woodson A.: (24); ditcher.

McCune, Robert H.: Enl. 18 September 1861 at Fairfax Court House; *shot* in the right arm (flesh wound) and *captured*; exchanged 1 August 1863.

Meadows, James F.: Enl. 7 May 1861 at Pamplin's Depot in Company "H"; (31); mason.

Meadows, Robert P.: Enl. 7 May 1861 at Pamplin's Depot in Company "H"; (30); mason.

Meredith, Wilson C.: (18); student; *wounded* in the right ankle and abdomen (flesh wound) and *captured*; died in a Federal hospital and buried to the rear of Isaac Diehl's barn, 2 1/2 miles down the Baltimore Pike by Rock Creek.

Murrell, Charles P.: Enl. 12 December 1862 at Fredericksburg; *wounded*.

Saunders, Samuel T.: (25); farmer; *wounded* in the lumbar region by the concussion of a shell.

Shorter, Woodson H.: Enl. 10 March 1862 at Charlotte Court House in Company "K."

Taylor, William R.: (20); gentleman; *captured*; exchanged 14 or 15 February 1865.

Whitehead, Joseph H.: Enl. 6 August 1862 at Richmond; *wounded* and *captured*; exchanged 21 January 1865.

Wilkerson, James T.: Enl. 5 March 1862; the company reports him successively as wounded and captured, then "supposed killed," and finally as captured and dying in prison 30 April 1864; there are no Federal records concerning him, however; *killed*.

Wilkerson, John W.: farmer.

Womack, Edmond L.: (27); farmer.

Woodson, Frederick W.: farmer.

Young, John H.: (19); farmer.

Company "E" ("Black Eagle Riflemen [or Rifles]")

This company enlisted 23 April 1861 at Walton's Mill, Cumberland County, Virginia for one year; was mustered into service 24 April 1861; and was reorganized 26 April 1862.

The following listing was obtained from the company's April/June 1863 muster roll captioned 1 July 1863 near Chambersburg, Pennsylvania.

The company reported the condition of its clothing as "fair," and that of its military appearance, arms, accouterments, discipline, and instruction as "good."

Cocke, Edmund Randolph (Captain): (20); farmer; slightly *wounded* in the head during the attack.

Weymouth, John E. (1st Lt.): (32); carpenter; slightly *wounded* in the chest, mouth, and left hand and *captured*; treated at U.S. XII Corps Hospital; paroled for exchange 21 March 1865.

Cocke, William F. (2nd Lt.): (24); farmer; born in Cumberland County; *killed* within 75 or 80 feet of the stone wall during the attack.

Austin, William C. (3rd Lt.): (21); farmer; *wounded* in the left knee and foot and *captured*; died at the Pennsylvania College Hospital and buried on the hospital's north side; disinterred to Richmond 17 May 1873 with 34 others in three large boxes marked "E."

Gilliam, Carter M. (1st Sgt.): (34); carpenter; born in Cumberland County; *killed*.

French, Hugh H. (1st Cpl.): (18); clerk; *wounded* in the testicles and both thighs (ball extracted from gluteal region) and *captured*; exchanged from West's Buildings Hospital 24 August 1863.

Bagby, William B.B. (2nd Cpl.): (29); carpenter.

Frayser, William R. (3rd Cpl.): Enl. 20 May 1861 at Richmond; (22); farmer; from Cartersville, Cumberland County; *shot* between the third and fourth ribs of the right chest, the ball passing through the upper lobe of the right lung and exiting through the inner margin of the right scapula, and *captured*; exchanged from West's Buildings Hospital 17 November 1863.

Anderson, Nathaniel D.: Enl. 23 July 1862 in camp.

Barker, John H.: (24); wheelwright; born in Cumberland County; *captured*; died of chronic diarrhea at Fort Delaware 19 October 1863; buried at Finns Point, N.J.

Boatwright, James A.: Enl. 1 April 1862 in camp; wife was Mrs. M. L. Boatwright; *shot* in the left leg (flesh wound) and *captured*; exchanged from West's Buildings Hospital 24 August 1863.

Brooks, George W.: Enl. 6 August 1862 in Fluvanna County; deserted 3 July 1863 probably while on the march to the battlefield and captured 4 or 5 July 1863; released on oath 11 May 1865.

Burge, J.E.: Enl. 10 February 1863 in Appomattox County; wife was Mrs. Francis S. Burge; the company reports him, initially, as missing in action and subsequently as killed; there are no Federal records concerning him; *killed.*

Carroll, John W.: Enl. 5 October 1862 in camp.

Clopton, Walter D.: Enl. 29 July 1861 in camp.

Covington, William H.: Enl. 24 February 1863 in Prince Edward County; received a flesh *wound* in the arm and *captured*; exchanged from DeCamp Hospital 28 August 1863.

Davis, S.H.: Enl. 24 February 1863 in Prince Edward County; *captured*; exchanged 20 or 21 February 1865.

Dowdy, James H.: Enl. 11 October 1861 in camp; born in Cumberland County; *shot* in the head and *captured*; died at the U.S. II Corps Hospital 16 July 1863 and buried in Row 3, Rard "D" of that hospital's cemetery in Jacob Schwartz's cornfield on Rock Creek; disinterred to Richmond 13 June 1872 with 110 others in ten large boxes marked "S."

Duncan, James W.: (22); farmer.

Gordon, J.W.: Enl. 10 February 1863 in Appomattox County; *shot* in the left leg and *captured*; exchanged from DeCamp Hospital 8 September 1863.

Moore, M.J.: Enl. 9 February 1863 in Lunenburg County.

Morton, James W.: Enl. 25 March 1862 in camp; born in Cumberland County; *wounded* in the thigh (lower third amputated) and *captured*; died at the U.S. II Corps Hospital 23 July 1863 and buried in Row 2 Yard "B" of that hospital's cemetery on the hill between Schwartz's and Bushman's under a walnut tree; disinterred to Richmond 13 June 1872 in Box #18.

Planck, A.: Enl. 1 September 1862 in Albemarle County; born in Austria; deserted probably while on the march to the field and captured 3 July 1863; joined U.S. 3rd Maryland Cavalry 5 September 1863.

Thomas, W.P.C.: Enl. 10 May 1863 at Palmyra; born in Fluvanna County; *captured*; died at Point Lookout 13 September 1864.

Whitehead, N.: Enl. 10 February 1863 in Appomattox County; born in Appomattox County; sent to the hospital sick in July 1863; died of diphtheria 24 August 1863.

Company "F" ("Farmville Guards")

Organized prior to April 1860, this company enlisted 23 April 1861 at Farmville, Prince Edward County, Virginia for one year; was mustered into service 25 April 1861; and was reorganized 23 April 1862.

The following listing was obtained from the company's April/June 1863 muster roll captioned 30 June 1863 near Chambersburg, Pennsylvania.

The company reported the condition of its clothing as "tolerable," and that of its arms as "minnie muskets in good order." Its military appearance, accouterments, discipline, and instruction were reported as "good."

Blanton, Zachariah Angel (Captain): (27); tobacconist; received a gunshot *wound* which fractured his upper right and lower left jaw and severely injured his tongue, and *captured*; exchanged 8 May 1864.

Miller, William A. (2nd Lt.): (18).

Fowlkes, Anderson J. (Bvt. 2nd Lt.): (26); clerk.

Elam, George W. (1st Sgt.): (22); clerk; born in Charlotte County; *killed*.

Hooton, Samuel C. (3rd Sgt.): (21); tinner; the company initially reports him as captured and subsequently as killed, there are no Federal records concerning him; *killed*.

Morton, Nathaniel S. (1st Cpl.): (22).

Setzer, George M. (2nd Cpl.): (18); carpenter; born in Shenandoah County; the company initially reports him as missing in action and subsequently as killed; there are no Federal records concerning him; *killed*.

Worsham, William T. (4th Cpl.): (23); father was Mr. John A. Worsham; *killed*.

Boatwright, Joseph R.: (19); carpenter.

Bryant, Thomas H.: (19); tailor; born in Buckingham County; *killed*.

Davis, John S.: (21); clerk; born in Chesterfield County; father was Mr. George B. Davis; *wounded*; died of his wounds at Williamsport, Maryland 7 July 1863.

East, Obadiah F.: Enl. 3 March 1862; *wounded* in the left hand.

Foster, Benjamin F.: (25); merchant.

Foster, John W.: Enl. 26 February 1862 at Chester Station; (37 in 1865); *captured*; died of chronic diarrhea at Point Lookout 31 January 1865.

Gilliam, Robert A.: (19); *wounded* by a shell fracturing the metatarsal bones of the great, second, and third toes.

Harvey, Henry H.: Enl. 28 February 1862.

Harvey, John Samuel: (35); coachmaker.

Hunt, Elisha B.: Enl. 25 February 1862; father was Mr. William P. Hunt; the company reports him, initially, as missing in action and subsequently as killed; there are no Federal records concerning him; *killed*.

Miller, Robert D.: Enl. 3 March 1862; *captured*; exchanged 21 January 1865.

Partin, Samuel B.: (20); *captured*; exchanged 20 or 21 February 1865.

Paulett, John T.: Enl. 6 March 1862 in Prince Edward County; received a flesh *wound* to his right leg and *captured*; exchanged from West's Buildings Hospital 24 August 1863.

Paulett, Samuel W.: Enl. 25 September 1861 at Fairfax Court House; *captured*; exchanged 28 December 1863.

Ranson, John: Enl. 20 March 1862 in Prince Edward County.

Riggins, John J.: Enl. 26 February 1862 at Chester Station; resided in Prince Edward County; *captured*; exchanged 8 May 1864.

Robinson, Jesse A.: Enl. 18 March 1862 in Cumberland County; *shot* in the right arm and left hand (lost middle finger) and *captured*; exchanged from DeCamp Hospital 16 September 1863.

Smith, William J.: Enl. 17 March 1862 in Prince Edward County.

Thackston, Richard D.: Enl. 17 August 1861 in Company "D"; *captured*; exchanged from Fort Delaware as Charles Ringold, 56th Virginia.

Walthall, Harrison: (19).

Walthall, John D.: Enl. 10 March 1862; *wounded* in the left hand.

Weaver, Thomas: (33); tailor.

Wells, Berry C.: (25); tinner.

Company "G" ("Nottoway Greys")

Organized in January 1861, this company enlisted 22 April 1861 at Blacks and Whites, Nottoway County, Virginia for one year; was mustered into service 23 April 1861; and was reorganized 23 April 1862.

The following listing was obtained from the company's April/June 1863 muster roll captioned 30 June 1863 near Chambersburg, Pennsylvania.

The company reported the condition of its clothing as "fair" and that of its military appearance, arms, accouterments, discipline, and instruction as "good." Regimental skirmish company during the assault.

Campbell, Archer (1st Lt.): (23); carpenter; *wounded* during the attack.

Muse, Edwin H. (2nd Lt.): Enl. 17 June 1861 at Manassas Junction; (20); student; *wounded.*

Hamilton, William M. (2nd Sgt.): (38); farmer; the company initially reports him as missing in action and subsequently as killed; there are no Federal records concerning him; *killed.*

Crenshaw, Archer D. (3rd Sgt.): Enl. 25 May 1861 at Richmond; (23); teacher.

Barrow, John E. (4th Sgt.): (19); student.

Goulder, Joseph A. (Sgt.): (25); bricklayer; *wounded.*

Jackson, George H. (Cpl.): (23); iron moulder; *wounded*; died of pyemia at the General Hospital at Staunton, Virginia 20 July 1863.

Morgan, Austin F. (Cpl.): (18); student; resided in Nottoway County; *wounded* in the right hand and thigh.

Tucker, Theophilus I. (Cpl.): (19); teacher.

Webb, Jordan C. (Cpl.): (22); student; *shot* in the left leg (flesh wound), and below the eye at the stone wall during the attack; *captured*; died at Fort Delaware 11 October 1863; buried at Finns Point, N.J.

Anderson, Abner W.: Enl. 28 February 1862.

Atkinson, Charles T.: (28); carpenter; *wounded* during the attack and *captured*; exchanged from Chester Hospital 23 September 1863.

Bowles, George S.: Enl. 28 February 1862; resided at Amelia Court House; *shot* in the middle third of the right leg below the knee (amputated) and *captured*; exchanged 20 March 1864.

Brown, Aaron V.: (18); student.

Campbell, John: (36); carpenter; the company initially reports him as wounded and subsequently as killed; there are no Federal records concerning him; *killed*.

Clay, James W.: Enl. 28 February 1862; *wounded* during the attack.

Eckles, James W.: Enl. 28 February 1862; wife was Mrs. Permelia A. Eckles; the company reports him as missing in action and there are no further records concerning him; *killed*.

Elder, Joseph A.: (20); carpenter; *killed*.

Evers, Christian: Enl. 22 August 1861; resided in Dinwiddie County; *captured*; exchanged 20 or 21 February 1865.

Farley, James C.: Enl. 28 February 1862; *wounded* and *captured*; exchanged from Chester Hospital 17 August 1863.

Foster, Horace H.: Enl. 1 April 1862 at Hardy's Bluff; *wounded* and *captured*; died at U.S. II Corps Hospital 17 July 1863 and buried in Row 1, Yard "D" of that hospital's cemetery in Jacob Schwartz's cornfield on Rock Creek; disinterred to Richmond 13 June 1872 with 110 others in ten large boxes marked "S."

Gunn, Thomas J.: (24); farmer; the company initially reports him as missing in action and subsequently as "supposed killed"; there are no Federal records concerning him; *killed*.

Hardaway, Junius W.: Enl. 28 February 1862; *wounded* in the right leg.

Hardaway, Robert N.: Enl. 25 April 1861 at Richmond; (25); farmer; *wounded*.

Hardy, John T.: Enl. 28 February 1862.

Hardy, Lewis E.: (19); farmer.

Irby, Edmund: Enl. 22 November 1862 at Fredericksburg.

Johnson, Lewis D.: Enl. 28 February 1862.

Marshall, Francis Q.: Enl. 28 February 1862.

Overby, Henry: Enl. 1 May 1861 at Richmond; (23); farmer; *killed*.

Reames, William H.: Enl. 28 February 1862; sick 4 July 1863 and sent to Winchester Hospital.

Seay, George B.: (22); teacher.

Stith, Cincinnatus: (22); clerk; *captured*; exchanged 22 September 1864.

Tunstill, James D.: (22); bricklayer.

Tunstill, John W.: (32); farmer; *wounded*.

Tunstill, Josephus M.: Enl. 28 February 1862.

Webb, John A.: Resided in Lunenburg County; *shot* in the left leg (flesh wound) and *captured*; exchanged 6 March 1864.

Webb, Lagiah E.: (20); farmer; *shot* in the right thigh (flesh wound) and *captured*; exchanged from DeCamp Hospital 28 August 1863.

Williams, William Ovid: Enl. 28 February 1862; *killed* during the retreat.

Winn, William H.: Enl. 28 February 1862.

Company "H" ("Appomattox Greys")

This company enlisted 7 May 1861 at Pamplin's Depot, Appomattox County, Virginia for one year; was mustered into service 7 May 1861; and was reorganized 29 March 1862.

The following listing was obtained from the company's April/June 1863 muster roll captioned 30 June 1863 near Chambersburg, Pennsylvania.

The company reported the condition of its clothing as "fair" and that of its military appearance, arms, accouterments, discipline, and instruction as "good."

Johnson, William T. (Captain): (23); farmer; *shot* in the left groin and *captured*; exchanged 15 December 1864.

Harvey, James G. (1st Lt.): (23); farmer; the company initially reports him as captured and subsequently as "supposed killed; there are no Federal records concerning him; *killed.*

Harvey, Edward B. (3rd Lt.): Enl. 8 March 1862 in Appomattox County; resided at Evergreen; married; (35 in 1863); *shot* in the thigh and *captured*; died at Camp Letterman Hospital 6 August 1863 of prostration fever and a second hemorrhage and buried in Section 3 Grave #13 of that hospital's cemetery; disinterred to Richmond 13 June 1872 in Box #45.

Elam, William R. (1st Sgt.): (24); merchant; *shot* in the lower third of the right thigh and *captured*; exchanged from West's Buildings Hospital 24 August 1863.

Pollard, George M. (2nd Sgt.): (22); teacher; *shot* in the right leg 3 inches below the knee joint, fracturing the tibia, and shot in the hand, and *captured*; exchanged from West's Buildings Hospital 27 September 1863.

Swan, Hugh B. (3rd Sgt.): (25); mechanic; born in Prince Edward County; the company initially lists him as captured and subsequently as "supposed killed"; there are no Federal records concerning him; *killed.*

Hamlet, James M. (5th Sgt.): (21); clerk; *killed.*

Hubbard, Samuel R. (5th Sgt.): (37); farmer; *shot* in the right hand, fracturing the metacarpal bones of the ring and middle fingers.

Dickerson, Daniel J. (3rd Cpl.): Teacher; *wounded.*

Farrar, Samuel H. (Cpl.): Enl. 8 March 1862 in Appomattox County; *shot* in the right shoulder between the spine and right scapula and *captured*; exchanged from DeCamp Hospital 28 August 1863.

Harvey, Holcomb P. (Cpl.): (21); farmer; *shot* in the lower third of the left thigh (flesh wound) and *captured*; exchanged form West's Buildings Hospital 27 September 1863.

Austin, John W.: (42); farmer; *shot* in the arm and *captured*; treated at the U.S. 1st Division, II Corps Hospital; exchanged from Chester Hospital 23 September 1863.

Baldwin, Charles W.: Enl. 29 January 1863 at Richmond; *captured*; exchanged 20 or 21 February 1865.

Cawthorn, Joel T.: Enl. 8 March 1862 in Appomattox County; *captured*; exchanged 20 or 21 February 1865.

Coleman, Addison: Enl. 8 September 1861 at Fairfax Court House.

Conner, Robert W.: Enl. 7 May 1861 at Pamplin's Store; (28); farmer; *captured*; exchanged sick with chronic diarrhea 31 July 1863.

Dews, Joshua S.: (33); shoemaker.

Dickerson, James D.: Enl. 8 March 1862 in Appomattox County.

Dickerson, John F.: Enl. 26 February 1862 in Appomattox County.

Dickerson, William J.: (22); farmer; *wounded*.

Ferguson, Daniel W.: (21); clerk; *wounded* in the face.

Ferguson, John R.: Enl. 8 March 1862 in Appomattox County.

Ferguson, William D.: Enl. 8 March 1862 in Appomattox County; *captured*; exchanged 14 or 15 February 1865.

Fitzgerald, Marcellus: Enl. 1 March 1862 in Appomattox County.

Fore, Joel P.: (23); carpenter.

Fore, John J.: Enl. 8 March 1862 in Appomattox County; (35 in 1863); *shot* in the right nates (flesh wound) in lower right portion of the pelvis exiting through the scrotum and left groin and *captured*; exchanged from West's Buildings Hospital 17 November 1863.

Fore, John L.L.: (19).

Fore, Julius L.: (26); carpenter; *wounded* in the perineum and bladder and *captured*; exchanged from West's Buildings Hospital 24 August 1863.

Fore, Leonidas P.: (18); *captured*; exchanged 14 or 15 February 1865.

Garrett, Joseph W.: Enl. 8 March 1862 in Appomattox County; resided at Evergreen; *shot* in the left foot and *captured*; exchanged from DeCamp Hospital 28 August 1863.

Gilliam, Henry E.: Enl. 5 May 1863 in Appomattox County.

Hamilton, Alonzo: (23); resided at Evergreen; *shot* in the right thigh and *captured*; exchanged from DeCamp Hospital 28 August 1863.

Hamilton, John T.: Enl. 15 May 1861 at Richmond; (24); mechanic.

Harvey, Thomas: (25); farmer; *wounded* and *captured*; exchanged from West's Buildings Hospital 27 September 1863.

Harvey, Thomas G.: Enl. 25 November 1862 at Fredericksburg; the company initially reports him as captured and subsequently as "supposed killed"; there are no Federal records concerning him; *killed*.

Hubbard, William J.: (36); farmer; *captured*; exchanged 14 or 15 February 1865.

Jennings, Henry C.: (22); farmer; received a *gunshot* fracture of the arm and *captured*; exchanged 20 March 1864.

Jennings, Robert P.: (21); farmer; *captured*; exchanged 20 or 21 February 1865.

Jennings, William W.: Enl. 1 March 1862 in Appomattox County; *captured*; exchanged 15 November 1864.

League, William S.: Enl. 8 March 1862 in Appomattox County.

Lee, John T.: Enl. 8 March 1862 in Appomattox County.

Lewis, J.D.: Enl. 10 February 1863 at Richmond; the company initially reports him as captured and subsequently as "supposed killed"; there are no Federal records concerning him; *killed*.

Martin, John C.: Enl. 8 September 1861 at Fairfax Court House; *shot* in the right side of the chest and *captured*; exchanged from DeCamp Hospital 28 August 1863.

Mitchell, Benjamin R.: (26); farmer; *wounded.*

Moses, Charles T.: Enl. 25 October 1862 near Winchester.

Paulett, Andrew J.: Enl. 8 March 1862 in Appomattox County; born in Appomattox County; wife was Mrs. Lucy A. Paulett; *killed.*

Roberts, Patrick H.: Enl. 8 March 1862 in Appomattox County.

Simms, William H.: Enl. 26 February 1863 in Company "C"; born in Campbell County; *killed.*

Williams, John P.: Enl. 8 March 1862 in Appomattox County.

Williams, Samuel T.: Enl. 8 March 1862 in Appomattox County; *captured*; exchanged 15 November 1864.

Woolridge, Joel L.: Enl. 8 March 1862 in Appomattox County; (29 in 1863); married; *shot* in the upper third of the left thigh (fractured) and *captured*; exchanged from West's Buildings Hospital 17 November 1863.

Company "I" ("Spring Garden Blues")

This company enlisted 24 April 1861 at Spring Garden, Pittsylvania County, Virginia for one year; was mustered into service 26 April 1861; and was reorganized 26 April 1862.

The following listing was obtained from the company's April/June 1863 muster roll captioned 1 July 1863 near Chambersburg, Pennsylvania.

The company reported the condition of its clothing as "tolerable" and that of its military appearance, arms, accouterments, discipline, and instruction as "good."

Oliver, Elisha D. (Captain): (20); farmer; *wounded* in the right arm (amputated) and *captured*; exchanged 8 May 1864.

Jones, George W. (1st Lt.): (29); farmer; *shot* in the leg and *captured*; exchanged 22 March 1865.

Fitzgerald, William, Jr. (2nd Lt.): (21); farmer.

Dodson, Isaac N. (1st Sgt.): (31); manufacturer; wife was Mrs. Jane Q. Dodson; recieved a *contusion* from a shell burst and *captured*; exchanged 30 April 1864; died of chronic diarrhea 20 May 1864.

Jennings, James (2nd Sgt.): (28); farmer; *wounded* and *captured*; died of his wounds at the U.S. II Corps Hospital 16 July 1863 and buried in that hospital's cemetery in back of Schwartz's barn.

Wade, Thomas M. (3rd Sgt.): Enl. 13 March 1862 at Aspen Grove; (18).

Womack, Polk Dallas (4th Sgt.): Enl. 9 August 1862 in Pittsylvania County; *wounded.*

Owen, Pleasant D. (5th Sgt.): (18); farmer; the company initially lists him as wounded and captured "supposed to be dead" but there are no Federal records concerning him; *killed.*

Yates, William T. (2nd Cpl.): (25); farmer; reported sick with chronic diarrhea 4 July 1863.

Echols, Henry E. (3rd Cpl.): (18); farmer.

Fitzgerald, Samuel, Jr. (4th Cpl.): (18); farmer; recieved a flesh *wound* in the thigh and *captured*; exchanged from DeCamp Hospital 8 September 1863.

Abbott, Charles S.: Enl. 14 March 1862 at Aspen Grove; (19); *captured*; died of typhoid fever at Fort Delaware 22 September 1863.

Abbott, Samuel A.: (24); farmer.

Adams, William H.: (24); farmer.

Allen, Augustine V.: (21); farmer.

Atkinson, Henry F.: (21); farmer; *wounded*.

Betterton, Nathan J.: (23); farmer; the company reports him as wounded and captured "supposed to be dead" but there are no Federal records concerning him; *killed*.

Burnett, Madison S.: (20); farmer; *captured*; exchanged 15 November 1864.

Burnett, Thomas T.: (25); farmer.

Burnett, William H.: Enl. 13 March 1862 at Aspen Grove; (30); the company initially reports him as wounded and captured and subsequently as captured but there are no Federal records concerning him; *killed*.

Clardy, William H.: Farmer.

Clark, James T.: (22); farmer; *captured*; released on oath 8 May 1865.

Coleman, James R.: Enl. 10 March 1862 at Aspen Grove; (18); *shot* in the neck and *captured*; treated at the U.S. 1st Division, I Corps hospital; exchanged 1 August 1863.

Corbin, Thompson: (28); farmer; *captured*; exchanged 20 or 21 February 1865.

Crowder, James: Enl. 14 May 1863 in Pittsylvania County; the company reports him as captured but there are no Federal records concerning him; *killed*.

Evans, Jackson: Enl. 17 March 1862; (34); *wounded*.

Ford, Layton N.: (19); farmer.

Haley, Peter: Enl. 17 March 1862; (43).

Hodnett, James D.: (20); farmer.

Hodnett, William: (25); farmer.

Ingram, Thomas E.: Enl. 17 March 1862; (26); *captured*; exchanged 20 or 21 February 1865.

Jennings, Joseph: (25); wheelwright.

Johnson, George W.: Enl. 17 March 1862; (35); *wounded* and *captured*; died of erysipelas at Fort Delaware 28 October 1863; buried at Finns Point, N.J.

Lewis, Benjamin G.: (21); farmer.

Lewis, John J.: (22); farmer.

Lovelace, John: (27); carpenter.

McNeally, William L.: (21); farmer.

Moon, William W.: Enl. 18 September 1862 in Pittsylvania County; the company reports him as having been captured but there are no Federal records concerning him; *killed*.

Neal, John W.: (27); farmer.

Power, William H.: (22); medical student; *wounded*.

Shields, William A.: (19); farmer.

Tosh, Samuel H.: Enl. 18 September 1862 in Pittsylvania County; *wounded*.

Walker, Nathan W.: (33); farmer; *wounded* in the middle third of his right femur (fractured) and *captured*; died at Camp Letterman Hospital 8 August 1863 and buried in Section 4, Grave #17 of that hospital's cemetery.

Womack, John W.: (20); farmer; *killed.*

Wood, William J.: (23); farmer.

Yates, John T.: Enl. 14 March 1862 at Aspen Grove; (20); the company initially reports him as captured and subsequently as "supposed dead"; there are no Federal records concerning him; *killed.*

Yates, Samuel E.: Enl. 15 January 1863 in Pittsylvania County.

Company "K" ("Charlotte Rifles")

Organized prior to February 1861, this company enlisted 24 April 1861 at Charlotte Court House, Charlotte County, Virginia for one year; was mustered into service 24 April 1861; and was reorganized 26 April 1862.

The following listing was obtained from the company's April/June 1863 muster roll captioned 12 August 1863 near Raccoon Ford, Virginia. There are no entries subsequent to 30 June 1863 on this roll, indicating that it was intended to reflect the company's status as of that date.

The company reported the condition of its clothing as "fair," and that of its military appearance, arms, accouterments, discipline, and instruction as "good."

Smith, John R. (1st Lt.): (21); farmer; *wounded* in the foot.

Stith, William W. (2nd Lt.): Enl. 5 June 1861 at Camp Pickens; (24); clerk.

Durphy, Thomas H.B. (Jr. 2nd Lt.): Enl. 7 May 1861 at Pamplin's Depot in Company "H"; (20); agent; *captured*; paroled for exchange 24 February 1865.

Harvey, Charles L. (3rd Sgt.): (21); teacher.

Spencer, Sion D. (5th Sgt.): (25); trader; *shot* in the right thigh and *captured*; exchanged from West's Buildings Hospital 24 August 1863.

Chappell, William J. (1st Cpl.): Mother was Mrs. Mary E. Chappell; *wounded* and *captured*; exchanged from Chester Hospital 23 September 1863.

Gaines, Henry F. (2nd Cpl.): Enl. 27 May 1861 at Richmond; (20); farmer; *captured*; died of chronic diarrhea at Point Lookout 29 January 1864.

Adams, E.V.: Enl. 10 March 1862; *captured*; exchanged sick with chronic diarrhea 8 May 1864.

Bailey, William H.: (27); farmer.

Bouldin, William D.: (21); clerk; probably *wounded*; *captured*; exchanged 20 or 21 February 1865.

Calhoun, John R.: Enl. 1 February 1862; *wounded* in the right shoulder joint and *captured*; exchanged from West's Buildings Hospital 24 August 1863.

Clark, John T.: Enl. 10 March 1862; *captured*; exchanged 14 or 15 February 1865.

Davis, Peter: Enl. 3 June 1862 near Richmond; *captured*; exchanged sick with dysentery 1 August 1863.

Davis, Robert R.: Farmer.

Davis, Temple T.: Enl. 3 June 1862 near Richmond; *captured*; died at Fort Delaware 7 April 1864.

Evans, P.L.: Enl. 10 March 1862.

Ford, Peyton R.: (19); saddler.

Franklin, John J.: Enl. 7 May 1861 at Pamplin's Depot in Company "H"; (19); *captured*; exchanged 20 or 21 February 1865.

Hagerman, John T.: (19); clerk; received a gunshot *fracture* of his left knee (left thigh amputated at middle third) and *captured*; treated at U.S. 2nd Division, II Corps Hospital; exchanged from West's Buildings Hospital 17 November 1863.

Haley, Samuel M.: (18); mechanic; *captured*; died of chronic diarrhea at Point Lookout 15 February 1864.

Harvey, J.C.: Enl. 28 June 1862 at Richmond; the company's April/June 1863 muster roll did not state whether he was present or absent and the unit's July/August 1863 roll reports him as AWOL; it is not certain that this man was at Gettysburg.

Holt, William D.: Enl. 23 April 1861 at Farmville in Company "F"; (21); bricklayer; *captured*; exchanged 20 March 1864.

Lindsey, Cincinnatus D.: Enl. 23 April 1861 at Farmville in Company "F"; (30); coachmaker; *captured*; exchanged 8 May 1864.

Maloney, Clem H.: Enl. 1 August 1862 at Camp Lee; (25 in 1863); received a severe gunshot *wound* to the back of the middle third of his left thigh and *captured*; exchanged from West's Buildings Hospital 24 August 1863.

Morrison, William A.: (19); wheelwright; the company reports him as having been captured but there are no Federal records concerning him; *killed*.

Preston, Edward T.: (19); farmer; *shot* in the left foot, the ball lodging in the arch.

Ransom, Henry C.: Enl. 7 May 1861 at Pamplin's Depot in Company "H"; (24).

Reames, Edward H.: Enl. 10 March 1862 in Charlotte County.

Roach, Elijah T.: Enl. 4 June 1861 in Halifax County; (transferred from Company "F," 38th Virginia).

Spencer, Samuel T.: (28); farmer; the company initially reports him as having been captured and subsequently as killed; there are no Federal records concerning him; *killed*.

Spencer, William H.: Enl. 1 February 1862.

Watkins, Joseph V.B.: (24); farmer; *wounded* in the left forearm with both bones being fractured immediately below the elbow joint and *captured*; exchanged from DeCamp Hospital 16 September 1863.

Weatherford, Philip Thomas J.: Enl. 4 February 1863 in Lunenburg County; *wounded* and *captured*; exchanged from Chester Hospital 17 August 1863.

Wilkes, Joseph W.: (23); wheelwright; *captured*; exchanged 21 January 1865.

Wilkinson, Thomas C.: (24); farmer.

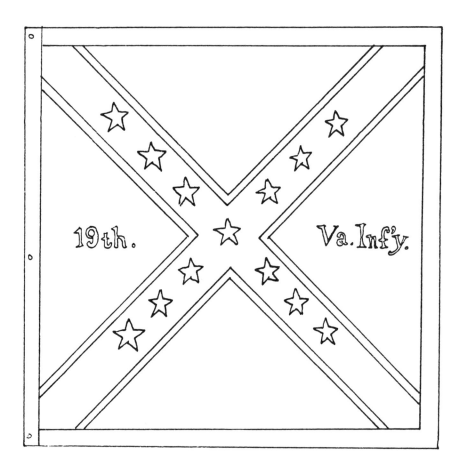

**Flag of the 19th Virginia Infantry
captured by the 19th Massachusetts Infantry
at the stone wall**

19th Virginia Volunteer Infantry Regiment

This regiment, the nucleus of which appears to have been the "Charlottesville and University Battalion," was organized at Manassas Junction in May 1861, accepted into Confederate service 1 July 1861 with ten companies, and reorganized 29 April 1862.

Field and Staff

The following listing was obtained from the unit's June/August 1863 muster roll captioned "camp near Somerville Ford, Virginia" 3 September 1863.

Gantt, Henry (Colonel): Born 1831; graduated VMI in 1851; from Scottsville, Va; married Pattie Eppes; farmer; Major 17 May 1861; promoted Colonel 14 September 1862; *wounded* in the face and left arm.

Ellis, John Thomas (Lt. Col.): Born in Amherst County, Va. 16 March 1827; merchant; graduated VMI in 1848; enl. 15 April 1861 at Amherst Court House as Captain of Company "H"; promoted Lt. Col. 14 September 1862; mortally *wounded* by a solid shot in the face during the cannonade; died at Pickett's Division Hospital 3 July; buried southeast of "Curn's" house at Bream's Mill on Marsh Creek in an orchard under an apple tree; disinterred to Richmond 3 August 1872 in Box #246.

Peyton, Charles Stephens (Major): Born in Albemarle County, Va. 21 January 1841; enl. 10 May 1861 at Stony Point as Captain of Company "E"; farmer; lost his left arm at 2nd Manassas; promoted Major 14 September 1862; slightly *wounded* in the leg.

Lewellyn, John A. (1st Lt.,. Adjutant): Enl. 17 April 1861 at Scottsville as 1st Lt. of Company "C"; (21); clerk; resigned 28 April 1862; appointed Adjutant 30 June 1862; resigned 24 July 1863.

Blair, James Edwin (Capt., AQM): Enl. 17 April 1861 at Scottsville as Jr. 2nd Lt. of Company "C"; (24); clerk; appointed AQM 1 January 1863; sick as of 27 July 1863.

Blair, John T. (1st Lt., ACS): Enl. 17 April 1861 at Scottsville as 5th Sgt. of Company "C"; (26); clerk; appointed ACS 29 January 1862.

Galt, James D. (Surgeon): Appointed Surgeon 24 June 1862.

Taylor, William H. (Asst. Surgeon): Appointed Asst. Surgeon and assigned to regiment 29 January 1862 at Centreville; three or four cubic inches of skin on buttock torn out by a shell fragment during the cannonade.

Wolfe, Luther T. (Sgt. Major): Enl. 8 May 1861 at Charlottesville; (23); clerk; wounded at 2nd Manassas 30 August 1862; sick with erysipelas September 1863, apparently from 30 August 1862 wound.

Gulley, George A. (Ordnance Sgt.): Enl. 16 April 1861 at Charlottesville in Company "A"; (22).

Mason, W.A. (QM Sgt.): Enl. 10 May 1862 at Amherst Court House in Company "H."

Lewellyn, Charles M. (Hospital Steward): Enl. 5 July 1861 at Centreville in Company "C."

Webb, George S. (Musician): Enl. 16 April 1861 at Charlottesville in Company "A"; (20).

Craig, James W. (Ambulance Driver): On extra-duty from Company "G"; enl. 1 May 1861 at Massie's Mill; (25); farmer.

Color Guard

Black, William (5th Cpl., Color Cpl.): Detailed from Company "K"; enl. 20 May 1861 at Hillsboro; (23).

Harvey, John (Color Cpl.): Detailed from Company "G"; enl. 1 May 1861 at Massie's Mill; (26); carpenter.

Company "A" ("Monticello Guard")

Organized 5 May 1857, this company enlisted 16 April 1861 at Charlottesville, Albemarle County, Virginia; was mustered in for one year 12 May 1861; and was reorganized 28 April 1862.

The following listing was obtained from the company's April/June 1863 muster roll captioned Orange County, Virginia and undated.

The company reported the condition of its arms as "rifle muskets"; that of its discipline as "good"; its instruction and military appearance as "fair"; accouterments "in good order"; and clothing as "indifferent."

Culin, John Charles (Captain): (27); *wounded.*

Wood, William Nathaniel (2nd Lt.): Enl. 9 July 1861; on extra or daily duty; received a *contusion* of the leg within 20 yards of the stone wall during the attack.

Hill, John Wesley (3rd Lt.): (27); VMI class of 1859; *captured*; died of pneumonia at Johnson's Island, Ohio 3 February 1864 and buried in Block 5, Grave #25 of that prison's cemetery.

Wingfield, Charles H. (1st Sgt.): (22).

Perley, James (2nd Sgt.): (27).

Maury, William Wirt (3rd Sgt.): (40).

Buck, James R., Jr. (5th Sgt.): (27); *captured*; exchanged sick with chronic diarrhea 8 May 1864.

Johnson, George T. (1st Cpl.): (23); *captured*; exchanged 20 or 21 February 1865.

Bacon, William O.: (18).

Birkhead, James G.: Enl. 19 March 1862.

Birkhead, Joseph F.: (27).

Birkhead, N.S.: Enl. 17 March 1862.

Bowen, John A.: The company reports him as missing in action but there are no Federal records concerning him; *killed.*

Brooks, A.J.:

Brown, James J.: Enl. 25 May 1861; (23).

Brown, William H.: (29).

Dennis, James M.:

Dobbins, Robert L.: (22).

Dodd, John B., Jr.: (19).

Dudley, James H.: Enl. 23 February 1863; probably *wounded*; *captured*; exchanged 1 August 1863.

Dudley, William M.: Enl. 23 February 1863; *captured*; died of acute diarrhea at Fort Delaware 28 September 1863; buried at Finns Point, N.J.

Durrett, John D.: (28); received a *contusion* of the right shoulder inflicted by a shell burst and *captured*; exchanged from West's Buildings Hospital 24 August 1863.

Harrison, Charles H.:

Houchens, John W.: (21); *wounded* and *captured*; exchanged from West's Buildings Hospital 24 August 1863.

Houchens, Thomas M.: (20).

Lane, Lorenzo: Enl. 9 March 1862.

McMullen, Richard L.: (19).

Mooney, Thomas J.: Enl. 9 July 1861.

Pierce, John N.: Enl. 7 July 1861.

Points, Joseph D.:

Points, Polk: Enl. 8 May 1861 in Company "B"; (17); *shot* in the neck and left shoulder and *captured*; exchanged from Chester Hospital 17 August 1863; died at Charlottesville General Hospital 12 May 1864.

Thomas, John W.: Enl. 29 August 1862.

Vandegrift, Christian W.: (20).

Vandegrift, Robert C.: (29).

Webb, William C.: (23).

Webb, William W.: (24).

Wingfield, Mathew W.: (30).

Company "B" ("The Albemarle Rifles")

Organized about November 1859, this company enlisted 8 May 1861 (actually enrolled 16 April 1861) at Charlottesville, Albemarle County, Virginia; was mustered into service 12 May 1861 for one year; and was reorganized 28 April 1862.

The following listing was obtained from the company's June/August 1863 muster roll, uncaptioned as to station or date.

Porter, Pulaski P. (1st Lt.): (19); student.

Hamner, William P. (2nd Lt.): (19); clerk; *wounded*.

Wood, Richard B. (Jr. 2nd Lt.): Enl. 11 June 1861 at Manassas; (19); clerk; the company initially lists him as captured and subsequently as missing in action but there are no Federal records concerning him; *killed*.

Taylor, Eugene G. (1st Sgt.): (18); student; received a flesh *wound* in the right thigh and *captured*; exchanged from West's Buildings Hospital 24 August 1863.

Robinson, Rufus W. (2nd Sgt.): (18); workman.

Bowyer, Leonidas R. (3rd Sgt.): (18); workman; the company reports him as missing in action but there are no Federal records concerning him; *killed*.

O'Brien, Timothy (4th Sgt.): Enl. 18 May 1861 at Culpeper Court House; (20); workman.

Whitesel, John W. (5th Sgt.): (24); workman; *wounded* by a shell which fractured his left ankle joint (leg amputated below the knee) and *captured*; treated at U.S. 2nd Division, I Corps Hospital; exchanged from West's Buildings Hospital 17 Novebmer 1863.

Jordan, John D. (1st Cpl.): Enl. 18 May 1861 at Culpeper Court House; (21); workman.

Harris, Bernard B. (2nd Cpl.): Enl. 25 May 1861 at Manassas; (22); farmer; *wounded.*

Keblinger, Wilber J. (3rd Cpl.): Enl. 16 January 1862 at Centreville; *wounded.*

Lumsden, Richard W. (4th Cpl.): Enl. 18 May 1861 at Culpeper Court House; (23); workman; apparently *wounded* in the left shoulder although this wound could have been inflicted at 2nd Manassas 30 August 1862; discharged due to wound 28 August 1863.

Bellamy, John H.: Enl. 23 March 1862; AWOL 10 July through 25 July 1863.

Dolin, James W.: (31); surveyor; *wounded.*

Dunaway, William: (30); workman; AWOL 26 through 30 August 1863.

Dunn, Albert S.: Enl. 3 March 1862; (18 in 1863); clerk.

Dunn, Luther M.: Enl. 3 March 1862.

Garth, James C.: Enl. 24 August 1861 at Centreville.

Huckstep, Jacob E.: Enl. 28 March 1862.

Hughes, John: Enl. 18 May 1861 at Culpeper Court House; (22); workman.

Humphreys, John H.: Enl. 23 March 1862; deserted 26 August 1863.

Johnson, Manoah D.:

Johnson, Marcellus: Enl. 24 March 1862 at Richmond; AWOL 12 July through 2 August 1863.

Jones, William H.: Enl. 17 March 1862; AWOL 10 July through 19 August 1863.

Morris, James E.: Enl. 18 May 1861 at Culpeper Court House; (23); workman; the company initially reports him as wounded and missing but there are no Federal records concerning him; *killed.*

O'Conner, M.: Enl. 1 November 1862 at Culpeper Court House; *wounded.*

Pearson, John T.: (23); workman.

Smith, Thomas: Enl. 20 December 1862 at Fredericksburg.

Sutler, John T.: Enl. 1 June 1863 at Anderson's; *wounded* and *captured*; exchanged from DeCamp Hospital 16 September 1863.

True, John M.: Enl. 18 March 1862; *wounded.*

Walton, Richmond T.: (27); workman; (present or absent not stated).

Company "C" ("The Scottsville Guard")

Organized prior to April 1861, this company enlisted 17 April 1861 at Scottsville, Albemarle County, Virginia; was mustered into service 11 May 1861 for one year; and was reorganized 28 April 1862.

The following listing was obtained from the company's June/August 1863 muster roll, captioned Chaffin's Farm, Virginia 28 October 1863.

Irving, Charles Scott (Captain): (24); farmer.

White, Samuel H. (1st Lt.): (30); druggist.

Harden, Hopkins (2nd Lt.): (22); farmer; *shot* through the back of the right thigh, the ball coming out through the privates; *captured*; treated at U.S. Cavalry Corps Hospital; released 12 June 1865.

Evans, Charles R. (3rd Lt.): (24); mechanic.

Stone, William B. (1st Sgt.): (21); clerk; *captured*; exchanged 14 or 15 February 1865.

Bowles, Robert S. (2nd Sgt.): (19); teacher; *wounded* and *captured*; exchanged from DeCamp Hospital 8 September 1863.

Omohundro, Thomas W. (3rd Sgt.): (21); farmer; *wounded.*

Quinn, James F. (4th Sgt.): (21); mechanic.

Clements, Joseph H. (5th Sgt.): (25); boatman; probably *wounded*; (at Scottsville General Hospital 21 July 1863).

Kent, James W. (1st Cpl.): (26); merchant; the company reports him as missing in action but there are no Federal records concerning him; *killed.*

Morris, William L. (2nd Cpl.): (18); mechanic.

Woodward, William A. (3rd Cpl.): (30); mechanic; *captured*; exchanged 20 or 21 February 1865.

Omohundro, Robert L. (4th Cpl.): (23); farmer; *captured*; released from Fort Delaware 7 June 1865.

Anderson, Richard M.: Enl. 10 September 1862 in Maryland; *wounded* and *captured*; exchanged from DeCamp Hospital 16 September 1863.

Burcher, James S.: (30); mechanic.

Campbell, Charles A.: (22); mechanic.

Clements, Benjamin F.: (20); mechanic.

Clements, Robert L.: Enl. 6 March 1862; (the last time this man recieved pay was 30 August 1862; he may not have been at Gettysburg but there is nothing conclusive establishing this fact).

Damron, William T.: (22); farmer.

Dawson, William D.: Enl. 27 February 1862.

Farish, Joseph: Enl. 18 January 1863 at Fredericksburg; (presence or absence not stated; last pay date not provided).

Ford, John P.: Enl. 13 March 1862.

Freeman, Charles: (24); mechanic.

Goode, John D.: (22); farmer.

Goodman, John P.: Enl. 10 April 1862 at Louisa Court House.

Hamner, Edward Bruce: (20); mechanic.

Harris, John W. (of Fluvanna): (20); mechanic; *captured*; exchanged sometime subsequent to 10 October 1864 and prior to 31 March 1865.

Heffernon, John: Enl. 23 November 1862 at Fredericksburg.

Irving, Robert R.: Enl. 6 March 1862; (presence or absence not stated).

Moon, Jacob N.: Enl. 10 April 1862 at Louisa Court House.

Moon, Samuel W.: Enl. 10 April 1862 at Louisa Court House; *captured*; exchanged 20 March 1864.

Morris, Nathaniel W.: (20); mechanic.

Napier, James M.: Enl. 10 April 1862 at Louisa Court House.

Napier, John R.: Enl. 13 March 1861; (last paid 30 April 1863; in hospital with lumbago 13 July 1863; deserted 7 August 1863; may not have been at Gettysburg).

Robertson, Thomas D.: Enl. 20 September 1862 at Winchester.

Snead, Pleasant A.: Enl. 17 March 1863 at Chester Station; the company reports him as missing in action but there are no Federal records concerning him; *killed*.

Spencer, Samuel T.: (21); mechanic.

Thomas, Granville Smith: Enl. 1 March 1862; *wounded*.

Thomas, Marion L.: (19); farmer.

Thompson, Charles E.: (38); mechanic; *captured*; exchanged 14 or 15 February 1865.

Vincent, John P.: (32); teacher; *captured*; released 21 June 1865.

Wright, Robert K.: Enl. at Charlottesville; (20); clerk.

Company "D" ("Howardsville Grays")

Organized in April 1861, this company enlisted 19 April 1861 at Howardsville, Albemarle County, Virginia; was mustered into service 10 May 1861 for one year; and was reorganized 1 May 1862.

The following listing was obtained from the company's June/August 1863 muster roll captioned "camp near Somerville Ford, Virginia" 7 September 1863.

Harlan, Richard J. (Captain): (23); boatman; *wounded*.

Baker, Henry (1st Lt.): (20).

Fortune, Joel M. (3rd Lt.): Enl. 8 August 1861 at Centreville.

Parrott, George W. (1st Sgt.): Enl. 15 July 1861 at Centreville; father was Mr. George Parrott; Sgt. Parrott had no wife or child at the time of his death; *wounded*; died at Charity Hospital, Gordonsville, Virginia 24 July 1863.

Ferguson, William H. (2nd Sgt.): (26); carpenter; *wounded*; captured at Greencastle, Pennsylvania 5 July 1863; exchanged from Fort Delaware 1 August 1863.

Patterson, George W. (3rd Sgt.): (21).

Brown, James A. (4th Sgt.): (25); farmer; *captured*; exchanged 20 or 21 February 1865.

Miles, Edward M. (5th Sgt.): (18).

Tindall, John (1st Cpl.): (26); farmer; *wounded* and *captured*; paroled and exchanged; absent wounded through at least 20 September 1864; no Federal or Confederate hospital records concerning him.

Fortune, Absalom M. (3rd Cpl.): Enl. 30 June 1861 at Camp Strange, Centreville, Virginia; (19); clerk; *killed*.

Londeree, William P. (4th Cpl.): (21).

Baker, John M.: (18).

Bugg, Samuel S., Jr.: (24).

Drumheller, Benjamin N.: Enl. 30 June 1861 at Camp Strange, Centreville, Virginia; (22); farmer; *killed*.

Duncan, William H.: (18)

Harding, John B.: (28); wheelwright.

Hughes, Henry H.: (24); well digger; the company reports him as wounded and missing in action but there are no Federal records concerning him; *killed*.

Johnson, James D.: Enl. 20 March 1862; the company reports him as wounded and captured but there are no Federal records concerning him; *killed*.

Maxwell, James W.: Enl. 6 July 1861 at Centreville; *wounded*.

O'Neill, John: Enl. 26 July 1862 at Richmond; *wounded*.

Patterson, John M.: (21); clerk; the company initially reports him as captured and subsequently as wounded and missing in action but there are no Federal records concerning him; *killed*.

Patterson, Robert H.: (23).

Stinnett, William T.: (26); moulder.

Strange, Jacob: Enl. 20 March 1862; the company reports him as wounded and captured but there are no Federal records concerning him; *killed*.

Straughan, Stafford H.: Enl. 25 July 1861 at Centreville.

Taylor, Joel F.: Enl. 26 September 1862 at Winchester; the company reports him as wounded and missing in action but there are no Federal records concerning him; *killed*.

Trevillian, E.C.: Enl. 17 February 1863 at Richmond; sick with epilepsy at Scottsville, Virginia hospital 4 August through 30 October 1863.

Walker, William J.: Enl. 30 June 1861 at Camp Strange, Centreville; (19).

Wood, George W.: Enl. 30 June 1861 at Camp Strange, Centreville; (22); *captured*; joined U.S. service 25 January 1864.

Wood, William H.: Enl. 30 June 1861 at Camp Strange, Centreville; (20).

Woody, Austin: (35); carpenter; *captured*; released from Fort Delaware 21 June 1865.

Company "E" ("Piedmont Guards")

Organized about April 1860, this company enlisted 10 May 1861 at Stony Point, Albemarle County, Virginia; was mustered into service 11 May 1861 for one year; and was reorganized 27 April 1862.

The following listing was obtained from the company's June/August 1863 muster roll captioned "near Somerville Ford, Virginia" 3 September 1863.

Goss, William Walker (Captain): (18); student; *shot* in the right lung and *captured*; died 18 July 1863.

Bragg, James Y. (1st Lt.): (21); farmer; probably *wounded*; *captured*; paroled for exchange 7 March 1865.

Le Tellier, William B. (2nd Lt.): Enl. 16 April 1861 at Charlottesville; (21); wife was Mrs. Molly S. Le Tellier; *shot* in the superior maxillary and *captured*; died of empyema at Chester Hospital 11 August 1863 and buried in Grave #137 of that hospital's cemetery.

Salmon, James (3rd Lt.): (24); mechanic.

Mundy, Thomas W. (2nd Sgt.): (22); farmer; the company reports him as missing in action but there are no Federal records concerning him; *killed*.

Gilbert, Robert W.: (4th Sgt.): (22); farmer; *wounded.*

Edwards, Samuel W. (1st Cpl.): (31); farmer; *shot* in the left tibia and *captured*; exchanged from West's Buildings Hospital 27 September 1863.

Sandridge, James J. (2nd Cpl.): Enl. 20 May 1861 at Culpeper Court House; (24); farmer; the company reports him as missing in action but there are no Federal records concerning him; *killed.*

Eastham, David C. (3rd Cpl.): (23); farmer.

Mahanes, Tavener O. (4th Cpl.): (22); farmer; *shot* in the neck and *captured*; exchanged 14 or 15 February 1865.

Brockman, James P.: Enl. 22 August 1862 at Frederick City.

Cardin, William B.: Enl. 20 May 1861 at Culpeper Court House; (20); miller; the company reports him as missing in action but there are no Federal records concerning him; *killed.*

Carpenter, John F.: Enl. 14 March 1862 at Orange Court House; (19); the company reports him as missing in action but there are no Federal records concerning him; *killed.*

Condry, Jerry: Enl. 1 August 1862 at Richmond.

Dowell, Major M.: (25); laborer; the company reports him as missing in action but there are no Federal records concerning him; *killed.*

Durrett, Thomas D.: Enl. 20 May 1861 at Culpeper Court House; (18); laborer; *wounded* and *captured*; exchanged from West's Buildings Hospital 24 August 1863.

Ehart, Adam G.: Enl. 20 May 1861 at Culpeper Court House; (32); farmer; *shot* in the right calf (flesh wound) and *captured*; exchanged 6 March 1864.

Flynt, James T.: (22); farmer.

Flynt, William D.: Enl. 14 March 1862 at Orange Court House; (24).

Hall, Henry J.: Enl. at Culpeper Court House; *killed.*

Hall, William S.: (26); mechanic.

Herring, John H.: (22); farmer; (presence or absence not stated).

Hill, William H.: Enl. 4 April 1862 at Orange Court House.

Leake, William J.: Enl. 14 July 1861 at Centreville.

Le Tellier, Joseph C.: Enl. 14 March 1862 at Orange Court House; (17); *wounded* and *captured*; exchanged from DeCamp Hospital 16 September 1863.

Madison, James A.: (18); farmer.

Meeks, Henry M.: (28); farmer.

Minor, Peter H.: (23); farmer; the company reports him as missing in action but there are no Federal records concerning him; *killed.*

Mooney, Madison: Enl. 15 April 1862 at Yorktown.

Mundy, Isaac L.: Enl. 20 May 1861 at Culpeper Court House; (26); farmer.

Mundy, Jonathan B.: Enl. 20 May 1861 at Culpeper Court House; (24); farmer; apparently *wounded*; (admitted to hospital with vulnus sclopeticum 3 August through 30 October 1863).

Nimmo, Hiram: Enl. 15 March 1862 at Orange Court House; *wounded.*

Norvell, Joseph B.: (29); miller; the company reports him as missing in action but there are no Federal records concerning him; *killed.*

Pritchett, Belfield: Enl. 7 June 1861 at Manassas Junction; (23); farmer; *wounded*.

Pritchett, James D.: (30); farmer.

Taylor, John R.: (23); farmer; the company reports him as missing in action but there are no Federal records concerning him; *killed*.

Vaughan, William F.: Enl. 13 May 1861 at Culpeper Court House; (24); farmer.

Wood, Alfred T.: Enl. 20 May 1861 at Culpeper Court House; (19); farmer.

Wood, James F.: Enl. 20 May 1861 at Culpeper Court House; (18); farmer; *wounded*.

Wood, Washington M.: Enl. 20 May 1861 at Culpeper Court House; (21); farmer.

Company "F" ("The Montgomery Guard")

This company enlisted 25 May 1861 at Charlottesville, Albemarle County, Virginia; was mustered into service 25 May 1861 for one year; and was reorganized 28 April 1862.

The following listing was obtained from the company's June/August 1863 muster roll captioned "camp near Chaffin's Farm, Virginia" 29 October 1863.

Taylor, Bennett (Captain): (24); teacher; *shot* in the side and *captured*; treated at U.S. 2nd Division, II Corps Hospital; exchanged from Johnson's Island, Ohio 22 March 1865.

McIntire, James Davis (2nd Lt.): (20); clerk; *wounded*.

Powell, Willard L. (3rd Lt.): (20); harness maker.

Jones, Lucien S. (1st Sgt.): Enl. 16 April 1861; (19); *shot* in the abdomen; died at Pickett's Division Hospital 4 or 5 July 1863 and buried at Bream's Mill above Myers' house at the side of a fence; disinterred to Richmond 3 August 1872 with 33 others in three large boxes marked "P Curns."

McLain, Abram S. (3rd Sgt.): (24); carpenter.

Melton, George S. (5th Sgt.): (21); carpenter.

Barnett, Charles: Enl. 1 March 1862.

Barnett, James A.: (22); laborer; recieved a shell *wound* in the right thigh (flesh wound) and *captured*; exchanged from West's Buildings Hospital 27 September 1863.

Barnett, William: Enl. 3 July 1861.

Brown, Richard: (23); laborer; AWOL 10 July through 13 September 1863.

Campbell, William B.: (18); laborer.

Clements, Thomas M.: (25); laborer; AWOL 8 August through November 1863.

Collins, James S.: (21); carpenter.

Comar, Michael: Enl. 1 March 1862.

Criddle, Patrick H.: Enl. 5 June 1861; (20); laborer; AWOL 10 July 1863.

Dayley, Jerry: (26); carpenter.

Dee, John: (25); carpenter.

Grace, James: (35); carpenter.

Hawley, James O.: (26); carpenter; *wounded*.

Herndon, Edward J.: Enl. 5 June 1861; (22); carpenter; *shot* in the right lung and arm (amputated) and *captured*; died 10 July 1863.

Herndon, Nicholas W.: (19); carpenter; deserted 4 July 1863 and captured; joined Capt. Ahl's U.S. Battery 27 July 1863.

Kennedy, Philip: (31); carpenter.

Langford, James: Enl. 5 June 1861.

Langford, William:

Madison, George D.: (22); laborer.

Madison, James: Enl. 5 June 1861; probably *wounded* (admitted to Charlottesville Hospital 22 July 1863 with vulnus sclopeticum; returned to duty 3 August 1863).

McDonald, Charles: (30); carpenter.

Meeks, James H.: (27); teacher; AWOL 8 through 23 July 1863.

Meeks, John F.: (18); laborer.

Meeks, John N.: Enl. 18 June 1861 at Manassas; (44); laborer.

Meeks, Lewis: (20); laborer; AWOL 8 through 11 August 1863.

Melton, Henry: Enl. 19 June 1861 at Manassas; (18); laborer.

Philmore, Samuel P.: Enl. 1 March 1862.

Rhodes, Andrew J.: Enl. 19 June 1861 at Manassas; (20); laborer.

Rhodes, Robert P.: Enl. 29 June 1861 at Centreville; (18); the company reports him as having been wounded and captured but there are no Federal records concerning him; *killed.*

Shiflett, James: (19); laborer.

Shope, John: Enl. 27 March 1863 at Hanover Junction; probably *wounded*; *captured*; joined U.S. service at Fort Delaware 29 January 1864.

Sprouse, Henry: Enl. 1 March 1862; *shot* in the leg and *captured*; treated at U.S. 1st Division, II Corps Hospital; exchanged from DeCamp Hospital 27 September 1863.

Strange, James A.: (22); laborer; *wounded.*

Taylor, James: Enl. 29 June 1861 at Centreville; (33); laborer; *wounded* and *captured*; died 4 July 1863.

Taylor, Joseph: Enl. 5 June 1861; (18); laborer.

Walton, Charles: Enl. 1 March 1862; *wounded* in the left thigh and knee and *captured*; exchanged 20 or 21 February 1865.

Willis, Rust W.: Enl. 25 May 1863 at Hanover Junction.

Company "G" ("Nelson Grays")

This company enlisted 1 May 1861 at Massie's Mill, Nelson County, Virginia; was mustered into service 20 May 1861 for one year; and was reorganized 28 April 1862.

The following listing was obtained from the company's June/August 1863 muster roll captioned "near Somerville Ford, Virginia" 31 August 1863.

Boyd, Waller M. (Captain): (18); farmer; VMI class of 1863; *wounded* in the thigh at the stone wall during the attack; *captured*; exchanged 6 March 1864.

Powell, John T. (1st Lt.): (20 or 22); student; *wounded* in the elbow requiring a resection.

McCrary, John H. (2nd Lt.): (19); clerk; (presence or absence not stated); signs 31 August 1863 muster roll as commanding company.

Gregory, Joseph F. (3rd Lt.): (32); cabinet maker.

Booz, William G. (1st Sgt.): (18); miller; the company reports him as missing in action but there are no Federal records concerning him; *killed.*

Purvis, Joseph E. (2nd Sgt.): (20); farmer; *captured*; exchanged 20 or 21 February 1865.

Monroe, Nelson (3rd Sgt.): (38); farmer; the company reports him as missing in action but there are no Federal records concerning him; *killed.*

Loving, William H. (4th Sgt.): (21); miller; *wounded.*

Wood, William D. (5th Sgt.): (18); farmer.

Loving, John J., Jr. (1st Cpl.): (27); farmer; *captured*; released from Fort Delaware 20 June 1865.

Stratton, Henry F. (2nd Cpl.): Enl. 10 June 1861 at Culpeper Court House; (25); farmer.

Hamilton, Jacob (3rd Cpl.): (21); farmer; *captured*; released 20 June 1865.

Smith, Abraham (4th Cpl.): (26); school master; *wounded* (admitted to a hospital with vulnus sclopeticum 19 September 1863).

Bolton, Thomas M.: Enl. 10 November 1862 at Culpeper Court House.

Bowles, William H.: (22); farmer; received a gunshot *wound* which resulted in a compound fracture of the middle third of his right thigh (femur) and knee and *captured*; exchanged 30 April 1864.

Bryant, Charles P.: (24); farmer.

Crist, Thomas J.:

Dillard, Oscar P.: (20); farmer; *captured*; died of chronic diarrhea at Fort Delaware 13 September 1863; buried at Finns Point, N.J.

Fitzgerald, Douglas: (23); carpenter.

Fortune, Meridith Winston: (38); distiller; the company reports him as missing in action but there are no Federal records concerning him; *killed.*

Fulks, James M.: (18); farmer; recieved a gunshot *wound* which fractured his right leg (amputated) and *captured*; died at Camp Letterman Hospital 6 August 1863 and buried in Sectino 3, Grave #7 of that hospital's cemetery.

Groves, William B.: Enl. 1 August 1861 at Centreville.

Hamilton, James M.: (19); farmer; probably *wounded* (admitted to a hospital 13 July 1863).

Hamilton, Varland, (24); carpenter.

Harlow, William N.: (25); farmer; the company reports him as missing in action but there are no Federal records concerning him; *killed.*

Harvey, James: (23); farmer; *captured*; exchanged 14 or 15 February 1865.

Hatter, Morgan A.: (26); farmer.

Hatter, Powhatan B.: Enl. 10 June 1861 at Culpeper Court House; (25); farmer.

Henderson, John L.: Enl. 11 November 1861 at Centreville; *shot* in the knee (tibia) and *captured*; exchanged from DeCamp Hospital 28 August 1863.

Higginbotham, James L.: (21); carpenter; the company reports him as missing in action but there are no Federal records concerning him; *killed.*

Hughes, Moses P.: (22); farmer; the company reports him as missing in action but there are no Federal records concerning him; *killed*.

Hughes, Samuel P.: (23); farmer; *captured*; died of chronic diarrhea at Point Lookout 22 January 1864.

Hundley, Joshua W.: (19); farmer.

Johnson, William: The company initially reports him as captured and subsequently as missing in action but there are no Federal records concerning him; *killed*.

Jones, William L.: (18); farmer; (admitted to Chimborazo Hospital #1 13 June 1863 with gonorrhea; present by 31 August 1863; may not have been at Gettsyburg).

Jordan, William F.: (25); farmer; the company reports him as missing in action but there are no Federal records concerning him; *killed*.

Kidd, Alexander B.: (22); farmer; AWOL in July or August 1863.

Kidd, Alexander R.: (25); farmer.

Kidd, Landon R.: (30); farmer.

Kidd, Lorenzo D.: (23); farmer; *wounded*.

Loving, James E.: (24); carpenter; *captured*; died of an inflammation of the lungs at Fort Delaware 30 May 1864; buried at Finns Point, N.J.

Loving, John J.W.: (19); farmer.

May, George P.: (18); blacksmith.

May, James M.: (21); carpenter.

Mays, Robert D.: (20); farmer; *shot* in both thighs and *captured*; treated at U.S. 1st Division, II Corps Hospital; exchanged from DeCamp Hospital 16 September 1863.

Meeks, John S.: Enl. 10 March 1862; AWOL in July or August 1863.

Monroe, Charles: (23); farmer.

Oliver, Samuel A.: (18); farmer.

Ponton, Henry E.: (30); carpenter; *wounded* and *captured*; exchanged sometime between 31 August and 31 December 1863.

Ponton, N.B.: Enl. 10 March 1862.

Ponton, Richard Hartwell: (20); carpenter; *wounded*.

Ponton, William H.: Enl. 10 March 1862; *captured*; released from Fort Delaware 20 June 1865.

Purvis, Albert A.: (20); miller.

Purvis, Clifford C.: (20); farmer.

Purvis, William H.: (19); farmer.

Stevens, Albert L.: *Captured*; exchanged 20 March 1864.

Stevens Richard P.: (21); farmer.

Stewart, John W.: (18); clerk; *shot* in the thigh and *captured*; treated at U.S. 1st Division, II Corps Hospital; exchanged from DeCamp Hospital 8 September 1863.

Thacker, Lafayette W.:

Whitehead, Kincaid: (25); dentist; *captured*; exchanged 20 or 21 February 1865.

Wills, Willis, C.: (27); schoolmaster.

Company "H" ("The Southern Rights Guard")

This company enlisted 15 April 1861 at Amherst Court House, Amherst County, Virginia; was mustered into service 24 May 1861 for one year; and was reorganized 28 April 1862.

The following listing was obtained from the company's June/August 1863 muster roll captioned "near Somerville Ford, Virginia" 31 August 1863.

Brown, Benjamin, Jr. (Captain): (19); farmer; VMI class of 1864; *wounded* in the right foot and *captured*; treated at U.S. 2nd Division, II Corps Hospital; paroled for exchange 24 February 1865.

Richeson, Jesse V. (1st Lt.): (30); farmer.

Garland, David S. (2nd Lt.): (19); student.

Landrum, James E. (Bvt. 2nd Lt.): (19); gentleman; the company reports him as missing in action but there are no Federal records concerning him; *killed.*

McGinnis, Thomas W. (1st Sgt.): (19); merchant.

Daniel, William S. (2nd Sgt.): (20); gentleman.

Going, George W. (3rd Sgt.): (21).

Mason, George B. (4th Sgt.): (21); clerk.

Mays, Nathaniel A. (5th Sgt.): (19); farmer.

Chiles, James M. (1st Cpl.): (22); farmer; *wounded* and *captured*; exchanged from DeCamp Hospital 28 August 1863.

Hite, Isaac W. (2nd Cpl.): (24); farmer.

Knight, Daniel C. (3rd Cpl.): Enl. 22 August 1861; the company reports him as missing in action but there are no Federal records concerning him; *killed.*

Jennings, Daniel R. (4th Cpl.): (20); farmer; *wounded.*

Barbour, John H.: (22); farmer; *captured*; exchanged 14 or 15 February 1865.

Bryant, John B.: Enl. 6 August 1861.

Burley, Thomas D.: Enl. 15 August 1861.

Christian, Charles A.: (22); farmer.

Cox, Breckenridge F.: (21); farmer; *wounded* in the superior maxillary and scalp and *captured*; exchanged 1 August 1863.

Daniel, James M.: (18); teacher.

Davidson, James: Enl. 21 June 1863 (exchanged from 2nd Virginia Cavalry); the company reports him as missing in action but there are no Federal records concerning him; *killed.*

Davidson, John: Enl. 1 March 1862.

Davies, John W.: (23); farmer.

Drumheller, Abram A.: (23); farmer; the company reports him as missing in action but there are no Federal records concerning him; *killed.*

Gilbert, Robert N.: (22); grocer.

Harvey, Marcellus B.: (19); farmer.

Henderson, J.J.: Enl. January 1863; *wounded* and *captured*; exchanged from DeCamp Hospital 28 August 1863.

Higginbotham, Clifton V.: Enl. 17 June 1861; (18); farmer.

Jennings, John T.: (23); farmer.

Joiner, Houston C.: (20); farmer.

Mason, Samuel E.: Enl. 17 June 1861; (18); farmer.

Mays, George W., Sr.: (22); farmer.

Mays, George W., Jr.: (21); farmer.

Mays, Marcellus H.: (24); farmer.

Proffit, Henry J.: (22); farmer.

Proffit, William N.: (20); farmer.

Stinnett, C.P.: Enl. 1 March 1862; the company reports him as missing in action but there are no Federal records concerning him; *killed.*

Stinnett, J.J.: Enl. in October 1862.

Stinnett, Paulus P.: (19); farmer; *wounded* in the right foot (fractured) and *captured*; exchanged 6 March 1864.

Tyree, Lucas P.: (23); farmer.

Ward, James: (23); farmer.

Company "I" ("The Amherst Rifle Grays")

This company enlisted 29 April 1861 at Buffalo Springs, Amherst County, Virginia; was mustered into service 29 May 1861 for one year; and was reorganized 29 April 1862.

The following listing was obtained from the company's June/August 1863 muster roll, uncaptioned as to station or date.

Henley, George W. (Captain): (32); farmer.

Smith, Horace (2nd Lt.): (31); farmer; slightly *wounded* in the face and *captured*; died at Point Lookout 12 August 1864.

Hill, Charles T. (3rd Lt.): Enl. 6 August 1861 at Centreville.

Myers, John W. (1st Sgt.): (30); farmer; *captured*; exchanged 20 or 21 February 1865.

Wilsher, Stafford K. (2nd Sgt.): (22); farmer; *wounded.*

Ware, Edwin S. (3rd Sgt.): Enl. 17 August 1861 at Fairfax Court House; *shot* in the right leg (amputated by surgeon C.S. Wood of the 66th New York 6 July 1863); and *captured*; treated at U.S. 1st Division, II Corps Hospital; exchanged from West's Buildings Hospital 17 November 1863.

Fulsher, Paul C. (4th Sgt.): (19); farmer; *wounded.*

Ware, Robert A. (1st Cpl.): Enl. 6 August 1861 at Centreville; *wounded*; died 21 August 1863.

Franklin, Abner M. (2nd Cpl.): (30); farmer.

Jennings, Leroy P. (3rd Cpl.): (19); farmer; *shot* in the right lung and *captured*; exchanged from West's Buildings Hospital 27 September 1863.

Burley, Alexander: Enl. 25 May 1861; (24); farmer; *captured*; died at Fort Delaware 5 October 1863; buried at Finns Point, N.J.

Campbell, Andrew: (24); farmer.

Campbell, Daniel G.: Enl. 3 June 1861 at Charlottesville; (20); farmer.

Campbell, James L.: Enl. 19 May 1861; (24); farmer.

Campbell, Josiah: Enl. 29 May 1861 at Charlottesville; (24); farmer.

Campbell, W.D.: Enl. 15 March 1862 at Amherst Court House; *wounded*.

Campbell, William H.: (31); farmer; *wounded*.

Campbell, William J.: Enl. 19 May 1861; (29); farmer.

Carpenter, Charles L.: Enl. 15 March 1862 at Amherst Court House; *captured*; sent to Point Lookout 26 October 1863 after which there are no further records concerning him; probably died at Point Lookout, date unrecorded.

Carter, Joseph C.: (25); farmer.

Cash, Otis: (30); farmer.

Cash, R.B.: (22); farmer.

Cash, William H.: Enl. 9 May 1861; (20); farmer; left at Hagerstown, Maryland 24 June 1863; returned to company in time for battle; *captured*; died of pericarditis at Fort Delaware 17 November 1863; buried at Finns Point, N.J.

Cash, Zeb: Enl. 15 March 1862 at Amherst Court House; AWOL 24 August 1863.

Evans, John T.: (25); farmer.

Fonkhowitzer, John M.: Enl. 20 May 1861; (41); tailor.

Franklin, Arthur W.: (32); farmer.

Hartless, Benjamin: Enl. 15 March 1862; *captured*; died of rheumatism at Fort Delaware 30 October 1863; buried at Finns Point, N.J.

Hawkins, Lucus P.: (26); farmer.

Higginbotham, Aaron L.: (33); farmer.

Higginbotham, Joseph A.: (33); farmer.

Higginbotham, Paul M.: (28); farmer.

Lawhorne, Edward P.: Enl. 20 May 1861; (20); farmer.

Lawhorne, Isham: Enl. 20 April 1861; the company reports him as missing in action but there are no Federal records concerning him; *killed*.

Logan, David T.: (19); farmer.

Logan, Samuel P.: (21); farmer.

Massie, John W.: Enl. 6 August 1861 at Centreville; *shot* in the leg and *captured*; treated at U.S. 1st Division, II Corps Hospital; died 10 July 1863.

Mays, Anderson: Enl. 20 January 1863 at Amherst Court House; the company reports him as missing in action but there are no Federal records concerning him; *killed*.

Page, D.D.: Enl. 20 January 1863 at Amherst Court House.

Page, Royal M.: Enl. 6 August 1861 at Centreville.

Powell, William H.: (22); farmer.

Quinn, Archibald S.: Enl. 6 August 1861 at Centreville; *captured*; exchanged 14 or 15 February 1865.

Seay, James C.: (18); farmer; *captured*; died of typhoid fever at Fort Delaware 29 December 1863; buried at Finns Point, N.J.

Thompson, Thomas J.: (20); farmer.

Thompson, William H.: Enl. 20 May 1861; (20); farmer; *wounded*.

Thompson, William M.: (23); farmer.

Tucker, Charles J.: (32); farmer.

Tyree, J.S.: Enl. 12 February 1863 at Amherst Court House.

Via, William: Enl. 15 March 1862 at Amherst Court House.

Ware, Paulus M.: Enl. 6 August 1861 at Centreville; captured while serving as a nurse at Gettysburg; exchanged 20 March 1864.

Wilsher, Charles T.: Enl. 3 June 1861 at Culpeper Court House; (18); farmer.

Wood, Teleman: Enl. 26 May 1861; (21); farmer.

Wright, Charles H.: Enl. 17 August 1861 at Fairfax Court House; AWOL 12 July 1863.

Wright, Paul C.: Enl. 26 May 1861; (27); farmer.

Wright, William: Enl. 15 March 1862 at Amherst Court House; *captured*; died of pneumonia at Point Lookout 10 or 12 January 1864.

Company "K" ("The Blue Ridge Rifles")

Organized 6 November 1860, this company enlisted 20 May 1861 at Hillsboro, Albemerle County, Virginia; was mustered into service 20 May 1861 for one year; and was reorganized 27 April 1862.

The following listing was obtained from the company's June/August 1863 muster roll, captioned Chaffin's Farm 29 October 1863.

Woodson, James Garland (Captain): (28).

Grinstead, James H. (1st Lt): (26); the company reports that he was wounded and captured but there are no Federal records concerning him; *killed*.

Martin, Sylvester G. (3rd Lt.): (28); *shot* in the intestines and *captured*; exchanged 22 March 1865.

Black, Nicholas (1st Sgt.): (20); received a severe gunshot *wound* to the right thigh and *captured*; exchanged from West's Buildings Hospital 24 August 1863.

Kennon, James H. (2nd Sgt.): (22).

Rea, William T. (3rd Sgt.): (18); *wounded* and *captured*; exchanged sometime prior to 31 October 1863.

Grinstead, Richard J. (4th Sgt.): (24).

Woods, John J. (5th Sgt.): (18); *wounded* in the right leg and *captured*; died 20 July or August 1863; buried on the north side of the Pennsylvania College Hospital.

Lindsay, Asberry D. (1st Cpl.): (28).

Wood, William D. (2nd Cpl.): (28).

Black, Robert (3rd Cpl.): (23).

Bailes, John T.: (31).

Bailes, Merritt G.: (22).

Ball, Charles H.: Enl. 12 March 1862 at Charlottesville; wife was Mrs. Harriett Ball; died of disease in Albemarle County 16 August 1863.

Black, Nicholas M.: (21).

Burton, Benjamin L.: Enl. 12 March 1862 at Charlottesville.

Cranwell, Henry: Enl. 25 May 1861 at Charlottesville in Compnay "F"; (40); carpenter.

Davis, George D.: (32).

Fisher, William J.: (19).

Foster, George A.: Enl. 12 March 1862 at Charlottesville; *captured*; exchanged 20 or 21 February 1865.

Gillum, Thomas Mann: Enl. 17 February 1863 at Charlottesville.

Hawkins, R.A., Sr.: (29).

Hawkins, Samuel A.: Enl. 12 March 1862 at Charlottesville; *captured*; exchanged 30 September 1864.

Hays, Thomas J.: Enl. 12 March 1862 at Charlottesville; *shot* in the foot and *captured*; died of tetanus 17 July 1863.

Johnson, James F.: Enl. 12 March 1862 at Charlottesville; the company reports him as missing in action but there are no Federal records concerning him; *killed*.

Lane, James B.: Enl. 12 March 1862 at Charlottesville.

Leathers, James A.: Enl. 19 January 1863 in the regiment; (24); *shot* in the left ankle (secondary amputation of the leg) and *captured*; exchanged from West's Buildings Hospital 17 November 1863.

Martin, Henry: Enl. 12 March 1862 at Charlottesville; *wounded*.

Martin, John A.: (22).

Martin, Samuel H.:

McCauley, Riland: Enl. 12 March 1862 at Charlottesville.

McMullen, William H.: Enl. 12 March 1862 at Charlottesville.

Moyer, Jacob: Enl. 12 March 1862 at Charlottesville.

Powell, Thomas A.: (28).

Reynolds, James R.: Enl. 12 March 1862 at Charlottesville.

Wood, John M.: (28).

Woods, Robert H.: (23).

Woolfert, Henry: Enl. 25 May 1861 at Charlottesville in Company "F."

Wyant, James D.: Enl. 1 September 1862 at Charlottesville.

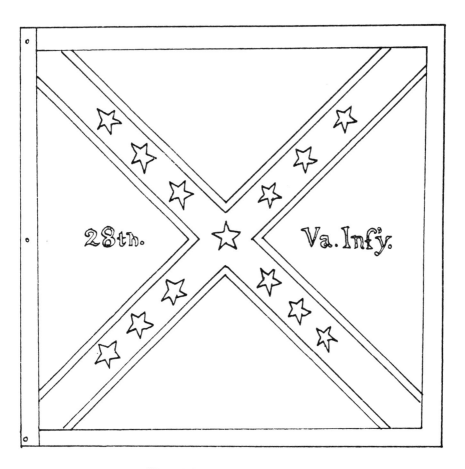

Flag of the 28th Virginia Infantry
captured by the 1st Minnesota Infantry
at Cushing's guns

28th Virginia Volunteer Infantry Regiment

This regiment was accpted in to Confederate service 1 July 1861 with ten companies designated "A" through "K." 1st Company "E" had been transferred from the regiment in June 1861 and subsequently became Company "C," 11th Virginia Infantry. 1st Company "C" was transferred to the artillery service about 20 August 1861 and finally became Captain John R. Johnston's Company Virginia Light Artillery. Company "H" was reorganized as an artillery organization 24 December 1861 and finally became Captain Douthat's Company Virginia Light Artillery. The regiment was reorganized with nine companies about 1 May 1862.

Field and Staff

The following listing was obtained from the unit's April/June 1863 muster roll dated 12 August 1863; no station was provided on the roll.

Allen, Robert Clotworthy (Colonel): Born in Shenandoah County, Va. 22 June 1834; graduated from VMI in 1855; lawyer at Salem, Va.; commissioned Colonel 20 April 1862; *killed* close to the stone wall during the attack.

Wilson, Nathaniel Claiborne (Major): Attended VMI; graduated from the University of Va.; enl. 15 May 1861 at Craig Court House as Captain of Company "B"; born at Fincastle, Virginia 12 September 1839; lawyer; had no wife or children at the time of his death; commissioned Major 1 May 1862; *wounded* by a grapeshot during the advance; died at Pickett's Division Hospital 3 July 1863 and buried in "Curn's" meadow under a walnut tree; his body was recovered prior to the general disinterrment of Confederates to the South in 1872 and 1873.

Allen, Henry C. (Adjutant): (27 in 1865); resided at Fincastle; appointed Adjutant 1 May 1862.

Holt, Joseph H. (Capt., AQM): Enl. 15 May 1861 at Liberty in 1st Company "C"; (30); planter; appointed Capt. and AQM 4 October 1861.

Wills, John R. (ACS): Enl. 15 May 1861 at Buchanan as a Private in Company "H"; appointed ACS 1 December 1862; on duty with the regiment 1 May 1863.

Rives, Edward (Surgeon): Appointed Surgeon 13 January 1863; assigned to the regiment 1 May 1863; captured 5 July 1863 while caring for the wounded at Gettysburg; exchanged 21 November 1863.

Tinsley, Peter (Chaplain): Enl. 13 May 1861 at Salem as a Private in Company "I"; captured 5 July while attending the wounded at Gettysburg; exchanged 5 October 1863.

Phelps, James H. (Sgt. Major): Enl. 20 May 1861 at Botetourt Springs in Company "E"; (36); *killed.*

Terry, Peyton L. (Ordnance Sgt.): Enl. 13 May 1861 at Salem as 3rd Cpl. in Company "I."

Smith, William F. (Hospital Steward): Enl. 23 April 1861 at Richmond in the 18th Virginia Infantry Regiment; transferred to the 28th Virginia 31 December 1862; captured 14 July 1863 while caring for the wounded at Williamsport, Maryland; exchanged 24 November 1863.

Belew, Edward A. (Colonel's Orderly): Detailed from Company "K"; enl. 15 May 1861 at Amsterdam.

Color Guard

Eakin, John J. (5th Sgt., Color Sgt.): Detailed from Company "B"; enl. 15 May 1861 at Craig Court House; farmer; *shot* in the upper third of the arm during the attack.

Britts, Dexter S. (5th Cpl., Color Cpl.): Detailed from Company "B"; enl. 12 March 1862 at Craig Court House.

Creasey, Lindsey S. (Color Cpl.): Detailed from Company "G"; enl. 27 April 1861 at Chestnut Fork; *shot* during the attack.

Hamilton, James H. (5th Cpl., Color Cpl.): Detailed from Company "K"; enl. 20 May 1861 at Amsterdam.

Company "A" ("Blue Ridge Rifles")

Organized in February 1860, this company enlisted 15 May 1861 at Blue Ridge, Botetourt County, Virginia; was mustered into service 16 May 1861 for one year; and was reorganized 21 April 1862.

The following listing was obtained from the company's April/June 1863 muster roll captioned "near Somerville Ford, Virginia" 12 August 1863.

Allen, Robert E. (Captain): (25); farmer.

Spangler, Clifton H. (1st Lt.): (24); boatman; *captured*; exchanged 8 May 1864.

Merritt, Charles D. (Bvt. 2nd Lt.): (20); miller.

Richardson, Edward G. (2nd Sgt.): (25); shoemaker.

Obenshain, James P. (4th Sgt.): (19); student; *captured*; exchanged 18 March 1865.

Richardson, Richard B. (2nd Cpl.): Enl. at Buchanan; (21).

Peters, John W. (3rd Cpl.): (20); farmer.

Thomas, James S. (4th Cpl.): (18); carpenter; the company initially reports him as captured and subsequently as missing in action but there are no Federal records concerning him; *killed*.

Burger, Philip T.: Enl. 8 March 1862 at Buchanan; (18).

Camper, William H.: Enl. 20 August 1861 at Centreville.

Coffman, Lewis: (25); laborer.

Coffman, Samuel A.: (23); laborer; wounded.

Creasy, James B.: Enl. 20 March 1863 at Bedford.

Fink, Elijah C.: (26); carpenter; *shot* in the right foot and *captured*; treated at U.S. 1st Division, II Corps Hospital; exchanged from DeCamp Hospital 28 August 1863; deserted Farmville, Virginia Hospital 14 September 1863.

Fout, Robert D.: (19); laborer.

Gordon, John R.: (18); laborer.

Heck, Martin Van: (20); farmer.

Honts, George D.: (21); farmer; the company initially reports him as captured and subsequently as missing in action but there are no Federal records concerning him; *killed*.

Hughes, Joseph H.: (21); laborer; received a gunshot *wound* which fractured his left leg (amputated) and *captured*; died at Camp Letterman Hospital 28 July 1863 and buried in Section 1, Grave #6 of that hospital's cemetery; disinterred to Richmond 13 June 1872 in box #89.

Kelley, George J.: (20); farmer.

Kern, Henry L.: (19); farmer; *captured*; joined U.S. service 24 January 1864.

McClure, Andrew J.: Enl. 5 August 1861 at the regimental camp on Cub Run; *wounded*; captured at Mercersburg (probably Greencastle) 5 July 1863; paroled from West's Buildings Hospital 22 August 1863.

Obenshain, Joel B.: (19); farmer; *captured*; exchanged 20 or 21 February 1865.

Obenshain, Samuel S.: (18); farmer.

Obenshain, William R.: Enl. 11 March 1862 at Fincastle; (18).

Ore, James P.: Enl. 20 March 1863 at Bedford; *wounded*.

Robinson, John E.W.: (19); farmer.

Swain, Rowlan B.: Enl. 20 March 1863 in Bedford County.

Trevey, William B.: (21); farmer.

Watson, Benjamin P.: Enl. 21 July 1861 on the Manassas Battlefield in Company "H."

Williamson, Slaughter D.: Enl. 20 March 1863 at Bedford.

<u>Company "B" ("Craig Rifles")</u>

This company enlisted 15 April 1861 at Craig Court House, Craig County, Virginia; was mustered into service 18 May 1861 for one year; and was reorganized 24 March 1862.

The following listing was obtained from the company's April/June 1863 muster roll captioned "near Culpeper, Virginia" 12 August 1863.

McCartney, Thomas Benton (Captain): (18); farmer; *captured*; exchanged 22 March 1865.

Goode, William M. (1st Lt.): Farmer; *wounded*.

Tucker, Owen H. (2nd Lt.): (34); farmer; *captured*; released from Fort Delaware 12 June 1865.

Snodgrass, Tilghman E. (3rd Lt.): (25); mechanic.

Walker, Thomas G. (1st Sgt.): Enl. 12 March 1862; slightly *wounded* in the face and *captured*; died of erysipelas of the face and diarrhea at Point Lookout 6 January 1864.

Caldwell, John B. (2nd Sgt.): Farmer; *wounded*.

Reynolds, Ralph C. (3rd Sgt.): Farmer.

Givens, John A. (1st Cpl.): *Wounded*.

Huston, John H. (2nd Cpl.): (23); farmer; *wounded*.

Lipes, John W. (3rd Cpl.): (18); farmer.

Carper, William L. (4th Cpl.): Enl. 16 August 1861 at Centreville; *wounded*.

Abbott, John: Enl. 12 March 1862.

Armstrong, Thomas: Enl. 12 March 1862.

Book, Henry L.: Mechanic; wife was Mrs. Mary Book; the company initially reports him as captured and subsequently as *killed*; there are no Federal records concerning him.

Brisentine, James R.: Laborer; *captured*; exchanged 20 or 21 February 1865.

Brisentine, John M.: Laborer; wife was Mrs. Sarah Jane Brisentine; the company initially reports him as wounded and captured and subsequently as *killed*; there are no Federal records concerning him.

Brisentine, William B.: Mechanic; *wounded.*

Caldwell, Alexander G.: Enl. 12 March 1862.

Craft, Samuel D.: Enl. 12 March 1862.

Crawford, John W.: Enl. 12 March 1862; *captured*; exchanged 15 November 1864.

Dooley, Marshal: Enl. 12 March 1862.

Elmore, James: Enl. 12 March 1862.

Fisher, Philip: Enl. 12 March 1862; wife was Mrs. Harriet A. Fisher; the company initially reports him as captured and subsequently as supposed *killed*; there are no Federal records concerning him.

Givens, Charles H.:

Givens, James M.: *Wounded.*

Givens, Texas P.: Enl. 12 March 1862; *captured*; died at Point Lookout 23 December 1863.

Huffman, Anderson: Enl. 12 March 1862.

Huffman, Thomas: Enl. 12 March 1862.

Kinzie, William C.: Enl. 22 February 1862 at Centreville; *captured*; exchanged sick with pneumonia 6 March 1864.

Miller, Erastus T.: Enl. 12 March 1862.

Myers, Alfred: Enl. 12 March 1862; *captured*; died of intermittent fever at Fort Delaware 12 September 1863; buried at Finns Point, N.J.

Myers, Charlton E.: (18); blacksmith.

Myers, Jacob W.: (17); blacksmith; *shot* in the lung and *captured*; treated at U.S. 1st Division, II Corps Hospital; died at II Corps Hospital, date not specified, and buried in Yard B, Row 2 of that hospital's cemetery on the hill between Schwartz's and Bushman's under a walnut tree; disinterred to Richmond 13 June 1872 with 110 others in ten large boxes marked "S."

Paitsel, Daniel E.: Enl. 12 March 1862.

Paxton, Samuel B.: (21); laborer; *wounded.*

Reynolds, John L.: Enl. 12 March 1862; *wounded.*

Slusser, Henry M.: Enl. 25 March 1863 at Greenville, North Carolina.

Steele, Charles T.: Distiller; *wounded* in the right thigh.

Surber, Levi: Enl. 12 March 1862; wife was Mrs. Amanda Surber; the company initially reports him as captured and subsequently as supposed *killed*; there are no Federal records concerning him.

Trenor, George W.: Enl. 29 August 1861 at Fairfax Court House; *wounded.*

Tucker, Andrew: Enl. 12 March 1862; *wounded* in the hip and thigh and *captured*; exchanged from DeCamp Hospital 28 August 1863; deserted from Farmville, Virginia Hospital 4 September 1863.

Vickars, James: Enl. 29 August 1861 at Fairfax Court House.

Second Company "C" ("Craig Mountain Boys")

Formerly called Company "D" until after the transfer of 1st Company "C" after 31 August 1861, this company enlisted 10 May 1861 at Newcastle, Craig County, Virginia, and was mustered into service 28 May 1861 for one year. The unit was reorganized 28 April 1862.

The following listing was obtained from the company's April/June 1863 muster roll captioned "near Orange Court House, Virginia" 12 August 1863.

Spessard, Michael Peters (Captain): (39); farmer.

Lee, John A.J. (Bvt. 2nd Lt.): (23); farmer; *captured*; released from Fort Delaware 12 June 1865; first man of Pickett's Division to cross the stone wall.

Leffel, John M. (2nd Sgt.): (24); farmer; *captured*; died at Point Lookout 25 August 1864.

Williams, Henry B. (3rd Sgt.): (24); farmer; *wounded*.

Webb, George W. (4th Sgt.): Farmer; *captured*; released from Fort Delaware 21 June 1865.

Hubbard, Alexander (1st Cpl.): (31); farmer; *wounded* and *captured*; treated at U.S. 1st Division, II Corps Hospital; died 9 or 19 July 1863.

McPherson, Thomas B. (2nd Cpl.): (20); farmer; *captured*; exchanged 8 May 1864.

Hendrickson, Elisha D. (3rd Cpl.): (18); farmer; *shot* in the right knee, the ball not entering the joint, and *captured*; exchanged from DeCamp Hospital 28 August 1863.

Miller, John J. (4th Cpl.): (23); farmer.

Camper, Peter A.: Mason; received flesh *wounds* in the leg and back and *captured*; paroled for exchange from West's Buildings Hospital 23 August 1863.

Carper, Oscar W.: *Captured*; exchanged 20 or 21 February 1865.

Drummond, George R.: (19); farmer; deserted about 15 July 1863 through 11 October 1864.

Dudding, James O.: (24); farmer; married; received a *gunshot* fracture of the middle third of his right humerus (resection required) and *captured*; died of tetanus at Letterman Hospital 13 September 1863 and buried in Section 7, Grave #30 of that hospital's cemetery; disinterred to Richmond 13 June 1872 in Box #115.

Eakin, Robert A.: (19); farmer; *wounded* and *captured*; exchanged 1 August 1863.

Elmore, James: (32); farmer; the company initially reports him as missing in action and subsequently as captured and then *killed*; there are no Federal records concerning him.

Givens, Jehu: (25); farmer; *captured*; exchanged 20 or 21 February 1865.

Huffman, Andrew, Jr.: (19); farmer.

Huffman, Andrew J.: (29); farmer; the company initially reports him as missing in action and subsequently as captured and then *killed*; there are no Federal records concerning him.

Huffman, Joseph: (34); farmer; captured while serving as a nurse at Gettysburg; exchanged 20 March 1864.

Huffman, Ransom P.: (22); farmer.

Looney, James M.: (24); farmer; the company initially reports him as missing in action and subsequently as captured and then "supposed to have died in hospital Maryland"; there are no Federal records concerning him; *killed*.

Lugar, James H.: (21); farmer; *wounded*.

Martin, James P.: Enl. 30 August 1861 at Fairfax Court House.

Matthews, Andrew J.: (19); blacksmith; had no wife or children at the time of his death; *shot* in the leg and *captured*; treated at U.S. 1st Division, II Corps Hospital; died at U.S. II Corps Hospital 23 July 1863 and buried in Yard B, Row 2 of that hospital's cemetery on the hill between Schwartz's and Bushman's under a walnut tree; disinterred to Richmond 13 June 1872 in Box #15.

McPherson, James R.: Enl. 30 August 1861 at Fairfax Court House; resided in Craig County, Virginia; *wounded* 100 yards from the stone wall.

Niday, David P.: (19); farmer.

Sarver, Adam A.: *Captured*; released from Fort Delaware 21 June 1865.

Sarver, Michael A.: (19); farmer.

Spessard, Hezekiah C.: Enl. 16 January 1863 at Guinea Station; father was Captain Michael P. Spessard; *wounded* during the advance; died 19 July 1863; father received $88.41 due his son for back pay, clothing allowances, etc.

Starks, William E.: (19); farmer; received a flesh *wound* in the thigh and *captured*; exchanged from West's Buildings Hospital 24 August 1863.

Steber, John: Enl. 3 May 1862 at Yorktown.

Taylor, Jacob S.: (33); carpenter; the company initially reports him as missing in action and subsequently as "supposed *killed*"; there are no Federal records concerning him.

Company "D" ("Piedmont Rifles")

Formerly Company "E" until after 31 August 1861, this company enlisted 20 May 1861 at Stewartsville, Bedford County, Virginia; was mustered into service 22 May 1861 for one year; and was reorganized 31 March 1862.

The following listing was obtained from the company's April/June 1863 muster roll uncaptioned as to date or station.

Wingfield, William Lewis (Captain): (24); VMI class of 1859.

Stewart, John S. (1st Lt.): (23).

Gooldy, William J. (2nd Lt.): (23); *wounded*.

Walrond, John P. (Jr. 2nd Lt.): (22); received a *gunshot* fracture of the lower third of his right thigh (leg amputated at middle third) and *captured*; died at Letterman Hospital 31 July 1863 and buried in Section 2, Grave #22 of that hospital's cemetery; disinterred to Richmond 13 June 1872 in Box #28.

Douglas, Abijah (1st Sgt.): (23).

Cooper, George W. (4th Sgt.): (20); the company initially reports him as wounded and captured and subsequently as missing in action, supposed *killed*; there are no Federal records concerning him.

Hale, John L. (5th Sgt.): (26).

Payne, Joseph H. (1st Cpl.): (21); *shot* in the leg and *captured*; exchanged from DeCamp Hospital 16 September 1863.

Draper, John L. (2nd Cpl.): (19); born in Botetourt County; father was Mr. Jackson Draper; *wounded.*

Camper, Henry L. (3rd Cpl.): (22); *wounded*; (admitted to Charlottesville, Virginia hospital 12 July 1863).

Feather, Marquis D. (4th Cpl.): (23).

Adams, James P.: (23).

Agnew, Thomas J.: Enl. 15 March 1862 at Bedford; (18).

Arnold, George: Enl. 1 May 1861; (22).

Barton, David, Sr.: Enl. 15 March 1862 at Bedford; (32).

Barton, John O.:

Bilbro, John W.: Enl. 27 April 1861 at Chestnut Fork in Company "G"; farmer.

Bryant, Reuben W.: Enl. 17 August 1861 at Centreville.

Bryant, William R.: Enl. 13 May 1861 at Salem in Company "I."

Burnett, John J.: (17); *wounded.*

Carroll, Joseph W.: (23).

Carroll, Nash J.: (25).

Chittum, Nathaniel A.: Enl. 15 March 1862 at Bedford; (22).

Corley, William L.: (24); the company reports him initially as captured and subsequently as missing in action supposed *killed*; there are no Federal records concerning him.

Debo, Lodevick C.: Enl. 27 July 1861 at Cub Run.

Dunithan, Andrew R.: (41).

Franklin, Joel M.: (25).

Franklin, Joseph D.: Enl. 27 April 1861 at Chestnut Fork in Company "G"; (22); shoemaker.

Gilwater, Preston H.: Enl. 13 March 1862 at Bedford; (44).

Hancock, Simon: Enl. 10 March 1862 at Bedford in Company "G"; (33); farmer.

Holdron, Henry H.: (28); *wounded.*

Maitlin, John: (32).

McDaniel, Charles T.: (20); the company intitally reports him as captured and subsequently as missing in action supposed *killed*; there are no Federal records concerning him.

Minter, Jesse L.: Enl. 10 March 1862 at Bedford in Company "G"; farmer; *captured*; died of acute diarrhea at Fort Delaware 26 October 1863; buried at Finns Point, N.J.

Neighbours, Green L.: Enl. 13 March 1862 at Bedford; (23).

Neighbours, Jonathan T.: Enl. 13 March 1862 at Bedford; (29).

Payne, John T.: (23).

Pearcy, William: Enl. 13 March 1862 at Bedford; (37).

Richardson, Peter: Enl. 31 March 1862 at Bedford; (17).

Rucker, Andrew J.: (24); deserted 3 July 1863 probably while on the march to the field; captured 4 July; died of pneumonia at Fort Delaware 14 February 1865.

Ryan, Obediah: (21); deserted 3 July 1863 probably while on the march to the field; captured 4, 5, or 6 July; joined U.S. 1st Connecticut Cavalry subsequent to 30 August 1863.

Settle, Fielding: (35); *wounded.*

Stewart, James R.F.: Enl. 12 August 1861 at Centreville; born in Botetourt County; clerk; discharged for disability 28 May 1862; re-enlisted in Company "G," 1st Virginia Infantry 9 February 1863; transferred to Company "D," 28th Virginia Infantry 23 May 1863; discharged for disability 9 August 1863.

Stone, Thomas A.: (34).

Thomas, William D.: Enl. 15 March 1862 at Bedford; (24).

Wade, Thaddeus M.: (26); *shot* in the hip (illum) and *captured*; died of exhaustion at Chester Hospital 16 September 1863 and buried in Grave #199 of that hospital's cemetery.

Walrond, Moses A.: (20).

Webb, Ferdinand H.: Enl. 13 March 1862 at Bedford; (18); received a *gunshot* compound fracture of the left thigh and *captured*; died of exhaustion at Chester Hospital 25 July 1863 and buried in Grave #77 of that hospital's cemetery.

Wheeler, Solomon: Enl. 13 March 1862 at Bedford; (40).

Wheeler, Thomas: Enl. 15 March 1862 at Bedford; (32).

Williamson, Robert W.: Enl. 14 March 1862 at Bedford; (18).

Third Company "E" ("Botetourt Springs Rifles")

Formerly Company "F" until after 31 August 1861, this company enlisted 20 May 1861 at Botetourt Springs, Botetourt County, Virginia. The unit was mustered 30 May 1861 and was reorganized 28 April 1862.

The following listing was obtained from the company's April/June 1863 muster roll uncaptioned as to date and station.

Whitten, Thomas L. (1st Sgt.): Enl. 13 May 1861 at Salem in Company "I"; *killed.*

Black, William T. (3rd Sgt.): (26); farmer; *wounded* and *captured*; exchanged 1 August 1863.

Lollis, Richard P. (1st Cpl.): (23); carpenter; resided in Roanoke County; *wounded.*

Simpson, William J. (2nd Cpl.): Enl. 13 May 1861 at Salem in Compnay "I"; *killed.*

Brown, Daniel M.: (29); carpenter; *wounded* in the left lung and forefinger of left hand (amputated) and *captured*; exchanged from West's Buildings Hospital 24 August 1863.

Bush, Gilla: Enl. 3 April 1863 at Washington, North Carolina; *captured*; exchanged 8 May 1864.

Collins, Michael: Enl. 20 March 1863 at Washington, North Carolina; *captured*; released on oath from Fort Delaware 10 July 1863.

Dooley, John: (28); farmer; *captured*; joined U.S. service at Point Lookout 24 January 1864.

316

Etter, Andrew James: (20); farmer; *killed.*

Fariss, George W.: (20); farmer.

Farriss, Charles H.: (22); farmer.

Fuqua, Charles D.: (24); farmer.

Kerns, John N.: Enl. 13 May 1861 at Salem in Company "I."

Lollis, George A.: (18); farmer; deserted 4 July 1863 and captured the next day; died of disease at Marine U.S.A. General Hospital, Baltimore, Maryland (smallpox hospital), 1 January 1864.

Michael, Daniel: (22); farmer.

Parish, Samuel: Enl. 8 August 1862 near Richmond; shot through the lungs; died at the U.S. II Corps Hospital, date unknown; (19); had a young sister; his mother died in 1862 or 1863.

Patterson, John T.: (21); farmer; *captured*; exchanged 20 or 21 February 1865.

Patterson, Thomas W.: Enl. 20 April 1863 at Washington, North Carolina; *captured*; exchanged 20 or 21 February 1865.

Perry, Addison: (19); farmer; *captured*; exchanged 20 or 21 February 1865.

Pollard, Sheppard: (36); farmer.

Roberts, John Lynch: (18); farmer; *captured*; exchanged 20 or 21 February 1865.

Ronk, Samuel: (31); wagon maker.

Webster, Henry L.: Enl. 7 September 1861 at regimental camp at Fairfax Court House.

Company "F" ("Bedford Greys")

Formerly Company "G" until after 31 August 1861, this company enlisted 26 April 1861 at Good's Crossing, Bedford County, Virginia; was mustered into service 22 May 1861 for one year; and was reorganized 27 April 1862.

The following listing was obtained from the company's April/June 1863 muster roll uncaptioned as to date or station.

Nelson, Hugh (Captain): Enl. 23 April 1861 at Lynchburg.

Leftwich, James B. (3rd Lt.): (26); farmer; *wounded.*

Lowry, Marshall M. (1st Sgt.): (20); farmer.

Ellis, James H. (2nd Sgt.): (32); farmer; the company initially reports him as captured and subsequently as missing in action "supposed *killed*"; there are no Federal records concerning him.

Bell, Leslie C. (3rd Sgt.): (20); farmer; *wounded.*

Schenks, Richard F. (4th Sgt.): (21); farmer.

Crank, James L. (2nd Cpl.): (19); farmer.

Rucker, John C. (3rd Cpl.): Enl. 11 March 1862 at Forest Depot; *wounded* in the left leg and wrist.

Mitchell, William H. (4th Cpl.): (21); farmer.

Anderson, James E.: (18); farmer.

Ballard, Robert: (20); farmer; deserted and captured 5 July 1863; joined U.S. 3rd Maryland Cavalry 5 September 1863.

Biby, E.P.: Enl. 1 March 1862 at Forest Depot.

Brooks, John: Enl. 11 March 1862 at Forest Depot.

Brown, James H.: (20); farmer.

Brown, R.R.: Enl. 1 March 1863 in Bedford County.

Campbell, D.P.: Enl. 11 March 1862 at Forest Depot; the last time this man's name appears on company muster rolls is 30 June 1863; there are no further records concerning him; probably *killed*.

Claytor, Moses B.: (22); farmer.

Coleman, Robert A.:

Dawson, Pleasant: (18); farmer.

Ellis, John R.: Enl. 1 March 1862 at Forest Depot.

Foster, Farris: Enl. 1 March 1862 at Forest Depot; the company initially reports him as wounded and left on the field and subsequently as "supposed *killed*"; there are no Federal records concerning him.

Gilbert, John C.: Enl. 1 March 1862 at Forest Depot.

Goodman, Alfred: Enl. 1 March 1862 at Forest Depot; the company initially reports him as missing in action and subsequently as "supposed *killed*"; there are no Federal records concerning him.

Goodman, John: Enl. 1 March 1862 at Forest Depot.

Howard, John A.: Enl. 1 March 1862 at Forest Depot.

Howard, Samuel J.: Enl. 1 March 1862 at Forest Depot; captured while serving as a nurse at Gettysburg 4 July 1863; exchanged from West's Buildings Hospital 17 November 1863.

Hunter, Joseph A.: Enl. 1 March 1862 at Forest Depot.

Jesse, William P.: Enl. 1 March 1862 at Forest Depot; *wounded* in the thigh.

Knight, Osson P.: Enl. 1 March 1862 at Forest Depot; *shot* in the forearm (radius) and *captured*; exchanged from Chester Hospital 17 August 1863.

Martin, A.J.: Enl. 1 March 1862 at Forest Depot.

Mason, John J.: Enl. 1 March 1862 at Forest Depot.

Mitchell, Albert T.: Enl. 1 March 1862 at Forest Depot.

Mitchell, Charles L.: Enl. 1 March 1862 at Forest Depot.

Mitchell, John W.: (18); farmer.

Moorman, William H.: Enl. 1 March 1862 at Forest Depot; (38 in 1864); farmer; *shot* in the upper third of the left thigh (flesh wound) and *captured*; exchanged from DeCamp Hospital 28 October 1863.

Padgett, Charles: (18); farmer; *wounded*.

Padgett, Joseph:

Powell, L.E.: Enl. 1 March 1862 at Forest Depot.

Robinson, E.H.: Enl. 1 March 1862 at Forest Depot; *wounded*.

Rucker, A. McD.: Enl. 1 March 1862 at Forest Depot; *shot* in the left wrist; captured at Greencastle, Pennsylvania 5 July 1863; exchanged from West's Buildings Hospital 24 August 1863.

Skinner, James H.: (25); farmer; *shot* in the upper anterior portion of the ileum (small intestine) and *captured*; exchanged form DeCamp Hospital 8 September 1863.

Tanner, Willis R.: (26); farmer.

Tinsley, H.B.: Enl. 1 March 1862 at Forest Depot; *wounded*; the company also reports him as captured but Federal records do not confirm this.

Turpin, Peter: Enl. 1 March 1862 at Good's Crossing.

Wade, James N.: Enl. 1 March 1862 at Forest Depot.

Whitten, James C.: Enl. 1 March 1862 at Forest Depot.

Whorley, William: Enl. 1 March 1862 at Forest Depot; the company initially reports him as captured and subsequently as missing in action "supposed *killed*"; there are no Federal records concerning him.

Wilson, Edward G.: Enl. 1 March 1862 at Forest Depot.

Wilson, George W.E.: Enl. 27 April 1861 at Chestnut Fork in Company "G"; (22); farmer; received a flesh *wound* in the thigh and *captured*; exchanged from DeCamp Hospital 8 September 1863.

Wilson, James E.: Enl. 1 March 1862 at Forest Depot.

Wilson, John R.: (19); farmer; received a flesh *wound* in the leg and *captured*; exchanged from DeCamp Hospital 28 August 1863.

Wilson, R.H.: Enl. 1 March 1862 at Forest Depot.

Wilson, Thomas J.: (33); farmer.

Wingfield, William: (23); farmer.

Wright, Archibald R.: (27); farmer.

Company "G" ("Patty Layne Rifles")

Formerly Company "H" until after 31 August 1861, this company enlisted 27 April 1861 at Chestnut Fork, Bedford County, Virginia; was mustered into service 1 June 1861 for one year; and was reorganized 28 April or 1 May 1862.

The following listing was obtained from the company's April/June 1863 muster roll captioned 12 August 1863. The company's station at the time of the muster was not provided.

Holland, Thomas C. (1st Lt.): (21); farmer; *shot* in the cheek and neck in the Angle and *captured*; exchanged 22 March 1865.

Wildman, Elisha S. (2nd Lt.): Enl. 10 March 1862 in Bedford County; (32); farmer; recieved a *gunshot* fracture of the right leg (amputated at the upper third) and *captured*; exchanged 30 April 1864.

Leftwich, James P. (2nd Sgt.): Enl. 1 August 1861 at regimental camp near the suspension bridge at Centreville; received a shell *wound* to the neck and *captured*; exchanged from Chester Hospital 17 August 1863.

Dowdy, Aldrige G. (3rd Sgt.): (35); farmer.

Gaines, Richard T. (4th Sgt.): (21); farmer; received a flesh *wound* in the right ankle and *captured*; exchanged 15 November 1864.

Debo, Reed P. (5th Sgt.): Enl. 10 March 1862 in Bedford County; (30); clerk; received a flesh *wound* in the right thigh and *captured*; exchanged from DeCamp Hospital 28 August 1863.

Mitchell, Robert D. (1st Cpl.): Enl. 1 March 1862 in Bedford County; (28); farmer.

Debo, Dabney C. (2nd Cpl.): (22); farmer; the company initially reports him as captured and subsequently as "supposed dead"; there are no Federal records concerning him; *killed*.

Dearing, Oliver V.B. (3rd Cpl.): (21); received a *gunshot* fracture of the lower jaw and *captured*; exchanged from West's Buildings Hospital 27 September 1863.

Creasey, Benjamin M. (4th Cpl.): Farmer; *captured*; died of rheumatism at Fort Delaware 27 October 1863; buried at Finns Point, N.J.

Ailiff, A.B. Tompkins: Enl. 8 March 1862 in Bedford County; (33); farmer.

Ailiff, George H.: Enl. 28 February 1862 in Bedford County; (22); farmer; received a compound *fracture* of the lower jaw and *captured*; exchanged 1 August 1863.

Ailiff, Philip C.: Enl. 10 March 1862 in Bedford County; (17); farmer; *wounded* in the humerus (arm amputated) and *captured*; exchanged from West's Buildings Hospital 24 August 1863.

Angel, Isaac N.: (25); farmer.

Ashwell, Pleasant T.: Enl. 8 March 1862 in Bedford County; (28); farmer.

Ayres, Uriah H.: Enl. 28 February 1862 in Bedford County; (26); farmer; the company reported him as captured but there are no Federal records concerning him; *killed*.

Barker, William H.: Enl. 1 March 1862; (31); farmer; *shot* in the leg and *captured*; exchanged from DeCamp Hospital 8 September 1863.

Burnett, David: Enl. 10 March 1862 in Bedford County; (33); farmer.

Cadwallader, Presley:

Creasey, David A.: (24); farmer; *shot* in the knee and *captured*; exchanged from DeCamp Hospital 8 September 1863.

Creasey, John H.: (23); farmer; *wounded* in the left foot and *captured*; exchanged from DeCamp Hospital 28 August 1863.

Creasey, Lewis G.: Enl. 10 February 1862 at Centreville.

Creasey, Robert H.: Farmer.

Creasey, Thomas G.: (25); farmer; *wounded* in the right foot (fractured metatarsal) and *captured*; exchanged 6 March 1864.

Creasey, William C.: Farmer.

Crouch, Joel: Enl. 10 March 1862 in Bedford County; (34); miller.

Cundiff, Marion J.: Enl. 28 February 1862 in Bedford County; (20); farmer; *captured*; exchanged 8 May 1864.

Dearing, Calvin P.: (19); farmer; *captured*; released from Fort Delaware 18 May 1865.

Dowdy, James T.: (18); farmer; *shot* in the bowels (ensiform cartilage), and *captured*; the ball entered the abdominal cavity and was passed in defecation; Dowdy saved the bullet for a souvenir; paroled for exchange from West's Buildings Hospital 25 September 1863.

Dowdy, Richard T.: Enl. 10 March 1862 in Bedford County; (19); farmer.

Drewry, Carey B.: Enl. 10 March 1862 in Bedford County; father was Mr. Isaac Drewry; *wounded* in the lung and *captured*; died 6 September 1863.

Ferguson, William C.: Enl. 10 March 1862 in Bedford County; (25); farmer; the company initially reports him as captured and subsequently as "supposed dead"; there are no Federal records concerning him; *killed*.

Frailing, William J.: Enl. 10 March 1862 in Bedford County; (32); farmer.

Hogan, James A.: Enl. 10 March 1862 in Bedford County; (26); farmer.

Houpt, George A.: Enl. 10 March 1862 in Bedford County; (33); stone mason; *captured*; released on oath from Fort Delaware 4 April 1864.

Hubbard, M.R.: Enl. 10 February 1863 at Fredericksburg; resided in Bedford County; (20 in 1865); farmer; *shot* in the leg and buttock and *captured*; exchanged from West's Buildings Hospital 24 August 1863.

Hubbard, Talifero G.: (18); farmer; *captured*; joined U.S. service 25 February 1864; deserted and rejoined regiment prior to 27 August 1864.

Johnson, A.P.: Enl. 14 August 1862 at Gordonsville.

Johnson, James T.: (21); farmer.

Leftwich, Preston L.: Enl. 1 March 1862 in Bedford County; (18); farmer.

Lewis, John E.: Enl. 1 March 1862 in Bedford County; (18) farmer; *shot* in the left foot and left ankle; captured at Greencastle, Pennsylvania 5 July 1863; exchanged from West's Buildings Hospital 17 November 1863.

Mathews, Spencer G.: Enl. 1 March 1862 in Bedford County; the company reports him as captured but there are no Federal records concerning him; *killed.*

McClary, William: Enl. 1 March 1862 in Bedford County; (18); farmer.

Mitchell, Lindith R.: Enl. 1 March 1862 in Bedford County; (21); farmer.

Morgan, Thomas C.: (18); farmer.

Morgan, William H.: (22); farmer.

Morris, Silas M.: (24); farmer; *captured*; exchanged 1 August 1863 sick with acute diarrhea.

Nance, Paschal J.: (23); farmer.

Overstreet, Benjamin F.: Enl. 10 March 1862 in Bedford County; (19); farmer; *captured*; died at Point Lookout 13 January 1864.

Overstreet, James V.: Enl. 1 March 1862 in Bedford County; *captured*; exchanged 20 or 21 February 1865.

Overstreet, Jesse W.: Enl. 1 March 1863 in Bedford County; father was Mr. Granville Overstreet; *shot* in the abdomen and *captured*; died at Chester Hospital 23 July 1863 and buried in Grave #46 of that hospital's cemetery.

Patterson, George W.: (22); farmer.

Powell, Henry M.: Enl. 10 March 1862 in Bedford County; (34); farmer.

Roach, John A.: Enl. 1 March 1862 in Bedford County; (29); tanner.

Roberts, John: Enl. 1 March 1862 in Bedford County; (32); farmer.

Scott, Auville L.: Enl. 10 March 1862 in Bedford County; (30); farmer; the company reports him as captured "supposed dead" but there are no Federal records concerning him; *killed.*

Simms, Alexander: Farmer; *shot* in the thigh and *captured*; died of exhaustion at Chester Hospital 22 July 1863 and buried in Grave #42 of that hospital's cemetery.

Stephens, Jesse C.: Enl. 10 March 1862 in Bedford County; (20); farmer.

Turner, George K.: (23); farmer.

Turner, James G.: Enl. 1 March 1862 in Bedford County; (27); carpenter.

Turner, Robert G.: Enl. 1 August 1861 at the regimental camp near the suspension bridge at Centreville.

Whorley, James W.: Enl. 1 March 1862 in Bedford County; (20); farmer.

Whorley, L. Tazwell: (22); farmer; *wounded* and *captured*; exchanged from Chester Hospital 17 August 1863.

Williams, Archibald W.: (28); farmer.

Williams, John D.: Enl. 10 March 1862 in Bedford County; (27); farmer.

Williams, Thomas P.: Enl. 1 August 1861 at the regimental camp near the suspension bridge at Centreville; (20 in 1863); farmer; resided in Bedford County; *wounded* in the right arm.

Williamson, Tinsley R.: Enl. 1 August 1861 at the regimental camp near the suspension bridge at Centreville.

Witt, James A.: Enl. 10 March 1862 in Bedford County; (28); farmer; *captured*; exchanged sick with diarrhea 8 May 1864.

Company "I" ("Deyerle's Battery")

Formerly Company "K" until 31 August 1861, this company enlisted 13 May 1861 at Salem, Roanoke County, Virginia

The following listing was obtained from the company's April/June 1863 muster roll captioned 3 August 1863 near Culpeper, Virginia.

Repass, Stephen A. (2nd Lt.): *Captured*; exchanged 22 March 1865.

Trout, Henry S. (2nd 2nd Lt.):

Roller, Albert H. (1st Sgt.):

Holland, Robert C. (2nd Sgt.): *Shot* in the right elbow joint and *captured*; treated at U.S. 1st Division, II Corps Hospital; exchanged from DeCamp Hospital 28 October 1863.

Loyd, Pleasant W. (1st Cpl.): *Captured*; joined U.S. service 24 January 1864.

Thrasher, James McD. (2nd Cpl.): Enl. 1 August 1861 at the suspension bridge at Centreville; *wounded*.

Persinger, John A. (3rd Cpl.): *Wounded* in the abdomen and *captured*; treated at the U.S. 1st Division, I Corps Hospital; exchanged from Chester Hospital 20 August 1863.

Danner, Jacob H. (4th Cpl.): Enl. 1 August in Fairfax County.

Baldwin, William Joseph:

Barnes, Willian B: Enl. 11 March 1862 near Richmond; mother was Mrs. Sarah Ruddell.

Brown, Samuel M.: Enl. 20 May 1861 at Botetourt Springs in Company "E"; (23); saddler; captured while serving as a nurse at Gettysburg; exchanged 14 or 15 February 1865.

Bryan, John L.: *Captured*; joined U.S. service at Point Lookout 23 January 1864.

Collins, David W.: Enl. 20 May 1861 at Botetourt Springs in Company "E"; (22); farmer; *wounded*.

Dangerfield, Luther: Enl. 5 February 1862 at Centreville; the company initially reports him as captured and subsequently as having "died in the hands of the enemy" but there are no Federal records concerning him; *killed*.

Doherty, James F.:

Gish, Jonas T.: Enl. 20 May 1861 at Botetourt Springs in Company "E"; (23); farmer.

Hardy, John R.: The company initially reports him as wounded and captured and subsequently as captured and "died of wounds in enemy hands" but there are no Federal records concerning him; *killed.*

Harkrider, John W.: Enl. 11 May 1862 near Richmond.

Hawley, Newton A.E.: Enl. 20 May 1861 at Botetourt Springs in Company "E"; (21); farmer; *shot* in the neck and received a flesh wound in the right side and leg, and *captured*; treated at the U.S. 2nd Division, II Corps Hospital; exchanged 20 or 21 February 1865.

Hix, John W.: *Killed.*

Lemon, Joseph P.:

McFalls, John:

Nichols, John G.: *Wounded*; died 18 July 1863.

Owens, John B.: Received a *contusion* of the abdomen and *captured*; exchanged from DeCamp Hospital 8 September 1863.

Reynolds, Terrill: Enl. 11 May 1862 near Richmond.

Rhodes, Aaron E.: Enl. 11 September 1861 in Amherst County in Kirkpatrick's Battery.

Ruddell, George W.: Enl. 1 August 1861 at the suspension bridge at Centreville.

Ruddell, James H.: Enl. 7 November 1862 at Culpeper; *shot* in the right side and *captured*; exchanged from DeCamp Hospital 28 August 1863; deserted from Farmville, Virginia Hospital 3 September 1863.

Ruddell, Michael: Enl. 1 August 1861 at the suspension bridge at Centreville; *wounded*; died of tetanus at Ladies' Relief Hospital at Lynchburg 19 July 1863.

Settle, Charles H.: Enl. 20 May 1861 at Stewartsville in Company "D"; (23).

Settle, Joseph N.: *Captured*; exchanged sick with chronic diarrhea 15 October 1864.

Shaver, Jacob H.: Enl. 11 May 1862 near Richmond.

Shaver, Madison P.: Enl. 20 May 1861 at Botetourt Springs in Company "E"; (25); farmer.

Short, Andrew J.: Enl. 11 May 1862 near Richmond.

Stump, Green B.:

Thompson, James H.: Enl. 16 April 1861 at Christiansburg; transferred from Company "E," 4th Virginia Infantry 30 August 1861; deserted 14 July 1863.

Turner, John:

Underwood, William B.: *Captured*; exchanged 20 or 21 February 1865.

Vinyard, N.J.: Enl. 11 May 1862 near Richmond; *shot* in the right thigh and *captured*; exchanged from DeCamp Hospital 28 August 1863; deserted from Farmville, Virginia Hospital 3 September 1863 and returned to the company.

Womack, James H.: *Killed.*

Woodward, James H.:

Company "K" ("Breckenridge Infantry")

Formerly Capt. Gilmer Breckenridge's Company Virginia Volunteers, this company enlisted 15 May 1861 at Amsterdam, Botetourt County, Virginia for one year; was organized 25 May 1861; mustered into service 16 August 1861; assigned to this regiment in place of First Company "C" 20 August 1861; and was reorganized sometime after 30 April 1862.

The following listing was obtained from the company's April/June 1863 muster roll captioned 2 August 1863 near Culpeper, Virginia.

Kelley, William H. (Captain): Enl. 1 May 1861.

Graybill, James A. (1st Lt.): Father was Mr. Michael Graybill; *killed.*

Sperry, John T. (1st Sgt.): Enl. 1 May 1861.

Minnich, William E. (4th Sgt.):

Painter, James B. (1st Cpl.): Enl. 20 July 1861; the company initially reports him as missing in action and subsequently as *killed*; there are no Federal records concerning him.

Lemon, Barnett E. (2nd Cpl.): Enl. 1 June 1861 at Glade Creek.

Graybill, Madison B. (3rd Cpl.): Enl. 13 July 1861; *killed.*

Kelley, William J. (4th Cpl.): Enl. 20 July 1861 at Fincastle; *wounded.*

Bigler, Mark: Enl. 25 July 1861 at Amsterdam.

Brown, Lewis E.: *Wounded.*

Caldwell, Robert T.: Enl. at Dasher's.

Cale, Leander:

Crawford, Josiah: Enl. 13 July 1861.

Cundiff, Lewis P.: Enl. 28 June 1861 at Glade Creek.

Dooley, Edward:

Dupree, Edward: Enl. 20 July 1861.

Fridley, John H.: Enl. 10 May 1861; *shot* in the leg and head and *captured*; died of meningitis from head wound at Chester Hospital 3 August 1863 and buried in Grave #114 of that hospital's cemetery.

Henderson, John S.: Enl. 1 May 1861.

Isaacs, George W.: Enl. 20 July 1861.

Kelley, Edward: Enl. 15 March 1862; (18); *shot* in the left foot and *captured*; treated at U.S. 2nd Division, II Corps Hospital; exchanged from Chester Hospital 17 August 1863.

Kessler, James G.: Enl. 15 July 1861 at Fincastle; (released from arrest by order of General Pickett 29 June 1863).

Linkenhoger, Mathew: Enl. 13 July 1861.

Mangas, William J.: Enl. 11 July 1861.

Otey, William Thomas: Enl. 11 July 1861; *wounded.*

Thomas, William Henry: Enl. 20 March 1862; (17).

Tyler, William A.: Enl. 27 July 1861; *wounded.*

Vest, James H.: Enl. 20 July 1861; *captured*; exchanged 20 or 21 February 1865.

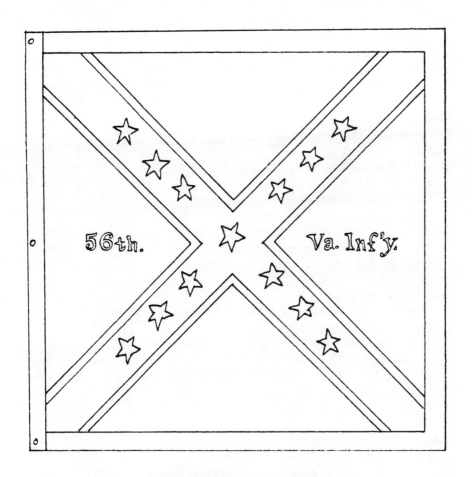

Flag of the 56th Virginia Infantry
captured inside the stone wall
by the 71st Pennsylvania Infantry

56th Virginia Volunteer Infantry Regiment

This regiment was organized 13 September 1861 with ten companies designated "A" through "K" and was reorganized 3 May 1862.

The following listing was obtained from a complete review of the service records of all 1,368 soldiers who served in the unit during the course of the war. Every effort was made to determine those men who definitely were not at Gettysburg. The residue are listed below. Some of these soldiers were probably not at the battle, but records do not definitively establish their absence from the 3 July assault.

Field and Staff

Stuart, William Dabney (Colonel): Born at Staunton, Va. 30 September 1830; graduated VMI in 1850; Richmond teacher and school official; Lt. Col. 15th Virginia July 1861; elected Colonel 56th Virginia 17 September 1861; *wounded* during the advance; died at Staunton 30 July 1863.

Wharton, Richard G. (1st Lt., Adjutant): VMI class of 1862; appointed Adjutant 26 November 1862; admitted to the hospital 24 July with scurvy and scabies.

Carter, Hilliard W. (AQM): Enl. 4 August 1861 as a 2nd Lt. in Company "A"; appointed AQM 25 March 1862; died 24 July 1863, cause unknown.

Davis, George W. (Capt., Quartermaster): Enl. 22 June 1861 at Tanner's Store as Captain of Company "B"; appointed QM 7 December 1862.

Nicholas, Robert C. (Capt., ACS): VMI class of 1861; enl. 8 July 1861 at Staunton Shop as 1st Lt. in Company "D"; appointed ACS 3 May 1862; admitted to the hospital with syphilis 26 July 1863; returned to duty 7 August 1863.

Baker, Philip P. (Surgeon): Appointed Surgeon 26 May 1863.

Harrison, B.C. (Asst. Surgeon): Appointed Asst. Surgeon 27 May 1863; captured 5 July 1863 while attending the wounded at Gettysburg; exchanged 21 November 1863.

Richards, John R. (2nd Lt., Asst. Surgeon): Enl. 29 July 1861 in Company "H"; appointed Asst. Surgeon 3 May 1862.

Waggoner, James R. (Chaplain): Appointed Chaplain 1 June 1862; resigned 10 July 1863.

Jones, Thomas T. (Sgt. Major): Enl. 10 July 1861 at Sturgeonville in Company "E"; admitted to a hospital at Petersburg; Virginia 13 July 1863, complaint not recorded; discharged from service 13 August 1863; probably *wounded.*

May, George W. (Ordnance Sgt.): Enl. 9 July 1861 at Louisa Court House in Company "C."

Overby, L.W. (Quartermaster Sgt.): Enl. 1 December 1861 at Clarksville, Virginia.

Trainham, Christopher C. (Hospital Steward): Enl. 26 July 1861 at Fork Church in Company "F."

Company "A" ("Mecklenburg Guards")

This company enlisted 8 July 1861 at Eph Church, Mecklenburg County, Virginia for one year and was reorganized 3 May 1862.

Nelson, Frank W. (1st Lt.): Born 25 December 1843; died 15 November 1936; last surviving officer of Pickett's Division who participated in the 3 July 1863 assault.

Garner, James A. (2nd Lt.):

Brooks, John R. (1st Sgt.):

Pattillo, John H. (2nd Sgt.):

Garner, Alfred H. (3rd Sgt.): Admitted to the hospital with chronic diarrhea 14 July 1863; reported as wounded as of 20 November 1863.

Nelson, William H. (4th Sgt.): Enl. in Mecklenburg County.

Calaham, James R. (1st Cpl.):

Apple, Flavius J. (2nd Cpl.): Enl. 25 August 1862 at Richmond; born at Clarksville, Virginia; (25 in 1865); farmer.

Maxey, Claiborne H. (3rd Cpl.): Enl. 18 July 1861.

Ellixson, James B. (4th Cpl.): The company reports him as "wounded and left at Gettysburg" and subsequently as "wounded, supposed mortally" but there are no Federal records concerning him; *killed.*

Dedman, William H. (5th Cpl.): Mother was Mrs. Amanda Dedman who filed a claim specifying that he died at Gettysburg; there are no Federal records concerning him; *killed.*

Adcock, John H.: Enl. 20 July 1861.

Apple, Lewis C.: Enl. 25 July 1862 at Richmond; the company reports him as "wounded, supposed mortally" and captured but there are no Federal records concerning him; *killed.*

Bevel, James T.: Enl. 29 August 1861 at Richmond; AWOL prior to 20 November 1863; presence at Gettysburg not certain.

Carter, James D.: Enl. 29 August 1861 at Richmond.

Chandler, Mathew L.: Enl. 21 July 1861; *wounded* by a shell in the lower third of the left scapula.

Clark, Alexander: Enl. 15 August 1862 in Mecklenburg County; captured while serving as a nurse at Gettysburg; exchanged from DeCamp Hospital 28 August 1863; possibly slightly *wounded.*

Clark, Rufus:

Clark, William C.: *Wounded* in the thigh and *captured*; exchanged from DeCamp Hospital 28 August 1863.

Collins, William H.:

Daniel, Zachariah: Admitted to the hospital 14 July 1863 with chronic rheumatism.

Dedman, John H.: Enl. 10 April 1863 in Mecklenburg County; *shot* in the left leg (primary amputation by Dr. B.C. Harrison of the 56th Virginia) and captured; exchanged from West's Buildings Hospital 27 September 1863.

Elliott, Alexander:

Hite, George W.:

Hudson, Mastin:

Keirson, Archer L.:

Vaughan, James M.:

Vaughan, Martin:

Yancy, Absalom: Enl. 15 August 1862 in Mecklenburg County; *shot* in the left forearm (radius) and back and *captured*; treated at U.S. XII Corps Hospital; exchanged from DeCamp Hospital 28 August 1863.

Company "B" ("Mecklenburg Spartans")

This company enlisted 22 June 1861 at Tanner's Store, Mecklenburg County, Virginia for one year, and was reorganized 3 May 1862.

Jones, John W. (Captain): VMI class of 1842; enl. 29 July 1861 at Richmond; *captured* at the stone wall.

Hamner, Robert M. (2nd Lt.): Date and place of enlistment not shown.

Moore, James H. (2nd Lt.): Enl. 29 July 1861 at Richmond.

Gee, Leonidas J. (1st Sgt.): Received a gunshot *wound* which fractured his arm and the middle third of his thigh (leg amputated) and *captured*; treated at U.S. 3rd Division, II Corps Hospital; died at U.S. II Corps Hospital 17 July 1863 and buried in Yard D, Row 2 of that hospital's cemetery in Jacob Schwartz's cornfield on Rock Creek; disinterred to Richmond 13 June 1872 with 110 others in ten large boxes labeled "S."

Lambert, George D. (4th Sgt.): *Wounded*; (admitted to the hospital with vulnus sclopeticum 13 July 1863).

Smith, Benjamin J. (5th Sgt.):

Tutor, Samuel A. (3rd Cpl.): Admitted to the hospital with debility 13 July 1863.

Drumwright, William R. (4th Cpl.):

Bacey, John W.:

Bennett, Silas J.: *Captured*; exchanged 1 August 1863 probably *wounded*.

Bingham, Allen W.: Enl. 3 May 1862 at Richmond.

Bowen, Hugh F.: Enl. 17 February 1863 at Richmond.

Bunch, Anderson H.: Enl. 3 May 1862 at Richmond.

Burton, Thomas J.:

Bush, John D.: Enl. 3 May 1862 at Richmond.

Cleaton, Charles L.:

Collins, Andrew J.: Enl. 3 May 1862 at Richmond.

Davis, Edward: Enl. 25 August 1862 at Richmond.

Dortch, James D.: *Wounded*; (admitted to the hospital with vulnus sclopeticum 13 July 1863).

Evans, John L.:

Evans, Wilson E.: Enl. 25 August 1862 at Richmond; *captured*; died of intermittent fever at Fort Delaware 4 November 1863; buried at Finns Point, N.J.

Floyd, Edward A.:

Gee, Benjamin C.: The company reports him initially as captured and subsequently

328

as missing in action supposed *killed*; there are no Federal records concerning him.

Gee, Walter A.: Enl. 25 August 1862 at Richmond.

George, Lewis W.: Enl. 19 October 1862 at Leetown; resided in Mecklenburg County.

Godsey, William H.: *Wounded*; (admitted to the hospital with vulnus sclopeticum 12 July 1863).

Hall, Anderson A.: Enl. 17 February 1863 at Richmond.

Hudson, Thomas J.: Enl. 1 July 1861 at Staunton Precinct in Company "D."

Hunter, William H.:

Jones, Francis: Possibly *wounded*; (issued clothing in a Richmond hospital 20 July 1863).

Kidd, Allen B.:

Kidd, Edward R.:

Kidd, William F.:

Lynch, Thomas J.: Enl. 17 February 1863 at Richmond.

Mitchell, William H.: Enl. 17 February 1863 at Richmond.

Moore, Joseph E.: Enl. 17 February 1863 at Richmond; possibly *wounded*; (received clothing at a Virginia hospital 29 July 1863).

Pleasants, Christopher S.: Enl. 3 May 1862 at Richmond; received a compound *fracture* of his right arm (ulna) and *captured*; treated at U.S. XII Corps Hospital; exchanged 20 or 21 February 1865.

Powell, Gilbert W.: Enl. 3 May 1862 at Richmond; (admitted to the hospital with "debilitas" 15 July 1863).

Purduy, William S.: Enl. 17 February 1863 at Richmond; *shot* in the face and foot and *captured*; exchanged from DeCamp Hospital 16 September 1863.

Rainey, Robert W.: Enl. 12 September 1861 at Richmond.

Ridout, David T.:

Simmons, Samuel:

Simmons, William:

Taylor, George W.: Enl. 3 May 1862 at Richmond; received a flesh *wound* in the right thigh; captured at Greencastle, Pennsylvania 5 July 1863; exchanged from Point Lookout 6 March 1864.

Taylor, Robert J.: The company reports him as a "prisoner at Gettysburg supposed to be dead" but there are no Federal records concerning him; *killed*.

Thomas, Charles W.:

Vaughan, John L.: Received a *gunshot* fracture of the left arm (amputated) and *captured*; died at Letterman Hospital 29 July 1863 and buried in Section 1 Grave #5 of that hospital's cemetery, disinterred to Richmond 13 June 1872 in Box #32.

Whittemore, Henry E.:

Widdifield, Martin V.: Enl. 3 May 1862 at Richmond; *captured*; exchanged 14 or 15 February 1865.

Williams, David P.: *Wounded* in the hip and *captured*; exchanged from DeCamp Hospital 16 September 1863.

Wingfield, Nimrod T.: Enl. 3 May 1862 at Richmond; *wounded* and *captured*; exchanged 1 August 1863 sick with vulnus sclopeticum and acute diarrhea.

Wright, Coleman F.: Enl. 17 February 1863 at Richmond.

Wright, James L.: *Wounded* in the head and *captured*; exchanged from West's Buildings Hospital 24 August 1863.

Wright, John W.: *Wounded* and *captured*; exchanged from West's Buildings Hosptal 24 August 1863.

Company "C" ("Louisa Holliday Guards")

This company enlisted 9 July 1861 at Louisa Court House, Louisa County, Virginia for one year and was reorganized 16 April 1862.

Smith, Timolean (Captain):

Ellis, Robert S. (1st Lt.): *Killed.*

Smith, Joseph H. (2nd Lt.): *Killed.*

Dickinson, Robert Pollard. (1st Sgt.):

Smith, Miles B. (2nd Sgt.): *Wounded*; (admitted to a Virginia hospital with vulnus sclopeticum 12 July 1863).

Smith, Robert S. (3rd Sgt.):

Smith, Leo C. (4th Sgt.):

Gibson, Bias P. (5th Sgt.):

Estis, Thomas B. (Sgt.): Enl. 12 September 1861 at Richmond; born in Louisa County; *shot* in the shoulder; died at General Hospial #1 at Richmond 8 August 1863.

Smith, George W. (1st Cpl.):

Kennon, William M. (2nd Cpl.):

Grubbs, William E. (3rd Cpl.):

Smith, John O. (4th Cpl.):

Bibb, Henry F.:

Branham, John:

Branham, Nathaniel, Jr.: The company reports him as supposed *killed* or taken prisoner at Gettysburg; there are no Federal records concerning him.

Brockman, John:

Fletcher, James:

Gibson, Churchwell: (absent wounded as of 20 November 1863).

Gibson, Granville R.:

Grady, James P.: *Captured*; exchanged 20 or 21 February 1865.

Harris, James W.: Captured while serving as a nurse at Gettysburg 5 July 1863; exchanged 20 March 1864.

Humphreys, Nathaniel:

Johnson, Richard:

Keeton, James P.: The company initially reports him as a "prisoner at Gettysburg" and subsequently as absent wounded; there are no Federal or Confederate hospital records concerning him; *killed.*

Kennon, Joseph:

Knighton, Albert: *Wounded*; (admitted to a Virginia hospital with vulnus sclopeticum 13 July 1863).

Lloyd, Robert H.: AWOL as of 20 November 1863.

Mathews, John H.: The company reports him as a "supposed prisoner" on its 20 November 1863 muster roll but there are no Federal records concerning him; *killed*.

May, John S.: Received a serious gunshot *wound* which fractured the middle third of his right leg (fibula) and *captured*; exchanged 20 March 1864.

McGehee, George V.: *Wounded*.

Mills, Nathaniel H.:

Mills, Thomas M.:

Mills, William H.:

Modena, Benjamin J.:

Poindexter, Edward W.:

Poindexter, William Thomas: *Shot* in the middle finger of the right hand (amputated) and *captured*; treated at U.S. 1st Division, I Corps Hospital; exchanged from DeCamp Hospital 16 September 1863.

Robinson, William A.: *Shot* in the head and *captured*; died 4 July 1863 at U.S. XII Corps Hospital at George Bushman's and buried there as Calvin Robinson.

Smith, Audubon C.: *Shot* in both shoulders and *captured*; given a drink and carried out of the line of fire by Albert N. Hamilton of the 72nd Pa. (the two men recognized each other at the 50th anniversary of the battle); exchanged from Chester Hospital 23 September 1863.

Smith, James C.:

Trainham, David C.: Received a *gunshot* in the right lung from a round ball (canister or buck-and-ball) and *captured*; exchanged from West's Buildings Hospital 24 August 1863.

Whitlock, John H.:

Young, Thomas J.:

Young, William H.: Tinner; *captured*; exchanged 20 or 21 February 1865.

Company "D" ("Buckingham Yancey Guards")

This company enlisted 8 July 1861 at Staunton Shop, Buckingham County, Virginia for one year and was reorganized 3 May 1862.

Jones, John P. (Captain): *Captured*; exchanged 22 March 1865.

Brown, Mathew (1st Lt.): (absent wounded as of 8 November 1863).

Rudisill, Jacob R. (2nd Lt.): Enl. 1 July 1861 in Staunton Precinct; *captured* at the stone wall; exchanged 22 March 1865.

Jones, William E. (3rd Lt.): The company reports him as "supposed to be dead" at Gettysburg; there are no further records concerning him; *killed*.

Tapscott, Vincent A. (1st Sgt.):

Brown, Richard H. (2nd Sgt.): *Captured*; exchanged 14 or 15 February 1865.

Goolsby, Alexander C. (4th Sgt.):

Spencer, James W. (2nd Cpl.): *Killed*.

Robertson, William J. (3rd Cpl.): *Captured*; exchanged 20 or 21 February 1865.

Cunningham, V. Hylton (4th Cpl.): Enl. 3 July 1861 in Staunton Precinct.

Abrahams, Samuel F.:

Adcock, Reuben T.:

Adcock, Walter H.:

Banton, James H.: Possibly *wounded*; (admitted to a Virginia hospital 12 July 1863, cause not recorded).

Banton, William J.: Possibly *wounded*; (admitted to a Virginia hospital 13 July 1863, cause not recorded).

Bishop, William J.: (admitted to a Virginia hospital 16 July 1863, cause not recorded; he was paid only through 30 June 1863 so was probably *wounded* at Gettysburg).

Branch, Curtis N.:

Brown, John R.:

Brown, Reuben R.: *Shot* in the face and neck and *captured*; exchanged from DeCamp Hospital sometime prior to 3 September 1863.

Brown, Richard H.: Enl. 23 July 1861; *wounded* and *captured*; exchanged from DeCamp Hospital 28 August 1863.

Bryant, James H.: AWOL as of 8 November 1863; apparently in hospital.

Cobbs, Robert A.: *Captured*; exchanged 30 April 1864.

Coffe, Andrew J.: Enl. 1 July 1861 in Staunton Precinct.

Damron, Robert B.: Enl. 1 July 1861 in Staunton Precinct; *shot* in the right shoulder and back in the angle and captured at Pickett's Division Hospital; exchanged from West's Buildings Hospital 17 November 1863.

Davis, J.J.: Enl. 3 July 1861 in Staunton Precinct; *shot* in the right thigh and *captured*; exchanged from West's Buildings Hospital 17 November 1863.

Denton, John T.: Enl. 1 July 1861 in Staunton Precinct; from Nelson County; (30 in 1863); *shot* in the right lung and *captured*; died at Letterman Hospital 2 August 1863 and buried in Section 2, Grave #4 of that hospital's cemetery; disinterred to Richmond 13 June 1872 in Box #52.

Dolen, John M.:

Eades, James H.:

Ferguson, Thomas E.: AWOL sometime between 31 October 1861 and 8 November 1863; may not have been at Gettysburg.

Fox, Samuel A.: Enl. 1 July 1861 in Staunton Precinct; *captured*; exchanged 16 March 1865.

Glover, George D.:

Goolsby, G.R.: Enl. 1 July 1861 in Staunton Precinct; AWOL as of 8 November 1863.

Gunter, Thomas J.: Enl. 23 July 1861.

Hackett, Francis M.: Enl. 28 July 1861; wife was Mrs. Mary F. Hackett who filed a claim for his back pay, etc., saying that he died at Williamsport, Maryland; the date and cause of death were not specified; probably mortally *wounded* at Gettysburg.

Maxey, Charles R.: Enl. 23 July 1861; *captured*; exchanged 20 or 21 February 1865.

Maxey, Edward L.: Enl. 23 July 1861.

Mooney, David G.:

Moore, Hartwell S.: Enl. 23 July 1861.

Moore, J.P.: Enl. 1 July 1861 in Staunton Precinct.

Moore, P.S.: Enl. 1 July 1861 in Staunton Precinct.

Neese, W.H.: Enl. 1 July 1861 in Staunton Precinct.

Newton, William J.: Enl. 1 July 1861 in Staunton Precinct; *captured*; died at Point Lookout 26 November 1863.

Newton, William W.:

Nicholas, Lorenzo D.:

Nicholas, William H.: AWOL as of 8 November 1863; paid to 31 August 1863.

Puggh, Joseph A.: Enl. 1 July 1861 in Staunton Precinct.

Robertson, Elisha Z.:

Scruggs, William G.:

Steger, Charles E.: Probably *wounded* and *captured*; exchanged from Fort Delaware 1 August 1863; admitted to a Virginia hospital 30 August 1863.

Tindall, Louis C.:

Wingfield, Albert B.: Enl. 1 July 1861 at Staunton Shop.

Yancy, John W.:

Company "E" ("Ebenezer Grays")

This company enlisted 10 July 1861 at Sturgeonville, Brunswick County, Virginia for one year and was reorganized 3 May 1862.

Frazer, Joseph A. (Captain): *Captured* at the stone wall; paroled for exchange from Johnson's Island, Ohio 24 February 1865.

Blick, William A. (2nd Lt.): *Killed.*

Burton, John T. (2nd Lt.): *Shot* in the face and *captured*; died.

Field, Richard (1st Sgt.): *Wounded* in the hip and *captured*; exchanged from DeCamp Hospital 16 September 1863.

Clayton, John K. (2nd Sgt.): The company reports him as a prisoner as of 21 November 1863 but there are no Federal or Confederate records concerning him; *killed.*

Lanier, Legrand H. (3rd Sgt.): *Captured*; exchanged 20 or 21 February 1865.

Jones, Francis G. (4th Sgt.):

Williams, Embren E. (5th Sgt.): (26 in 1865); born in Brunswick County; farmer; *wounded* in the left arm (amputated above the elbow) and *captured*; exchanged from West's Buildings Hospital 24 August 1863.

Trotter, Isham E. (1st Cpl.): *Captured*; exchanged 8 May 1864.

Bishop, James A. (2nd Cpl.):

Flournoy, Jacob M. (3rd Cpl.): *Wounded* in the right forearm fracturing the ulna.

Stainback, George W. (4th Cpl.): (22 in 1865).

McClarin, James W. (Musician): Enl. 1 August 1862 in Brunswick County.

Abernathy, John E.: *Wounded* and *captured*; exchanged from Chester Hospital 23 September 1863.

Abernathy, William M.:

Archer, Benjamin J.:

Birdsong, Nathaniel A.:

Birdsong, Thomas M.: Enl. 9 February 1863 in Brunswick County.

Blick, George R.: Enl. 9 February 1863 in Brunswick County.

Drake, Joel T.:

Epperson, David J.: Enl. 9 February 1863 in Brunswick County.

Epperson, James E.: Enl. 9 February 1863 in Brunswick County; wife was Mrs. Jane E. Epperson who filed a claim for his back pay, etc.; *captured*; at Point Lookout 2 October 1863 after which there is no further record of him; apparently died in prison, date not recorded.

Gray, William H.: The company reports him as a prisoner on its muster rolls dated 21 November 1863 through 31 August 1864 and subsequently records him as having died in prison; there are no Federal records concerning him, however; *killed*.

House, James: Enl. 9 February 1863 in Brunswick County; *captured*; died at Point Lookout 24 January 1864.

Johnson, Peter B.: Enl. 9 February 1863 in Brusnwick County.

Lanier, Charles H.:

Lanier, Wesley: Received a flesh *wound* in the thigh from a gunshot.

Lewis, James W.: Enl. 9 February 1863 in Brunswick County.

Lewis, Philip J.: (admitted to a Virginia hospital sick with chronic diarrhea 14 July 1863).

Maitland, Hartwell J.:

Maitland, James M.:

Maitland, William H.:

Maiton, William R.: Enl. 9 February 1863 in Brunswick County; *wounded*; (admitted to a Richmond hospital 15 July 1863 and reported as wounded on company's 21 November 1863 muster roll).

Martin, Richard: *Captured*; died at Fort Delaware 12 October 1863; buried at Finns Point, N.J.

Moore, William R.: Enl. 9 February 1863 in Brunswick County.

Morris, William E.:

Parish, William D.: Enl. 9 February 1863 in Brunswick County.

Parsons, Cornelius: *Captured*; died of chronic diarrhea at Fort Delaware 2 November 1863.

Sadler, John F.: Enl. 9 February 1863 in Brunswick County.

Sadler, Samuel C.:

Sanders, Thomas L.: Enl. 9 February 1863 in Brunswick County.

Saunders, John T.: *Captured*; died of chronic diarrhea at Point Lookout 31 January 1864.

Short, William B.: Enl. 9 February 1863 in Brunswick County; *captured*; died of scurvy at Chester Hospital 8 September 1863 and buried in Grave #184 of that hospital's cemetery.

Slate, William P.:

Stainback, George W.:

Williams, Benjamin H.: Enl. 9 February 1863 in Brunswick County; (40 in 1864); wife was Mrs. Margaret Williams.

Williams, Green W.: Enl. 9 February 1863 in Brunswick County; *shot* in the right thigh (flesh wound) and *captured*; exchanged 20 March 1864.

Williams, James A.: Received a gunshot *wound* which fractured his hip and *captured*; died at U.S. II Corps Hospital 19 July 1863 and buried in Row 1, Yard D of that hospital's cemetery in Jacob Schwartz's cornfield on Rock Creek; disinterred to Richmond 13 June 1872 with 110 others in ten large boxes labeled "S."

Williams, James H.: Enl. 9 February 1863 in Brunswick County.

Williams, Jesse: Enl. 9 February 1863 in Brunswick County; *captured*; died of rubeola at Fort Delaware 26 August 1863; buried at Finns Point, N.J.

Williams, Richard:

Williams, Starling J.:

Wilmoth, Richard H.: Enl. 9 February 1863 in Brunswick County; (24 in 1865); farmer; born in Brunswick County.

Wray, William A.: Enl. 9 February 1863 in Brunswick County; *captured*; released from Fort Delaware 20 June 1865.

Company "F" ("Louisa Nelson Greys")

This company enlisted 26 July 1861 at Fork Church, Louisa County, Virginia for one year and was reorganized 16 April 1862.

Richardson, John (Captain):

Talley, William H. (1st Lt.):

Garnett, Thomas M. (2nd Sgt.):

Terrell, Richmond Q. (3rd Sgt.): *Wounded.*

McGehee, James E. (5th Sgt.): *Captured*; died of "congestion of the brain" at Fort Delaware 6 August 1863; buried at Finns Point, N.J.

Perkins, Henry J.W. (2nd Cpl.):

Hughson, Aubrey (3rd Cpl.): Enl. 25 July 1861.

Henderson, Robert (4th Cpl.):

Acors, Thomas:

Amos, James P.:

Bagby, William S.:

Barrett, John W.: Farmer.

Cocke, Thomas E.:

Corker, James H.:

Corker, Thomas J.: Enl. 25 July 1861.

Cross, William B.: Enl. 25 July 1861.

Grubbs, Frederick J.:

Hall, Edmund N.:

Hall, George W.: *Captured*; died at Fort Delaware 5 October 1863; buried at Finns Point, N.J.

Hall, Timothy T.:

Harris, James L.: *Shot* in the left leg (amputated) and *captured*; died at U.S. II Corps Hospital 16 July 1863 and buried in Yard D, Row 3 of that hospital's cemetery in Jacob Schwartz's cornfield on Rock Creek; disinterred to Richmond 13 June 1872 with 110 others in ten large boxes labeled "S."

Higgason, William B.:

Hollins, George T.:

Hollins, William C.: Enl. 25 July 1861.

Kennon, Robert W.:

Kersey, Thomas F.: Enl. 25 July 1861.

Lockhart, Ashburn: Enl. 25 July 1861.

Lowry, Wyatt:

Meridith, James T.:

Mills, John J.:

Richardson, William:

Strong, Nathaniel H.:

Talley, George F.:

Talley, Robert B.:

Tate, Calvin O.:

Tate, Fleming D.:

Tate, John S.:

Tate, Nathan G.:

Terrell, John E.: Enl. 25 July 1861.

Thompson, Charles:

Waldrop, William D.: Possibly *wounded*; (on sick furlough 13 July through 13 August 1863).

Wash, Robert D.: *Wounded.*

Wilshire, Robert A.: (deserted 13 September 1863).

<u>Company "G" ("Charlotte Defenders")</u>

This company enlisted 12 July 1861 at Wylliesburg, Charlotte County, Virginia for one year and was reorganized 16 April 1862.

Thomas, Robert N. (Captain): Enl. 26 July 1861 at Fork Church in Company "F."

Barnes, Francis C. (2nd Lt.): *Captured* at the stone wall; released 12 June 1865.

Purcell, John P. (3rd Sgt.): (22 in 1862); farmer; born in Charlotte County.

Eudailey, Samuel P. (Sgt.): (died sometime prior to 18 June 1864).

Jones, William T. (1st Cpl.):

Jones, John L. (2nd Cpl.): *Captured*; exchanged 20 or 21 February 1865.

Eudailey, John T. (3rd Cpl.):

Blake, John T.:

Canada, John M.:

Dickerson, Peter C.:

Estes, James E.: Enl. 18 July 1861; *captured*; joined U.S. 1st Connecticut Cavalry about 4 October 1863.

Eudailey, Francis C.:

Gregory, Charles G.:

Hawthorn, Peter W.: Enl. 25 July 1862 at St. John, Lunenburg County.

Jones, Isham H.: *Wounded*; (admitted to a Virginia hospital with vulnus sclopeticum 12 July 1863).

Jones James W.:

Lipscomb, Edward T.:

Loafman, James H.:

Locke, James W.: *Shot* in the right leg (flesh wound).

Newcomb, Henry J.:

Newcomb, James H.: Enl. 18 July 1861; *wounded*; (admitted to a Virginia hospital with vulnus sclopeticum 12 July 1863).

Palmore, John T.: *Captured*; joined U.S. serivce at Point Lookout 11 February 1864.

Redd, Richard L.:

Yates, James W.:

Company "H" ("White Hall Guards")

This company enlisted 15 July 1861 at White Hall, Albemarle County, Virginia for one year, was accepted into Confederate service 29 July 1861, and was reorganized 3 May 1862.

Wyant, James C. (Captain): Enl. 3 May 1862 at Richmond; wife was Mrs. S.A. Wyant; *shot* in the face and *captured*; treated at U.S. 1st Division, I Corps Hospital; died of erysipelas at Chester Hospital 31 July 1863 and buried in Grave #90 of that hospital's cemetery.

Michie, Henry Clay (1st Lt.): Slightly *wounded* during the attack; *captured* at the stone wall; exchanged 22 March 1865.

Miller, Ira A. (2nd Lt.): *Wounded* and *captured*; exchanged 22 March 1865.

Blackwell, James W. (1st Sgt.): (23 in 1863); received a *gunshot* fracture of the right humerus and *captured*; exchanged from West's Buildings Hospital 24 August 1863.

Wood, William R. (2nd Sgt.): *Captured*; exchanged 15 November 1864.

Jones, John (4th Sgt.): *Captured*; exchanged 20 or 21 February 1865.

Michie, Orin (2nd Cpl.): *Wounded* and *captured*; exchanged from DeCamp Hospital 16 September 1863; died of wound sometime thereafter.

Maupin, David G. (3rd Cpl.): The company reports him as "supposed to be captured at Gettsyburg" but there are no Federal records concerning him; *killed*.

Sandridge, G.W. (4th Cpl.): Enl. 3 May 1862 at Richmond; the company reports him as "supposed captured at Gettysburg" but there are no Federal records concerning him; *killed*.

Ballard, John T.: (AWOL sometime between 5 August 1862 and 25 October 1863); may not have been at Gettsyburg.

Ballard, William G.: The company reports him as missing in action, "supposed captured" but there are no Federal records concerning him; *killed*.

Blackwell, Robert B.: Enl. 3 May 1862 at Richmond; *wounded* and *captured*; exchanged from West's Buildings Hospital 27 September 1863.

Bowen, Lucius M.: *Captured*; exchanged 16 March 1865.

Brown, Richard T.:

Brown, William G.: Enl. 3 May 1862 at Richmond.

Craig, John: Enl. 15 August 1862 at Gordonsville; *wounded* in the thigh and *captured*; exchanged from DeCamp Hospital 16 September 1863.

Craig, Robert F.: Enl. 3 May 1862 at Richmond.

Dunn, John T.:

Dunn, Thomas W.: Enl. 3 May 1862 at Richmond; *killed*.

Estes, L.E.: Enl. 3 May 1862 at Richmond.

Estes, Robert G.: The company reports him as "absent prisoner" for the period 25 October 1863 through 16 October 1864 but there are no Federal records concerning him; *killed*.

Estes, W.J.: Enl. 3 May 1862 at Richmond; the company reports him as a "prisoner" and subsequently as *killed*; there are no Federal records concerning him.

Gardner, Ira T.: Enl. 3 May 1862 at Richmond.

Garrison, H. White:

Gibson, H.T.: Date and place of enlistment not recorded; single; (27 in 1863); received a *gunshot* fracture of the right humerus and shot in the right chest and *captured*; died at West's Buildings Hospital 19 August 1863.

Gibson, William C.: Enl. 3 May 1862 at Richmond.

Gibson, William W.: Enl. 3 May 1862 at Richmond; *captured*; exchanged sick with tonsilitas 1 August 1863.

Hall, James F.: Enl. 3 May 1862 at Richmond; *captured*; exchanged 20 or 21 February 1865.

Harlow, Samuel: Enl. 3 May 1862 at Richmond; AWOL as of 25 October 1863; paid through 31 March 1863; may not have been at Gettysburg.

Harris, William H.: Enl. 3 May 1862 at Richmond; AWOL as of 25 October 1863; may not have been at Gettysburg.

Harris, Z.P.: Enl. 3 May 1862 at Richmond; AWOL as of 25 October 1863; may not have been at Gettysburg.

Henkle, John: Enl. 3 May 1862 at Richmond; the company reports him as a "prisoner" but there are no Federal records concerning him; *killed*.

Herring, B. Franklin:

Keaster, L.B.: Enl. 3 May 1862 at Richmond.

Keyton, S.F.: *Wounded* and *captured*; exchanged from DeCamp Hospital 16 September 1863.

Lane, John H.: Enl. 3 May 1862 at Richmond.

Layne, Nehemiah: Enl. 18 March 1862 at Charlottesville.

Layne, Robert C.: Wife was Mrs. C.A. Layne; (29 in 1863); the company initially reports him as a "prisoner" and subsequently as *killed*; there are no Federal records concerning him.

Marsh, John C.: Enl. 6 March 1863 at Petersburg.

Marsh, William F.: Enl. 3 May 1862 at Richmond; *shot* in the thigh and *captured*; exchanged from Chester Hospital 23 September 1863.

Maupin, C.B.: Enl. 3 May 1862 at Richmond; the company reports him as "absent prisoner" for the period 31 October 1863 through January 1864 but there are no further Federal or Confederate records concerning him; *killed.*

Maupin, James R.: Enl. 3 May 1862 at Richmond; *wounded* and *captured*; exchanged from DeCamp Hospital 28 August 1863.

McCauley, Robert W.: (30); enl. 3 May 1862 at Richmond; wife was Mrs. Margaret J. McCauley; *wounded* in the left elbow and *captured*; died of chronic diarrhea at Point Lookout 19 August 1864.

Norris, James H.: Enl. 3 May 1862 at Richmond; *captured*; released from Fort Delaware 15 June 1865.

Pritchett, Peter: (absent under arrest for desertion as of 25 October 1863).

Rhodes, Franklin:

Rhodes, Hezekiah:

Summerson, J.E.: Enl. 22 August 1862 at Richmond; *captured*; exchanged 8 May 1864.

Taylor, David M.: Enl. 3 May 1862 at Richmond.

Thomas, William E.:

Via, Manoah G.: Admitted to a Virginia hospital 17 July 1863; probably *wounded.*

Via, Waller T.: AWOL as of 25 October 1863.

Wood, C.C.: Enl. 22 Augsut 1862 at Richmond; (20 in 1864); born in Albemarle County; farmer; *shot* in the right forearm and *captured*; exchanged from Chester Hospital 23 September 1863.

Wood, William H.: Enl. 3 May 1862 at Richmond; *captured*; exchanged sick with "debility" 1 August 1863.

<u>Company "I" ("Charlotte Greys")</u>

This company enlisted 18 July 1861 at Reece's Church, Charlotte County, Virginia for one year and was reorganized 3 May 1862.

Clarke, Charles J. (Captain): *Wounded*; (admitted to a Virginia hospital with vulnus sclopeticum 12 July 1863).

Cronin, Stephen D. (1st Lt.): Enl. 1 August 1861 at Richmond; *shot* in the chest and *captured*; paroled for exchange 24 February 1865.

Price, William H. (2nd Lt.):

Mason, John R. (1st Sgt.): The company reports him as a "supposed prisoner" but there are no Federal records concerning him; *killed.*

Holt, Robert A. (2nd Sgt.):

Berkley, William W. (1st Cpl.):

Hardiman, John Edward (3rd Cpl.): *Shot* in the thigh and *captured*; exchanged from DeCamp Hospital 8 September 1863.

Williams, Alexander L.P. (4th Cpl.): *Shot* in the thigh and *captured*; exchanged from Chester Hospital 23 September 1863.

Baker, Elijah W.: *Shot* in the middle third of the left thigh and *captured*; died at

Letterman Hospital 7 August 1863 and buried in Section 4, Grave #22 of that hospital's cemetery; disinterred to Richmond 13 June 1872 in Box #53.

Beasley, William D.:

Booker, Robert S.:

Breedlove, John W.: *Shot* in the left forearm two inches below the elbow.

Calhoun, Adam N.:

Daniel, George C.:

Dixon, John T.:

Driscoll, Larkin R.: Date and place of enlistment not recorded; *wounded* in the foot and *captured*; died of pyemia at Chester Hospital 28 July 1863 and buried in Grave #63 of that hospital's cemetery.

Ellington, Branch A.:

Gaines, John C.:

Garrison, John R.:

Garrison, Joseph W.: *Shot* in the lower third of the left leg.

Guill, John R.:

Hamblett, Edward W.:

Hamblett, Jesse W.:

Hamblett, Thomas P.: Enl. 12 February 1863 at Guinea Depot.

Hamersley, William R.: Enl. 3 September 1862 in Charlotte County; *captured*; exchanged 20 or 21 February 1865.

Harvey, Jesse R.: Enlisted in Georgia; transferred to this company in October 1862.

Harvey, William D.:

Harvey, William H.: Enlisted in June 1862 in Tennessee.

Holt, Burwell N.M.: *Wounded*; (admitted to a Virginia hospital 13 July 1863; reported as wounded 24 October 1863).

Holt, James P.: *Shot* in the hip and *captured*; exchanged from Chester Hospital 20 August 1863.

Holt, John Lea: The company reports him as "supposed to be prisoner" during the period 24 October 1863 through 19 January 1864 but there are no Federal records concerning him; *killed*.

Holt, Richard M.:

Lawson, Thomas G.: *Wounded* in the left side (groin) and *captured*; exchanged from DeCamp Hospital 28 August 1863; deserted hospital 4 September 1863.

Lester, Hartwell F.:

Lester, William T.: (returned to duty from hospital 23 June 1863).

Morton, Jacob W.: *Captured*; exchanged 14 or 15 February 1865.

Pugh, Presley A.:

Rash, James S.:

Smith, Thomas B.: Received a gunshot *wound* which fractured his right ankle and *captured*; exchanged from Point Lookout 30 April 1864.

Smith, William Lee: (27 in 1862); born in Campbell County; wife was Mrs. Sarah K. Smith; *killed*.

Steel, Adison P.: *Captured*; exchanged 20 or 21 February 1865.

St. John, Alexander A.: Enl. 3 September 1862 in Charlotte County; *shot* below and back of the right shoulder and *captured*; died at U.S. 1st Division, I Corps hospital 26 July 1863.

Wilkes, Benjamin H.: (29 in 1865); *captured*; exchanged 28 December 1863.

Williams, Clement W.: Deserted near Gettysburg 3 July 1863 probably while on the march to the field and captured two days later; took oath of allegiance to the U.S. 7 July 1863.

Company "K" ("Harrison's Guards")

This company enlisted 6 August 1861 at Mechanicsville, Hanover County, Virginia for one year and was reorganized 5 May 1862.

Finley, George W. (1st Lt.): Date and place of enlistment not recorded; *captured* at the stone wall; released from Fort Delaware 14 May 1865.

Via, Harrison (1st Sgt.):

Via, Edward (3rd Sgt.): *Wounded*; (admitted to a Virginia hospital with vulnus sclopeticum 17 July 1863).

Tucker, Bentley H. (4th Sgt.): *Wounded* in the right humerus (arm amputated at the shoulder joint) and captured; exchanged from West's Buildings Hospital 27 September 1863.

Wood, William H. (1st Cpl.): *Captured*; released from Fort Delaware 21 June 1865.

McGhee, William A. (4th Cpl.):

Bailey, William:

Baskett, Reuben: Resided in King and Queen County.

Cox, Charles B.: Enl. 1 May 1862 at Richmond.

Earnest, Henry C.: Resided in Hanover County.

Fields, John A.: *Wounded* in the heel and *captured*; exchanged 20 or 21 February 1865.

Garthright, John E.: Enl. 26 June 1862 at Richmond; *captured*; exchanged 8 May 1864.

Garthright, Philip T.:

Heath, Logan W.: *Shot* in the right thigh and *captured*; exchanged from West's Buildings Hospital 24 August 1863.

Ingram, William:

Jackson, Thomas: Enl. 13 August 1861 at Richmond.

Kelley, Edward W.: (22); received a *gunshot* fracture of the left elbow joint (arm amputated at upper third by Surgeon J.M.G. McGuire, CSA) and *captured*; treated at U.S. XII Corps Hospital; exchanged from West's Buildings Hospital 27 September 1863.

Kelley, Henry P.:

Marshall, Benjamin F.: Resided in Henrico County.

Martin, William T.: (46 in 1863); farmer.

McGhee, John L.:

McGhee, Peter C.: Captured while serving as a nurse at Gettysburg; exchanged 20 or 21 February 1865.

Peace, Edwin M.: Resided in Hanover County.

Richardson, William T.: (on detached service as of 24 October 1863).

Smithee, Joseph J.: *Captured*; exchanged 20 or 21 February 1865.

Truman, Thomas J.:

Tucker, James E.:

Tucker, John T.:

White, William: *Captured*; died of chronic diarrhea at Fort Delaware 30 October 1863; buried at Finns Point, N.J.

Woody, Pleasant J.:

Wright, George H.:

Armistead's Brigade

Brigadier General Armistead, appointed 1 April 1862, was in command of a brigade organized during the Peninsula Campaign, consisting of the 9th, 14th, 38th, 53rd and 57th Virginia, and the 5th Virginia Battalion. On 6 September 1862, the 5th Battalion was disbanded and the men transferred to the 53rd Virginia. With this exception, there was no change in the composition of the brigade until Appomattox.

Armistead, Lewis Addison (Brig. Gen.): Born at New Berne, North Carolina 18 February 1817; dismissed from West Point in 1836 for breaking a messhall plate over the head of Jubal A. Early; Lt. 6th U.S. Infantry 1839; Seminole War service; twice brevetted for Mexican War service; wounded at Chapultepec; resigned from U.S. Army as Capt. 26 May 1861; widower; Major of Confederate infantry 1861; appointed Col. of the 57th Virginia Infantry Regiment 25 September 1861; promoted to Brig. Gen. 1 April 1862; commanding brigade Dept. of Norfolk about 1 through 12 April 1862; relieved of regimental command to assume generalship 14 April 1862; commanding bgd. Huger's Division, Dept. of Northern Virginia 12 April through July 1862; commanding bgd., Anderson's Division, 1st Corps, Army of Northern Virginia July through 17 September 1862; wounded at Sharpsburg, Maryland 17 September 1862; commandng brigade Pickett's Division, 1st Corps, Army of Northern Virginia October 1862 through 25 February 1863; in Dept. of Virginia and North Carolina 25 February through 1 April 1863; in Dept. of Southern Virginia 1 April through May 1863; commanding bgd. Pickett's Division, 1st Corps, Army of Northern Virginia May through 3 July 1863; *shot* in the arm and leg below the knee and *captured*; died of exhaustion at 9 AM 5 July 1863 at the U.S. 2nd Division, XI Corps Hospital and buried there; disinterred about the end of July 1863 and finally placed in St. Paul's Cemetery in Baltimore, Maryland.

Armistead, W. Keith (1st Lt., ADC): Born at St. Davids Parsonage, Alabama 11 December 1844; enl. 10 May 1862 at Richmond as a Private in Company "A," 6th Virginia Cavalry; student; appointed 1st Lt. and ADC on Armistead's staff 30 April 1863.

Carter, Richard H. (Major, Quartermaster): Appointed Major and QM on Armistead's staff 4 October 1862; served in this post 26 November 1862 through 25 August 1863; relieved from duty with the brigade 1 September 1863.

Darden, James D. (Capt., AAG): (37 in 1865); merchant; VMI class of 1867; appointed Captain and AAG on Armistead's staff 31 July 1862; *wounded.*

Herbert, William W. (Major, Commissary of Subsistence): Appointed Captain and ACS of the 57th Virginia 4 October 1861; appointed Major and Commissary of Subsistence on Armistead's staff 8 May 1862.

Randolph, Peyton (Temporary Capt., AIG): (28 in 1861); assigned to Armistead's staff as Assistant Provost Marshal 7 September 1862; Lt. and Acting Inspector General on Armistead's staff 2 December 1862; appointed temporary Capt. on Armistead's staff as an Engineer officer 26 May 1863; reported as a Captain of Engineers on Inspection duty on Armistead's staff 30 July 1863.

Randolph, William L. (1st Lt., Ordnance Officer): (23 in 1865); VMI class of 1864; appointed 1st Lt. and Ordnance Officer on Armistead's staff 9 May 1862.

McAlpine, James N. (Surgeon): Appointed Surgeon 3 June 1861.

Hawthorne, Benjamin J. (Capt. serving temporarily on Armistead's staff at Gettysburg): Formerly Captain of Company "G," 38th Virginia, prior to arrival of Captain Henderson L. Lee who assumed command of that company just prior to the battle; date and place of enlistment not shown; *shot* in the left arm.

Armistead's Orderlies

Haden, John W.: On extra duty from Company "I," 53rd Virginia; enl. 22 April 1861 at Pittsylvania Court House.

Moseley, James E.: On extra duty from Company "A," 57th Virginia; enl. 29 May 1861 at Gravel Hill.

Owens, Albert B.: On extra duty from Company "G," 9th Virginia; enl. 26 March 1862 at Portsmouth.

Guards for Armistead's Wagon

Beale, Terry: Detailed from Company "A," 9th Virginia; enl. 23 April 1862 at Craney Island.

Lawrence, George W. (4th Sgt.): Detailed from Company "A," 9th Virginia; enl. 23 April 1862 at Craney Island.

Brigade Surgeon's Department

Bilisoly, Joseph: Detailed from Company "K," 9th Virginia; enl. 20 April 1861 at Portsmouth.

Upton, Thomas W.: Detailed from Company "F," 38th Virginia; enl. 4 June 1861 at Republican Grove.

Quartermaster's Department

Cocke, John N. (3rd Cpl.): Detailed from Company "K," 9th Virginia; enl. 20 April 1861 at Portsmouth.

Brigade Mail Carrier

Anglea, Samuel R.: Detailed from Company "K," 38th Virginia; enl. 20 February 1862 at Cascade.

Brigade Commissary Department

Ayres, Nathan W.: Detailed from Company "A," 57th Virginia; enl. 29 May 1861 at Gravel Hill.

Ford, William J.: On extra duty from Company "A," 57th Virginia; enl. 29 May 1861 at Gravel Hill.

Leath, John W.: Detailed from Company "D," 53rd Virginia; enl. 6 May 1861 at Fort Powhatan.

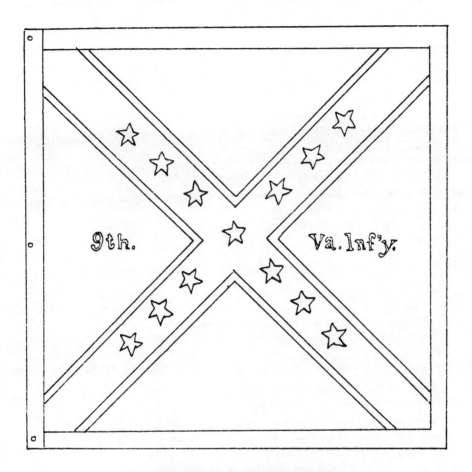

**Flag of the 9th Virginia Infantry
captured at the stone wall
by the 71st Pennsylvania Infantry**

345

9th Virginia Volunteer Infantry Regiment

This regiment was organized 7 July 1861 with ten companies designated "A" through "K" which had previously been accepted into Confederate service. Prior to the organization of this regiment and while in the service of the State of Virginia, some of these companies had taken part in an ineffective attempt to form an artillery regiment. At the time the regiment was formed, the companies composing it were distributed among the various fortifications around the harbor of Portsmouth and Norfolk doing duty as heavy artillery as well as infantry. Second Company "A" was attached to the regiment by special order 28 November 1863 and joined the unit 1 May 1864. First Company "H" became Company "C," 28th Battalion Virginia Infantry on 24 September 1862. Second Company "H" was attached to this regiment by special order dated 28 November 1863.

The following listing was obtained from company April/June 1863 muster rolls captioned 30 June 1863, Chambersburg, Pennsylvania. All rifle companies reported the condition of their arms as "rifle muskets"; that of their clothing as "inferior"; and their accouterments, military appearance, discipline and instruction as "good." The Field and Staff unit reported all aspects of its condition as "good."

Field and Staff

Owens, John Crowder (Major): Born in Mathews County, Va. 19 March 1830; pharmacist or ship carpenter in Portsmouth; enl. 20 April 1861 at Portsmouth as Captain of Company "G"; promoted Major 24 May 1862; promoted Col. 1 July 1863 to rank from 30 October 1862; *wounded* in the groin during the attack; died at Pickett's Division Hospital 4 July 1863 and buried in the woods across the creek form Bream's Mill; his body was removed sometime prior to the general disinterment of Confederates to the South in 1872 and 1873; buried in Oakwood Cemetery, Portsmouth.

Crocker, James F. (1st Lt., Adjutant): Appointed Adjutant 24 May 1862; *shot* in the right leg and *captured*; treated at U.S. XII Corps Hospital; paroled for exchange 24 February 1865.

Compton, James (AQM): Appointed AQM 14 November 1861.

Chamberlain, George (Capt., ACS): VMI class of 1853; appointed ACS 24 September 1861.

Barry, Arthur R. (Surgeon): Appointed Assistant Surgeon 28 October 1861; promoted to Surgeon 16 March 1863.

Howard, Thomas R. (Asst. Surgeon): Appointed Asst. Surgeon 27 June 1862; assigned to the regiment 17 April 1863.

Phillips, Charles T. (Sgt. Major): Enl. 20 April 1861 at Portsmouth in Company "G"; (23); teacher; captured while serving as a nurse at Gettysburg; exchanged 20 March 1864.

Gilliam, James S., Jr. (Ordnance Sgt.): Enl. 9 May 1861 at Petersburg in Company "C."

Edwards, Amos W. (Quartermaster Sgt.): Enl. 20 April 1861 at Portsmouth in Company "G"; (31); boiler maker.

Grimes, Joshua M. (4th Sgt., Color Bearer): Detailed from Company "I"; enl. 15 May 1861 at Churchland; (20); farmer; *wounded* and *captured*; exchanged from DeCamp Hospital 16 September 1863.

Whitehurst, Marshall P. (Hospital Orderly): On extra daily duty from Company "G"; enl. 20 April 1861 at Portsmouth; (28); painter.

Collins, William B. (QM Dept.): Detailed from Company "K"; enl. 1 January 1862 at Pinner's Point.

Thompson, John W. (Commissary of Subsistence Dept.): On extra duty from Company "D"; enl. 27 April 1861 at the Naval Hospital in Porstmouth; (19); clerk.

Williams, Samuel L. (Ambulance Corps): On daily duty from Company "D"; enl. 27 April 1861 at the Naval Hospital in Portsmouth; (27); carpenter; captured at Waterloo, Maryland (?) 5 July 1863; released on oath from Fort Delaware 30 November 1864.

Company "B" ("Baltimore Artillery")

This company enlisted 5 June 1861 at Norfolk, mustered 8 June 1861, and was reorganized 8 May 1862.

Wilkinson, Henry S. (Jr. 2nd Lt.): (26 in 1862); clerk; *shot* in the head and *captured*; treated at U.S. 2nd Division, II Corps Hospital; died of chronic diarrhea at Johnson's Island, Ohio 21 April 1864 and buried in Block 23, Grave #4 of that prison's cemetery.

Jenkins, John W. (2nd Sgt.): (23); waterman; *wounded.*

Kivet, Alexander L. (3rd Sgt.): Enl. 13 May 1862 at Petersburg; *captured*; died of smallpox at Point Lookout 30 December 1863.

McLaughlin, William (1st Cpl.): Enl. 23 April 1862 at Craney Island; *shot* in the right shoulder and *captured*; treated at U.S. XII Corps Hospital; exchanged from DeCamp Hospital 28 October 1863.

Beale, Nathaniel L.: Enl. 23 April 1862 at Craney Island; the company reports him as "wounded in enemy hands" through the 31 August 1864 muster but there are no Federal records concerning him; *killed.*

Bluhm, Fritz: Enl. 23 April 1862 at Craney Island; *captured*; released on oath from Fort Delaware 10 May 1865.

Eans, John: (34); laborer.

Fagan, William T.: Enl. 10 May 1862 at Petersburg; captured with wagon train near Gettysburg 4 July 1863.

Johnson, Zachariah T.: Enl. 23 April 1862 at Craney Island; (under arrest for desertion since 8 June 1863).

Kello, James R.: Enl. 23 April 1862 at Craney Island.

Knight, Benjamin F.: Enl. 23 April 1862 at Craney Island; (listed as present 30 June 1863, but reported as a deserter since 13 April 1863).

Lowe, James J.: Enl. 23 April 1862 at Craney Island.

McClenny, James M.: Enl. 23 April 1862 at Craney Island; *captured*; released from Fort Delaware 20 June 1865.

Rayford, Albert N.: Enl. 23 April 1862 at Craney Island.

Thorp, Walter C.: Enl. 21 August 1862 in Southampton County.

Company "C" ("Yellow Jacket Artillery" or "Chesterfield Yellow Jackets")

This company enlisted 27 May 1861 at Chesterfield Court House, Chesterfield County, Virginia for one year and was reorganized 20 March 1862.

Gregory, John Marcus (Captain): (23); farmer; *captured*; died of a "putrid sore throat" at Johnson's Island, Ohio 21 November 1863 and buried in Block 10 of that prison's cemetery.

Clay, Mathew B. (1st Lt.): (20); farmer; *captured*; exchanged 15 October 1864.

Varnier, Edward (2nd Lt.): (32); farmer; *captured*; exchanged 22 March 1865.

Britton, Henry Clay (3rd Lt.): (22); farmer; *captured*; exchanged 20 March 1864.

Dyson, Benjamin (1st Sgt.): (27); farmer; born in Chesterfield County; mother was Mrs. Martha C. Dyson; Sgt. Dyson had no father, wife or child at the time of his death; *killed*.

Howlett, Thomas A. (2nd Sgt.): (26); farmer.

Hatcher, Richard G. (3rd Sgt.): (35); farmer.

Varnier, John W. (4th Sgt.): (18); farmer; *wounded* (compound fracture).

Stuart, Ralph H. (5th Sgt.): Enl. 13 July 1861 at Craney Island; *wounded* and *captured*; exchanged from West's Buildings Hospital 24 August 1863.

Graves, Robert H. (1st Cpl.): Enl. 24 September 1861 at Craney Island; born in Amelia County; *wounded*; died of his wound at Chimborazo Hospital in Richmond 14 September 1863.

Cheatham, Richard D. (4th Cpl.): (40); farmer; *wounded*.

Adkins, William J.: Enl. 27 June 1861 at Craney Island; (20); cooper.

Bennett, John A.: (22); farmer.

Britton, Richard J.: Enl. 26 July 1861 at Craney Island; born in Chesterfield County; *captured*; died at Fort Delaware 23 July 1863; buried at Finns Point, N.J.

Brooks, Camillus: (20); farmer; *captured*; exchanged 30 September 1864.

Brown, Robert J.: Enl. 15 March 1862 at Craney Island; born in Chesterfield County; (33); *captured*; exchanged 1 August 1863; died of chronic diarrhea at Petersburg, Virginia hospital 4 August 1863.

Brown, Sydney K.: (19); farmer.

Bruce, Richard T.: Enl. 27 June 1861 at Craney Island; (20); farmer.

Chalkley, Lemuel F.: Enl. 31 July 1861 at Craney Island; *wounded*.

Childress, John C.: Enl. 7 December 1862 near Fredericksburg; (sick with chronic cystitis since 3 July 1863); probably not in assault.

Cox, Christopher C.: (20); farmer; *wounded*.

Dodson, John E.J.: (20); toll collector.

Dunnavant, Charles F.: (27); farmer; wife was Mrs. Julia A. Dunnavant; had two children; *captured*; died of chronic diarrhea at Fort Delaware 18 September 1863; buried at Finns Point, N.J.

Dyer, George W.: Enl. 16 June 1861 at Craney Island; (18); farmer.

Ellett, William T.: (20); shoemaker; *captured*; died of chronic diarrhea at Fort Delaware 23 August 1863.

Ellis, Robert: (30); farmer; *captured*; exchanged 20 or 21 February 1865.

Farmer, Joseph L.: (29); mason.

Forloine, Thomas G.: (22); merchant; *captured*; exchanged 20 or 21 February 1865.

Gannon, Daniel: Probably *wounded*; *captured*; exchanged 1 August 1863.

Gill, Larkin M.: Enl. 10 December 1861 at Craney Island; *captured*; exchanged 14 or 15 February 1865.

Graves, Charles F.: Enl. 9 September 1861 at Craney Island.

Gregory, James M.: (19); student.

Hobbs, Richard M.: (23); farmer; *captured*; exchanged 15 November 1864.

Hurt, George T.: (29); farmer; *wounded* in the upper lobe of the left lung and *captured*; exchanged 6 March 1864.

Jackson, William M.: Enl. 29 September 1861 at Craney Island; *captured*; released from Fort Delaware 20 June 1865.

Mackey, John H.: Enl. 11 July 1862 at Drewry's Bluff; the company initially reports him as missing in action and subsequently as having died of wounds but there are no Federal records concerning him; *killed*.

Morris, Uriah C.: (27); farmer.

Morrisett, John T.: (18); farmer; *wounded* and *captured*; exchanged from DeCamp Hospital 8 September 1863.

Nunnally, William T.: (20); cooper; *captured*; exchanged 14 or 15 February 1865.

Puckett, John T.: Enl. 5 August 1861 at Craney Island.

Reames, Isham D.: Enl. 14 August 1861 at Craney Island; probably *wounded*; *captured*; exchanged 1 August 1863.

Rowlett, James T.: (18); farmer.

Rowlett, Peter A.: (18); farmer; *captured*; exchanged 15 November 1864.

Russell, Samuel C.: (19); farmer; *captured*; exchanged 1 August 1863 sick with typhoid fever; died at Petersburg, Virginia hospital 9 August 1863.

Smith, William T.: (35); carpenter; (present in arrest).

Totty, George W.: Enl. 9 April 1862 at Craney Island; *captured*; exchanged 30 September 1864.

Totty, John: Enl. 14 August 1861 at Craney Island; *wounded* in the hip and *captured*; exchanged 15 November 1864.

Turner, Velerius: (18); cooper; *shot* in the right knee and *captured*; treated at U.S. XII Corps Hospital; exchanged from DeCamp Hospital 16 September 1863.

Vest, Chastine H.: Enl. 15 March 1862 at Craney Island; (21).

Wilkinson, John T.: (24); farmer.

Company "D" ("Virginia Artillery")

Organized about 12 April 1861, this company was enrolled for service 27 April 1861 at the Naval Hospital at Portsmouth, Virginia for one year and was reorganized 8 May 1862.

Richardson, William James (Captain): (33); carpenter; *captured*; exchanged 22 March 1865.

Weaver, Samuel W. (1st Lt.): (30); tinner; *captured*; released from Fort Delaware 12 June 1865.

Vermillion, Richard (2nd Lt.): (23); boat builder.

Culpepper, William A. (1st Sgt.): (20); carpenter; *shot* in the wrist and *captured*; exchanged from Chester Hospital 23 September 1863.

Myers, Thomas H. (Sgt.): (27); moulder.

Walton, George W. (Sgt.): (22); printer; *captured*; released on oath from Fort Delaware 30 November 1864.

Brown, James (Musician): (17); laborer.

Bailey, Thomas B.: Enl. 12 June 1861 at Craney Island; (24); laborer; *captured*; released on oath from Fort Delaware 5 March 1865.

Bird, Daniel: Enl. 30 April 1863 in Nansemond County.

Bland, George: (24); laborer.

Cross, John D.: Enl. 27 February 1862 at Craney Island; mother was Mrs. Nancy H. Austin; *captured*; died of smallpox at Point Lookout 29 November 1863.

Cutherell, Leonard: (25); butcher.

Hampton, Augustus F.: (19); boat builder.

Hansford, James: (19); painter.

Kirby, John P.: Enl. 12 March 1863 at Richmond.

McCoy, Rufus K.: (26); carpenter; *shot* in the chest and *captured*; exchanged from Chester Hospital 23 September 1863.

Miltier, Daniel: Enl. 30 April 1863 in Nansemond County; received a *contusion* and *captured*; exchanged from DeCamp Hospital 28 August 1863.

Morgan, William: Enl. 30 Apirl 1863 in Nansemond County; *captured*; died of smallpox at Point Lookout 2 November 1863.

Reid, Robert E.: (23); stone mason; the company reports him initially as missing in action and subsequently as having died of wounds, but there are no Federal records concerning him; *killed*.

Skinner, Abraham: Enl. 30 April 1863 in Nansemond County.

Urquhart, William J.: Enl. 5 February 1862 at Craney Island; *shot* in the side and *captured*; exchanged from DeCamp Hospital 28 August 1863.

Yates, Josiah D.: (22); farmer; *wounded* through both thighs and *captured*; exchanged from DeCamp Hospital 8 September 1863.

Company "E" ("Isle of Wight Rifle Blues")

This company enlisted 27 May 1861 at Smithfield, Isle of Wight County, Virginia for one year and was reorganized 3 May 1862.

Chapman, Richard F. (Bvt. 2nd Lt.): Enl. 9 April 1863 at Broad Water Bridge; *wounded* in the right leg (amputated below the knee) and *captured*; the company reports him as having died of wounds 15 or 16 July 1863; there are no Federal records of his death.

Hack, John W. (Jr. 2nd Lt.): Enl. 18 May 1861 at Chuckatuck in Company "F"; (22); received a gunshot *wound* which fractured his ulna and *captured*; treated at U.S. XII Corps Hospital; exchanged 22 March 1865.

Hall, Mathew (1st Sgt.):

Vellines, Marsden J. (2nd Sgt.): Enl. 28 February 1862 at Fort Boykin; *shot* in the thigh and *captured*; exchanged from DeCamp Hospital 28 August 1863.

Russell, Jacob P. (3rd Sgt.): *Captured*; released on oath from Fort Delaware 25 April 1864.

Hall, George W. (4th Sgt.): Enl. 18 July 1861 at Barrett's Point; *captured*; exchanged 20 or 21 February 1865.

Garrison, James R. (2nd Cpl.):

Powell, Cornelius (3rd Cpl.): *Wounded* in the thigh (leg amputated) and *captured*; died at U.S. II Corps Hospital 21 July 1863 and buried back of Schwartz's barn in Grave #17.

Driver, William H. (4th Cpl.):

Archer, Levi: Enl. 28 February 1862 at Fort Boykin; born in Isle of Wight County; *captured*; died at Fort Delaware 7 October 1863.

Atkins, James:

Battin, Monroe: Enl. 28 February 1862 at Fort Boykin.

Battin, William H.: Enl. 29 July 1861 at Barrett's Point; received a *wound* which fractured his left leg and *captured*; exchanged from Point Lookout 20 March 1864.

Betts, John D.:

Brock, Joel D.: Born in Isle of Wight County.

Cutchens, Thomas E.:

Doyles, William H.: Enl. 22 May 1863 in Isle of Wight County; *killed*.

Edwards, Joshua: Enl. 5 March 1863 at Mill Swamp Church; *wounded* and *captured*; exchanged from Chester Hospital 23 September 1863.

Edwards, Richard C.: Enl. 5 March 1863 at Mill Swamp Church.

Edwards, Richard H.: Enl. 28 February 1862 at Fort Boykin; born in Isle of Wight County; *killed*.

Garner, David: Enl. 10 May 1862 at Fort Boykin; *shot* in the shoulder and *captured*; exchanged 20 or 21 February 1865.

Garrison, Albert: Enl. 15 May 1862 at Dunn's Hill; (present in arrest at brigade guardhouse); *captured*; exchanged 22 March 1865 when mistakenly identified as an officer.

Garrison, John: Enl. 16 February 1862 at Fort Boykin; *captured*; sent to Fort Delaware 7 July 1863 after which there are no further records concerning him; probably died in prison.

Godwin, Jonathan: Enl. 4 October 1861 at Barrett's Point.

Godwin, Mills: Enl. 4 March 1862 at Fort Boykin.

Gray, Edwin: Enl. 10 March 1862 at Fort Boykin; *captured*; died of chronic diarrhea and scorbutus (scurvy) at Point Lookout 12 December 1863.

Holfoot, Robert: Enl. 13 March 1862 at Fort Boykin.

Holland, Samuel H.: Enl. 29 August 1861 at Barrett's Point.

Johnson, Benjamin R.: Enl. 21 June 1861 at Barrett's Point; *captured*; exchanged 20 or 21 February 1865.

Johnson, James A.: Enl. 28 February 1862 at Fort Boykin; (sick in hospital with lumbago since 3 July 1863); probably not in assault.

Johnson, William A.:

Nelms, Elijah: Enl. 8 May 1863 at Mill Swamp.

Parkerson, William J.: Enl. 8 May 1863 at Mill Swamp.

Pitman, John D.:

Powell, Charles W.: Enl. 28 February 1862 at Fort Boykin.

Powell, Henry J.: *Captured*; exchanged 8 May 1864.

Stephens, Jesse: Enl. 14 May 1862 at Fort Boykin; *captured*; died of smallpox at Point Lookout 26 February 1864.

Sykes, William H.: Enl. 1 July 1861 at Barrett's Point; *wounded.*

Taylor, Enos: Enl. 4 March 1862 at Fort Boykin; *shot* in the back and arm and *captured*; exchanged from DeCamp Hospital 27 September 1863.

Turner, Henry: *Captured*; exchanged 6 March 1864.

Vellines, Isaac: Enl. 28 February 1862 at Fort Boykin.

Walters, Edwin: Enl. 26 July 1861 at Barrett's Point; born in Nansemond County; *shot* in the foot and side and *captured*; exchanged from West's Buildings Hospital 24 August 1863.

Company "F"

This company enlsited 18 May 1861 at Chuckatuck, Nansemond County, Virginia for one year and was reorganized 3 May 1862.

Phillips, James Jasper (Captain): (29); VMI class of 1853; (promoted to Colonel 4 July 1863.).

Gwynn, Henry (1st Lt.): (24); *captured*; exchanged 22 March 1865.

Butts, Walter (Jr. 2nd Lt.): (20); *shot* in the lung and *captured*; treated at U.S. 1st Division, II Corps Hospital; died 11 July 1863 and buried in Yard D, Row 1 of that hospital's cemetery in Jacob Schwartz's cornfield on Rock Creek; disinterred to Richmond 13 June 1872 with 110 others in ten large boxes labeled "S."

Cowling, John E. (1st Sgt.): (23).

Bailey, Francis M. (2nd Sgt.): (19); *captured*; exchanged 15 November 1864.

Gray, Francis M. (5th Sgt.): (18).

Barradall, William J. (2nd Cpl.): (23); *captured*; died of diarrhea at Point Lookout 25 March 1864.

Beach, John T. (4th Cpl.): (23); *shot* in the leg and arm and *captured*; exchanged from West's Buildings Hospital 24 August 1863.

Boykin, James J.: Enl. 27 July 1861 at the Cedar Point Battery; (present in arrest on a charge of desertion).

Boykin, Jeremiah M.: Enl. 28 February 1862 at Cedar Point.

Brock, Benjamin F.: Enl. 22 April 1862 at Cedar Point.

Brock, James J.: Enl. 13 June 1861 at Barrett's Point; (18).

Corbell, Richard S.: Enl. 21 May 1861; (19).

Daniel, Augustus W.: Enl. 7 May 1862 at Cedar Point; *wounded.*

Daniel, Robert T.: Enl. 7 May 1862 at Cedar Point.

Dann, Silas: (21); *captured*; exchanged 20 or 21 February 1865.

Davis, George W.: Enl. 7 May 1862 at Cedar Point; *captured*; died of smallpox at Fort Delaware 17 Novebmer 1863; buried at Finns Point, N.J.

Edmonds, Henry: Enl. 20 May 1861; (19); *wounded.*

Fletcher, Stephen G.: (21); *captured*; exchanged 20 or 21 February 1865.

Godwin, Lucien J.B.: (27); *captured*; exchanged 20 or 21 February 1865.

Hodsden, Wilfred J.: (18); *shot* in the left foot and *captured*; exchanged from West's Buildings Hospital 17 November 1863.

Holladay, Joseph H.: Enl. 3 April 1863 at Ivor Station; the company reports him as "in the hands of the enemy" through August 1864 but there are no Federal records concerning him; *killed.*

Holland, Exum: (23); *captured*; exchanged 20 or 21 February 1865.

Matthews, Barnaba B.: Enl. 22 April 1862 at Cedar Point; *killed.*

Matthews, David: Enl. 22 April 1862 at Cedar Point.

Metcalf, Jesse T.: (29).

Moody, Thomas D.: (21).

Powell, Matthew W.: Enl. 17 July 1861 at the Cedar Point Battery.

Pruden, Keeney: Enl. 27 April 1862 at Cedar Point.

Purcell, Thomas: Enl. 17 March 1862 at Cedar Point; (36); *captured*; exchanged 15 November 1864.

Schwartz, Ernest: (25).

Smith, John B.: (25).

Walters, Bray: (19); seaman.

Wilson, George W.: Enl. 29 April 1862 at Cedar Point.

Company "G" ("Portsmouth Rifles")

This company was enrolled 20 April 1861 at Portsmouth and was mustered into service 30 April 1861. It was transferred to the 9th Virginia from the 3rd Regiment Virginia Volunteers sometime after 30 June 1861. This unit was reorganized 1 May 1862.

Tonkin, William F. (1st Lt.): (25); ship carpenter.

Gayle, Nathaniel G. (2nd Lt.): (26); ship carpenter.

Lewis, John H.: (Jr. 2nd Lt.): (29); carpenter; *captured* at the stone wall; released from Fort Delaware 12 June 1865.

Beaton, John K. (1st Sgt.): Enl. 21 April 1861; (26); ship carpenter.

Ballentine David W. (Sgt.): (23); house joiner; *captured*; exchanged 14 or 15 February 1865.

Dunn, John R. (Sgt.): Enl. 24 April 1861; (26); laborer; *killed.*

Gayle, Levin C. (Sgt.): Enl. 24 April 1861; (28); brick mason; *captured* at the stone wall; released on oath from Fort Delaware 9 June 1865.

Wood, John W. (Sgt.): Enl. 13 June 1861 at Pig Point; (19); ship carpenter.

Ashe, Theophilus F. (Cpl.): (21); blacksmith.

Brittingham, William H. (Cpl.): Enl. 15 May 1861 at Pig Point; (24); house joiner.

George, Thomas (Cpl.): (40); rigger.

Williams, Lemuel H. (Cpl.): Enl. 10 May 1862; *killed.*

Bennett, William B.: (18); plasterer; father was Mr. William Bennett; Pvt. Bennett had no wife or children at the time of his death; *killed.*

Bourke, Joseph B.: (25); grocer.

Boyed, Henry C.: (28); carpenter; *shot* in the knee and *captured*; exchanged from DeCamp Hospital 16 September 1863.

Brownley, William K.: (25); ship carpenter; *captured*; died of smallpox at Fort Delaware 6 November 1863; buried at Finns Point, N.J.

Burton, Robert P.: Enl. 30 April 1862; *captured*; exchanged 14 or 15 February 1865.

Buxton, John T.: (25); laborer; (sick 3 July 1863); captured at Greencastle, Pennsylvania 6 July; died of typhoid fever at Fort Delaware 15 August 1863; probably not in the assault; buried at Finns Point, N.J.

Creecy, George A.: Enl. 5 August 1861 at Pig Point; (24); carpenter.

Edwards, Oney H.: Enl. 24 April 1861; (34); cooper.

Edwards, William T.: (20); boat builder.

Emmerson, George W.: Enl. 26 March 1862; *captured*; released on oath from Fort Delaware 20 April 1865.

Etheredge, Samuel R.: Enl. 24 April 1861; (25); carpenter.

Ferebee, George W.: Enl. 24 April 1861; (25); carpenter; *captured*; exchanged 8 May 1864.

Ferebee, Joseph K.: Enl. 26 March 1862; *captured*; ; released on oath from Fort Delaware 20 April 1865.

Fiendley, James W.: Enl. 16 June 1861 at Pig Point; (25); carpenter.

Gaskins, Thomas J.: Enl. 24 April 1861; (30); cooper; *captured*; released on oath from Point Lookout 21 February 1864.

Grant, Jordan W.: Enl. 24 April 1861; (23); ship carpenter; *captured*; died of chronic diarrhea at Point Lookout 1 January 1864.

Harding, Milton: (22); carpenter; *captured*; exchanged 14 or 15 February 1865.

Hargroves, John R.: Enl. 21 April 1861; (26); mason; *shot* in the chest and *captured*; exchanged from West's Buildings Hospital 27 September 1863.

Harvey, Arthur W.: (19); clerk; *captured*; exchanged 14 or 15 February 1865.

Johnston, Theophilus: (30); painter; captured while serving as a nurse at Gettysburg 5 July 1863; exchanged from West's Buildings Hospital 27 September 1863.

Kelsic, John R.: Enl. 15 May 1861 at Pig Point; (28); painter.

Land, James W.T.: Enl. 24 April 1861; (25); blacksmith; *shot* in the right thigh and *captured*; exchanged from DeCamp Hospital 28 October 1863.

Lattimer, John W.: (25); clerk; married; received a *wound* which fractured his left leg (amputated) and *captured*; treated at U.S. 1st Division, II Corps Hospital; died at Letterman Hospital 18 September 1863 of gangrene and buried in Section 8, Grave #9 of that hospital's cemetery.

Lewis, George W.: (25); blacksmith.

Monte, William G.: Enl. 21 April 1861; (30); barber; *killed.*

Moreland, James B.: Enl. 30 April 1861; *captured*; took oath and released from Point Lookout.

Murphy, Enos; Enl. 10 May 1862.

Myers, Stephen A.: Enl. 26 March 1862.

Nash, Richard James: Enl. 20 July 1861 at Pig Point; (28 in 1863); single; *shot* in the right knee (leg amputated at thigh) and *captured*; died at Letterman Hospital 16 August 1863 and buried in Section 2, Grave #27 of that hospital's cemetery; disinterred to Richmond 13 June 1872 in Box #75.

Neville, William S.: (23); ship carpenter; *captured*; released from Fort Delaware 5 May 1865.

Owens, Thomas C.: Enl. 24 April 1861; (24); ship carpenter; *shot* in the neck; died at Pickett's Division Hospital 9 July 1863 and buried in the woods across the creek from Bream's Mill; his body was recovered prior to the general disinterment of Confederates to the South in 1872 and 1873.

Peed, Samuel S.: (24); tinner; (sick 3 July 1863); captured at Greencastle, Pennsylvania 5 July 1863; exchanged 20 or 21 February 1865; probably not in the assault..

Phillips, Henry O.: (19); ship carpenter; *shot* in the abdomen and *captured*; exchanged from DeCamp Hospital 16 September 1863.

Revell, George A.: Enl. 15 May 1861 at Pig Point; (21); carpenter; *captured*; exchanged 14 or 15 February 1865.

Revell, Randall: Enl. 26 March 1862; *wounded*.

Sale, John E.: (28); painter; received a *gunshot* in the arm resulting in a compound fracture of the right humerus and *captured*; treated at U.S. XII Corps Hospital; exchanged from DeCamp Hospital 16 September 1863.

Stewart, James T.: (28).

Tompkins, Thomas G.: (22); carpenter; left with the wounded at Williamsport, Maryland and captured the next day; exchanged 14 or 15 February 1865.

White, George D.: Enl. 26 March 1862.

Williams, Millard C.: Enl. 24 April 1863 in Nansemond County; (34 in 1864); clerk; *wounded*.

Woodhouse, Thomas C.: (19); spar maker.

Company "I" ("Craney Island Light Artillery")

This company enrolled 15 May 1861 at Churchland, Norfolk County, Virginia; was mustered into service 12 June 1861 for one year as Kilby's Battery Virginia Light Artillery; and was accepted into Confederate service 1 July 1861. The unit was reorganized 17 March 1862.

Crocker, Jules O.B. (Captain): (34); farmer; *captured*; released from Fort Delaware 10 June 1865.

Niemeyer, John C. (1st Lt.): (21 in 1863); VMI class of 1863; *shot* in the head and *killed* during the attack.

Vermillion, John (2nd Lt.): Enl. 20 April 1861 at Portsmouth in Company "K"; *captured*; released from Fort Delaware 12 June 1865.

Lewis, McKemmy (1st Sgt.): (28); farmer.

Grimes, Thomas J. (2nd Sgt.): (18); farmer.

Arthur, Francis M. (3rd Sgt.): Enl. 17 April 1862 at Pinner's Point; (23 in 1865); *captured*; exchanged 15 November 1864.

Humphlet, John T. (1st Cpl.): Enl. 11 June 1861; (18); farmer.

Capps, Josiah (Cpl.): (23); farmer; *captured*; died of smallpox at Point Lookout 24 December 1863.

Barnes, Belson: (33); farmer.

Bidgood, Willis D.: (19); student; *captured*; exchanged 15 November 1864.

Brinkley, Daniel: Enl. 19 February 1862 at Pinner's Point; (33).

Brinkley, Granville: Enl. 19 February 1862 at Pinner's Point; (22); father was Mr. David Brinkley; the company reports him as captured but there are no Federal records concerning him; *killed*.

Brinkley, Mills: Enl. 19 February 1862 at Pinner's Point; (21); the company reports him as captured but there are no Federal records concerning him; *killed*.

Carney, Richard R.: Farmer; *wounded*.

Gwynn, George W.L.: (23); farmer; *shot* through the lower third of the right leg, the ball slightly fracturing the tibia.

Harrell, Reuben: Enl. 26 April 1863 near Suffolk; *captured*; died of acute diarrhea at Fort Delaware 9 September 1863; buried at Finns Point, N.J.

Herring, Robert H.: Enl. 19 February 1862 at Pinner's Point.

Jones, Nathan E.K.: (18); farmer; *shot* in the hip and *captured*; treated at U.S. 1st Division, II Corps Hospital; exchanged from DeCamp Hospital 8 September 1863.

Jordan, John L.: (27); farmer.

Lassiter, Richard: Enl. 19 February 1862 at Pinner's Point.

Norfleet, Jesse: Enl. 19 February 1862 at Pinner's Point; (18); *captured*; died of chronic diarrhea at Fort Delaware 18 October 1863.

Parker, William J.: Enl. 19 February 1862 at Pinner's Point.

Rabey, Thomas: Enl. 19 February 1862 at Pinner's Point; *captured*; released from Fort Delaware 7 June 1865.

Riddick, Amos: Enl. 20 April 1863 at Suffolk; *wounded* and *captured*; exchanged from Chester Hospital 23 September 1863.

Skeeter, William J.: Farmer.

Stallings, Javan: Enl. 19 February 1862 at Pinner's Point; (36).

Taylor, William Benjamin: Enl. 19 February 1862 at Pinner's Point; (18); *captured*; exchanged 20 or 21 February 1865.

Taylor, Williamson B.: Enl. 19 February 1862 at Pinner's Point; (20).

Vann, William H.: Enl. 19 February 1862 at Pinner's Point; (22).

Walton, Henry: (20); farmer; *shot* in the foot and *captured*; exchanged from West's Buildings Hospital 24 August 1863.

Wilkins, George: Enl. 19 February 1862 at Pinner's Point; (35).

Wilkins, Henry: Enl. 19 February 1862 at Pinner's Point; (25).

Company "K" ("Old Dominion Guards")

This company enlisted 20 April 1861 at Portsmouth, Virginia, was mustered 30 April 1861, and was reorganized 9 May 1862..

Allen, Henry A. (Captain): *Captured*; released from Fort Delaware 11 June 1865.

Hudgins, Henry C. (1st Lt.): Enl. 27 May 1861 at Pinner's Point.

Robinson, James H. (2nd Lt.): (23 in 1863); received a flesh *wound* in the right forearm and side and *captured*; treated at U.S. 1st Division, I Corps Hospital; exchanged 15 November 1864.

Walker, James H. (1st Sgt.): *Captured*; exchanged 15 November 1864.

Bilisoly, Adolphus (2nd Sgt.):

Dashiell, Thomas J. (3rd Sgt.): *Captured*; exchanged 22 September 1864.

Williams, William Wallace (4th Sgt.): *Captured*; exchanged 14 or 15 February 1865.

Cutherell, George (2nd Cpl.): (sent to the rear sick with secondary syphilis and chronic rheumatism 4 July 1863); probably not in the assault.

James, Randolph B. (4th Cpl.):

Barnes, George D.: Enl. 23 April 1862 at Pinner's Point; received *contusions* of both shoulders and *captured*; exchanged from DeCamp Hospital 16 September 1863.

Bilisoly, Eugene E.: Enl. 20 September 1861 at Pinner's Point.

Borland, Thomas R.: Enl. 27 May 1861 at Pinner's Point.

Brooks, Eugene K.: *Captured*; exchanged 14 or 15 February 1865.

Daughtrey, Robert T.: Enl. 10 March 1862 at Pinner's Point; *captured*; exchanged 14 or 15 February 1865.

Davis, John C.A.:

Dunderdale, John A.F.: (23); druggist; father was Mr. John Dunderdale; had no wife or children at the time of his death; *wounded* in the groin; died at Pickett's Division Hospital 21 July 1863 and buried in the woods across from Bream's Mill.

Dyson, Walter:

Host, Andrew C.: Enl. 10 March 1862 at Pinner's Point; *shot* in the leg and *captured*; exchanged from West's Buildings Hospital 24 August 1863.

Jordan, Joseph W.: Enl. 18 September 1861 at Pinner' Point; *shot* in the leg and *captured*; exchanged from Chester Hospital 17 August 1863.

Williams, Edward B.: Enl. 10 March 1862 at Pinner's Point; *wounded* in the jaw and *captured*; treated at U.S. 1st Division, I Corps Hospital; exchanged 1 August 1863.

SEVEN PINES!

**Flag of the 14th Virginia Infantry
captured at one of Cushing's guns
by the 72nd Pennsylvania Infantry**

14th Virginia Volunteer Infantry Regiment

This regiment was organized 23 May 1861; was mustered into service 8 June 1861; was accepted into Confederate service 1 July 1861 with ten companies designated "A" through "K"; and was reorganized 6 May 1862. First Company "G" was transferred to the 1st Regiment Virginia Artillery as Third Company "C" about 1 May 1862. Second Company "G" of this regiment was formerly First Company "I" of the 38th Regiment Virginia Infantry.

The following listing was obtained from company April/June 1863 muster rolls captioned 30 June 1863, Chambersburg, Pennsylvania.

Company "K" reported the condition of its clothing as "not well supplied"; its military appearance as "not as good as formerly"; and its arms, accouterments, discipline and instruction as "good."

Field and Staff

Hodges, James Gregory (Colonel): Born at Portsmouth, Va. 28 December 1829; physician and Mayor of Portsmouth; wife was Mrs. Sallie W. Hodges; commissioned Colonel 17 May 1861; *killed* within 4 feet of the enemy line.

White, William (Lt. Col.): Born in Norfolk County, Va 7 January 1820; attended Yale and Medical College of Va.; graduated from the University of Pennsylvania; doctor; married Henrietta Kemp Turner; doctor at Deep Creek, Va.; Major 14th Va. 17 May 1861; promoted to Lt. Col 26 August 1862; promoted to Colonel 3 July 1863; *wounded.*

Poore, Robert Henry (Major): Born 31 May 1823; attended University of Va.; married Janetta Bankhead Magruder; lawyer; enl. 10 May 1861 at Palmyra as Captain of Company "C"; promoted Major 26 August 1862; *wounded* with Colonel Hodges within four feet of the enemy line; died at Pickett's Division Hospital and buried at Francis Bream's "north of the tavern near the burial place"; his body was subsequently removed to the U.S. XII Corps Hospital.

Jenkins, John Summerfield (Adjutant): Enl. 20 April 1861 at Portsmouth as a Private in Company "C," 16th Virginia; (28); lawyer; transferred to the 14th Virginia and appointed Adjutant 10 November 1862; *killed* with Colonel Hodges within four feet of the enemy line.

Clark, Montilla (1st Lt., AQM): Enl. 10 May 1861 at Palmyra as a Lt. in Company "C"; (35); farmer; appointed AQM 25 May 1861.

Tuttle, Ezra B. (ACS): Enl. 22 April 1861 at Paineville as a Cpl. in Company "A"; (33); teacher; appointed ACS 12 April 1862.

Leftwich, John S. (Sgt. Major): Enl. 24 April 1861 at Fancy Grove in Company "B"; (27); farmer.

Smith, John P. (QM Sgt.): Enl. 12 May 1861 at Lombardy Grove as a Private in Company "F"; (23); clerk.

Clack, John R. (Ordnance Sgt.): Detailed from Company "E"; enl. 12 May 1861 at Clarksville; (21): tobacconist.

Moorefield, William A. (Commissary Sgt.): Detailed from Company "H"; enl. 29 April 1861 at Meadville; (21); teacher.

Alvis, William J.: On extra-duty from Company "C"; enl. 10 May 1861 at Palmyra; (18); scholar.

Barbour, Shadrach H.: Detailed from Company "E"; enl. 12 May 1861 at Clarksville; (32); mason.

King, Elias W.: On extra-duty from Company "C"; enl. 27 March 1862 at Richmond.

Company "A" ("Paineville Rifles")

This company existed in 1858; was enlisted 22 April 1861 at Paineville, Amelia County, Virginia for one year; was mustered into service at Richmond 23 April 1861; and was reorganized 5 May 1862.

Chappell, Alpheus M. (Captain): (33); merchant; *wounded* in the left knee joint.

Scott, Sidney (1st Lt.): (30); carpenter.

Hatcher, Thomas A. (2nd Lt.): Enl. 12 May 1861 at Lombardy Grove in Company "F"; (23); planter; VMI class of 1858; *wounded* and *captured*; exchanged 22 March 1865.

Perrin, John I. (3rd Lt.): (22); farmer; *killed.*

Lester, Giles W. (1st Sgt.): (27); carpenter.

Wingo. Benjamin M. (3rd Sgt.): (31); carpenter.

Atkins, Thomas S. (4th Sgt.): (25); farmer.

Bell, Nathan W. (1st Cpl.): (29); carpenter; *shot* in the left shoulder joint and left humerus (fractured), and *captured*; treated at U.S. XII Corps Hospital; exchanged from West's Buildings Hospital 17 November 1863.

Foster, James M. (3rd Cpl.): (28); overseer.

Ashburn, Thomas J.: Enl. 5 May 1862 at Suffolk.

Bell, Christopher C.: (27); carpenter; *killed.*

Bell, Samuel E.: Enl. 13 June 1861 at Jamestown; (31); wife was Mrs. Maria E. Bell; *captured*; died of smallpox at Point Lookout 9 December 1863.

Burton, John A.: Enl. 23 March 1862 at Petersburg.

Collins, Elliott E.: Enl. 5 May 1862 at Suffolk; *captured*; released from Fort Delaware 22 June 1865.

Davis, William S.: Enl. 12 March 1862.

Deaton, John H.: (24); farmer.

Dowdy, Richard B.: (24); carpenter.

Dowdy, Robert M.: (27); carpenter.

Ellis, James T.:

Farriss, John A.: Enl. 31 July 1862 in Amelia County.

Gills, Peter M.: Enl. 9 August 1861 at Spratley's; *shot* in the thigh and *captured*; paroled for exchange from West's Buildings Hospital 22 August 1863.

Holland, Zachary T.: Enl. 5 May 1862 at Suffolk.

Jackson, William: Enl. 5 May 1862 at Suffolk; *captured*; died of chronic diarrhea at Point Lookout 10 November 1863.

Johnson, Robert J.: Enl. 5 May 1862 at Suffolk; resided in Nansemond County.

O'Kennon, Peter: Enl. 23 April 1861 at Richmond; (17); laborer.

Perrin, James V.: Enl. 19 August 1862 in Amelia County; captured sick at Gettysburg; treated at U.S. 1st Division, II Corps Hospital; exchanged from Chester Hospital 23 September 1863; may not have been in the assault.

Pollard, James E.: (17); laborer; (present under arrest for desertion).

Pollard, Joseph R.: Enl. 12 March 1862.

Rawls, Francis H.: Enl. 5 May 1862 at Suffolk.

Roberts, John C.: (22); carpenter.

Roberts, William H.: (17); carpenter; (present under arrest for desertion).

Rucker, Alfred R.: (37); overseer; *captured*; exchanged 14 or 15 February 1865.

Russell, William T.: Enl. 5 May 1862 at Suffolk.

Scott, Albert S.: Enl. 12 March 1862; *captured*; exchanged sick with acute rheumatism 30 April 1864.

Scott, James M.: Enl. 11 March 1863 in Amelia County; born in Amelia County; *killed.*

Scott, William H.: (19); farmer; *captured*; exchanged 8 May 1864.

Seay, Bernard A.: (20); laborer; *captured*; exchanged 8 May 1864.

Seay, Richard D.: (23); overseer; *shot* in the right arm (amputated at the shoulder), and *captured*; exchanged from West's Buildings Hospital 27 September 1863.

Sheffield, George W.: Enl. 4 July 1862 at Amelia.

Thompson, John W.: Enl. 6 June 1861 at Jamestown; (22); laborer.

Company "B" ("Bedford Rifle Greys")

This company enlisted 24 April 1861 at Fancy Grove, Bedford County, Virginia; was mustered into service at Richmond 26 April 1861; and was reorganized 6 May 1862.

Smith, James A. (Captain): (24); farmer; *killed.*

Turner, Alexander W. (1st Lt.): Enl. 2 July 1861 at Jamestown Island; *captured*; exchanged 22 March 1865.

Smith, Benjamin H. (2nd Lt.): Enl. 2 July 1861 at Jamestown Island; *killed.*

Burnett, Elisha C. (3rd Lt.): (30); farmer.

Goad, Vincent C. (1st Sgt.): Enl. 2 July 1861 at Jamestown Island; *shot* in the thigh and *captured*; treated at U.S. 1st Division, II Corps Hospital; exchanged from Chester Hospital 23 September 1863.

Owen, William O. (2nd Sgt.): (23); farmer.

Tinsley, Thomas H. (3rd Sgt.): (25); clerk; *wounded* in both feet and *captured*; exchanged from West's Buildings Hospital 24 August 1863.

Hackworth, Uriah (4th Sgt.): (39); farmer.

Rover, Armistead D. (5th Sgt.): (27); farmer; *shot* in the right arm (amputated at upper third); and *captured*; treated at U.S. XII Corps Hospital; exchanged from West's Buildings Hospital 27 September 1863.

Terry, John W. (1st Cpl.): (22); farmer.

Wilson, Alpheus S. (2nd Cpl.): Enl. 12 July 1861 at Jamestown Island; *wounded* in the mouth and *captured*; exchanged from West's Buildings Hospital 24 August 1863.

Overstreet, Jesse W. (3rd Cpl.): Enl. 26 July 1861 at Jamestown Island; died of unknown causes at Winchester, Virginia hospital 29 July 1863 and buried in Grave #1171 of the Winchester Cemetery; possibly mortally *wounded* at Gettsyburg.

Arthur, Elkana: Enl. 26 February 1863 at Chester Station; *captured*; died of smallpox at Fort Delaware 13 December 1863; buried at Finns Point, N.J.

Ashwell, John B.: (33); farmer.

Ashwell, William B.: (34); farmer.

Ayres, Nathaniel M.: (24); farmer; *captured*; died at Point Lookout 6 April 1864.

Bates, John C.: Enl. 2 July 1861 at Jamestown Island.

Burnett, James C.: (23); farmer.

Cundiff, Alfred B.: Enl. 29 September 1862 at Winchester; *captured*; exchanged 21 January 1865.

Cundiff, John B.: (22); farmer.

Dobyns, Colita W.: (28); farmer.

Dowdy, John A.: Enl. 1 April 1862 at Suffolk; *killed.*

Gregory, James R.: (30); farmer; wife was Mrs. Matilda Gregory.

Hackworth, Elijah: Enl. 1 April 1862 at Suffolk; *shot* in the leg and *captured*; exchanged from DeCamp Hospital 16 September 1863.

Hackworth, George D.: Enl. 1 April 1862 at Suffolk; *captured*; died of an inflammation of the liver at Fort Delaware 21 May 1864; buried at Finns Point, N.J.

Hackworth, Taswell W.: Enl. 5 March 1863 at Petersburg.

Harris, John W.: (31); shoemaker.

Hogan, James E.: Enl. 1 April 1862 at Suffolk; *wounded.*

Hogan, William H.: Enl. 15 May 1861 at Richmond; mother was Mrs. M.M. Hogan; (25); farmer; *killed.*

Howell, Alexander F.: (35); farmer.

Howell, Nicodemus L.: (24); farmer; AWOL 25 July through 26 October 1863.

Jacobs, Thomas A.: (31); farmer; *captured*; exchanged sick with acute diarrhea 1 August 1863; died at a Petersburg hospital 13 August 1863.

Johnson, James T.: (20); *captured*; exchanged 14 or 15 February 1865.

Johnson, William W.: Enl. 29 September 1862 at Winchester; sick with chronic diarrhea 3 July 1863 and subsequently captured; exchanged from DeCamp Hospital 8 September 1863; probably not in the assault.

Langhon, Isham: (38); farmer; received a gunshot *wound* of the left shoulder which fractured the clavicle.

Leftwich, Lynch A.: Enl. 10 June 1862 at Richmond; AWOL 18 July through 27 October 1863.

Mitchell, William W.: (23); farmer.

Musgrove, Christopher A.: Enl. 25 May 1862 at Petersburg.

Newman, Callohill M.: Enl. 26 July 1861 at Jamestown Island; wife was Mrs. Julia A. Newman; *captured*; died at Point Lookout 21 August 1864.

Overstreet, Samuel W.: Enl. 5 September 1862 at Leesburg; deserted 18 July 1863 and captured 30 July 1863; at U.S. hospital at Winchester, Virginia; exchanged prior to 20 September 1863.

Scott, John D.: (24); farmer.

Sims, William B.: Enl. 26 April 1862 at Suffolk; *killed*.

Snow, William J.: (28); farmer; *shot* in the shoulder, hand, and leg and *captured*; treated at U.S. 2nd Division, II Corps Hospital; exchanged from Chester Hospital 23 September 1863.

Tinsley, Homer: Enl. 1 April 1862 at Suffolk; reported as "sick since 3 July 1863"; probably *wounded* as most of the soldiers noted as sick on this company's rolls turned out to be wounded.

Tinsley, Jerome: Enl. 15 May 1861 at Richmond; (22); farmer; *captured*; at West's Buildings Hospital 26 July 1863 cause not recorded; exchanged 14 or 15 February 1865.

Tuck, Davis: Enl. 19 March 1863 at Petersburg.

Tuck, George: Enl. 26 February 1863 at Chester Station.

Tuck, Joseph D.: Enl. 1 April 1862 at Suffolk.

Tuck, Stephen H.: Enl. 19 March 1863 at Petersburg.

Tuck, Thomas: Enl. 19 March 1863 at Petersburg.

Updike, William A.: Enl. 1 April 1862 at Suffolk.

West, John A.: Enl. 1 April 1862 at Suffolk.

West, Robert G.: Enl. 1 April 1862 at Suffolk.

Woodford, William S.: (19); farmer.

Company "C" ("Fluvanna Rifle Guard")

Organized in January 1860, this company enlisted 10 May 1861 at Palmyra, Fluvanna County, Virginia; was mustered into service at Richmond 12 May 1861; and was reorganized 6 May 1862.

Perkins, Archelaus (Captain): (31); clerk; *captured*; exchanged sick with chronic diarrhea 8 May 1864.

Morris, Thomas C. (1st Lt.): (22); clerk; *captured*; exchanged 22 March 1865.

Frith, William M. (2nd Lt.): (23); coach painter.

Seay, Philip G. (Jr. 2nd Lt.): Enl. 26 May 1861 at Richmond; (23); merchant; *shot* in the abdomen and *captured*; exchanged 22 March 1865.

Martin, Joseph H. (1st Sgt.): (18); clerk; *captured*; exchanged 20 or 21 February 1865.

Payne, Benjamin H. (2nd Sgt.): (19); farmer.

Richardson, Richard J. (3rd Sgt.): (21); clerk; *captured*; exchanged 20 or 21 February 1865.

Payne, Tucker W. (4th Sgt.): (21); farmer; *captured*; exchanged 14 or 15 February 1865.

Taylor, John W. (5th Sgt.): (30); carpenter.

Sclater, Morton T. (2nd Cpl.): (28); farmer; *captured*; exchanged 20 or 21 February 1865.

Martin, James B. (3rd Cpl.): (22); farmer; born in Fluvanna County; *shot* in the right arm (amputated), and *captured*; died at U.S. XII Corps Hospital 10 July 1863.

Smith, Nathaniel H. (4th Cpl.): (26); miller; *captured*; exchanged 16 March 1865.

Ballenger, Isaac: Enl. 7 October 1862 at Winchester; received a *wound* which fractured his right scapula, and *captured*; exchanged 6 March 1864.

Bugg, Lucius T.: (17); miller; *killed*.

Busby, Edward M.: (22); farmer.

Chiles, John C.: Enl. 8 August 1862 at Richmond; (19 in 1863); father was Mr. Alfred H. Chiles; born in Fluvanna County; *shot* in the head and *captured*; treated at U.S. 2nd Division, II Corps Hospital: died at Chester Hospital 9 August 1863 of a hemorrhage, and buried in Grave #128 of that hospital's cemetery.

Denton, James M.: Enl. 3 April 1862 at Orange Court House; transferred from Company "E," 28th Virginia 28 June 1863; *captured*; exchanged 28 December 1863.

Foster, James A.: (18); farmer; *captured*; released from Fort Delaware 22 June 1865.

Glass, John: (30); farmer; born in Fluvanna County; the company reports him as missing in action "supposed *killed*"; there are no Federal records concerning him.

Haley, James M.: (20); farmer.

Hobbs, Eldbridge L.: Enl. 3 March 1863 at Petersburg; born in Prince George County.

Houchens, Joseph W.: (23); farmer.

Hunter, George F.:

Johnson, Henry M.: (23); coach maker; born in Louisa County; *shot* in the thigh and *captured*; exchanged from Chester Hospital 17 August 1863.

Kirtley, Bushrod C.: (18); coach maker.

Kirtley, Samuel C.: (23); school teacher; *captured*; joined U.S. service 24 January 1864.

Lane, William G.: Born in Fluvanna County; the company reports him as missing in action, and subsequently as captured, then "supposed *killed*"; there are no Federal records concerning him.

Lewis, John R.: (23); farmer.

Loving, Richard J.: Enl. 8 August 1862 at Richmond; born in Fluvanna County; *captured*; died of typhoid fever at Fort Delaware 25 August 1863; buried at Finns Point, N.J.

Mathews, John J.: (30); brickmason; born in Goochland County; *captured*; died of typhoid fever at Fort Delaware 10 September 1863; buried at Finns Point, N.J.

McLain, James E.:

Moon, Julian K.: (23); carpenter; severely *wounded* in the hip and *captured*; there are no further records of him after 15 October 1863; probably died in prison.

Morris, George H.: (23); clerk; *wounded.*

Morris, John Henry: Enl. 27 March 1862 at Richmond; deserted near Culpeper Court House 26 July 1863.

Morris, John Hillary: Enl. 8 August 1862 at Richmond.

Morris, John W.: Enl. 27 March 1862 at Richmond; *captured*; died at Point Lookout 26 December 1863.

Morris, Robert B.: (19); farmer.

Murray, Lafayette: (18); farmer.

Noel, Thomas F.: (32); farmer; *wounded.*

Pace, Archibald B.: Enl. 27 March 1862 at Richmond; the company reports him as missing in action "supposed *killed*"; there are no Federal records concerning him.

Pace, William J.: Enl. 27 March 1862 at Richmond.

Parrish, William G.: (28); farmer; received a *gunshot* fracture of the right elbow (arm amputated), and *captured*; treated at U.S. 1st Division, I Corps Hospital; exchanged from West's Buildings Hospital 17 November 1863.

Payne, George A.: (18); farmer.

Richardson, John S.: (18); farmer; the company reports him initially as missing in action and subsequently as captured, then "supposed *killed*"; there are no Federal records concerning him.

Richardson, Robert S.: Enl. 12 May 1861; (19); scholar.

Ross, James E.: Enl. 27 March 1862 at Richmond; the company reports him as missing in action "supposed *killed*"; there are no Federal records concerning him.

Ross, William D.: (24); farmer; the company reports him as missing in action "supposed *killed*"; there are no Federal records concerning him.

Seay, Fleming P.: (23); cooper.

Seay, Richard B.: Enl. 26 May 1861 at Richmond; (19); farmer; *captured*; exchanged 8 May 1864.

Shepherd, Abraham, Jr.: (18); farmer.

Shiflett, Thomas: (23); farmer; born in Albemarle County; *wounded* in the arm and cheek near the eye (bone fractured), and *captured*; exchanged from Chester Hospital 23 September 1863.

Thomas, James J.: (32); carpenter.

Thurmond, Merideth B.: Enl. 17 May 1861 at Richmond; (36); boatman; born in Chesterfield County; deserted near Culpeper Court House 26 July 1863; returned to his company 6 March 1864.

Wescoat, James R.: (20); carpenter.

White, William M.: Enl. 8 August 1862 at Richmond.

Wren, William O.: (22); farmer; *wounded* and *captured*; exchanged from Chester Hospital 23 September 1863.

Company "D" ("Chesterfield Central Guards")

Organized by mid-February 1860, this company enlisted 24 April 1861 at Chesterfield Court House, Chesterfield County, Virginia; was mustered into service at Richmond 25 April 1861; and was reorganized 5 May 1862.

Cogbill, W.W.T. (Capt.): (39); clerk; *killed.*

Taylor, John S. (1st Lt.): Farmer, *shot* in the thigh and *captured*; treated at U.S. 2nd Division, II Corps Hospital; released from Fort Delaware 12 June 1865.

Adkins, Sydenham P. (2nd Lt.): Farmer; *killed.*

Chalkley, Gideon P. (3rd Lt.): Merchant; *shot* in the right knee (leg amputated at the lower third of the right thigh) and *captured*; exchanged 13 December 1864.

Godsey, Hiram W. (1st Sgt.): Farmer; *killed.*

Perkinson, John E. (2nd Sgt.): Bricklayer.

Wilkinson, William L. (3rd Sgt.): Farmer.

Wilkinson, George C. (4th Sgt.): Farmer.

Adkins, John T. (5th Sgt.): Enl. 29 May 1861 at Hermitage Fairgrounds; farmer; *wounded* in the leg and *captured*; exchanged from DeCamp Hospital 16 September 1863.

Wells, William W. (2nd Cpl.): Farmer; probably *wounded* and *captured*; exchanged 1 August 1863.

Sculley, Charles I. (3rd Cpl.): Enl. 18 June 1861 at Jamestown Island; farmer; *captured*; died at Point Lookout 29 March 1865.

Moore, George T.: (4th Cpl.): Enl. 2 August 1861 at Camp Hodges; *killed.*

Cogbill, John A. (Musician): Enl. 25 March 1862 at Camp Randolph.

Gill, William C. (Musician): Enl. 18 January 1863 near Guinea Station.

Jackson, Andrew (Musician): Enl. 15 March 1862 at Camp Randolph.

Baugh, William F.: Enl. 15 August 1862; *wounded* and *captured*; exchanged from DeCamp Hospital 8 September 1863.

Chalkley, Alonzo M.: Farmer.

Cheatham, Newton F.: Enl. 21 July 1861 at Jamestown Island; *captured*; died at Point Lookout 20 January 1864.

Cheatham, Samuel O.: Enl. 29 May 1861 at Hermitage Fairgrounds; *shot* in both legs and *captured*; died at U.S. II Corps Hospital 17 July 1863 and buried in Yard D, Row 1 of that hospital's cemetery; disinterred to Richmond with 110 others in ten large boxes lableled "S" 13 June 1872.

Childress, William Y.: Farmer; the company reports him as having been captured but there are no Federal records concerning him; *killed.*

Cogbill, Marcus Aurelius: Farmer.

Cotton, Charles W.: Farmer; born in Chesterfield County; *captured*; exchanged sick with chronic diarrhea 31 July 1863; died at a Petersburg, Virginia hospital 9 August 1863.

Dunnavant, William A.: Enl. 26 April 1861; bricklayer.

Dunston, Fielding T.: Enl. 25 July 1861 at Camp Hodges; *captured*; died at Point Lookout 11 August 1864.

Dunston, James H.: Enl. 29 May 1861 at Hermitage Fairgrounds; (25 in 1863); cabinet maker; *wounded* in the right hip (illium), and *captured*; died at Letterman Hospital 12 September 1863 and buried in Section 7, Grave #35 of that hospital's cemetery; disinterred to Richmond 13 June 1872 in Box #78.

Dunston, John N.: Farmer.

Everett, Isaac W.: Enl. 6 May 1862 at Camp Randolph; resided in Nansemond County.

Fuqua, William R.: (22 in 1862); carpenter.

Gill, William F., Jr.: Enl. 4 June 1861 at Jamestown Island; farmer; *shot* in the shoulder and *captured*; exchanged 1 August 1863.

Gregory, Gustavus C.: Enl. 15 August 1862.

Hall, William T.: Enl. 4 May 1862 at Camp Randolph; resided in Chesterfield County.

Howlett, Thomas T.: Enl. 8 March 1862 at Camp Randolph.

Hughes, Anthony T.: Enl. 4 March 1862 at Suffolk; *shot* in the arm, leg, and thigh and *captured*; exchanged from DeCamp Hospital 27 September 1863.

Jackson, Joseph A.: Enl. 29 May 1861 at Hermitage Fairgrounds; farmer; resided in Chesterfield County.

Johnson, Henry B.: Railroad hand.

McGee, Richard H.: Farmer.

Partin, Daniel W.: Farmer; *shot* in the left arm above the elbow, and *captured*; treated at U.S. 1st Division, I Corps Hospital; died at Penn College Hospital 23 July 1863 and buried in the hospital's cemetery on the north side of the college; disinterred to Richmond 17 May 1873 with 34 others in three large boxes labeled "E."

Perdue, Everett M.: Enl. 25 March 1862 at Camp Randolph; *killed*.

Perdue, William Thomas: Miller; *killed*.

Perkinson, Andrew B.: Bricklayer; *captured*; exchanged sick with acute diarrhea 22 September 1864.

Phillips, Samuel F.: Enl. 29 August 1861 at Camp Hodges.

Rogers, Jesse W.: Enl. 1 August 1862 in Chesterfield County.

Rowlett, John F.: Farmer.

Taylor, Benjamin:

Wilkinson, Henry C.: Enl. 20 May 1862 at Camp Hare; *captured*; died of diphtheria at Point Lookout 3 December 1863.

Wilkinson, Joseph H.: Farmer.

Winfree, George: Farmer; *captured*; exchanged 15 November 1864.

Winfree, Joseph: Tobacconist; shot in the leg and *captured*; exchanged from DeCamp Hospital 16 September 1863.

Company "E" ("Clarksville Blues")

This company enlisted 12 May 1861 at Clarksville, Mecklenburg County, Virginia; was mustered into service at Richmond 17 May 1861; and was reorganized 6 May 1862.

Yancey, William H. (1st Lt.): (20); farmer; *killed*.

Finch, George B. (2nd Lt.): (23); teacher; *wounded* in the hip joint.

Lewis, John T. (Jr. 2nd Lt.): (20); farmer; *shot* in the finger and hips, and *captured*; treated at U.S. 1st Division, II Corps Hospital; released from Fort Delaware 12 June 1865.

Lewis, Richard B. (1st Sgt.): Enl. 7 April 1862 at Suffolk (transferred from Company "I," 14th Virginia); *shot* in the hips and *captured*; treated at U.S. 1st Division, II Corps Hospital; exchanged 1 August 1863.

Elam, William A. (2nd Sgt.): (23); farmer; *captured*; exchanged 20 or 21 February 1865.

Swann, James M. (3rd Sgt.): (18); jeweler.

Pool, John E.P. (4th Sgt.): Enl. 18 October 1861 at Land's End; born in Halifax County; the company reports him as missing in action "supposed *killed*"; there are no Federal records concerning him.

Taylor, Robert H. (1st Cpl.): (18); farmer; born in Mecklenburg County; the company reports him as missing in action "supposed *killed*"; there are no Federal records concerning him.

Yancey, Charles D. (3rd Cpl.): *Wounded* and *captured*; exchanged from Chester Hospital 17 August 1863.

Harris, William A. (4th Cpl.): (18); farmer; *shot* in the right hip and *captured*; treated at U.S. XII Corps Hospital; exchanged 20 or 21 February 1865.

Allcott, Philo E.: (22); teacher.

Averett, William J.: (22); farmer; *wounded*.

Binford, James L.: (22); farmer; born in Mecklenburg County; *killed*.

Blanks, John L.: (19); farmer; received a *gunshot* fracture of the lower third of the right thigh, and *captured*; exchanged from West's Buildings Hospital 24 August 1863.

Brewer, Edward B.: (21); farmer.

Duncum, Richard: Enl. 7 April 1862 at Suffolk; resided in Halifax County; *wounded* and *captured*; treated at U.S. 1st Division, II Corps Hospital; died of smallpox at Point Lookout 1 December 1863.

Duncum, Thomas: Enl. 7 April 1862 at Suffolk; resided in Halifax County; *captured*; died of smallpox at Point Lookout 5 December 1863.

Easley, Frederick B.: (25); clerk; *wounded* and *captured*; died at U.S. II Corps Hospital and buried on Jacob Schwartz's lane, near the creek, under a walnut tree.

Geoghegan, Joel W.: (25); tabacconist; *captured*; exchanged 15 November 1864.

Glasscock, James, Jr.: Enl. 7 April 1862 at Suffolk; born in Mecklenburg County; *captured*; died at Fort Delaware 21 July 1863.

Graves, George R.: (21); mechanic.

Green, Eli T.: (22); saddler; single; (23 in 1863); recieved a *gunshot* fracture of the right arm below the elbow (arm amputated at shoulder joint) and shot in the right hip, and *captured*; treated at U.S. 1st Division, I Corps Hospital; died at Letterman Hospital 15 August 1863 and buried in an unknown grave; currently buried in Section D, Grave 61, Pennsylvania plot, Soldiers' National Cemetery, Gettysburg.

Jones, George W.: Enl. 16 May 1862 at Petersburg; *wounded* and *captured*; exchanged 1 August 1863.

Lackey, Samuel L.: (26); millwright; born at Lincoln, North Carolina.

Loafman, Allen C.: (23); farmer; *shot* in the left wrist and *captured*; exchanged from West's Buildings Hospital 27 September 1863.

Martin, William G.: *Wounded.*

McFarlin, William H.: (23); merchant.

Neal, James H.: Enl. 7 April 1862 at Suffolk.

Newton, Joseph: (23); farmer; *wounded* in the left foot (leg amputated), and *captured*; exchanged from West's Buildings Hospital 17 November 1863.

Oakes, Thomas H.: Enl. 23 April 1861 at Richmond; *shot* and *captured*; treated at U.S. 3rd Division, II Corps Hospital; exchanged from Chester Hospital 17 August 1863.

Park, Charles T.: (23); carpenter; *wounded* in the right arm (amputated at forearm) and right hip, and *captured*; exchanged from West's Buildings Hospital 27 September 1863.

Park, Thomas A.: (20); carpenter; *captured*; exchanged 15 November 1864.

Puryear, Isaiah: (22); farmer; *wounded.*

Ramsey, James Y.: (25); farmer; *shot* in the left knee and *captured*; exchanged from West's Buildings Hospital 17 November 1863.

Ramsey, William B.: (23); farmer; born in Mecklenburg County; received a *wound* which fractured his thigh, and *captured*; died at U.S. II Corps Hospital 25 July 1863 and buried in Grave #3 in back of Schwartz's barn.

Reynolds, Samuel T.: (29); farmer; *wounded* and *captured*; exchanged from West's Buildings Hospital 27 September 1863.

Richardson, John T.: (21); tobacconist.

Scott, Robert Graham: *Killed*; currently buried under a separate grave stone in Hollywood cemetery, Richmond, Va.

Smith, James C.: Enl. 26 March 1863 at Richmond.

Smith, William J.A.: (20); farmer; possibly *wounded*; admitted to Danville Virginia Hospital 21 July 1863.

Twisdale, George W.: Enl. 7 April 1862 at Suffolk; *captured*; exchanged 20 or 21 February 1865.

Woltz, Thomas H.: Enl. 1 May 1863 near Suffolk.

Yancey, Jordan L.: (24); farmer.

Company "F" ("Chambliss Grays")

This company enlisted 12 May 1861 at Lombardy Grove, Mecklenburg County, Virginia; was mustered into service at Richmond 17 May 1861; and was reorganized 5 May 1862.

Farrar, John P. (Capt.): (25); planter.

Read, Stephen P. (1st Lt.): (20); merchant.

Curtis, William C. (2nd Lt.): (26); school teacher; *wounded.*

Johnson, John L. (Jr. 2nd Lt.): Enl. 17 July 1861 at Jamestown; born in Mecklenburg County; *wounded*; died at Pickett's Division Hospital 3 July 1863 and buried at Bream's Mill on the hill; disinterred to Richmond 3 August 1872 with 33 others in three large boxes marked "P Curns."

Smith, Henry E. (1st Sgt.): (25); planter; *shot* in the arm, the ball injuring the spine, and *captured*; treated at U.S. 2nd Division, II Corps Hospital; exchanged from Chester Hospital 17 August 1863.

Farrar, Robert R. (2nd Sgt.): (22); planter.

Cliborne, Darius (3rd Sgt.): (23); *captured*; exchanged 21 January 1865.

May, Charles E. (4th Sgt.): (23); teacher.

Curtis, Charles A. (1st Cpl.): (21); planter; *shot* in the neck and *captured*; exchanged from DeCamp Hospital 28 August 1863.

Curtis, Zachariah W. (3rd Cpl.): (23); overseer; *wounded* in the left arm and *captured*; exchanged 1 August 1863.

Smith, Richard J. (4th Cpl.): Enl. 1 April 1862.

Andrews, Varney O.: (19); student; *captured*; exchanged 14 or 15 February 1865.

Bracey, Virginius S.: Enl. 16 May 1861 at Petersburg; (23); clerk.

Burton, Lucas: Enl. 1 May 1862 at Suffolk.

Carroll, H.B.: Enl. 1 April 1862; *captured*; exchanged 5 October 1864.

Crowder, George W.: Enl. 1 November 1861 at Land's End; born in Mecklenburg County; *wounded*; died of his wounds 22 or 31 July 1863; there are no Federal hospitals records concerning him; probably died in an unknown Confederate hospital.

Crowder, Richard W.: (23); planter.

Farrar, Alexander J.: Enl. 26 May 1861 at Richmond; (21); clerk.

Farrar, William H.: Enl. 21 July 1862 at Boydton; *shot* in the arm and *captured*; exchanged from Chester Hospital 17 August 1863.

Fennell, Joseph J.C.: Enl. 6 August 1862 at Osborne's.

Gregory, Richard H.: Enl. at Clarksville in Company "E"; born in Mecklenburg County; (19); clerk; *killed.*

Hazlewood, Robert R.R. Enl. 17 July 1861 at Jamestown.

Heath, James E.: (20); student; *shot* in the left arm and *captured*; treated at U.S. XII Corps Hospital; exchanged 18 September 1864.

House, Richard J.: Enl. 1 May 1862 at Suffolk; born in Mecklenburg County; died of "debilitas" at Blacks and Whites Hospital, Virginia 31 August 1863.

Insco, Isaac: Enl. 1 May 1862 at Suffolk; *captured*; died of scurvy at Fort Delaware 25 November 1863; buried at Finns Point, N.J.

Insco, Robert O.: Enl. 1 May 1862 at Suffolk; (25 in 1862); mechanic; *captured*; died of pneumonia at Fort Delaware 28 August 1863.

Jones, Edward C.: Enl. 1 May 1862 at Suffolk.

Jones, John C.: Enl. 1 May 1862 at Suffolk.

Jones, Walter L.: (23); planter; *shot* in the thigh and *captured*; exchanged from West's Buildings Hospital 24 August 1863.

Jones, Williamson: Enl. 1 April 1862; father was Mr. Zack Jones.

Langley, John, Jr.: (21); planter; *captured*; exchanged 15 October 1864.

McNulley, James: Enl. 27 October 1862 at Winchester; (46 in 1865); laborer; received a *contusion* of the ankle, and *captured*; exchanged 20 or 21 February 1865.

Nicholson, Richard H.: (21); planter; born in Mecklenburg County; *killed.*

Phillips, William H.: (25); planter.

Rainey, P.L.: Enl. 1 August 1862 at Falling Creek; born in Mecklenburg County; *killed.*

Rudd, George W.: (24); carpenter.

Simmons, Benjamin W.: (19); clerk; died of typhoid fever at Chimborazo Hosptial #1, Richmond 26 July 1863.

Smith, John A.: Enl. 3 August 1861 at Camp Hodges.

Thompson, George W.: Enl. 1 May 1862 at Suffolk; born in Mecklenburg County; *killed.*

Thompson, Richard C.: Enl. 17 July 1861 at Jamestown; born in Mecklenburg County; father was Mr. Nicholas C. Thompson; *captured*; died at Point Lookout 17 February 1864.

Thompson, Thomas B.: Enl. 19 April 1863 at Suffolk.

Tucker, William R.: Enl. 9 July 1861 at Jamestown.

Vaughan, S.L.: Enl. 1 May 1862 at Suffolk.

Wade, William F.: Enl. 1 April 1862.

Walker, Chastain C.: (23); planter.

Warren, John J.: (19); clerk.

<u>Second Company "G"</u>

This company enlisted 20 June 1861 at Clarksville, Mecklenburg County, Virginia for one year, and was reorganized 29 April 1862. The company was transferred from the 38th Virginia Infantry Regiment 27 June 1862.

Wood, William Walter (Capt.): Enl. 12 May 1861 as a 2nd Lt. in Company "E"; (22); attorney.

Yancey, Joseph S. (1st Lt.): Enl. 29 April 1862; *wounded*; died 4 July 1863.

Vaughan, Peter G. (Jr. 2nd Lt.):

Talley, Henry M. (1st Sgt.): *Wounded* in both feet and *captured*; exchanged from DeCamp Hospital 8 September 1863.

Griffin, William L. (3rd Sgt.):

Overbey, P.H. (5th Sgt.): Enl. 20 April 1862 in New Orleans, Louisiana; transferred to this regiment from the 14th Louisiana Regiment 24 September 1862; *killed.*

Moore, Henry M. (1st Cpl.): Enl. 20 February 1862; born in Mecklenburg County; *wounded* in the right side and thigh and *captured*; exchanged from Chester Hospital 17 August 1863.

Nelson, William G. (2nd Cpl.): Enl. 28 February 1862; wife was Mrs. Susan M. Nelson, the couple had one child; slightly *wounded.*

Yancey, A.C. (3rd Cpl.): Enl. 1 August 1862; *killed.*

Averett, James Y.: Enl. 8 March 1862; *captured*; exchanged 22 September 1864.

Chandler, L.B.: Enl. 10 March 1862; *shot* in the left thigh (flesh wound), and head, and *captured*; treated at U.S. XII Corps Hospital; exchanged from DeCamp Hospital 28 August 1863.

Chandler, M.C.: *Shot* in the shoulder and *captured*; exchanged from West's Buildings Hospital 24 August 1863.

Clark, James M.: Enl. 12 March 1862; (appointed 5th Sgt. from the ranks 3 July 1863).

Cook, Benjamin S.: Enl. 26 April 1861 at Townesville, North Carolina in Company "B," 12th North Carolina Regiment; transferred to the 14th Virginia 5 March 1863; AWOL 5 August through 26 August 1863.

Cook, William H.:

Cox, Eli: Enl. 17 March 1862; *wounded* in the left hand.

Cox, Elijah H.: Enl. 1 March 1862; *killed.*

Cox, James: Enl. 12 March 1862.

Cox, William:

Daniel, Lat A.: *Captured*; released from Fort Delaware 7 June 1865.

Daniel, Lewis T.: Enl. 28 February 1862; (40 in 1863); farmer; *wounded* in the sixth right rib and thigh, and *captured*; exchanged from West's Buildings Hospital 17 November 1863.

Daniel, Stephen A.: *Captured*; released from Fort Delaware 19 June 1865.

Earles, Rufus: *Captured*; apparently slightly *wounded*; served as a nurse at Gettysburg; exchanged from DeCamp Hospital 28 August 1863.

Garrett, James W.: Enl. 18 March 1862.

Gold, John B.:

Gold, William:

Gregory, Theodore B.: Enl. 19 March 1862.

Griffin, Andrew J.: Enl. 6 March 1862; *killed.*

Griffin, John R.:

Griffin, Ralph: Enl. 1 March 1862; probably *wounded*; *captured*; released from Fort Delaware 22 June 1865.

Hendrick, Lucius J.: Enl. 20 March 1862; captured sick 5 July 1863; exchanged from DeCamp Hospital 28 August 1863.

Hopgood, Albert:

James, Richard: Enl. 4 March 1862; *shot* in the upper left arm (amputated) and *captured*; treated at U.S. 1st Division, I Corps Hospital; there are no further records concerning him; he apparently died in a Federal hospital or prison.

Jones, Peter: Enl. 12 March 1862.

Jones, Thomas Jefferson: Born in Mecklenburg County; *captured*; died at Fort Delaware 7 March 1864.

Keeter, James: Enl. 5 March 1862.

Lockett, Philip: Enl. 12 May 1861 at Lombardy Grove in Company "F"; (19); student; *wounded* and *captured*; exchanged 1 August 1863.

Matthews, J. Kemp: Born in Mecklenburg County; *wounded* and *captured*; exchanged from DeCamp Hospital 16 September 1863.

Moore, John B.: Enl. 1 March 1862; *captured*; died of typhoid pneumonia at Fort Delaware 4 August 1863; buried at Finns Point, N.J.

Murray, R.A.: *Killed.*

Nethery, George D.: Severely *wounded.*

Newton, Henry J.: Enl. 15 March 1862.

Newton, John: Born in Mecklenburg County; *wounded* and *captured*; died of scurvy at Fort Delaware 22 September 1863; buried at Finns Point, N.J.

Newton, Patrick, J.: (29 in 1865); farmer; born in Mecklenburg County; received a *wound* which fractured his right leg (tibia).

Newton, William T.:

Noblin, John H.: *Wounded* and *captured*; exchanged from Chester Hospital 17 August 1863.

Owen, William J.:

Parrott, Lewis:

Phillips, Howell: *Wounded.*

Phillips, James D.: Enl. 12 March 1862.

Pinckman, Thomas:

Pinson, Allen: (24 in 1862); farmer; discharged for disability 27 August 1861; re-enlisted 15 May 1863 at Clarksville; *shot* in the head and *captured*; died 5 July 1863.

Ramsey, Warren: Born in Mecklenburg County; *captured*; died at Point Lookout 19 January 1864.

Richardson, Robert H.:

Sizemore, Thomas L.: *Shot* in the shoulder and *captured*; exchanged from Chester Hospital 23 September 1863.

Thomas, John T.: Slightly *wounded.*

Vaughan, James T.: Enl. 1 March 1862; born in Mecklenburg County; father was Mr. Grandison Vaughan; *wounded* and *captured*; exchanged 1 August 1863.

Watkins, George D.: *Wounded.*

Wilkerson, Thomas C.: Enl. 12 March 1862; *captured*; released from Fort Delaware 21 June 1865.

Wilkerson, William P.: Enl. 12 March 1862; *captured*; exchanged 20 March 1864.

Wilkins, James F.: Enl. 8 March 1862.

Wilkinson, John H.: Enl. 5 March 1862.

Williamson, Absalom:

Williamson, Robert:

Wilson, James: Born in Mecklenburg County.

Wilson, Lee: Probably *wounded*; *captured*; exchanged 20 or 21 February 1865.

Wilson, Richard: Enl. 14 March 1862; *shot* in the right foot and *captured*; exchanged from West's Buildings Hospital 27 September 1863.

Yancey, Edward H.: Enl. 8 March 1862.

Company "H" ("Meadville Greys")

This company enlisted 29 April 1861 at Meadville, Halifax County, Virginia; was mustered into service 2 May 1861; and was reorganized 6 May 1862.

Logan, Richard, Jr. (Capt.): (31); farmer; VMI class of 1849; *killed* by artillery fire during the advance or by a gunshot near the heart during the attack.

Logan, John A. (1st Lt.): Enl. 24 March 1862 at Suffolk; *captured*; released from Fort Delaware 12 June 1865.

Guerrant, Philip P. (2nd Lt.): (21); clerk; probably *wounded*; *captured*; exchanged 22 March 1865.

White, John L. (2nd Lt.): (19); clerk.

Barksdale, Robert M. (1st Sgt.): (21).

Garner, Calvin (3rd Sgt.): (22); overseer; *shot* in the right leg and *captured*; treated at U.S. 1st Division, II Corps Hospital; exchanged 6 March 1864.

Easley, Drewry B. (5th Sgt.): (17); student; *captured*; exchanged 14 or 15 February 1865.

Ives, Richard W. (1st Cpl.): (23); mechanic; *wounded* in the upper jaw and *captured*; died, date and location unknown.

Moorefield, John W. (2nd Cpl.): Enl. 18 October 1861 at Catawba; *captured*; exchanged 14 or 15 February 1865.

Sydnor, Eppa (3rd Cpl.): (20); teacher.

Brooks, James G. (4th Cpl.): (21); mechanic; the company reports him as having been captured but there are no Federal records concerning him; *killed*.

Bickle, James A.: Enl. 14 July 1862 at Falling Creek; *wounded*.

Booth, John S.: *Wounded*.

Clay, George W.: (22); mechanic.

Covington, David G.: Enl. 17 July 1861; *killed*.

Crowder, Daniel: (21); farmer; *captured*; exchanged sick with debilitas 1 August 1863.

Epps, Thomas W.: (30); farmer.

Farmer, Chesley M.: (20); moulder; *wounded* in the left shoulder and *captured*; died at U.S. 3rd Division, I Corps Hospital at Widow Young's four miles down the Baltimore Pike, and buried there.

Garrett, Albert D.: Father was Mr. John J. Garrett; *killed*.

Guerrant, Clayton M.: (24); mechanic.

Harter, Henry: Enl. 15 May 1863 at Manchester.

Irby, Samuel T.: Enl. 22 March 1862 at Suffolk; the company initially reports him as captured, and subsequently as having died of wounds, but there are no Federal records concerning him; *killed*.

Light, George W.: (26); farmer; *shot* in the back, and suffering from chronic diarrhea, and *captured*; died at West's Buildings Hospital 16 July 1863.

Light, John R.: (20); farmer.

Light, William S.: (21); farmer; *shot* in the thigh and *captured*; exchanged from DeCamp Hospital 8 September 1863.

Lovelace, John T.: Enl. 17 July 1861 at Jamestown; *captured*; exchanged 21 January 1865.

Motley, George M.: Enl. 1 August 1861.

Motley, Joseph: (18); carpenter.

Motley, Robert D.: Enl. 24 March 1862 at Suffolk.

Neal, James H.: (18); farmer.

Ousley, Thomas: (27); overseer.

Owen, James W.: Enl. 1 August 1861.

Perkins, John: (23); farmer; *captured*; died of chronic diarrhea at Fort Delaware 27 October 1863.

Perkins, Robert: (22); farmer; *captured*; died of chronic diarrhea at Fort Delaware 12 September 1863.

Petty, Robert J.: Enl. 26 March 1862 at New Market; *wounded*; died, date and location unknown; there are no Federal records concerning him; probably died in a Confederate hospital.

Rodenhizer, John W.: Enl. 1 September 1861 at Mulberry Island; *captured*; joined U.S. service 24 January 1864.

Shaw, James J.: (28); farmer.

Smart, Charles W.: (22); carpenter.

Smart, David C.: Enl. 28 May 1862 at Petersburg.

Snead, Charles O.: (18); farmer; *captured*; joined U.S. service at Point Lookout 23 January 1864.

White, George W.: Enl. 5 May 1862 at Suffolk; *shot* over the stomach and *captured*; exchanged from West's Buildings Hospital 24 August 1863; deserted Farmville, Virginia hospital 4 September 1863 and returned to his company.

White, James L.: (17); student.

Williams, Erasmus: Enl. 5 May 1862 at Suffolk; wrist and fingers of left hand *wounded* by a shell burst.

Womack, Charles H.: (26); farmer; received a *gunshot* fracture of the left thigh and shot in the side, and *captured*; died at Letterman Hospital 16 August 1863 and buried in Section 2, Grave #30 of that hospital's cemetery; disinterred to Richmond 13 June 1872 in Box #60.

Womack, James K.: (18); student; *shot* in the left foot (amputated), and *captured*; exchanged from West's Buildings Hospital 27 September 1863.

<u>Company "I" ("Chester Grays"; also "Southern Braves")</u>

This company enlisted 11 May 1861 at Chester, Chesterfield County, Virginia; was mustered into service 11 May 1861; and was reorganized 5 May 1862.

Smith, Richard P. (1st Lt.): (25); farmer.

Snead, James L. (2nd Lt.): (26); farmer.

Snead, John H. (3rd Lt.): (21); farmer.

Ashbrook, James L. (1st Sgt.): (18); farmer.

Robertson, William B. (2nd Sgt.): (28); farmer; *disabled* by the concussion of a shell during the advance.

Patram, Edward F. (3rd Sgt.): (34); farmer.

Bennett, William T. (5th Sgt.): Enl. 21 May 1861 at Camp Lee near Richmond; (18); farmer; *captured*; exchanged 15 November 1864.

Coleman, Samuel A. (2nd Cpl.): *Shot* in the thigh and *captured*; exchanged from DeCamp Hospital 28 August 1863.

Jewitt, Andrew (4th Cpl.): (21); fireman.

Condrey, James L.: (23); farmer.

Connard, John H.: (28); miner; the company reports him as captured and subsequently as "supposed *killed*"; there are no Federal records concerning him.

Davis, Philip: (23); carpenter; received a *wound* which fractured his thigh and *captured*; died at U.S. II Corps Hospital 24 July 1863 and buried in back of Schwartz's barn.

Duke, James M.: Enl. 6 May 1862 at Suffolk.

Ellis, Joseph F.: (20); farmer.

Golden, Michael: (19); miner; *captured*; escaped from Fort Delaware in September 1863; there is no further record of him.

Hancock, Charles: (17); farmer.

Jordan, John: Enl. 15 August 1862 in regimental camp near Falling Creek.

Laprade, Cornelius B.: (19); farmer; the company reports him as wounded and captured and subsequently as "supposed *killed*"; there are no Federal records concerning him.

Laprade, Everett G.: (22); carpenter.

O'Brian, Hugh: (24); miner.

Pollard, Eugene M.: (17); farmer.

Puckett, James A.: (24); sawyer; *wounded*; *captured* as a nurse at Gettysburg; deserted hospital at Gettysburg 6 September 1863.

Puckett, John H.: Enl;. 21 July 1862 at regimental camp near Falling Creek.

Puckett, John W.: (17); cooper; AWOL 28 July through 1 September 1863.

Traylor, Thomas: (18); farmer.

Watkins, Thomas: (38); wheelwright; AWOL 4 August through 16 September 1863.

<u>Company "K" ("Dan River Rifles")</u>

This company enlisted 14 May 1861 at South Boston, Halifax County, Virginia; was mustered into service 14 May 1861; and was reorganized 6 May 1862.

Sutphin, James S. (Capt.): (19); clerk; *wounded.*

Tuck, Edward A. (1st Lt.): (19); artist.

Sternberger, Moses (2nd Lt.): Farmer.

Thaxton, William E. (1st Sgt.): (18); clerk; the company initially reports him as wounded and captured, and subsequently as missing in action but there are no Federal records concerning him; *killed.*

Elliott, John A. (2nd Sgt.): (25); carpenter; *shot* in the right leg and hip, and *captured*; treated at the U.S. XII Corps Hospital; exchanged from DeCamp Hospital 8 September 1863.

Howard, John W. (3rd Sgt.): (18); farmer; *wounded.*

Palmer, Henry (4th Sgt.): (23); farmer; probably *wounded*; *captured*; exchanged 15 November 1864.

Clark, James G. (5th Sgt.): Enl. 12 July 1861 at Jamestown.

Spencer, James A. (1st Cpl.): (27); plasterer; *wounded* and *captured*; exchanged from DeCamp Hospital 8 September 1863.

Wilkins, Richard B. (2nd Cpl.): Enl. 12 July 1861 at Jamestown.

Whitt, John T. (3rd Cpl.): Enl. 12 July 1861 at Jamestown; probably *wounded*; *captured*; exchanged 8 March 1864.

Tuck, Joseph P. (4th Cpl.): Enl. 12 July 1861 at Jamestown.

Ryan, Patrick P. (Musician): Enl. 17 March 1862 in Halifax County.

Bowen, Berry A.: (18); farmer; the company reports him as having been captured but there are no Federal records concerning him; *killed.*

Bowen, Marshall: (25); farmer; *captured*; records show him at Fort Delaware but there are no further records concerning him; probably died in prison.

Boyd, James G.: Enl. 12 July 1861 at Jamestown; *captured*; exchanged from DeCamp Hospital sick with chronic diarrhea 16 September 1863.

Bray, William Y.: (22); miller; *captured*; died of chronic diarrhea at Fort Delaware 24 October 1863; buried at Finns Point, N.J.

Chandler, William: (23); farmer.

Clark, Ellis A.: (26); farmer; mother was Mrs. Henrietta Clark; born in Mecklenburg County; the company reports him as having been captured but there are no Federal records concerning him; *killed*.

Davenport, William T.: (20); farmer.

Edwards, Christopher B.: Enl. 12 July 1861 at Jamestown; *captured*; exchanged 18 September 1864.

Edwards, Richard T.: (18); carpenter; *captured*; exchanged 22 September 1864.

Elliott, John W.: (21); farmer.

Elliott, William L.: Enl. 6 June 1863 at Hanover Junction; mother was Mrs. Elizabeth Elliott; *captured*; exchanged 1 August 1863 apparently sick; died at City Point, Virginia, 1 August 1863.

Fletcher, George W.: Enl. 12 July 1861 at Jamestown.

Fletcher, Henry Y.: (20); farmer; *shot* in the right foot and *captured*; treated at U.S. XII Corps Hospital where he died, 13 July 1863, and was buried.

Goode, John H.: (21); farmer.

Gravitt, Thomas: Enl. 12 July 1861 at Jamestown.

Hite, Edward S.: (21); farmer.

Ladd, Robert T.: (18); farmer; *wounded*.

Loftis, James M.: Enl. 12 July 1861 at Jamestown.

Lowry, John W.: Enl. 12 July 1861 at Jamestown.

McCann, Isham: Enl. 1 April 1862 at Suffolk.

Morris, James W.: (27); farmer.

Nethery, Richard E.: (30); farmer.

Noblin, Alexander: (27); mason.

Overbey, Warren: (19); farmer; mother was Mrs. Elizabeth Overbey; *captured*; died at Point Lookout 23 December 1863.

Parrott, James: (25); carpenter; the company reports him as having been captured but there are no Federal records concerning him; *killed*.

Peck, James William: Enl. 12 July 1861 at Jamestown.

Powell, Richard M.: Enl. 20 June 1861 at Jamestown Island; (18); farmer.

Reaves, Thomas L.: (22); farmer.

Rickman, Jennings: (23); carpenter; does not appear on any company muster rolls subsequent to the 30 June 1863 muster; *killed*.

Satterfield, Onslow J.: Enl. 12 July 1861 at Jamestown; *captured*; exchanged 14 or 15 February 1865.

Sizemore, John B.: (22); boatman.

Smith, William J.: (24); farmer.

Terry, John D.: (18); farmer.

Whitt, John A.: (21); farmer; *shot* across the back between the scapulae and *captured*; exchanged 8 March 1864.

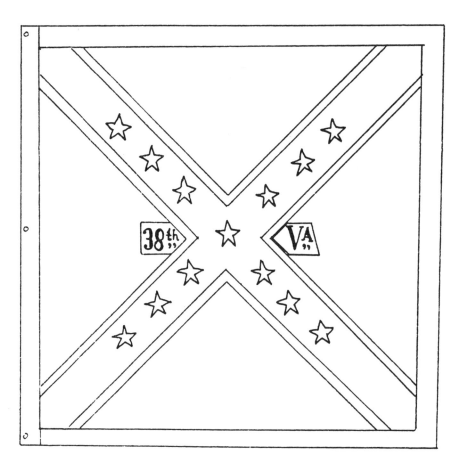

**Flag of the 38th Virginia Infantry
captured by the 8th Ohio Infantry
during the retreat**

38th Virginia Volunteer Infantry Regiment
(The "Pittsylvania Regiment")

This regiment was organized 12 June 1861 for 12 months; was accepted into Confederate service 1 July 1861; and was reorganized 12 May 1862.

First Company "I" was transferred to the 14th Virginia Infantry as Second Company "G" 27 June 1862. Company "B," 20th Battalion Virginia Heavy Artillery was transferred to this regiment as Second Company "I" 3 May 1864.

The following listing was obtained from a complete review of the service records of all men who served in the regiment during the course of the war. Those who could definitely be established as having been absent from the battle were deleted. The residue are provided here.

Field and Staff

Edmonds, Edward Claxton (Colonel): Born at Paris, Va. 21 January 1835; graduated from VMI in 1858; Principal Danville Military Academy; commissioned Colonel 12 June 1861; *killed* during the attack.

Whittle, Powhatan Bolling (Lt. Col.): Born in Mecklenburg County, Va. 26 June 1829; attended University of Va.; lawyer in Macon, Georgia; his mother's fifteenth child; 6 feet 4 inches tall; commissioned Lt. Col. 12 June 1861; *shot* through the right arm and left thigh.

Cabell, Joseph Robert (Major): Born 28 May 1840; married Mary Elizabeth Irby in 1863; enl. 8 June 1861 at Danville as Captain of Company "E"; promoted to Major 28 May 1861; promoted to Lt. Col. 3 July 1863.

Smith, Albert G. (Adjutant): Appointed Adjutant 20 September 1861.

Averett, John T. (Capt., AQM): Enl. 30 May 1861 at Kentuck as a 2nd Lt. in Company "A"; appointed AQM 24 December 1861.

Edmonds, William B. (ACS): Appointed ACS 20 September 1861.

Trevillian, James G. (Surgeon): Appointed Asst. Surgeon 15 October 1861; appointed Surgeon 12 June 1863.

Nowlin, William S. (Asst. Surgeon): Appointed 6 March 1863; captured 5 July 1863 while attending wounded at Gettysburg; exchanged 21 November 1863.

Cridlin, Ransel W. (Chaplain): Appointed 9 June 1863.

Waddill, Charles M. (Ordnance Sgt.): Enl. 30 May 1861 at Kentuck in Company "A"; appointed Ordnance Sgt. 11 September 1862.

Penick, Charles C. (QM Sgt.): Enl. 24 May 1861 at Whitmell in Company "D."

Blackwell, Moore C. (Commissary Sgt.): Enl. 12 October 1862 at Winchester in Company "D."

Thompson, Joseph S. (Teamster): Detailed from Company "F"; enl. 4 June 1861 at Republican Grove.

Color Guard

Bullington, John R. (Color Cpl.): Detailed from Company "K"; enl. 2 June 1861 at Cascade; *wounded.*

Singleton, Joseph (Color Cpl.): Detailed from Company "F"; enl. 4 June 1861 at Republican Grove.

Ambulance Corps

Peake, Mark L. (Litter Bearer): Detailed from Company "F"; enl. 4 June 1861 at Republican Grove.

Stone, John M. (Litter Bearer): Detailed from Company "F"; enl. 4 June 1861 at Republican Grove.

Company "A"

This company was organized in State service 20 August 1860; enlisted 30 May 1861 at Kentuck, Pittsylvania County, Virginia for one year; and was reorganized 29 April 1862.

Townes, Daniel C. (Capt.): Born in Pittsylvania County; *killed.*

Joyce, Richard J. (1st Lt.):

Turner, Thomas J. (2nd Lt.):

Butler, Thomas J. (Bvt. 2nd Lt.): (28 in 1864); received *gunshot* fractures of the left leg (amputated at the knee), and of the upper third of the right tibia, and *captured*; exchanged 3 September 1864.

Carter, Edward A. (Sgt.): (20 in 1864); farmer; born in Pittsylvania County; *shot* in the left foot and *captured*; exchanged from DeCamp Hospital 28 August 1863.

Gardner, Joseph C. (Sgt.):

Lindsey, John S. (Sgt.): Father was Mr. James H. Lindsey; *killed.*

Logan, John K. (Sgt.):

Marshall, James M. (Sgt.): Probably *wounded*; *captured*; exchanged 1 August 1863.

Blair, William T. (Cpl.):

Bradley, Robert (Cpl.): Received a slight *wound* in the right foot and *captured*; exchanged 8 May 1864.

Bradley, Thomas D. (Cpl.):

Wiles, James T. (Cpl.): Enl. 10 March 1862.

Allen, Henry C.: Enl. 10 March 1862.

Barker, Clark H.: Captured while attending the wounded at Gettysburg; exchanged 14 or 15 February 1865.

Bennett, Charles D.: *Wounded.*

Bennett, J. Samuel: Enl. 1 January 1863; *wounded.*

Bryant, Charles W.: Born in Pittsylvania County; father was Mr. William Bryant; had no wife or children at the time of his death; *killed.*

Carter, Charles S.: Enl. 7 March 1862.

Carter, Jesse L.: Enl. 5 March 1862; *wounded.*

Chatten, William B.: Received a *gunshot* fracture of the left arm; captured at South Mountain 4 July 1863; died of variola at Fort Delaware 24 August 1863; buried at Finns Point, N.J.

Clement, Parham B.: Enl. 13 March 1862; *wounded.*

Clements, Green W.: Date and place of enlistment not shown; born in Halifax County; *killed.*

Conway, Alexander F.: Born in Pittsylvania County; *killed.*

Dix, Tanda W.: Born in Pittsylvania County; *killed.*

Echols, Joseph W.:

Evans, George W.: *Captured*; died at Point Lookout 19 November 1863.

Evans, Robert H.: *Shot* in the back and shoulder and *captured*; exchanged from West's Buildings Hospital 24 August 1863.

Evans, William M.: Enl. 13 March 1862; *shot* in the inside of the right tibia, the ball ranging up to the knee and remaining lodged in the wound, and *captured*; exchanged from West's Buildings Hospital 24 August 1863.

Ferrell, James M.: (24 in 1863):

Finch, Marcellus L.: Enl. 13 March 1862.

Gosney, James L.: *Shot* in the thigh and *captured*; exchanged from DeCamp Hospital 28 August 1863.

Green, Thomas C.: Enl. 27 February 1862; *captured*; died at Point Lookout 11 August 1864.

Gunnell, Joseph L.: Born in Pittsylvania County; *killed.*

Haley, Thomas J.: Date and place of enlistment not shown; *killed.*

Hawker, Thomas S.: Enl. 13 March 1862.

Hill, John R.:

Hill, Joseph W.:

Hundley, Jason B.:

Jackson, Green M.: Enl. 13 March 1862.

Jackson, Lewis: Date and place of enlistment not shown; *wounded* and *captured*; died of pyemia at Chester Hospital 1 August 1863 and buried in Grave #100 of that hospital's cemetery.

Marshall, George M.:

McDowell, Robert A.: Enl. 12 March 1862.

Motley, William D.: Enl. 15 January 1863.

Murrell, James W.: Captured while serving as a nurse at Gettysburg 5 July 1863; exchanged 20 March 1864.

Myers, Robert:

Myers, Wilson P.:

Owen, Beverly B.: Enl. 30 August 1862; the company reports him as having been captured but there are no Federal records concerning him; *killed.*

Owen, Thomas W.:

Owen, William R.: Enl. 30 August 1862.

Posey, Benjamin:

Posey, George W.:

Ray, George F.:

Richards, Jesse H.:

Richardson, William D.H.:

Smith, James W.: Received a flesh *wound* in the right thigh, and *captured*; exchanged 6 March 1864.

Warf, William G.: Deserted and captured near Gettysburg 4 July 1863; released from Fort Delaware 4 May 1865.

Warren, George W.: Enl. 7 March 1862; *wounded* and *captured*; exchanged from Chester Hospital 17 August 1863.

Williams, William C.G.: Enl. 27 February 1862; born in Pittsylvania County; wife was Mrs. Sarah Williams; *killed*.

Yeaman, William H.: Enl. 13 March 1862 in Pittsylvania County; born in Pittsylvania County; father was Mr. John Yeaman; had no wife or children at the time of his death; *killed*.

Company "B"

This company was organized for State service 23 May 1861; enlisted 4 June 1861 at Callands, Pittsylvania County, Virginia for one year; and was reorganized 1 May 1862.

Prichard, William B. (Capt.): Enl. 7 July 1861 at Richmond.

Clement, Benjamin F. (1st Lt.): (24 in 1862).

Warren, James P. (2nd Lt.):

Adkins, Whitmell T. (Jr. 2nd Lt.):

Blair, George W. (1st Sgt.): (21 in 1862); *captured*; exchanged 20 or 21 February 1865.

Berger, James H. (2nd Sgt.): (20 in 1862); *shot* in the right elbow joint, and *captured*; exchanged from DeCamp Hospital 28 October 1863.

Oakes, Thomas C. (3rd Sgt.): Received a *fractured* thigh and *captured*; died 2 August 1863 at U.S II Corps Hospital and buried in Yard B, Row 2 of that hospital's cemetery on the hill between Schwartz's and Bushman's; disinterred to Richmond 13 June 1872 in Box #213.

Fuller, Josiah E. (4th Sgt.): *Captured*; died of chronic diarrhea at Point Lookout 1 January 1864.

Robertson, William E.F. (1st Cpl.):

Dunn, Samuel B. (2nd Cpl.):

Oakes, John K. (3rd Cpl.):

Uhles, David (4th Cpl.): *Shot* in the leg and thigh, and *captured*; exchanged from DeCamp Hospital 16 September 1863.

Adkins, Bartlett E.: Enl. 10 July 1861 at Winchester; (25 in 1862); *captured*; released on oath from Point Lookout 14 March 1864.

Adkins, Henry: Enl. 11 June 1861.

Adkins, Richard: *Captured*; sent to Point Lookout from Fort Delaware 26 October 1863; no further record; apparently died in prison.

Allen, Ferdinand R.: (22 in 1862).

Allen, James W.: Enl. 10 March 1862.

Bates, Jordan: Enl. 10 March 1862; *captured*; exchanged 20 or 21 February 1865.

Blair, Suter F.: Enl. 10 March 1862; born in Pittsylvania County; *wounded* in the thigh (leg amputated) and *captured*; died 15 July 1863.

Bradner, Thomas H.: Enl. 10 March 1862; the company reports him as wounded and captured "supposed to be dead" but there are no Federal records concerning him; killed.

Casey, Thomas W.: Enl. 16 June 1861; (26 in 1862).

Chatten, Nathaniel: Enl. 10 March 1862.

Collins, Ira: Enl. 10 March 1862.

Craddock, Daniel S.: Enl. 10 March 1862.

Craddock, William B.:

Dodd, James W.: Enl. 10 March 1862.

Dodd, Thomas W.: (20 in 1862).

Dodd, William S.: Enl. 14 August 1862 at Danville; admitted to Danville Hospital with vulnus sclopeticum 12 August 1863; probably *wounded*.

Emerson, John D.: Enl. 17 June 1861.

Foust, Bolling G.: Enl. 10 March 1862; *captured*; died of smallpox at Point Lookout 17 November 1863.

Foust, Fountain J.: Enl. 10 March 1862; *shot* in the leg and *captured*; exchanged from West's Buildings Hospital 24 August 1863.

Fuller, Berryman: Enl. 10 March 1862; *captured*; died of remittent fever at Fort Delaware 25 September 1863; buried at Finns Point, N.J.

Fuller, Brittain: Captured while serving as a nurse at Gettysburg; released on oath from Point Lookout 29 January 1864 and joined U.S. service.

Fuller, Henry B.: Enl. 10 March 1862; *captured*; exchanged 6 March 1864.

Fuller, Waddy Thompson: Enl. 10 March 1862.

Gaulden, Jabez S.: Wife was Mrs. Cynthia A. Gaulden; *killed*.

Gibson, Harrison H.: *Captured*; joined U.S. service 29 January 1864.

Grant, Isaac S.: Enl. 10 March 1862; *captured*; exchanged 30 April 1864.

Gregory, John B.: Enl. 10 July 1861 at Winchester; born in Pittsylvania County; wife was Mrs. Martha J. Gregory; had three children at the time of his death; *killed*.

Hankins, Henry C.: Enl. 9 June 1863 at Danville.

Hodges, Edward P.: *Captured*; exchanged 20 or 21 February 1865.

Jones, Green W.:

Keatts, Lawson S.: Enl. 14 August 1862 at Danville.

Lewis, William L.: Enl. 16 June 186

Mayham, John W.: Enl. 1 August 1862 at Danville; wife was Mrs. Matilda A. Mayham; *captured*; died at Fort Delaware 2 October 1863; buried at Finns Point, N.J.

Meade, Wiley W.: Deserted prior to 19 May 1863; may not have been at Gettysburg.

Meadows, James R.: Received a *fractured* clavicle, and *captured*; exchanged from West's Buildings Hospital 24 August 1863.

Midkiff, William R.:

Motley, Daniel J.: Enl. in April 1862 at Pittsylvania Court House.

Nuchols, James A.: Enl. 14 June 1861; (22 in 1863); single; received a *gunshot* fracture of the right arm (lower third amputated), and *captured*; died at Letterman Hospital 21 September 1863, and buried in Section 8, Grave #21 of that hospital's cemetery; disinterred to Richmond 13 June 1872 in Box #95.

Nucholds, David R.: Enl. 10 March 1862; (20 in 1863); married; received a dissection *wound* of the left hand, and *captured*; died at Letterman Hospital 17

September 1863 and buried in Section 8, Grave #13 of that hospital's cemetery; disinterred to Richmond 13 June 1872 in Box #113.

Oakes, James A.: Enl. 10 March 1862; wife was Mrs. M.C. Oakes; *shot* in the leg (amputated at upper third) and *captured*; died 15 July 1863.

Oakes, James L.: Enl. 14 August 1862 at Danville; admitted to a Southern hospital 13 July 1863; probably *wounded*.

Owen, David L.: (24); *shot* in the right humerus (amputated at joint), and *captured*; exchanged from West's Buildings Hospital 24 August 1863.

Parsons, Spencer: Enl. 12 April 1862 at Richmond.

Reynolds, Coleman: Born in Pittsylvania County; *wounded*; died at home in Pittsylvania County 30 July 1863.

Reynolds, Joseph D.: *Captured*; exchanged 15 November 1864.

Riddle, John A.:

Shelton, George J.: Enl. 12 June 1861.

Shelton, Ralph S.:

Stokes, Allen W.: *Captured*; died of typhoid fever at Fort Delaware 17 September 1863; buried at Finns Point, N.J.

Tatum, John T.: Reported as a deserter as of 19 May 1863 and again in August 1863; probably not at Gettysburg.

Towler, Joseph L.: Enl. 10 July 1861 at Winchester.

Woodall, James S.: Enl. 12 June 1861; (26 in 1862); *captured*; exchanged sick with debilitas 5 October 1864.

Company "C" ("Laurel Grove Riflemen")

This company was organized for State service 11 May 1861; enlisted 30 May 1861 at Laurel Grove, Pittsylvania County, Virginia for one year; was mustered into Confederate service 3 June 1861; and was reorganized 29 April 1862.

Grubbs, John T. (Capt.):

Gibson, John T. (2nd Lt.): (47 in 1865); *wounded* in the left foot.

Walters, Charles W. (2nd Lt.): Elected 31 May 1862; *killed*.

Turner, William W. (1st Sgt.): Slightly *wounded*.

Vernon, William T. (2nd Sgt.): Slightly *wounded*.

Durham, James A. (Sgt.): *Shot* in the left shoulder and *captured*; treated at U.S. XII Corps Hospital; exchanged 22 September 1864.

Norman, James M. (Sgt.):

White, Jerrie M. (2nd Cpl.): *Shot* in the right leg below the knee, and in the left shoulder and *captured*; exchanged from West's Buildings Hospital 27 September 1863.

Chaney, Daniel S. (Cpl.):

Alderson, James A.: (25 in 1863); slightly wounded four times.

Alderson, John C.:

Alderson, Thomas M.: Enl. 18 March 1862.

Barker, Josiah: Enl. 19 March 1862; *captured*; exchanged 20 March 1864 suffering from swelling of the right leg.

Barker, William H.: *Captured*; exchaned 20 March 1864.

Bohannon, William: (26 in 1864); *shot* in the thigh and *captured*; exchanged from DeCamp Hospital 28 August 1863.

Boothe, Benjamin: *Hit* on the forehead by a grapeshot.

Bryant, Fleming B.W.: *Captured*; *wounded* and sick with chronic diarrhea; exchanged from DeCamp Hospital 8 September 1863.

Burton, John M.:

Cassada, O.F.: Enl. 4 March 1863 at Petersburg.

Crews, Samuel T.: Enl. 15 March 1862.

Dodson, James A.:

Dodson, Josephus B.: Date and place of enlistment not shown; *wounded* in the thigh (primary amputation) and *captured*; died of shock 6 July 1863.

Dooley, Jesse:

Durham, John H.: Enl. 14 April 1863.

Finch, Nathaniel B.: Enl. 27 June 1861 at Richmond.

Greenwood, Robert H.:

Hardy, Robert T.: (24); *wounded* in the right foot (amputated); and *captured*; exchanged 20 March 1864.

Hodges, Joseph H.: *Shot* in the forehead fracturing the eye socket.

Johns, Thomas J.:

Lovelace, William A.:

McCormick, John B.: Received a *contusion* from a shell explosion near his head, and suffering from chronic diarrhea, and subsequently captured; exchanged from DeCamp Hospital 28 August 1863.

McCormick, William L.: (24 in 1862); born in Halifax County; *shot* in the leg and *captured*; exchanged from DeCamp Hospital 28 August 1863.

Meeks, John T.: *Shot* in the left thigh and *captured*; treated at U.S. XII Corps Hospital; exchanged from DeCamp Hospital 16 September 1863.

Owen, George R.: *Shot* in the thigh and *captured*; exchanged from Chester Hospital 23 September 1863.

Payne, John R.:

Payne, Joseph T.: *Wounded* and captured; died 22 July 1863 at U.S. II Corps Hospital and buried in Yard B, Row 2 of that hospital's cemetery on the hill between Schwartz's and Bushman's; disinterred to Richmond 13 June 1872 with 110 others in 10 large boxes marked "S."

Richardson, John S.: Slightly *wounded.*

Rives, Abram:

Rives, Ephraim: Enl. 19 March 1862; *wounded* in the neck and *captured*; exchanged from West's Buildings Hospital 24 August 1863.

Shelton, William T.:

Simpson, Archer M.: Date and place of enlistment not shown; born in Pittsylvania County; *shot* in the abdomen and leg, and *captured*; died 6 July 1863.

Sneed, Robert L.: The company reports him as having been captured but there are no Federal records concerning him; *killed.*

Strickland, James L.: Enl. 19 March 1862.

Tankersley, Alexander: Enl. 14 March 1862.

Tucker, Richard:

Turner, Joseph H.: *Captured*; exchanged 20 or 21 February 1865.

Vernon, James D.: Enl. 18 March 1862.

Vernon, James H.: Enl. 22 April 1862 at Fort Dillard, North Carolina; *captured*; exchanged sick with chronic rheumatism 20 March 1864.

White, Abram: *Wounded* in both legs, and *captured*; exchanged from West's Buildings Hospital 27 September 1863.

Wilkerson, David A.: Enl. 1 August 1862 at Falling Creek; slightly *wounded*.

Wilkerson, Robert W.:

Wilkerson, Walter S.:

Williams, David L.:

<h3 style="text-align:center;">Company "D" ("Whitmell Guards")</h3>

This company enlisted in State service 27 April 1861; enlisted in Confedeate service 24 May 1861 at Whitmell, Pittsylvania County, Virginia for one year; was mustered into Confederate service 11 June 1861; and was reorganized 1 May 1862.

Herndon, John A. (Capt.):

Lanier, Adolphus M. (1st Lt.): *Shot* in both legs, and *captured*; released from Fort Delaware 12 June 1865.

Burton, William J. (2nd Lt.): (30 in 1865).

Harris, Samuel J. (2nd Lt.): *Captured*; exchanged 22 March 1865.

Harris, William O. (Sgt.): Enl. 11 March 1862; paid on descriptive roll 1 May through 30 June 1863; admitted to a Richmond hospital 13 July 1863; may not have been at Gettysburg.

Hutcherson, William H. (Sgt.):

Booker, James (Cpl.):

Anglin, Samuel H.: Enl. 1 March 1862 at Whitmell; *shot* in the right arm and *captured*; treated at U.S. XII Corps Hospital; died at Fort Delaware 8 October 1863; buried at Finns Point, N.J.

Barber, James A.: *Killed*.

Booker, John:

Collins, John W.:

Davis, John G.: Enl. 9 February 1863 at Mount Jackson.

Eanes, William T.: *Killed*.

Easley, Henry W.: Received a *gunshot* fracture of the right thigh, and captured while serving as a nurse at Gettysburg; exchanged 14 or 15 February 1865.

Easley, James C.: Received a *fractured* left humerus, and *captured*; exchanged from West's Buildings Hospital 17 November 1863.

Emmerson, Elisha W.: *Captured*; released on oath from Fort Delaware 5 May 1865.

Fargusson, James M.: *Captured*; joined U.S. service at Point Lookout 29 January 1864.

Gaulding, James H.:

Gregory, James F.: Admitted to a Richmond hospital 13 July 1863; on sick furlough 20 July through 29 August 1863; may have been *wounded* at Gettysburg.

Hastings, Robert H.: Enl. 11 March 1862.

Hundley, Charles W.: Enl. 15 June 1861; *shot* in the head fracturing the left temporal bone, and *captured*; exchanged 20 March 1864.

Inman, Memory A.:

McCarthy, Daniel: Enl. 5 March 1862.

Meade, Harrison W.: *Shot* in the leg and right arm (amputated) and *captured*; exchanged from DeCamp Hospital 28 August 1863.

Meadows, Francis D.: Enl. 13 March 1862.

Mills, Caleb W.:

Mitchell, Henry C.:

Myers, Stephen R.:

Newton, George W.:

Norton, Hugh:

Oakes, Edward B.:

Payne, Leroy:

Powell, Joseph W.: Enl. 11 March 1862.

Powell, Robert H.:

Prewett, David D.:

Prewett, Ephraim:

Prewitt, Abel: Enl. 14 August 1862 at Danville; *wounded*.

Read, James W.: Enl. 11 March 1862; *shot* in the left arm below the shoulder and *captured*; treated at U.S. 1st Division, I Corps Hospital; died 25 July 1863.

Robertson, John S.: Enl. 24 April 1861 at Tuskegee, Alabama; *shot* in the arm (amputated) and *captured*; exchanged from DeCamp Hospital 8 September 1863.

Stokes, William C.:

Thomas, Abraham J.: Father was Mr. Abraham Thomas; *wounded* and *captured*; died 9 July 1863 at U.S. II Corps Hospital and buried in Yard D of that hospital's cemetery in Jacob Schwartz's cornfield on Rock Creek; disinterred to Richmond 13 June 1872 with 110 others in 10 large boxes labeled "S."

Thomas, Campbell H.:

Walker, John: *Shot* in the right buttock, and *captured*; exchanged 1 August 1863.

Walton, William J.:

Company "E"

This company was organized for state service 28 May 1861; enlisted in Confederate service 8 June 1861 at Danville, Pittsylvania County, Virginia for one year; and was reorganized 29 April or 1 May 1862.

The following listing was obtained from the company's April/June 1863 muster roll dated 30 June 1863.

Tyree, Thomas M. (Capt.): (24 in 1865).

Carter, William S. (1st Lt.): *Wounded*.

Knight, Henry C. (2nd Lt.):

Miller, Joseph T. (3rd Lt.): *Shot* in the right leg (amputated below the knee 3 July by Surgeon McAlpine of the 38th Virginia) and *captured*; exchanged 6 March 1864.

Shackleford, James T. (1st Sgt.): Severely *wounded* in the leg.

Rice, James P. (2nd Sgt.): Born in Pittsylvania County; father was Mr. Joseph L. Rice; *killed.*

Anglea, Allen C. (3rd Sgt.): Born in Pittsylvania County; father was Mr. Allen C. Anglea.

Howerton, William H. (4th Sgt.): Enl. 13 March 1862.

Howerton, Joseph T. (5th Sgt.):

Brown, John T. (1st Cpl.): *Shot* in the arm and leg, and *captured*; exchanged from West's Buildings Hospital 24 August 1863.

Cox, Bedford B. (2nd Cpl.):

Ashby, William F. (Musician): Enl. 1 November 1861.

Brady, William (Musician): Enl. 1 December 1861; *captured*; joined U.S. 3rd Maryland Cavalry at Fort Delaware 22 September 1863.

Wynn, Robert S. (Musician): Captured while serving as a nurse at Gettysburg 5 July 1863; exchanged 15 November 1864.

Adkins, Edward J.: Enl. 11 March 1862.

Adkins, James: Enl. 11 March 1862.

Adkins, John O.: Born in Pittsylvania County; *wounded*; died at Pickett's Division Hospital and buried at Bream's Mill on the hill; disinterred to Richmond 3 August 1872 with 33 others in three large boxes marked "P Curns."

Ashby, Henry S.: Enl. 1 January 1862 at Manassas.

Barber, Thomas L.: Enl. 14 March 1862.

Bays, David E.: (present under arrest for being AWOL 1 March though 18 May 1863.)

Bolton, Hilry: Enl. 21 March 1862; deserted 4 July 1863 and captured the same day; died of chronic diarrhea at Fort Delaware 17 August 1863; buried at Finns Point, N.J.

Brown, William L.: Enl. 7 March 1862; *captured*; died of chronic diarrhea at Point Lookout 12 December 1863.

Burks, Joseph:

Clayton, James C.: Enl. 19 February 1862.

Clayton, William R.:

Cox, William S.:

Crawley, William R.: Enl. 8 March 1862.

Davis, Creed O.:

Davis, James: Enl. 25 February 1862.

Davis, John H.: Enl. 3 March 1862; *shot* in the thigh and *captured*; exchanged from DeCamp Hospital 8 September 1863.

Dillard, Henry J.: Enl. 15 August 1862.

Elliott, John K.:

Elliott, William A.: Severely *wounded.*

Ferrell, Joseph B.:

Gaines, Robert R.:

Hall, Beverly B.: Enl. 15 August 1862.

Hall, John O.: Enl. 24 February 1862; *killed.*

Hardy, James H.: Enl. 13 March 1862.

Hardy, Samuel H.:

Harris, George W.: Severely *wounded*.

Harris, John S.:

Hughes, Walter B.: Enl. 15 August 1862.

McCarty, James M.: Enl. 13 March 1862.

Mitchell, William R.:

Morgan, Lafayette:

Oaks, Robert J.: Born in Pittsylvania County; died of typhoid pneumonia at Williamsport, Maryland 11 July 1863.

Orrender, Mathew T.: Enl. 10 March 1862.

Owen, James J.: Enl. 28 February 1862.

Powell, James A.: Enl. 21 March 1862.

Ricketts, Reuben: Enl. 19 March 1862.

Robinson, John H.:

Shackleford, Francis S.: Enl. 12 March 1862; born in Pittsylvania County; wife was Mrs. Elizabeth Shackleford; *killed*.

Shelton, Robert M.: Enl. 12 March 1862.

Slayton, Daniel T.: Enl. 19 March 1862.

Sledge, Francis L.: Enl. 12 March 1862; possibly *wounded*; *captured*; exchanged 1 August 1863.

True, Levi: Enl. 5 March 1862.

True, Lewis, J.:

Voss, William H.: Enl. 24 February 1862; born in Pittsylvania County; *killed*.

Warf, Thomas A.: Enl. 15 March 1862.

Watkins, Linnaeus D.: Born in Pittsylvania County.

Westbrooks, James S.:

Company "F" ("Davis Rifle Guard")

This company was organized 7 May 1861; enlisted 4 June 1861 at Republican Grove, Halifax County, Virginia for one year; and was reorganized 29 April 1862.

The following listing was obtained from the company's April/June 1863 muster roll captioned 1 July 1863, Chambersburg, Pennsylvania.

Jennings, Lafayette (Capt.): *Wounded* by a grape shot in the face which fractured his upper jaw.

Thornton, Robert F. (2nd Lt.):

Jones, Joel T. (Jr. 2nd Lt.): *Captured*; exchanged 22 March 1865.

Clement, Charles H. (1st Sgt.): *Wounded*.

Pierce, Edgar T. (2nd Sgt.):

Clay, Charles M. (3rd Sgt.):

Coates, John C. (4th Sgt.):

Carr, John R. (5th Sgt.):

Hankins, William D. (1st Cpl.): *Captured*; died of chronic diarrhea at Point Lookout 18 December 1863.

Hunt, John W. (2nd Cpl.):

Jennings, John B. (3rd Cpl.): Enl. 5 July 1861 at Hermitage Camp; *wounded* in the left chest and *captured*; exchanged from DeCamp Hospital 28 August 1863.

Jones, Samuel J. (4th Cpl.):

Funkhouser, James D. (Musician):

Adams, James W.: Enl. 20 June 1861 at Hermitage Camp.

Bates, Nathaniel: *Shot* in the left side and thigh, and *captured*; treated at U.S. XII Corps Hospital; exchanged 1 August 1863.

Bates, Thomas: *Wounded.*

Guthery, James T.: Reported as absent 1 July 1863 (sick at hospital since 11 April 1863); *shot* in the side and *captured*; exchanged from DeCamp Hospital 8 September 1863.

Guthrie, Paul W.: Enl. 14 March 1862; present on April/June 1863 muster roll; no further record thereafter; probably *killed.*

Guthrie, William T.: Enl. 15 March 1862.

Hall, James D.:

Hancock, Lafayette: Born in Halifax County; *captured*; died of smallpox at Point Lookout 8 January 1864.

Hancock, Samuel: Enl. 4 March 1862; *captured*; exchanged 21 January 1865.

Light, Charles M.: Enl. 20 June 1861 at Hermitage Camp; *shot* in the shoulder and *captured*; died of vulnus sclopeticum at DeCamp Hospital 30 July 1863 and buried in Grave #710 of the Cypress Hill Cemetery on Long Island.

Martin, Robert W.: Enl. 20 June 1861 at Hermitage Camp; *captured*; released from Fort Delaware 20 June 1865.

McGregor, William H.: Enl. 17 March 1862.

McHaney, William R.:

Oliver, John J.: Enl. 1 March 1862; the company reports him as having been captured but there are no Federal records concerning him; *killed.*

Peake, Luke R.:

Peake, Thomas L.: Enl. 13 March 1862.

Roark, Booker: Received a *gunshot* wound which fractured his third rib, the ball exiting near the upper and external edge of the scapula.

Roark, William P.:

Robey, Austin:

Robey, George W.:

Saunders, James B.: Enl. 5 March 1862; *wounded.*

Saunders, William: Enl. 20 June 1861 at Hermitage Camp.

Singleton, Abram:

Smith, Marcellus W.:

Stevens, James W.: Enl. 20 June 1861 at Hermitage Camp; received a *fractured* thigh and *captured*; died 29 July 1863 at U.S. II Corps Hospital and buried in Yard B, Row 2 of that hospital's cemetery on the hill between Schwartz's and Bushman's; disinterred to Richmond 13 June 1872 in Box #200.

Tucker, James W.:

Waller, Woodley: Born in Halifax County; *captured*; died at Point Lookout 3 September 1864.

Company "G" ("Mecklenburg Rifles")

This company enlisted 18 May 1861 at Boydton, Mecklenburg County, Virginia; was mustered into Confederate service 3 June 1861; and was reorganized 29 April 1862.

Lee, Henderson L. (Capt.): Date and place of enlistment not shown; (35); *shot* in the head of the humerus (resection required).

Carter, William J. (2nd Lt.):

Carter, George W. (3rd Lt.): *Captured*; released from Fort Delaware 12 June 1865.

Gill, Thomas J. (1st Sgt.): *Shot* in the right ankle (flesh wound) and *captured*; treated at U.S. XII Corps Hospital; exchanged 6 March 1864.

Moore, Henry H. (2nd Sgt.):

Willard, Benjamin B. (4th Sgt.): The company reports him as missing in action but there are no Federal records concerning him; *killed*.

Bugg, James R. (5th Sgt.):

Roffe, Lewis J. (1st Cpl.): *Wounded* by a grapeshot in the external hamstring of the right leg injuring the knee, and *captured*; exchanged from DeCamp Hospital 28 August 1863.

Mackasey, Robert F. (4th Cpl.): Enl. 24 March 1862.

Hutcherson, James F. (Cpl.):

Pitt, Julian V. (Musician): Enl. 6 May 1861 at Clarksville.

Algood, William T.: Enl. 4 February 1863 in Mecklenburg County.

Bevell, Charles D.: Enl. 4 February 1863 in Mecklenburg County.

Burnett, Edwin H.: *Shot* in the side and *captured*; died of chronic diarrhea at Point Lookout 8 March 1865.

Burton, Giles A.:

Burton, Hillery G.: Enl. 23 August 1862.

Coleman, Thomas B.: Enl. 27 April 1862 at Yorktown.

Cumby, Edward G.:

Gill, John R.: Enl. 6 March 1862.

Hendrick, Murray: Enl. 4 February 1863 in Mecklenburg County.

Hendrick, William L.:

Hendrick, William T.: *Wounded* and *captured*; exchanged from Chester Hospital 23 September 1863.

Holmes, Robert:

Hotelen, Henry:

Mackasey, Thomas S.: Enl. 26 January 1863 at Richmond.

Mallett, Beverly:

Mallett, Horace L.: Enl. 13 March 1862.

Mallett, Silas C.: Enl. 12 March 1862.

Mitchell, George W.:

Morgan, George T.: Deserted 10 April 1863; last paid to 31 December 1862; may not have been at Gettysburg.

Morgan, John J.: Deserted 10 April 1863; last paid to 31 December 1862; may not have been at Gettysburg.

Nethery, Alexander:

Newcomb, William T.: Enl. 24 August 1862.

Owen, William T.: Enl. 10 March 1862; *shot* in the left leg (flesh wound) and *captured*; exchanged 6 March 1864.

Palmer, William: Deserted 10 April 1863; may not have been at Gettysburg.

Rainey, Mathew J.:

Reese, Joseph M.:

Riggins, Robert D.:

Singleton, James: *Wounded.*

Sneed, John J.: Enl. 15 March 1862.

Ward, John W.: Enl. 29 March 1862; *shot* in the left thigh.

Wilmoth, John A.:

Wynne, William H.: Enl. 24 February 1862; *captured*; served as a nurse at a Gettysburg hospital; died of chronic diarrhea at Fort Delaware 5 August 1863; buried at Finns Point, N.J.

Company "H" ("Secession Guards")

This company was organized and mustered into State service 7 June 1861; enlisted and was mustered into Confederate service 2 July 1861 at Pittsylvania Court House, Pittsylvania County, Virginia for twelve months; and was reorganized 29 April 1862.

Poindexter, James E. (Captain): *Captured*; exchanged 22 March 1865.

Segar, Arthur S. (1st Lt.): Enl. 14 May 1861 at Hampton.

Perkins, James R. (Sr. 2nd Lt.):

Burnett, Achilles H. (1st Sgt.):

Scruggs, Powhatan B. (2nd Sgt.): The company reports him as having been captured but there are no Federal records concerning him; *killed.*

Poindexter, William R. (3rd Sgt.): Enl. 22 March 1862 in Orange County; *wounded.*

Segar, John A. (4th Sgt.): Enl. 10 March 1862 at Craney Island.

Adkins, James C.:

Arthur, Berry: Enl. 19 March 1862 at Lynchburg.

Crews, Armstead C.: The company initially reported him as missing in action and subsequently as captured but there are no Federal records concerning him; *killed.*

Dalton, Richard:

Dudley, Chiswell:

Farthing, James: *Wounded.*

Garton, James H.: Enl. 9 March 1863 at Orange Court House; (21 in 1863); farmer; *shot* below and in front of the tibia, the ball passing through the leg, and *captured*; exchanged from West's Buildings Hospital 27 September 1863.

Griffith, Andrew J.: Enl. 2 June 1861 at Cascade in Company "K."

Hardy, Obadiah:

Hardy, Presley: Enl. 22 March 1862 at Orange Court House; father was Mr. Banister Hardy; had no wife or children at the time of his death; *wounded*; died of his wound at Staunton, Virginia hospital 4 October 1863.

Harris, William J.: Enl. 10 November 1862 in Henry County.

Hill, James O.: Enl. 9 March 1863 at in Pittsylvania County.

Hoofman, Moses:

Humphrey, Joseph R.: Enl. 9 March 1863 at Orange Court House.

Jacobs, John D.: Enl. 17 March 1862 at Lynchburg.

Jones, Asa W.:

Jones, James T.: Enl. March 1862 in Pittsylvania County.

Jones, Yancey B.: Detailed 11 June 1863 for an undetermined period of time; may not have been at Gettysburg.

Kindrick, Linwood: Enl. 8 February 1863 at Guinea Station; the company intitally reported him as missing in action and subsequently as wounded and captured but there are no Federal records concerning him; *killed*.

Lawson, John O.: Enl. 9 March 1863 in Green County; the company initially reported him as missing in action, and subsequently as having "deserted the battlefield at Gettysburg"; there is no further record of him; probably *killed* during the battle.

Mann, John T.: Enl. 2 June 1861 at Cascade in Company "K"; *captured*; released from Fort Delaware 20 June 1865.

Martin, Mallory: Enl. 9 March 1863 in Orange County; the company's 1 April 1864 muster roll reported him as sick with leave, but the July/August 1864 muster roll reported him as having been captured at Gettysburg; there are no Federal or Confederate hospital records concerning him; probably *killed* at Gettysburg.

McCormick, John: Enl. 3 March 1863 in Campbell County; received a *wound* which fractured his hip, and *captured*; died 23 July 1863 at U.S. II Corps Hospital and buried in Yard B, Row 2 of that hospital's cemetery on the hill between Schwartz's and Bushman's; disinterred to Richmond 13 June 1872 in Box #211.

Mitchell, David W.:

Motley, Richard W.:

Owen, Wilson: The company initially reported him as missing in action and subsequently as captured but there are no Federal records concerning him; *killed*.

Powell, Thomas J.:

Rice, James J.: Enl. 3 March 1863 in Campbell County; single; born in North Carolina; (39 in 1863); *shot* in the right side of the thorax and abdomen and *captured*; died at West's Buildings Hospital 13 January 1864 and buried in Baltimore's Loudon Park Cemetery.

Scott, William L.: Enl. 22 March 1862 in Orange County.

Scruggs, John W.:

Toler, John D.: Enl. 17 March 1862 at Lynchburg.

Williamson, Joshua: Enl. 22 March 1862 in Orange County.

Company "K" ("Cascade Rifles")

Organized and mustered into state service 24 April 1861, this company enlisted 2 June 1861 at Cascade, Pittsylvania County, Virginia, and was mustered into Confederate service the next day.

Griggs, George K. (Capt.): VMI class of 1862; *wounded.*

Cabaniss, William G. (1st Lt.):

Cabaniss, James M. (2nd Lt.): *Wounded.*

Estes, Joseph H. (2nd Lt.): *Wounded.*

Hatcher, Richard J. (2nd Sgt.):

Marshall, Clement C. (4th Sgt.): *Wounded.*

Shumate, James L. (5th Sgt.):

Anthony, Phillip S.P. (Sgt.): *Captured;* died of pneumonia at Point Lookout 11 Februray 1865.

Estes, Edward H. (Sgt.);

Davis, Augustine H. (2nd Cpl.): The company reported him as missing in action "supposed prisoner" but there are no Federal records concerning him; *killed.*

Anderson, James R. (Cpl.):

Gauldin, John J. (Cpl.):

Adams, James M.: Enl. 1 March 1862; *captured;* joined U.S. service at Point Lookout 24 January 1864.

Adams, John Q.:

Austin, Joseph H.: Enl. 6 January 1863.

Bowe, Henry C.:

Bray, Ellis H.: *Wounded.*

Bray, John:

Bray, Madison H.: *Captured;* exchanged 14 or 15 February 1865.

Burton, James W.: Enl. 12 March 1862; (26 in 1864); farmer.

Burton, William T.:

Christian, William E.:

Cox, Thomas P.: Enl. 10 March 1862.

Davis, Thomas J.: *Wounded.*

Dillion, William D.: Enl. 10 March 1862.

Dixon, William:

Gammon, James A.:

Gauldin, William: Enl. 10 March 1862.

Gibbs, Joseph W.: *Killed.*

Goodman, Silas: Enl. 6 March 1862.

Grant, William C.:

Gravely, Isaac: Enl. 28 February 1862.

Gray, Thomas W.: (32 in 1863); single; *shot* in the back of the right shoulder, the ball piercing the lung, and *captured;* died of exhaustion at Letterman Hospital 4 October 1863 and buried in Section 8, Grave #35 of that hospital's cemetery; disinterred to Richmond 13 June 1872 in Box #98.

Hailey, James T.: Enl. 1 March 1862.

Harris, Joel: Enl. 6 March 1862.

Harville, George A.: *Killed.*

Holland, Constantine:

Holland, John: Enl. 10 March 1862; the company reported him as having been captured but there are no Federal records concerning him; *killed.*

Hopper, George W.: Enl. 24 February 1862; *killed.*

Hopper, John H.: Enl. 6 March 1862; *killed.*

Hughey, A.T.: Enl. 24 February 1862.

Hundley, James M.: *Shot* in the right foot, the ball injuring the bones.

Jefferson, Haily R.:

Land, Henry M.: Enl. 10 March 1862.

Law, George W.C.: The company reported him as missing in action "supposed dead" but there are no Federal records concerning him; *killed.*

Mahon, Pleasant:

Mahon, Plyant: *Captured*; released from Fort Delaware 20 June 1865.

Marshall, Humphrey:

Matherly, Madison: Enl. 3 March 1862; *wounded.*

McDonald, George C.: *Wounded.*

McDowell, Joseph M.: Enl. 10 March 1862.

McDowell, Robert B.: *Shot* in the shoulder and *captured*; died 22 July 1863.

Meakes, Powhatan J.: Enl. 10 March 1862.

Meaks, George W.: Enl. 10 March 1862.

Millner, James W.:

Morrison, John R.: Enl. 10 March 1862.

Muck, Daniel H.: Enl. 28 February 1862.

Muck, Samuel H.: Enl. 28 February 1862.

Norman, Henry J.: Enl. 10 March 1862.

Owen, Joseph T.:

Robertson, Daniel C.: *Killed.*

Robertson, Henry H.: *Wounded*; died at Winder Hospital in Richmond, Virginia 5 August 1863.

Robertson, William T.:

Scearce, Richard: Paid only through 31 December 1862; may not have been at Gettysburg.

Shelton, Tavenor S.:

Shumate, Samuel H.:

Slaughter, Peter D.:

Stallings, Archibald A.: (21 in 1863); farmer; received flesh *wounds* in the right thigh and left shoulder, and *captured*; exchanged from West's Buildings Hospital 17 November 1863.

Stephens, Benjamin F.: (25 in 1862).

Stokes, Collins: *Shot* in the right lung and *captured*; exchanged from West's Buildings Hospital 24 August 1863.

Thornton, Moses T.: *Captured*; exchanged 20 or 21 February 1865.

Trent, William J.: Enl. 5 March 1862.

Turner, Willis W.: Enl. 5 March 1862; *captured*; joined U.S. service at Point Lookout 29 January 1864.
Wilson, William C.:
Wright, Andrew J.: (32 in 1864); *wounded.*

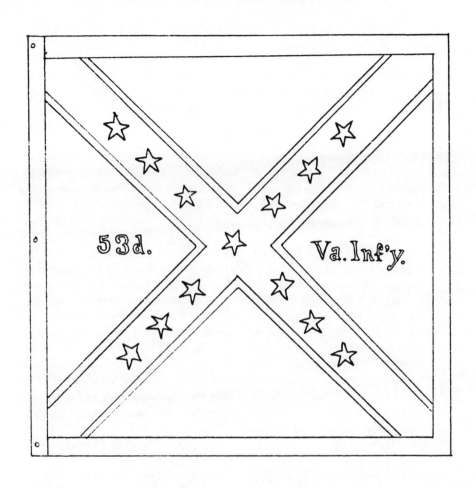

**Flag of the 53rd Virginia Infantry
captured at one of Cushing's guns**

53rd Virginia Volunteer Infantry Regiment

This regiment was organized 1 December 1861 by the amalgamation of Majors Tomlin's and Montague's Battalions Virginia Infantry and Waddill's Company Virginia Infantry. The regiment was reorganized in May 1862. The 5th Battalion Virginia Volunteers was disbanded 6 September 1862 and men of this unit aged 18 to 35 were enrolled and transferred to the 53rd Virginia in September and October 1862.

Field and Staff

Aylett, William Roane (Colonel): Born in King William County, Va. 14 May 1833; attended University of Va.; lawyer; married Alice Brockenbrough in 1860; 5 feet 9 inches tall; enl. 13 May 1861 at West Point as Captain of Company "D"; promoted to Major 13 May 1861; promoted to Lt. Col. 2 February 1863; promoted to Col. 5 March 1863; *wounded* during the cannonade.

Martin, Rawley White (Lt. Col.): Born in Pittsylvania County 20 September 1835; attended University of Va.; graduated University of New York; physician; enl. 22 April 1861 at Pittsylvania Court House as 1st Lt. of Company "I"; promoted to Lt. Col. 5 March 1863; received a *wound* in the Angle which fractured the upper third of his right thigh; and wounds in the left leg (flesh wound), left thigh, and left foot (shell wound) and *captured*; treated at U.S. 2nd Division, II Corps Hospital; exchanged from Point Lookout 30 April 1864; retired as Lt. Col. 22 October 1864.

Timberlake, John Corbett (Major): Born in 1829; lived at New Kent Court House; 5 feet 8 inches tall; enl. 8 July 1861 at West Point as Captain of Company "E"; promoted to Major 10 March 1863; *captured*; exchanged sick with chronic diarrhea 8 May 1864.

Coalter, Henry T. (1st Lt. and Adjutant): Appointed Adjutant October 1862; *captured*; exchanged 7 March 1865.

Moon, Ransom B. (Captain and AQM): Appointed AQM 1 December 1862.

Eaimes, James L. (ACS): Appointed ACS 1 December 1862.

Temple, Thomas P. (Surgeon): Appointed Surgeon 16 October 1862.

Parsons, Zorobald (Commissary Sgt.): Detailed from Company "K"; enl. 18 July 1861 at Charles City Court House in Company "K"; (36); farmer.

Worsham, Exet D. (Colonel's Orderly): Detailed from Company "G"; enl. 28 August 1861 at Pittsylvania Court House.

Keen, David S. (Hospital Cook): On extra-duty from Company "I"; enl. 8 May 1861 at Richmond.

Color Guard

Blackburn, Leander C. (Color Sgt.): Detailed from Company "E"; enl. 8 July 1861 at West Point; *wounded* and *captured*; died at a Gettysburg hospital in July 1863.

Carter, Thomas T. (5th Sgt.): Detailed from Company "A"; enl. 24 April 1861 at Halifax Court House; *shot* in the left shoulder and *captured*; treated at U.S. XII Corps Hospital; exchanged from Chester Hospital 17 August 1863.

Scott, John B. (4th Cpl.): Detailed from Company "G"; enl. 11 September 1861 at Pittsylvania Court House; shot and *killed* during the attack.

Carter, James, Jr. (1st Cpl.): Detailed from Company "I"; enl. 22 April 1861 at Pittsylvania Court House; *wounded* during the attack.

Jones, Robert Tyler (1st Cpl.): Detailed from Company "K"; enl. 25 June 1861 at Jamestown; (18); farmer; *wounded* twice (once in the arm) near the stone wall while carrying the colors after the color bearer had fallen.

Ambulance Corps

Hazlewood, Payton A. (Ambulance Driver): On extra-duty from Company "B"; enl. 11 May 1861 at West Point.

Company "A" ("Halifax Light Infantry")
(formerly Company "A," Montague's Battalion)

This company enlisted 24 April 1861 at Halifax Court House, Halifax County, Virginia for one year, and was reorganized 5 May 1862.

The following listing was obtained from the company's April/June 1863 muster roll, captioned 30 June 1863, near Chambersburg, Pennsylvania.

The company reported the condition of its clothing as "indifferent," its military appearance as "fair," its arms as "in good order and condition," its accouterments as "incomplete," and its instruction and discipline as "good."

Edmondson, Henry A. (Capt.):

Ragland, Evan J. (2nd Lt.): Enl. 12 June 1861 at Yorktown; (43 in 1865); *wounded* in the neck.

Green, Alexander R. (1st Sgt.): *Wounded* in the right lung and *captured*; exchanged from West's Buildings Hospital 24 August 1863.

Noell, James D. (2nd Sgt.):

Carrington, Clement R. (3rd Sgt.): *Captured*; exchanged 14 or 15 February 1865.

Willingham, Andrew B. (4th Sgt.): (23 in 1865); *shot* in the right thigh and *captured*; treated at U.S. 1st Division, I Corps Hospital; exchanged prior to 31 August 1863.

Gilliland, Lewis B. (1st Cpl.): *Captured*; exchanged 20 or 21 February 1865.

Neathery, Joseph H. (2nd Cpl.): *Captured*; released from Fort Delaware 20 June 1865.

McMillan, James W. (3rd Cpl.):

Abbott, William H.: Enl. 18 September 1861 at Deep Creek; AWOL 4 July 1863.

Adams, Robert E.: Enl. 6 June 1861 at Richmond; *shot* in the right shoulder joint, and *captured*; exchanged from DeCamp Hospital 27 September 1863.

Altick, Alexander R.: Enl. 21 April 1862 at Suffolk.

Booth, Samuel D.: *Wounded.*

Carlton, Thomas N.:

Carter, Elias: Enl. 16 July 1861 at Fort Powhatan; mother was Mrs. Martha Carter; had no wife, child, or father at the time of his death subsequent to Gettysburg.

Cumby, Elisha B.: *Captured*; died at Point Lookout 2 February 1864.

Drean, John F.: (26 in 1863); single, nearest relative was Sarah Palmer of Whitesville, Virginia; received a *gunshot* fracture of the middle third of his left thigh (leg amputated) and *captured*; leg reamputated 9 October; died of exhaustion at Letterman Hospital 4 November 1863 and buried in Section 9, Grave #13 of that hospital's cemetery; disinterred to Richmond 13 June 1872 in Box #99.

Drean, William T.: *Captured*; exchanged 15 November 1864.

Foster, John H.: Enl. 17 April 1862 at Hardy's Bluff.

Gilliland, George W.:

Morton, Jacob T.: (22 in 1862); *captured*; exchanged 14 or 15 February 1865.

Neathawk, Edward S.: Enl. 21 April 1862 at Suffolk.

Owen, Albert H.: Enl. 12 June 1861 at Yorktown.

Perkerson, William H.:

Sharp, William H.: Enl. 16 July 1861 at Fort Powhatan.

Skelton, Alexander: Enl. 6 June 1861 at Richmond; *shot* in the left hip and *captured*; treated at U.S. 1st Division, II Corps Hospital; died of wound and chronic diarrhea at Fort Wood, Bedloe's Island, New York Harbor 4 December 1863, and buried in Grave #953 of the Cypress Hill Cemetery, Long Island, New York.

Smith, Henry S.: Enl. 21 April 1862 at Suffolk.

Smith, Richard G.: Enl. 5 June 1861 at Yorktown.

Tucker, Archer B.: Enl. 6 June 1861 at Richmond.

Tucker, Samuel E.:

Turner, Albert C.: Enl. 6 June 1861 at Richmond; *captured*; released from Fort Delaware 21 June 1865.

Wirtz, Noah: Enl. 21 April 1862 at Suffolk.

Wirtz, Samuel: Enl. 21 April 1862 at Suffolk.

Witt, James R.: Enl. 21 April 1862 at Suffolk.

Company "B" ("Barhamsville Grays")
(formerly Company "A," Tomlin's Battalion)

This company enlisted 11 May 1861 at West Point, King William County, Virginia for one year, and was reorganized 5 May 1862.

The following listing was obtained from the company's April/June 1863 muster roll captioned 25 August 1863 near Culpeper Court House, Virginia.

Richardson, Sylvester H. (2nd Lt.): *Captured*; exchanged 22 March 1865.

Woodward, William H. (3rd Lt.):

Hockaday, John R. (1st Sgt.): (22 in 1862); mechanic; born in New Kent County.

King, George N. (2nd Sgt.): Enl. 30 July 1861; (18 in 1862); student; born in Henrico County; *wounded* in the right leg, and suffered a fractured left tibia, and *captured*; exchanged from Point Lookout 6 March 1864.

Hockaday, James H. (3rd Sgt.): (30 in 1862); farmer; born in New Kent County; *captured*; exchanged 20 or 21 February 1865.

Gilliam, West M. (4th Sgt.): Enl. 4 June 1861.

Woodward, Roland H. (5th Sgt.): *Captured*; exchanged prior to 21 March 1865.

Reames, Peter S. (1st Cpl.): Enl. 22 May 1861 at Dinwiddie.

Woodward, William J. (2nd Cpl.): *Captured*; died of chronic diarrhea at Point Lookout 18 April 1864.

Hicks, Andrew S. (3rd Cpl.):

Jennings, William G. (4th Cpl.):

Aaron, John B.: Enl. 20 April 1862 at Suffolk.

Abernathy, William D.: Enl. 22 May 1861 at Dinwiddie.

Blankenship, William W.: Enl. 20 April 1862 at Suffolk; *shot* in the foot and *captured*; exchanged from DeCamp Hospital 28 August 1863.

Butler, Thomas J.: Enl. 22 May 1861 at Dinwiddie; *wounded.*

Conally, Thomas B.: Enl. 6 July 1861 at Fort Powhatan; captured 5 July 1863 at Cashtown, Pa., apparently sick; released from Fort Delaware 19 June 1865.

Cross, James S.: Enl. 22 May 1861 at Dinwiddie; probably *wounded*; *captured*; exchanged 1 August 1863.

Cross, Thomas W.: Enl. 22 May 1861 at Dinwiddie; (22 in 1863); *wounded* in the left thigh, two inches below the groin, the ball lodging in the buttock, and *captured*; exchanged from West's Buildings Hospital 27 September 1863.

Davis, H.G.: Enl. 22 May 1861 at Dinwiddie.

Davis, Peter: Enl. 20 July 1861 at Fort Powhatan; the company reported him as having been captured, but there are no Federal records concerning him; *killed.*

Farinholt, John L.:

Ford, John A.: Enl. 22 May 1861 at Dinwiddie.

Gittman, Francis C.: Enl. 22 May 1861 at Dinwiddie; the company reported him as having been captured but there are no Federal records concerning him; *killed.*

Greer, Charles P.: Enl. 20 April 1862 at Suffolk.

Hawkins, Thomas H.: Enl. 22 May 1861 at Dinwiddie; *wounded.*

Hogwood, John: Enl. 22 May 1861 at Dinwiddie.

Hogwood, Joseph T.: Enl. 22 May 1861 at Dinwiddie; *captured*; exchanged sick with "debilitas" 8 May 1864.

Howle, Isaac H.: Enl. 7 June 1861.

Hudson, William T.: Enl. 22 May 1861 at Dinwiddie.

Knewstep, Miles: Enl. 8 July 1861 in Company "E"; AWOL 2 July 1863; reported to Provost Marshal's office in Washington, D.C., took oath of allegiance and sent to Fort Delaware; no further records pertaining to him; may have died in prison.

Manning, Armstead R.: (45 in 1862); farmer; born in New Kent County.

McGuire, James E.: Enl. 20 April 1862 at Suffolk; AWOL 1 August 1863; present with his company by 31 October 1863.

Rash, William H.: Enl. 22 May 1861 at Dinwiddie; father was Robert Rash; *killed.*

Robbins, Daniel: Enl. 18 July 1861 Company "E"; (22 in 1863); *shot* in the back of the left shoulder, the ball lodging in the wound, and in the neck (flesh wound), and *captured*; treated at U.S. 1st Division, I Corps Hospital; died at Letterman Hospital 29 July 1863 and buried in Section 1, Grave #7 of that hospital's cemetery; disinterred to Richmond 13 June 1872 in Box #34.

Robbins, James P.: (21 in 1862); farmer; born in New Kent County; *shot* in the leg (amputated) and *captured*; treated at U.S. 3rd Division, II Corps Hospital; died at U.S. II Corps Hospital 20 July 1863 and buried in Yard B, Row 2 of that hospital's cemetery; disinterred to Richmond 13 June 1872 with 110 others in ten large boxes labeled "S."

Smith, William M.:

Sweeney, Stephen B.:

Timberlake, Albert: (28 in 1862); farmer; born in New Kent County.

Timberlake, James W.: (36 in 1862); farmer; born in New Kent County; discharged 9 August 1862; re-enlisted 16 January 1863.

Tosh, Josiah: Enl. 20 April 1862 at Suffolk; (24 in 1863); *wounded* in the right hip, and *captured*; treated at U.S. 1st Division, II Corps Hospital; exchanged from DeCamp Hospital 27 September 1863.

Tyree, John:

Vaiden, Page H.: Enl. 22 May 1861 at Dinwiddie; *captured*; died at Fort Delaware 14 October 1863; buried at Finns Point, N.J.

Williams, Beverly W.: *Killed.*

Williams, David M.: Enl. 22 May 1862 at Dinwiddie; *captured*; exchanged sick with "piles" from Point Lookout, 6 March 1864.

Williams, Joseph B.: Enl. 22 May 1861 at Dinwiddie.

Williams, Joseph S.: Enl. 22 May 1861 at Dinwiddie.

Woody, James H.: Enl. 20 April 1862 at Suffolk.

Company "C" ("Old Dominion Riflemen")
(formerly Company "D," Montague's Battalion)

This company enlisted 4 May 1861 at Richmond, Henrico County, Virginia and was reorganized 14 May 1862.

The following listing was obtained from the company's April/June 1863 muster roll captioned 30 June 1863, near Chambersburg, Pennsylvania.

The company reported the condition of its clothing as "indifferent," its military appearance as "satisfactory"; its arms as "in good order and condition but deficient in bayonets," its accouterments as "incomplete," and its instruction and discipline as "fair."

Ligon, John T. (2nd Lt.): Mother was Mrs. Agnes B. Ligon: born in Prince Edward County; *captured*; died at Johnson's Island, Ohio 11 December 1863.

Walton, Joseph E. (Jr. 2nd Lt.): *Captured*; released from Fort Delaware 12 June 1865.

Harper, Creed H. (1st Sgt.):

Bradshaw, Richard B. (2nd Sgt.):

Harper, Robert A. (3rd Sgt.):

Weaver, William S. (4th Sgt.):

Walthall, Lindsey B. (5th Sgt.): *Captured*; exchanged sick with chronic diarrhea 20 March 1864.

Bradshaw, Robert M. (1st Cpl.):

Bradshaw, William P. (2nd Cpl.):

Crute, Christopher C. (3rd Cpl.): Enl. 10 March 1862 at Spratly Farm; *captured*; died of rubeola at Fort Delaware 28 August 1863; buried at Finns Point, N.J.

Scarborough, John Douglas (4th Cpl.): Enl. 6 May 1861 at Fort Powhatan; *wounded*.

Fowlkes, Patrick H. (Musician):

Ritchie, Francis H. (Musician):

Arthur, Thomas J.: *Captured*; exchanged 20 or 21 February 1865.

Borum, Henry M.: Enl. 17 July 1861 at Camp Page.

Carter, James L.: The company reported him as missing in action; there are no Federal records concerning him; *killed*.

Cumby, William W.: Enl. 10 March 1862 at Spratly Farm.

Daniel, James E.: Enl. 6 May 1861 at Fort Powhatan.

Duell, Littleton J.: Enl. 21 April 1862 at Hardy's Bluff; *shot* in the left thigh (flesh wound) and *captured*; released from Point Lookout in May 1865.

Ellett, Beverly H.: Enl. 6 May 1861 at Fort Powhatan; *shot* in the left shoulder, and *captured*; treated at U.S. XII Corps Hospital; exchanged from DeCamp Hospital 28 August 1863.

Ellette, James T.: Enl. 21 April 1862 at Suffolk.

Ellette, Thomas M.: Enl. 1 August 1862.

Eppes, Edwin T.: Enl. 6 May 1861 at Fort Powhatan.

Farley, George A.: Enl. 25 October 1861 at Spratly Farm.

Finn, Percival: Enl. 14 March 1862 at Hardy's Bluff; *shot* in the face and *captured*; exchanged from Chester Hospital 23 September 1863.

Flippin, James A.: Enl. 1 September 1862; *captured*; released on oath from Fort Delaware 16 November 1864.

Harper, Richard M.: Enl. 1 September 1862.

Harville, John R.: Enl. 5 August 1861 at Hardy's Bluff.

Hobbs, William E.: Enl. 2 April 1862 at Hardy's Bluff.

Lanier, Virginius W.: Enl. 6 August 1861 at Fort Powhatan.

Marker, Thomas J.: Enl. 10 March 1862 at Spratly Farm; *captured*; he was exchanged sick with dysentery 8 May 1864.

Marks, Samuel C.: Enl. 6 May 1861 at Fort Powhatan; AWOL near Bunker Hill, Virginia 21 July 1863; present with his company by 31 August 1863.

Marron, Bernard: Enl. 12 July 1861.

Marshall, Quintin A.: Enl. 10 March 1862 at Spratly Farm.

Morgan, James W.: Enl. 10 March 1862 at Spratly Farm; wife was Mrs. Mary J. Morgan; *captured*; died of anemia at Fort Delaware 24 October 1863; buried at Finns Point; N.J.

Moring, Floyd C.: Enl. 10 March 1862 at Spratly Farm; *captured*; released from Fort Delaware 20 June 1865.

Newcomb, Winfield T.: Enl. 6 May 1861 at Fort Powhatan; *captured*; died of anemia at Fort Delaware 17 November 1863; buried at Finns Point, N.J.

Nunnally, Samuel E.:

Overton, John W.:

Pettaway, James R.: Enl. 6 May 1861 at Fort Powhatan; probably *wounded*; *captured*; exchanged 1 August 1863.

Pettaway, James W.: Enl. 6 May 1861 at Fort Powhatan; *captured*; exchanged 20 or 21 February 1865.

Phillips, Henry T.: Enl. 1 March 1863 at Chester Depot.

Temple, Elverton E.: Enl. 6 May 1861 at Fort Powhatan.

Tucker, Hillery: Enl. 6 May 1861 at Fort Powhatan.

Tucker, William S.: Enl. 6 June 1861 at Fort Powhatan.

Wade, Charles A.:

Warren, Thomas G.: Enl. 6 May 1861 at Fort Powhatan; *captured*; died at Fort Delaware 1 October 1863; buried at Finns Point, N.J.

Weaver, Charles G.: *Captured*; exchanged sick with chronic diarrhea 15 October 1864.

Wingo, Lawrence H.: Captured while serving as a nurse at Gettysburg; exchanged sick with chronic diarrhea 30 April 1864.

Womack, Benjamin T.: Enl. 6 May 1861 at Fort Powhatan; *captured*; died at Point Lookout 3 November 1863.

Wood, Robert W.: Enl. 15 March 1862 at Hardy's Bluff.

Company "D" ("Taylor Grays")
(formerly Company "B," Tomlin's Battalion)

This company enlisted 13 May 1861 at West Point, King William County, Virginia for one year.

The following listing was obtained from the company's April/June 1863 muster roll captioned 30 June 1863, near Chambersburg, Pennsylvania.

The company reported the condition of its clothing as "indifferent," its military appearance as "good," its arms as "in good order and condition," its accouterments as "incomplete," and its instruction and discipline as "fair."

Turner, William J. (Capt.): *Wounded.*

Robinson, Eugene D. (1st Lt.): *Captured*; exchanged 22 March 1865.

Campbell, Robert C. (2nd Lt.): Enl. 15 May 1861; *captured*; exchanged 21 October 1864.

Hill, James B.: (3rd Lt.): Enl. 30 June 1861; (24 in 1865).

Slaughter, John B. (1st Sgt.):

Lipscomb, Thomas A. (2nd Sgt.): *Wounded.*

Cobb, William T. (3rd Sgt.):

Davis, Parks B. (4th Sgt.): Enl. 30 June 1861.

George, William H. (5th Sgt.): *Shot* in the leg (flesh wound) and *captured*; died of acute dysentery 13 July 1863.

Redd, Thomas (1st Cpl.):

Tuck, Anderson (2nd Cpl.): *Wounded.*

Burch, James H. (3rd Cpl.): *Captured*; exchanged 20 or 21 February 1865.

Parry, Richard L. (4th Cpl.): Enl. 30 June 1861; *captured*; released from Fort Delaware 20 June 1865.

Alley, E.B.: Enl. 6 May 1861 at Fort Powhatan; *captured*; exchanged sick with chronic diarrhea 6 March 1864.

Bains, Julian D.: Enl. 11 June 1861 at Fort Powhatan.

Bishop, John: Enl. 21 April 1862 at Suffolk.

Bray, Charles: Enl. 13 May 1861 at West Point; the company reported him as wounded and captured but there are no Federal records concerning him; *killed.*

Brown, Archie B.: Enl. 30 June 1861 at West Point.

Burch, John F.: Enl. 30 June 1861; *wounded.*

Carlton, Milton:

Carneal, Henry: Enl. 30 June 1861; *killed.*

Chick, James T.:

Crow, Robert W.:

Crutchfield, Charles C.: Enl. 30 June 1861.

Dallas, Robert G.: Enl. 21 April 1862 at Suffolk.

Griffin, Benjamin: Enl. 6 May 1861 at Fort Powhatan; there is no further record of this soldier subsequent to 30 June 1863; probably *killed.*

Howell, John H.: Enl. 1 March 1863 at Petersburg.

Kimbrough, Cary A.:

Lewis, John R.: (22 in 1863); farmer; *shot* in the arm and right leg, and *captured*; exchanged from DeCamp Hospital 16 September 1863.

Littlepage, Lewis L.: *Captured*; exchanged 25 or 26 February or 2 or 3 March 1865.

Morris, James E.: Enl. 11 June 1861 at Fort Powhatan.

Padgett, John F.: Enl. 6 May 1861 at Fort Powhatan; *shot* in the right tibia, and *captured*; exchanged from West's Buildings Hospital 24 August 1863.

Pointer, William B.: *Wounded.*

Pollard, Robert C.: Enl. 21 April 1862 at Richmond; *wounded.*

Powell, Thomas: Enl. 30 June 1861.

Powell, William H.:

Prewett, Joseph: Enl. 21 April 1862 at Suffolk.

Robinson, Albert:

Robinson, Lorimer B.: *Wounded* and *captured*; exchanged 1 August 1863.

Saunders, Robert W.: Enl. 13 March 1862 at Hardy's Bluff.

Seigle, John Henry: Deserted and captured 5 July 1863; died of chronic diarrhea at Fort Delaware 27 November 1863; buried at Finns Point, N.J.

Slaughter, Selim: Enl. 10 July 1861; *wounded.*

Sullens, James W.: The company initially reported him as wounded, and subsequently as captured but there are no Federal records concerning him; *killed.*

Sweet, Patrick H.: AWOL 10 July through 15 August 1863.

Tucker, Eli B.: (26 in 1862); farmer; born in King William County.

Wilson, James F.: *Captured*; died of disease at sea 14 November 1864 en route to prisoner exchanged at Savannah, Georgia; buried at Hilton Head, South Carolina.

Wood, Henry William: Enl. 16 March 1862 at Hardy's Bluff; the company reported him as having been captured but there are no Federal records concerning him; *killed.*

Company "E" ("Pamunkey Rifles")
(formerly Company "C," Tomlin's Battalion)

This company enlisted 8 July 1861 at West Point, King William County, Virginia for one year, and was reorganized 5 May 1862.

The following listing was obtained from the company's April/June 1863 muster roll captioned 30 June 1863, near Chambersburg, Pennsylvania.

The company reported the condition of its clothing as "indifferent," its military appearance and instruction as "fair," its arms as "in good order and condition," its accouterments as "insufficient," and its discipline as "good."

Farinholt, Benjamin L. (Capt.): *Wounded* in the thigh in the Angle and *captured*; escaped from Johnson's Island, Ohio in February 1864 and returned to his company; promoted to Lt. Col. in the reserve forces in August 1864.

Bray, William Harvie (1st Lt.): Enl. 21 April 1862 at Suffolk; VMI class of 1861; *wounded* in the thigh (leg amputated) and *captured*; died at U.S. II Corps Hospital 14 July 1863 and buried in Yard D of that hospital's cemetery; disinterred to Richmond 13 June 1872 with 110 others in ten large boxes labled "S."

Apperson, Richard Crump (2nd Lt.): Enl. 7 March 1862 at Williamsburg.

Timberlake, George A. (3rd Lt.): Enl. 11 May 1861 in Company "B."

Vaiden, Algernon S. (1st Sgt.): Enl. 6 July 1861 at Fort Powhatan.

Odell, Thomas M. (2nd Sgt.):

Jones, Lewis A. (4th Sgt.): Enl. 11 May 1861 in Company "B"; *captured*; died of chronic diarrhea at Point Lookout 3 January 1864.

Timberlake, Benjamin N. (2nd Cpl.): Enl. 11 May 1861 in Company "B"; (28 in 1862); farmer; born in New Kent County; *shot* in the thigh and *captured*; died 13 July 1863.

Wilkerson, Richard A. (3rd Cpl.): Enl. 30 July 1861 at Fort Powhatan; captured sick with diarrhea following the battle; exchanged from West's Buildings Hospital 24 August 1863.

Masters, Edward N. (Musician):

Aaron, Willis C.: Enl. 20 April 1862 at Suffolk.

Adams, William E.:

Atkinson, Richard O.: *Wounded* in the shoulder.

Austin, William S.: Enl. 16 January 1863 at Camp Lee.

Brushwood, Washington:

Cox, Henry W.: Enl. 16 May 1861 at Cumed.

Crowdis, Miles C.: (19 in 1862); *wounded.*

Fretwell, Samuel L.: Enl. 20 April 1862 at Suffolk.

Gilliam, John C.: Enl. 18 July 1861; (22 in 1862).

Hodnett, Thomas B.: Enl. 20 April 1862 at Suffolk.

Holfoot, Robert: Enl. 13 March 1862 at Fort Boykin.

Jones, Richard S.: Enl. 10 March 1861 at Cumed.

Law, Samuel S.: Enl. 20 April 1862 at Suffolk; *killed.*

Lutze, Theodore E.: Enl. 10 June 1861 near Richmond; AWOL 4 July 1863.

Moody, Joseph D.: Enl. 13 March 1861 at Cumed.

Patterson, Cornelius: Enl. 11 May 1861 in Company "B."

Powell, Algernon W.: Enl. 16 March 1861 at Petersburg.

Sullivan, John H.: Enl. 23 July 1861; (28 in 1862); mechanic; born in Richmond.

Thompson, Edwyn B.: Enl. 9 July 1861 at Fort Powhatan.

Wade, William H.:

Company "F" ("Edmunds Guards")
(fomerly Company "C," Montague's Battalion)

This company enlisted 10 July 1861 at Union Church, Halifax (?) County, Virginia for one year, and was reorganized 5 May 1862

The following listing was obtained from the company's April/June 1863 muster roll captioned 30 September 1863, near Petersburg, Virginia.

The company reported the condition of its clothing as "indifferent," its military appearance and instruction as "fair," its arms as "in good order and condition," its accouterments as "incomplete," and its discipline as "good."

Edmunds, Henry (Capt.):

Anderson, Andrew B. (2nd Lt.): *Wounded.*

Younger, Joseph G. (Bvt. 2nd Lt.):

Tucker, James G. (1st Sgt.): Received a *fractured* left leg and *captured*; died at Letterman Hospital 12 August 1863 and buried in Section 5, Grave #7 of that hospital's cemetery.

Stephens, Robert W. (2nd Sgt.): *Captured*; exchanged 5 October 1864.

Ferguson, Joel D. (3rd Sgt.): *Captured*; exchagned 15 November 1864.

Jarratt, Theophilus (4th Sgt.): Enl. 4 May 1861 at Hicksford; *wounded.*

Ferguson, Stephen P. (5th Sgt.): *Captured*; exchanged 15 November 1864.

Bass, William A. (1st Cpl.):

Jones, William R. (2nd Cpl.):

Meador, Calvin H. (3rd Cpl.): Enl. 21 April 1862 at Suffolk; *killed.*

Walton, James W. (4th Cpl.): Enl. 4 May 1861 at Hicksford.

Allen, William B.: Enl. 15 June 1861 at Jamestown; *captured*; exchanged sick with chronic rheumatism 30 April 1864.

Austin, James: Enl. 21 April 1862 at Suffolk; AWOL 19 July 1863.

Bendall, Benjamin F.: Enl. 4 May 1861 at Hicksford; (23 in 1863); single; received a *gunshot* fracture of his left arm and right leg (both amputated) and *captured*; died at Letterman Hospital 6 August 1863 and buried in Section 3, Grave #6 of that hospital's cemetery; disinterred to Richmond 13 June 1872 in Box #57.

Boitnott, Josiah: Enl. 21 April 1862 at Suffolk; *captured*; released from Fort Delaware 19 June 1865.

Brooks, Rufus M.: Enl. 21 April 1862 at Suffolk; *shot* in the right thigh, and *captured*; exchanged from West's Buildings Hospital 27 September 1863.

Chappell, Jesse A.: The company initially reported him as captured and subsequently as missing in action "supposed killed"; there are no Federal records concerning him; *killed*.

Compton, William R.:

Crank, Joseph H.:

Cumbie, Edwin W.: (28 in 1863); wheelwright.

Duane, Thomas F.: Enl. 4 May 1861 at Hicksford.

Gilliland, Robert J.:

Guill, Charles: Enl. 21 April 1862 at Suffolk.

Guill, Henry P.: Date and place of enlistment not shown.

Guill, Robert L.:

Harding, Junius: Enl. 13 May 1862 at Richmond; *captured*; died of chronic diarrhea at Fort Delaware 21 September 1863.

Henderson, John E.: *Wounded*.

Hopkins, John O.: Enl. 21 April 1862 at Suffolk; *captured*; exchanged 15 November 1864.

McComac, Edward P.W.: (24 in 1863); *wounded* in the leg.

McComac, John W.: *Wounded*.

Meador, William D.: Enl. 21 April 1862 at Suffolk; received a buckshot *wound* in the lower third of his left thigh, and *captured*; exchanged 14 or 15 February 1865.

Myrick, Walter: Enl. 15 July 1861 at Jamestown.

Newman, Mills N.: Enl. 8 April 1863 at Ivor; (47); *shot* in the left elbow (arm amputated 4 July by Assistant Surgeon W.F. Richardson, CSA), and captured; exchanged from West's Buildings Hospital 27 September 1863.

Northcross, Richard W.M.: Enl. 4 May 1861 at Hicksford; *captured*; released from Fort Delaware 10 June 1865.

Old, William B.:

Reese, Abner R.:

Reese, William:

Rooke, Martin V.: Enl. 4 May 1861 at Hicksford.

Taylor, Thomas W.: Enl. 13 May 1862 at Richmond.

Thomason, James H.: Enl. 4 May 1861 at Hicksford; *killed*.

Walton, John H.:

Williams, David R.: Enl. 5 February 1863 at Guinea Station; *shot* in the arm (amputated), and leg, and *captured*; transferred 25 July; no further record concerning him; probably died in a Federal hospital or prison.

Williams, Nathan T.: Enl. 13 May 1862 at Hicksford.

Younger, Nathan B.:

Company "G" ("Davy Logan Guards" or "Logan Guards")
(formerly in Montague's Battalion)

This company enlisted 28 August 1861 at Pittsylvania Court House, Pittsylvania County, Virginia for one year, and was reorganized 5 May 1862.

The following listing was obtained from the company's April/June 1863 muster roll captioned 30 June 1863, Chambersburg, Pennsylvania.

The company reported the condition of its clothing as "indifferent," its military appearance, instruction, and discipline as "good," its arms as "in good order and condition," and its accouterments as "incomplete."

Mustain, R.A. (Capt.):

Moses, Joseph M. (Jr. 2nd Lt.):

Millam, James E. (1st Sgt.): Enl. 11 September 1861; *shot* in the arm, and *captured*; treated at U.S. 1st Division, II Corps Hospital; died of pneumonia at Chester Hospital 6 August 1863 and buried in Grave #123 of that hospital's cemetery.

Hopkins, John W. (2nd Sgt.): *Captured*; exchanged 14 or 15 February 1865.

Thurman, William H. (3rd Sgt.): The company initially reported him as missing in action, and subsequently as captured but there are no Federal records concerning him; *killed.*

Witt, E.J. (4th Sgt.): Enl. 11 September 1861; *captured*; exchanged 20 or 21 Feburary 1865.

Moses, John T. (5th Sgt.): *Captured*; exchanged 20 or 21 February 1865.

Knight, H.D. (1st Cpl.): Enl. 16 May 1861 at Crimea.

Blair, Samuel B. (2nd Cpl.):

Sweeney, James T. (3rd Cpl.):

Angle, Benjamin: Enl. 17 April 1862 at Norfolk; AWOL 19 July 1863 through 30 May 1864.

Baldwin, R. William: Enl. 16 May 1861 at Crimea; born in Dinwiddie County; mother was Mrs. Caroline Baldwin; *captured*; died of chronic diarrhea at Point Lookout 15 November 1863.

Clark, G.W.: Enl. 24 January 1863 at Petersburg; the company reported him as missing in action and there are no Federal records concerning him; *killed.*

Crowder, Thomas: *Captured*; released from Fort Delaware in May 1865.

Davis, George C.: Enl. 16 May 1861 at Crimea.

Drewry, L.M.: *Captured*; exchanged sick with chronic diarrhea 30 September 1864; died at Chimborazo Hospital #4 in Richmond 19 November 1864.

Echols, R.C.B.: Enl. 16 May 1861 at Crimea.

Farthing, Joel:

Gibbs, John A.: Enl. 24 January 1863 at Petersburg.

Gibbs, John B.: Enl. 16 May 1861 at Crimea.

Grinstead, T.H.: Enl. 10 April 1863 at Franklin; the company reported him as missing in action and there are no Federal records concerning him; *killed.*

Gunn, Richard A.: Enl. 20 July 1861 at Fort Powhatan.

Hawks, J.H.: Enl. 6 March 1862 at Hardy's Bluff.

Hobbs, N.R.: Enl. 16 May 1861 at Crimea.

Howerton, W.W.: Enl. 16 May 1861 at Crimea; (22 in 1865); born in Brunswick County; farmer.

Hudgins, B.P.: Enl. 16 May 1861 at Crimea; *captured*; exchanged sick with scurvy 30 April 1864.

Hudgins, R.R.: Enl. 6 March 1862 at Hardy's Bluff; *wounded.*

Lovelace, Charles H.:

Mustain, J.C.: Enl. 19 March 1863 at Danville.

Neal, Abraham Thomas: *Shot* in the shoulder, and *captured*; exchanged from Chester Hospital 23 September 1863.

Robinson, Jacob T.: The company reported him as missing in action and there are no Federal records concerning him; *killed.*

Scruggs, James H.:

Shell, R.C.: Enl. 6 March 1862 at Hardy's Bluff; *wounded.*

Shelton, James J.: *Captured*; exchanged 20 or 21 February 1865.

Thomas, E.B.: Enl. 9 July 1861 at Fort Powhatan; *wounded.*

Thurman, W.R.: AWOL in July or August 1863.

Tuck, Joseph: Enl. 17 April 1862 at Norfolk; *shot* in the thigh.

Vaughan, Raleigh T.:

Westmoreland, D.H.: Enl. 16 May 1861 at Crimea; *captured*; died at Point Lookout 11 February 1864.

Westmoreland, Jesse H.: Enl. 16 May 1861 at Crimea.

White, George W.:

Whitlow, John R.: Enl. 17 April 1862 at Norfolk; *captured*; exchanged 20 or 21 February 1865.

Wills, E.A.: Enl. 25 March 1862 at Hardy's Bluff.

Womack, Charles: Enl. 17 April 1862 at Norfolk; *captured*; died of scurvy at Fort Delaware 26 April 1864; buried at Finns Point, N.J.

Worley, C.R.: (19 in 1863); farmer; *wounded* in the hand.

Worsham, A.D.: *Shot* in the right heel.

Worsham, Thomas:

Company "H" ("Mattapony Guards")
(formerly Company "D," Tomlin's Battalion)

This company enlisted 26 July 1861 at West Point, King William County, Virginia for one year, and was reorganized 5 May 1862.

The following listing was obtained from the company's April/June 1863 muster roll captioned 28 July 1863, near Culpeper Court House, Virginia.

The company reported the condition of its clothing as "indifferent," its military appearance as "fair," its arms as "in good order and condition," its accouterments as "incomplete," and its instruction and discipline as "good."

Latane, John L. (Capt.): *Captured*; released from Fort Delaware 12 June 1865.

Burruss, William H. (1st Lt.): *Wounded* and *captured*; died 15 August 1863.

Sale, James Irving (2nd Lt.): *Captured*; exchanged 22 March 1865.

Graves, Benjamin B. (1st Sgt.): Enl. 4 May 1861 at Lawrenceville; the company reported him as having been captured, but there are no Federal records concerning him; *killed.*

Campbell, Marius G. (2nd Sgt.): Enl. 7 August 1861; *captured*; died of chronic diarrhea at Point Lookout 17 September 1864.

Stith, Benjamin A. (5th Sgt.): Enl. 4 May 1861 at Lawrenceville; *shot* in the leg and *captured*; exchanged 20 or 21 February 1865.

Floyd, Americus (2nd Cpl.): *Wounded.*

Gary, William J. (3rd Cpl.): *Shot* in the right hand and *captured*; exchanged from West's Buildings Hospital 17 November 1863.

Moser, Charles (Musician):

Ancarrow, Charles E.:

Atkins, Thomas L.:

Buford, James Walter: Enl. 25 May 1861 at Lawrenceville; shot in the left leg (flesh wound).

Clayton, Benjamin D.: Enl. 6 August 1862 at Richmond.

Clayton, John R.: Enl. 4 May 1861 at Lawrenceville; *shot* in the middle third of the left thigh (flesh wound) and *captured*; exchanged 6 March 1864.

Crow, Preston: Captured at Falling Waters, Maryland 14 July 1863; joined U.S. service at Point Lookout 21 January 1864.

Flora, Samuel B.: Enl. 4 May 1862 at Suffolk.

George, Robert W.: (26 in 1862).

Guthrow, John F.:

Hagood, John H.: Enl. 4 May 1861 at Lawrenceville; the company reported him as having been captured but there are no Federal records concerning him; *killed.*

Hall, Robert W.: Enl. 4 May 1861 at Lawrenceville.

Hammonds, Alonzo W.: Enl. 31 May 1861 at Lawrenceville; *captured*; exchanged 20 or 21 February 1865.

Hammonds, James T.: Enl. 13 February 1863 at Guinea Station; *wounded.*

Hammonds, William E.: Enl. 31 May 1861 at Lawrenceville; *shot* in the right big toe.

Hargrove, James A.:

Johnson, Lucanus A.: Enl. 4 May 1861 at Lawrenceville; the company reported him as having been captured but there are no Federal records concerning him; *killed.*

Johnson, Richard A.: Enl. 6 August 1862 at Richmond.

Kelly, Henry C.: Enl. 18 December 1862 at Fredericksburg.

Kesler, John: Enl. 4 May 1862 at Suffolk; *wounded* in the side and *captured*; died of erysipelas and chronic diarrhea at Point Lookout 5 January 1864.

Kirkland, James M.: Enl. 4 May 1861 at Lawrenceville; received a *gunshot* fracture of the right leg, and shot in the left side, and *captured*; exchanged from West's Buildings Hospital 24 August 1863.

Lewis, Richard S.: Enl. 9 March 1863 at Petersburg; *captured*; died of an inflammation of the stomach at Fort Delaware 22 August 1864.

Maclin, Thomas B.: Enl. 4 May 1861 at Lawrenceville; *wounded.*

Michael, George E.: Enl. 4 May 1861 at Lawrenceville; recieved a *gunshot* fracture of the right clavicle, the ball passing through the scapula, and *captured*; exchanged from West's Buildings Hospital 17 November 1863.

Montague, Charles P.: Enl. 4 May 1861 at Lawrenceville.

Organ, Marcellus: Enl. 8 March 1862 at Lawrenceville.

Organ, William A.: Enl. 6 August 1862 at Richmond.

Peters, Noah: Enl. 4 May 1862 at Suffolk; AWOL 4 July 1863.

Poyner, William H.: Enl. 28 May 1862 at Lawrenceville; the company reported him as having been captured but there are no Federal records concerning him; *killed.*

Reynolds, George W.: Enl. 1 May 1862 at Hardy's Bluff.

Rice, William A.: (28 in 1862); overseer; born in King William County.

Robertson, George W.: Enl. 4 September 1861 at Hardy's Bluff.

Short, Gideon A.: Enl. 15 July 1862 at Falling Creek.

Slaughter, William: *Shot* in the left thumb (amputated), the left hand, and the head, and *captured*; treated at U.S. 1st Division, I Corps Hospital; exchanged prior to 31 August 1863.

Stith, William E.: Enl. 8 March 1862 at Lawrenceville.

Traylor, James A.: Enl. 8 March 1862 at Lawrenceville.

Tuck, George P.: *Captured*; exchanged 15 November 1864.

Walker, Benjamin J.: Enl. 8 July 1862 near Richmond; (19); received a *gunshot* fracture of the right humerus (arm amputated at the upper third 3 July by Surgeon C.S. Wood of the 66th New York), and *captured*; exchanged from West's Buildings Hospital 27 September 1863.

Williams, Leonidas F.: Enl. 4 May 1861 at Lawrenceville; the company reported him as having been captured but there are no Federal records concerning him; *killed.*

Young, Henry E.: Enl. 4 May 1861 at Lawrenceville.

Company "I" ("Chatham Grays")
(formerly Company "B," Montague's Battalion)

This company enlisted 22 April 1861 at Pittsylvania Court House, Pittsylvania County, Virginia for one year, and was reorganized 5 May 1862.

The following listing was obtained from the company's April/June 1863 muster roll captioned 28 July 1863, near Culpeper Court House, Virginia.

The company reported the condition of its clothing as "indifferent," its military appearance as "fair," its arms as "in good order and condition," its accouterments as "incomplete," and its instruction and discipline as "good."

Tredway, William Marshall, Jr. (Capt.): *Shot* in the Angle.

Carter, Hutchings L. (1st Lt.): *Captured* in the Angle; exchanged 20 March 1864.

Bilharz, Charles (Sr. 2nd Lt.):

Whitehead, James Wyatt (Jr. 2nd Lt.): *Wounded* in the left leg, and *captured*; released from Fort Delaware 12 June 1865.

Walker, Zebedee P. (1st Sgt.): *Captured*; died of chronic diarrhea at Point Lookout 20 August 1864.

Ferguson, Robert D. (2nd Sgt.):

Tredway, Thomas B. (3rd Sgt.): *Shot* and *captured*; died 13 July 1863.

Dyer, Walter C. (4th Sgt.): *Captured*; released from Fort Delaware 19 June 1865.

Coleman, James T. (5th Sgt.): The company reported him as having been captured but there are no Federal records concerning him; *killed.*

Cook, Fortunatus S. (2nd Cpl.):

Jones, John E. (3rd Cpl.): *Wounded.*

Fackler, Abraham (4th Cpl.): (36 in 1862); farmer.

Bradley, William T.: Enl. 21 March 1862 at Suffolk.

Bradner, John:

Chism, George W.: Enl. 8 May 1861 at Richmond; *shot* in the right leg below the knee.

Coleman, James C.;

Corbin, James D.G.: Enl. 21 March 1862 at Suffolk.

Cousins, Jabez S.:

Daniel, Demarcus L.: AWOL 3 August through 6 October 1863.

Easley, Robert C.: Enl. 2 March 1862 at Suffolk; the company reported him as having been captured but there are no Federal records concerning him; *killed.*

East, George W.: Enl. 21 March 1862 at Suffolk; father was Mr. Thomas C. East; had no wife or children at the time of his death; *captured*; died at Point Lookout 6 February 1864.

Glass, Jennings C.T.: *Captured*; exchanged 20 or 21 February 1865.

Haden, Daniel W.: Enl. 21 March 1862 at Suffolk; AWOL 3 July 1863, probably while on the march to the battlefield.

Harris, William S.:

Hatchett, Augustus F.:

Hatchett, Logan A.:

Holley, William H.: Probably *wounded*; *captured*; exchanged prior to 31 August 1863.

Jones, Benjamin W.: Enl. 21 March 1862 at Suffolk; *captured*; exchanged 15 October 1864.

Lacey, Robert M.: Enl. 21 March 1862 at Suffolk; (35 in 1862); *shot* in the right leg, and *captured*; treated at U.S. XII Corps Hospital; exchanged from DeCamp Hospital 28 August 1863.

Meadows, John H, Sr.: Enl. 21 March 1862 at Suffolk.

Meadows, John H, Jr.: Enl. 21 March 1862 at Suffolk.

Mills, Walter C.:

Mitchell, John S.: (28 in 1862); stone mason; born in Pittsylvania County; AWOL 3 August through 6 October 1863.

Moon, Daniel P.: Enl. 21 March 1862 at Suffolk.

Parsons, Joseph: Enl. 21 March 1862 at Suffolk.

Phillips, John W.:

Pillow, Samuel B.: Enl. 26 February 1863 at Petersburg; *captured*; exchanged 30 September 1864.

Pruitt, Elijah:

Ramsey, William S.: Enl. 12 February 1863 at Guinea Station.

Riddle, George W.: Enl. 8 May 1861 at Richmond; *wounded* and *captured*; exchanged from DeCamp Hospital 28 August 1863.

Riddle, Thomas C.: Enl. 21 March 1862 at Suffolk; *shot* in the thigh, and *captured*; exchanged from DeCamp Hospital 28 August 1863.

Shelhorse, James M.: Enl. 21 March 1862 at Suffolk.

Shelhorse, John B.: Enl. 21 March 1862 at Suffolk; *shot* in the right leg near the ankle, the ball lodging in the wound, and *captured*; treated at U.S. 1st Division, I Corps Hospital; exchanged from West's Buildings Hospital 27 September 1863.

Simpson, William R.: Enl. 21 April 1862 at Suffolk; *shot* in the thigh, and *captured*; exchanged from DeCamp Hospital 28 August 1863.

Sowers, Edward L.:

Taylor, William H.: Enl. 8 May 1861 at Richmond.

Ward, Robert A.: Enl. 1 November 1861 at the mouth of Deep Creek; the company reported him as having been captured but there are no Federal records concerning him; *killed.*

Warren, Columbus: Enl. 21 March 1862 at Suffolk.

Watson, Shimi: Enl. 21 March 1862 at Suffolk; (22 in 1862); *captured*; exchanged 20 or 21 February 1865.

White, George W.:

Yeatts, Andrew J.: Enl. 21 March 1862 at Suffolk; *captured*; released from Fort Delaware 21 June 1865.

Yeatts, Mark A.: Enl. 21 April 1862 at Suffolk; (28 in 1864); (present confined in guard house for being AWOL).

Company "K" ("Charles City Southern Guards")
(formerly Waddill's Company)

This company enlisted and was mustered 9 May 1861 at Charles City Court House, Charles City County, Virginia.

The following listing was obtained from the company's April/June 1863 muster roll captioned 9 September 1863, near the Rapidan River, Virginia.

The company reported the condition of its clothing as "indifferent," its military appearance as "fine," its arms as "in good order and condition," its accouterments as "incomplete," and its instruction and discipline as "good."

Lipscomb, James H. (Capt.): (30); lumber merchant; *killed.*

Ferguson, Robert R. (1st Lt.): (26); farmer; recieved a *gunshot* fracture of the middle third of his left thigh, and *captured*; exchanged 30 September 1864.

Harwood, James A. (Sr. 2nd Lt.): Captured sick with debilitas 5 July 1863 at the School House Hospital at Chambersburg, Pennsylvania; exchanged 22 March 1865.

Major, John E. (Jr. 2nd Lt.): (18); farmer.

McLees, John (1st Sgt.): (27); mason; *wounded*; captured 5 or 6 July 1863 at the School House Hospital at Chambersburg, Pennsylvania; exchanged from West's Buildings Hospital 24 August 1863.

Pierce, William W. (2nd Sgt.): (22); carpenter; *captured*; exchanged 14 or 15 February 1865.

Marable, Edward W. (3rd Sgt.): (19); farmer.

Southall, Henry M. (1st Cpl.): Enl. 18 July 1861; (31); mechanic.

Ammons, George W., Sr. (2nd Cpl.): (23); farmer; *wounded* in both thighs and *captured*; exchanged from West's Buildings Hospital 17 November 1863.

Duane, David C. (3rd Cpl.): Enl. 4 May 1861 at Hicksford.

Binns, Jordan T. (4th Cpl.): (17); farmer.

Adams, Alexander C.: Enl. 20 May 1861; (18); farmer; *shot* in the neck (flesh wound), and left shoulder (fractured humerus), and *captured*; exchanged from West's Buildings Hospital 17 November 1863.

Ammons, Francis A.: Enl. 18 July 1861; (21); farmer.

Ammons, George W., Jr.: Enl. 29 June 1861 at Jamestown; (18); farmer; the company reported him as having been captured but there are no Federal records concerning him; *killled*.

Ammons, John W.: (25); farmer.

Backhurst, George T.: Enl. 8 July 1861; (31); farmer; the company reported him as having been wounded and captured but there are no Federal records concerning him; *killed*.

Beckett, William F.: Enl. 28 February 1862; the company reported him as having been captured but there are no Federal records concerning him; *killed*.

Binns, Benjamin F.: Enl. 18 July 1861; (28); farmer; probably *wounded, captured*; exchanged 24 August 1863.

Binns, Charles D.: Enl. 18 July 1861; (18); farmer; single; received a *fractured* left leg (lower third amputated), and *captured*; died at Letterman Hospital 3 October 1863 and buried in Section 8, Grave #32 of that hospital's cemetery; disinterred to Richmond 13 June 1872 in Box #84.

Binns, Christopher J.: Enl. 18 July 1861; (31); farmer.

Binns, Fleming J.: Enl. 18 July 1861; (29); farmer.

Binns, Major E.: Enl. 18 July 1861; (23); farmer; mother was Mrs. Susan Binns; *shot* in the hand and knee (leg amputated at upper third of the femur); died at Pickett's Division Hospital 23 July 1863 and buried at Bream's Mill above Myers' house at the side of a fence; disinterred to Richmond 3 August 1872 with 33 others in three large boxes labeled "P Curns."

Bowery, James H.: (27); architect; *killed*.

Bullifant, John A.: Enl. 17 May 1861 at Jamestown; (17); farmer.

Camp, Joseph: Enl. 28 February 1862.

Clark, Joseph W.: Enl. 4 May 1861 at Hicksford.

Crafford, Edmund C.: Enl. 28 February 1862; *captured*; exchanged 20 or 21 February 1865.

Daniel, W.R.: Enl. 7 September 1862 at Greensville.

Davis, Robert E.: (16); farmer.

Fowler, William A.: (24); farmer; *shot* in the left hip, the ball lodging in the abdomen, and *captured*; exchanged from Point Lookout 20 March 1864.

Harwood, Christopher E.: (19); teacher; *shot* twice; died of his wounds at Chimborazo Hospital #1, Richmond, 15 August 1863.

Hayes, Richard H.: (24); farmer; the company reported him as having been captured but there are no Federal records concerning him; *killed*.

Haynes, William B.: (32); farmer; *captured*; exchanged 27 April 1864.

415

Holmes, George W.: Enl. 28 February 1862; *shot* in the leg, and *captured*; exchanged from Chester Hospital 23 September 1863.

Hubbard, J.S.: Enl. 7 September 1862 in Greenville County.

Jones, Fred: Enl. 4 May 1861 at Hicksford.

Ladd, Henry L.: Enl. 18 July 1861; (20); farmer; *killed*.

Lamkin, Oliver P.: Enl. 10 July 1861 at Jamestown; (17); farmer.

Lee, William E.: Enl. 4 May 1862 at Hicksford.

Marable, Albert W.: (22); farmer.

Marable, Richard H.: Enl. 5 July 1861 at Jamestown; (18); farmer.

Martin, Robert J.: Enl. 1 February 1863.

Martin, William J.: Enl. 14 June 1861 at Jamestown; (24); farmer; captured 5 or 6 July 1863 sick with typhoid fever and debilitas at the School House Hospital in Chambersburg, Pennsylvania; died of debility and bronchitis at Point Lookout 8 January 1864.

McLemore, Junius: Enl. 4 May 1861 at Hicksford; *captured*; exchanged 5 October 1864.

Morecock, Albert M.: Enl. 28 February 1862.

Mountcastle, John L.: Enl. 1 May 1862.

New, James W.: Enl. 15 December 1861.

New, Thomas W.: Enl. 28 February 1862.

Penny, James E.: Enl. 25 June 1861 at Jamestown; (20); farmer; *captured*; exchanged in February 1865.

Penny, William H.: Enl. 25 June 1861 at Jamestown; (25); farmer.

Phillips, W.H.: Enl. 1 May 1862.

Pierce, Edward W.: Enl. 18 July 1861; (18); farmer; *wounded* in the scalp; captured 5 or 6 July 1863 at the School House Hospital in Chambersburg, Pennsylvania; exchanged from West's Buildings Hospital 24 August 1863.

Pond, Robert T.: Enl. 15 April 1862.

Vaughan, James E.: Enl. 18 July 1861; *wounded*; captured 5 or 6 July 1863 at the School House Hospital in Chambersburg, Pennsylvania; exchanged 14 or 15 February 1865.

Walker, Henry T.: Enl. 5 July 1861 at Jamestown; (40); farmer.

Walker, William M.: Enl. 5 July 1861 at Jamestown; (18); farmer.

Watson, William H.: Enl. 7 September 1862 at Greensville; *captured*; died of chronic diarrhea and bronchitis at Point Lookout 7 December 1863.

Weaver, Peter B.: Enl. 4 May 1861 at Hicksford.

Woodcock, William E.: Enl. 15 April 1861; *wounded*; captured 5 or 6 July 1863 at the School House Hospital in Chambersburg, Pennsylvania; exchanged from West's Buildings Hospital 24 August 1863.

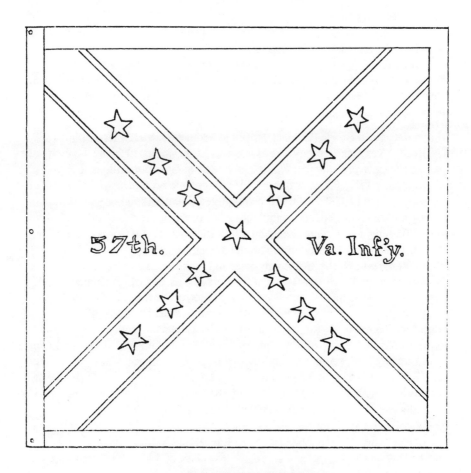

**Flag of the 57th Virginia Infantry
captured at the stone wall
by the 19th Massachusetts Infantry**

57th Virginia Volunteer Infantry Regiment

This regiment was organized 25 September 1861 by the addition of five independent companies to the five companies of Keen's Battalion Virginia Volunteers. Company "A" saw prior service as Company "F," 20th Regiment Virginia Infantry. The regiment was reorganized 7 May 1862.

The following listing for the Field and Staff, and Companies "A," "B," "C," "F," and "I" were obtained from company muster rolls captioned 30 June 1863, near Chambersburg, Pennsylvania. Listings for the remaining units were obtained from the company July/August muster rolls dated 31 August 1863.

Magruder, John Bowie (Colonel): Born at Scottsville, Va. 24 November 1839; lived at Keswick Depot, Va.; VMI class of 1864; graduated from University of Va.; teacher at Culpeper; enl. 22 July 1861 at Charlottesville as Captain of Company "H"; father was Mr. B.H. Magruder; promoted Major in 1862; promoted to Lt. Col. 31 July 1862; promoted Colonel 12 January 1863; *shot* in the left chest and upper right arm (the balls crossing in the chest) within 20 steps of Cushing's guns; *captured*; died 5 July 1863 at U.S. XII Corps Hospital and buried there; disinterred to Richmond in October 1863.

Wade, Benjamin H. (Lt. Col.): Physician in Franklin County, Va. in 1860 at the age of 30; enl. 5 August 1861 at Sydnorsville as 2nd Lt. of Company "G"; promoted to Capt. 17 October 1861; promoted to Major 13 October 1862; promoted to Lt. Col. 2 February 1863; *wounded*; died 5 July 1863.

Fontaine, Clement R. (Major): Born in Buckingham County, Va. in 1832; attended University of Va.; enl. 29 May 1861 at Gravel Hill as 1st Lt. of Company "A"; promoted Capt. 24 April 1862; promoted Major 4 February 1863; promoted Col. 5 July 1863; *wounded*.

Watson, John Davis (Adjutant): (24 in 1865); VMI class of 1864; appointed Adjutant 21 January 1863; wounded.

Phillips, Joseph P. (Capt. and ACS): Enl. 29 May 1861 at Gravel Hill as 3rd Lt. of Company "A"; appointed ACS 10 June 1862.

Smith, William B. (Capt. and AQM): VMI class of 1861; appointed AQM 2 October 1861.

Lippitt, Charles E. (Surgeon): Appointed surgeon 29 October 1861.

Carter, William G. (Asst. Surgeon): Appointed Assistant Surgeon 7 July 1862.

Smith, William W. (Sgt. Major): Enl. 10 July 1861 at Mount Vernon Church in Company "F"; *wounded*; captured at Greencastle, Pennsylvania 5 July 1863; exchanged from Chester Hospital 23 September 1863.

Jones, Philip D. (Ordnance Sgt.): Enl. 8 March 1862 at Charlottesville in Company "H."

Lee, Charles D. (Quartermaster Sgt.): Enl. 10 March 1862 at Bachelor's Hall in Company "I"; appointed QM Sgt. 16 May 1862.

Wood, George A. (Hospital Steward): Enl. 22 July 1861 at Charlottesville in Company "H."

Holman, Samuel D. (Commissary Dept.): Detailed from Company "A"; enl. 29 May 1861 at Gravel Hill.

Lavender, Joseph G. (Adjutant's Office): Detailed from Company "A"; enl. 17 April 1862 at Norfolk.

Legwin, William A. (Wagon Master): On extra-duty from Company "G"; enl. 13 July 1861 at Sydnorsville.

Matthews, Wiley J. (QM Forage Master): On extra-duty from Company "G"; enl. 20 July 1861 at Sydnorsville.

Fitch, Robert H. (Colonel's Orderly): On daily-duty from Company "H"; enl. 15 March 1862 at Charlottesville.

Ambulance Corps

Ayres, James E. (Ambulance Driver): Detailed from Company "A"; enl. 29 May 1861 at Gravel Hill.

Paul, James E. (Ambulance Driver): On extra-duty from Company "F"; enl. 10 July 1861 at Mount Vernon Church.

Teamsters

Melton, John H.: On extra-duty from Company "H"; enl. 24 July 1861 at Charlottesville.

Nichols, James W.: Detailed from Company "C"; enl. 21 June 1861 at Higg's Old Field.

Phelps, Andrew J.: Detailed from Company "G"; enl. 17 April 1862 at Norfolk.

Ray, Eusibeous: On extra-duty from Company "B"; enl. 15 June 1861 at Young's Store.

Stanley, Burwell: On extra-duty from Company "B"; enl. 24 June 1861 at Young's Store.

Stanley, Ferdinand: On extra-duty from Company "B"; enl. 24 June 1861 at Young's Store.

Thomas, George H.: On extra-duty from Company "D"; enl. 22 June 1861 at Gumsprings.

Zeigler, William A.: On extra-duty from Company "E"; enl. 22 April 1862 at Fort Dillard, North Carolina.

Company "A" ("Jeff Davis Guard")
(formerly Company "F," 20th Virginia Infantry)

This company enlisted 29 May 1861 at Gravel Hill, Buckingham County, Virginia for one year, and was reorganized 16 April 1862.

Ford, P. Fletcher (Jr. 2nd Lt.): Born in Buckingham County; *killed.*

Meador, Wyatt S. (1st Sgt.): *Shot* in the right lower jaw.

Agee, Garland P. (2nd Sgt.): *Shot* in the inner upper third of the right arm, the ball passing under the scapula and exiting between the scapula and the spine.

Seay, John R. (4th Sgt.): *Killed.*

Shepard, Samuel M. (5th Sgt.): *Killed.*

Morgan, John J. (1st Cpl.): *Captured*; exchanged 15 November 1864.

Duncan, Stephen A. (2nd Cpl.): *Shot* in the middle third of the left leg; *captured*; exchanged from DeCamp Hospital 28 August 1863.

Maxey, Frederick C. (3rd Cpl.): *Killed.*

Lewis, Samuel M. (4th Cpl.): Enl. 7 November 1861; *killed.*

Adcock, Thomas A.: Enl. 10 March 1862 at Gary's Store; *captured*; died at Point Lookout 24 February 1864.

Adkins, Robert: Enl. 17 April 1862 at Norfolk.

Blackwell, Houston L.: Enl. 22 August 1861; *captured*; exchanged February 1865.

Blackwell, John D.: Enl. 29 March 1863 at Fort Powhatan; *captured*; exchanged prior to 1 May 1864.

Brooks, William R.: Enl. 25 February 1862.

Coleman, Chapman J.: Enl. 17 April 1862 at Norfolk; *captured*; exchanged sick with acute diarrhea 1 August 1863.

Drake, Robert B.: Enl. 22 August 1861; born in Buckingham County; received a *fractured* thigh, and *captured*; died 8 July 1863.

Dunkum, Richard L.: Enl. 22 August 1861; *shot* in the left shoulder and *captured*; treated at U.S. XII Corps Hospital; exchanged from DeCamp Hospital 8 September 1863.

Dunkum, William B.: Enl. 22 August 1861; *wounded* and *captured*; died of erysipelas at Fort Delaware 26 October 1863; buried at Finns Point, N.J.

England, Benjamin M.: Enl. 10 May 1863 near Drewry's Bluff.

Harris, Alexander B.:

Hodges, William A.: Enl. 17 April 1862 at Norfolk.

Hodges, William H.: Enl. 17 April 1862 at Norfolk; (19 in 1865); farmer; born in Franklin County; *shot* in the right groin and *captured*; exchanged from DeCamp Hospital 27 September 1863.

Huddleston, William T.: Enl. 8 March 1862 at Farmville.

Janney, Isaac: Enl. 17 April 1862 at Norfolk; *shot* in the thigh and leg.

Lavender, Tazwell C.: Enl. 17 April 1862 at Norfolk.

Lee, James G.: Enl. 11 September 1861 at Richmond; (19 in 1861); born in Buckingham County; *killed.*

Lee, William A.: Enl. 1 August 1862 at Drewry's Bluff; born in Buckingham County; *killed.*

Lewis, Benjamin W.: Enl. 5 October 1861.

Meador, Jesse L.: Born in Buckingham County; *shot* in the abdomen; died 9 July 1863 at Pickett's Division Hospital; buried at Bream's Mill on the hill; disinterred to Richmond 3 August 1872 with 33 others in three large boxes labeled "P Curns."

Meador, Thomas B.: Enl. 18 June 1862 at Drewry's Bluff.

Merriman, James A.: Enl. 17 April 1862 at Norfolk; *killed.*

Miles, Drury L.: Enl. 17 February 1862; *killed.*

O'Bryant, Thomas H.: Enl. 10 March 1862 at New Store.

Parsel, William: Enl. 17 April 1862 at Norfolk.

Richards, King D.: Enl. 17 April 1862 at Norfolk; born in Franklin County; *killed.*

Seay, Benjamin:

Seay, William B., Sr.: *Killed.*

Seay, William B., Jr.: Enl. 28 March 1863 ar Fort Powhatan; *killed.*

Smith, Arthur L.: Enl. 1 March 1862 at Well Water; *shot* in the right side and arm, and *captured*; exchanged from West's Buildings Hospital 24 August 1863.

Smith, John W.: Enl. 8 March 1862; *killed.*

Smith, Lineas B.: Enl. 20 July 1862 at Drewry's Bluff.

Smith, Nathan L.: Enl. 22 August 1861; *captured*; exchanged 14 or 15 February 1865.

Snoddy, Lorenzo L.: *Killed.*

Southall, Delbert T.: Enl. 5 October 1861.

Stinson, George M.: *Killed.*

Stone, William R.: Enl. 17 April 1862 at Norfolk; *killed.*

Thomas, John T.: *Captured*; exchanged 20 or 21 February 1865.

Thompson, George W.: Enl. 17 April 1862 at Norfolk.

Wade, Alfred J.: *Captured*; exchanged with acute diarrhea 1 August 1863.

Walden, William T.: Enl. 22 August 1861.

Whitlow, James H.: Enl. 17 April 1862 at Norfolk; (25 in 1865); born in Franklin County; *shot* in the right leg (lower third amputated), and *captured*; exchanged from West's Buildings Hospital 27 September 1863.

Williams, James E.: *Captured*; exchanged 20 or 21 February 1865.

Williams, William:

Wilson, George W.: *Captured*; exchanged sick with scurvy 22 September 1864.

Wilson, Robert M.:

Wootton, Anderson:

<u>Company "B" ("Franklin Sharpshooters")</u>

This company enlisted 15 June 1861 at Young's Store, Franklin County, Virginia for twelve months, and was reorganized 7 May 1862.

Smith, John H. (Capt.): Enl. 23 July 1861 at Big Lick; born in Franklin County; *killed.*

Ward, John L. (1st Lt.): Enl. 23 July 1861 at Big Lick.

Prillaman, Chrisitian S. (2nd Lt.): Enl. 6 March 1862 in Franklin County; *wounded.*

Prillaman, Isaac C. (2nd Lt.): Born in Franklin County; *killed.*

Helms, George T. (2nd Sgt.): *Captured*; exchanged 20 or 21 February 1865.

Davis, Solomon K. (4th Sgt.): Born in Franklin County; *wounded.*

Prillaman, Fleming M. (5th Sgt.): *Shot* in the lower third of the left thigh, and *captured*; exchanged from West's Buildings Hospital 17 November 1863.

Starkey, Robert M. (2nd Cpl.):

Thornton, Addison H. (3rd Cpl.):

Thornton, John S. (4th Cpl.)

Bowles, Daniel M.: *Wounded.*

Brown, Charles H.:

Cox, Joseph: Enl. 6 March 1862 in Franklin County.

Davis, Thomas: Enl. 11 July 1861.

Eggleton, Armistead J.: Enl. 17 April 1862 at Fort Dillard, North Carolina; *wounded* and *captured*; exchanged from DeCamp Hospital 8 September 1863.

Goode, Jonas: Enl. 12 July 1861; *captured*; exchanged sick with debility 6 March 1864.

Goode, William P.: Enl. 6 March 1862 in Franklin County; *captured*; released from Fort Delaware 20 June 1865.

Jacobs, David P.: Enl. 6 March 1862 in Franklin County; (present in arrest for desertion).

Lackey, George: Born in Franklin County; *killed*.

Lackey, Josiah:

Mason, Joseph W.: Enl. 2 July 1861.

Massey, William B.:

Maxey, Bruce E.: Enl. 6 March 1862 in Franklin County.

Maxey, Levi P.: Enl. 6 March 1862 in Franklin County.

Maxey, William W.:

McMellon, John W.: Enl. 20 June 1861; *shot* in the right side, and *captured*; exchanged 1 August 1863.

McMellon, William H.: Enl. 6 March 1862 in Franklin County; *shot* in the scalp, and *captured*; no further record beyond 15 October 1863; may have died in a Federal hospital or prison.

Meeks, Robert S.: *Wounded.*

Mullins, Andrew J.:

Mullins, Booker: Enl. 6 March 1862 in Franklin County.

Mullins, Henry M.: Enl. 6 March 1862 in Franklin County.

Otey, John M.: Enl. 12 July 1861; born in Franklin County; *wounded* and *captured*; died of wounds in a hospital near Gettysburg; date unknown.

Ramsey, Henry C.:

Ramsey, William B.: Enl. 1 September 1861 at Richmond.

Ray, Abner: Enl. 22 June 1861.

Ray, John: Enl. 15 August 1862 in Franklin County; (29 in 1863); farmer; received a *fractured* right knee (amputated at middle third of leg 6 July) and *captured*; exchanged 20 March 1864.

Ray, William R.:

Scott, Samuel H.: Enl. 22 June 1861.

Shelton, Josiah W.: Enl. 20 June 1861; born in Patrick County; received a *gunshot* fracture of the thigh, and *captured*; died at U.S. II Corps Hospital 27 July 1863, and buried in Grave #5 in back of Schwartz's barn.

Spencer, Andrew J.: Enl. 22 June 1861.

Stanley, Dennis P.: *Shot* in the left thigh, and *captured*; exchanged from West's Buildings Hospital 24 August 1863.

Stone, Moses H.: Enl. 6 March 1862 in Franklin County.

Stone, Stephen B.: Enl. 22 June 1861; *captured*; exchanged from Chester Hospital 23 September 1863.

Thornton, Joseph A.: Enl. 6 March 1862 in Franklin County; born in Franklin County; *killed.*

Thornton, Samuel W.: *Wounded* in the right side and thigh (flesh wound), and *captured*; treated at U.S. 1st Division, I Corps Hospital; exchanged 6 March 1864.

Company "C" ("Franklin Fire Eaters")

This company enlisted 21 June 1861 at Higg's Old Field, Franklin County, Virginia for twelve months; joined Keen's Battalion, probably as Company "D," 16 September 1861; and was reorganized 7 May 1862.

Heckman, David P. (Captain): (34 in 1865); *wounded.*

Jones, Charles H. (1st Lt.): (28 in 1865); VMI class of 1850.

Miles, James E. (2nd Lt.): Wife was Mrs. Jane Miles.

Cannaday, Giles L. (3rd Lt.): Enl. 22 June 1861 at Pig River.

Vest, Samuel (1st Sgt.):

Adkins, William H. (2nd Sgt.):

Vest, Willis M. (4th Sgt.): (21 in 1863); born in Franklin County; wife was Mrs. M.J. Vest; *shot* in both shoulders injuring the lungs and *captured*; died at West's Buildings Hospital 18 August 1863.

Hill, James R. (5th Sgt.): Enl. 7 July 1861 at Long Branch.

Hale, Robert (1st Cpl.): (23 in 1865); received a *gunshot* fracture of the right tibia, and *captured*; exchanged 6 March 1864.

Via, Samuel (2nd Cpl.):

Payne, Jefferson (3rd Cpl.): Enl. 21 July 1861 at Pig River; sick 4 July 1863; died of diarrhea in Floyd County, Virginia 23 October 1863.

Heckman, Joseph W. (4th Cpl.): Enl. 10 July 1861 at Pig River; born in Franklin County; *killed.*

Bowles, Middleton G. (Musician): Enl. 17 April 1862 at Norfolk.

Delancy, John P. (Musician): Enl. 20 July 1861 at Pig River.

Adkins, Peter H.: Enl. 23 July 1861 at Pig River; *wounded* and *captured*; died at Gettysburg 8 July 1863.

Adkins, Robert:

Bird, Samuel W.: Enl. 17 April 1862 at Norfolk; born in Henry County; *wounded*; died 3 July 1863.

Bowles, Henry C.: Enl. 4 February 1863 at Guinea Station; (present sick in camp).

Bowles, William R.: Enl. 11 February 1863 at Guinea Station.

Davis, William H.: (36 in 1862); farmer; born in Franklin County.

Dowdy, Thomas W.: Enl. 7 March 1862 at Long Branch; *captured*; died of acute diarrhea at Fort Delaware 12 September 1863; buried at Finns Point, N.J.

Draper, John H.: Enl. 17 April 1862 at Norfolk; *captured*; exchanged 20 or 21 February 1865.

Edwards, James D.: Enl. 17 April 1862 at Norfolk; *shot* in the left lung and *captured*; died of exhaustion at Chester Hospital 25 July 1863 and buried in Grave #76 of that hospital's cemetery.

Geer, Alexander: *Shot* in the side, and *captured*; died 7 July 1863.

Harris, James: Enl. 17 April 1862 at Norfolk; *wounded* in the right shoulder and *captured*; exchanged 1 August 1863.

Heckman, James A.: Enl. 17 April 1862 at Norfolk.

Jones, Fleming:

Jones, William: Enl. 23 July 1861 at Pig River; mechanic.

Martin, Mathew: Enl. 1 March 1862 at Long Branch.

Martin, Robert: AWOL 4 August through 19 September 1863.

Miles, John H.:

Montgomery, John B.: Enl 17 April 1862 at Norfolk; *wounded* and *captured*; exchanged from West's Buildings Hospital 24 August 1863.

Moran, William: Enl. 17 April 1862 at Norfolk; *shot* in the righ arm; died of his wounds at General Hospital #1 at Richmond 30 July 1863.

Nichols, Charles: Enl. 17 March 1862 at Long Branch; (23 in 1863); single; received a compound *fracture* of the right thigh, and *captured*; died at Letterman Hospital 11 September 1863 and buried in Section 7, Grave #29 of that hospital's cemetery; disinterred to Richmond 13 June 1872 in Box # 93.

Pate, John B.:

Peters, William: Enl. 21 July 1861 at Pig River; wife was Mrs. Rachel Peters; *wounded*; died 4 July 1863.

Poff, William B.: Enl. 22 June 1861 at Pig River.

Radford, Greenville R.:

Rakes, Sparrel:

Richerson, Peter: Enl. 15 March 1862 at Long Branch; AWOL 4 August through 19 September 1863.

Roberson, Benjamin S.: Enl. 11 January 1863 at Guinea Station; *wounded* and *captured*; died of his wounds at West's Buildings Hospital 16 August 1863.

Shively, William: Enl. 20 July 1861 at Pig River.

Smith, Willis: Enl. 15 March 1862 at Long Branch; *wounded*.

Terry, Peter: Enl. 20 July 1861 at Pig River.

Trail, Creed V.: Enl. 15 March 1863 at Fort Powhatan; AWOL 4 August through 19 September 1863.

Trail, William V.: Enl. 15 March 1862 at Long Branch; (27 in 1865); farmer; born in Franklin County; *shot* in the left thigh fracturing the femur, and *captured*; exchanged from Chester Hospital 23 September 1863.

Webb, John W.: AWOL 4 August through 19 September 1863.

Company "D" ("Galveston Tigers")
(formerly Company "A," Keen's Battalion)

This company enlisted 22 June 1861 at Gumsprings, Pittsylvania County, Virginia for twelve months, and was reorganized 7 May 1862.

Dickinson, David V. (Captain): *Captured*; exchanged 24 February 1865.

Rowles, Wilford G. (1st Lt.): Enl. 6 July 1861 at Springfield; (38 in 1865).

Dyer, Leroy S. (2nd Lt.): *Captured*; exchanged 24 February 1865.

Robertson, Edward S. (2nd Lt.): Enl. 6 July 1861 at Springfield; *captured*; exchanged 22 March 1865.

Haden, John T. (1st Sgt.): Enl. 6 July 1861 at Springfield.

Abbott, John C. (4th Sgt.): Enl. 22 April 1862 at Fort Dillard, North Carolina; *captured*; exchanged 20 or 21 February 1865.

Haden, Thomas D. (5th Sgt.): Enl. 21 July 1861 at Galveston; *shot* in the face, and *captured*; exchanged from Chester Hospital 23 September 1863.

Goad, Richard (Cpl.): Enl. 24 July 1861 at Galveston; *captured*; exchanged 20 or 21 February 1865.

Hancock, John H. (Cpl.): Enl. 5 March 1862 at Pittsylvania Court House.

Tosh, Daniel (Cpl.): Enl. 6 July 1861 at Springfield.

Adams, William H.: Enl. 5 March 1862 at Pittsylvania Court House.

Austin, John H.: Enl. 22 April 1862 at Fort Dillard, North Carolina; wife was Mrs. S.A. Austin; *wounded*; died in Franklin County December 1863.

Barber, Charles H.: Enl. 11 March 1862 at Pittsylvania Court House.

Butcher, James T.: Enl. 14 March 1862 at Pittsylvania Court House; deserted and captured at South Mountain 5 July 1863; exchanged 20 or 21 February 1865.

Compton, John W.: Enl. 10 March 1862 at Pittsylvania Court House.

Dalton, John A.: Enl. 10 August 1861 at Galveston; *wounded*.

Dalton, Jubal: Enl. 13 March 1862 at Pittsylvania Court House.

Dalton, Winchester W.:

Doss, Charles L.: Enl. 5 September 1861 at Richmond; *wounded* in the right leg.

Gray, William W.: Enl. 22 April 1862 at Fort Dillard, North Carolina.

Gregory, William R.: Enl. 10 March 1862 at Pittsylvania Court House; the company reported him as missing in action but there are no Federal records concerning him; *killed*.

Haizlip, Jefferson: Enl. 22 April 1862 at Fort Dillard, North Carolina; *captured*; died of remittent fever at Fort Delaware 25 September 1863; buried at Finns Point, N.J.

Hines, Thomas H.: Enl. 14 March 1862 at Pittsylvania Court House; *wounded*.

Kissee, John H.: Enl. 5 September 1861 at Richmond.

Manuel, John: Enl. 2 February 1862 at Richmond; (probably present in the division guard house).

Manuel, Robert W.: Enl. 29 August 1861 at Danville.

Mayhue, William H.: Enl. 4 March 1862 at Pittsylvania Court House.

Murphy, John W.: Enl. 28 February 1862 at Pittsylvania Court House.

Murphy, Robert B.: Enl. 1 August 1861 at Galveston; *captured*; exchanged sick with bronchitis 23 September 1864.

Murphy, Wyatt B.: Enl. 1 August 1861 at Galveston.

Mustain, Creed G.: Enl. 9 March 1862 at Pittsylvania Court House; born in Pittsylvania County; *shot* in the left hip and foot, and *captured*; died 23 July 1863.

Mustain, Thomas N.: Enl. 28 February 1862 at Pittsylvania Court House; *wounded* in the head and neck, and *captured*; treated at U.S. 1st Division, I Corps Hospital; exchanged from Chester Hospital 17 August 1863.

Owen, James W.:

Payne, Richard J.:

Pugh, Columbus C.: Enl. 5 March 1862 at Pittsylvania Court House; deserted and captured 5 July 1863; exchanged 20 or 21 February 1865.

Robertson, Joel T.: Enl. 28 February 1862 at Pittsylvania Court House.

Robertson, John T.: Enl. 10 August 1861 at Galveston; *captured*; exchanged 20 or 21 February 1865.

Saunders, James D.: Enl. 22 July 1861 at Galveston.

Shelton, James C.:

Shelton, Thomas: (19 in 1863); farmer; *shot* in the side, and *captured*; exchanged from West's Buildings Hospital 27 September 1863.

Shelton, William T.: Enl. 30 May 1861 at Laurel Grove; *captured*; died of chronic diarrhea at Fort Delaware 14 November 1863; buried at Finns Point, N.J.

Simpson, Ulum B.: Enl. 13 March 1862 at Pittsylvania Court House.

Tinsley, Samuel H.: Enl. 22 April 1862 at Fort Dillard, North Carolina; captured while serving as a nurse at Gettysburg; exchanged prior to 31 August 1863.

Townsend, James C.: Enl. 13 March 1862 at Pittsylvania Court House; *captured*; exchanged 20 or 21 February 1865.

Company "E" ("Pig River Greys")
(formerly Company "B," Keen's Battalion)

This company enlisted 29 June 1861 at Rorer's, Pittsylvania County, Virginia for twelve months, and was reorganized 16 April 1862.

Ramsey, William Henry (Captain): *Wounded* in the right shoulder.

Woody, Ralph S. (1st Lt.):

Lawrence, James H. (2nd Lt.): Enl. 21 July 1861.

Boswell, John L.C. (1st Sgt.): Born in Pittsylvania County; received a *gunshot* fracture of the hip and thigh, and *captured*; died at U.S. II Corps Hospital 14 July 1863 and buried in Yard D of that hospital's cemetery; disinterred to Richmond 13 June 1872 with 110 others in ten large boxes labeled "S."

Wright, Thomas R. (2nd Sgt.): Enl. 8 July 1861.

Mahan, Joseph C. (3rd Sgt.): Enl. 10 July 1861; *shot* in the left and right sides of the face, and *captured*; treated at U.S. XII Corps Hospital; exchanged from DeCamp Hospital 28 August 1863.

Anderson, James (4th Sgt.): Enl. 25 July 1861.

McDowell, Joseph T. (5th Sgt.): Enl. 15 July 1861; *wounded.*

Young, Thomas S. (1st Cpl.): Enl. 22 April 1862 at Fort Dillard, North Carolina; *captured*; released from Fort Delaware 10 June 1865.

Young, Charles P. (2nd Cpl.): Enl. 22 April 1862 at Fort Dillard, North Carolina; (33); *shot* in the left arm (amputated) and *captured*; exchanged from West's Buildings Hospital 24 August 1863.

Jefferson, James T. (3rd Cpl.): Enl. 28 February 1863 at Fort Powhatan; *wounded* and *captured*; died of his wounds at West's Buildings Hospital 16 August 1863.

Deboe, Joseph (4th Cpl.): The company reported him as missing in action but there are no Federal records concerning him; *killed.*

426

Adkins, Henry: Enl. 1 July 1861; *captured*; died of chronic diarrhea at Fort Delaware 7 August 1863; buried at Finns Point, N.J.

Adkins, Ralph: Enl. 1 July 1861; *captured*; exchanged 20 or 21 February 1865.

Barber, George W.: Enl. 20 March 1862 at Fort Powhatan.

Blankenship, Elijah P.: Enl. 22 April 1862 at Fort Dillard, North Carolina; *shot* in the leg (amputated) and *captured*; exchanged from DeCamp Hospital 8 September 1863.

Brown, Burwell B.: Enl. 22 April 1862 at Fort Dillard, North Carolina.

Carter, James M.: Enl. 10 December 1862 at Fredericksburg; *wounded* in the left shoulder, and *captured*; exchanged from Chester Hospital 23 September 1863.

Crider, John H.: Enl. 22 April 1862 at Fort Dillard, North Carolina; *shot* in the shoulder and *captured*; exchanged from Chester Hospital 23 September 1863.

Custard, Alexander: Enl. 17 August 1861; the company reported him as missing in action, and subsequently as captured but there are no Federal records concerning him; *killed*.

Doss, Christopher C.: Enl. 22 April 1862 at Fort Dillard, North Carolina; *captured*; joined U.S. 1st Connecticut Cavalry at Fort Delaware 30 August 1863.

English, James H.: Enl. 22 April 1862 at Fort Dillard, North Carolina.

George, William: Enl. 15 March 1862 at Sandy Level; *shot* in both legs, and *captured*; died of tetanus 17 July 1863.

Gilbert, Solomon P.: Enl. 22 April 1862 at Fort Dillard, North Carolina; *wounded* and *captured*; exchanged from DeCamp Hospital 8 September 1863.

Guthrie, John H.: Enl. 22 April 1862 at Fort Dillard, North Carolina.

Haley, McMurry:

Hardy, Henry C.: Enl. 8 August 1861; *shot* in the abdomen.

Headrick, Columbus: Enl. 22 April 1862 at Fort Dillard, North Carolina.

Headrick, Jacob, Jr.: Enl. 22 April 1862 at Fort Dillard, North Carolina; *killed*.

Hines, John H.: Enl. 15 March 1862 at Sandy Level; *captured*; died of disease at Fort Delaware 20 October 1863.

Jefferson, William Taze: Enl. 21 July 1861; possibly *wounded*; sick in hospital 15 July 1863.

Jefferson, William Thomas: *Wounded* and *captured*; exchanged from West's Buildings Hospital 24 August 1863.

Julius, John: The company reported him as missing in action but there are no Federal records concerning him; *killed*.

Kennett, James F.: Enl. 22 April 1862 at Fort Dillard, North Carolina; *wounded*.

Kesler, Peter: Enl. 22 April 1862 at Fort Dillard, North Carolina; born in Franklin County; *killed*.

Lawrence, George W.: Enl. 11 March 1862 at Danbury, North Carolina.

Mahan, Abner A.: Enl. 15 March 1862 at Sandy Level; received a contusion *fracture* of the cheek and nose, and *captured*; exchanged from DeCamp Hospital 28 August 1863.

McGhee, William H.: (25 in 1865); farmer; *shot* in the left ankle, and *captured*; exchanged from West's Buildings Hospital 24 August 1863.

Mease, John R.: *Captured*; released from Fort Delaware 20 June 1865.

Oakes, Charles H.: Enl. 22 April 1862 at Fort Dillard, North Carolina.

Osborn, John H.: Enl. 15 March 1862 at Sandy Level.

Owen, Coleman B.: Enl. 13 March 1862 at Sandy Level.

Owen, William T.: Enl. 14 March 1862 at Sandy Level; captured 5 July 1863 while serving as a nurse at Gettysburg; exchanged sick with chronic rheumatism 20 March 1864.

Rigna, Henry:

Rowles, William: Enl. 6 July 1861 at Springfield in Company "D"; received a flesh *wound* in the right leg.

Smith, William H.: Enl. 12 March 1862 at Sandy Level.

Stevens, Isaac D.:

Toler, John J.:

Willis, Count D.A.: Enl. 13 March 1862 at Sandy Level; the company reported him as missing in action but there are no further records concerning him; *killed*.

Willis, James E.: Enl. 11 March 1862 at Sandy Level; left sick near Falling Waters, Maryland 10 July 1863; no further record.

Young, George W.: Enl. 18 August 1861; (25 in 1865); *wounded* in the back and *captured*; exchanged from West's Buildings Hospital 24 August 1863.

Company "F" ("Henry and Pittsylvania Rifles")

This company enlisted 10 July 1861 at Mount Vernon Church, Henry County, Virginia for twelve months, and was reorganized 7 May 1862.

Griggs, Green T. (Captain): Enl. 1 March 1862 at Bachelor's Hall in Company "I"; (20 in 1865).

Philpott, Benjamin W.L. (1st Lt.): *Captured*; exchanged 22 March 1865.

Slaydon, John T. (Jr. 2nd Lt.):

Stokes, Benton H. (1st Sgt.):

Belcher, Henry S. (2nd Sgt.):

Dyer, Thomas S. (3rd Sgt.): Born in Henry County; *killed*.

Hodges, Richard S. (4th Sgt.): Enl. 17 April 1862 at Fort Dillard, North Carolina; *shot* in the right thigh and shoulder, left hip, and right hand, and *captured*; treated at U.S. VI Corps Hospital; exchanged from DeCamp Hospital 27 September 1863.

Naff, Abram I. (5th Sgt.): Enl. 17 April 1862 at Fort Dillard, North Carolina.

McVey, Chesley (2nd Cpl.): Enl. 17 April 1862 at Fort Dillard, North Carolina; *wounded*.

Brock, Tarlton F. (3rd Cpl.): Born in Henry County; *killed*.

Elliott, Abraham F. (4th Cpl.): *Shot* in the leg, and *captured*; died of chronic diarrhea at Fort Delaware 21 September 1863.

Arthur, John W.: Enl. 17 April 1862 at Fort Dillard, North Carolina; (30 in 1863); farmer; *shot* in the face, and received a fractured left arm (amputated) and *captured*; treated at U.S. 1st Division, I Corps Hospital; exchanged from West's Buildings Hospital 27 September 1863.

Belcher, Granville W.:

Billings, Pierce W.: *Shot* in the right foot (flesh wound) and *captured*; treated at U.S. VI Corps Hospital; exchanged from Chester Hospital 23 September 1863.

Bouldin, Nathaniel H.: (33 in 1864); farmer; wife was Mrs. Sally Ann Bouldin; *wounded* and *captured*; exchanged sick with scurvy 20 March 1864.

Brown, James H.: Enl. 15 May 1862 at Petersburg.

Clift, Zachariah M.:

Donnahoo, Aaron: Enl. 17 April 1862 at Fort Dillard, North Carolina; AWOL 18 July through 27 September 1863.

Gardner, James R.:

Goode, Thomas B.: *Killed.*

Griggs, Lewis S.: Enl. 1 February 1863 at Guinea Station.

Horsely, George W.:

Jones, Creed F.: Enl. 17 April 1862 at Fort Dillard, North Carolina; AWOL 18 July 1863 through 5 January 1864.

Jones, Samuel: Enl. 17 April 1862 at Fort Dillard, North Carolina; *captured*; died at Point Lookout 2 August 1864.

Lester, John C.: *Wounded.*

Martin, Brice E.:

Murphy, Pleasant: Enl. 17 April 1862 at Fort Dillard, North Carolina; *shot* in the penis and *captured*; exchanged from DeCamp Hospital 28 August 1863.

Naff, Isaac M.: Enl. 17 April 1862 at Fort Dillard, North Carolina.

Overfelt, Merit: Enl. 17 April 1862 at Fort Dillard, North Carolina; AWOL 7 August through 27 September 1863.

Overfelt, Robert: Enl. 17 April 1862 at Fort Dillard, North Carolina; AWOL 7 August through 27 September 1863.

Paul, William L.:

Richardson, Benjamin E.:

Robertson, Granville W.: Enl. 17 April 1862 at Fort Dillard, North Carolina.

Robertson, John J.: Enl. 17 April 1862 at Fort Dillard, North Carolina; born in Franklin County; *killed.*

Shaon, John T.: Enl. 17 April 1862 at Fort Dillard, North Carolina.

Shaon, Singleton K.: Enl. 17 April 1862 at Fort Dillard, North Carolina; born in Franklin County; *killed.*

Stockton, Thomas K.:

Thomas, Jackson:

Turner, William J.: Enl. 17 April 1862 at Fort Dillard, North Carolina.

Wagner, William G.: Enl. 17 April 1862 at Fort Dillard, North Carolina.

Warren, Joseph W., Jr.: (present in arrest in the Brigade Guardhouse for desertion).

Wyatt, Richard S.:

Company "G" ("Ladies Guard")
(formerly Company "E," Keen's Battalion)

This company enlisted 13 July 1861 at Sydnorsville, Franklin County, Virginia for twelve months, and was reorganized 7 May 1862.

Arrington, Daniel (Captain): *Captured*; released from Fort Delaware 12 June 1865.

Boon, Marquis D.L. (1st Lt.): Enl. 5 August 1861; *shot* in the hip and thigh, and *captured*; exchanged 5 October 1864.

Holland, Abram F. (2nd Lt.): *Shot* in the left thigh.

Hutcherson, John D. (1st Sgt.): *Killed.*

Boon, Beverly B. (2nd Sgt.): Enl. 1 November 1862 at Rocky Mount.

Angle, Daniel (Sgt.): Enl. 5 August 1861; deserted near Smithfield, Virginia 19 July 1863.

Angle, John W. (Sgt.): Enl. 5 August 1861; deserted near Smithfield, Virginia 19 July 1863.

Martin, John C. (Sgt.): Enl. 26 July 1861; *shot* in the right leg, and *captured*; exchanged 1 August 1863.

Miles, William S. (Sgt.): Enl. 10 August 1861; *shot* in the left lung, and *captured*; exchanged from West's Buildings Hospital 24 August 1863.

Akers, Henry S. (Cpl.): Enl. 17 April 1862 at Norfolk; deserted near Smithfield, Virginia 19 July 1863.

Feasel, Joab R. (Cpl.): *Wounded.*

Parsel, Isaiah (Cpl.): Enl. 26 July 1861; *killed.*

Amos, John N.: Enl. 27 July 1861; (on detached service as of 31 August 1863; paid to 30 April 1863; may not have been at Gettysburg).

Amos, William F.: Enl. 26 July 1861; (on detached service as of 31 August 1863; paid to 30 April 1863; may not have been at Gettysburg).

Bennett, Franklin: Enl. 29 July 1861; received a grapeshot *wound* in the left leg (amputated at middle third), and *captured*; exchanged from West's Buildings Hospital 17 November 1863.

Bird, Obadiah W.: Enl. 17 July 1861; *shot* in the left leg, and *captured*; exchanged from DeCamp Hospital 8 September 1863.

Bird, Wilson T.: Enl. 17 July 1861; *killed.*

Boon, Norman T.: Enl. 17 April 1862 at Norfolk, (20 in 1863); *wounded* in both arms (left humerus resected).

Bowles, William A.: Enl. 17 April 1862 at Norfolk.

Clingingheel, Jacob: Enl. 14 August 1861; AWOL 17 July through 26 September 1863.

Craig, James C.: Enl. 13 August 1861; AWOL 17 July through 10 September 1863.

Crum, John B.: Enl. 20 March 1862 at Rocky Mount; AWOL 19 July through 4 October 1863.

Crum, John S.: AWOL 19 July 1863 through 14 January 1864.

Custer, Hiram: Enl. 20 March 1862 at Rocky Mount; AWOL 23 July through 26 September 1863.

Dalton, James L.:

Dunman, Achilles J.: Enl. 20 March 1862 at Rocky Mount.

Ferguson, Charles D.: Enl. 20 March 1862 at Rocky Mount; (40 in 1865); teacher.

Fowler, Thomas H.: Enl. 20 March 1862 at Rocky Mount; *wounded.*

Hodges, Landon: Enl. 26 July 1861.

Hodges, William R.: (37 in 1863); farmer; *killed*.

Horsley, Thomas: Born in Franklin County; mother was Mrs. Sally Horsley; *wounded* and *captured*; died of his wounds 5 July 1863.

Hutts, John W.T.: Enl. 26 July 1861; *killed*.

Jones, William L.: Enl. 19 August 1861; *captured*; died of acute diarrhea at Point Lookout 14 July 1864.

Kirks, William A.: AWOL 23 July 1863 through 10 April 1864.

La Praid, William W.: Enl. 13 August 1861; AWOL 23 July through 24 October 1863.

Lavender, Robert R.: Enl. 17 April 1862 at Norfolk.

Law, Amos B.:

Law, Joseph: Enl. 26 July 1861; *captured*; died of chronic diarrhea at Fort Delaware 15 September 1863; buried at Finns Point, N.J.

Law, Peter C.: Enl. 17 July 1861; *shot* in the thigh and *captured*; exchanged from Chester Hospital 17 August 1863.

Lynch, James H.: Enl. 5 August 1861; AWOL 23 July through 26 September 1863.

Mason, John K.: *Captured*; died at Point Lookout 9 February 1864.

Matthews, John T.: Enl. 20 July 1861.

McBride, William T.: Enl. 20 March 1862 at Rocky Mount; *wounded*.

McGhee, Elkanah T.: Enl. 20 March 1862 at Rocky Mount; (27 in 1863); farmer.

Parsel, Benjamin F.:

Roberson, Hezekiah: AWOL 19 July through 24 September 1863.

Shorter, Tazewell C.: Deserted 19 July 1863.

Smith, Wyatt H.: Enl. 17 April 1862 at Norfolk.

Ward, William A.: Enl. 17 April 1862 at Norfolk; *killed*.

White, Henry P.: Born in Franklin County; *shot* in the leg and arm (amputated) and *captured*; died at U.S. II Corps Hospital 27 July 1863, and buried in Yard B, Row 2 of that hospital's cemetery; disinterred to Richmond 13 June 1872 in Box #3.

White, John W.: Enl. 1 October 1862 at Winchester; received a *contusion*.

Wilkes, Richard F.: *Shot* in the right calf and *captured*; treated at U.S. 1st Division, I Corps Hospital; exchanged from West's Buildings Hospital 27 September 1863.

Willis, George C.: Enl. 19 August 1861.

Company "H" ("Rivanna Guards")

This company enlisted 22 July 1861 at Charlottesville, Albemarle County, Virginia for one year, and was reorganized 7 May 1862.

Thompson, William (1st Lt.): *Wounded*.

Thompson, Thomas W. (2nd Lt.): Enl. 4 April 1862 at Orange Court House.

Wood, Christopher C. (1st Sgt.): *Wounded* and *captured*; exchanged from Chester Hospital 17 August 1863.

Gillispy, David M. (2nd Sgt.): Enl. 20 September 1861 at Richmond; *captured*; released on oath from Point Lookout, date unknown.

Shifflett, Octavius M. (3rd Sgt.): *Shot* in the arm, and *captured*; died at U.S. II Corps Hospital 13 July 1863 and buried in Yard D, Row 1 of that hospital's cemetery; disinterred to Richmond 13 June 1872 with 110 others in ten large boxes labeled "S."

Eddins, Theodore F. (4th Sgt.): Enl. 8 March 1862; *shot* in the shoulder, and *captured*; exchanged from West's Buildings Hospital 24 August 1863.

Bailey, John C. (5th Sgt.): *Captured*; released from Fort Delaware 19 June 1865.

Norris, James B. (1st Cpl.): Enl. 3 March 1862; farmer; *captured*; released from Point Lookout 14 May 1865.

Tyler, Joseph W. (2nd Cpl.): Received a *gunshot* fracture of the cranium.

Adams, Edward R. (3rd Cpl.): Received a *fractured* humerus.

Jones, Schuyler H. (4th Cpl.):

Bellomy, George W.: Enl. 15 March 1862; received a *gunshot* fracture of a thigh, and *captured*; died at U.S. II Corps Hospital 10 July 1863 and buried in Yard C of that hospital's cemetery; disinterred to Richmond 13 June 1872 with 110 others in ten large boxes labeled "S."

Bragg, Henry Lewis: *Shot* in the left thorax and right arm and *captured*; exchanged from West's Buildings Hospital 17 November 1863.

Bragg, Horatio C.: Enl. 30 March 1862 at Fredericksburg; *shot* in the right thigh and arm and *captured*; treated at U.S. XII Corps Hospital; exchanged from DeCamp Hospital 28 August 1863.

Bragg, Robert T.:

Butler, James O.: Transferred from Company "D," 23rd Virginia 16 October 1862 near Winchester.

Butler, William K.: Enl. 17 June 1862 at camp Drewry; *captured*; exchanged 20 or 21 February 1865.

Bybee, John A.:

Cason, William G.: Enl. 13 March 1862; born in Greene County; *wounded* and *captured*; died at U.S. II Corps Hospital 17 July 1863 and buried in Yard D, Row 3 of that hospital's cemetery; disinterred to Richmond 13 June 1872 with 110 others in ten large boxes labeled "S."

Catterton, Albert M.: Enl. 25 April 1862; received a *contusion* from a shell fragment.

Dudley, Nelson P.: Enl. 9 December 1862 in camp near Fredericksburg.

Eades, James: Enl. 5 March 1862.

Fore, John A.: Enl. 6 February 1862 at Richmond.

Gianniny, Horace M.: Enl. 5 September 1861 at Richmond; AWOL 31 July through 26 August 1863.

Hall, William F.: Enl. 8 March 1862.

Harlow, James M.: *Captured*; exchanged 15 November 1864.

Kegan, Martin: Enl. 24 November 1862 in camp near Fredericksburg.

Lupton, Jacob C.: Enl. 12 March 1862; accidentally shot in the left shoulder at Williamsport, Maryland 12 July 1863; captured 14 July 1863; exchanged from West's Buildings Hospital 17 November 1863.

Maupin, Gabriel O.: *Wounded*.

Mayo, James M.: Enl. 12 March 1862; AWOL 1 August through 18 August 1863.

Meeks, George W.: AWOL 31 July through 18 August 1863.

Melton, William G.: Enl. 8 March 1862; *killed.*

Morris, John R.: AWOL 31 July through 20 August 1863.

Morris, Robert J.: AWOl 31 July through 20 August 1863.

Naylor, John T.: Enl. 13 July 1861 at Stony Point.

Norris, James R.:

Norris, William H.: Enl. 13 July 1861 at Stony Point.

Pace, Benjamin H.: AWOL 31 July through 18 August 1863.

Powell, Edward: Enl. 26 August 1861 at Richmond; *captured*; exchanged 20 or 21 February 1865.

Priddy, William B.:

Reinhart, William W.: Received *gunshot* flesh wounds in both thighs inflicted by a bullet passing through the left and hitting the right thigh, and *captured*; exchanged from West's Buildings Hospital 24 August 1864.

Snow, Pulaski P.: Captured while serving as a nurse at Gettysburg 5 July 1863; joined U.S. service at Point Lookout 14 October 1864.

Tyler, Thomas R.: Enl. 1 March 1862.

Via, Thompson S.:

Company "I" ("Pittsylvania Life Guards")
(formerly Company "C," Keen's Battalion)

This company enlisted 17 July 1861 at Bachelor's Hall, Pittsylvania County, Virginia for twelve months, and was reorganized 16 April 1862.

Ransom, Robert Smith (Captain): Enl. 1 June 1861.

Martin, Richard S. (1st Sgt.): Enl. 20 July 1861; *shot* in the knee, and *captured*; exchanged from DeCamp Hospital 8 September 1863.

Keen, Daniel F. (2nd Sgt.): Enl. 1 March 1862; (sick and not in 3 July 1863 assault).

Payne, Remus M. (3rd Sgt.): Enl. 10 July 1861; *killed.*

Lynsky, Martin C. (4th Sgt.): Enl. 6 March 1862; *captured*; exchanged 20 or 21 February 1865.

Watson, John S. (2nd Cpl.): Enl. 9 March 1862; severly *wounded* in the right chest, and *captured*; exchanged from West's Buildings Hospital 24 August 1863.

Gammon, Levi J. (3rd Cpl.): Enl. 1 March 1862; *wounded* in the face, and *captured*; exchanged from West's Buildings Hospital 24 August 1863.

Turpin, Alfred S. (Musician): Enl. 20 July 1861.

Barber, John E.: Enl. 1 March 1862.

Beggerly, Joel A.: Enl. 1 March 1862; *wounded* in the right eye, and *captured*; exchanged from West's Buildings Hospital 24 August 1863.

Brooks, John T.: Enl. 1 March 1862.

Brown, John P.: Enl. 15 June 1861.

Bryant, Peter: Enl. 1 March 1862; *killed.*

Bullington, James H.: Enl. 1 March 1862; *captured*; exchanged sick with chronic diarrhea 22 September 1864.

Childress, William J.: Enl. 1 March 1862; *wounded.*

Cobler, John S.: Enl. 28 February 1862.

Cook, Evans T.: Enl. 20 August 1861.

Cook, John R.: Enl. 1 March 1862; *shot* in the head, and wounded by a shell fragment in the right thigh, and *captured*; treated at U.S. 1st Division, I Corps Hospital; exchanged sick with rheumatism 6 March 1864.

Davis, Jackson: Enl. 18 February 1862; born in Pittsylvania County; *killed.*

Earles, Jesse: Enl. 10 June 1861; *captured*; exchanged sick 1 August 1863.

Earles, Uriah C.: Enl. 10 June 1861; possibly *wounded*; *captured*; exchanged 1 August 1863.

Frazier, William M.: Enl. 28 February 1862.

Gammon, John C.: Enl. 10 June 1861; (22 in 1861); farmer; *captured*; exchanged 15 October 1864.

Gaulding, John R.: Enl. 15 August 1861; (26 in 1863); farmer; *wounded* in the back,and *captured*; exchanged from West's Buildings Hospital 17 November 1863.

Gilley, Edward: Enl. 6 March 1862; (absent in arrest for desertion).

Gilly, James M.: Enl. 6 March 1862; (present in arrest for desertion; also sick and not in 3 July 1863 assault).

Griffith, Isham T.: Enl. 15 June 1861; (28 in 1863); farmer; *wounded* in the right thigh (flesh wound) and *captured*; exchanged from West's Buildings Hospital 17 November 1863.

Hiler, Peter S.: Enl. 24 February 1862.

Hodges, Willis T.: Enl. 4 March 1862; *wounded.*

Jones, Erasmus D.: Enl. 6 March 1862.

Jones, John R.: Enl. 20 August 1861.

Lee, Richard H.: Enl. 20 February 1862; received a *gunshot* fracture of the knee, and *captured*; died at U.S. II Corps Hospital 15 July 1863 and buried in Yard D, Row 3 of that hospital's cemetery; disinterred to Richmond 13 June 1872 with 110 others in ten large boxes labeled "S."

Lewis, Joseph S.: Enl. 28 February 1862.

Lynsky, Patrick H.: Enl. 1 March 1862.

Mahon, Gideon: Enl. 28 February 1862; *captured*; released from Fort Delaware 20 June 1865.

May, William H.: Enl. 22 July 1861.

McBride, Robert: Enl. 21 February 1862; admitted to a Richmond hospital 19 July 1863, possibly *wounded.*

McDaniel, Major W.: Enl. 15 August 1861.

McDaniel, William H.: Enl. 1 March 1862.

Mullins, William: Enl. 16 September 1861.

Ooles, Uriah: Enl. 1 March 1862; *wounded.*

Overby, Thomas: Enl. 10 July 1861.

Pyron, John H.: Enl. 1 March 1862.

Ragan, John J.: Enl. 28 February 1862.

Ragsdale, James J.: Enl. 10 July 1861.

Robertson, Samuel A.: Enl. 24 August 1861.

Scearce, Joseph: Enl. 1 March 1862; *captured*; released from Fort Delaware 15 June 1865.

Slaughter, John M.: Enl. 22 February 1862; deserted near Bunker Hill, West Virginia 29 July 1863.

Southard, William R.: Enl. 15 August 1861.

Taylor, Newton: Enl. 15 June 1861.

Tomlinson, William J.: Enl. 10 June 1861; (36 in 1861); farmer; born in Pittsylvania County; *killed.*

Trammel, Andrew J.: Enl. 20 June 1861; *captured*; died of chronic diarrhea at Fort Delaware 1 November 1863; buried at Finns Point, N.J.

Williams, Robert H.: Enl. 4 March 1862.

Wilson, William, Jr.: Enl. 15 August 1861.

Wootton, Monroe T.: Enl. 1 March 1862.

Company "K" ("Botetourt Guards")

This company was organized in Botetourt County 20 July 1861 for twelve months, and was reorganized 7 May 1862.

Taylor, John B. (Captain): Enl. at Jackson; wife was Mrs. Mary M. Taylor; *wounded.*

Styne, James M. (1st Lt.): Enl. 24 June 1861 at Jackson; born in Botetourt County; mother was Mrs. Sarah A. Styne; *killed.*

Brewbaker, William (2nd Lt.): Enl. 27 July 1861 at Fincastle (32 in 1865).

Styne, Andrew J. (2nd Lt.): Enl. 15 July 1861 at Jackson; mother was Mrs. Sarah A. Styne; *killed.*

Mays, Thomas L. (1st Sgt.): Enl. 10 July 1861; *wounded.*

Shickel, Theophilus J.H. (2nd Sgt.): Enl. 18 July 1861 at Waskey's Mill.

Moore, Tilford J. (3rd Sgt.): Enl. 18 July 1861 at Waskey's Mill.

Rowland, William P. (4th Sgt.): Enl. 24 July 1861 at Fincastle.

Ripley, Martin V.B. (5th Sgt.): Enl. 18 July 1861 at Jackson.

Dill, John (Cpl.): Enl. 18 July 1861 at Jackson; (30 in 1865).

Givens, Oliver H. (Cpl.): Enl. 1 August 1861 in Craig County; *wounded.*

Hawkins, William S. (Cpl.): Enl. 4 March 1862; *captured*; exchanged 20 or 21 February 1865.

Mullen, Henry W. (Cpl.):

Allen, Andrew J.B.: Enl. 22 February 1862; born in Botetourt County; *killed.*

Allmond, James F.: Enl. 17 April 1872 at Fort Dillard, North Carolina.

Bierly, Andrew J.: Enl. 1 July 1861 at Jackson; discharged 2 September 1861; re-enlisted 25 March 1862 in Botetourt County; *killed.*

Bierly, Samuel D.: Enl. 25 February 1862; *wounded.*

Booze, William H.: Enl. 5 May 1862; *shot* in the thigh and foot, and *captured*; exchanged from DeCamp Hospital 8 September 1863.

Broughman, Andrew J.: Enl. 24 July 1861 at Fincastle.

Broughman, James K.: Enl. 1 May 1862; *wounded.*

Bryant, James: Enl. 10 June 1861; deserted; reported to the Provost Marshal's Office in Washington, DC 7 July 1863; sent to Fort Delaware between 7 and 12 July 1863; no further record; probably not in 3 July assault.

Burger, Abraham: Enl. 18 July 1861 at Waskey's Mill; born in Botetourt County; *captured*; died of typhoid fever at Fort Delaware 22 September 1863; buried at Finns Point, N.J.

Cofer, Joseph E.: Enl. 15 June 1861 at Jackson.

Craft, Jacob M.: Enl. 1 July 1861 at Jackson.

Dolman, Achilles M.: Enl. 20 July 1861 at Jackson.

Driskill, Dennis: Enl. 19 July 1861.

Dupree, James R.: Enl. 1 August 1861 at Fincastle.

Emberson, Allison W.: Enl. 17 April 1862 at Fort Dillard, North Carolina; *shot* in the right thigh, and *captured*; exchanged sick with debilitas 30 April 1864.

Fryer, James P.: Enl. 4 March 1862.

Grilley, Albert: Enl. 18 July 1861 at Jackson.

Hartsville, Jacob A.J.: Enl. 25 March 1862; the company reported him initially as missing in action and subsequently as captured but there are no Federal records concerning him; *killed*.

Hill, James W.: Enl. 6 July 1861; *captured*; died 22 December 1863.

Hill, William: Enl. 6 July 1861 ; born in Alleghany County; *killed*.

Housman, George C.: Enl. 15 June 1861.

Hunt, John C.: Enl. 17 April 1862 at Fort Dillard, North Carolina.

Huse, Jesse H.: Enl. 23 July 1861; born in Botetourt County; *captured*; died at Fort Delaware 15 October 1863; buried at Finns Point, N.J.

Huse, Samuel B.: Enl. 22 February 1862; *shot* in the right hip, the ball carrying away the right testicle, and shot in the finger (amputated), and *captured*; exchanged 30 April 1864.

Johnson, Austin H.: Enl. 20 July 1861; born in Botetourt County; *killed*.

Johnson, Francis: Enl. 18 July 1861.

Johnson, Thaddeus C.S.: Enl. 30 April 1862.

Lemon, William: Enl. 24 July 1861 at Fincastle; born in Botetourt County; *shot* in the foot, and *captured*; died of chronic diarrhea at DeCamp Hospital 24 August 1863 and buried in Grave #823 of the Cypress Hill Cemetery on Long Island.

Linkinhoker, Abraham Thomas: Enl. 5 May 1862.

Linkinhoker, Cary B.: Enl. 18 July 1861 at Jackson.

Linkinhoker, Phillip S.: Enl. 20 June 1861 at Blue Ridge: born in Botetourt County.

Lipes, Harvey D.: Enl. 17 July 1861 at Waskey's Mill.

Lipes, John M.: Enl. 27 July 1861 at Waskey's Mill.

Lipes, William L.: Enl. 24 June 1861 at Jackson; *wounded*.

Lockett, John T.: Enl. 20 June 1861 at Blue Ridge; *wounded*.

Mahone, Edward: Enl. 22 July 1861 at Jackson; born in Botetourt County; *killed*.

McAlister, Jehu H.: Enl. 6 July 1861; *shot* in the side and arm (amputated) and *captured*; exchanged from West's Buildings Hospital 24 August 1863.

McCommac, James M.: Enl. 18 July 1861 at Jackson; *shot* in the testicles, and *captured*; exchanged from Chester Hospital 17 August 1863.

Page, Andrew L.: Enl. 18 July 1861 at Waskey's Mill.

Page, John J.A.: Enl. 20 June 1861 at Blue Ridge.

Peery, Abraham W.: Enl. 25 March 1862.

Peery, John M.: Enl. 27 July 1861 at Fincastle; *shot* in the arm and hand, and *captured*; exchanged from Chester Hospital 17 August 1863.

Peery, Mathew M.: Enl. 25 March 1862; *wounded*.

Redman, Stephen: Enl. 24 July 1861 at Fincastle; born in Botetourt County; *captured*; died of typhoid fever at Fort Delaware 8 September 1863.

Scott, James A.: Enl. at Jackson; the company reported him as wounded, and subsequently as captured but there are no Federal records concerning him; *killed*.

Scott, William W.: Enl. 25 March 1862; born in Botetourt County; *killed*.

Shanks, John R.: Enl. 20 June 1861 at Blue Ridge.

Sheets, French E.: Enl. 15 July 1861 at Fincastle.

Stanley, Charles T.: Enl. 27 March 1862; *wounded*.

Whitmore, John: Enl. 19 July 1861.

Wilcher, William J.: Enl. 18 July 1861 at Waskey's Mill; born in Botetourt County; *killed*.

Winger, Christopher C.: Enl. 12 June 1861 at Waskey's Mill; born in Botetourt County; *killed*.

Winger, Martin V.B.: Enl. 20 June 1861 at Waskey's Mill; born in Botetourt County; *killed*.

Young, Samuel S.: Enl. 10 June 1861 at Jackson.

38th Battalion Virginia Volunteer Light Artillery

This battalion was organized about June 1863 with four companies designated "A" through "D" which had previously been serving as independent batteries.

Field and Staff

The following listing was obtained from a complete review of the service records of all men who served in the unit during the course of the war. Those who could definitely be established as not having been at the battle were deleted, and the residue are listed below.

Dearing, James (Major): Born in Campbell County, Va. 25 April 1840; graduated from Hanover Academy, Va.; entered West Point in 1858; resigned from West Point 22 April 1861; entered Confederate service as a Lt. of the Washington Artillery of New Orleans, La.; Capt. of Company "D" (Lynchburg Artillery) 1862; Major of Artillery 3 December 1862; commanding artillery battalion, Pickett's Division, Dept. of Southern Va. 16 April through May 1863; commanding artillery battalion Pickett's Divison, 1st Corps, Army of Northern Virginia May through July 1863.

Read, John Postell Williamson (Major): Born at Savannah, Georgia 21 April 1829; Savannah Chief of Police 1856-1858; enl. 18 May 1861 at Savannah, Georgia as Captain of Company "K," 10th Georgia Infantry which became the Pulaski (Georgia) Artillery at Savannah, Georgia; promoted Major 4 April 1863; *wounded* in the head by a shell fragment.

Lewis, Thomas (1st Lt. and Adjt.): Enl. 15 May 1861 at Salem as Sgt. Major of the 28th Virginia Infantry; appointed Adjutant of the 28th Virginia 18 March 1862; appointed Adjutant of the 38th Battalion Virginia Light Artillery 13 March 1863.

Meade, Hodijah (1st Lt. and Ordnance Officer): (23 in 1865); promoted 1st Lt. and Ordnance Officer from Private in the 1st Richmond Howitzers 1 March 1863.

Shackelford, J.F. (Surgeon): Appointed Surgeon 4 March 1862.

Marshall, Edward C. (Ordnance Sgt.): Enl. 17 April 1861 at Alexandria in Company "A"; (23 in 1865).

Cable, John W. (Quartermaster Sgt.): Enl. 15 July 1861 at Markham Station; (detailed from Company "A").

Aunspaugh, Joseph (Clerk): Enl. 22 July 1861 or 1862 at Liberty; (on extra-duty from Company "D").

Pendleton, Benjamin (Ambulance Driver): Detailed from Company "D"; enl. 8 June 1861 or 1862 at Lynchburg.

Company "A" ("Fauquier Artillery")
(formerly 1st Company "G," 49th Regiment Virginia Infantry)

This company was organized 22 June 1861 as the Markham Guards; enlisted 1 July 1861 at Markham Station, Fauquier County, Virginia for one year; detached from the 49th Virginia in September or October 1861 to become an independent artillery battery; and was reorganized 12 May 1862.

The following listing was obtained from a complete review of the service records of all men who served in the unit during the course of the war. Those who could definitely be established as not having been at the battle were deleted, and the residue are listed below.

The battery had four Napoleon Smoothbores, and two 20-pounder Parrott Rifles at Gettysburg.

Stribling, Robert Mackey. (Captain): Enl. 22 June 1861.

Marshall, William C. (1st Lt.): Enl. 12 May 1862 at Chickahominy.

Rogers, M.M. (1st Lt.): Enl. 14 May 1862 at Chickahominy.

Archer, Thomas M. (2nd Lt.):

Carroll, Gray (2nd Lt.):

Phillips, A.W. (Quartermaster Sgt.): Enl. 15 September 1862; (34 in 1865).

Powell, F.W. (3rd Sgt.): Enl. 10 March 1862 at Orange Court House.

Howser, William C. (Sgt.): Enl. 12 June 1861 at Leesburg.

Marshall, Jacquelin A. (Sgt.): Enl. 1 November 1861; (21 in 1865).

Mason, Daniel M. (Sgt.):

Norris, James L. (Sgt.): Enl. 6 April 1862 at Yorktown.

Phillips, Wallace A. (Sgt.): Enl. 1 September 1862.

Stribling, Henry C. (Sgt.): Enl. 15 March 1862 in Rappahannock County; (27 in 1864); farmer; born in Fauquier County.

Fouch, John H. (6th Cpl.): Enl. 12 June 1861 at Leesburg.

Heath, J. Brent (10th Cpl.): Enl. 10 April 1862 at Richmond.

Birkby, John M. (12th Cpl.): Enl. 16 April 1862 at Yorktown.

Cable, James F. (Cpl.):

Jett, Peter (Cpl.): (27 in 1865).

Kemper, John J. (Cpl.): Enl. 16 July 1861; (27 in 1865).

Lane, William A. (Cpl.): Enl. 15 July 1861 in Leesburg.

Marshall, Martin P. (Cpl.):

Megeath, James T. (Cpl.): (23 in 1865).

Pearson, James W. (Cpl.):

Smith, William F. (Cpl.): Enl. 12 June 1861 at Leesburg; (40 in 1865).

Thomas, Presley P. (Cpl.):

Ankers, Samuel W.: Enl. 1 June 1861 at Leesburg.

Ashe, H.: Enl. 15 September 1862.

Ashe, James W.:

Ashe, Joseph A.D.: Enl. 15 July 1861.

Ashe, Richard H.: Enl. 15 July 1861.

Aylor, J.F.: Enl. 8 September 1862 at Leesburg.

Ayres, William S.: Enl. 12 June 1861 at Leesburg.

Ball, B.F.: Enl. 12 February 1863 at Fredericksburg.

Barbee, William H.:

Barron, James E.: Date and place of enlistment not shown.

Beales, Joel E.: Enl. 7 September 1862 at Leesburg.

Benedum, James H., Jr.: Enl. 2 March 1863 at Petersburg; born in Loudoun

County; father was Mr. James H. Benedum; had no wife or children at the time of his death in 1864.

Benjamin, William H.: Enl. 12 June 1861 at Leesburg.

Berryman, D.: Enl. 15 September 1862.

Bowden, D.F.: Enl. 18 May 1861 at Prince George Court House.

Brent, Heath J.: Enl. 15 April 1862 at Richmond.

Brierwood, Robert: Enl. 20 September 1862.

Brown, John W.: Enl. 16 April 1863 in Nansemond County.

Bussey, James Henry:

Canard, James W.:

Carruthers, John E.: Enl. 6 April 1862 at Orange Court House.

Carruthers, Thomas N.: Enl. 6 April 1862 at Orange Court House.

Carter, John E.:

Caylor, Samuel T.: Enl. 16 April 1862 at Orange Court House.

Chamberlayne, William C.: Enl. 14 March 1863 at Petersburg.

Cockrell, R.E.: Enl. 15 July 1861 at Leesburg.

Coleman, John: Enl. 1 October 1862; (21 in 1865).

Conner, George: Enl. 9 March 1863 at Petersburg; (25 in 1865).

Cornwell, Jonas: Enl. 1 March 1863 at Petersburg.

Cornwell, Joseph: (31 in 1865).

Cornwell, Thornton: Enl. 1 March 1863 at Petersburg; possibly *wounded*; captured at Martinsburg, Virginia 24 July 1863; exchanged from West's Buildings Hospital 24 August 1863.

Cridler, John W.: Enl. 16 April 1862 at Orange Court House.

Dove, Thomas: Enl. 15 July 1861 at Leesburg.

Dyke, Nathan: Enl. 16 July 1861.

Ford, James: Captured at Chester Gap, Virginia 21 July 1863; released on oath from Old Capitol Prison, Washington, D.C. 19 March 1864 and sent to Philadelphia.

Franklin, Henry T.: Enl. 15 July 1861 at Leesburg.

Freeman, James G.: (31 in 1865).

Freeman, William T.: Enl. 13 February 1863 at Fredericksburg; (20 in 1865).

Gentle, David L.: Enl. 15 July 1861 at Leesburg; (24 in 1865); farmer; born in Washington, DC.

Glasscock, John F.:

Glasscock, Leroy B.: (23 in 1865).

Grimes, John T.: Enl. 12 June 1861 at Leesburg.

Groves, Albert:

Harding, William H.: Enl. 12 June 1861 at Leesburg.

Heffran, Stephen: Enl. 15 July 1861 at Leesburg.

Heflin, J. Thomas: Enl. 13 September 1862; (23 in 1865).

Hoffman, Francis W.:

Hunt, James L.: Enl. 12 June 1861 at Leesburg.

Iden, Abner:

Iden, John N.: Enl. 23 October 1862; (23 in 1865).

Jenkins, Charles T.: Enl. 12 June 1861 at Leesburg.

Johnston, Thomas: Enl. 15 September 1862.

Kane, William A.: Enl. 15 March 1862 in Rappahannock County; (21 in 1865).

Kemper, Joshua: (31 in 1865).

Kendal, George: Enl. 15 July 1861; (23 in 1865); captured at Boonsboro, Maryland 7 July 1863; exchanged 20 March 1864.

Kerrick J.T.: Enl. 9 March 1863 at Petersburg; (20 in 1865).

Kerrick, W.T.: Enl. 15 March 1862 in Rappahannock County.

Kines, Daniel: Enl. 15 September 1862.

Lefever, Samuel C.: Enl. 12 June 1861 at Leesburg.

Major, George C.: Enl. 16 March 1862 at Orange Court House.

Marshall, William: Enl. 17 July 1861 at Gauley Bridge; (24 in 1865).

Mathers, George W.: Date and place of enlistment not shown.

Mathers, T.J.: Date and place of enlistment not shown.

Moore, John: (44 in 1865).

Moore, R.S.: Enl. 2 March 1863 at Petersburg.

Moore, Thomas: Enl. 15 July 1861.

Moran, A.F.: Enl. 14 April 1862 at Orange Court House.

Payne, Arthur: Enl. 15 July 1861; (22 in 1865).

Payne, Bernard:

Payne, Jesse F.: Enl. 14 February 1863 at Fredericksburg.

Payne, William E.:

Payne, William H.:

Pearson, James: Enl. 16 July 1861; (27 in 1864); farmer.

Pearson, Richard E.: Enl. 16 July 1861.

Phillips, John T.: Enl. 10 July 1861; (33 in 1865).

Pritchard, Henry J.:

Rector, Albin: Enl. 15 July 1861.

Rector, Charles H.: Enl. 15 July 1861.

Rector, Marion: Enl. 15 July 1861.

Riley, William H.:

Robinson, John: Enl. 15 July 1861; (27 in 1865).

Saunders, George F.: Enl. 2 March 1863 at Petersburg.

Sillman, Charles L.:

Suddith, Martin:

Swain, Thomas H.: Enl. 25 January 1863 at Fredericksburg.

Thayer, John R.: (23 in 1865).

Thorp, Martin F.: Enl. 15 July 1861.

Underwood, Bushrod: Date and place of enlistment not shown.

Weeks, Joseph: Enl. 15 July 1861.

Welch, Elias W.: Enl. 9 March 1863 at Petersburg.

White, George W.: Enl. 12 June 1861 at Leesburg.

Wines, Elias: Enl. 9 March 1863 at Fredericksburg.

Wright, J.H.: Enl. 15 September 1862.

Wright, William: Enl. 15 September 1862.

Wynkoop, P.H.: Enl. 12 June 1861 at Leesburg; (battery forage driver).
Wynkoop, Simeon: Enl. 6 September 1862 at Leesburg.
Wyser, Joseph: Enl. 15 September 1862.

Company "B" ("Richmond Fayette Artillery")
(formerly Company "I," 1st Regiment Virginia Artillery)

This company enlisted 25 April 1861 at Richmond, Henrico County, Virginia; became an independent battery in the latter half of 1862; and was assigned to this battalion in early 1863.

The following listing was obtained from the company's July/August 1863 muster roll, uncaptioned as to date and station.

The battery had two Napoleon Smoothbores, and two 10-pounder Parrott Rifles at Gettysburg.

Macon, Miles C. (Captain): VMI class of 1856.
Clopton, William I. (Sr. 1st Lt.):
Jones, William Winston, Jr. (Jr. 1st Lt.):
Robinson, Benjamin H. (Sr. 2nd Lt.):
Johnston, Peyton, Jr. (Jr. 2nd Lt.): VMI class of 1864; enl. 25 April 1862; father was Mr. Peyton Johnston, Sr.
Fleming, Robert J. (Sgt. Major):
Carter, Leonard H. (Quartermaster Sgt.):
Newton, George A. (1st Sgt.):
Jones, A.H. (2nd Sgt.): (26 in 1865); painter.
Brown, George W. (3rd Sgt.):
Edwards, A.C. (6th Sgt.): Enl. 2 September 1861 at Gloucester Point; *killed.*
Martin, William T. (1st Cpl.):
McCann, Daniel C. (2nd Cpl.): (30 in 1865); residence in 1865 was 2nd Street between Canal and Byrd Streets in Richmond.
Williams, Milton G. (3rd Cpl.): Enl. 10 March 1862.
Pope, Charles W. (4th Cpl.): Enl. 1 April 1862.
Leary, John H. (5th Cpl.):
Shell, Richard (6th Cpl.):
Spencer, William B. (Artificer): (forage master).
White, James P. (Artificer):
Allen, William A.: Enl. 1 September 1861 at Norfolk.
Benton, George: Enl. 6 July 1861 at Norfolk.
Bohannon, George W.:
Bruce, James: Enl. 20 April 1863 in Rockbridge County; deserted and captured 4 July 1863; joined Capt. Ahl's U.S. Battery 27 July 1863.
Brumfield, John M.:
Butler, Isham: Enl. 20 April 1863 in Nansemond County.
Butler, Solomon: Enl. 20 April 1863 in Nansemond County.
Carr, Jesse: Enl. 20 April 1863 in Nansemond County.
Carter, Thomas R.: Enl. 5 August 1861 at Gloucester Point.

Clements, William: Enl. 13 March 1863 at Wyoming.

Cocke, Edwin: Enl. 11 March 1862.

Cole, Haley:

Dowden, Richard B.: (30 in 1865); laborer.

Doyle, Thomas: (39 in 1864).

Dunn, James: Enl. 6 May 1863.

Epperson, Joseph B.: Enl. 1 April 1863 in Campbell County.

Eubank, Carter H.: *Wounded.*

Fercron, Archer: Enl. 6 March 1862.

Ford, Frederick W.: Enl. 10 March 1862.

Fowlkes, Richard H.: Enl. 10 March 1862.

Fritz, Peter: Enl. 5 September 1861.

Gaines, E.W.:

Gay, William C.: Enl. 18 August 1861 at Gloucester Point.

Gilliam, Robert: (18 in 1862); teamster; born in Richmond.

Hartsberger, Peter A.:

Hawkins, Charles H.C.:

Heath, W.L.:

Herndon, G.A.: Enl. 15 January 1863 in Pittsylvania County.

Hix, A.L.: Enl. 29 September 1861 at Gloucester Point.

Hix, George F.:

Hogan, Joseph: Enl. 31 March 1863 in Pittsylvania County.

Holmes, Julius C.:

Hood, John T.: Enl. 31 July 1861 at Gloucester Point.

Hunt, Michael:

Ingraham, S.H.: Enl. 18 March 1863 in Lunenberg County.

Irby, Morgan G.: Enl. 30 March 1863 in Pittsylvania County.

Jarvis, Ottaway:

Jennings, George F.: Enl. 12 March 1862.

Kane, John: Enl. 18 March 1863.

Keene, James H.: Enl. 20 March 1863 in Nansemond County.

Lampkin, J.W.: Enl. 4 March 1863 in Culpeper County.

Long, Reuben:

Manning, William T.:

Martin, Patrick K.: Enl. 30 September 1861 at Gloucester Point.

Martin, Washington O.:

McCrea, William H.: Enl. 16 February 1863 in Caroline County; *killed*; buried on
   Felix's farm in the woods by the road near the house; disinterred to Richmond
   3 August 1872 in Box #256.

McCurdey, Peter: Enl. 14 July 1861 at Gloucester Point.

McKennon, William: Enl. 21 April 1862.

McNamara, Thomas S.:

Morris, George P.: Enl. 12 March 1862.

Moseley, Thomas F.:

Munda, James E.: Enl. 21 April 1862.

Myers, C.A.: Enl. 15 January 1863 in Pittsylvania County.

Newman, Alexander: (21 in 1862); carpenter.

Perdue, Andrew J.: Enl. 26 July 1861 at Gloucester Point; (45 in 1864); painter; born in Chesterfield County.

Phoeny, Anthony: Enl. 20 April 1863.

Pippin, Elijah: (21 in 1865).

Ramy, T.G.: Enl. 25 April 1863 in Mecklenburg County.

Rayford, A.C.: Enl. 20 April 1863 in Nansemond County.

Reese, Richard:

Reeves, Daniel D.: Enl. 4 April 1863 in Pittsylvania County.

Robinson, James C.: Enl. 2 September 1861 at Gloucester Point.

Robinson, William H.:

Rogers, William H.: Enl. 5 March 1862.

Roper, Edwin:

Rourke, John: Enl. 30 September 1861 at Gloucester Point.

Shell, William:

Shook, James B.:

Sneed, Thomas W.: Enl. 6 March 1862.

Southard, Richard: Enl. 1 April 1862.

Sutton, John C.: (22 in 1865); gas fitter.

Thompson, J.S.: Enl. 15 April 1863 at Danville.

Tyree, James H.:

Udurley, Moses: Enl. 1 April 1863 in Charlotte County; *killed.*

Vaughan, James C.: Enl. 20 April 1863 in Nansemond County.

Walsh, William R.: Enl. 15 March 1862.

West, William H.: Enl. 20 April 1863 in Nansemond County.

Wilson, Alexander J.:

Wilson, Andrew J.: Enl. 30 March 1863 in Pittsylvania County.

Woodward, Robert A.: Enl. 17 April 1863 in New Kent County.

Wright, Pleasant: (28 in 1865), carpenter.

Company "C" ("Hampden Light Artillery")

Organized as "Hampden Guard" in April 1861. Named for English statesman John Hampden (1594-1643). The company enlisted and was mustered into state service 11 May 1861 at Richmond, Henrico County, Virginia for one year as Captain Lawrence S. Marye's Battery Virginia Light Artillery and was reorganized 21 April 1862 as Captain William H. Caskie's Battery Virginia Light Artillery.

The following listing was obtained from a complete review of the service records of all soldiers who served with the unit during the course of the war. Those who could definitely be established as not having been at the battle were deleted and the residue are listed below.

The battery had two Napoleon Smoothbores, one 3-inch Rifle, and one 10-pounder Parrott Rifle at Gettysburg.

Caskie, William Henderson (Captain): (29 in 1865), merchant; residence in 1865 was at the corner of 4th and Franklin Streets in Richmond; elected Captain 21 April 1862.

Sullivan, J.E. (1st Lt.): Date and place of enlistment not shown.

Booker, Lewis (2nd Lt.): Date and place of enlistment not shown.

Beers, Henry H. (Quartermaster Sgt.): Enl. 22 April 1861.

Baughman, Greer H. (1st Sgt.): Enl. 2 August 1862.

Dunn, Woodson (2nd Sgt.):

Trewolla, Samuel P. (3rd Cpl.):

McCook, William H. (4th Cpl.): Enl. 10 May 1861.

Sutton, William (5th Cpl.): Enl. 15 August 1861.

Jones, Reuben A. (6th Cpl.):

Nichols, George H. (Bugler): Enl. 10 May 1861.

McLaughlin, John D. (Artificer): Enl. 10 May 1861.

Allen, John: Enl. 10 May 1861.

Barker, William C.: Date and place of enlistment not shown.

Baughman, E.A.: Enl. 1 May 1863.

Blain, Joseph A.: Enl. 18 May 1861.

Bowe, George A.: Enl. 10 May 1861.

Bradley, Johnston T.: Enl. 10 May 1861.

Breadlouv, William F.: Enl. 21 March 1862 at Fredericksburg.

Bridgewater, O.C.: Enl. 10 May 1861.

Brooks, Albert: Enl. 25 March 1862 at Fredericksburg.

Brown, George W.: Enl. 21 March 1862 at Fredericksburg.

Brown, Thomas J.:

Brunt, Robert W.: Enl. 10 May 1861.

Champion, Z.: Enl. 10 May 1861.

Clayton, George B.:

Cocke, John B.: Enl. 18 July 1861.

Congdon, George W.: Enl. 1 August 1861.

Cottrell, William R.: Enl. 10 May 1861.

Davidson, Robert S.: Enl. 10 May 1861.

Davis, Robert S.:

Doherty, Matthew: Enl. 10 May 1861.

Dunn, James: Enl. 10 May 1861.

Duvall, Melville J.:

Eve, E. Dorsay: (30 in 1862); born in Fredericksburg.

Fields, Thomas B.:

Fisher, Samuel: Enl. 25 March 1862 at Fredericksburg.

Ford, Robert M.:

Ford, Simon Peter:

Gill, James A.: Enl. 10 July 1861; deserted and captured 5 July 1863; joined U.S. 3rd Maryland Cavalry 22 September 1863.

Glass, Anthony: Enl. 21 March 1862 at Fredericksburg.

Glass, Thomas: Enl. 21 March 1862 at Fredericksburg.

Green, William: Enl. 10 May 1861.

Halsey, Charles A.: Enl. 22 August 1862.

Herndon, L.T.:

Hughes, William H.: Enl. 21 March 1862 at Fredericksburg.

Johnson, Charles: Enl. 10 May 1861.

Jones, David N.:

Jones, Eli H.: Enl. 21 March 1862 at Fredericksburg.

Jones, Richard: Enl. 25 March 1862 at Fredericksburg.

Jones, Thomas: Enl. 25 March 1862 at Fredericksburg.

Jones, Walter D.: Enl. 21 March 1862 at Fredericksburg.

Kelley, William H.: Enl. 21 March 1862 at Fredericksburg.

Lindsey, Jeter J.:

Loving, Benjamin V.: Enl. 25 March 1862 at Fredericksburg.

Luck, John H.: Enl. 25 March 1862 at Fredericksburg.

Mahone, James H.:

Mantle, Henry: Enl. 10 May 1861.

Martin, George D.: Enl. 21 March 1862 at Fredericksburg.

Mastern, James: Enl. 25 March 1862 at Fredericksburg.

Matthews, Thomas: Enl. 25 March 1862 at Fredericksburg.

McCurdey, John H.: Enl. 10 May 1861.

McGhee, Richard: Enl. 20 March 1862 at Fredericksburg.

McGinness, Phillip B.: Laborer; mother was Mrs. Ann McGinness; had no wife, children, or father in 1864.

Melton, Benjamin B.:

Melton, Matthew: Enl. 16 July 1861.

Melton, Reuben: Enl. 21 March 1862 at Fredericksburg.

Melton, Samuel M.:

Meyer, Charles: Enl. 9 February 1862.

Miller, David: Enl. 9 January 1863 in Henrico County; (26 in 1865).

Miller, John R.:

Morris, Joseph B.:

Nunnally, Edward D.:

Oakley, James K.: Enl. 10 May 1861.

Otey, George: (22 in 1865); nailer.

Pates, John A.: Enl. 25 March 1862 at Fredericksburg.

Phillips, Richard W.: Enl. 7 March 1862 at Fredericksburg.

Powell, James E.: Enl. 25 March 1862 at Fredericksburg.

Ragland, Joseph H.: Enl. 10 May 1861; (24 in 1865); seaman; residence in 1865 was Origan Hill.

Rey, William T.: Enl. 10 May 1861.

Roberts, Richard F.: Enl. 25 March 1862 at Fredericksburg.

Robertson, Joseph R.: Enl. 10 May 1861.

Rogers, John: Enl. 10 May 1861.

Rountree, Daniel R.:

Schleiser, Conrad: Enl. 25 March 1862.

Smith, Emmett P.:

Snellings, George T.: Enl. 25 March 1862 at Fredericksburg.

Stewart, Charles: Enl. 25 March 1862 at Fredericksburg.

Sullings, Richard: Enl. 21 March 1862 at Fredericksburg.

Sullivan, Woodson J.: Enl. 25 March 1862 at Fredericksburg.

Tennent, Charles B.: Enl. 10 March 1862.

Tennent, Julian R.: Enl. 10 March 1862.

Terrell, Berry: Enl. 10 May 1861.

Thorp, James H.:

Trewolla, Alfred P.: Enl. 17 July 1861.

Tucker, Thomas: Enl. 21 March 1862 at Fredericksburg.

Tucker, William: Enl. 21 March 1862 at Fredericksburg.

Tyler, Samuel G.:

Vaughan, John T.: Enl. 25 March 1862 at Fredericksburg.

Warbritton, Major:

West, James T.: Enl. 25 March 1862 at Fredericksburg.

Wheeler, John H.: Enl. 24 March 1862 at Fredericksburg.

Wicker, Elisha: Enl. 21 March 1862 at Fredericksburg.

Woodson, Aylett R.: Enl. 10 May 1861.

Wright, Carter: Enl. 21 March 1862 at Fredericksburg.

Company "D"

This company enlisted 23 April 1861 at Lynchburg, Campbell County, Virginia for one year as Captain H. Grey Latham's Company Virginia Light Artillery; was reorganized 3 April 1862 as Captain James Dearing's Company Virginia Light Artillery; and became Captain Joseph G. Blount's Company Virginia Light Artillery on 23 January 1863.

The following listing was obtained from the company's May/June 1863 muster roll captioned 30 June 1863, in camp near Chambersburg, Pennsylvania.

The company had four Napoleon Smoothbores at Gettysburg.

Blount, Joseph Gray (Captain): Appointed Captain and assigned to the company 23 January 1863.

Dickerson, James Woodson (1st Lt.):

Blackwell, William H. (2nd Lt.):

Thompson, Joseph L. (2nd Lt.):

Percival, Maurice L. (Quartermaster Sgt.):

Hazlewood, Newton H. (1st Sgt.): Enl. 26 May 1861 at Liberty; (24 in 1865).

Perry, Charles M. (2nd Sgt.):

Ross, Thomas H. (3rd Sgt.): (32 in 1865).

Adams, Samuel W. (4th Sgt.): Enl. 15 May 1861 at Liberty.

Patterson, William H. (5th Sgt.):

Walden, Elijah H. (2nd Cpl.):

Jones, Albert (3rd Cpl.): Enl. 15 May 1861 at Liberty.

Stanley, George W. (4th Cpl.):

Merriman, John E. (5th Cpl.): *Killed*; buried on Crawford's farm in the corner of the woods under a white oak tree near a fence.

Jeter, Tinsley W. (6th Cpl.): Enl. 15 May 1861 at Liberty.

Merriman, Harvey L. (7th Cpl.): Enl. 15 May 1862 at Liberty.

Wright, Gilliam R. (8th Cpl.): (21 in 1864); harness maker; *wounded*.

Arthur, James W.A.: Enl. 18 March 1861 or 1862 at Liberty.

Biby, George W.: Deserted near Hagerstown, Maryland 8 July 1863.

Bush, Eugene: Enl. 10 May 1863 at Hanover Junction.

Cain, Thomas: Enl. 1 September 1862 at Richmond.

Calloway, Charles C.: Enl. 16 February 1863.

Camden, Samuel H.:

Camden, William A.:

Campbell, Elcanah M.: Enl. 22 May 1861 or 1862 at Richmond; mortally wounded in the thigh during the cannonade; buried on George Arnold's farm on the Mummasburg Road on a bluff near a little house along Willoughby Run.

Chenault, Churchwell O.:

Childress, Thomas J.: Enl. 25 August 1861 or 1862 at Richmond.

Coleman, Clifton S.:

Coleman, Robert H.:

Cox, William F.:

Creasy, James T.:

Day, Charles R.:

Dean, James E.: Enl. 8 June 1861 at Manassas.

Deaton, Edward T.:

Dunbar, Elisha: Enl. 24 October 1862 at Winchester; (52 in 1864); merchant; born in Loudoun County.

Earley, Henry T.: Enl. 15 May 1861 at Liberty; (22 in 1864).

Earley, John M.: Enl. 14 May 1863 at Richmond.

Farrell, Michael: Enl. 26 May 1861 or 1862 at Richmond.

Ferguson, Martin P.: Enl. 15 May 1861 at Liberty; *killed* during the cannonade.

Fitzsimons, John: Enl. 1 September 1862 at Richmond.

Foster, Edward B.: Enl. 2 August 1862 at Richmond.

Gibbs, David C.: Enl. 17 March 1862 at Liberty.

Gilliam, James D.:

Goff, Thomas H.:

Hackworth, Lewis C.:

Hewitt, William L.: Enl. 15 May 1861 at Liberty.

Houseman, Joseph: Enl. 22 March 1862 at Shenandoah.

Hudson, Joseph D.: Enl. 20 August 1862.

Hyman, William P.: Enl. 16 February 1863 at Leesburg.

Kelley, Bryant: Enl. 8 June 1861 at Manassas.

Lane, John H.:

Latham, Albert: Enl. 15 May 1861 at Liberty.

Lawless, William L.: Enl. 15 May 1861 at Liberty.

Lindsay, William Daniel: Born in Bedford County; wife was Mrs. Hester A. Lindsay.

Lloyd, Benjamin S.: Enl. 8 June 1861 at Manassas.

Loving, Michael: Enl. 10 March 1863.

Lowry, Granville N.: Enl. 15 May 1861 at Liberty; (30 in 1864); born in Bedford County; father was Mr. Elliott Lowry.

Marks, Thomas V.:

Mason, John W.:

Mays, Joseph R.: Enl. 15 May 1861 or 1862 at Liberty.

Mays, William C.: *Wounded.*

McCory, James C.: Enl. 15 May 1861 or 1862 at Liberty; (AWOL 4 through 19 August 1863).

McCory, Thomas D.: Enl. 19 May 1861 or 1862 at Liberty; (AWOL 4 through 19 August 1863).

McDaniel, Alexander: Enl. 12 March 1862 at Liberty.

McGhee, John B.: Enl. 1 September 1862 at Richmond.

McGruley, James B.:

Mead, Samuel R.: Enl. 15 May 1862 at Liberty; (24 in 1863); farmer; born in Bedford County; *shot* in both legs.

Merriman, George S.: Enl. 15 May 1862 at Liberty.

Moore, Hiram: Enl. 21 March 1862; (59 in 1864); born in Campbell County.

Moore, Jerry: Deserted 5 July 1863.

Moore, William S.: (20 in 1864); baker; born in Kingston, Canada West.

Noell, William T.: Enl. 15 May 1861 or 1862 at Liberty.

Oliver, William H.:

Orndorff, Mason D.: Enl. 1 July 1861 or 1862 at Richmond.

Parker, Lewis C.: Enl. 15 May 1861 or 1862 at Liberty.

Phelps, James B.: Deserted and captured near Fayetteville, Pennsylvania 5 July 1863; released 5 May 1865.

Reynolds, Benjamin J.:

Ross, Robert Budds: Enl. 1 July 1861 at Centreville.

Saunders, Robert A.: Enl. 15 May 1861 or 1862 at Liberty; possibly *wounded*; captured at Greencastle, Pennsylvania 3 (?) July 1863; exchanged 15 November 1864.

Saunders, Wesley M.: Enl. 15 May 1861 or 1862 at Liberty.

Scruggs, Charles O.: Enl. 15 May 1861 or 1862 at Liberty.

Skinnell, Joseph: Enl. 20 July 1861 or 1862 at Liberty.

Smith, Samuel H.: Enl. 4 July 1861 or 1862 at Liberty.

Smoot, James H.: Enl. 1 September 1861 or 1862 at Richmond.

Spencer, Albert G.:

Spencer, Silas:

Spencer, William A.: (25 in 1863); carpenter; born in Nelson County; wife was Mrs. Rebecca Spencer; *killed.*

Stoughton, Francisco P.: Enl. 1 October 1861 or 1862 at Winchester.

Taylor, Charles A.:

Terry, Thomas J.: Enl. 15 May 1861 or 1862 at Liberty.

Torgee, George W.: *Killed.*

Turpin, Sanford: Enl. 1 February 1863.

Turpin, William A.: Enl. 1 February 1863; (31 in 1864); harness maker.
Wells, James M.: Enl. 1 April 1863 at Liberty.
Wells, Jesse W.: Enl. 15 May 1861 or 1862 at Liberty.
Wells, William H.L.: Enl. 15 May 1861 or 1862 at Liberty.
Wicker, Robert Tate:
Wicker, William E.:
Wright, Samuel L.: Enl. 19 August 1862 at Richmond.
Wyatt, Charles Newton:

Appendix I
Strengths and Losses

The following tabulation is a statistical representation of the engaged strength and losses of Pickett's Division on a company by company basis during the cannonade and assault of 3 July 1863. Engaged strengths are intended to reflect those who actually were present under fire during the division's combat at Gettysburg. Some of the units' personnel, while present on the field, did not actually take part in the assault or its preliminaries. Such men would include those detailed to the commissary department, division trains, and the like. While it is impossible to determine from the records exactly who advanced and who stayed behind during the attack, logic would assume that such men would have no reason to advance in the assault. They have, therefore, been excluded from the tabulation. Other individuals, such as teamsters, provost guards, wagon guards, musicians and cooks, have been similarly excluded from the attacking force. These men were occupied in their various duties behind the lines and did not take part in the advance. Cooks are excluded based upon the service records of several individuals which specified that the men were designated as "unfit for field service" and, therefore, assigned as cooks for their units. Their absence from the assault is confirmed by the fact that no man designated as a cook became a casualty during the attack.

Casualties are broken down into the categories of "killed," "wounded," "wounded and captured," and "captured." "Killed" indicates those soldiers who were actually killed on the field of battle. (This category includes those who were listed as "missing in action" but for whom no further record could be found in their service records. It also includes men who were listed by their companies as "wounded and captured" or "captured" but for whom no corroborating Union records could be found.) "Wounded" are those who were hit during the combat but were able to return to their own lines, or who were later recovered by Confederate search parties and were treated in Southern hospitals. Some of these men were captured later when their hospital(s) fell into Union hands on 5 July. "Wounded and captured" indicates those who were hit, captured by Union forces on the field, and subsequently treated in Union hospitals. "Captured" specifies those unwounded Virginians taken by the enemy both during the assault on and retreat from Cemetery Ridge on 3 July.

Engaged and casualty figures are broken down by Officer, Non-Commissioned Officer (NCO) and Private categories in an effort to provide some idea of the magnitude of losses to the division's leadership and combat power. This study indicates that the division as a whole lost 59.7% of its officers, 53.4% of its NCOs and 38.2% of its privates during the cannonade and assault. Deaths from wounds and the ordeals of prison life are also provided in parentheses to indicate the horrors associated with becoming these types of casualties during the Civil War period. 15.8% of Pickett's wounded subsequently died of their injuries, while 29.2% of the division's losses to capture resulted in deaths due to disease in squalid Federal prisons. Fully 928 (35%) of the division's 2,655 casualties died before the end of the war as a result of this assault (498 killed, 233 died of wounds, 197 died in captivity).

Strengths and Losses
Cannonade and Assault Casualties

Unit	Engaged O+NCO+PVT=T	Killed O+NCO+PVT=T	Wounded O+NCO+PVT=T	Wounded & Captured O+NCO+PVT=T	Captured O+NCO+PVT=T	Total O+NCO+PVT=T	Percentage Loss O+NCO+PVT=T
Division Staff	6 + 0 + 4 = 10	0 + 0 + 0 = 0	0 + 0 + 0 = 0	0 + 0 + 0 = 0	0 + 0 + 0 = 0	0 + 0 + 0 = 0	0 + 0 + 0 = 0
Kemper & Staff	5 + 0 + 1 = 6	1 + 0 + 0 = 1	0 + 0 + 0 = 0	2 + 0 + 0 = 2 (1 1)	0 + 0 + 0 = 0	3 + 0 + 0 = 3 (2 2)	60.0 + 0 + 0 = 50.0
1st VA F & S	3 + 1 + 0 = 4	1 + 0 + 0 = 1	1 + 0 + 0 = 1	0 + 0 + 0 = 0	0 + 0 + 0 = 0	2 + 0 + 0 = 2 (1 1)	66.7 + 0 + 0 = 50.0
Color Guard	0 + 3 + 2 = 5	0 + 0 + 1 = 1	0 + 1 + 1 = 2	0 + 2 + 0 = 2	0 + 0 + 0 = 0	0 + 3 + 2 = 5 (1 1)	0 + 100.0 + 100.0 = 100.0
Company "B"	3 + 5 + 19 = 27	0 + 0 + 1 = 1	1 + 0 + 4 = 5	1 + 1 + 4 = 6	0 + 0 + 2 = 2	2 + 1 + 11 = 14 (1 1)	66.7 + 20.0 + 57.9 = 51.9
Company "C"	2 + 4 + 21 = 27	1 + 2 + 4 = 7	0 + 0 + 0 = 0	1 + 1 + 9 = 11 (2 2)	0 + 0 + 0 = 0	2 + 3 + 13 = 18 (1 2 8 11)	100.0 + 75.0 + 61.9 = 66.7
Company "D"	4 + 9 + 30 = 43	0 + 0 + 2 = 2	3 + 2 + 7 = 12	1 + 1 + 5 = 7 (1 1)	0 + 1 + 0 = 1	4 + 4 + 14 = 22 (3 3)	100.0 + 44.4 + 46.7 = 51.2
Company "G"	2 + 7 + 36 = 45	0 + 0 + 1 = 1	2 + 4 + 8 = 14 (1 1)	0 + 0 + 7 = 7	0 + 1 + 4 = 5 (1 1)	2 + 5 + 20 = 27 (1 2 3)	100.0 + 71.4 + 55.6 = 60.0
Company "H"	3 + 4 + 26 = 33	0 + 1 + 1 = 2	3 + 0 + 3 = 6	0 + 2 + 15 = 17 (1 3 4)	0 + 0 + 1 = 1	3 + 3 + 20 = 26 (2 4 6)	100.0 + 75.0 + 76.9 = 78.8
Company "I"	3 + 8 + 23 = 34	0 + 0 + 1 = 1	0 + 2 + 5 = 7	1 + 3 + 5 = 9 (1 1 2 4)	0 + 3 + 2 = 5	1 + 8 + 13 = 22 (1 1 3 5)	33.3 + 100.0 + 56.5 = 64.7
Total 1st VA	20 + 41 + 157 = 218	2 + 3 + 11 = 16	10 + 9 + 28 = 47 (1 1)	4 + 10 + 45 = 59 (1 2 8 11)	0 + 5 + 9 = 14 (3 3)	16 + 27 + 93 = 136 (3 6 22 31)	80.0 + 65.9 + 59.2 = 62.4

Unit	Engaged O+NCO+PVT=T	Killed O+NCO+PVT=T	Wounded O+NCO+PVT=T	Wounded & Captured O+NCO+PVT=T	Captured O+NCO+PVT=T	Total O+NCO+PVT=T	Percentage Loss O+NCO+PVT=T
3rd VA F & S	4 + 0 + 0 = 4	1 + 0 + 0 = 1	1 + 0 + 0 = 1	0 + 0 + 0 = 0	0 + 0 + 0 = 0	2 + 0 + 0 = 2 (1 1)	50.0 + 0 + 0 = 50.0
Color Guard	0 + 0 + 1 = 1	0 + 0 + 1 = 1	0 + 0 + 0 = 0	0 + 0 + 0 = 0	0 + 0 + 0 = 0	0 + 0 + 1 = 1 (1 1)	0 + 0 + 100.0 = 100.0
Company "A"	3 + 8 + 16 = 27	0 + 0 + 0 = 0	2 + 1 + 0 = 3	0 + 1 + 1 = 2	1 + 1 + 1 = 3 (1 1)	3 + 3 + 2 = 8 (1 1)	100.0 + 37.5 + 12.5 = 29.6
Company "B"	3 + 7 + 11 = 21	0 + 0 + 0 = 0	1 + 0 + 1 = 2 (1 1)	0 + 0 + 1 = 1	1 + 3 + 1 = 5	2 + 3 + 3 = 8 (1 1)	66.7 + 42.9 + 27.3 = 38.1
Company "C"	3 + 4 + 15 = 22	0 + 0 + 0 = 0	1 + 1 + 1 = 3	1 + 1 + 2 = 4 (1 1)	0 + 0 + 2 = 2	2 + 2 + 5 = 9 (1 1 2)	66.7 + 50.0 + 33.3 = 40.9
Company "D"	3 + 8 + 45 = 56	0 + 3 + 4 = 7	0 + 0 + 1 = 1	0 + 0 + 0 = 0	2 + 0 + 5 = 7 (1 1)	2 + 3 + 10 = 15 (3 5 8)	66.7 + 37.5 + 22.2 = 26.8
Company "E"	3 + 6 + 20 = 29	0 + 0 + 0 = 0	1 + 0 + 0 = 1	0 + 0 + 1 = 1	0 + 1 + 1 = 2	1 + 1 + 2 = 4	33.3 + 16.7 + 10.0 = 13.8
Company "F"	4 + 5 + 14 = 23	2 + 0 + 1 = 3	2 + 1 + 2 = 5 (1 1 2 4)	0 + 1 + 2 = 3	0 + 0 + 2 = 2	4 + 2 + 7 = 13 (3 1 3 7)	100.0 + 40.0 + 64.3 = 56.5
Company "G"	2 + 8 + 33 = 43	0 + 0 + 1 = 1	0 + 1 + 1 = 2 (1 1 2)	0 + 0 + 1 = 1	0 + 2 + 1 = 3 (1 1)	0 + 3 + 4 = 7 (1 3 4)	0 + 37.5 + 12.1 = 16.3
Company "H"	2 + 7 + 23 = 32	1 + 0 + 0 = 1	0 + 0 + 0 = 0	0 + 0 + 2 = 2	1 + 1 + 1 = 3	2 + 1 + 3 = 6 (1 1)	100.0 + 14.3 + 13.0 = 18.8
Company "I"	3 + 6 + 41 = 50	1 + 0 + 3 = 4	0 + 0 + 2 = 2 (1 1)	0 + 1 + 3 = 4	0 + 3 + 5 = 8 (3 4 7)	1 + 4 + 13 = 18 (1 3 8 12)	33.3 + 66.7 + 31.7 = 36.0
Company "K"	3 + 9 + 31 = 43	0 + 0 + 0 = 0	1 + 0 + 3 = 4 (3 3)	0 + 3 + 1 = 4	2 + 1 + 4 = 7 (1 2 3)	3 + 4 + 8 = 15 (1 5 6)	100.0 + 44.4 + 25.8 = 34.9
Total 3rd VA	33 + 68 + 250 = 351	5 + 3 + 10 = 18	9 + 4 + 11 = 24 (2 2 7 11)	1 + 7 + 14 = 22 (1 1)	7 + 12 + 23 = 42 (5 9 14)	22 + 26 + 58 = 106 (7 11 26 44)	66.7 + 38.2 + 23.2 = 30.2

Unit	Engaged O+NCO+PVT=T	Killed O+NCO+PVT=T	Wounded O+NCO+PVT=T	Wounded & Captured O+NCO+PVT=T	Captured O+NCO+PVT=T	Total O+NCO+PVT=T	Percentage Loss O+NCO+PVT=T
7th VA F & S	3 + 1 + 1 = 5	0 + 0 + 0 = 0	1 + 0 + 0 = 1	1 + 0 + 1 = 2 (1 1 2)	0 + 0 + 0 = 0	2 + 0 + 1 = 3 (1 1 2)	66.7 + 0 + 100.0 = 60.0
Color Guard	0 + 3 + 0 = 3	0 + 0 + 0 = 0	0 + 2 + 0 = 2	0 + 1 + 0 = 1	0 + 0 + 0 = 0	0 + 3 + 0 = 3	0 + 100.0 + 0 = 100.0
Company "A"	3 + 6 + 31 = 40	0 + 0 + 1 = 1	0 + 1 + 3 = 4	0 + 1 + 2 = 3	0 + 0 + 2 = 2	0 + 2 + 8 = 10 (1 1)	0 + 33.3 + 25.8 = 25.0
Company "B"	2 + 7 + 31 = 40	0 + 0 + 2 = 2	0 + 0 + 2 = 2	0 + 0 + 5 = 5 (1 1)	0 + 0 + 2 = 2 (1 1)	0 + 0 + 11 = 11 (4 4)	0 + 0 + 35.5 = 27.5
Company "C"	4 + 9 + 39 = 52	0 + 1 + 1 = 2	0 + 1 + 2 = 3 (1 1)	2 + 1 + 7 = 10 (1 1)	1 + 0 + 1 = 2 (1 1)	3 + 3 + 11 = 17 (2 3 5)	75.0 + 33.3 + 28.2 = 32.7
Company "D"	4 + 7 + 21 = 32	0 + 1 + 3 = 4	1 + 0 + 2 = 3	0 + 0 + 3 = 3	1 + 0 + 2 = 3	2 + 1 + 10 = 13 (1 3 4)	50.0 + 14.3 + 47.6 = 40.6
Company "E"	1 + 4 + 22 = 27	0 + 0 + 3 = 3	0 + 0 + 0 = 0	0 + 1 + 0 = 1	0 + 0 + 2 = 2	0 + 1 + 5 = 6 (3 3)	0 + 25.0 + 22.7 = 22.2
Company "F"	1 + 4 + 22 = 27	0 + 1 + 2 = 3	1 + 0 + 1 = 2 (1 1)	0 + 0 + 2 = 2	0 + 1 + 2 = 3 (2 2)	1 + 2 + 7 = 10 (1 5 6)	100.0 + 50.0 + 31.8 = 37.0
Company "G"	4 + 6 + 34 = 44	1 + 0 + 1 = 2	1 + 0 + 8 = 9 (1 1)	0 + 1 + 2 = 3 (1 1)	0 + 1 + 3 = 4 (1 1)	2 + 2 + 14 = 18 (1 1 3 5)	50.0 + 33.3 + 41.2 = 40.9
Company "I"	4 + 9 + 36 = 49	0 + 0 + 3 = 3	0 + 2 + 2 = 4	2 + 1 + 6 = 9 (1 1 2)	0 + 2 + 1 = 3	2 + 5 + 12 = 19 (1 4 5)	50.0 + 55.6 + 33.3 = 38.8
Company "K"	3 + 8 + 29 = 40	0 + 0 + 0 = 0	1 + 2 + 1 = 4	0 + 1 + 1 = 2 (1 1)	0 + 2 + 0 = 2 (1 1)	1 + 5 + 2 = 8 (2 2)	33.3 + 62.5 + 6.9 = 20.0
Total 7th VA	29 + 64 + 266 = 359	1 + 3 + 16 = 20	5 + 8 + 21 = 34 (3 3)	5 + 7 + 29 = 41 (2 2 4 8)	2 + 6 + 15 = 23 (2 4 6)	13 + 24 + 81 = 118 (3 7 27 37)	44.8 + 37.5 + 30.5 = 32.9

Unit	Engaged O+NCO+PVT=T	Killed O+NCO+PVT=T	Wounded O+NCO+PVT=T	Wounded & Captured O+NCO+PVT=T	Captured O+NCO+PVT=T	Total O+NCO+PVT=T	Percentage Loss O+NCO+PVT=T
11th VA F & S	2+1+0=3	0+0+0=0	1+0+0=1	0+0+0=0	0+0+0=0	1+0+0=1	50.0+0+0=33.3
Color Guard	0+2+0=2	0+0+0=0	0+2+0=2	0+0+0=0	0+0+0=0	0+2+0=2	0+100.0+0=100.0
Company "A"	4+3+28=35	0+0+1=1	1+0+6=7	0+1+2=3	0+0+1=1	1+1+10=12 (1 1)	25.0+33.3+35.7=34.3
Company "B"	4+8+30=42	0+0+2=2	3+1+6=10	0+1+6=7 (1 1)	0+0+1=1	3+2+15=20 (3 3)	75.0+25.0+50.0=47.6
Company "C"	2+7+43=52	1+1+4=6	0+3+4=7 (2 2)	0+0+2=2	0+0+2=2	1+4+12=17 (1 1 6 8)	50.0+57.1+27.9=32.7
Company "D"	4+7+35=46	0+0+0=0	1+1+2=4 (1 1)	0+1+1=2	0+0+1=1	1+2+4=7 (1 1)	25.0+28.6+11.4=15.2
Company "E"	3+5+39=47	0+1+3=4	0+1+5=6	0+1+4=5	1+0+2=3	1+3+14=18 (1 3 4)	33.3+60.0+35.9=38.3
Company "F"	3+8+41=52	0+0+3=3	1+2+4=7 (1 1)	1+1+3=5 (1 1)	0+0+3=3 (1 1)	2+3+13=18 (6 6)	66.7+37.5+31.7=34.6
Company "G"	1+5+26=32	0+0+4=4	1+2+5=8 (1 1)	0+1+4=5 (1 1)	0+0+1=1	1+3+14=18 (6 6)	100.0+60.0+53.8=53.6
Company "H"	1+6+14=21	0+0+0=0	0+2+2=4 (1 1)	1+0+1=2	0+0+2=2 (1 1)	1+2+5=8 (1 1 2)	100.0+33.3+35.7=38.1
Company "I"	3+3+36=42	0+1+2=3	0+0+7=7 (1 1)	1+0+5=6 (2 2)	0+0+5=5 (3 3)	1+1+19=21 (1 8 9)	33.3+33.3+52.8=50.0
Company "K"	3+6+22=31	0+2+1=3	0+2+0=2	2+0+3=5	0+0+3=3 (2 2)	2+4+7=13 (2 3 5)	66.7+66.7+31.8=41.9
Total 11th VA	30+61+314=405	1+5+20=26	8+16+41=65 (1 1 5 7)	5+6+31=42 (5 5)	1+0+21=22 (7 7)	15+27+113=155 (2 6 37 45)	50.0+44.3+36.0=38.3

Unit	Engaged O+NCO+PVT=T	Killed O+NCO+PVT=T	Wounded O+NCO+PVT=T	Wounded & Captured O+NCO+PVT=T	Captured O+NCO+PVT=T	Total O+NCO+PVT=T	Percentage Loss O+NCO+PVT=T
24th VA F & S	3 + 0 + 0 = 3	0 + 0 + 0 + 0 = 0	2 + 0 + 0 = 2	0 + 0 + 0 = 0	0 + 0 + 0 = 0	2 + 0 + 0 = 2	66.7 + 0 + 0 = 66.7
Color Guard	0 + 0 + 1 = 1	0 + 0 + 0 + 0 = 0	0 + 0 + 0 = 0	0 + 0 + 0 = 0	0 + 0 + 0 = 0	0 + 0 + 0 = 0	0 + 0 + 0 = 0
Company "A"	2 + 7 + 36 = 45	0 + 0 + 1 = 1	1 + 3 + 2 = 6 (1 1 2)	1 + 0 + 0 = 1	0 + 1 + 5 = 6 (2 2)	2 + 4 + 8 = 14 (1 4 5)	100.0 + 57.1 + 22.2 = 31.1
Company "B"	3 + 8 + 47 = 58	0 + 2 + 3 = 5	0 + 0 + 1 = 1	1 + 1 + 4 = 6	1 + 0 + 5 = 6 (4 4)	2 + 3 + 13 = 18 (2 7 9)	66.7 + 37.5 + 27.7 = 31.0
Company "C"	4 + 6 + 56 = 66	1 + 1 + 3 = 5	1 + 0 + 11 = 12	0 + 0 + 8 = 8 (5 5)	0 + 0 + 4 = 4 (3 3)	2 + 1 + 26 = 29 (1 1 11 13)	50.0 + 16.7 + 46.4 = 43.9
Company "D"	4 + 8 + 44 = 56	0 + 1 + 7 = 8	1 + 2 + 3 = 6 (2 2)	1 + 2 + 7 = 10 (1 1)	0 + 1 + 1 = 2 (1 1)	2 + 6 + 18 = 26 (1 1 10 12)	50.0 + 75.0 + 40.9 = 46.4
Company "E"	3 + 7 + 18 = 28	0 + 0 + 0 = 0	1 + 0 + 3 = 4	0 + 0 + 1 = 1	0 + 2 + 0 = 2	1 + 2 + 4 = 7	33.3 + 28.6 + 22.2 = 25.0
Company "F"	4 + 8 + 32 = 44	0 + 4 + 0 = 4	2 + 0 + 5 = 7	1 + 2 + 2 = 5	0 + 0 + 2 = 2	3 + 6 + 9 = 18 (4 4)	75.0 + 75.0 + 28.1 = 40.9
Company "G"	3 + 7 + 18 = 28	0 + 1 + 1 = 2	1 + 0 + 6 = 7 (2 2)	1 + 3 + 0 = 4 (1 1)	0 + 0 + 1 = 1 (1 1)	2 + 4 + 8 = 14 (2 4 6)	66.7 + 57.1 + 44.4 = 50.0
Company "H"	4 + 6 + 48 = 58	0 + 0 + 5 = 5	0 + 1 + 1 = 2	0 + 1 + 4 = 5	0 + 1 + 0 = 1	0 + 3 + 10 = 13 (5 5)	0 + 50.0 + 20.8 = 22.4
Company "I"	2 + 5 + 31 = 38	0 + 1 + 1 = 2	0 + 1 + 5 = 6 (1 1)	1 + 1 + 3 = 5	0 + 0 + 2 = 2 (1 1)	1 + 3 + 11 = 15 (1 3 4)	50.0 + 60.0 + 35.5 = 39.5
Company "K"	2 + 3 + 12 = 17	0 + 0 + 1 = 1	0 + 0 + 0 = 0	0 + 1 + 2 = 3 (1 1)	0 + 0 + 0 = 0	0 + 1 + 3 = 4 (2 2)	0 + 33.3 + 25.0 = 23.5
Total 24th VA	34 + 65 + 343 = 442	1 + 10 + 22 = 33	9 + 7 + 37 = 53 (1 6 7)	6 + 11 + 31 = 48 (1 1 6 8)	1 + 5 + 20 = 26 (12 12)	17 + 33 + 110 = 160 (2 12 46 60)	50.0 + 50.8 + 32.1 = 36.2
Total Kemper	151+299+1331=1781	11+24+79=114	41+44+138=223 (3 5 21 29)	23+41+150=214 (5 6 23 34)	11+28+88=127 (7 35 42)	86+137+455=678 (19 42 158 219)	57.0 + 45.8 + 34.2 = 38.1

Unit	Engaged O+NCO+PVT=T	Killed O+NCO+PVT=T	Wounded O+NCO+PVT=T	Wounded & Captured O+NCO+PVT=T	Captured O+NCO+PVT=T	Total O+NCO+PVT=T	Percentage Loss O+NCO+PVT=T
Garnett & Staff	4 + 0 + 2 = 6	1 + 0 + 0 = 1	1 + 0 + 0 = 1	1 + 0 + 0 = 1 (1 1)	1 + 0 + 0 = 1	4 + 0 + 0 = 4 (2 2)	100.0 + 0 + 0 = 66.7
8th VA F & S	4 + 0 + 1 = 5	0 + 0 + 0 = 0	2 + 0 + 0 = 2	1 + 0 + 0 = 1	0 + 0 + 0 = 0	3 + 0 + 0 = 3	75.0 + 0 + 0 = 60.0
Color Guard	0 + 1 + 0 = 1	0 + 0 + 0 = 0	0 + 0 + 0 = 0	0 + 0 + 0 = 0	0 + 0 + 0 = 0	0 + 0 + 0 = 0	0 + 0 + 0 = 0
Company "A"	3 + 3 + 16 = 22	0 + 0 + 4 = 4	0 + 0 + 0 = 0	1 + 0 + 3 = 4 (1 1 2)	2 + 1 + 5 = 8 (1 1)	3 + 1 + 12 = 16 (1 6 7)	100.0 + 33.3 + 75.0 = 72.7
Company "B"	2 + 4 + 16 = 22	0 + 2 + 3 = 5	0 + 1 + 4 = 5	1 + 0 + 5 = 6 (1 1)	0 + 1 + 1 = 2	1 + 4 + 13 = 18 (1 2 3 6)	50.0 + 100.0 + 81.3 = 81.8
Company "C"	1 + 7 + 21 = 29	0 + 0 + 3 = 3	0 + 1 + 0 = 1	0 + 1 + 4 = 5 (1 1)	1 + 3 + 6 = 10 (2 2)	1 + 5 + 13 = 19 (6 6)	100.0 + 71.4 + 61.9 = 65.5
Company "D"	4 + 4 + 28 = 36	0 + 0 + 5 = 5	0 + 0 + 1 = 1	2 + 2 + 7 = 11 (1 1)	2 + 1 + 5 = 8 (1 1)	4 + 3 + 18 = 25 (1 6 7)	100.0 + 75.0 + 64.3 = 69.4
Company "E"	3 + 2 + 14 = 19	0 + 0 + 1 = 1	2 + 0 + 3 = 5	0 + 0 + 1 = 1 (1 1)	0 + 2 + 2 = 4	2 + 2 + 7 = 11 (2 2)	66.7 + 100.0 + 50.0 = 57.9
Company "F"	2 + 6 + 11 = 19	1 + 1 + 2 = 4	0 + 1 + 1 = 2	1 + 0 + 1 = 2 (1 1)	0 + 2 + 5 = 7 (1 1)	2 + 4 + 9 = 15 (2 1 3 6)	100.0 + 66.7 + 81.8 = 78.9
Company "G"	4 + 7 + 18 = 29	0 + 2 + 2 = 4	1 + 1 + 6 = 8	1 + 4 + 3 = 8 (1 1)	0 + 0 + 3 = 3 (1 2 3)	2 + 7 + 14 = 23 (1 3 4 8)	50.0 + 100.0 + 77.8 = 79.3
Company "H"	3 + 6 + 13 = 22	0 + 0 + 1 = 1	1 + 1 + 2 = 4	0 + 0 + 2 = 2 (1 1)	0 + 3 + 1 = 4 (1 1)	1 + 4 + 6 = 11 (1 2 3)	33.3 + 66.7 + 46.2 = 50.0
Company "I"	2 + 3 + 10 = 15	1 + 1 + 2 = 4	0 + 0 + 0 = 0	1 + 0 + 2 = 3 (1 1)	0 + 2 + 3 = 5	2 + 3 + 7 = 12 (2 1 2 5)	100.0 + 100.0 + 70.0 = 80.0
Company "K"	3 + 6 + 14 = 23	0 + 0 + 3 = 3	1 + 1 + 3 = 5	1 + 1 + 4 = 6 (1 1)	0 + 1 + 0 = 1	2 + 3 + 10 = 15 (1 3 4)	66.7 + 50.0 + 71.4 = 65.2
Total 8th VA	31 + 49 + 162 = 242	2 + 6 + 26 = 34	7 + 6 + 20 = 33	9 + 8 + 32 = 49 (5 2 4 11)	5 + 16 + 31 = 52 (1 1 7 9)	23 + 36 + 109 = 168 (8 9 37 54)	74.2 + 73.5 + 67.3 = 69.4

Unit	Engaged O+NCO+PVT=T	Killed O+NCO+PVT=T	Wounded O+NCO+PVT=T	Wounded & Captured O+NCO+PVT=T	Captured O+NCO+PVT=T	Total O+NCO+PVT=T	Percentage Loss O+NCO+PVT=T
18th VA F & S	2 + 1 + 0 = 3	0 + 0 + 0 = 0	0 + 0 + 0 = 0	1 + 1 + 0 = 2 (1 1)	1 + 0 + 0 = 1	2 + 1 + 0 = 3 (1 1)	100.0 + 100.0 + 0 = 100.0
Company "A"	3 + 6 + 31 = 40	0 + 0 + 6 = 6	0 + 1 + 7 = 8	1 + 2 + 4 = 7	0 + 1 + 3 = 4 (2 2)	1 + 4 + 20 = 25 (8 8)	33.3 + 66.7 + 64.5 = 62.5
Company "B"	4 + 4 + 18 = 26	0 + 0 + 0 = 0	1 + 3 + 5 = 9	2 + 0 + 2 = 4	0 + 0 + 1 = 1 (1 1)	3 + 3 + 8 = 14 (1 1)	75.0 + 75.0 + 44.4 = 53.8
Company "C"	2 + 7 + 23 = 32	1 + 0 + 1 = 2	0 + 1 + 3 = 4	0 + 4 + 5 = 9 (1 1)	0 + 1 + 2 = 3 (1 2 3)	1 + 6 + 11 = 18 (1 2 3 6)	50.0 + 85.7 + 47.8 = 56.3
Company "D"	2 + 9 + 32 = 43	0 + 2 + 2 = 4	1 + 1 + 6 = 8	1 + 3 + 8 = 12 (2 2)	0 + 0 + 3 = 3 (1 1)	2 + 6 + 19 = 27 (2 5 7)	100.0 + 66.7 + 59.4 = 62.8
Company "E"	4 + 4 + 15 = 23	1 + 1 + 1 = 3	1 + 0 + 0 = 1	2 + 2 + 5 = 9 (1 2 3)	0 + 0 + 3 = 3 (2 2)	4 + 3 + 9 = 16 (2 1 5 8)	100.0 + 75.0 + 60.0 = 69.6
Company "F"	3 + 5 + 23 = 31	0 + 4 + 2 = 6	0 + 0 + 4 = 4 (1 1)	1 + 0 + 2 = 3	0 + 0 + 6 = 6 (1 1)	1 + 4 + 14 = 19 (4 4 8)	33.3 + 80.0 + 60.9 = 61.3
Company "G"	2 + 8 + 30 = 40	0 + 1 + 6 = 7	2 + 3 + 4 = 9 (1 1)	0 + 1 + 6 = 7 (1 1)	0 + 0 + 2 = 2 (1 1)	2 + 5 + 18 = 25 (3 7 10)	100.0 + 62.5 + 60.0 = 62.5
Company "H"	3 + 8 + 40 = 51	1 + 2 + 4 = 7	0 + 2 + 3 = 5	2 + 4 + 9 = 15 (1 1)	0 + 0 + 9 = 9	3 + 8 + 25 = 36 (2 2 4 8)	100.0 + 100.0 + 62.5 = 70.6
Company "I"	3 + 8 + 36 = 47	0 + 1 + 6 = 7	0 + 1 + 4 = 5	2 + 3 + 3 = 8 (1 2 3)	0 + 0 + 5 = 5 (1 1)	2 + 5 + 18 = 25 (2 9 11)	66.7 + 62.5 + 50.0 = 53.2
Company "K"	3 + 4 + 28 = 35	0 + 0 + 2 = 2	1 + 0 + 1 = 2	0 + 2 + 6 = 8	1 + 1 + 9 = 11 (1 2 3)	2 + 3 + 18 = 23 (1 4 5)	66.7 + 75.0 + 64.3 = 65.7
Total 18th VA	31 + 64 + 276 = 371	3 + 11 + 30 = 44	6 + 12 + 37 = 55 (1 1 2)	12 + 22 + 50 = 84 (2 3 7 12)	2 + 3 + 43 = 48 (3 12 15)	23 + 48 + 160 = 231 (5 18 50 73)	74.2 + 75.0 + 58.0 = 62.3

Unit	Engaged O+NCO+PVT=T	Killed O+NCO+PVT=T	Wounded O+NCO+PVT=T	Wounded & Captured O+NCO+PVT=T	Captured O+NCO+PVT=T	Total O+NCO+PVT=T	Percentage Loss O+NCO+PVT=T
19th VA F & S	4 + 1 + 0 = 5	0 + 0 + 0 = 0	3 + 0 + 0 = 3 (1 1)	0 + 0 + 0 = 0	0 + 0 + 0 = 0	3 + 0 + 0 = 3 (1 1)	75.0 + 0 + 0 = 60.0
Color Guard	0 + 2 + 0 = 2	0 + 0 + 0 = 0	0 + 0 + 0 = 0	0 + 0 + 0 = 0	0 + 0 + 0 = 0	0 + 0 + 0 = 0	0 + 0 + 0 = 0
Company "A"	3 + 5 + 29 = 37	0 + 0 + 1 = 1	2 + 0 + 0 = 2	0 + 0 + 4 = 4	1 + 2 + 1 = 4 (1 1 2)	3 + 2 + 6 = 11 (1 2 3)	100.0 + 40.0 + 20.7 = 29.7
Company "B"	3 + 9 + 19 = 31	1 + 1 + 1 = 3	1 + 3 + 3 = 7	1 + 2 + 1 = 4	0 + 0 + 0 = 0	3 + 6 + 5 = 14 (1 1 1 3)	100.0 + 66.7 + 26.3 = 45.2
Company "C"	4 + 9 + 29 = 42	0 + 1 + 1 = 2	0 + 2 + 1 = 3	1 + 1 + 1 = 3	0 + 3 + 4 = 7	1 + 7 + 7 = 15 (1 1 2)	25.0 + 77.8 + 24.1 = 35.7
Company "D"	3 + 8 + 20 = 31	0 + 1 + 6 = 7	1 + 2 + 2 = 5 (1 1)	0 + 1 + 0 = 1	0 + 1 + 2 = 3	1 + 5 + 10 = 16 (2 6 8)	33.3 + 62.5 + 50.0 = 51.6
Company "E"	4 + 6 + 30 = 40	0 + 2 + 7 = 9	1 + 0 + 4 = 5	3 + 2 + 3 = 8 (2 2)	0 + 0 + 0 = 0	3 + 5 + 14 = 22 (2 2 7 11)	75.0 + 83.3 + 46.7 = 55.0
Company "F"	3 + 3 + 37 = 43	0 + 0 + 1 = 1	1 + 1 + 3 = 5 (1 1)	1 + 0 + 6 = 7 (2 2)	0 + 0 + 0 = 0	2 + 1 + 10 = 13 (1 3 4)	66.7 + 33.3 + 27.0 = 30.2
Company "G"	4 + 9 + 48 = 61	0 + 2 + 6 = 8	1 + 2 + 3 = 6	1 + 0 + 6 = 7 (1 1)	0 + 3 + 7 = 10 (3 3)	2 + 7 + 22 = 31 (2 10 12)	50.0 + 77.8 + 45.8 = 50.8
Company "H"	4 + 9 + 27 = 40	1 + 1 + 3 = 5	0 + 1 + 0 = 1	1 + 1 + 3 = 5	0 + 0 + 1 = 1	2 + 3 + 7 = 12 (1 1 3 5)	50.0 + 33.3 + 25.9 = 30.0
Company "I"	3 + 7 + 45 = 55	0 + 0 + 2 = 2	0 + 3 + 3 = 6 (1 1)	1 + 2 + 1 = 4 (1 1)	0 + 1 + 7 = 8 (1 6 7)	1 + 6 + 13 = 20 (1 1 9 11)	33.3 + 85.7 + 28.9 = 36.4
Company "K"	3 + 8 + 28 = 39	1 + 0 + 1 = 2	0 + 0 + 1 = 1	1 + 3 + 2 = 6 (1 1 2)	0 + 0 + 2 = 2	2 + 3 + 6 = 11 (1 1 2 4)	66.7 + 37.5 + 21.4 = 28.2
Total 19th VA	38 + 76 + 312 = 426	3 + 8 + 29 = 40	9 + 15 + 20 = 44 (1 3 4)	10 + 12 + 27 = 49 (2 1 5 8)	1 + 10 + 24 = 35 (2 10 12)	23 + 45 + 100 = 168 (8 12 44 64)	60.5 + 59.2 + 32.1 = 39.4

459

Unit	Engaged O+NCO+PVT=T	Killed O+NCO+PVT=T	Wounded O+NCO+PVT=T	Wounded & Captured O+NCO+PVT=T	Captured O+NCO+PVT=T	Total O+NCO+PVT=T	Percentage Loss O+NCO+PVT=T
28th VA F & S	3 + 1 + 0 = 4	1 + 1 + 0 = 2	1 + 0 + 0 = 1 (1 1)	0 + 0 + 0 = 0	0 + 0 + 0 = 0	2 + 1 + 0 = 3 (2 1 3)	66.7 + 100.0 + 0 = 75.0
Color Guard	0 + 3 + 1 = 4	0 + 0 + 0 = 0	0 + 1 + 1 = 2	0 + 0 + 0 = 0	0 + 0 + 0 = 0	0 + 1 + 1 = 2	0 + 33.3 + 100.0 = 50.0
Company "A"	3 + 5 + 23 = 31	0 + 1 + 1 = 2	0 + 0 + 3 = 3	0 + 0 + 2 = 2 (1 1)	1 + 1 + 2 = 4	1 + 2 + 8 = 11 (1 2 3)	33.3 + 40.0 + 34.8 = 35.5
Company "B"	4 + 7 + 31 = 42	0 + 0 + 4 = 4	1 + 4 + 5 = 10	0 + 1 + 2 = 3 (1 1 2)	2 + 0 + 5 = 7 (2 2)	3 + 5 + 16 = 24 (1 7 8)	75.0 + 71.4 + 51.6 = 57.1
Company "C"	2 + 7 + 23 = 32	0 + 0 + 4 = 4	0 + 1 + 3 = 4 (1 1)	0 + 2 + 5 = 7 (1 2 3)	1 + 3 + 3 = 7 (1 1)	1 + 6 + 15 = 22 (2 7 9)	50.0 + 85.7 + 65.2 = 68.8
Company "D"	4 + 7 + 38 = 49	0 + 1 + 2 = 3	1 + 2 + 3 = 6	1 + 1 + 2 = 4 (1 2 3)	0 + 0 + 1 = 1 (1 1)	2 + 4 + 8 = 14 (1 1 5 7)	50.0 + 57.1 + 21.1 = 28.6
Company "E"	0 + 4 + 19 = 23	0 + 2 + 1 = 3	0 + 1 + 0 = 1	0 + 1 + 2 = 3 (1 1)	0 + 0 + 7 = 7	0 + 4 + 10 = 14 (2 2 4)	0 + 100.0 + 52.6 = 60.9
Company "F"	2 + 7 + 46 = 55	0 + 1 + 4 = 5	1 + 2 + 5 = 8	0 + 0 + 5 = 5	0 + 0 + 0 = 0	1 + 3 + 14 = 18 (1 4 5)	50.0 + 42.9 + 30.4 = 32.7
Company "G"	2 + 8 + 58 = 68	0 + 1 + 4 = 5	0 + 0 + 2 = 2	2 + 4 + 12 = 18 (3 3)	0 + 1 + 8 = 9 (1 1 2)	2 + 6 + 26 = 34 (2 8 10)	100.0 + 75.0 + 44.8 = 50.0
Company "I"	2 + 6 + 33 = 41	0 + 0 + 4 = 4	0 + 1 + 2 = 3 (2 2)	0 + 2 + 4 = 6	1 + 1 + 4 = 6	1 + 4 + 14 = 19 (6 6)	50.0 + 66.7 + 42.4 = 46.3
Company "K"	2 + 6 + 19 = 27	1 + 2 + 0 = 3	0 + 1 + 3 = 4	0 + 0 + 2 = 2 (1 1)	0 + 0 + 1 = 1	1 + 3 + 6 = 10 (1 2 1 4)	50.0 + 50.0 + 26.3 = 33.3
Total 28th VA	24 + 61 + 291 = 376	2 + 9 + 24 = 35	4 + 13 + 27 = 44 (1 3 4)	3 + 11 + 36 = 50 (1 2 11 14)	5 + 6 + 31 = 42 (2 4 6)	14 + 39 + 118 = 171 (4 13 42 59)	58.3 + 63.9 + 40.5 = 45.5

Unit	Engaged O+NCO+PVT=T	Killed O+NCO+PVT=T	Wounded O+NCO+PVT=T	Wounded & Captured O+NCO+PVT=T	Captured O+NCO+PVT=T	Total O+NCO+PVT=T	Percentage Loss O+NCO+PVT=T
56th VA F & S	2 + 1 + 0 = 3	0 + 0 + 0 = 0	1 + 1 + 0 = 2 (1 1)	0 + 0 + 0 = 0	0 + 0 + 0 = 0	1 + 1 + 0 = 2 (1 1)	50.0 + 100.0 + 0 = 66.7
Company "A"	2 + 9 + 18 = 29	0 + 2 + 1 = 3	0 + 0 + 3 = 3	0 + 0 + 2 = 2	0 + 0 + 0 = 0	0 + 2 + 6 = 8 (2 1 3)	0 + 22.2 + 33.3 = 27.6
Company "B"	3 + 5 + 46 = 54	0 + 0 + 2 = 2	0 + 1 + 5 = 6	0 + 1 + 8 = 9 (1 1 2)	1 + 0 + 2 = 3 (1 1)	1 + 2 + 17 = 20 (1 4 5)	33.3 + 40.0 + 37.0 = 37.0
Company "C"	3 + 10 + 31 = 44	2 + 0 + 3 = 5	0 + 2 + 2 = 4 (1 1)	0 + 0 + 5 = 5 (1 1)	0 + 0 + 2 = 2	2 + 2 + 12 = 16 (2 1 4 7)	66.7 + 20.0 + 38.7 = 36.4
Company "D"	4 + 6 + 42 = 52	1 + 1 + 0 = 2	0 + 0 + 5 = 5 (1 1)	0 + 0 + 5 = 5 (1 1)	2 + 2 + 4 = 8 (1 1)	3 + 3 + 14 = 20 (1 1 3 5)	75.0 + 50.0 + 33.3 = 38.5
Company "E"	3 + 9 + 41 = 53	1 + 1 + 1 = 3	0 + 1 + 2 = 3	1 + 2 + 3 = 6 (1 1 2)	1 + 2 + 8 = 11 (7 7)	3 + 6 + 14 = 23 (2 1 9 12)	100.0 + 66.7 + 34.1 = 43.4
Company "F"	2 + 6 + 35 = 43	0 + 0 + 0 = 0	0 + 1 + 2 = 3	0 + 0 + 1 = 1 (1 1)	0 + 1 + 1 = 2 (1 1 2)	0 + 2 + 4 = 6 (1 2 3)	0 + 33.3 + 11.4 = 14.0
Company "G"	2 + 5 + 17 = 24	0 + 0 + 0 = 0	0 + 0 + 3 = 3	0 + 0 + 0 = 0	1 + 1 + 2 = 4	1 + 1 + 5 = 7	50.0 + 20.0 + 29.4 = 29.2
Company "H"	3 + 6 + 45 = 54	0 + 2 + 7 = 9	0 + 0 + 1 = 1	3 + 2 + 8 = 13 (1 1 1 3)	0 + 2 + 6 = 8 (1 1)	3 + 6 + 22 = 31 (1 3 9 13)	100.0 + 100.0 + 48.9 = 57.4
Company "I"	3 + 5 + 35 = 43	0 + 1 + 2 = 3	1 + 0 + 3 = 4	1 + 2 + 6 = 9 (3 3)	0 + 0 + 4 = 4	2 + 3 + 15 = 20 (1 5 6)	66.7 + 60.0 + 42.9 = 46.5
Company "K"	1 + 5 + 25 = 31	0 + 0 + 0 = 0	0 + 1 + 1 = 2	0 + 1 + 2 = 3	1 + 1 + 3 = 5 (1 1)	1 + 3 + 6 = 10 (1 1)	100.0 + 60.0 + 24.0 = 32.3
Total 56th VA	28 + 67 + 335 = 430	4 + 7 + 16 = 27	2 + 7 + 27 = 36 (1 1 1 3)	5 + 8 + 40 = 53 (2 2 9 13)	6 + 9 + 32 = 47 (1 12 13)	17 + 31 + 115 = 163 (7 11 38 56)	60.7 + 46.3 + 34.3 = 37.9
Total Garnett	156+317+1378=1851	15+41+125=181	29+53+131=213 (3 5 5 13)	40+61+185=286 (13 10 36 59)	20+44+161=225 (3 7 45 55)	104+199+602=905 (34 63 211 308)	66.7 + 62.8 + 43.7 = 48.9

Unit	Engaged O+NCO+PVT=T	Killed O+NCO+PVT=T	Wounded O+NCO+PVT=T	Wounded & Captured O+NCO+PVT=T	Captured O+NCO+PVT=T	Total O+NCO+PVT=T	Percentage Loss O+NCO+PVT=T
Armistead & Staff	4 + 0 + 0 = 4	0 + 0 + 0 = 0	2 + 0 + 0 = 2	1 + 0 + 0 = 1 (1 1)	0 + 0 + 0 = 0	3 + 0 + 0 = 3 (1 1)	75.0 + 0 + 0 = 75.0
9th VA F & S	2 + 1 + 0 = 3	0 + 0 + 0 = 0	1 + 0 + 0 = 1 (1 1)	1 + 0 + 0 = 1	0 + 0 + 0 = 0	2 + 0 + 0 = 2 (1 1)	100.0 + 0 + 0 = 66.7
Color Guard	0 + 1 + 0 = 1	0 + 0 + 0 = 0	0 + 0 + 0 = 0	0 + 1 + 0 = 1	0 + 0 + 0 = 0	0 + 1 + 0 = 1	0 + 100.0 + 0 = 100.0
Company "B"	1 + 3 + 11 = 15	0 + 0 + 1 = 1	0 + 1 + 0 = 1	1 + 1 + 0 = 2	0 + 1 + 2 = 3 (1 1 2)	1 + 3 + 3 = 7 (1 1 1 3)	100.0 + 100.0 + 27.3 = 46.7
Company "C"	4 + 7 + 38 = 49	0 + 1 + 1 = 2	0 + 3 + 2 = 5 (1 1)	0 + 1 + 6 = 7	4 + 0 + 14 = 18 (1 3 4)	4 + 5 + 23 = 32 (1 2 4 7)	100.0 + 71.4 + 60.5 = 65.3
Company "D"	3 + 3 + 15 = 21	0 + 0 + 1 = 1	0 + 0 + 0 = 0	0 + 1 + 4 = 5	2 + 1 + 3 = 6 (2 2)	2 + 2 + 8 = 12 (3 3)	66.7 + 66.7 + 53.3 = 57.1
Company "E"	2 + 7 + 32 = 41	0 + 0 + 2 = 2	0 + 0 + 1 = 1	2 + 2 + 5 = 9 (1 1 2)	0 + 2 + 8 = 10 (4 4)	2 + 4 + 16 = 22 (1 1 6 8)	100.0 + 57.1 + 50.0 = 53.7
Company "F"	3 + 5 + 26 = 34	0 + 0 + 2 = 2	0 + 0 + 2 = 2	1 + 1 + 1 = 3 (1 1)	1 + 2 + 6 = 9 (1 1 2)	2 + 3 + 11 = 16 (1 1 3 5)	66.7 + 60.0 + 42.3 = 47.1
Company "G"	3 + 9 + 39 = 51	0 + 2 + 2 = 4	0 + 0 + 3 = 3 (1 1)	0 + 0 + 7 = 7 (2 2)	1 + 2 + 12 = 15 (2 2)	1 + 4 + 24 = 29 (2 7 9)	33.3 + 44.4 + 61.5 = 56.9
Company "I"	3 + 5 + 24 = 32	1 + 0 + 2 = 3	0 + 0 + 2 = 2	0 + 0 + 3 = 3	2 + 2 + 5 = 9 (1 2 3)	3 + 2 + 12 = 17 (1 1 4 6)	100.0 + 40.0 + 50.0 = 53.1
Company "K"	3 + 5 + 11 = 19	0 + 0 + 0 = 0	0 + 0 + 1 = 1 (1 1)	1 + 0 + 4 = 5	1 + 3 + 2 = 6	2 + 3 + 7 = 12 (1 1)	66.7 + 60.0 + 63.6 = 63.2
Total 9th VA	24 + 46 + 196 = 266	1 + 3 + 11 = 15	1 + 4 + 11 = 16 (1 1 2 4)	6 + 7 + 30 = 43 (2 1 2 5)	11 + 13 + 52 = 76 (2 3 14 19)	19 + 27 + 104 = 150 (6 8 29 43)	79.2 + 58.7 + 53.1 = 56.4

Unit	Engaged O+NCO+PVT=T	Killed O+NCO+PVT=T	Wounded O+NCO+PVT=T	Wounded & Captured O+NCO+PVT=T	Captured O+NCO+PVT=T	Total O+NCO+PVT=T	Percentage Loss O+NCO+PVT=T
14th VA F & S	4+1+0=5	2+0+0=2	2+0+0=2 (1 1)	0+0+0=0	0+0+0=0	4+0+0=4 (3 3)	100.0+0+0=80.0
Company "A"	4+5+30=39	1+0+2=3	1+0+0=1	1+1+2=4	0+0+7=7 (2 2)	3+1+11=15 (1 4 5)	75.0+20.0+36.7=38.5
Company "B"	4+8+41=53	2+0+3=5	0+1+3=4 (1 1)	0+4+2=6	1+0+8=9 (4 4)	3+5+16=24 (2 1 7 10)	75.0+62.5+39.0=45.3
Company "C"	4+8+44=56	0+0+7=7	0+0+2=2	1+1+7=9 (1 1 2)	2+5+7=14 (4 4)	3+6+23=32 (1 12 13)	75.0+75.0+52.3=57.1
Company "D"	4+8+33=45	2+2+3=7	0+0+0=0	2+2+7=11 (3 3)	0+1+6=7 (1 3 4)	4+5+16=25 (2 3 9 14)	100.0+62.5+48.5=55.6
Company "E"	3+7+33=43	1+2+2=5	1+0+4=5	1+3+12=16 (3 3)	0+1+5=6 (3 3)	3+6+23=32 (1 2 8 11)	100.0+85.7+69.7=74.4
Company "F"	4+7+35=46	0+0+4=4	2+0+1=3 (1 1 2)	0+3+4=7	0+1+6=7 (3 3)	2+4+15=21 (1 8 9)	50.0+57.1+42.9=45.7
Company "G"	3+6+59=68	0+2+3=5	1+1+6=8 (1 1)	0+2+15=17 (2 2)	0+0+8=8 (4 4)	1+5+32=38 (1 2 9 12)	33.3+83.3+54.2=55.9
Company "H"	4+7+34=45	1+1+3=5	0+0+4=4 (1 1)	1+2+6=9 (1 3 4)	1+2+6=9 (2 2)	3+5+19=27 (1 2 9 12)	75.0+71.4+55.9=60.0
Company "I"	3+6+17=26	0+0+2=2	0+1+0=1	0+1+2=3 (1 1)	0+1+1=2	0+3+5=8 (3 3)	0+50.0+29.4=30.8
Company "K"	3+9+34=46	0+1+4=5	1+1+1=3	0+4+2=6 (1 1)	0+0+8=8 (3 3)	1+6+15=22 (1 8 9)	33.3+66.7+44.1=47.8
Total 14th VA	40+72+360=472	9+8+33=50	8+4+21=33 (3 1 2 6)	6+23+59=88 (2 14 16)	4+11+62=77 (1 28 29)	27+46+175=248 (12 12 77 101)	67.5+63.9+48.6=52.5

Unit	Engaged O+NCO+PVT=T	Killed O+NCO+PVT=T	Wounded O+NCO+PVT=T	Wounded & Captured O+NCO+PVT=T	Captured O+NCO+PVT=T	Total O+NCO+PVT=T	Percentage Loss O+NCO+PVT=T
38th VA F & S	4 + 0 + 0 = 4	1 + 0 + 0 = 1	1 + 0 + 0 = 1	0 + 0 + 0 = 0	0 + 0 + 0 = 0	2 + 0 + 0 = 2 (1 1)	50.0 + 0 + 0 = 50.0
Color Guard	0 + 2 + 0 = 2	0 + 0 + 0 = 0	0 + 1 + 0 = 1	0 + 0 + 0 = 0	0 + 0 + 0 = 0	0 + 1 + 0 = 1	0 + 50.0 + 0 = 50.0
Company "A"	4 + 9 + 47 = 60	1 + 1 + 9 = 11	0 + 0 + 5 = 5	1 + 3 + 6 = 10 (1 1)	0 + 0 + 2 = 2 (2 2)	2 + 4 + 22 = 28 (1 1 12 14)	50.0 + 44.4 + 46.8 = 46.7
Company "B"	4 + 8 + 51 = 63	0 + 0 + 3 = 3	0 + 0 + 3 = 3 (1 1)	0 + 3 + 7 = 10 (1 4 5)	0 + 2 + 13 = 15 (1 5 6)	0 + 5 + 26 = 31 (2 13 15)	0 + 62.5 + 51.0 = 49.2
Company "C"	3 + 6 + 44 = 53	1 + 0 + 1 = 2	1 + 2 + 7 = 10	0 + 2 + 10 = 12 (3 3)	0 + 0 + 4 = 4	2 + 4 + 22 = 28 (1 4 5)	66.7 + 66.7 + 50.0 = 52.8
Company "D"	4 + 3 + 37 = 44	0 + 0 + 2 = 2	0 + 0 + 3 = 3	1 + 0 + 8 = 9 (2 2)	1 + 0 + 2 = 3 (1 1)	2 + 0 + 15 = 17 (5 5)	50.0 + 0 + 40.5 = 38.6
Company "E"	4 + 7 + 49 = 60	0 + 1 + 3 = 4	2 + 1 + 3 = 6 (1 1)	0 + 1 + 2 = 3	0 + 0 + 2 = 2 (1 1)	2 + 3 + 10 = 15 (1 5 6)	50.0 + 42.9 + 20.4 = 25.0
Company "F"	3 + 9 + 27 = 39	0 + 0 + 2 = 2	1 + 1 + 3 = 5	0 + 1 + 4 = 5 (2 2)	1 + 1 + 4 = 6 (1 2 3)	2 + 3 + 13 = 18 (1 6 7)	66.7 + 33.3 + 48.1 = 46.2
Company "G"	3 + 7 + 32 = 42	0 + 1 + 0 = 1	1 + 0 + 2 = 3	0 + 2 + 3 = 5	1 + 0 + 1 = 2 (2 2)	2 + 3 + 6 = 11 (1 2 3)	66.7 + 42.9 + 18.8 = 26.2
Company "H"	3 + 4 + 32 = 39	0 + 1 + 5 = 6	0 + 1 + 2 = 3 (1 1)	0 + 0 + 3 = 3 (2 2)	1 + 0 + 1 = 2	1 + 2 + 11 = 14 (1 8 9)	33.3 + 50.0 + 34.4 = 35.9
Company "K"	4 + 8 + 63 = 75	0 + 1 + 7 = 8	3 + 1 + 7 = 11 (1 1)	0 + 0 + 4 = 4 (2 2)	0 + 1 + 5 = 6 (1 1)	3 + 3 + 23 = 29 (2 10 12)	75.0 + 37.5 + 36.5 = 38.7
Total 38th VA	36 + 63 + 382 = 481	3 + 5 + 32 = 40	9 + 7 + 35 = 51 (4 4)	2 + 12 + 47 = 61 (1 16 17)	4 + 4 + 34 = 42 (3 13 16)	18 + 28 + 148 = 194 (3 9 65 77)	50.0 + 44.4 + 38.7 = 40.3

Unit	Engaged O+NCO+PVT=T	Killed O+NCO+PVT=T	Wounded O+NCO+PVT=T	Wounded & Captured O+NCO+PVT=T	Captured O+NCO+PVT=T	Total O+NCO+PVT=T	Percentage Loss O+NCO+PVT=T
53rd VA F & S	4 + 0 + 0 = 4	0 + 0 + 0 = 0	1 + 0 + 0 = 1	1 + 0 + 0 = 1	2 + 0 + 0 = 2	4 + 0 + 0 = 4	100.0 + 0 + 0 = 100.0
Color Guard	0 + 3 + 2 = 5	0 + 1 + 0 = 1	0 + 1 + 1 = 2	0 + 1 + 1 = 2 (1 1)	0 + 0 + 0 = 0	0 + 3 + 2 = 5 (1 1 2)	0 + 100.0 + 100.0 = 100.0
Company "A"	2 + 7 + 25 = 34	0 + 0 + 0 = 0	1 + 0 + 1 = 2	0 + 2 + 3 = 5 (2 2)	0 + 3 + 4 = 7 (1 1)	1 + 5 + 8 = 14 (3 3)	50.0 + 71.4 + 32.0 = 41.2
Company "B"	2 + 9 + 35 = 46	0 + 0 + 4 = 4	0 + 0 + 2 = 2	0 + 1 + 6 = 7 (2 2)	1 + 3 + 3 = 7 (1 1 2)	1 + 4 + 15 = 20 (1 7 8)	50.0 + 44.4 + 42.9 = 43.5
Company "C"	2 + 9 + 38 = 49	0 + 0 + 1 = 1	0 + 1 + 0 = 1	0 + 0 + 4 = 4	2 + 2 + 10 = 14 (1 1 4 6)	2 + 3 + 15 = 20 (1 1 5 7)	100.0 + 33.3 + 39.5 = 40.8
Company "D"	4 + 9 + 34 = 47	0 + 0 + 5 = 5	1 + 2 + 4 = 7	0 + 1 + 3 = 4	2 + 2 + 3 = 7 (1 1)	3 + 5 + 15 = 23 (6 6)	75.0 + 55.6 + 44.1 = 48.9
Company "E"	4 + 5 + 20 = 29	0 + 0 + 1 = 1	0 + 0 + 2 = 2	2 + 1 + 0 = 3 (1 1 2)	0 + 1 + 0 = 1 (1 1)	2 + 2 + 3 = 7 (1 2 1 4)	50.0 + 40.0 + 15.0 = 24.1
Company "F"	3 + 9 + 33 = 45	0 + 1 + 2 = 3	1 + 1 + 4 = 6	0 + 1 + 4 = 5 (1 2 3)	0 + 3 + 5 = 8 (1 1)	1 + 6 + 15 = 22 (2 5 7)	33.3 + 66.7 + 45.5 = 48.9
Company "G"	2 + 8 + 37 = 47	0 + 1 + 3 = 4	0 + 0 + 6 = 6	0 + 1 + 1 = 2	0 + 3 + 8 = 11 (1 3 4)	0 + 5 + 18 = 23 (2 6 8)	0 + 62.5 + 48.6 = 48.9
Company "H"	3 + 5 + 39 = 47	0 + 1 + 4 = 5	0 + 1 + 4 = 5	1 + 2 + 6 = 9 (1 1 2)	2 + 1 + 3 = 6 (1 1 2)	3 + 5 + 17 = 25 (1 2 6 9)	100.0 + 100.0 + 43.6 = 53.2
Company "I"	4 + 8 + 39 = 51	0 + 1 + 2 = 3	1 + 1 + 2 = 4	1 + 1 + 6 = 8 (1 1)	1 + 2 + 6 = 9 (1 1 2)	3 + 5 + 16 = 24 (3 3 6)	75.0 + 62.5 + 41.0 = 47.1
Company "K"	4 + 7 + 48 = 59	1 + 0 + 6 = 7	0 + 1 + 5 = 6 (2 2)	1 + 1 + 5 = 7 (1 1)	0 + 1 + 5 = 6 (1 1)	2 + 3 + 21 = 26 (1 10 11)	50.0 + 42.9 + 43.8 = 44.1
Total 53rd VA	34 + 79 + 350 = 463	1 + 5 + 28 = 34	5 + 8 + 31 = 44 (2 2)	6 + 12 + 39 = 57 (2 3 9 14)	10 + 21 + 47 = 78 (1 6 14 21)	22 + 46 + 145 = 213 (4 14 53 71)	64.7 + 58.2 + 41.4 = 46.0

Unit	Engaged O+NCO+PVT=T	Killed O+NCO+PVT=T	Wounded O+NCO+PVT=T	Wounded & Captured O+NCO+PVT=T	Captured O+NCO+PVT=T	Total O+NCO+PVT=T	Percentage Loss O+NCO+PVT=T
57th VA F & S	4 + 1 + 0 = 5	0 + 0 + 0 = 0	3 + 1 + 0 = 4 (1 1)	1 + 0 + 0 = 1 (1 1)	0 + 0 + 0 = 0	4 + 1 + 0 = 5 (2 2)	100.0 + 100.0 + 0 = 100.0
Company "A"	1 + 8 + 47 = 56	1 + 4 + 11 = 16	0 + 2 + 2 = 4 (1 1)	0 + 1 + 6 = 7 (2 2)	0 + 1 + 9 = 10 (1 1)	1 + 8 + 28 = 37 (1 4 15 20)	100.0 + 100.0 + 59.6 = 66.1
Company "B"	4 + 6 + 35 = 45	2 + 0 + 2 = 4	1 + 1 + 2 = 4	0 + 1 + 8 = 9 (3 3)	0 + 1 + 3 = 4	3 + 3 + 15 = 21 (2 5 7)	75.0 + 50.0 + 42.9 = 46.7
Company "C"	4 + 8 + 33 = 45	0 + 1 + 0 = 1	1 + 0 + 4 = 5 (3 3)	0 + 2 + 8 = 10 (1 5 6)	0 + 0 + 2 = 2 (1 1)	1 + 3 + 14 = 18 (2 9 11)	25.0 + 37.5 + 42.4 = 40.0
Company "D"	4 + 6 + 34 = 44	0 + 0 + 1 = 1	0 + 0 + 4 = 4 (1 1)	0 + 1 + 3 = 4 (1 1)	3 + 2 + 5 = 10 (2 2)	3 + 3 + 13 = 19 (5 5)	75.0 + 50.0 + 38.2 = 43.2
Company "E"	3 + 9 + 39 = 51	0 + 1 + 5 = 6	1 + 1 + 4 = 6	0 + 4 + 9 = 13 (2 1 3)	0 + 1 + 5 = 6 (1 1)	1 + 7 + 23 = 31 (3 7 10)	33.3 + 77.8 + 59.0 = 60.8
Company "F"	3 + 8 + 31 = 42	0 + 2 + 3 = 5	0 + 1 + 1 = 2	0 + 2 + 4 = 6	1 + 0 + 1 = 2 (1 1 2)	1 + 5 + 9 = 15 (3 4 7)	33.3 + 62.5 + 29.0 = 35.7
Company "G"	3 + 9 + 41 = 53	0 + 2 + 4 = 6	1 + 1 + 4 = 6	1 + 2 + 6 = 9 (2 2)	1 + 0 + 3 = 4 (3 3)	3 + 5 + 17 = 25 (2 9 11)	100.0 + 55.6 + 41.5 = 47.2
Company "H"	2 + 9 + 33 = 44	0 + 0 + 1 = 1	1 + 2 + 2 = 5	0 + 3 + 5 = 8 (1 2 3)	0 + 3 + 3 = 6	1 + 8 + 11 = 20 (1 3 4)	50.0 + 88.9 + 33.3 = 45.5
Company "I"	1 + 5 + 45 = 51	0 + 1 + 3 = 4	0 + 0 + 4 = 4	0 + 3 + 6 = 9 (1 1)	0 + 1 + 6 = 7	0 + 5 + 19 = 24 (1 4 5)	0 + 100.0 + 42.2 = 47.1
Company "K"	4 + 9 + 53 = 66	2 + 0 + 11 = 13	1 + 2 + 6 = 9	0 + 0 + 7 = 7	0 + 1 + 4 = 5 (5 5)	3 + 3 + 28 = 34 (2 16 18)	75.0 + 33.3 + 52.8 = 51.5
Total 57th VA	33 + 78 + 391 = 502	5 + 11 + 41 = 57	9 + 11 + 33 = 53 (1 5 6)	2 + 19 + 62 = 83 (1 4 17 22)	5 + 10 + 41 = 56 (1 14 15)	21 + 51 + 177 = 249 (7 16 77 100)	63.6 + 65.4 + 45.3 = 49.6
Total Armistead	171+338+1679=2188	19+32+145=196	34+34+131=199 (5 2 15 22)	23+73+237=333 (6 11 58 75)	34+59+236=329 (3 14 83 100)	110+198+749=1057 (33 59 301 393)	64.3 + 58.6 + 44.6 = 48.3

Unit	Engaged O+NCO+PVT=T	Killed O+NCO+PVT=T	Wounded O+NCO+PVT=T	Wounded & Captured O+NCO+PVT=T	Captured O+NCO+PVT=T	Total O+NCO+PVT=T	Percentage Loss O+NCO+PVT=T
38th Bn F & S	3 + 0 + 0 = 3	0 + 0 + 0 = 0	1 + 0 + 0 = 1	0 + 0 + 0 = 0	0 + 0 + 0 = 0	1 + 0 + 0 = 1	33.3 + 0 + 0 = 33.3
Company "A"	5 + 20 + 97 = 122	0 + 0 + 0 = 0	0 + 0 + 1 = 1	0 + 0 + 0 = 0	0 + 0 + 0 = 0	0 + 0 + 1 = 1	0 + 0 + 1.0 = 0.8
Company "B"	5 + 12 + 83 = 100	0 + 1 + 2 = 3	0 + 0 + 1 = 1	0 + 0 + 0 = 0	0 + 0 + 0 = 0	0 + 1 + 3 = 4 (1 2 3)	0 + 8.3 + 3.6 = 4.0
Company "C"	3 + 7 + 95 = 105	0 + 0 + 0 = 0	0 + 0 + 0 = 0	0 + 0 + 0 = 0	0 + 0 + 0 = 0	0 + 0 + 0 = 0	0 + 0 + 0 = 0
Company "D"	4 + 13 + 83 = 100	0 + 1 + 3 = 4	0 + 1 + 4 = 5 (1 1)	0 + 0 + 0 = 0	0 + 0 + 0 = 0	0 + 2 + 7 = 9 (1 4 5)	0 + 15.4 + 8.4 = 9.0
Total 38th Bn	20 + 52 + 358 = 430	0 + 2 + 5 = 7	1 + 1 + 6 = 8 (1 1)	0 + 0 + 0 = 0	0 + 0 + 0 = 0	1 + 3 + 11 = 15 (2 6 8)	5.0 + 5.8 + 3.1 = 3.5
Total Pickett	504+1006+4750=6260	45+99+354=498	105+132+406=643 (11 12 42 65)	86+175+572=833 (24 27 117 168)	65+131+485=681* (6 28 163 197)	301+537+1817=2655 (86 166 676 928)	59.7 + 53.4 + 38.3 = 42.4

Survivors: 203+469+2933=3605

* The discrepancy between the 197 total given here and the 208 total given on the Roll of Honor list in Appendix II is caused by the inclusion on the Roll of Honor list of noncombatant soldiers who were captured while serving as hospital nurses and subsequently died in prison.

Appendix II

Pickett's Roll of Honor

This nominal listing depicts those soldiers of Pickett's Division who were killed on the field, mortally wounded, or who died in Union prison camps. The listing of the killed is provided alphabetically by surname. The soldiers' ranks and units are also specified. All men listed were killed during the cannonade and the various stages of the division's assault on 3 July 1863.

The listing of those who were wounded during the attack but survived for a period of time before succumbing to their injuries, are provided alphabetically by surname and are segregated by the locality of their deaths. Ranks and units are also specified, as well as the dates of death. All dates are meant to indicate the year 1863 unless otherwise specified. 126 of Pickett's wounded Virginians died in Federal hospitals (91 at or near Gettysburg), and 50 more died in Southern hospitals (31 at the division's hospital near Bream's Mill at Gettysburg). Another 55 died in unknown hospitals, the majority (judging from the dates of their deaths) somewhere in the vicinity of the battlefield.

The final portion of the roll lists those of Pickett's unwounded and captured soldiers who died of disease in Union prisons. Again, ranks and units are provided together with dates of death. Where no year is specified, it can be assumed that the death occurred in 1863. Causes of death are provided in the individual soldier's listing in the main portion of the roster. the overwhelming number of deaths occurred in the famous Union prisons of Fort Delaware, Delaware, and Point Lookout, Maryland. 191 of Pickett's men died in these prisons, 96 in Fort Delaware and 95 in Point Lookout. Two of the division's soldiers (Private Howson M. Hall of the 3rd Virginia and James F. Wilson of the 53rd) suffered the supreme tragedy of fate as prisoners of war. Both, having survived the horrors of battle and the squalid existence of prison life, died of their debilitating experiences on a ship enroute to Savannah, Georgia, where they were to be exchanged. All the hopes and promises of a renewed life, which would begin at their exchange, died with them on the rolling Atlantic swells in November 1864. Private Wilson was buried at Hilton Head, South Carolina. Private Hall's body, however, decayed too rapidly to await proper burial. His remains were relegated to the sea sometime shortly after 9 November 1864. A sad ending for one of "Pickett's men."

Pickett's Roll of Honor

Killed in Action (498)

Adkins, Sydenham P. (2nd Lt.)	D, 14
Akers, David C.	D, 7
Allen, Andrew J.B.	K, 57
Allen, Robert Clotworthy (Col.)	28
Ambroselle, John J.	I, 7
Ammons, George W., Jr.	K, 53

Amos, Charles D.	D, 24
Apple, Lewis C.	A, 56
Arthur, Patrick H. (2nd Lt.)	F, 3
Ashby, James S.	B, 8
Ayres, Uriah H.	G, 28
Backhurst, George T.	K, 53
Bailey, Edwin S.	D, 8
Bailey George H.	D, 3
Bailiss, William R.	A, 18
Ballard, William G.	H, 56
Barber, James A.	D, 38
Barrett, Jesse	D, 7
Batten, Archer J.	I, 3
Beale, Nathaniel L.	B, 9
Beckett, William F.	K, 53
Bell, Christopher C.	A, 14
Bell, L.L.	F, 7
Bennett, Charles Henry (3rd Sgt.)	I, 24
Bennett, William B.	G, 9
Betterton, Nathan J.	I, 18
Bierly, Andrew J.	K, 57
Binford, James L.	E, 14
Bird, Wilson T.	G, 57
Bish, Daniel (Cpl.)	D, 7
Blick, William A. (2nd Lt.)	E, 56
Book, Henry L.	B, 28
Booz, William G. (1st Sgt.)	G, 19
Bowen, Berry A.	K, 14
Bowen, John A.	A, 19
Bowery, James H.	K, 53
Bowyer, Leonidas R. (3rd Sgt.)	B, 19
Bradner, Thomas H.	B, 38
Branch, John H.	D, 3
Branham, Nathaniel, Jr.	C, 56
Bray, Charles	D, 53
Briggs, Henry L.	C, 24
Brinkley, Granville	I, 9
Brinkley, Mills	I, 9
Brisentine, John M.	B, 28
Brock, Tarlton F. (3rd Cpl.)	F, 57
Brooks, James G. (4th Cpl.)	H, 14
Bryant, Charles W.	A, 38
Bryant, Peter	I, 57
Bryant, Thomas H.	F, 18

Bugg, Lucius T.	C, 14
Burch, James R.	A, 18
Burge, J.E.	E, 18
Burnett, William H.	I, 18
Byrnes, Edward (2nd Sgt.)	C, 1
Calhoun, John L.	D, 18
Callcote, Alexander Daniel (Lt. Col.)	3
Campbell, D.P.	F, 28
Campbell, John	G, 18
Canaday, John D.	E, 7
Cardin, William B.	E, 19
Carneal, Henry	D, 53
Carpenter, John F.	E, 19
Carter, James L.	C, 53
Chappell, Jesse A.	F, 53
Childress, William Y.	D, 14
Clark, Ellis A.	K, 14
Clark, G.W.	G, 53
Clayton, John K. (2nd Sgt.)	E, 56
Clayton, Julian T. (3rd Sgt.)	D, 3
Clements, Green W.	A, 38
Clements, Mathew J.	I, 7
Cocke, William F. (2nd Lt.)	E, 18
Coffee, William H.	E, 11
Cogbill, W.W.T. (Capt.)	D, 14
Coleman, James M.	H, 24
Coleman, James T. (5th Sgt.)	I, 53
Connard, John H.	I, 14
Connelly, James D. (Sr. 2nd Lt.)	C, 11
Conway, Alexander F.	A, 38
Cooper, George W. (4th Sgt.)	D, 28
Cooper, Taswell T.	D, 24
Corley, William L.	D, 28
Coulter, George	I, 3
Covington, David G.	H, 14
Cox, Charles L.	D, 8
Cox,. Elijah H.	G, 14
Craig, Chester	K, 24
Crenshaw, William H.	C, 1
Crews, Armstead C.	H, 38
Crowder, James	I, 18
Cundiff, Albert A.	D, 24
Cundiff, Samuel C.	D, 24
Custard, Alexander	E, 57

Dalton, John A.	A, 18
Dangerfield, Luther	I, 28
Davidson, James	H, 19
Davies, Arthur B. (Cpl.)	E, 11
Davis, Augustine H. (2nd Cpl.)	K, 38
Davis, Jackson	I, 57
Davis, Peter	B, 53
Davis, Thomas	C, 7
Dear, Thomas A. (1st Cpl.)	I, 8
Debo, Dabney C. (2nd Cpl.)	G, 28
Deboe, Joseph (4th Cpl.)	E, 57
Dedman, William H. (5th Cpl.)	A, 56
DeHart, Jesse H.	A, 24
Dix, Tanda W.	A, 38
Dodson, Albert	G, 7
Doss, Gehu	G, 1
Dowdy, John A.	B, 14
Dowell, Major M.	E, 19
Doyles, William H.	E, 9
Drumheller, Abram A.	H, 19
Drumheller, Benjamin N.	D, 19
Dugger, C.C.	C, 8
Dunford, Robert J.	F, 3
Dunn, John R. (Sgt.)	G, 9
Dunn, Thomas W.	H, 56
Dyer, Thomas S. (3rd Sgt.)	F, 57
Dyson, Benjamin (1st Sgt.)	C, 9
Eakin, Jotham W.	F, 11
Eanes, William T.	D, 38
Easley, Robert C.	I, 53
Eckles, James W.	G, 18
Edmonds, Edward C. (Col.)	38
Edwards, A.C. (6th Sgt.)	B, 38 Bn.
Edwards, Joseph R. (1st Cpl.)	D, 3
Edwards, Richard H.	E, 9
Einstein, Harvey	F, 11
Elam, George W. (1st Sgt.)	F, 18
Elder, Joseph A.	G, 18
Elliotte, James O.	B, 7
Ellis, James H. (2nd Sgt.)	F, 28
Ellis Robert S. (1st Lt.)	C, 56
Ellixson, James B. (4th Cpl.)	A, 56
Elmore, James	C, 28

Estes, Robert G.	H, 56
Estes, W.J.	H, 56
Etter, Andrew James	E, 28
Evans, T.L.	A, 7
Everett, Richard B.L. (4th Sgt.)	D, 3
Fair, William H.	C, 8
Felts, Richard A.	G, 3
Ferguson, Martin P.	D, 38 Bn.
Ferguson, William C.	G, 28
Finch, Charles H.	B, 11
Fisher, Philip	B, 28
Flinn, George W.	I, 8
Ford P. Fletcher (Jr. 2nd Lt.)	A, 57
Fortune, Absalom M. (3rd Cpl.)	D, 19
Fortune, Meridith Winston	G, 19
Foster, Farris	F, 28
Foushee, David M. (Cpl.)	C, 7
Fowlkes, Andrew J.	C, 18
Franklin, Fendall	B, 1
Freeman, J.W.	D, 1
Furr, Henry C. (3rd Cpl.)	F, 8
Gardner, William J.	D, 3
Garnett, Richard B. (Brig. Gen.)	
Garrett, Albert D.	H, 14
Gaulden, Jabez S.	B, 38
Gee, Benjamin C.	B, 56
Gibbs, Joseph W.	K, 38
Gilbert, Samuel S.	I, 24
Gilliam, Carter M. (1st Sgt.)	E, 18
Gittman, Francis C.	B, 53
Glass, John	C, 14
Glenn, Isaac S. (2nd Sgt.)	D, 18
Godsey, Hiram W. (1st Sgt.)	D, 14
Goode, Thomas B.	F, 57
Goodman, Alfred	F, 28
Graves, Benjamin B. (1st Sgt.)	H, 53
Gray, William H.	E, 56
Graybill, James A. (1st Lt.)	K, 28
Graybill, Madison B. (3rd Cpl.)	K, 28
Grayson, Alexander (Capt.)	F, 8
Green, John Thomas (Capt.)	I, 8
Gregory, John B.	B, 38
Gregory, Richard H.	F, 14

Gregory, William R.	D, 57
Griffin, Andrew J.	G, 14
Griffin, Benjamin	D, 53
Grinstead, James H. (1st Lt.)	K, 19
Grinstead, T.H.	G, 53
Gunn, Thomas J.	G, 18
Gunnell, Joseph L.	A, 38
Gunnell, William A.	H, 24
Guthrie, Paul W.	F, 38
Hagood, John H.	H, 53
Haley, Thomas J.	A, 38
Hall, Henry J.	E, 19
Hall, John O.	E, 38
Hallinan, James (Capt.)	C, 1
Hamilton, William M. (2nd Sgt.)	G, 18
Hamlet, James M. (4th Sgt.)	H, 18
Hansford, Calvin P. (5th Sgt.)	H, 1
Hardy, John R.	I, 28
Hardy, William H. (3rd Sgt.)	K, 11
Harlow, William N.	G, 19
Harper, John T.	H, 8
Harrison, Asbury	G, 8
Hartsville, Jacob A.J.	K, 57
Harvey, James G. (1st Lt.)	H, 18
Harvey, Thomas G.	H, 18
Harville, George A.	K, 38
Hayes, Richard H.	K, 53
Haynes, Robert L.	E, 11
Headrick, Jacob, Jr.	E, 57
Heckman, Joseph W. (4th Cpl.)	C, 57
Henkle, John	H, 56
Higginbotham, James L.	G, 19
Hill, William	K, 57
Hinson, George	K, 8
Hix, John W.	I, 28
Hodges, George R. (1st Cpl.)	D, 24
Hodges, James Gregory (Col.)	14
Hodges, William R.	G, 57
Hodnett, Phillip	H, 24
Hogan, William H.	B, 14
Holladay, Joseph H.	F, 9
Holland, John	K, 38
Holt, John Lea	I, 56
Honts, George D.	A, 28

Hooton, Samuel C. (3rd Sgt.)	F, 18
Hopper, George W.	K, 38
Hopper, John H.	K, 38
Hoy, James M.	B, 24
Huffman, Andrew J.	C, 28
Huffman, Thomas	I, 11
Hughes, Henry H.	D, 19
Hughes, Moses P.	G, 19
Hunt, B.B.	K, 11
Hunt, Elisha B.	F, 18
Hutcherson, John D. (1st Sgt.)	G, 57
Hutcheson, John F. (3rd Sgt.)	F, 24
Hutts, John W.T.	G, 57
Hyden, Joseph L. (2nd Cpl.)	F, 24
Irby, Samuel T.	H, 14
Jackson, Benjamin E.	D, 8
James, Townsend A.	A, 8
Jelks, James K.	D, 3
Jenkins, John Summerfield (Adjt.)	14
Jennings, Thomas	G, 11
Jennings, William	G, 11
Johnson, Austin H.	K, 57
Johnson, James D.	D, 19
Johnson, James F.	K, 19
Johnson, Lucanus A.	H, 53
Johnson, William	G, 19
Jones, Charles W.	C, 11
Jones, Walker W.	C, 11
Jones, William E. (3rd Lt.)	D, 56
Jordan, William F.	G, 19
Julius, John	E, 57
Kean, Charles (4th Sgt.)	C, 1
Keeton, James P.	C, 56
Kenney, Nicholas J. (2nd Cpl.)	C, 24
Kent, James W. (1st Cpl.)	C, 19
Kercheval, John W.	F, 8
Kesler, Peter	E, 57
Kindrick, Linwood	H, 38
Kinney, James	G, 24
Kitterman, J.A.	I, 8
Knight, Daniel C. (3rd Cpl.)	H, 19

Lackey, George	B, 57
Ladd, Henry L.	K, 53
Landrum, James E. (Bvt. 2nd Lt.)	H, 19
Lane, William G.	C, 14
Laprade, Cornelius B.	I, 14
Law, George W.C.	K, 38
Law, Samuel S.	E, 53
Lawhorne, Isham	I, 19
Lawson, John O.	H, 38
Layne, Robert C.	H, 56
Lee, James G.	A, 57
Lee, William A.	A, 57
Legg, Alexander F.	E, 7
LeGrand, Peter A. (3rd Cpl.)	C, 11
Leslie, William A.	A, 8
Lewis J.D.	H, 18
Lewis, Samuel M. (4th Cpl.)	A, 57
Lindsey, John S. (Sgt.)	A, 38
Lipscomb, James H. (Capt.)	K, 53
Logan, Richard, Jr. (Capt.)	H, 14
Looney, James M.	C, 28
Lynn, Joseph F. (Sgt.)	G, 8
Mackey, John H.	C, 9
Mahone, Edward	K, 57
Maier, John	E, 11
Mansfield, James D. (4th Sgt.)	B, 24
Marshall, Ballard	C, 24
Martin, Mallory	H, 38
Mason, John R. (1st Sgt.)	I, 56
Mason, Morris W.	C, 11
Mathews, John H.	C, 56
Mathews, Spencer G.	G, 28
Matthews, Barnaba B.	F, 9
Maupin, C.B.	H, 56
Maupin, David G. (3rd Cpl.)	H, 56
Maxey, Frederick C. (3rd Cpl.)	A, 57
Mays, Anderson	I, 19
McArtor, John R. (3rd Sgt.)	B, 8
McCarty, William F.	E, 8
McConchie, William	I, 11
McCrea, William H.	B, 38 Bn.
McDaniel, Charles T.	D, 28
Meador, Calvin H. (3rd Cpl.)	F, 53
Meadors, William C.	B, 24

Melton, William G.	H, 57
Merriman, James A.	A, 57
Merriman, John E. (5th Cpl.)	D, 38 Bn.
Midkiff, Levi T.	A, 18
Miles, Drury L.	A, 57
Milton, William L.	K, 8
Minor, Peter H.	E, 19
Mitchel, William L. (Col. Gd.)	1
Mitchell, George William (1st Lt.)	H, 3
Money, E. Frank (Sgt.)	G, 8
Monroe, Nelson, (3rd Sgt.)	G, 19
Monte, William G.	G, 9
Moon, William W.	I, 18
Moore, George T. (4th Cpl.)	D, 14
Morris, Albert J.	D, 8
Morris, James E.	B, 19
Morrison, William A.	K, 18
Mundy, Thomas W. (2nd Sgt.)	E, 19
Murden, Joshua (Col. Bearer)	3
Murray, R.A.	G, 14
Myers, Joseph S.	F, 11
Newlon, James M. (4th Cpl.)	B, 8
Newman, William R.	D, 8
Nicholson, Richard H.	F, 14
Niemeyer, John C. (1st Lt.)	I, 9
Norvell, Joseph B.	E, 19
O'Brien, Bat	K, 8
Oliver, John J.	F, 38
Overbey, P.H. (5th Sgt.)	G, 14
Overby, Henry	G, 18
Overstreet, Alexander	G, 11
Owen, Beverly B.	A, 38
Owen, Pleasant D. (5th Sgt.)	I, 18
Owen, Wilson	H, 38
Owens, Thomas E.	F, 8
Pace, Archibald B.	C, 14
Painter, James B. (1st Cpl.)	K, 28
Parkerson, Mills D.	I, 3
Parks, Charles P. (1st Cpl.)	K, 11
Parrott, James	K, 14
Parsel, Isaiah (Cpl.)	G, 57

Patterson, John M.	D, 19
Paulett, Andrew J.	H, 18
Payne, John F.	A, 18
Payne, Remus M. (3rd Sgt.)	I, 57
Peck, Benjamin W. (3rd Sgt.)	G, 24
Pedigo, Elisha F.	H, 24
Pennington, John	B, 8
Pennington, Levi	B, 8
Perdue, Everett M.	D, 14
Perdue, William Thomas	D, 14
Perrin, John I. (3rd Lt.)	A, 14
Phelps, James H. (Sgt. Maj.)	28
Phillips, C. Crawley (Capt.)	F, 3
Phillips, John N.	B, 11
Pillow, Daniel A.	C, 11
Pollock, Thomas Gordon (Capt.)	Kemper
Pool, John E.P. (4th Sgt.)	E, 14
Porter, William S. (5th Sgt.)	I, 11
Porterfield, David H. (1st Sgt.)	F, 24
Poyner, William H.	H, 53
Price, George H. (4th Cpl.)	F, 24
Prillaman, Isaac C. (2nd Lt.)	B, 57
Rainey, P.L.	F, 14
Rash, William H.	B, 53
Reid, Robert E.	D, 9
Rhodes, Robert P.	F, 19
Rice, James P. (2nd Sgt.)	E, 38
Richards, King D.	A, 57
Richardson, John S.	C, 14
Rickman, Jennings	K, 14
Robertson, Daniel C.	K, 38
Robertson, John J.	F, 57
Robinson, Jacob T.	G, 53
Rollins, Alfred F.	A, 8
Ross, James E.	C, 14
Ross, William D.	C, 14
Sandbower, John D.	B, 7
Sandridge, G.W. (4th Cpl.)	H, 56
Sandridge, James J. (2nd Cpl.)	E, 19
Scott, Auville L.	G, 28
Scott, James A.	K, 57
Scott, James M.	A, 14
Scott, John B. (4th Cpl., Col. Gd.)	53

Scott, Robert G.	E, 14
Scott, William W.	K, 57
Scruggs, Powhatan B. (2nd Sgt.)	H, 38
Seay, John R. (4th Sgt.)	A, 57
Seay, William B., Jr.	A, 57
Seay, William B., Sr.	A, 57
Semones, William G.	D, 24
Setzer, George M. (2nd Cpl.)	F, 18
Shackleford, Francis S.	E, 38
Shaon, Singleton K.	F, 57
Shepard, Samuel M. (5th Sgt.)	A, 57
Sheppard, Josiah (4th Cpl.)	D, 18
Shrigley, Jacob R.	A, 8
Simms, William H.	H, 18
Simpson, William J. (2nd Cpl.)	E, 28
Sims, William B.	B, 14
Sink, John H. (4th Cpl.)	B, 24
Smith, Alexander E.	A, 18
Smith, Benjamin H. (2nd Lt.)	B, 14
Smith, James A. (Capt.)	B, 14
Smith, John H. (Capt.)	B, 57
Smith, John W.	A, 57
Smith, Joseph H. (2nd Lt.)	C, 56
Smith, William Lee	I, 56
Snead, Pleasant A.	C, 19
Sneed, Robert L.	C, 38
Snoddy, Lorenzo L.	A, 57
Spencer, James W. (2nd Cpl.)	D, 56
Spencer, Samuel T.	K, 18
Spencer, William A.	D, 38 Bn.
St. Clair, B.S.	H, 1
Steel, O. Frank	G, 8
Stephens, William O.	C, 24
Stewart, Philip H.	A, 11
Stinnett, C.P.	H, 19
Stinson, George M.	A, 57
Stone, William R.	A, 57
Story, Columbus (Jr. 2nd Lt.)	G, 7
Strange, Jacob	D, 19
Stunz, Charles W.	H, 24
Styne, Andrew J. (2nd Lt.)	K, 57
Styne, James M. (1st Lt.)	K, 57
Sublett, John P.	D, 7
Suddith, Oscar F.	C, 8
Sullens, James W.	D, 53

Surber, Levi	B, 28
Swan, Hugh B. (3rd Sgt.)	H, 18
Taliaferro, Edwin	I, 1
Taylor, Jacob S.	C, 28
Taylor, Joel F.	D, 19
Taylor, John R.	E, 19
Taylor, Robert H. (1st Cpl.)	E, 14
Taylor, Robert J.	B, 56
Teel, Josiah W.	B, 24
Thaxton, William E. (1st Sgt.)	K, 14
Thomas, James	C, 1
Thomas, James S. (4th Cpl.)	A, 28
Thomason, James H.	F, 53
Thompson, George W.	F, 14
Thornton, Joseph A.	B, 57
Thurman, William H. (3rd Sgt.)	G, 53
Tomlinson, William J.	I, 57
Tompkins, John	C, 1
Torgee, George W.	D, 38 Bn.
Townes, Daniel C. (Capt.)	A, 38
Udurley, Moses	B, 38 Bn.
Valentine, Edward W.	G, 11
Vernon, Alexander	F, 7
Voss, William H.	E, 38
Walker, George H. (2nd Lt.)	C, 24
Walker, John B. (Cpl.)	F, 7
Walters, Charles W. (2nd Lt.)	C, 38
Ward, Robert A.	I, 53
Ward, William A.	G, 57
Watkins, Aurelius A. (Bvt. 2nd Lt.)	C, 18
Welsh, Willis W.	E, 7
White, James O.	D, 24
Whitten, Thomas L. (1st Sgt.)	E, 28
Whorley, William	F, 28
Wilcher, William J.	K, 57
Wilkerson, James T.	D, 18
Willard. Benjamin B. (4th Sgt.)	G, 38
Williams, Beverly W.	B, 53
Williams, Lemuel H. (Cpl.)	G, 9
Williams, Leonidas F.	H, 53
Williams, Louis B., Jr. (Col.)	1

Williams, William C.G.	A, 38	
Williams, William O.	G, 18	
Willis, Count D.A.	E, 57	
Winger, Christopher C.	K, 57	
Winger, Martin V.B.	K, 57	
Wingfield, M.J.	D, 1	
Womack, James H.	I, 28	
Womack John W.	I, 18	
Wood, Henry William	D, 53	
Wood, Richard B. (Jr. 2nd Lt.)	B, 19	
Wood, William T.	I, 7	
Worsham, William T. (4th Cpl.)	F, 18	
Wrenn, Fenton Eley (Sr. 2nd Lt.)	I, 3	
Yancey, A.C. (3rd Cpl.)	G, 14	
Yancey, William H. (1st Lt.)	E, 14	
Yates, John T.	I, 18	
Yeaman, William H.	A, 38	
Youell, Robert	C, 1	
Zeigler, William G.	D, 24	

Died of Wounds (233)

At United States Hospitals (127)

Chester Hospital, Chester, Pennsylvania: (16)

Ayre, William Thomas (2nd Lt.)	F, 8	25 July
Caho, William A. (2nd Lt.)	I, 1	31 July
Chiles, John C.	C, 14	9 August
Driscoll, Larkin R.	I, 56	28 July
Edwards, James D.	C, 57	25 July
Fridley, John H.	K, 28	3 August
Hitt, Paskill A.	G, 7	27 July
Jackson, Lewis	A, 38	1 August
Le Tellier, William B. (2nd Lt.)	E, 19	11 August
Miller, James B. (1st Lt., Provost Marshal)	Garnett	5 August
Overstreet, Jesse W.	G, 28	23 July
Simms, Alexander	G, 28	22 July
Waddell, William D.	H, 1	12 August
Wade, Thaddeus M.	D, 28	16 September
Webb, Ferdinand H.	D, 28	25 July
Wyant, James C. (Capt.)	H, 56	31 July

DeCamp Hospital, David's Island, New York Harbor: (4)

Giles, Richard E.	C, 1	21 August
Good, Albert H. (2nd Lt.)	I, 7	29 August
Light, Charles M.	F, 38	30 July
McDaniel, David E.	K, 24	31 July

Eleventh Corps Hospital, Gettysburg: (1)

Armistead, Lewis A. (Brig. Gen.)		5 July

First Corps Hospital, Gettysburg: (3)

Farmer, Chesley M.	H, 14	?
Read, James W.	D, 38	25 July
St. John, Alexander A.	I, 56	26 July

Fort Delaware, Delaware: (2)

Dunkum, William B.	A, 57	26 October
Johnson, George W.	I, 18	28 October

Fort Wood, Bedloe's Island, New York Harbor: (1)

Skelton, Alexander	A, 53	4 December

Harrisburg, Pennsylvania: (1)
Chestnut Street General Hospital

Hicks, Jeremiah	C, 24	23 July

Letterman General Hospital, Gettysburg: (31)

Alley, D.S.	F, 11	29 July
Baker, Elijah W.	I, 56	7 August
Bendall, Benjamin F.	F, 53	6 August
Binns, Charles D.	K, 53	3 October
Bowen, John	B, 7	15 August
Bresnaham, Mathew	H, 1	1 August
Burress, Charles W. (4th Cpl.)	G, 24	3 August
Denton, John T.	D, 56	2 August
Drean, John F.	A, 53	4 November
Dudding, James O.	C, 28	13 September
Dunston, James H.	D, 14	12 September
Edwards, David S.	D, 1	11 September

Fulks, James M.	G, 19	6 August
Gaskins, William H. (1st Sgt.)	K, 8	5 November
Gray, Thomas W.	K, 38	4 October
Gray, William G. (1st Sgt.)	C, 3	6 October
Green, Eli T.	E, 14	15 August
Harvey, Edward B. (3rd Lt.)	H, 18	6 August
Harvey, Stephen R.	D, 18	28 July
Hughes, Joseph H.	A, 28	28 July
Lattimer, John W.	G, 9	18 September
Nash, Richard James	G, 9	16 August
Nichols, Charles	C, 57	11 September
Nuchols, James A.	B, 38	21 September
Nuckolds, David R.	B, 38	17 September
Robbins, Daniel	B, 53	29 July
Tucker, James G. (1st Sgt.)	F, 53	12 August
Vaughan, John L.	B, 56	29 July
Walker, Nathan W.	I, 18	8 August
Walrond, John P. (Jr. 2nd Lt.)	D, 28	31 July
Womack, Charles H.	H, 14	16 August

Pennsylvania College, Gettysburg: (4)

Austin, William C. (3rd Lt.)	E, 18	?
Partin, Daniel W.	D, 14	23 July
Patton, Waller Tazewell (Col.)	7	21 July
Woods, John J. (5th Sgt.)	K, 19	20 July or August

Point Lookout, Maryland: (2)

Harrold, Daniel B.	C, 24	7 January 1864
Kesler, John	H, 53	5 January 1864

Second Corps Hospital, Gettysburg: (48)

Adams, Edwin Thomas (2nd Lt.)	D, 8	18 July
Bellomy, George W.	H, 57	10 July
Boss, James P.	H, 8	?
Boswell, John L.C. (1st Sgt.)	E, 57	14 July
Bray, William H. (1st Lt.)	E, 53	14 July
Butts, Walter (Jr. 2nd Lt.)	F, 9	11 July
Cason, William G.	H, 57	17 July
Cheatham, Samuel O.	D, 14	17 July
Cooper, Giles H. (2nd Lt.)	D, 24	27 July
Davis, Joseph	E, 8	11 July
Davis, Philip	I, 14	24 July
Dawson, Leroy T.	C, 24	21 July

Dowdy, James H.	E, 18	16 July
Easley, Frederick B.	E, 14	?
Ellett, Lemuel O. (2nd Cpl.)	I, 1	12 July
Foster, Horace H.	G, 18	17 July
Gee, Leonidas J. (1st Sgt.)	B, 56	17 July
Gill, James C. (Sgt. Maj.)	18	11 July
Glassell, James S.	I, 11	5 July
Harris, James L.	F, 56	16 July
Herring, N.B.	I, 7	27 or 29 July
Hubbard, Alexander (1st Cpl.)	C, 28	9 or 19 July
Jennings, James (2nd Sgt.)	I, 18	16 July
Jones, John O.	I, 11	15 July
Lee, Richard H.	I, 57	15 July
Massie, John W.	I, 19	10 July
Matthews, Andrew J.	C, 28	23 July
McCormick, John	H, 38	23 July
Moore, James M.	G, 11	19 July
Morton, James W.	E, 18	23 July
Myers, Jacob W.	B, 28	?
Oakes, Thomas C. (3rd Sgt.)	B, 38	2 August
Parish, Samuel	E, 28	?
Payne, Fielding F. (2nd Lt.)	B, 8	13 July
Payne, Joseph T.	C, 38	22 July
Powell, Cornelius (3rd Cpl.)	E, 9	21 July
Presgraves, John R. (2nd Lt.)	I, 8	8 or 15 July
Racer, James O.B. (1st Sgt.)	K, 7	15 July
Ramsey, William B.	E, 14	25 July
Reed, Charles W. (1st Sgt.)	G, 8	17 July
Robbins, James P.	B, 53	20 July
Robertson, Robert A. (Cpl.)	C, 18	24 July
Shelton, Josiah W.	B, 57	27 July
Shifflett, Octavius M. (3rd Sgt.)	H, 57	13 July
Stevens, James W.	F, 38	29 July
Thomas, Abraham J.	D, 38	9 July
White, Henry P.	G, 57	27 July
Williams, James A.	E, 56	19 July

Seminary Hospital, Gettysburg: (1)

Farson, Stephen	H, 1	29 August

Sixth Corps Hospital, Gettysburg: (1)

McHone, Micajah	C, 24	?

Twelfth Corps Hospital, Gettysburg: (4)

Fletcher, Henry Y.	K, 14	13 July
Magruder, John B. (Col.)	57	5 July

Martin, James B. (3rd Cpl.)	C, 14	10 July
Robinson, William A.	C, 56	4 July

West's Buildings Hospital, Baltimore, Maryland: (8)

Gibson, H.T.	H, 56	19 August
Jefferson, James T. (3rd Cpl.)	E, 57	16 August
Lancaster, William Thomas (2nd Cpl.)	F, 3	11 August
Light, George W.	H, 14	16 July
Raber, Henry L.	A, 8	14 August
Rice, James J.	H, 38	13 January
Roberson, Benjamin S.	C, 57	16 August
Vest, Willis M. (4th Sgt.)	C, 57	18 August

At Confederate Hospitals (50)

Gordonsville, Virginia: (1)
Charity Hospital

Parrott, George W. (1st Sgt.)	D, 19	24 July

At Home: (3)

Austin, John H.	D, 57	December
Reynolds, Coleman	B, 38	30 July
Shockley, William	C, 24	19 November

Lynchburg, Virginia: (3)

Cooper, William S.	D, 24	18 July
Lovins, Arthur J.	I, 24	7 August, Gen. Hosp. #2
Ruddell, Michael	I, 28	19 July, Ladies Relief Hosp.

Montgomery White Sulpher Springs, Virginia: (1)

Griffith, Elkanah B.	A, 24	10 August

Pickett's Division Hospital, Gettysburg: (31)

Adkins, John O.	E, 38	?
Ames, Benjamin Franklin (3rd Cpl.)	F, 3	3 July
Arthur, John C. (3rd Lt.)	F, 3	3 July
Binns, Major E.	K, 53	23 July
Calfee, Henderson F.	G, 24	7 July

Daniel, John P. (1st Cpl.)	H, 11	28 or 30 July
Dunderdale, John A.F.	K, 9	21 July
Ellis, John Thomas (Lt Col.)	19	3 July
Guy, Robert F. (3rd Lt.)	B, 3	4 July
Harris, W.T.	F, 7	?
Houston, David Gardiner, Jr. (Capt.)	D, 11	4 July
Johnson, John L. (Jr. 2nd Lt.)	F, 14	3 July
Jones, Lineous	C, 11	8 July
Jones, Lucien S. (1st Sgt.)	F, 19	4 or 5 July
Jordan, John Chappell	F, 3	12 July
McKinney, George W.	K, 3	3 July
Meador, Jesse L.	A, 57	9 July
Murray, Elisha	F, 3	21 July
Owens, John C. (Maj.)	9	4 July
Owens, Thomas C.	G, 9	9 July
Poore, Robert Henry (Maj.)	14	?
Pope, Joseph W. (2nd Cpl.)	G, 3	11 July
Thomas, John William	K, 3	3 July
Tweedy, George Dabney	C, 11	3 July
Vellines, John A.	I, 3	26 July
Vermillion, Levi H.	G, 24	9 July
West, Henry G.	G, 3	16 July
Wier, John A.	K, 3	8 July
Williamson, James	F, 11	4 July
Wilson, Nathaniel Claiborne (Maj.)	28	3 July
Zeigler, Thomas F.	D, 24	16 July

Richmond, Virginia: (5)

Estis, Thomas B. (Sgt.)	C, 56	8 August, Gen Hosp. #1
Graves, Robert H. (1st Cpl.)	C, 9	14 September, Chimborazo
Harwood, Christopher E.	K, 53	15 August, Chimborazo #1
Moran, William	C, 57	30 July, Gen. Hosp. #1
Robertson, Henry H.	K, 38	5 August, Winder Hosp.

Staunton, Virginia: (2)

Hardy, Presley	H, 38	4 October
Jackson, George H. (Cpl.)	G, 18	7 July

Williamsport, Maryland: (2)

Davis, John S.	F, 18	7 July
Hackett, Francis M.	D, 56	?

Winchester, Virginia: (2)

Overstreet, Jesse W. (3rd Cpl.)	B, 14	29 July
Woodward, William W.	G, 7	15 July

Died of Wounds at Unknown Hospitals (55)

Adkins, Peter H.	C, 57	8 July
Agnew, William H.	G, 11	?
Bird, Samuel W.	C, 57	3 July
Bissell, William R. (Capt.)	A, 8	16 July
Blackburn, Leander C. (Col. Sgt.)	53	July
Blair, Suter F.	B, 38	15 July
Burruss, William H. (1st Lt.)	H, 53	15 August
Burton, John T. (2nd Lt.)	E, 56	?
Campbell, Elcanah M.	D, 38th Bn.	?
Chadick, Richard (3rd Cpl.)	H, 1	13 July
Chapman, Richard F. (Bvt. 2nd Lt.)	E, 9	15 or 16 July
Crowder, George W.	F, 14	22 or 31 July
Dodson, Josephus B.	C, 38	6 July
Drake, Robert B.	A, 57	8 July
Drewry, Carey B.	G, 28	6 September
Geer, Alexander	C, 57	7 July
Geiger, George E. (1st Lt., ADC)	Kemper	about 17 July
George, William	E, 57	17 July
Goss, William Walker (Capt.)	E, 19	18 July
Griffin, E.J.	I, 1	18 July
Hansbrough, Elijah T.	I, 11	?
Hays, Thomas J.	K, 19	17 July
Herndon, Edward J.	F, 19	10 July
Hill, William H. (Cpl.)	C, 7	?
Horsley, Thomas	G, 57	5 July
Ives, Richard W. (1st Cpl.)	H, 14	?
James, Richard	G, 14	?
Loving, Cleophas A.	C, 8	7 July
McDowell, Robert B.	K, 38	22 July
McLaughlan, Hugh	I, 1	?
Meredith, Wilson C.	D, 18	?
Michie, Orin (2nd Cpl.)	H, 56	?
Miller, William T. (1st Cpl.)	G, 1	?
Moorman, Samuel E.	B, 11	17 July
Mustain, Creed G.	D, 57	23 July
Nichols, John G.	I, 28	18 July
Oakes, James A.	B, 38	15 July
Otey, John M.	B, 57	?

Payne, Francis M. (4th Sgt.)	A, 24	?
Peters, William	C, 57	4 July
Petty, Robert J.	H, 14	?
Pinson, Allen	G, 14	5 July
Schammel, John H.	C, 1	?
Shadrack, Abraham W.	C, 7	30 August
Simpson, Archer M.	C, 38	6 July
Somerville, Robert B. (Adjt.'s Clerk)	7	?
Spessard, Hezekiah C.	C, 28	19 July
Stuart, William D. (Col.)	56	30 July
Taylor, James	F, 19	4 July
Timberlake, Benjamin N. (2nd Cpl.)	E, 53	13 July
Tredway, Thomas B. (3rd Sgt.)	I, 53	13 July
Wade, Benjamin H. (Lt. Col.)	57	5 July
Ware, Robert A. (1st Cpl.)	I, 19	21 August
Williams, David R.	F, 53	?
Yancey, Joseph S. (1st Lt.)	G, 14	7 July

Died in Union Prisons (208)

Chester, Pennsylvania Hospital: (3)

Dulaney, William E. (Sgt.)	F, 7	12 August of typhoid fever
Millam, James E. (1st Sgt.)	G, 53	6 August of pneumonia
Short, William B.	E, 56	8 September of scurvy

DeCamp Hospital, David's Island, New York Harbor: (1)

Lemon, William	K, 57	24 August of chronic diarrhea

Elmira, New York: (1)

James, John B.	I, 11	10 February 1865

Fort Delaware, Wilmington, Delaware: (96)

Abbott, Charles S.	I, 18	22 September
Adkins, Henry	E, 57	7 August
Adkins, Wilson J.	B, 18	15 October
Anglin, Samuel H.	D, 38	8 October
Archer, Levi	E, 9	7 October
Arthur, Elkana	B, 14	13 December

Barker, John H.	E, 18	19 October
Bowen, Marshall	K, 14	?
Bray, William Y.	K, 14	24 October
Britton, Richard J.	C, 9	23 July
Brownley, William K.	G, 9	6 November
Burger, Abraham	K, 57	22 September
Burley, Alexander	I, 19	5 October
Carter, Robert O.	C, 8	21 September
Cash, William H.	I, 19	17 November
Chatten, William B.	A, 38	24 August
Clarke, James D.	C, 1	22 July
Creasey, Benjamin M. (4th Cpl.)	G, 28	27 October
Crute, Christopher C. (3rd Cpl.)	C, 53	28 August
Davis, George W.	F, 9	17 November
Davis, Temple T.	K, 18	7 April 1864
Dawson, James F. (5th Sgt.)	K, 7	30 August
Dempsey, Levi J.	C, 7	3 October
Dillard, Oscar P.	G, 19	13 September
Donohoe, Lewis J.	C, 8	27 October
Dowdy, Thomas W.	C, 57	12 September
Dudley, William M.	A, 19	28 September
Dunnavant, Charles F.	C, 9	18 September
Ellett, William T.	C, 9	23 August
Elliott, Abraham F. (4th Cpl.)	F, 57	21 September
Evans, Wilson E.	B, 56	4 November
Follin, William R. (4th Sgt.)	H, 8	27 October
Fowlkes, James T.	C, 18	6 October
Fuller, Berryman	B, 38	25 September
Fuller, James R.	G, 1	9 October
Furgusson, Eldridge	K, 11	26 September
Garrison, John	E, 9	?
Glasscock, James, Jr.	E, 14	21 July
Hackworth, George D.	B, 14	21 May 1864
Haizlip, Jefferson	D, 57	25 September
Hall, George W.	F, 56	5 October
Harding, Junius	F, 53	21 September
Harrell, Reuben	I, 9	9 September
Hartless, Benjamin	I, 19	30 October
Hines, John H.	E, 57	20 October
Holt, William J.	C, 18	4 September
Huse, Jesse H.	K, 57	15 October
Insco, Isaac	F, 14	25 November
Insco, Robert O.	F, 14	28 August
Jarrell, J.E., Jr.	F, 7	21 September
Johnson, James D.	K, 11	23 October

488

Jones, Thomas Jefferson	G, 14	7 March 1864
Kean, Christopher C.	A, 18	21 November
Law, Joseph	G, 57	15 September
Law, Nathaniel C.	D, 24	18 September
Lewis, Richard S.	H, 53	22 August 1864
Loving, James E.	G, 19	30 May 1864
Loving, Richard J.	C, 14	25 August
Lunceford, James D.	F, 8	11 or 12 March 1864
Lynch, Christopher	B, 24	20 December
Martin, Richard	E, 56	12 October
Mathews. John, J.	C, 14	10 September
Mayham, John w.	B, 38	2 October
McGehee, James E. (5th Sgt.)	F, 56	6 August
Minter, Jesse L.	D, 28	26 October
Mitchell, R.O.	F, 7	3 October
Moore, John B.	G, 14	4 August
Morgan, James W.	C, 53	24 October
Myers, Alfred	B, 28	12 September
Newcomb, Winfield T.	C, 53	17 November
Newton, John	G, 14	22 September
Norfleet, Jesse	I, 9	18 October
Palmer., Isaac	A, 24	23 May 1864
Parsons, Cornelius	E, 56	2 November
Perkins, John	H, 14	27 October
Perkins, Robert	H, 14	12 September
Ramsey, Jesse H.	D, 24	17 January 1864
Redman, Stephen	K, 57	8 September
Seay, James C.	I, 19	29 December
Semones, James S.	C, 24	6 October
Shelton, William T.	D, 57	14 November
Simmons, Peter	G, 3	7 September
Sparks, Champ C. (1st Cpl.)	G, 7	3 October
Stokes, Allen W.	B, 38	17 September
Taylor, John Wade	F, 11	28 September
Trammel, Andrew J.	I, 57	1 November
Trent, John	B, 24	4 December
Turner, Charles H.	H, 11	10 January 1865
Vaiden, Page H.	B, 53	14 October
Vipperman, Nicholas T.	I, 24	7 October
Warren, Thomas G.	C, 53	1 October
Webb, Jordan C. (Cpl.)	G, 18	11 October
White, William	K, 56	30 October
Williams, Jesse	E, 56	26 August
Womack, Charles	G, 53	26 April 1864
Wynne, William H.	G, 38	5 August

Johnson's Island, Ohio: (5)

Gregory, John M. (Capt.)	C, 9	21 November
Hill, John Wesley (3rd Lt.)	A, 19	3 February 1864
Ligon, John T. (2nd Lt.)	C, 53	11 December
Swink, George W. (2nd Lt.)	G, 8	13 February 1864
Wilkinson, Henry S. (Jr. 2nd Lt.)	B, 9	21 April 1864

Point Lookout, Maryland: (95)

Abshire, Robert T.	B, 24	12 or 27 February 1864
Adcock, Thomas A.	A, 57	24 February 1864
Adkins, Richard	B, 38	?
Anthony, Phillip S.P. (Sgt.)	K, 38	11 February 1865
Arnett, Samuel M.	A, 8	6 January 1864
Ashworth, William O.	C, 24	10 February 1864
Ayres, Nathaniel M.	B, 14	6 April 1864
Baldwin, R. William	G, 53	15 November
Barradall, William J. (2nd Cpl.)	F, 9	25 March 1864
Bell, Samuel E.	A, 14	9 December
Bell, Thomas	D, 8	10 February 1864
Brown, William L.	E, 38	12 December
Burnett, Edwin H.	G, 38	8 March 1865
Campbell, Marius G. (2nd Sgt.)	H, 53	17 September 1864
Capps, Josiah (Cpl.)	I, 9	24 December
Carpenter, Charles L.	I, 19	?
Chapman, Robert J. (1st Sgt.)	I, 3	31 July 1864
Cheatham, Newton F.	D, 14	20 January 1864
Corran, Edgar	I, 3	15 July 1864
Courtney, Bazil	I, 11	1 February 1864
Cross, John D.	D, 9	29 November
Cumby, Elisha B.	A, 53	2 February 1864
Dews, Edwin (5th Sgt.)	I, 3	7 September 1864
Duncom, Richard	E, 14	1 December
Duncom, Thomas	E, 14	5 December
Dunston, Fielding T.	D, 14	11 August 1864
Early, John W.	C, 24	4 February 1864
East, George W.	I, 53	6 February 1864
Edwards, James	I, 3	19 February 1865
Embrey, James T.	I, 11	14 April 1864
Epperson, James E.	E, 56	?
Evans, George W.	A, 38	19 November
Foster, John W.	F, 18	31 January 1865
Foust, Bolling G.	B, 38	17 November
Fuller, Josiah E. (4th Sgt.)	B, 38	1 January 1864

Gaines, Henry F. (2nd Cpl.)	K, 18	29 January 1864
Gardner, Charles S.	D, 3	23 December
Ghent, Emmett M. (3rd Cpl. Med. Dept.)	3	18 September
Givens, Texas P.	B, 28	23 December
Grant, Jordan W.	G, 9	1 January 1864
Gray, Edwin	E, 9	12 December
Green, Thomas C.	A, 38	11 August 1864
Gwaltney, Benjamin L.W.	I, 3	6 March 1865
Haley, Samuel M.	K, 18	15 February 1864
Hall, John (3rd Cpl.)	I, 3	25 February 1864
Hancock, Lafayette	F, 38	8 January 1864
Hankins, William D. (1st Cpl.)	F, 38	18 December
Harris, Thomas F.	A, 18	11 March 1864
Hodges, Nathan H. (1st Sgt.)	A, 3	18 January 1864
Holland, Matthew	F, 3	2 February 1865
House, James	E, 56	24 January 1864
Hubbard, William A.	D, 18	27 December 1864
Hughes, Samuel P.	G, 19	22 January 1864
Hutchison, J.L.	G, 8	31 March 1865
Jackson, William	A, 14	10 November
Johnson, John W.	B, 7	21 January 1864
Jones, Lewis A. (4th Sgt.)	E, 53	3 January 1864
Jones, Samuel	F, 57	2 August 1864
Jones, William L.	G, 57	14 July 1864
Kivet, Alexander L. (3rd Sgt.)	B, 9	30 December
Leffel, John M. (2nd Sgt.)	C, 28	25 August 1864
Mason, John K.	G, 57	9 February 1864
McCauley, Robert W.	H, 56	19 August 1864
McClanahan, James T. (4th Cpl.)	K, 8	15 February 1864
Mealler, Willian L.	K, 3	26 November
Morgan William	D, 9	2 November
Morris, John W.	C, 14	26 December
Newman, Callohill M.	B, 14	21 August 1864
Newton, William J.	D, 56	26 November
Overbey, Warren	K, 14	23 December
Overstreet, Benjamin F.	G, 28	13 January 1864
Parkerson, George W.	I, 3	20 August 1864
Ramsay, Warren	G, 14	19 January 1864
Saunders, John T.	E, 56	31 January 1864
Scott, Walter or William F.A.	C, 3	23 January 1864
Sculley, Charles I. (3rd Cpl.)	D, 14	29 March 1865
Smith, Horace (2nd Lt.)	I, 19	12 August 1864
Stephens, Jesse	E, 9	26 February 1864
Stribling, Robert H.	I, 11	31 October

Thomas, John P.	G, 24	12 September 1864
Thomas W.P.C.	E, 18	13 September 1864
Thompson, Armistead	G, 8	23 November 1864
Thompson, Richard C.	F, 14	17 February 1864
Verser, Cicero A. (Sgt.)	C, 18	27 March 1864
Walker, Thomas G. (1st Sgt.)	B, 28	6 January 1864
Walker, Zebedee P. (1st Sgt.)	I, 53	20 August 1864
Waller, Woodley	F, 38	3 September 1864
Watson, William H.	K, 53	7 December
Weddle, Ahab	A, 24	7 March 1864
West, Napoleon B. (1st Cpl.)	K, 3	2 March 1864
Westmoreland, D.H.	G, 53	11 February 1864
Wilkinson, Henry C.	D, 14	3 December
Womack, Benjamin T.	C, 53	3 November
Woodward, William J. (2nd Cpl.)	B, 53	18 April 1864
Wright, William	I, 19	10 or 12 January 1864

At Sea (enroute to exchange at Savannah, Georgia): (2)

Hall, Howson M.	K, 3	9 November 1864
Wilson, James F.	D, 53	14 November 1864

Prison Location Unknown: (5)

George, William H. (5th Sgt.)	D, 53	13 July
Hill, James W.	K, 57	22 December
McMellon, William H.	B, 57	?
Moon, Julian K.	C, 14	?
Sloan, Samuel H.	C, 1	29 November

492

Appendix III
Known Burial Locations

Specific burial locations are provided for 217 of Pickett's dead. The majority of these (114) were located in the Gettysburg area, primarily in the vicinity of Confederate and Union hospitals. These Gettysburg burials, as previously stated, were documented by Dr. J.W.C. O'Neal and Rufus B. Weaver of Gettysburg. Locations are specified using the terms provided by these two men and may not always be compatible with battle maps of the period owing to changes in property ownership, etc. The listing is provided alphabetically by location and surname of soldier. The overwhelming majority of the dead, initially buried at Gettysburg, now rest in Richmond's Hollywood Cemetery. This listing is provided in an effort to instill in the reader a sense of compassion for these heroic men. To realize that a life, with all of its victories, defeats, joys, sorrows, loves, and hatreds, concluded "in the corner of the woods under a white oak tree near a fence" is both humbling and sorrowful, indeed.

Known Burial Locations (217)

Baltimore, Maryland: (2)

Loudon Park Cemetery: (1)
Rice, James J.	H, 38	

St. Paul's Cemetery: (1)
Armistead, Lewis A. (Brig. Gen.)

Chester, Pennsylvania Hospital Cemetery: (19)		Grave #
Ayre, William Thomas (2nd Lt.)	F, 8	49
Caho, William A. (2nd Lt.)	I, 1	92
Chiles, John C.	C, 14	128
Driscoll, Larkin R.	I, 56	63
Dulaney, William E. (Sgt.)	F, 7	145
Edwards, James D.	C, 57	76
Fridley, John H.	K, 28	114
Hitt, Paskill A.	G, 7	70
Jackson, Lewis	A, 38	100
Le Tellier, William B. (2nd Lt.)	E, 19	137
Millam, James E. (1st Sgt.)	G, 53	123
Miller, James B. (1st Lt., Prov. Marshal)	Garnett	119
Overstreet, Jesse W.	G, 28	46
Short, William B.	E, 56	184
Simms, Alexander	G, 28	42

Waddell, William D.	H, 1	146
Wade, Thaddeus M.	D, 28	199
Webb, Ferdinand H.	D, 28	77
Wyant, James C. (Capt.)	H, 56	90

Finns Point, New Jersey: (70)

Adkins, Henry	E, 57
Anglin, Samuel H.	D, 38
Arthur, Elkana	B, 14
Barker, John H.	E, 18
Bray, William Y.	K, 14
Britton, Richard J.	C, 9
Brownley, William K.	G, 9
Burger, Abraham	K, 57
Burley, Alexander	I, 19
Carter, Robert O.	C, 8
Cash, William H.	I, 19
Chatten, William B.	A, 38
Clarke, James D.	C, 1
Creasey, Benjamin M. (4th Cpl.)	G, 28
Crute, Christopher C. (3rd Cpl.)	C, 53
Davis, George W.	F, 9
Dawson, James F. (5th Sgt.)	K, 7
Dempsey, Levi J.	C, 7
Dillard, Oscar P.	G, 19
Dowdy, Thomas W.	C, 57
Dudley, William M.	A, 19
Dunkum, William B.	A, 57
Dunnavant, Charles F.	C, 9
Elliott, Abraham F. (4th Cpl.)	F, 57
Evans, Wilson E.	B, 56
Follin, William R. (4th Sgt.)	H, 8
Fowlkes, James T.	C, 18
Fuller, Berryman	B, 38
Fuller, James R.	G, 1
Hackworth, George D.	B, 14
Haizlip, Jefferson	D, 57
Hall, George W.	F, 56
Harrell, Reuben	I, 9
Hartless, Benjamin	I, 19
Holt, William J.	C, 18
Huse, Jesse H.	K, 57
Insco, Isaac	F, 14

Jarrell, J.E., Jr.	F, 7
Johnson, James D.	K, 11
Johnson, George W.	I, 18
Kean, Christopher C.	A, 18
Law, Joseph	G, 57
Loving, James E.	G, 19
Loving, Richard J.	C, 14
Lunceford, James D.	F, 8
Martin, Richard	E, 56
Mathews, John J.	C, 14
Mayham, John W.	B, 38
McGehee, James E. (5th Sgt.)	F, 56
Minter, Jesse L.	D, 28
Mitchell, R.O.	F, 7
Moore, John B.	G, 14
Morgan, James W.	C, 53
Myers, Alfred	B, 28
Newcomb, Winfield T.	C, 53
Newton, John	G, 14
Seay, James C.	I, 19
Shelton, William T.	D, 57
Simmons, Peter	G, 3
Sparks, Champ C.(1st Cpl.)	G, 7
Stokes, Allen W.	B, 38
Taylor, John Wade	F, 11
Trammel, Andrew J.	I, 57
Vaiden, Page H.	B, 53
Warren, Thomas G.	C, 53
Webb, Jordan C. (Cpl.)	G, 18
White, William	K, 56
Williams, Jesse	E, 56
Womack, Charles	G, 53
Wynne, William H.	G, 38

Gettysburg, Pennsylvania: (114)

George Arnold's Farm on the Mummasburg Road: (1)
On a bluff near a little house along Willoughby Run
    Campbell, Elcanah M.   D, 38 Bn.

Crawford's Farm: (1)
In the corner of the woods under a white oak tree near a fence
    Merriman, John E. (5th Cpl.)   D, 38 Bn.

Isaac Diehl's Farm 2 1/2 miles down the Baltimore Pike: (1)
In the rear of the barn
    Meredith, Wilson C.   D, 18

Eleventh Corps Hospital (U.S.): (1)
    Armistead, Lewis A. (Brig. Gen.)

Felix's Farm: (1)
In the woods by the road near the house
    McCrea, William H.   B, 38 Bn.

First Corps Hospital (U.S.): (1)
    Farmer, Chesley M.   H, 14

Letterman General Hospital: (31)		Section #	Grave #
Alley, D.S.	F, 11	1	3
Baker, Elijah W.	I, 56	4	22
Bendall, Benjamin F.	F, 53	3	6
Binns, Charles D.	K, 53	8	32
Bowen, John	B, 7	1	35
Bresnaham, Mathew	H, 1	2	10
Burress, Charles W. (4th Cpl.)	G, 24	3	24
Denton, John T.	D, 56	2	4
Drean, John F.	A, 53	9	13
Dudding, James O.	C, 28	7	30
Dunston, James H.	D, 14	7	35
Edwards, David S.	D, 1	7	28
Fulks, James M.	G, 19	3	7
Gaskins, William H. (1st Sgt.)	K, 8	9	14
Gray, Thomas W.	K, 38	8	35
Gray, William G. (1st Sgt.)	C, 3	9	5
Green, Eli T.	E, 14	?	
Harvey, Edward B. (3rd Lt.)	H, 18	3	13
Harvey, Stephen R.	D, 18	1	10
Hughes, Joseph H.	A, 28	1	6
Lattimer, John W.	G, 9	8	9
Nash, Richard James	G, 9	2	27
Nichols, Charles	C, 57	7	29
Nuchols, James A.	B, 38	8	21
Nuckolds, David R.	B, 38	8	13
Robbins, Daniel	B, 53	1	7
Tucker, James G. (1st Sgt.)	F, 53	5	7
Vaughan, John L.	B, 56	1	5
Walker, Nathan W.	I, 18	4	17

| Walrond, John P. (Jr. 2nd Lt.) | D, 28 | 2 | 22 |
| Womack, Charles H. | H, 14 | 2 | 30 |

Pennsylvania College Hospital: (3)
On the north side of the hospital

Austin, William C. (3rd Lt.)	E, 18
Partin, Daniel W.	D, 14
Woods, John J. (5th Sgt.)	K, 19

Pickett's Division Hospital: (24)
At Bream's Mill above Myers' house at the side of a fence

Binns, Major E.	K, 53
Daniel, John P. (1st Cpl.)	H, 11
Jones, Lineous	C, 11
Jones, Lucien S. (1st Sgt.)	F, 19
Jordan, John Chappell	F, 3
Pope, Joseph W. (2nd Cpl.)	G, 3
Vermillion, Levi H.	G, 24
Wier, John A.	K, 3
Zeigler, Thomas F.	D, 24

At Bream's Mill on the hill

Adkins, John O.	E, 38
Guy, Robert F. (3rd Lt.)	B, 3
Houston, David Gardiner, Jr. (Capt.)	D, 11
Johnson, John L. (Jr. 2nd Lt.)	F, 14
Meador, Jesse L.	A, 57
Williamson, James	F, 11

In the woods across the creek from Bream's Mill

Dunderdale, John A.F.	K, 9
Owens, John C. (Maj.)	9
Owens, Thomas C.	G, 9

In the corner of "Curn's" garden west of the house

| Harris, W.T. | F, 7 |

Northeast of "Curn's" house in the corner of a field in the edge of the woods on the south bank of Bream's Mill dam

| Tweedy, George Dabney | C, 11 (buried by one of his brothers) |

Southeast of "Curn's" house at Bream's Mill on Marsh Creek in orchard under an apple tree

| Ellis, John Thomas (Lt. Col.) | 19 |

In "Curn's" meadow under a walnut tree
    Wilson, Nathaniel Claiborne (Maj.)   28

At Francis Bream's, north of the tavern near the burial place
    Poore, Robert Henry (Maj.)   14

Exact location unknown
    Ames, Benjamin Franklin (3rd Cpl.)   F, 3

Presbyterian Graveyard: (1)
    Bissell, William R. (Capt.)   A, 8

U.S. 2nd Corps Hospital: (44)

Yard "B," on the hill between Schwartz's and Bushman's under a walnut tree;
Row 2

Cooper, Giles H. (2nd Lt.)	D, 24	
Dawson, Leroy T.	C, 24	
Matthews, Andrew J.	C, 28	
McCormick, John	H, 38	
Morton, James W.	E, 18	
Myers, Jacob W.	B, 28	
Oakes, Thomas C. (3rd Sgt.)	B, 38	
Payne, Joseph T.	C, 38	
Robbins, James P.	B, 53	
Stevens, James W.	F, 38	
White, Henry P.	G, 57	

Yard "C"

Bellomy, George W.	H, 57	

Yard "D," Jacob Schwartz's cornfield on Rock Creek

Adams, Edwin Thomas (2nd Lt.)	D, 8	Row 1
Boswell, John L.C. (1st Sgt.)	E, 57	
Bray, William H. (1st Lt.)	E, 53	
Butts, Walter (Jr. 2nd Lt.)	F, 9	Row 1
Cason, William G.	H, 57	Row 3
Cheatham, Samuel O.	D, 14	Row 1
Davis, Joseph	E, 8	Row 2
Dowdy, James H.	E, 18	Row 3
Ellett, Lemuel O. (2nd Cpl.)	I, 1	
Foster, Horace H.	G, 18	Row 1
Gee, Leonidas J. (1st Sgt.)	B, 56	Row 2
Gill, James C. (Sgt. Maj.)	18	Row 2

Harris, James L.	F, 56	Row 3
Jones, John O.	I, 11	
Lee, Richard H.	I, 57	Row 3
Payne, Fielding F. (2nd Lt.)	B, 8	
Racer, James O.B. (1st Sgt.)	K, 7	Row 3
Shifflett, Octavius M. (3rd Sgt.)	H, 57	Row 1
Thomas, Abraham J.	D, 38	
Williams, James A.	E, 56	Row 1

In back of Schwartz's barn

Davis, Philip	I, 14	
Herring, N.B.	I, 7	Grave # 6
Jennings, James (2nd Sgt.)	I, 18	
Moore, James M.	G, 11	
Powell, Cornelius (3rd Cpl.)	E, 9	Grave #17
Ramsey, William B.	E, 14	Grave # 3
Reed, Charles W. (1st Sgt.)	G, 8	Grave #14
Robertson, Robert A. (Cpl.)	C, 18	Grave # 9
Shelton, Josiah W.	B, 57	Grave # 5

West of Schwartz's house, near Yard "C," in the woods on the "red hill" above the creek

Presgraves, John R. (2nd Lt.)	I, 8

Jacob Schwartz's lane near the creek under a walnut tree

Easley, Frederick B.	E, 14

Exact location unknown

Glassell, James S.	I, 11

Seminary Hospital: (1)
In the southwest corner of Seminary Woods

Farson, Stephen	H, 1

U.S. 6th Corps Hospital: (1)
Forty feet east of grave in northeast corner of Trostle's field on the south bank of Rock Creek four miles southeast of Gettysburg

McHone, Micajah	C, 24

U.S. 12th Corps Hospital: (3)

Fletcher, Henry Y.	K, 14
Magruder, John B. (Col.)	57
Robinson, William A.	C, 56

Hilton Head, South Carolina: (1)
    Wilson, James F.   D, 53

Johnson's Island, Ohio: (3)
    Gregory, John M. (Capt.)   C, 9   Block 10
    Hill, John Wesley (3rd Lt.)   A, 19   Block 5 Grave #25
    Wilkinson, Henry S. (Jr. 2nd Lt.)   B, 9   Block 23 Grave # 4

Long Island, New York: (5)
Cypress Hill Cemetery
    Giles, Richard E.   C, 1   Grave #815
    Lemon, William   K, 57   Grave #823
    Light, Charles M.   F, 38   Grave #710
    McDaniel, David E.   K, 24   Grave #707
    Skelton, Alexander   A, 53   Grave #953

New York City: (1)
Brady's Receiving Tomb, 2nd Avenue
    Good, Albert H. (2nd Lt.)   I, 7

At Sea: (1)
    Hall, Howson M.   K, 3

Winchester, Virginia: (1)
Cemetery
    Overstreet, Jesse W. (3rd Cpl.)   B, 14   Grave #1171

Appendix IV

Disinterments from the Battlefield

This listing provides information concerning the disinterments of identified Confederate soldiers of Pickett's Division from the battlefield in 1872 and 1873. The data were obtained from the records of Rufus B. Weaver of Gettysburg who was responsible for disinterring, boxing, and shipping Southern remains from the field to Richmond's Hollywood Cemetery in the early 1870s. The information is provided in a chronological order of shipments and thence by box number where appropriate. Only 83 names are listed here. Remaining unidentified dead of the division were boxed, ten remains to a container, prior to shipment from their original burial locations on the field. In such boxes lie, today, those of the division who fell in the heat of combat along the stone wall, in the "slashing," and near Cushing's guns in "the Angle." Visitors to the Hollywood Cemetery, who locate the final resting place of these men, should remember their sacrifice, and honor the courage and devotion to duty exhibited by these soldiers on that oppressively hot 3rd of July 1863.

Disinterments from the Battlefield: (83)

Prior to general disinterments to Richmond's Hollywood Cemetery: (5)

Armistead, Lewis A. (Brig. Gen.)	End of July 1863	
Owens, John C. (Maj.)	9	
Owens, Thomas C.	G, 9	
Presgraves, John R. (2nd Lt.)	I, 8	
Wilson, Nathaniel Claiborne (Maj.)	28	

Disinterments to Richmond's Hollywood Cemetery: (78)

13 June 1872: (55)

Box #

3	White, Henry P.	G, 57
10	Dawson, Leroy T.	C, 24
15	Matthews, Andrew J.	C, 28
18	Norton, James W.	E, 18
28	Walrond, John P. (Jr. 2nd Lt.)	D, 28
32	Vaughan, John L.	B, 56
34	Robbins, Daniel	B, 53
45	Harvey, Edward B. (3rd Lt.)	H, 18
50	Bresnaham, Mathew	H, 1
52	Denton, John T.	D, 56

53	Baker, Elijah W.	I, 56
54	Alley, D.S.	F, 11
57	Bendall, Benjamin F.	F, 53
60	Womack, Charles H.	H, 14
63	Harvey, Stephen R.	D, 18
75	Nash, Richard James	G, 9
76	Edwards, David S.	D, 1
77	Gray, William G. (1st Sgt.)	C, 3
78	Dunston, James H.	D, 14
84	Binns, Charles D.	K, 53
89	Hughes, Joseph H.	A, 28
93	Nichols, Charles	C, 57
95	Nuchols, James A.	B, 38
97	Burress, Charles W. (4th Cpl.)	G, 24
98	Gray, Thomas W.	K, 38
99	Drean, John F.	A, 53
113	Nuckolds, David R.	B, 38
115	Dudding, James O.	C, 28
200	Stevens, James W.	F, 38
202	Cooper, Giles H. (2nd Lt.)	D, 24
211	McCormick, John	H, 38
213	Oakes, Thomas C. (3rd Sgt.)	B, 38

With 88 others in 10 large boxes labeled "S"

Adams, Edwin Thomas (2nd Lt.)	D, 8
Bellomy, George W.	H, 57
Boswell, John L.C. (1st Sgt.)	E, 57
Bray, William H. (1st Lt.)	E, 53
Butts, Walter (Jr. 2nd Lt.)	F, 9
Cason, William G.	H, 57
Cheatham, Samuel O.	D, 14
Davis, Joseph	E, 8
Dowdy, James H.	E, 18
Ellett, Lemuel O. (2nd Cpl.)	I, 1
Foster, Horace H.	G, 18
Gee, Leonidas J. (1st Sgt.)	B, 56
Gill, James C. (Sgt. Maj.)	18
Harris, James L.	F, 56
Jones, John O.	I, 11
Lee, Richard H.	I, 57
Myers, Jacob W.	B, 28
Payne, Fielding F. (2nd Lt.)	B, 8
Payne, Joseph T.	C, 38
Robbins, James P.	B, 53

Shifflett, Octavius M. (3rd Sgt.)		H, 57
Thomas, Abraham J.		D, 38
Williams, James A.		E, 56

3 August 1872: (20)

Box #

246	Ellis, John Thomas (Lt. Col.)	19
248	Tweedy, George Dabney	C, 11
250	Harris, W.T.	F, 7
251	McHone, Micajah	C, 24
256	McCrea, William H.	B, 38 Bn.

With 19 others in 3 large boxes labeled "P Curns"

Adkins, John O.	E, 38
Ames, Benjamin Franklin (3rd Cpl.)	F, 3
Binns, Major E.	K, 53
Daniel, John P. (1st Cpl.)	H, 11
Guy, Robert F. (3rd Lt.)	B, 3
Johnson, John L. (Jr. 2nd Lt.)	F, 14
Jones, Lineous	C, 11
Jones, Lucien S. (1st Sgt.)	F, 19
Jordan, John Chappell	F, 3
Meador, Jesse L.	A, 57
Pope, Joseph W. (2nd Cpl.)	G, 3
Vermillion, Levi H.	G, 24
Wier, John A.	K, 3
Williamson, James	F, 11
Zeigler, Thomas F.	D, 24

17 May 1873: (3)

With 33 others in 3 large boxes labeled "E"

Austin, William C. (3rd Lt.)	E, 18
Partin, Daniel W.	D, 14

With 5 others in one box labeled "U"

Farson, Stephen	H, 1

Appendix V
Unengaged Personnel

The following information provides an alphabetical listing of those soldiers of the division who were present with the unit at the time of the assault but who were detailed to other duties which prevented their participation in the attack itself. Included here are cooks, teamsters, pioneers, blacksmiths, cattle herders, and the like. The format for each soldier is the same as that used in the roster. Of the 118 names listed here, only one soldier is noted as having been wounded during the battle. This man, Corporal John Hutchison of the 8th Virginia, was on provost guard duty at the time and may have been hit by a Union artillery overshot or while attempting to stem the tide of fugitives from the division following the assault. Since only one casualty was sustained among these men, it is apparent that they did not participate in the actual attack itself. This listing is provided in an attempt to account, as completely as possible, for all of Pickett's men at the battle.

Alexander, James F. (Company Cook): Detailed im Company "F," 8th Virginia; enl. 19 June 1861 at Bloomfield; deserted at Williamsport, Maryland 9 July 1863.

Alexander, William (Company Cook): Detailed in Company "I," 8th Virginia; enl 13 July 1861 at Mount Gilead; captured with some of Mosby's men near Mountsville, Virginia 21 November 1863.

Allder, Joseph F. (Cattle Herd): Detailed from Company "A," 8th Virginia; enl. 13 May 1861 at Leesburg; AWOL July 1863; captured at Snakesville, Virginia 28 November 1863.

Ashley, William (Teamster): Detailed from Company "I," 19th Virginia; enl. 20 May 1861 at Buffalo Springs; (23); farmer.

Bailey, James M. (Company Cook): Extra-duty in Company "G," 9th Virginia; enl. 26 March 1862 at Portsmouth; born in James City County.

Barker, John M. (Pioneer): Detailed from Company "D," 8th Virginia; enl. 13 May 1861 at Aldie.

Barner, Mark A. (Company Cook): Detailed in Company "E," 14th Virginia; enl. 12 May 1861 at Clarksville; (27); tobacconist.

Bellomy, Benjamin F. (Teamster): Extra-duty from Company "H," 57th Virginia; enl. 22 July 1861 at Charlottesville.

Benton, Thomas H. (Pioneer): Detailed from Company "F," 8th Virginia; enl. 19 June 1861 at Bloomfield; AWOL 9 July through 18 August 1863.

Berry, George T. (Company Cook): Extra-duty in Company "G," 9th Virginia; enl. 20 April 1861 at Portsmouth; (25); housejoiner.

Betterton, James W. (Teamster): Detailed from Company "F," 38th Virginia; enl. 4 June 1861 at Republican Grove.

Bishop, James H. (Company Cook): Detailed in Company "K," 28th Virginia; enl. 15 May 1861 at Amsterdam.

Blunt, James T. (Blacksmith): Detailed from Company "B," 38th Virginia Battalion of Artillery; enl. 25 April 1861 at Richmond.

Blunt, Joseph E. (Blacksmith): Detailed from Company "B," 38th Virginia Battalion of Artillery; enl. 25 April 1861 at Richmond.

Bowman, William H. (Teamster): Detailed from Company "A," 14th Virginia; enl. 30 June 1861 at Jamestown; (36); boatman.

Brooks, John B. (Wagon Guard): Detailed from Company "F," 9th Virginia; enl. 18 May 1861 at Chuckatuck; (24).

Brooks, Joseph N. (Teamster): Detailed from Company "C," 3rd Virginia; enl. 23 May 1861 at Dinwiddie Court House; (38); farmer.

Brown, James E. (Teamster): Extra-duty from Company "D," 38th Battalion Virginia Artillery; enl. 17 March 1861 or 1862 at Liberty.

Brownley, Charles D. (Company Cook): Extra-duty in Company "G," 9th Virginia; enl. 30 April 1862 at Portsmouth.

Bugg, John W. (Ordnance Wagon Guard): Detailed from Company "G," 38th Virginia, Enl. 18 March 1862 at Boydton.

Bush, Edward (Ordnance Train Guard): Detailed from Company "F," 9th Virginia; enl. 18 May 1861 at Chuckatuck; (19).

Carlisle, Reynold R. (Pioneer): Detailed from Company "A," 8th Virginia; enl. 15 September 1861 at Camp Johnson.

Carter, Alexander (Company Cook): Detailed in Company "B," 8th Virginia; enl. 17 May 1861 at Rectortown; deserted 12 July 1863; captured by Buford's cavalry at Chester Gap, Virginia 21 July 1863.

Childress, Edward (Teamster): Detailed from Company "C," 38th Virginia Artillery Battalion; enl. 11 May 1861 at Richmond.

Cogbill, William C. (Teamster): Extra-duty from Company "C," 9th Virginia; enl. 16 June 1861 at Craney Island; (32); blacksmith.

Collins, William G. (Company Cook): Extra-duty in Company "C," 1st Virginia; enl. 17 September 1862 at Richmond.

Creel, Elijah (Company Cook): Detailed in Company "B," 8th Virginia; enl. 16 October 1862 in camp eight miles north of Winchester.

Crowder, Coleman D. (Blacksmith): Detailed from Company "B," 53rd Virginia; enl. 22 May 1861 at Dinwiddie.

Crowder, John N. (Teamster): Detailed from Company "C," 3rd Virginia; enl. 23 May 1861 at Dinwiddie Court House; (36); farmer.

Croy, James B. (Cattle Herd): Detached from Company "D," 7th Virginia; enl. 13 May 1861 at Giles Court House.

Cullen, John W. (Teamster): Extra-duty from Company "D," 38th Virginia Artillery Battalion; enl. 23 April 1861 at Lynchburg.

Daniel, John M. (Unknown assignment): Extra-duty from Company "I," 57th Virginia; enl. 1 March 1862 at Bachelor's Hall.

Davis, Henry W. (Company Cook): Detailed in Company "F," 38th Virginia; enl. 4 June 1861 at Republican Grove.

Dennis, Francis (Company Cook): Detailed in Company "K," 8th Virginia; enl. 8 March 1862 at Salem.

Dillon, James Dabney (Teamster): Extra-duty from Company "D," 38th Virginia Artillery Battalion; enl. 1 July 1861 at Centreville; (50 in 1864); blacksmith.

Dillon, James E. (Teamster): Extra-duty from Company "C," 9th Virginia; enl. 26 July 1861 at Craney Island.

Dooley, Jacob (Company Cook): Detailed in Company "K," 28th Virginia; enl. 20 July 1861 at Amsterdam.

Dove, Avry M. (Wheelwright, Armistead's Brigade): Extra-duty from Company "E," 57th Virginia; enl. 29 June 1861 at Rorer's.

Eanes, Silas W. (Butcher, Armistead's Brigade): Detailed from Company "E," 57th Virginia; enl. 22 April 1862 at Fort Dillard, North Carolina.

Edwards, James H. (Teamster): Detailed from Company "B," 38th Virginia Artillery Battalion; enl. 24 July 1862 at Richmond.

Edwards, Newit J. (Company Cook): Extra-duty in Company "B," 9th Virginia; enl. 23 April 1862 at Craney Island.

Evans, Charles O. (Blacksmith): Detailed from Company "K," 24th Virginia; enl. 14 May 1861 at Lynchburg.

Garrison, Ira P. (Teamster): Detailed from Company "B," 19th Virginia; enl. 18 May 1861 at Culpeper Court House; (18); farmer.

Garrison, James T. (Wagoner): Detailed from Company "I," 7th Virginia; enl. 3 June 1861 at White Hall; (25); farmer.

Gilliam, Cornelius B. (Teamster): Extra-duty from Company "D," 38th Virginia Artillery Battalion; enl. 23 April 1861 at Lynchburg.

Gilliam, Robert A. (Teamster): Detailed from Company "E," 53rd Virginia; enl. 8 July 1861 at West Point.

Gilliam, William A. (Teamster): Extra-duty from Company "D," 38th Virginia Artillery Battalion; enl. 23 April 1861 at Lynchburg.

Grant, George W. (Company Cook): Daily-duty in Company "D," 9th Virginia; enl. 27 April 1861 at the Naval Hospital, Portsmouth; (22); confectioner.

Grant, Leander H. (Company Cook): Detailed in Company "K," 9th Virginia; enl. 20 April 1861 at Portsmouth.

Gunn, Robert C. (Company Cook): Detailed in Company "G," 18th Virginia; enl. 22 April 1861 at Blacks and Whites; (32); farmer.

Haines, Henry G. (Pioneer): Detailed from Company "K," 18th Virginia; enl. 23 April 1861 at Farmville in Company "F," 18th Virginia (27); carpenter.

Hamilton, James P. (Butcher): Detailed from Company "I," 19th Virginia; enl. 29 April 1861 at Buffalo Springs; (34); farmer.

Hawley, William R. (Unknown assignment): Extra-duty from Company "H," 57th Virginia; enl. 22 July 1861 at Charlottesville.

Haws, William (Company Cook): Extra-duty in Company "E," 8th Virginia; enl. 29 May 1861 at Philomont.

Heckman, Creed T. (Wagoner): Detailed from Company "B," 24th Virginia; enl. 25 April 1861 at Gogginsville.

Herring, Henry A. (Teamster): Detailed from Company "E," 19th Virginia; enl. 28 March 1862 at Orange Court House.

Hicks, William R. (Teamster): Detailed from Company "E," 53rd Virginia; enl. 8 July 1861 at West Point.

Hopkins, John D. (Teamster): Detailed from Company "C," 38th Virginia Artillery Battalion; enl. 23 July 1861 at Staunton; (41 in 1865).

Horner, Charles A. (Teamster): Extra-duty from Company "C," 9th Virginia; enl. 27 May 1861 at Chesterfield Court House; (21); farmer.

Horner, Joseph B. (Wagon Guard): Extra-duty from Company "C," 9th Virginia; enl. 27 May 1861 at Chesterfield Court House; (19); farmer.

Hughes, John W. (Company Cook): Detailed in Company "K," 53rd Virginia; enl. 15 December 1861 at Charles City Court House.

Hutchison, John (3rd Cpl. Provost Guard): Detailed from Company "D," 8th Virginia; enl. 13 May 1861 at Aldie; *wounded.*

Inge, Caswell F. (Blacksmith): Detailed from Company "F," 38th Virginia; enl. 21 June 1861 at Republican Grove.

Jackson, David W. (Company Cook): Detailed in Company "F," 38th Virginia; enl. 4 June 1861 at Republican Grove.

Jackson, E.M. (Cattle Herd): Detailed from Company "K," 18th Virginia; enl. 9 August 1862 near Richmond.

Jenkins, Ira W. (Blacksmith): Detailed from Company "A," 38th Virginia Artillery Battalion; enl. 12 June 1861 at Leesburg.

Kearns, John W. (Teamster): Detailed from Company "A," 38th Virginia Artillery Battalion; enl. 15 July 1861 at Markham Station; (47 in 1865).

Keatts, John R. (Blacksmith): Detailed from Company "C," 38th Virginia Artillery Battalion; enl. 11 May 1861 at Richmond.

Kermick, Benjamin F. (Teamster): Detailed from Company "A," 38th Virginia Artillery Battalion; enl. 1 July 1861 at Markham Station; (26 in 1865).

Kermick, Francis M. (Teamster): Detailed from Company "A," 38th Virginia Artillery Battalion; enl. 1 July 1861 at Markham Station; (26 in 1865).

Knight, William (Company Cook): Detailed in Company "B," 8th Virginia; enl. 17 April 1861 at Orlean.

Larkins, John (Company Cook): Detailed in Company "F," 9th Virginia; enl. 18 May 1861 at Chuckatuck; (25).

Lewis, William (Company Cook): Detailed in Company "I," 9th Virginia; enl. 15 May 1861 at Churchland; (22); farmer.

Litchfield, Jacob (Company Cook): Detailed in Company "I," 9th Virginia; enl. 15 May 1861 at Churchland; (35); farmer.

Lockridge, Calvin (Teamster): Detailed from Company "D," 53rd Virginia; enl. 6 May 1861 at Fort Powhatan.

Lucas, William D. (Blacksmith): Detailed from Company "B," 38th Virginia Artillery Battalion; enl. 6 March 1862 at Richmond.

Marable, James E. (Wagoner): Detailed from Company "K," 53rd Virginia; enl. 9 May 1861 at Charles City Court House; (25); farmer.

Martin, John S. (Teamster): Detailed from Company "D," 24th Virginia; enl. 13 May 1861 at Rocky Mount.

Martin, Joseph W. (Provost Guard): Detailed from Company "A," 53rd Virginia; enl. 24 April 1861 at Halifax Court House.

McCory, Craven P. (Blacksmith): Extra-duty from Company "D," 38th Virginia Artillery Battalion; enl. 15 May 1861 or 1862 at Liberty.

McCoy, William H. (Teamster): Detailed from Company "I," 3rd Virginia; enl. 23 June 1861 at Smithfield; (19); farmer.

Moffitt, Robert F. (Company Cook): Detailed in Company "K," 8th Virginia; enl. 30 July 1861 at Warrenton; AWOL 13 July to 10 November 1863.

Moore, George H. (Company Cook): Detailed in Company "E," 14th Virginia; enl. 12 May 1861 at Clarksville; (26); carpenter.

Morefield, P.H. (Teamster): Detailed from Company "B," 38th Virginia Artillery Battalion; enl. 2 April 1863 in Pittsylvania County.

Morris, Charles S. (Ordnance Train Guard): Detailed from Company "K," 9th Virginia; enl. 1 April 1862 at Pinner's Point.

Myers, Peter C. (Wagoner): Detailed from Company "H," 8th Virginia; enl. 13 July 1861 at Leesburg.

Newman, Robert (Teamster): Detailed from Company "D," 53rd Virginia; enl. 6 May 1861 at Fort Powhatan.

Oakley, Thomas (Teamster): Detailed from Company "C," 38th Virginia Artillery Battalion; enl. 10 May 1861 at Richmond; (38 in 1865).

Owen, Drury (Teamster, Armistead's Brigade): Extra-duty form Company "D," 57th Virginia; enl. 16 August 1862 at Richmond.

Owens, Charles (Company Cook): Detailed in Company "K," 9th Virginia; enl. 20 April 1861 at Portsmouth.

Parker, George W. (Company Cook): Detailed in Company "G," 24th Virginia; enl. 4 May 1861 at Lynchburg.

Pruden, Joseph H. (Company Cook): Detailed in Company "F," 9th Virginia; enl. 23 March 1862 at Cedar Point.

Riley, William (Teamster): Detailed from Company "A," 38th Virginia Artillery Battalion; enl. 15 July 1861 at Markham Station.

Roane, Alonzo B. (Ordnance Train): Extra-duty from Company "G," 9th Virginia; enl. 26 March 1862 at Portsmouth.

Singleton, James F. (Teamster): Detailed from Company "H," 14th Virginia; enl. 29 April 1861 at Meadville; (23); wagoner.

Smith, Thomas L. (Teamster): Detailed from Company "B," 38th Virginia Artillery Battalion; enl. 25 April 1861 at Richmond.

Sneed, John (Wagoner): Detailed from Company "I," 7th Virginia; enl. 3 June 1861 at White Hall; (27); farmer.

Sneed, Richard E. (Wagoner): Detailed from Company "I," 7th Virginia; enl. 3 June 1861 at White Hall; (23); farmer.

Stone, Samuel M. (Blacksmith): Extra-duty from Company "D," 38th Virginia Artillery Battalion; enl. 15 May 1861 or 1862 at Liberty.

Stultz, Peyton W. (Butcher, Armistead's Brigade): Detailed from Company "F," 57th Virginia; enl. 10 July 1861 at Mount Vernon Church.

Swain, William E. (Pioneer): Detailed from Company "K," 8th Virginia; enl. 30 July 1861 at Salem.

Tompkins, James E. (Provost Guard): Detailed from Company "B," 11th Virginia; enl. 23 April 1861 at Yellow Branch; (25); teacher.

Trussell, Howard (Company Cook): Detailed in Company "F," 8th Virginia; enl. 19 July 1861 at Bloomfield; AWOL about 12 July 1863.

Twyford, Revel T. (Teamster): Detailed from Company "B," 38th Virginia Artillery Battalion; enl. 2 September 1861 at Gloucester Point.

Wade, John T. (Teamster): Detailed from Company "F," 38th Virginia; enl. 17 March 1862 at Republican Grove.

Waldron, Hiram (Teamster): Detailed from Company "G," 11th Virginia; enl. 15 March 1862 at Lynchburg; (46).

Waller, William G. (Teamster): Detailed from Company "C," 3rd Virginia; enl. 23 May 1861 at Dinwiddie Court House; (35); mechanic.

West, William (Teamster): Extra-duty from Company "B," 14th Virginia; enl. 1 April 1862 at Suffolk.

Wilkerson, George P. (Butcher, Armistead's Brigade): Extra-daily duty from Company "G," 9th Virginia; enl. 20 April 1861 at Portsmouth; (27); carpenter.

Williams, Granderson (Teamster): Extra-duty from Company "C," 9th Virginia; enl. 19 March 1862 at Craney Island.

Winn, George W. (Company Cook): Detailed in Company "G," 18th Virginia; enl. 1 August 1862 at Richmond.

Wiseman, Henry (Blacksmith): Extra-duty from Company "D," 53rd Virginia; enl. 6 May 1861 at Fort Powhatan.

Wolf, Thomas B. (Wagoner): Detailed from Company "I," 7th Virginia; enl. 3 June 1861 at White Hall; (24); farmer.

Wortman, J.W. (Teamster): Detailed from Company "A," 38th Virginia Artillery Battalion; enl. 12 June 1861 at Leesburg.

Wright, Robert B. (Teamster): Detailed from Company "E," 53rd Virginia; enl. 8 July 1861 at West Point.

Wright, Robert J. (Teamster): Extra-duty from Company "C," 14th Virginia; enl. 27 March 1862 at Richmond.

Wright, William B. (Teamster): Extra-duty from Company "C," 14th Virginia; enl. 10 May 1861 at Palmyra; (31); carpenter.

Yancey, Richard H. (Quartermaster Wagon Guard): Detailed from Company "E," 14th Virginia; enl. 12 May 1861 at Clarksville; (19); farmer.

Appendix VI

Unit Synonym Index

(All units are infantry unless otherwise specified.)

Albemarle Rifles, The (B, 19)
Amherst Rifle Grays, The (I, 19)
Appomattox Greys (H, 18)
Baltimore Artillery (B, 9)
Barhamsville Grays (B, 53)
Bedford Greys (F, 28)
Bedford Rifle Greys (B, 14)
Black Eagle Riflemen (E, 19)
Black Eagle Rifles (E, 19; See Black Eagle Riflemen)
Blue Mountain Boys (F, 8)
Blue Ridge Rifles, The (K, 19)
Blue Ridge Rifles (A, 28)
Botetourt Guards (K, 57)
Botetourt Springs Rifles (3rd E, 28)
Breckenridge Infantry (K, 28)
Buckingham Yancy Guards (D, 56)
Bull Run Rangers (C, 8; see Evergreen Guards)
Carroll Boys (C, 24)
Cascade Rifles (K, 38)
Chambliss Grays (F, 14)
Champe Rifles (D, 8)
Charles City Southern Guards (K, 53)
Charlotte Defenders (G, 56)
Charlotte Greys (I, 56)
Charlotte Rifles (K, 18)
Chatham Grays (I, 53)
Chester Grays (I, 14)
Chesterfield Central Guards (D, 14)
Chesterfield Yellow Jackets (C, 9; see Yellow Jacket Artillery)
Clarksville Blues (E, 14)
Clifton Greys (C, 11)
Cockade Rifles (E, 3)
Craney Island Light Artillery (I, 9)
Craig Mountain Boys (2nd C, 28)
Craig Rifles (B, 28)
Dan River Rifles (B, 28)
Danville Blues (A, 18)
Danville Greys (B, 18)
Davis Rifle Guard (F, 38)
Davy Logan Guards (G, 53)

Deyerle's Battery (I, 28)
Dinwiddie Grays (C, 3)
Dismal Swamp Rangers (A, 3)
Ebenezer Grays (E, 56)
Edmunds Guards (F, 53)
Evergreen Guards (C, 8)
Farmville Guards (F, 18)
Fauquier Artillery (A, 38 Bn.)
Fincastle Rifles (D, 11)
Floyd Riflemen (A, 24)
Fluvanna Rifle Guard (C, 14)
Franklin Fire Eaters (C, 57)
Franklin Sharpshooters (B, 57)
Galveston Tigers (D, 57)
Giles Volunteers (D, 7)
Halifax Light Infantry (A, 53)
Halifax Rifles (2nd K, 3)
Hampden Guard (C, 38 Bn.; see Hampden Lt. Art.)
Hampden Light Artillery (C, 38 Bn.)
Harrison's Guards (K, 56)
Hazelwood Volunteers (E, 7)
Henry Guards (H, 24)
Henry and Pittsylvania Rifles (F, 57)
High Hill Rifles (2, K 3; see Halifax Rifles)
Hillsboro Border Guards (A, 8)
Holcombe Guards (I, 7)
Home Guard (G, 11)
Howardsville Greys (D, 19)
Isle of Wight Rifle Blues (E, 9)
James River Artillery (2nd I, 3)
Jeff Davis Guard (H, 11)
Jeff Davis Guard (A, 57)
Jefferson Davis Riflemen (H, 11; see Jeff Davis Guard)
Ladies' Guard (G, 57)
Laurel Grove Riflemen (C, 38)
Logan Guards (G, 53; see Davy Logan Guards)
Louisa Holliday Guards (C, 56)
Louisa Nelson Greys (F, 56)
Lynchburg Rifle Grays (A, 11)
Lynchburg Rifles (E, 11)
Madison Grays (K, 7)
Markham Guards (A, 38 Bn.; see Fauquier Art.)
Mattapony Guards (H, 53)
Meadville Greys (H, 14)
Mecklenburg Guards (A, 56)

Mecklenburg Rifles (G, 38)
Mecklenburg Spartans (B, 56)
Montgomery Guard, The (C, 1)
Montgomery Guard, The (F, 19)
Montgomery Guards (F, 11; see Preston Guards)
Monticello Guard (A, 19)
Nansemond Rangers (F, 3)
Nelson Grays (G, 19)
New River White Rifles (F, 24)
Nottoway Greys (G, 18)
Nottoway Rifle Guards (C, 18)
Old Dominion Guard (D, 1)
Old Dominion Guards (K, 9)
Old Dominion Riflemen (C, 53)
Paineville Rifles (A, 14)
Pamunkey Rifles (E, 53)
Patty Layne Rifles (G, 28)
Piedmont Guards (E, 19)
Piedmont Rifles (B, 8)
Piedmont Rifles (D, 28)
Pig River Greys (E, 57)
Pittsylvania Life Guards (I, 57)
Portsmouth National Greys (H, 3)
Portsmouth Rifles (G, 9)
Potomac Greys (H, 8)
Preston Guards (F, 11)
Prospect Rifle Grays (D, 18)
Prospect Rifle Guards (D, 18; see Prospect Rifle Grays)
Rappahannock Guards (G, 7)
Richardson Guards (A, 7)
Richmond City Guard (B, 1; see Riflemen)
Richmond Fayette Artillery (B, 38 Bn.)
Richmond Grays Number 2 (H, 1)
Riflemen (B, 1)
Rivanna Guards (H, 57)
Rough and Ready Guards (G, 3)
Rough and Ready Rifles (I, 11)
Scottsville Guard, The (C, 19)
Secession Guards (H, 38)
Solomon Grays (H, 8; see Potomac Greys)
Southampton Greys (D, 3)
Southern Braves (I, 14; see Chester Grays)
Southern Guards (B, 11)
Southern Rights Guard, The (H, 19)
Spring Garden Blues (I, 18)

Taylor Grays (D, 53)
Valley Regulators (K, 11)
Virginia Artillery (D, 9)
Virginia Rifles (B, 3)
Washington Grays (B, 7)
Washington Volunteers (H, 7)
White Hall Guards (H, 56)
Whitmell Guards (D, 38)
Williams' Rifles (1st)
Yellow Jacket Artillery (C, 9)

Bibliography

Manuscripts

Aiken, David. Letter to unidentified captain, n.d., [1863]. South Caroliniana Library, University of South Carolina.

Alexander, Colonel E. Porter. Letter to Adam L. Alexander, 17 July 1863. Alexander-Hillhouse Papers, University of North Carolina.

Armistead, Mrs. Lewis A. Letter to Frederick J. Tilberg, 20 January 1939 [?]. Gettysburg National Military Park files.

Berkeley, Edmund. Letter to John W. Daniel, 26 September n.d., John W. Daniel Papers, University of Virginia Library.

Brinton, D. G. Letter to John B. Bachelder, 22 March 1869. J. B. Bachelder, Gettysburg Correspondence, New Hampshire Historical Society.

Carrington, Colonel Henry A. Biographical Sketch. John W. Daniel Papers, University of Virginia Library.

Coleman, Clayton, Letter to John W. Daniel, 1 July 1904. John W. Daniel Papers, University of Virginia Library.

Confederate Civil War Records: National Archives, Washington, DC; Record Group 109, War Department Collection of Confederate Records: Entry 18. Muster and Pay Rolls 1861-65; Register of Staff Assignments 1862-64 (Chapter 1, Volume 122); Entry 193. Records of the Adjutant General's Office Relating to the Military and Naval Service of Confederates, "Carded" Records Showing Military Service.

Cowan, Andrew. Letter to Colonel John P. Nicholson, 27 July 1913. *Gettysburg Newspaper Clippings Relating to the Battle*, Gettysburg National Military Park.

_____ ."Remarks," in Alexander S. Webb Papers. Yale University.

Damron, Robert B. "Recollections of some of the incidents of the Battle of Gettysburg." John W. Daniel Papers, University of Virginia Library.

Dearing, James. Biographical Sketch. John W. Daniel Papers, University of Virginia Library.

Easley, D. B. Letter to Howard Townsend, 24 July 1913. D. B. Easley Papers, U.S. Army Military History Institute.

Farinholt, Benjamin L. Letter to John W. Daniel, 15 April 1904. John W. Daniel Papers, University of Virginia Library.

Garnett, Richard B. Letters to Mrs. Dandridge, 21 June, 25 June 1863. Bedinger-Dandridge Family Correspondence, Duke University Library.

Gates, Theodore B. Letter to P. F. Rothermel, 28 April 1868. Peter F. Rothermel Papers, Pennsylvania Historical and Museum Commission.

Gayle, Sergeant Levin C. Diary, typescript portion. Gettysburg National Military Park.

Georg-Harrison, Kathleen. May 4,1993 letter to John Busey citing information concerning Pvt. Samuel Parish of Company "E", 28th Virginia found in United States Christian Commission "Second Report of the Committee of Maryland, September 1, 1863," (Baltimore: Sherwood & Co., 1863).

_____. August 31, 1993 letter to John Busey citing information concerning Col. Waller Tazewell Patton of the 7th Virginia found in the Surgeon's Folder, Box 7 of the Robert Blake Collection, U.S. Army Military History Institute.

Granbery, J. C. Letter to John W. Daniel, 25 March 1905. John W. Daniel Papers, University of Virginia Library.

Hunton, Eppa. Letter to John W. Daniel, 15 July 1904. John W. Daniel Papers, University of Virginia Library.

Hurt, James J. Letter to John W. Daniel, 28 October 1904. John W. Daniel Papers, University of Virginia Library.

Hutter, James R. Letter to John W. Daniel, n.d., John W. Daniel Papers, University of Virginia Library.

Jesse, William P. Account. John W. Daniel Papers, University of Virginia Library.

Kemper James L. Letter to E. P. Alexander, 20 September 1869. Dearborn Collection of Confederate Civil War Papers. Houghton Library, Harvard University.

_____. Letter to John B. Bachelder, 4 February 1886. J. B. Bachelder, Gettysburg Correspondence, New Hampshire Historical Society.

Longstreet, James A. Letter to Colonel J. B. Walton, 6 November 1877. Historic New Orleans Collection, Tulane University.

Mayo, Colonel Joseph C. "Report," for Kemper's Brigade to Major Charles Pickett, 25 July 1863. George E. Pickett Papers, Duke University Library.

Michie, Henry C. Letter to John W. Daniel, 27 January 1904. John W. Daniel Papers, University of Virginia Library.

_____. Letter to Vincent Tapscott, 21 February 1904. John W. Daniel Papers, University of Virginia Library.

Musser, John D. Letter, 15 September 1863. John D. Musser Papers, Ronald Boyer Collection, Military History Institute.

O'Brien, H. D. Letter to John B. Bachelder, 23 March 1883. J. B. Bachelder, Gettysburg Correspondence, New Hampshire Historical Society.

O'Connor-Moulder, Rebecca. Letter to Superintendent, Gettysburg National Cemetery, with 18 May 1864 enclosure. Gettysburg National Military Park.

Plaisted, A. D. Letter to John B. Bachelder, 11 June 1870. J. B. Bachelder, Gettysburg Correspondence, New Hampshire Historical Society.

Rawls, S. Waite, III. Letter to John W. Busey dated 23 June 1992 citing information from Jennings C. Wise's Military History of VMI and the 1989 Roster of Former Cadets of the Virginia Military Institute.

Report of ? for 24th Virginia Infantry, 9 July 1863. George E. Pickett Papers, Duke University Library.

Rider, A. J. Letter to John B. Bachelder, 2 October 1885. J. B. Bachelder, Gettysburg Correspondence, New Hampshire Historical Society.

Robertson, William B. Letter to Mattie _____, 18 July 1863. John W. Daniel Papers, University of Virginia Library.

Stribling, Robert. Letter to John W. Daniel, 7 March 1904. John W. Daniel Papers, University of Virginia Library.

Thompson, Joseph L. Letter to John W. Daniel, n.d., John W. Daniel Papers, University of Virginia Library.

Webb, Alexander S. Letter to his father, 17 July 1863. Alexander S. Webb Papers, Yale University.

Wilcox, Cadmus M. "Report" for Wilcox's Brigade to Major Thomas A. Mills, July 1863. Virginia Historical Society

Williams, Erasmus. "A Private's Experience in the 14th Virginia Infantry at Gettysburg." John W. Daniel Papers, University of Virginia Library.

Winston, William H. H. Account. John W. Daniel Papers, University of Virginia Library.

Woodworth, Madison J. C. Letter to Theodore B. Gates, 13 October 1888. Seward Osborne, Jr. Collection, photocopy in Gettysburg National Military Park files.

Wray, James W. Account. John W. Daniel Papers, University of Virginia Library.

Newspapers

Bachelder, John B. "The Third Day's Battle," *The Philadelphia Weekly Times*, 15 December 1877. In *Gettysburg Newspaper Clippings*, I, 35-37.

Balch, William Ralton. "Pickett's Charge," Gettysburg *Compiler*, 11 August 1887, 1.

Baltimore *American*, "To Rest With Pickett," 16 February, 1896.

Corbin, Elbert. "Pettit's Battery at Gettysburg," *The National Tribune*, 3 February 1910.

Cowan, Andrew. "When Cowan's Battery Withstood Pickett's Splendid Charge," *New York Herald*, 2 July 1911.

Finley, George W. "Bloody Angle," *Buffalo Evening News*, 29 May 1894. In *Gettysburg Newspaper Clippings*, IV, 43.

Friend, Thomas R. "Pickett's Position," Richmond *Times-Dispatch*, 29 November 1903.

Gettysburg *Compiler*, 23 September 1902, 4.

Huston, Thomas D. "Storming Cemetery Hill," *The Philadelphia Weekly Times*, 21 October 1882. In *Gettysburg Newspaper Clippings Relating to the Battle*, 21, 23.

Jacobs, Rev. Dr. [Henry.] "Meteorology of the Battle," in *Gettysburg Newspaper Clippings Relating to the Battle*, 35.

Latrobe, R. Steuart. "The Pinch of the Fight. Gettysburg, July 2, '63," Gettysburg *Compiler*, 7 December 1877, 1.

"Lee Statue Site," *Industrial School News* (Scotland, PA) n.d., in *Virginia Monument Correspondence*, Gettysburg National Military Park.

[McCullough, Captain Robert.] "St. Louisians Among Gettysburg Heroes," *St. Louis Globe-Democrat*, 9 March 1913, 15.

Moore, J. H. "Longstreet's Assault," *The Philadelphia Weekly Times*, 4 November 1882. In *Gettysburg Newspaper Clippings Relating to the Battle*, 28-31.

Nesbit, John W. "Recollections of Pickett's Charge," *The National Tribune*, 29 January 1914.

Otey, Kirkwood. "Some War History," Richmond *Times*, 7 November 1894.

Owen, H. T. "Pickett's Charge," Gettysburg *Compiler*, 6 April 1881, 1.

Owen, William M. "Pickett's Charge," Gettysburg *Star and Sentinel*, 6 July 1886.

Pennsylvania Daily Telegraph, 7 July 1863.

"Pickett's Charge," *The Philadelphia Press*, 4 July 1887, 1.

Smith, Christopher and [G. W. Finley.] "Bloody Angle," *Buffalo Evening News*, 29 May 1894. In *Gettysburg Newspaper Clippings*, IV, 41-44.

Smith, R. Penn. "The Battle—The Part Taken by the Philadelphia Brigade in the Battle," *Gettysburg Compiler*, 7 June 1887.

"Terrific Fight of Third Day," *The Scranton Truth*, 3 July 1913.

Wood, Col. William W. "Pickett's Charge at Gettysburg," Gettysburg *Compiler*, 22 August 1887, 1.

Periodicals

"About the Death of General Garnett," *Confederate Veteran Magazine*, XIV (February 1905), 81.

Address query in *Confederate Veteran Magazine*, V (1897), 162.

Berkeley, Edmund. "Rode with Pickett," *Confederate Veteran Magazine*, XXXVIII (May 1930), 175.

Bright, R. A. "Pickett's Charge at Gettysburg," *Confederate Veteran Magazine*, XXXVII (July 1930), 263-266.

Carter, James T. "Flag of the Fifty-third Va. Regiment," *Confederate Veteran Magazine*, X (June 1902), 263.

"Col & Dr. R. W. Martin, of Virginia," *Confederate Veteran Magazine*, V (1897), 70.

"Colonel E. P. Alexander's Report of the Battle of Gettysburg," *Southern Historical Society Papers*, IV (1877), 235-239.

Crocker, James F. "Colonel James Gregory Hodges," *Southern Historical Society Papers*, XXXVII (1909), 184-197.

_____ . "Gettysburg — Pickett's Charge," *Southern Historical Society Papers*, XXXIII (1905), 118-134.

Easley, D. B. "With Armistead When he was Killed," *Confederate Veteran Magazine*, XX (August 1912), 379.

Farinholt, Col. B. L. "Battle of Gettysburg—Johnson's Island," *Confederate Veteran Magazine*, V (September 1897), 467-470.

Gomer, A. P. "Service of Third Virginia Infantry," *Confederate Veteran Magazine*, XVIII (1910), 228.

Griggs, Colonel George K. "Memorandum of Thirty-eighth Virginia Infantry," *Southern Historical Society Papers*, XIV (1886), 252-253.

Hazelwood, Martin W. "Gettysburg Charge. Paper as to Pickett's Men," *Southern Historical Society Papers*, XXIII (1895), 229-237.

Holland, Captain T. C. "With Armistead at Gettysburg," *Confederate Veteran Magazine*, XXIX (February 1921), 62.

Johnson, Ida Lee. "Over the Stone Wall at Gettysburg," *Confederate Veteran Magazine*, XXXI (July 1923), 248-249.

Loehr, Charles T. "The 'Old First' at Gettysburg," *Southern Historical Society Papers*, XXXII (1904), 33-40.

Martin, Rawley W. "Armistead at the Battle of Gettysburg," *Southern Historical Society Papers*, XXXIX (1914), 186-187.

_____ . and John H. Smith. "The Battle of Gettysburg and the Charge of Pickett's Division," *Southern Historical Society Papers*, XXXII (1904), 183-195.

Mayo, Colonel Joseph C. "Pickett's Charge at Gettysburg," *Southern Historical Society Papers*, XXXIV (1906), 327-335.

McPherson, J. R. "A Private's Account of Gettysburg," *Southern Veteran Magazine*, VI (1898) 148-149.

Owen, H. T. Letter, *Confederate Veteran Magazine*, XII (January 1904), 7.

Peters, Winfield. "The Lost Sword of Gen. Richard B. Garnett, Who Fell at Gettysburg," *Southern Historical Society Papers*, XXXIII (1905), 26-31.

Poindexter, James E. "General Armistead's Portrait Presented," *Southern Historical Society Papers*, XXXVII (1909), 144-151.

Reeve, E. P. "Casualties in the Old First at Gettysburg," *Southern Historical Society Papers*, XVII (1889), 407-409.

Rollins, Richard. "Black Confederates at Gettysburg - 1863." *The Gettysburg Magazine*, No. 6 (January 1992) 97.

Shotwell, Randolph A. "Virginia and North Carolina in the Battle of Gettysburg," *Our Living and Our Dead*, IV, No. 1 (January 1876), 80-97.

Stewart, William H. "Col. John Bowie M'Gruder," *Confederate Veteran Magazine*, VIII (1900), 329.

Swallow, W. H. "The Third Day at Gettysburg," *The Southern Bivouac*, IV (February 1886), 562-572.

Taylor, William H. "Some Experiences of a Confederate Assistant Surgeon," *Transactions of the College of Physicians of Philadelphia*, XXVIII, 91-121.

Walker, James H. "The Charge of Pickett's Division," *The Blue and the Gray*, I (1893), 221-223.

Books

Alexander, E. P. "The Great Charge and Artillery Fighting at Gettysburg," *Battles and Leaders of the Civil War*, Vol. 3. New York: Thomas Yoseloff, 1956.

Andrews, C. C., ed. *Minnesota in the Civil and Indian Wars 1861-1865*. St. Paul: Pioneer Press Co., 1891.

Benedict, George Greenville. *A Short History of the 14th Vermont Regt*. Bennington, VT: Press of C. A. Pierce, 1887.

Boatner, Mark M., III. *The Civil War Dictionary*. Revised Edition. New York, NY: David McKay Co., Inc., 1988.

Busey, John W., and David G. Martin. *Regimental Strengths and Losses at Gettysburg*. Hightstown, NJ: Longstreet House, 1986.

Clement, Maude Carter, ed. *The History of Pittsylvania County, Va*. Lynchburg, 1929.

Coco, Gregory A. *On the Bloodstained Field*. Gettysburg, PA: Thomas Publications, 1987.

_____. *War Stories*. Gettysburg, PA: Thomas Publications, 1992.

Cook, Captain John S. D. "Personal Reminiscences of Gettysburg," read 12 December 1903 before the Kansas Commandery of the Military Order of the Loyal Legion of the United States, War Paper No. 24.

Crocker, James F. *Gettysburg—Pickett's Charge and Other War Addresses*. Portsmouth, VA: W. A. Fiske, 1915.

Durkin, Joseph T., ed. *John Dooley: Confederate Soldier—His War Journal*. South Bend, IN: University of Notre Dame Press, 1963.

Faust, Patricia L., ed. *Historical Times Illustrated Encyclopedia of the Civil War*. New York, NY: Harper Collins Publishers, 1991.

Fox, William F., ed. *New York at Gettysburg*. 3 Vols. Albany, NY: J. B. Lyon Company, 1900.

Gates, Theodore B. *The "Ulster Guard" and the War of the Rebellion*. New York: B. H. Tyrrel, 1879.

Gibbon, John. *Personal Recollections of the Civil War*. Dayton: Morningside Books, 1978 reprint.

Govan, Gilbert E. and James W. Livingood, eds. *The Haskell Memoirs, John Cheves Haskell.* New York: G. P. Putnam's Sons, 1960.

Harrison, Walter. *Pickett's Men: A Fragment of War History.* New York: D. Van Nostrand, 1870.

Heaps, Willard A. and Porter W. *The Singing Sixties. The Spirit of Civil War Days Drawn from the Music of the Times.* Norman, OK: University of Oklahoma Press, 1960.

Hoke, Jacob. *The Great Invasion.* New York: Thomas Yoseloff, 1959.

Hunton, Eppa. *Autobiography of Eppa Hunton.* Richmond: William Byrd Press, 1933.

Irby, Richard. *Historical Sketch of the Nottoway Grays, afterwards Company G, Eighteenth Virginia Regiment, Army of Northern Virginia.* Richmond: J. W. Ferguson and Son, 1878.

Johnson, Rev. John Lipscomb. *The University Memorial Biographical Sketches of Alumni of the University of Virginia who fell in the Confederate War.* Baltimore: Turnbull Brothers, 1871.

Johnston, David E. *Four Years a Soldier.* Princeton, WV, 1887.

Jones, John T. "Pettigrew's Brigade at Gettysburg," *Histories of the Several Regiments and Battalions from North Carolina in the Great War 1861-1865,* ed. Walter Clark, V. Raleigh: E. M. Uzzell, 1901.

Kane, John F. *The Medal of Honor.* Washington: G. P. O., 1948.

Krick, Robert K. *The Gettysburg Death Roster. The Confederate Dead at Gettysburg.* Second Edition, Revised. Dayton, OH: Press of Morningside Bookshop, 1985.

_____. *Lee's Colonels. A Biographical Register of the Field Officers of the Army of Northern Virginia.* 3rd Edition, Revised. Dayton, OH: Press of Morningside House, Inc., 1991.

Lewis, John H. *Recollections from 1860 to 1865.* Portsmouth, VA, 1893.

Moore, Frank, ed. *The Rebellion Record: A Diary of American Events.* VII. New York: D. Van Nostrand, 1864.

Morgan, William H. *Personal Reminiscences of the War of 1861-65.* Lynchburg: J. P. Bell and Co., Inc., 1911.

New York Monuments Commission. *In Memoriam Alexander Stewart Webb 1835-1911.* Albany, NY: J. B. Lyon Company, 1916.

Official Records of the War of the Rebellion, Series I, XXVII, 3 parts. Washington: Government Printing Office, 1889.

Poindexter, Rev. James E. "Address on the Life and Services of Gen. Lewis A. Armistead, delivered ... before R. E. Lee Camp, No. 1, Confederate Veterans." Richmond, 29 January 1909.

Reed, John, Sylvester Byrne, Frederick Middleton, et al., representing the survivors of the Seventy-second Regiment of Pennsylvania Volunteers, Plaintiffs vs. Gettysburg Battlefield Memorial Association, and John P. Taylor, J. P. S. Gobin, John P. Nicholson, and R. B. Ricketts, Commissioners appointed by the Governor of the State of Pennsylvania, Defendants. Testimony in the Court of Common Pleas of Adams Co. In equity, No. 1. January Term, 1889.

Reply of the Philadelphia Brigade Association to the Foolish and Absurd Narrative of Lieutenant Frank A. Haskell, which Appears to be Endorsed by the Military Order of the Loyal Legion Commandery of Massachusetts, and the Wisconsin History Committee. Philadelphia: Bowers Printing Co., 1910.

Rice, Edmund. "Repelling Lee's Last Blow at Gettysburg," *Battles and Leaders of the Civil War*, III. New York: Thomas Yoseloff, 1956.

Sifakis, Stewart. *Who Was Who in the Confederacy.* New York, NY: Facts on File, Inc. 1988.

Skelly, Daniel Alexander. *A Boy's Experiences During the Battles of Gettysburg.* Gettysburg: D. A. Skelly, 1932.

Sorrel, G. Moxley. *Recollections of a Confederate Staff Officer.* New York: Neale Publishing Co., 1905.

Stine, J. H. *History of the Army of the Potomac.* 2nd ed. Washington: Gibson Brothers, 1893.

Sturtevant, Ralph Orson. *Pictorial History Thirteenth Regiment Vermont Volunteers War of 1861-1865.* Burlington: Regimental Association, 1910.

Waitt, Ernest Linden. *History of the Nineteenth Regiment Massachusetts Volunteer Infantry 1861-1865.* Salem, MA: The Salem Press Co., 1906.

Walker, Charles D. *Memorial, Virginia Military Institute. Biographical Sketches of the Graduates and Eleves of the Virginia Military Institute who Fell During the War Between the States.* Philadelphia: J. B. Lippincott & Co., 1875.

Wallace, Lee A., Jr. *A Guide to Virginia Military Organizations.* Lynchburg, VA: H.E. Howard, Inc., 1986.

Wert, J. Howard. *A Complete Hand-Book of the Monuments and Indications and Guide to the Positions on the Gettysburg Battlefield.* Harrisburg: R. M. Sturgeon & Co., 1886.

_____ . *Poems of Camp and Hearth.* Harrisburg: Harrisburg Publishing Co., 1887.

Wood, Lieutenant William Nathaniel. *Reminiscences of Big I.* ed. Bell I. Wiley. Wilmington, NC: Broadfoot Publishing Co., 1987.

General Index

Hampden (Va) Artillery See Virginia
    Troops, Caskie's Bat.
Hanover Junction, 2
Harrisburg, Pa., 140
Harrison, Maj. Walter, 10, 15, 23, 68,
    79, 131
Harrow's Brigade (USA), 12, 88, 92,
    97, 98, 102, 109, 119
Haymarket, Va., 4
Hays' Brigade (CSA), 60
Hays' Division (USA), 86, 134
Henry, Patrick, 6
Henry's Artillery Battalion (CSA), 132
Hereter's Mill Road (Gettysburg), 13
Herr Ridge (Gettysburg), 13
Heth's Division (CSA), 13, 15
High Water Mark of the Rebellion
    Monument (Gettysburg), 78
Hill, Lt. Gen. A.P., 2, 5, 12, 13, 20, 21,
    32, 127
Hill's Corps (CSA), 3
Hodges, Col. James G., 6, 30, 54, 88,
    89, 111, 112, 127
Hollywood Cemetery (Richmond), 29
Hood's Division (CSA), 1, 12, 13, 75
Hunt, Gen. Henry, 79, 88, 89, 98
Hunton, Col. Eppa, 2, 5, 18, 21, 28, 29,
    34, 49, 50, 52, 60, 77, 103, 123,
    130, 132
Hutter, Capt. James R., 5, 13, 16, 43,
    44, 45, 47, 98

-I-
Imboden, Gen. John, 122
Imboden's Brigade (CSA), 123, 124

-J-
Jackson, Benjamin E., 28
Jackson, Gen. T.J., 5, 8
James River, 6
Jellison, Sgt. Benjamin, 115
Jenkins' Brigade (CSA), 1
Johnston, Corp. David, 17, 26, 27, 48
Jones, Pvt. Robert Tyler, 6, 91, 113

-K-
Kemper, Gen. James L., 2, 17, 24, 25,
    27, 39, 42, 43, 49, 50, 51, 60, 65,
    66, 69, 70, 75, 76, 80, 116, 122,

131, 133, 134
Kemper's Brigade (CSA), 2, 4, 5, 8, 11,
    13, 15, 17, 21, 26, 29, 31, 38, 41,
    44, 48, 52, 54, 56, 57, 58, 59, 67,
    68, 81, 87, 89, 92, 93, 98, 100,
    101, 102, 104, 110, 111, 121, 129
Klingel Farm (Gettysburg), 67
Knoxlyn Road (Gettysburg), 13

-L-
Ladies' Memorial Association, 139
Lafayette, Marquis de, 8
Lang's Brigade (CSA), 68, 70, 76, 134
Lee, Gen. Robert E., 3, 12, 13, 16, 17,
    18, 19, 21, 30, 34, 37, 55, 60, 61,
    72, 95, 97, 108, 117, 118, 119,
    120, 121, 123, 124, 129
Lewis, Lt. John H., 31, 55, 112
Little Round Top (Gettysburg), 17, 24,
    29, 48, 49, 53, 56, 63
Loehr, Corp. Charles T., 17, 18, 73, 74,
    100, 120, 121, 122
Logan, Capt. Richard, 30, 54, 89
Long, Col. A.L., 13
Longstreet, Lt. Gen. James, 5, 10, 13,
    15, 16, 19, 23, 24, 25, 30, 33, 39,
    60, 61, 62, 72, 100, 128
Longstreet's Corps (CSA), 11, 12
Lynchburg, Va., 4, 8

-M-
Macon, Capt. Miles C., 8, 11
Magruder, Col. John B., 6, 91
Malvern Hill, Va., 115
Marsh Creek (Gettysburg), 1, 11, 13,
    14, 15, 122
Martin, Lt. Col. Rawley, 31, 56, 90, 91,
    110, 113, 114, 119, 125
Martinsburg, Va., 2
Mason-Dixon line, 2
Massachusetts Troops
    15th Inf., 98
    19th Inf., 35, 105, 112, 115, 117,
    118
Mayo, Col. Joseph, Jr., 5, 16, 17, 18,
    27, 34, 48, 49, 66, 70, 74, 75, 78,
    98, 99, 100, 101, 102
McGilvery's Guns (USA), 35, 41, 67,
    97, 133

McLaws' Division (CSA), 12, 13, 69,
75
Meade, Maj. Gen. George G., 12, 49,
55, 68, 118
Medal of Honor, 105, 115
Michigan Troops
7th Inf., 111
Miller, Sgt. Daniel, 115
Miller, Capt. M.B., 23, 61
Millerstown Road, 11
Minnesota Troops
1st Inf., 106
Morris, Albert, 28
Myres, Jeff, 139

-N-
Nansemond River, Va., 7
Nesbit, John, 58
New York Troops
1st Bat. (Cowan's), 88, 98, 102,
105, 109, 116, 119
Bat. B, 1st Art. (Rorty's), 98, 116
59th Inf., 111
111th Inf., 129
20th Militia, 88, 109, 111, 119
Norfolk, Va., 1, 3, 4, 6

-O-
Ohio Troops
8th Inf., 115, 129
107th Inf., 115
O'Neal, Dr. John W.C., 139
Otey, Maj. Kirkwood, 5, 16, 43, 44, 72,
98, 101, 129, 130
Owens, Maj. John C., 6, 54, 89, 90, 112

-P-
Patton, Col. Walter Tazewell, 5, 16, 17,
26, 27, 34, 73, 74, 75, 85, 101
Peach Orchard (Gettysburg), 11, 19,
61, 132
Pender's Division (CSA), 13
Pendleton, Gen. Edmund, 32, 33, 61
Pennsylvania Troops
69th Inf., 85, 88, 89, 93, 109, 111,
116, 119, 127
71st Inf., 85, 88, 109, 112
72nd Inf., 86, 112
143rd Inf., 35, 60

Petersburg, Va., 1
Pettigrew, Brig. Gen. J.J., 23, 39, 50,
86, 120, 134
Pettigrew's Division (CSA), 83, 133
Philadelphia, Pa., 112, 115, 140
Philippoteaux, Paul, 130
Pickett, Gen. George, 2, 7, 9, 10, 15,
16, 20, 23, 30, 32, 33, 34, 36, 39,
40, 42, 45, 49, 53, 68, 69, 106,
107, 115, 121, 122, 123, 124, 129,
130, 131, 132, 133, 134
Pickett's Brigade (CSA), 67, 68
Pickett's Division (CSA), 1, 3, 4, 5, 8,
9, 12, 13, 16, 17, 24, 26, 37, 38,
44, 51, 58, 60, 61, 63, 65, 74, 78,
80, 81, 83, 87, 89, 92, 94, 95, 97,
104, 115, 117, 118, 120, 127, 128
Pickettt's Division Hospital See
Bream's Mill (Gettysburg)
Pitzer, Samuel, 11
Pitzer Farm (Gettysburg), 13, 15, 18,
95, 122
Pitzer's Lane (Gettysburg), 122
Pitzer's Run (Gettysburg), 18, 120
Polak, J.R., 26, 46, 73, 100
Portsmouth, Va., 6, 48
Potomac River, 5, 123, 124
Prospect Depot, Va., 4

-R-
Red Hill (Gettysburg), 140
Rice, Edmund, 117
Richardson, Maj. Charles, 32
Richmond, Va., 1, 2, 4, 8, 47, 125
Rider, A.J., 115
Riley, D.A., 138
Rock Creek (Gettysburg), 140
Rogers Farmhouse (Gettysburg), 43
Rorty, Capt., 98, 102, 116

-S-
St. Paul's Cemetery, Baltimore, Md.,
115
Sandusky, Oh., 125
Schwartz Farm (Gettysburg), 140
Scotland, Pa., 3
Second Corps (USA), 35, 54, 68, 86,
108
Second Corps Hospital (Gettysburg),
140

57th Inf., Flag, 417
57th Inf., Co. H, 6

-W-

Walton, Col. J.B., 19, 23
Walton's Mill, Va., 4
Washington Artillery (CSA), 20, 24,
  33, 61, 98
Webb, Brig. Gen. Alexander, 75, 78,
  92, 112
Webb's Brigade (USA), 86, 98
Wentz Farm (Gettysburg), 133
Westminster, Md., 123
Wheatfield Road (Gettysburg), 132,
  133
White Run (Gettysburg), 140
Wilcox, Brig. Gen. Cadmus, 32, 69, 70,
  128
Wilcox's Brigade (CSA), 13, 21, 68,
  76, 134
Williams, Col. Louis B., Jr., 5, 18, 26,
  28, 42, 46, 47, 48, 73, 101
Williamsburg, Va., 42
Williamsport, Md., 2
Willoughby Run (Gettysburg), 13, 35,
  121, 122, 131
Winchester, Va., 124
Withers, Col. R.E., 5
Wolf Farm (Gettysburg), 141
Wood, Lt. William N., 18, 29, 51, 52,
  83, 84, 105, 106
Wright's Brigade (CSA), 12, 116

-Y-

York Pike (Gettysburg), 3

-Z-

Ziegler's Grove (Gettysburg), 40, 57,
  63

Roster Index

[Pickett], 174
Baker, Elijah W. [I, 56], 339
    Henry (1st Lt.) [D, 19], 296
    John M. [D, 19], 296
    Philip P. (Surg.) [F&S, 56], 326
Baldwin, Caleb T. [C, 18], 276
    Charles W. [H, 18], 284
    R. William [G, 53], 409
    William Joseph [I, 28], 322
Ball, B.F. [A, 38 Bn.], 439
    Charles H. [K, 19], 306
    George W. (1st Sgt.) [G, 1], 187
Ballard, Albert [B, 8], 262
    John T. [H, 56], 337
    Robert [F, 28], 317
    William G. [H, 56], 337
Ballenger, Isaac [C, 14], 364
Ballentine, David W. (Sgt.) [G, 9], 353
Ballow, Henry C. (1st Lt.) [I, 1], 190
Balthrope, James F. [B, 8], 262
Bane, Robert H. (Capt.) [D, 7], 213
    William H.L. (Jr. 2nd Lt.) [F, 24], 248
Banks, Solomon [H, 1], 189
Banton, James H. [D, 56], 332
    William J. [D, 56], 332
Barbee, William H. [A, 38 Bn.], 439
Barber, Charles H. [D, 57], 425
    George W. [E, 57], 427
    James A. [D, 38], 386
    John E. [I, 57], 433
    Thomas L. [E, 38], 388
    William D. [D, 11], 222
Barbour, John H. [H, 19], 303
    Shadrach H. [E, 14], 360
Barden, William D. [D, 3], 197
Barger, James W. [F, 24], 249
Barham, George A. [D, 3], 197
Barker, Clark H. [A, 38], 380
    John H. [E, 18], 280
    John M. [D, 8], 504
    Josiah [C, 38], 384
    William C. [C, 38 Bn.], 445
    William H. [G, 28], 320
    William H. [C, 38], 384
Barksdale, John J. [A, 18], 273
    Robert M. (1st Sgt.) [H, 14], 374
Barner, Mark A. [E, 14], 504
Barnes, Belson, [I, 9], 356

Edward [A, 3], 194
Edward C. [G, 11], 179
Francis C. (2nd Lt.) [G, 56], 336
George D. [K, 9], 357
William B. [I, 28], 322
Barnett, Charles [F, 19], 299
    Charles T.S. (1st Sgt.) [K, 24], 254
    James A. [F, 19], 299
    William [F, 19], 299
    William H. [F, 11], 230
Barr, E.M. [E, 8], 265
Barradall, William J. (2nd Cpl.) [F, 9], 352
Barrett, George W. [H, 3], 201
    Jesse [D, 7], 213
    John H. [D, 3], 197
    John W. [F, 56], 335
    Solomon H. [H, 3], 201
Barron, James E. [A, 38 Bn.], 439
Barrow, John A. [D, 24], 246
    John E. (4th Sgt.) [G, 18], 282
    Orren W. (Capt.) [H, 24], 251
    William W. [H, 24], 251
Barry, Arthur R. (Surg.) [F&S, 9], 346
Barter, Thomas B. (5th Sgt.) [A, 3], 194
Bartley, Nathan T. (2nd Lt.) [C, 7], 211
Barton, David, Sr. [D, 28], 315
    John O. [D, 28], 315
Bashaw, John W. [C, 7], 212
Baskett, Reuben [K, 56], 341
Bass, William A. (1st Cpl.) [F, 53], 407
Bates, John C. [B, 14], 362
    Jordan [B, 38], 382
    Nathaniel [F, 38], 390
    Thomas [F, 38], 390
Batten, Archer J. [2nd I, 3], 203
    Edmond [2nd I, 3], 203
    Junius [F, 3], 199
Battin, Monroe [E, 9], 351
    William H. [E, 9], 351
Baugh, William A. (1st Sgt.) [A, 18], 273
    William F. [D, 14], 366
Baughman, E.A. [C, 38 Bn.], 445
    Greer H. (1st Sgt.) [C, 38 Bn.], 445
Bayliss, James W. [B, 7], 210

Bayne, George W. [K, 8], 270
Bays, David E. [E, 38], 388
Beach, John T. (4th Cpl.) [F, 9], 352
    Richard R. [B, 24], 242
Beale, Nathaniel L. [B, 9], 347
    Terry [B, 9], 344
Beales, Joel E. [A, 38 Bn.], 439
Beans, Oscar M. [A, 8], 261
Beasley, William D. [I, 56], 340
Beaton, John K. (1st Sgt.) [G, 9], 353
Beckett, William F. [K, 53], 415
Beckham, Abner Camp (Vol ADC)
    [Kemper], 178
Beckwith, Henry Clay [A, 11], 222
Bedsaul, Friel [C, 24], 244
Beedle, Andrew P. [E, 8], 176
Beeks, William H. [H, 3], 201
Beers, Henry H. (QM Sgt.) [C, 38 Bn.],
    445
Beggerly, Joel A. [I, 57], 433
Belcher, Charles P. (3rd Cpl.) [D, 24],
    246
    George P. [G, 24], 239
    Granville W. [F, 57], 429
    Henry S. (2nd Sgt.) [F, 57], 428
    William J. [D, 24], 246
    William McH. [G, 24], 250
Belew, Edward A. [K, 28], 310
    John T. [I, 7], 218
Bell, Christopher C. [A, 14], 360
    James W. [C, 24], 244
    L.L. [F, 7], 215
    Leslie C. (3rd Sgt.) [F, 28], 317
    Nathan W. (1st Cpl.) [A, 14], 360
    Samuel E. [A, 14], 360
    Theophilus [A, 8], 261
    Thomas [D, 8], 264
Bellamy, John H. [B, 19], 294
Bellomy, Benjamin F. [H, 57], 504
    George W. [H, 57], 432
Bendall, Benjamin F. [F, 53], 407
Benedum, James H., Jr. [A, 38 Bn.],
    439
Benjamin, William H. [A, 38 Bn.], 440
Bennett, Charles D. [A, 38], 380
    Charles Henry (3rd Sgt.) [I, 24],
    252
    Franklin [G, 57], 430
    J. Samuel [A, 38], 380

John A. [C, 9], 348
Oscar A. (4th Cpl.) [I, 11], 234
Silas J. [B, 56], 328
William B. [G, 9], 354
William T. (5th Sgt.) [I, 14], 375
Bentley, William W. (Capt.) [E, 24],
    247
Benton, George [B, 38 Bn.], 442
    Joseph J. [A, 3], 194
    Thomas H. [F, 8], 504
Berger, James H. (2nd Sgt.) [B, 38],
    382
Berkeley, Charles F. (1st Lt.) [D, 8],
    263
    Edmund (Maj.) [F&S, 8], 259
    Norborne (Lt. Col.) [F&S, 8], 259
    William N. (Capt.) [D, 8], 263
Berkley, R.C. (QM Sgt.) [F&S, 7], 207
    William W. (1st Cpl.) [I, 56], 339
Bernard, John A. (Capt.) [B, 24], 241
Berry, George T. [G, 9], 504
    James (Capt.) [G, 8], 266
    James F. [G, 7], 216
Berryman, D. [A, 38 Bn.], 440
Bersch, Benjamin H. [D, 18], 277
Betterton, James W. [F, 38], 504
    Nathan J. [I, 18], 287
Betts, John D. [E, 9], 351
Bevel, James T. [A, 56], 327
Bevell, Charles D. [G, 38], 391
Bibb, Henry F. [C, 56], 330
Biby, E.P. [F, 28], 317
    George W. [D, 38 Bn.], 448
Bickle, James A. [H, 14], 374
Bicksler, H.B. (1st Lt.) [G, 8], 266
Bidgood, Willis D. [I, 9], 356
Bierly, Andrew J. [K, 57], 435
    Samuel D. [K, 57], 435
Bigler, Mark [K, 28], 324
Bilbro, John W. [D, 28], 315
Bilharz, Charles (Sr. 2nd Lt.) [I, 53],
    412
Bilisoly, Adolphus (2nd Sgt.) [K, 9],
    357
    Eugene E. [K, 9], 357
    Joseph L. [K, 9], 344
Billings, Charles H. [A, 18], 273
    Pierce W. [F, 57], 429
Binford, James L. [E, 14], 368

Joseph T. [D, 18], 277
Bingham, Allen W. [B, 56], 328
Binns, Benjamin F. [K, 53], 415
   Charles D. [K, 53], 415
   Christopher J. [K, 53], 415
   Fleming J. [K, 53], 415
   Jordan T. (4th Cpl.) [K, 53], 415
   Major E. [K, 53], 415
Bird, Bluford W. [G, 24], 250
   Daniel [D, 9], 350
   Daniel M. [D, 24], 246
   Obadiah W. [G, 57], 430
   Samuel W. [C, 57], 423
   Wilson T. [G, 57], 430
Birdsong, Nathaniel A. [E, 56], 334
   Solomon T. (1st Lt.) [E, 3], 198
   Thomas M. [E, 56], 334
Birkby, John M. (12th Cpl.) [A, 38
   Bn.], 439
Birkhead, James G. [A, 19], 292
   Joseph F. [A, 19], 292
   N.S. [A, 19], 292
Biscoe, William E. [C, 7], 212
Bish, Daniel (Cpl.) [D, 7], 213
Bishop, Elijah E. [F, 8], 266
   James A. (2nd Cpl.) [E, 56], 333
   James H. [K, 28], 504
   John [D, 53], 405
   Obediah [F, 11], 230
   William J. [D, 56], 332
Bissell, William R. (Capt.) [A, 8], 260
Bitzer, George W. [A, 8], 260
Black, Nicholas (1st Sgt.) [K, 19], 306
   Nicholas M. [K, 19], 306
   Robert (3rd Cpl.) [K, 19], 306
   William (5th and Col. Cpl.) [K,
   19], 292
   William T. (3rd Sgt.) [E, 28], 316
Blackburn, Leander C. (Col. Sgt.) [E,
   53], 398
Blackwell, Henry Clay [I, 7], 218
   Houston L. [A, 57], 420
   James W. (1st Sgt.) [H, 56], 337
   John D. [A, 57], 420
   Joseph D. [H, 3], 202
   Moore C. (Com. Sgt.) [F&S, 38],
   379
   Robert B. [H, 56], 338
   Robert G. [2nd I, 3], 193

William H. (2nd Lt.) [D, 38 Bn.],
   447
Blain, Joseph A. [C, 38 Bn.], 445
Blair, Adolphus (Jr. 2nd Lt.) [D, 1],
   185
   George W. (1st Sgt.) [B, 38], 382
   James Edwin (Capt., AQM) [F&S,
   19], 291
   John T. (1st Lt., ACS) [F&S, 19],
   291
   Samuel B. (2nd Cpl.) [G, 53], 409
   Suter F. [B, 38], 382
   William T. [A, 38], 380
Blake, John T. [G, 56], 336
Bland, George [D, 9], 350
Blankenbeker, Elias F. [A, 7], 209
   George M. [A, 7], 209
Blankenship, Charles T. [C, 11], 225
   Elijah P. [E, 57], 427
   Joseph R. (4th Sgt.) [E, 3], 198
   Leslie C. [C, 11], 225
   William W. [B, 53], 401
Blankinship, Thomas [B, 24], 242
Blanks, John L. [E, 14], 368
Blanton, Lee M. (2nd Sgt.) [D, 1], 185
   Zachariah Angel (Capt.) [F, 18],
   281
Blick, George R. [E, 56], 334
   William A. (2nd Lt.) [E, 56], 333
Blount, Joseph Gray (Capt.) [D, 38
   Bn.], 447
Bluhm, Fritz [B, 9], 347
Blunt, James R. [F, 24], 249
   James T. [B, 38 Bn.], 504
   Joseph E. [B, 38 Bn.], 505
Boatwright, James A. [E, 18], 280
   Joseph R. [F, 18], 281
Bocock, Thomas M. [H, 24], 251
Bohannon, George W. [B, 38 Bn.], 442
   Thomas A. [A, 7], 209
   William [C, 38], 385
Boitnott, John H. [B, 24], 242
   Josiah F. [F, 53], 407
Boland, John [H, 11], 233
Boler, George W. [I, 1], 191
Bolton, Alexander H. [D, 7], 213
   Hilry [E, 38], 388
   Thomas M. [G, 19], 301
Bond, Antrobus (Capt.) [E, 3], 198

Bondurant, Jacob W. [B, 11], 224
Bones, Joseph E. [F, 11], 230
Book, Henry L. [B, 28], 312
Booker, James (1st Cpl.) [D, 38], 386
    John [D, 38], 386
    Lewis (2nd Lt.) [C, 38 Bn.], 445
    Robert S. [I, 56], 340
    Thomas L. [H, 24], 251
Boon, Beverly B. (2nd Sgt.) [G, 57], 430
    Marquis D.L. (1st Lt.) [G, 57], 430
    Norman T. [G, 57], 430
Booth, John S. [H, 14], 374
    Peter B. (1st Lt.) [D, 24], 245
    Richard H. [E, 3], 198
    Samuel D. [A, 53], 399
Boothe, Benjamin [C, 38], 385
Booton, Sinclair [A, 7], 209
Booz, William G. (1st Sgt.) [G, 19], 301
Booze, William H. [K, 57], 435
Borden, George W. [F, 11], 230
Borland, Thomas R. [K, 9], 357
Borum, Henry M. [C, 53], 403
    Joseph Z. (Cpl.) [C, 18], 276
    Samuel T. [C, 18], 276
Boryer, Fred A. (5th Sgt.) [D, 8], 264
Boss, James P. [H, 8], 268
Bosserman, William B. [D, 11], 227
Boswell, John L.C. (1st Sgt.) [E, 57], 426
    Whitmel T. [I, 24], 253
Bouldin, Nathaniel H. [F, 57], 429
    William D. [K, 18], 288
Bourke, Joseph B. [G, 9], 354
Bousman, George W. [H, 24], 251
    Josiah [B, 24], 242
Bowden, D.F. [A, 38 Bn.], 440
Bowe, George A. [C, 38 Bn.], 445
    Henry C. [K, 38], 394
    N.W. [D, 1], 185
Bowen, Berry A. [K, 14], 376
    Henry E. [B, 7], 210
    Henry L. [A, 8], 261
    Hine [B, 3], 195
    Hugh F. [B, 56], 328
    John [B, 7], 210
    John A. [A, 19], 292

    Lucius M. [H, 56], 338
    Marshall [K, 14], 376
Bower, Robert H. (2nd Sgt.) [A, 24], 240
Bowery, James H. [K, 53], 415
Bowler, Napoleon B. [A, 7], 209
Bowles, Daniel M. [B, 57], 421
    George S. [G, 18], 283
    Henry C. [C, 57], 423
    Middleton G. (Mus.) [C, 57], 423
    Robert S. (2nd Sgt.) [C, 19], 295
    William A. [G, 57], 430
    William H. [G, 19], 301
    William R. [C, 57], 423
Bowman, William H. [A, 14], 505
Bowyer, David W. (2nd Sgt.) [K, 11], 236
    Leonidas R. (3rd Sgt.) [B, 19], 293
Boyd, Charles F. [2nd K, 3], 204
    James G. [K, 14], 377
    Waller M. (Capt.) [B, 19], 300
Boyed, Henry C. [G, 9], 354
Boykin, James J. [F, 9], 352
    Jeremiah M. [F, 9], 352
Bracey, Virginius S. [F, 14], 370
Bradford, Osmond (1st Cpl.) [A, 7], 209
Bradley, Johnston T. [C, 38 Bn.], 445
    Robert (Cpl.) [A, 38], 380
    Thomas D. (Cpl.) [A, 38], 380
    William T. [I, 53], 413
Bradner, John [I, 53], 413
    Thomas H. [B, 38], 382
Bradshaw, Richard B. (2nd Sgt.) [C, 53], 402
    Robert M. (1st Cpl.) [C, 53], 403
    William P. (2nd Cpl.) [C, 53], 403
Brady, William (Mus.) [E, 38], 388
Brafford, Marcellus [K, 11], 236
Bragg, Henry Lewis [H, 57], 432
    Horatio C. [H, 57], 432
    James Y. (1st Lt.) [E, 19], 297
    Robert T. [H, 57], 432
Branch, Curtis N. [D, 56], 332
    John H. [D, 3], 197
    Patrick B. [D, 3], 197
Branham, John [C, 56], 330
    Nathaniel, Jr. [C, 56], 330
Brawner, James F. [D, 8], 264

Bray, Charles [D, 53], 405
  Ellis H. [K, 38], 394
  John [K, 38], 394
  Madison H. [K, 38], 394
  Richard [2nd K, 3], 204
  William Harvie (1st Lt.) [E, 53], 406
  William J. [2nd K, 3], 204
  William Y. [K, 14], 377
Brazzlia, Lewis [A, 18], 273
Breadlouv, William F. [C, 38 Bn.], 445
Breedlove, John W. [I, 56], 340
Brent, Heath J. [A, 38 Bn.], 440
Bresnaham, Mathew [H, 1], 189
Brewbaker, William (2nd Lt.) [K, 57], 435
Brewer, Alexander B. [D, 24], 246
  Edward B. [E, 14], 368
Bridgewater, O.C. [C, 38 Bn.], 445
Brierwood, Robert [A, 38 Bn.], 440
Briggs, Henry L. [C, 24], 244
Bright, Robert A. (Vol. ADC) [Pickett], 174
  Thomas J. [A, 3], 194
Brightwell, Thomas H. (1st Sgt.) [D, 18], 277
Brinkley, Daniel [I, 9], 356
  Granville, [I, 9], 356
  Mills, [I, 9], 356
Brisentine, James R. [B, 28], 312
  John M. [B, 28], 312
  William B. [B, 28], 312
Brittingham, William H. (Cpl.) [G, 9], 353
Britton, Henry Clay (3rd Lt.) [C, 9], 348
  Richard J. [C, 9], 348
Britts, Dexter S. (5th & Col. Cpl.) [B, 28], 310
Brock, Benjamin F. [F, 9], 352
  James J. [F, 9], 352
  Joel D. [E, 9], 351
  Tarlton F. (3rd Cpl.) [F, 57], 428
Brockman, James P. [E, 19], 298
  John [C, 56], 330
Brooks, A.J. [A, 19], 292
  Albert [C, 38 Bn.], 445
  Camillus [C, 9], 348
  Cicero W. [B, 11], 224

Eugene K. [K, 9], 357
George W. [E, 18], 280
Ira W. [C, 3], 196
James G. (4th Cpl.) [H, 14], 374
John [F, 28], 318
John B. [F, 9], 505
John R. (1st Sgt.) [A, 56], 327
John T. [I, 57], 433
Joseph N. [C, 3], 505
Rufus M. [F, 53], 407
William R. [A, 57], 420
Broughman, Andrew J. [K, 57], 435
  James K. [K, 57], 435
Broughton, Joseph E. (Cpl.) [B, 3], 195
Brown, Aaron V. [G, 18], 283
  Alfred N. [D, 11], 227
  Archie B. [D, 53], 405
  Benjamin, Jr. (Capt.) [H, 19], 303
  Beverly W. [E, 7], 214
  Bezaliel G. (Capt.) [I, 7], 217
  Bezaliel G., Jr. (2nd Cpl.) [I, 7], 218
  Burwell B. [E, 57], 427
  Charles B. (2nd Lt.) [I, 7], 217
  Charles H. [B, 57], 421
  Daniel M. [E, 28], 316
  Daniel T. [E, 7], 214
  Douglas B. [C, 24], 244
  George P. [E, 7], 214
  George W. (3rd Sgt.) [B, 38 Bn.], 442
  George W. [C, 38 Bn.], 445
  Hillary B. [E, 11], 228
  J.V. [G, 7], 216
  James (Mus.) [D, 9], 350
  James A. [C, 11], 225
  James A. (4th Sgt.) [D, 19], 296
  James E. (Sr. 2nd Lt.) [C, 3], 196
  James E. [B, 24], 242
  James E. [D, 38 Bn.], 505
  James H. [F, 28], 318
  James H. [F, 57], 429
  James J. [A, 19], 292
  James M. [B, 7], 210
  James W. (Sr. 2nd Lt.) [G, 7], 216
  James W. [I, 11], 234
  Jesse [I, 11], 234
  John C. [H, 11], 233
  John P. [I, 57], 433

John R. [D, 56], 332
John T. (1st Cpl.) [E, 38], 388
John W. [A, 38 Bn.], 440
Lemuel F. [E, 7], 214
Leslie C. [A, 11], 222
Lewis E. [K, 28], 324
Mathew (1st Lt.) [D, 56], 331
Paul C. [G, 7], 216
R.R. [F, 28], 318
Reuben R. [D, 56], 332
Richard [F, 19], 299
Richard H. (2nd Sgt.) [D, 56], 331
Richard H. [D, 56], 332
Richard T. [H, 56], 338
Robert C. [I, 7], 218
Robert J. [C, 9], 348
Samuel M. [I, 28], 322
Sydney K. [C, 9], 348
Thomas J. [C, 38 Bn.], 445
Thornton S. [E, 7], 214
W.T. [G, 7], 216
Watkins L. (5th Sgt.) [C, 11], 225
William G. [H, 56], 338
William H. (Mus.) [F&S, 7], 108
William H. (1st Cpl.) [B, 7], 210
William H. [A, 19], 292
William H.C. [A, 18], 273
William H.H. [I, 7], 218
William L. [E, 38], 388
Brownley, Charles D. [G, 9], 505
Daniel T. (1st Sgt.) [B, 3], 195
William K. [G, 9], 354
Bruce, James [B, 38 Bn.], 442
Richard T. [C, 9], 348
Brumfield, John M. [B, 38 Bn.], 442
Brummett, Jonathan M. [B, 8], 262
Brunt, Robert W. [C, 38 Bn.], 445
Brushwood, Washington [E, 53], 406
Bryan, John L. [I, 28], 322
Bryant, Charles P. [G, 19], 301
Charles W. [A, 38], 380
Fleming B.W. [C, 38], 385
James [K, 57], 436
James H. [D, 56], 332
John B. [H, 19], 303
Peter [I, 57], 433
Reuben W. [D, 28], 315
Samuel H. (4th Cpl.) [E, 3], 198
Thomas H. [F, 18], 281

William C. [I, 24], 253
William R. [D, 28], 315
Buchannan, Mungo P. [B, 1], 182
Buck, James R., Jr. (5th Sgt.) [A, 19], 292
William M. [E, 3], 198
Buford, James Walter [H, 53], 411
Bugg, James R. (5th Sgt.) [G, 38], 391
John W. [G, 38], 505
Lucius T. [C, 14], 364
Samuel S., Jr. [D, 19], 296
Bullifant, John A. [K, 53], 415
Bullington, James H. [I, 57], 433
Jasper [A, 18], 273
John R. (Col. Cpl.) [K, 38], 379
Bunch, Anderson H. [B, 56], 328
Burch, James H. (3rd Cpl.) [D, 53], 404
James R. [A, 18], 273
John F. [D, 53], 405
John L. (3rd Sgt.) [H, 8], 268
Burcher, James S. [C, 19], 295
Robert E. [E, 3], 198
Burchett, James M. [K, 8], 270
William H. [K, 8], 270
Burford, William H. (2nd Cpl.) [H, 11], 233
Burge, J.E. [E, 18], 280
Burger, Abraham [K, 57], 436
Philip T. [A, 28], 310
Burk, John R. [F, 11], 230
Burke, Arthur W. [G, 7], 216
Edwin J. [C, 18], 276
John L. [B, 18], 275
John R. [G, 7], 216
John W. [B, 7], 210
John W. [D, 24], 246
Michael [E, 3], 198
William A. [C, 18], 276
Burks, Joseph [E, 38], 388
Solomon C. [E, 11], 228
Burley, Alexander [I, 19], 304
Thomas D. [H, 19], 303
Burnett, Achilles H. (1st Sgt.) [H, 38], 392
David [G, 28], 320
Edwin H. [G, 38], 391
Elisha C. (3rd Lt.) [B, 14], 361
James C. [B, 14], 362
John J. [D, 28], 315

Madison S. [I, 18], 287
Thomas T. [I, 18], 287
William H. [I, 18], 287
Burns, John W. [C, 18], 276
William [2nd I, 3], 203
Burress, Charles W. (4th Cpl.) [G, 24], 250
Burrows, Franics M. (Mus.) [F&S, 7], 208
Henry C. [E, 7], 214
Burruss, Thomas G. [B, 11], 224
William H. (1st Lt.) [H, 53], 410
Burton, Benjamin L. [K, 19], 306
Giles A. [G, 38], 391
Hillery G. [G, 38], 391
James W. [K, 38], 394
John A. [A, 14], 360
John M. [C, 38], 385
John T. (2nd Lt.) [E, 56], 333
Lucas [F, 14], 370
Robert P. [G, 9], 354
Robert W. (4th Cpl.) [F, 11], 230
Thomas J. [B, 56], 328
William J. (2nd Lt.) [D, 38], 386
William T. [K, 38], 394
Burwell, Blair (Surg.) [F&S, 8], 259
Busby, Edward M. [C, 14], 364
Bush, Edward [F, 9], 505
Eugene [D, 38 Bn.], 448
Gilla [E, 28], 316
John D. [B, 56], 328
Bussey, James Henry [A, 38 Bn.], 440
James O. [G, 24], 240
Butcher, James T. [D, 57], 425
Butler, Hezekiah [B, 3], 195
Isham [B, 38 Bn.], 442
James O. [H, 57], 432
John [B, 3], 195
John W. [G, 8], 267
Marcus A. (Asst. Surg.) [F&S, 1], 181
Napoleon [G, 7], 216
Robert [G, 7], 216
Solomon [B, 38 Bn.], 442
Thomas J. (Bvt. 2nd Lt.) [A, 38], 380
Thomas J. [B, 53], 401
William K. [H, 57], 432
Butts, Walter (Jr. 2nd Lt.) [F, 9], 352

Buxton, John T. [G, 9], 354
Bybee, John A. [H, 57], 432
Byram, Edward [C, 7], 212
James N. [E, 7], 214
Byrd, William H. [B, 24], 242
Byrnes, Edward (2nd Sgt.) [C, 1], 183

-C-

Cabaniss, James M. (2nd Lt.) [K, 38], 394
William G. (1st Lt.) [K, 38], 394
Cabell, Joseph Robert (Maj.) [F&S, 38], 379
Paul Carrington (2nd Lt.) [H, 1], 188
Cable, James F. (Cpl.) [A, 38 Bn.], 439
John W. [A, 38 Bn.], 438
Cadwallader, Presley [G, 28], 320
Cage, Fielding (1st Lt.) [2nd K, 3], 204
Thomas W. (2nd Cpl.) [2nd K, 3], 204
Caho, William A. (2nd Lt.) [I, 1], 190
Cain, Thomas [D, 38 Bn.], 448
Calaham, James R. (1st Cpl.) [A, 56], 327
Caldwell, Alexander G. [B, 28], 312
Daniel R. [C, 11], 225
John B. (2nd Sgt.) [B, 28], 311
Robert T. [K, 28], 324
Cale, Leander [K, 28], 324
Calfee, Henderson F. [G, 24], 250
Calhoun, Adam N. [I, 56], 340
John L. [D, 18], 278
John R. [K, 18], 288
Callaham, Charles M. [C, 11], 225
Callahan, Ezekiel W. [B, 11], 224
Callcote, Alexander D. (Lt. Col.) [F&S, 3], 193
Calloway, Charles C. [D, 38 Bn.], 448
Camden, Samuel H. [D, 38 Bn.], 448
William A. [D, 38 Bn.], 448
Camp, James W. [H, 1], 189
Joseph [K, 53], 415
Campbell, Alexander J. (4th Cpl.) [D, 24], 246
Andrew [I, 19], 304
Archer (1st Lt.) [G, 18], 282
Carter [I, 8], 269
Charles A. [C, 19], 295

D.P. [F, 28], 318
Daniel G. [I, 19], 304
Elcanah M. [D, 38 Bn.], 448
James L. [I, 19], 304
John [D, 8], 264
John [G, 18], 283
Josiah [I, 19], 304
Marius G. (2nd Sgt.) [H, 53], 410
Martin V. [G, 19], 177
Richard [G, 7], 216
Robert C. (2nd Lt.) [D, 53], 404
Samuel L. [K, 11], 236
W.D. [I, 19], 305
William B. [F, 19], 299
William H. [I, 19], 305
William J. [I, 19], 305
Z.C. [D, 8], 264
Camper, Henry L. (3rd Cpl.) [D, 28],
    315
    John H. (2nd Lt.) [D, 11], 227
    Newton L. [D, 11], 227
    Peter A. [2nd C, 28], 313
    William H. [A, 28], 310
Canada, John M. [G, 56], 336
    Marshall [E, 24], 248
Canaday, John D. [E, 7], 214
Canard, James W. [A, 38 Bn.], 440
Cannaday, Giles L. (3rd Lt.) [C, 57],
    423
Capps, Josiah (Cpl.) [I, 9], 356
Carder, Joshua W. (Mus.) [F&S, 7],
    208
    Silas B. [G, 7], 216
Cardin, William B. [E, 19], 298
Carlisle, Reynold R. [A, 8], 505
Carlton, Milton [D, 53], 405
    Thomas N. [A, 53], 400
Carneal, Henry [D, 53], 405
Carney, Richard R. [I, 9], 356
Carpenter, Albert W. [A, 7], 209
    Charles L. [I, 19], 305
    Cumberland G. [A, 7], 209
    James H. [A, 7], 209
    Jeremiah A. [E, 7], 214
    John A. [A, 7], 209
    John F. [E, 19], 298
    Robert F. [A, 7], 209
    William B. (1st Sgt.) [A, 7], 209
Carper, John C. (4th Cpl.) [E, 24], 248

John T. [E, 24], 248
Oscar W. [2nd C, 28], 313
William L. (4th Cpl.) [B, 28], 311
Wyndham R. (3rd Cpl.) [D, 11],
    227
Carr, Jesse [B, 38 Bn.], 442
    John R. (5th Sgt.) [F, 38], 389
Carrington, Clement R. (3rd Sgt.) [A,
    53], 399
    Henry Alexander (Lt. Col.) [F&S,
    18], 272
Carroll, Gray (2nd Lt.) [A, 38 Bn.], 439
    H.B. [F, 14], 370
    John W. [E, 18], 280
    Joseph W. [D, 28], 315
    Nash J. [D, 28], 315
Carruthers, John E. [A, 38 Bn.], 440
    Thomas N. [A, 38 Bn.], 440
Carter, Albert [B, 8], 262
    Alexander [B, 8], 505
    Charles S. [A, 38], 380
    Edward (Capt.) [K, 8], 269
    Edward A. (Sgt.) [A, 38], 380
    Elias [A, 53], 400
    George W. (3rd Lt.) [G, 38], 391
    Hilliard W. (AQM) [F&S, 56],
    326
    Hutchings L. (1st Lt.) [I, 53], 412
    James, Jr. (1st Cpl.) [I, 53], 399
    James D. [A, 56], 327
    James L. [C, 53], 403
    James M. [E, 57], 427
    Jesse L. [A, 38], 380
    John E. [A, 38 Bn.], 440
    Joseph C. [I, 19], 305
    Landon E. [C, 8], 263
    Leonard H. (QM Sgt.) [B, 38 Bn.],
    442
    Richard H. (Maj. QM)
    [Armistead], 343
    Robert O. [C, 8], 263
    Thomas J. (3rd Cpl.) [C, 8], 263
    Thomas R. [B, 38 Bn.], 442
    Thomas T. (5th Sgt.) [A, 53], 399
    William G. (Asst. Surg.) [F&S,
    57], 418
    William Irvin (1st Cpl.) [B, 1],
    182
    William J. (2nd Lt.) [G, 38], 391

George P. (5th Sgt.) [I, 7], 218
J.L. [I, 7], 218
James D. [C, 1], 184
James W. [B, 7], 210
Thomas C. [I, 7], 208
William N. [I, 7], 218
Clary, Thomas L. [D, 3], 197
Clatterbuck, William J. [F, 7], 215
Claxton, Henry H. [I, 11], 234
  Robert P. [I, 11], 234
Clay, Charles M. (3rd Sgt.) [F, 38], 389
  Charles T. [B, 18], 272
  George W. [H, 14], 374
  James W. [G, 18], 283
  Mathew B. (1st Lt.) [C, 9], 348
  Thomas J. [F, 38], 176
Clayton, Allen O. [H, 1], 189
  Benjamin D. [H, 53], 411
  George B. [C, 38 Bn.], 445
  James C. [E, 38], 388
  James K.P. [D, 3], 197
  John A. [D, 3], 197
  John K. (2nd Sgt.) [E, 56], 333
  John R. [H, 53], 411
  John W. [K, 7], 219
  Julian T. (3rd Sgt.) [D, 3], 197
  William R. [E, 38], 388
Claytor, Moses B. [F, 28], 318
Cleaton, Charles L. [B, 56], 328
Clement, Benjamin F. (1st Lt.) [B, 38], 382
  Charles B.J. (2nd Sgt.) [C, 11], 225
  Charles H. (1st Sgt.) [F, 38], 389
  Parham B. [A, 38], 380
  William T. (1st Sgt.) [B, 11], 223
Clements, Benjamin F. [C, 19], 295
  Green W. [A, 38], 380
  Joseph H. (5th Sgt.) [C, 19], 295
  Mathew J. [I, 7], 218
  Miles E. [I, 7], 218
  Robert L. [C, 19], 295
  Thomas M. [F, 19], 299
  William [B, 38 Bn.], 443
Cliborne, Darius (3rd Sgt.) [F, 14], 370
Clift, Zachariah M. [F, 57], 429
Clifton, William J. [I, 24], 253
Clingingheel, Jacob [G, 57], 430
Clopton, Walter D. [E, 18], 280

William I. (Sr. 1st Lt.) [B, 38 Bn.], 442
Clore, Charles L. [K, 7], 219
  Robert W. [A, 7], 209
Coalter, A.M. (Cpl.) [G, 8], 267
  Henry T. (1st Lt., Adjt.) [F&S, 53], 398
Coates, John C. (4th Sgt.) [F, 38], 389
Cobb, William T. (3rd Sgt.) [D, 53], 404
Cobbs, Robert A. [D, 56], 332
Cobler, John S. [I, 57], 434
Coburn, John D. [G, 24], 250
Cochran, Robert T. [I, 8], 269
Cock, James B. [C, 11], 225
  Robert M. (4th Sgt.) [C, 11], 225
Cocke, Edmund Randolph (Capt.) [E, 18], 279
  Edwin [B, 38 Bn.], 443
  John B. [C, 38 Bn.], 445
  John N. (3rd Cpl.) [K, 9], 344
  Thomas E. [F, 56], 335
  William F. (2nd Lt.) [E, 18], 279
Cockrell, R.E. [A, 38 Bn.], 440
Coe, Robert (2nd Lt.) [E, 8], 265
Cofer, Joseph E. [K, 57], 436
Coffe, Andrew J. [D, 56], 332
Coffee, William H. [E, 11], 228
Coffman, Lewis [A, 28], 310
  Samuel A. [A, 28], 310
Cogbill, John A. (Mus.) [D, 14], 366
  Marcus Aurelius [D, 14], 366
  W.W.T. (Capt.) [D, 14], 366
  William C. [C, 9], 505
Cogsdale, James [D, 3], 197
Cole, Haley [B, 38 Bn.], 443
Coleman, Addison [H, 18], 285
  Chapman J. [A, 57], 420
  Clayton G., Jr. (Asst. Surg.) [24], 239
  Clifton S. [D, 38 Bn.], 448
  James C. [I, 53], 413
  James M. [H, 24], 251
  James R. [I, 18], 287
  James T. (5th Sgt.) [I, 53], 412
  John [A, 38 Bn.], 440
  Joseph A. [C, 7], 212
  Robert A. [F, 28], 318
  Robert H. [D, 38 Bn.], 448

Samuel A. (2nd Cpl.) [I, 14], 375
Stephen M. [A, 18], 273
Thomas B. [G, 38], 391
Thomas P. [C, 7], 212
William [A, 18], 273
William [I, 24], 253
Collins, Andrew J. [B, 56], 328
David W. [I, 28], 322
Elliott E. [A, 14], 360
Franklin C. [B, 18], 275
Hillery W. [C, 1], 184
Ira [B, 38], 383
James S. [F, 19], 299
John W. [D, 38], 386
Michael [E, 28], 316
Van Buren [C, 7], 208
William B. [K, 9], 347
William G. [C, 1], 505
William H. [A, 56], 327
Colvin, Henry H. [E, 11], 228
William O. [E, 11], 228
Comar, Michael [F, 19], 299
Compton, Alexander H. (1st Sgt.) [C, 8], 262
Edward H. (4th Sgt.) [B, 7], 210
James (AQM) [F&S, 9], 346
John R. [A, 18], 273
John W. [D, 57], 425
Marshall [B, 18], 275
William G. [H, 24], 251
William R. [F, 53], 408
Conally, Thomas B. [B, 53], 401
Conaway, Benjamin D. [I, 24], 253
Condrey, James L. [I, 14], 375
Condry, Jerry [E, 19], 298
Congdon, George W. [C, 38 Bn.], 445
Conley, James T. [G, 3], 200
John H. [G, 11], 231
Connard, John H. [I, 14], 375
Connelly, James D. (2nd Lt.) [C, 11], 225
Conner, Benjamin E. [2nd K, 3], 204
George [A, 38 Bn.], 440
James R. [2nd K, 3], 204
Robert W. [H, 18], 285
Consadine, Michael [C, 1], 184
Conway, Alexander F. [A, 38], 381
Catlett (5th Sgt.) [A, 7], 209
Charles C. (3rd Cpl.) [A, 7], 209

Cook, Benjamin S. [2nd G, 14], 372
Evans T. [I, 57], 434
Fortunatus S. (2nd Cpl.) [I, 53], 413
John R. [I, 57], 434
Samuel [F, 24], 240
William H. [2nd G, 14], 372
Cooper, Andrew L. [G, 24], 250
Charles H. [D, 24], 246
George W. (2nd Sgt.) [D. 24], 246
George W. (4th Sgt.) [D, 28], 315
Giles H. (2nd Lt.) [D, 24], 246
Haley A. [D, 24], 246
John B. [B, 7], 210
Joseph (Bvt. 2nd Lt.) [G, 8], 267
Josiah [D, 24], 246
Lowry M. [D, 24], 246
Taswell T. [D, 24], 246
William S. [D, 24], 246
William W. [D, 24], 246
Coppage, Lewis J. [I, 11], 234
Robert [K, 7], 219
Corbell, Richard S. [F, 9], 352
Corbin, James D.G. [I, 53], 413
Thompson [I, 18], 287
Corker, James H. [F, 56], 335
Thomas J. [F, 56], 335
Corley, William L. [D, 28], 315
Cornelius, Thomas R. [G, 3], 200
Cornell, John T. [E, 8], 265
Cornwell, Hezekiah [B, 7], 210
Jonas [A, 38 Bn.], 440
Joseph [A, 38 Bn.], 440
Thornton [A, 38 Bn.], 440
Corran, Edgar [2nd I, 3], 203
Costello, Timothy (2nd Cpl.) [C, 1], 184
Cotton, Charles W. [D, 14], 366
Cottrell, William R. [C, 38 Bn.], 445
Coulter, George [2nd I, 3], 203
James [2nd I, 3], 203
John [2nd I, 3], 203
Courtney, Bazil [I, 11], 234
Calvin [I, 11], 234
James E. [I, 11], 234
Cousins, Jabez S. [I, 53], 413
Covington, David G. [H, 14], 374
William H. [E, 18], 280
Cowling, John E. (1st Sgt.) [F, 9], 352

Cox, Bedford B. (2nd Cpl.) [E, 38], 388
  Breckenridge F. [H, 19], 303
  Charles B. [K, 56], 341
  Charles L. [D, 8], 264
  Christopher C. [C, 9], 348
  Daniel [F, 11], 230
  Eli [2nd G, 14], 372
  Elijah H. [2nd G, 14], 372
  Evelton M. [E, 3], 198
  Henry W. [E, 53], 406
  J.E.N. [I, 7], 218
  James [2nd G, 14], 372
  Joseph [B, 57], 421
  Samuel L. [D, 8], 264
  Thomas P. [K, 38], 394
  William [2nd G, 14], 372
  William F. [D, 38 Bn.], 448
  William Henry [F, 7], 215
  William S. [E, 38], 388
Craddock, Daniel S. [B, 38], 383
  William B. [B, 38], 383
  William T. [B, 24], 242
Crafford, Edmund C. [K, 53], 415
Craft, Jacob M. [K, 57], 436
  Samuel D. [B, 28], 312
Craig, Chester [K, 24], 254
  George E. (3rd Cpl.) [D, 1], 185
  James C. [G, 57], 430
  James T.F. [F, 11], 230
  James W. [G, 19], 292
  John [H, 56], 338
  John G. (4th Cpl.) [D, 11], 227
  Robert F. [H, 56], 338
Crank, James L. (2nd Cpl.) [F, 28], 317
  Joseph H. [F, 53], 408
Cranwell, Henry [K, 19], 306
Crawford, John R. [D, 7], 213
  John W. [B, 28], 312
  Josiah [K, 28], 324
  Thomas E. (4th Cpl.) [G, 24], 243
Crawley, William R. [E, 38], 388
Creasey, Benjamin M. (4th Cpl.) [G,
  28], 320
  David A. [G, 28], 320
  Gustavus A. (4th Cpl.) [C, 11],
  225
  John H. [G, 28], 320
  John W. (2nd Cpl.) [B, 24], 242
  Lewis G. [G, 28], 320

Lindsey S. (Col. Cpl.) [G, 28], 310
Robert H. [G, 28], 320
Thomas C. [C, 11], 225
Thomas G. [G, 28], 320
Thomas H. [B, 24], 242
William C. [G, 28], 320
Creasy, James B. [A, 28], 310
  James T. [D, 38 Bn.], 448
Creecy, George A. [G, 9], 354
Creekmore, Malachi [A, 3], 194
Creel, Elijah [B, 8], 505
Crenshaw, Archer D. (3rd Sgt.) [G, 18],
  282
  James M. [B, 18], 275
  William H. [C, 1], 184
Crew, John T. (2nd Sgt.) [I, 1], 190
Crews, Armstead C. [H, 38], 392
  Samuel T. [C, 38], 385
Crichton, Robert H. [D, 3], 197
Criddle, Patrick H. [F, 19], 299
Crider, John H. [E, 57], 427
Cridler, John W. [A, 38 Bn.], 440
Cridlin, Ransel W. (Chap.) [F&S, 38],
  379
Crigger, W.H. [B, 1], 182
Crisler, Nelson W. (Maj., AQM)
  [Kemper], 178
Crist, Thomas J. [G, 19], 301
Crocker, James F. (1st Lt., Adjt.) [F&S,
  9], 346
  Joel [2nd I, 3], 194
  Jules O.B. (Capt.) [I, 9], 355
Crockett, John G. (1st Cpl.) [C, 24],
  243
Cromer, Charles D. [K, 24], 254
  Samuel W. (3rd Sgt.) [F, 11], 230
Cronin, Stephen D. (1st Lt.) [I, 56], 339
Cross, Alfred B. [F, 3], 199
  James S. [B, 53], 401
  John D. [D, 9], 350
  Nimrod [I, 8], 269
  Thomas W. [B, 53], 401
  William B. [F, 56], 335
Crouch, Joel [G, 28], 320
Crow, Benjamin M. (2nd Sgt.) [B, 1],
  182
  Preston [H, 53], 411
  Robert W. [D, 53], 405
Crowder, Coleman D. [B, 53], 505

Darnold, Richard Z. [A, 7], 209
Darr, Tim P. [D, 7], 213
Dashiell, Thomas J. (3rd Sgt.) [K, 9], 357
Daughtrey, Robert T. [K, 9], 357
Davenport, John W. [2nd K, 3], 204
    Joseph [H, 11], 233
    William T. [K, 14], 377
Davidson, E.F. [H, 1], 189
    James [H, 19], 303
    John [H, 19], 303
    Robert S. [C, 38 Bn.], 445
Davies, Arthur B. (Cpl.) [E, 11], 228
    John W. [H, 19], 303
Davis, Augustine H. (2nd Cpl.) [K, 38], 394
    Benjamin [E, 8], 265
    Charles W. [H, 24], 251
    Creed O. [E, 38], 388
    Edward [B, 56], 328
    Eli M. [C, 1], 184
    George [G, 8], 267
    George C. [G, 53], 409
    George D. [K, 19], 306
    George W. [F, 9], 353
    George W. (QM) [F&S 56], 326
    H.G. [B, 53], 401
    Henry T. [I, 7], 218
    Henry W. [F, 38], 505
    J.J. [D, 56], 332
    Jackson [I, 57], 434
    James [E, 38], 388
    James E. [B, 18], 275
    Joel [B, 24], 242
    John C.A. [K, 9], 357
    John G. [D, 38], 386
    John H. [E, 38], 388
    John J. [B, 18], 275
    John L. [D, 8], 264
    John R. [H, 11], 233
    John S. [F, 18], 281
    John W. [A, 7], 209
    Joseph [E, 8], 265
    Labon J. [H, 24], 251
    Parks B. (4th Sgt.) [D, 53], 404
    Peter [K, 18], 288
    Peter [B, 53], 401
    Peter L. [I, 7], 218
    Peter P., Jr. (1st Lt.) [H, 24], 251

Philip [I, 14], 375
Robert E. [K, 53], 415
Robert R. [K, 18], 288
Robert S. [C, 38 Bn.], 445
S.H. [E, 18], 280
Solomon K. (4th Sgt.) [B, 57], 421
Temple T. [K, 18], 288
Thomas [C, 7], 212
Thomas [B, 57], 422
Thomas Herbert (Capt.) [B, 1], 182
Thomas J. [K, 38], 394
Volney [D, 11], 227
William [K, 7], 219
William [E, 8], 265
William A. [C, 7], 212
William H. [C, 57], 423
William S. [A, 14], 360
Dawson, Charles G. (2nd Lt.) [H, 8], 268
    James F. (5th Sgt.) [K, 7], 219
    Leroy T. [C, 24], 244
    Pleasant [F, 28], 318
    William D. [C, 19], 295
    William F. (5th Sgt.) [C, 8], 262
Day, Charles R. [D, 38 Bn.], 448
    Thomas E. [E, 11], 228
Dayley, Jerry [F, 19], 299
Deal, Charles T. [G, 7], 217
Dean, James E. [D, 38 Bn.], 448
    William H. (QM Sgt.) [F&S, 1], 182
Deane, William H. (2nd Sgt.) [G, 1], 187
Dear, Thomas A. (1st Cpl.) [I, 8], 269
Dearing, Calvin P. [G, 28], 320
    James (Maj.) [F&S, 38 Bn.], 438
    Oliver V.B. (3rd Cpl.) [G, 28], 320
Deaton, Edward T. [D, 38 Bn.], 448
    John H. [A, 14], 360
Debo, Dabney C. (2nd Cpl.) [G, 28], 319
    Lodevick C. [D, 28], 315
    Reed P. (5th Sgt). [G, 28], 319
Deboe, Joseph (4th Cpl.) [E, 57], 426
Dedman, John H. [A, 56], 327
    William H. (5th Cpl.) [A, 56], 327
Dee, John [F, 19], 299

DeGaribody, John [F, 3], 199
De Hart, Henry [A, 24], 240
　　Jesse H. [A, 24], 240
Dehaven, Wesley [C, 24], 244
DeJarnette, Albert [2nd K, 3], 204
Delanay, John P. (Mus.) [C, 57], 423
Delk, Owighton G. (Capt.) [2nd I, 3], 202
　　Sidney E. [2nd I, 3], 203
Delph, W.S. [K, 7], 219
Dempsey, Coleman H. [C, 7], 212
　　Levi J. [C, 7], 212
Dennis, Francis [K, 8], 505
　　George E. (Capt., ACS) [F&S, 24], 239
　　James M. [A, 19], 292
　　Jasper [E, 7], 214
Denton, James M. [C, 14], 364
　　John T. [D, 56], 332
Derby, Alonzo T. [D, 3], 197
　　Junius N. [D, 3], 197
Desmond, Michael [F, 7], 215
Dews, Demarquis P. [B, 11], 224
　　Edwin (5th Sgt.) [2nd I, 3], 202
　　Joshua S. [H, 18], 285
Diamond, Thomas J. (4th Sgt.) [F, 24], 248
Dickens, Franklin C. [C, 24], 244
Dickenson, Edward D. [F, 7], 215
Dickerson, Daniel J. (3rd Cpl.) [H, 18], 284
　　James D. [H, 18], 285
　　James Woodson (1st Lt.) [D, 38 Bn.], 447
　　John F. [H, 18], 285
　　Peter C. [G, 56], 336
　　William J.[H, 18], 285
Dickey, James H. [G, 8], 267
Dickinson, David V. (Capt.) [D, 57], 424
　　Robert Pollard (1st Sgt.) [C, 56], 330
Dignum, Robert E. [H, 1], 189
Dill, John (Cpl.) [K, 57], 435
Dillard, Henry J. [E, 38], 388
　　Oscar P. [G, 19], 301
Dillen, John Edward [D, 11], 227
Dillion, William D. [K, 38], 394
Dillon, James Dabney [D, 38], 505

James E. [C, 9], 506
　　William F. [B, 24], 242
Dinguid, Edward S. [A, 11], 223
Dinwiddie, John W. (3rd Cpl.) [B, 11], 223
Dix, Austin (Drum) [F&S, 18], 272
　　Tanda W. [A, 38], 381
Dixon, John T. [I, 56], 340
　　William [K, 38], 394
Dixson, W.H. [K, 7], 219
Dobbins, Robert L. [A, 19], 292
Dobyns, Colita W. [B, 14], 362
　　Frazier O. (2nd Cpl.) [A, 24], 240
Dodd, James W. [B, 38], 383
　　John B., Jr. [A, 19], 293
　　Thomas W. [B, 38], 383
　　William S. [B, 38], 383
Dodson, Albert [G, 7], 217
　　Alexander S. [H, 24], 251
　　Isaac N. (1st Sgt.) [I, 18], 286
　　James A. [C, 38], 385
　　John E.J. [C, 9], 348
　　Josephus B. [C, 38], 385
　　Reuben [B, 7], 210
Doggett, Basil M. (Sgt.) [E, 7], 214
Doherty, James F. [I, 28], 322
　　Matthew [C, 38 Bn.], 445
Dolen, John M. [D, 56], 332
Dolin, James W. [B, 19], 294
Dolman, Achilles M. [K, 57], 436
Donnahoo, Aaron [F, 57], 429
Donohoe, Lewis J. [C, 8], 263
Dooley, Edward [K, 28], 324
　　Jacob [K, 28], 506
　　Jesse [C, 38], 385
　　John [E, 28], 316
　　John E. (1st Lt.) [C, 1], 183
　　Marshal [B, 28], 312
　　William H. [F, 11], 230
Dooly, Andrew A. [K, 11], 236
　　James P. [K, 11], 236
Dorrell, Archibald P. [H, 8], 268
Dortch, James D. [B, 56], 328
Doss, Charles L. [D, 57], 425
　　Christopher C. [E, 57], 427
　　Gehu [G, 1], 198
Doud, Sylvester J. (2nd Sgt.) [F, 11], 229
Dougherty, Charles E. (5th Sgt.) [B,

18], 272
John [H, 8], 260
Douglas, Abijah (1st Sgt.) [D, 28], 314
Douthat, Robert W. (Capt.) [F, 11], 229
Dove, Avry M. [E, 57], 506
   Thomas [A, 38 Bn.], 440
Dowden, Richard B. [B, 38 Bn.], 443
Dowdy, Albert G. [F, 24], 249
   Aldrige G. (3rd Sgt.) [G, 28], 319
   James H. [E, 18], 280
   James T. [G, 28], 320
   John A. [B, 14], 362
   Richard B. [A, 14], 360
   Richard T. [G, 28], 320
   Robert M. [A, 14], 360
   Thomas W. [C, 57], 423
Dowell, Major M. [E, 19], 298
Downs, Cicero [C, 8], 263
   William H. [C, 8], 263
Doyle, Benjamin H. (Drum) [D, 1], 185
   Henry (5th Sgt.) [H, 11], 233
   John [D, 8], 264
   Thomas [B, 38 Bn.], 443
Doyles, William H. [E, 9], 351
Drake, Joel T. [E, 56], 334
   Robert B. [A, 57], 420
Draper, Elkanah B. [H, 24], 251
   Jackson [D, 1], 185
   Jesse H. (1st Cpl.) [H, 24], 251
   John H. [C, 57], 423
   John L. (2nd Cpl.) [D, 28], 315
Drean, John F. [A, 53], 400
   William T. [A, 53], 400
Drewry, Carey B. [G, 28], 320
   Joseph H. [D, 3], 197
   L.M. [G, 53], 409
   Robert A. [D, 3], 197
   Samuel T. (Jr. 2nd Lt.) [D, 3], 197
Driscoll, Larkin R. [I, 56], 340
Driskill, Dennis [K, 57], 436
Driver, William H. (4th Cpl.) [E, 9], 351
Drumheller, Abram A. [H, 19], 303
   Benjamin N. [D, 19], 296
Drummond, George R. [C, 28], 313
Drumwright, William R. (4th Cpl.) [B, 56], 328
Duane, David C. (3rd Cpl.) [K, 53], 415

Thomas F. [F, 53], 408
Dudding, James O. [C, 28], 313
Dudley, Chiswell [H, 38], 392
   James H. [A, 19], 293
   John A. [B, 11], 224
   John S. [D, 7], 213
   Nelson P. [H, 57], 432
   William H. [B, 11], 224
   William M. [A, 19], 293
Duell, Littleton J. [C, 53], 403
Duerson, William H. [H, 1], 189
Dugger, C.C. [C, 8], 263
Duke, Gideon [A, 3], 194
   Henry T. [I, 1], 191
   James M. [I, 14], 376
Dulaney, William E. (Sgt.) [F, 7], 215
Dunaway, William [B, 19], 294
Dunbar, Elisha [D, 38 Bn.], 448
Duncan, James F. [C, 24], 244
   James W. [E, 18], 280
   Stephen A. (2nd Cpl.) [A, 57], 420
   William H. [D, 19], 297
Duncum, Richard [E, 14], 368
   Thomas [E, 14], 368
Dunderdale, John A.F. [K, 9], 357
Dunford, Robert J. [F, 3], 199
Dunithan, Andrew R. [D, 28], 315
Dunivant, Leroy W. [C, 11], 225
Dunkum, Richard L. [A, 57], 420
   William B. [A, 57], 420
Dunman, Achilles J. [G, 57], 430
Dunn, Albert S. [B, 19], 294
   James [B, 38 Bn.], 443
   James [C, 38 Bn.], 445
   John R. (1st Sgt.) [G, 9], 353
   John T. [H, 56], 338
   Luther M. [B, 19], 294
   Robert N. [H, 1], 189
   Samuel B. (2nd Cpl.) [B, 38], 382
   Thomas W. [H, 56], 338
   Woodson (2nd Sgt.) [C, 38 Bn.], 445
Dunnavant, Charles F. [C, 9], 348
   William A. [D, 14], 366
Dunston, Fielding T. [D, 14], 366
   James H. [D, 14], 367
   John N. [D, 14], 367
Dupree, Edward [K, 28], 324
   James R. [K, 57], 436

547

Durham, James A. (Sgt.) [C, 38], 384
    John H. [C, 38], 385
    Thomas H. (5th Sgt.) [G, 1], 187
Durphy, Thomas H.B. (Jr. 2nd Lt.) [K,
    18], 288
Durrett, John D. [A, 19], 293
    Thomas D. [E, 19], 298
Durrow, William [F, 7], 215
Duval, Edmund [A, 11], 223
Duvall, Melville J. [C, 38 Bn.], 445
Dyer, Charles C. [G, 8], 267
    George W. [C, 9], 349
    Hardin H. [H, 24], 251
    Leroy S. (2nd Lt.) [D, 57], 424
    Thomas G. [H, 24], 239
    Thomas S. (3rd Sgt.) [F, 57], 428
    Walter C. (4th Sgt.) [I, 53], 412
    William C. (3rd Sgt.) [H, 24], 251
Dyke, Nathan [A, 38 Bn.], 440
Dyson, Benjamin (1st Sgt.) [C, 9], 348
    Walter [K, 9], 357

-E-

Eades, James [H, 57], 432
    James H. [D, 56], 332
Eaimes, James L. (ACS) [F&S, 53],
    398
Eakin, John J. (5th & Col. Sgt.) [B, 28],
    310
    Jotham W. [F, 11], 230
    Robert A. [C, 28], 313
Eanes, Silas W. [E, 57], 506
    William T. [D, 38], 386
Eans, John [B, 9], 347
Earles, Hyram [I, 57], 176
    Jesse [I, 57], 434
    Rufus [2nd G, 14], 372
    Uriah C. [I, 57], 434
Earley, Henry T. [D, 38 Bn.], 448
    John M. [D, 38 Bn.], 448
Earls, Gordon C. [A, 24], 240
Early, John W. [C, 24], 244
Earnest, Henry C. [K, 56], 341
Easley, Drewry B. (5th Sgt.) [H, 14],
    374
    Frederick B. [E, 14], 368
    Henry W. [D, 38], 386
    James C. [D, 38], 386
    Robert C. [I, 53], 413

Eason, George F. [F, 3], 199
East, George W. [I, 53], 413
    Obadiah F. [F, 18], 281
    Richard J. [F, 11], 230
    Samuel A. [G, 24], 250
Eastham, David C. (3rd Cpl.) [E, 19],
    298
Echols, Henry E. (3rd Cpl.) [I, 18], 286
    Jeremiah G. [F, 24], 249
    Joseph W. [A, 38], 381
    R.C.B. [G, 53], 409
Eckles, James W. [G, 18], 283
Eddins, Theodore F. (4th Sgt.) [H, 57],
    432
Eddy, John C. [B, 24], 242
Edmonds, Edward Claxton (Col.)
    [F&S, 38], 379
    Henry [F, 9], 353
    William B. (ACS) [F&S, 38], 379
Edmondson, Henry A. (Capt.) [A, 53],
    399
Edmunds, Henry (Capt.) [F, 53], 407
Edwards, A.C. (6th Sgt.) [B, 38 Bn.],
    442
    Amos W. (QM Sgt.) [F&S, 9], 347
    Benjamin [A, 18], 274
    Benjamin F. [2nd I, 3], 203
    Benjamin K. [2nd I, 3], 203
    Charles [2nd I, 3], 203
    Creed H. [C, 24], 244
    Christopher B. [K, 14], 377
    David S. [D, 1], 185
    Henry [I, 11], 234
    Inman R. [I,11], 234
    James [C, 1], 184
    James [2nd I, 3], 203
    James D. [C, 57], 423
    James H. [B, 38 Bn.], 506
    John E. (3rd Sgt.) [B, 18], 275
    Joseph R. (1st Cpl.) [D, 3], 197
    Joseph W. [I, 24], 253
    Joshua [E, 9], 351
    Miles [2nd I, 3], 302
    Newit J. [B, 9], 506
    Oney H. [G, 9], 354
    Patrick H. [2nd I, 3], 203
    Richard C. [E, 9], 351
    Richard H. [E, 9], 351
    Richard M. [C, 24], 244

Richard T. [K, 14], 377
Samuel W. (1st Cpl.) [E, 19], 298
William E. [D, 3], 197
William T. [G, 9], 354
Eggleton, Armistead J. [B, 57], 422
George W. [H, 24], 251
Henry H. [H, 24], 251
Thomas J. [H, 24], 251
Ehart, Adam G. [E, 19], 298
Einstein, Harvey [F, 11], 230
Elam, George W. (1st Sgt.) [F, 18], 281
William A. (2nd Sgt.) [E, 14], 368
William R. (1st Sgt.) [H, 18], 284
Elder, Hiram [E, 11], 228
Joseph A. [G, 18], 283
Eley, James M. [2nd I, 3], 203
John M. [2nd I, 3], 203
Eliason, George P. (1st Sgt.) [C, 7], 211
Ellett, Beverly H. [C, 53], 403
Lemuel O. (2nd Cpl.) [I, 1], 190
William T. [C, 9], 349
Ellette, James T. [C, 53], 403
Thomas M. [C, 53], 403
Ellington, Branch A. [I, 56], 340
Elliott, Abraham F. (4th Cpl.) [F, 57],
428
Alexander [A, 56], 327
Henry E. [D, 18], 278
John A. (2nd Sgt.) [K, 14], 376
John K. [E, 38], 388
John W. [K, 14], 377
Joshua L. [B, 24], 242
Richard T. [2nd K, 3], 204
Samuel H. [G, 11], 231
Washington A. (3rd Lt.) [B, 11],
223
William A. [E, 38], 388
William L. [K, 14], 377
Willis [C, 18], 276
Elliotte, James O. [B, 7], 211
William [B, 7], 211
Ellis, James H. (2nd Sgt.) [F, 28], 317
James T. [A, 14], 360
John R. [F, 28], 318
John Thomas (Lt. Col.) [F&S, 19],
291
Joseph F. [I, 14], 376
Richard P. [G, 3], 200
Robert [C, 9], 349

Robert S. (1st Lt.) [C, 56], 330
Ellixson, James B. (4th Cpl.) [A, 56],
327
Elmore, James [B, 28], 312
James [2nd C, 28], 313
Emberson, Allison W. [K, 57], 436
Embrey, Charles O. [I, 11], 234
James T. [I, 11], 234
Jesse C. [I, 11], 234
Judson J. (2nd Lt.) [I, 11], 234
Norman D. (2nd Sgt.) [I, 11], 234
Robert E. [I, 11], 234
Sandford E. [E, 7], 214
Thomas R. [I, 11], 234
Emerson, John D. [B, 38], 383
Emmerson, Elisha W. [D, 38], 386
George W. [G, 9], 354
James M. (2nd Sgt.) [F, 3], 199
England, Benjamin M. [A, 57], 420
Robert M. [C, 7], 212
English, George W.S. [D, 24], 246
James H. [E, 57], 427
William W. [D, 24], 246
Epling, Floyd [F, 24], 249
William A. [F, 24], 249
Epperson, David J. [E, 56], 334
James E. [E, 56], 334
Joseph B. [B, 38 Bn.], 443
Eppes, Edwin T. [C, 53], 403
Epps, James Ryland [G, 1], 187
Thomas W. [H, 14], 374
Estes, Edward H. (Sgt.) [K, 38], 394
James D. (AS) [F&S, 8], 259
James E. [G, 56], 336
Joseph H. (2nd Lt.) [K, 38], 394
L.E. [H, 56], 338
Robert G. [H, 56], 338
W.J. [H, 56], 338
Estis, Cornelius W. (4th Sgt.) [K, 7],
219
Thomas B. (Sgt.) [C, 56], 330
Etcher, Charles L. (1st Sgt.) [I, 8], 269
James C. [I, 8], 257
Etheredge, Samuel R. [G, 9], 354
Etheridge, John E. [H, 3], 202
Etter, Andrew James [E, 28], 317
Eubank, Carter H. [B, 38 Bn.], 443
George W. [I, 1], 191
Eudailey, Francis C. [G, 56], 337

549

John T. (3rd Cpl.) [G, 56], 336
Samuel P. (Sgt.) [G, 56], 336
Evans, Charles O. [K, 24], 506
Charles R. (3rd Lt.) [C, 19], 295
George W. [A, 38], 381
Jackson [I, 18], 287
John L. [B, 56], 328
John R. [I, 11], 235
John T. [I, 19], 305
P.L. [K, 18], 289
Robert H. [A, 38], 381
T.L. [A, 7], 209
William M. [A, 38], 381
Wilson E. [B, 56], 328
Eve, E. Dorsay [C, 38 Bn.], 445
Everett, Isaac W. [D, 14], 367
Richard B.L. (4th Sgt.) [D, 3], 197
Evers, Christian [G, 18], 283

-F-

Fackler, Abraham (4th Cpl.) [I, 53], 413
Fadeley, Charles W. (2nd Sgt.) [H, 8], 268
Fagan, William T. [B, 9], 347
Fair, William H. [C, 8], 263
Fairfax, Raymond (Capt., Chief Pioneer Corps) [Pickett], 174
Fargusson, James M. [D, 38], 386
Farinholt, Benjamin L. (Capt.) [E, 53], 406
John L. [B, 53], 401
Farish, Joseph [C, 19], 295
Fariss, George W. [E, 28], 317
Reuben W. [C, 11], 179
Farley, George A. [C, 53], 403
James C. [G, 18], 283
Farmer, Arthur [B, 11], 224
Chesley M. [H, 14], 374
Edward [B, 11], 224
Isaac L. [C, 24], 244
John T. [D, 1], 186
Joseph L. [C, 9], 349
William (Cpl.) [B, 11], 223
William H. [B, 11], 224
Farrar, Alexander J. [F, 14], 370
James [G, 1], 187
John P. (Capt.) [F, 14], 369
Robert R. (2nd Sgt.) [F, 14], 370

Samuel H. (Cpl.) [H, 18], 284
William H. [F, 14], 370
Farrell, Michael [D, 38 Bn.], 448
Farrer, Robert H. [H, 11], 233
Farriss, Charles H. [E, 28], 317
John A. [A, 14], 360
Farson, Stephen [H, 1], 189
Farthing, James [H, 38], 392
Joel [G, 53], 409
William F. [B, 11], 224
Faulkner, Jacob B. [K, 24], 254
Feagans, George W. [I, 24], 253
Feasel, Joab. R. (Cpl.) [G, 57], 430
Feather, Marquis D. (4th Cpl.) [D, 28], 315
Feazle, Frank H. [A, 11], 223
Fellers, Zachariah (3rd Cpl.) [G, 24], 250
Felts, Benjamin F. [D, 3], 197
Richard A. [G, 3], 200
Fennell, Joseph J.C. [F, 14], 370
Fentress, Batson [A, 3], 194
Fercron, Archer [B, 38 Bn.], 443
Ferebee, George W. [G, 9], 354
Joseph K. [G, 9], 354
Fergerson, William [A, 24], 240
Ferguson, Benjamin [G, 3], 200
Charles D. [G, 57], 430
Colin J. [G, 3], 200
Daniel W. [H, 18], 285
James E. (Asst. Surg.) [18], 272
Joel D. (3rd Sgt.) [F, 53], 407
John R. [H, 18], 285
Martin P. [D, 38 Bn.], 448
Richard (1st Lt., Adjt.) [18], 272
Robert D. (2nd Sgt.) [I, 53], 412
Robert R. (1st Lt.) [K, 53], 414
Stephen P. (5th Sgt.) [F, 53], 407
Thomas E. [D, 56], 332
William C. [G, 28], 320
William D. [H, 18], 285
William H. (2nd Sgt.) [D, 19], 296
Fergusson, Henry C. [G, 1], 187
William J. [G, 1], 187
Ferrell, James M. [A, 38], 381
Joseph B. [E, 38], 388
Fewell, Charles H. (4th Sgt.) [K, 8], 270
Field, Richard (1st Sgt.) [E, 56], 333

Fielding, Eppa (4th Cpl.) [I, 7], 218
  William B. [I, 7], 218
Fields, Charles W. [K, 8], 270
  George M. (2nd Cpl.) [E, 3], 198
  John A. [K, 56], 341
  Thomas B. [C, 38 Bn.], 445
Fiendley, James W. [G, 9], 354
Figg, John Q. (4th Sgt.) [B, 1], 182
Fignor, Alphonzo A. [I, 1], 191
Finch, Charles H. [B, 11], 224
  George B. (2nd Lt.) [E, 14], 368
  James M. [B, 11], 224
  Marcellus L. [A, 38], 381
  Nathaniel B. [C, 38], 385
  Thomas R. [B, 24], 242
Fincham, Green S. [B, 7], 211
  Jonas [B, 7], 211
Finchman, William T. [K, 7], 219
Fink, Elijah C. [A, 28], 310
Finks, Henry L. [C, 7], 212
Finley, George W. (1st Lt.) [K, 56], 341
Finn, James M. (4th Sgt.) [D, 1], 185
  Percival [C, 53], 403
Fiser, E.C. [H, 1], 189
Fisher, George R. [I, 7], 218
  Philip [B, 28], 312
  Samuel [C, 38 Bn.], 445
  William J. [K, 19], 306
Fiske, William A. [B, 3], 195
Fitch, Robert H. [H, 57], 419
Fitz-James, James (Capt., ACS) [18], 272
Fitzgerald, Cyrus [H, 11], 233
  Douglas [G, 19], 301
  Marcellus [H, 18], 285
  Samuel, Jr. (4th Cpl.) [I, 18], 287
  William, Jr. (2nd Lt.) [I, 18], 286
Fitzsimons, John [D, 38 Bn.], 448
Fizer, Peter M. [K, 24], 254
Flake, Joseph D. [I, 3], 203
Fleig, Joseph A. [D, 11], 227
Fleming, Robert J. (Sgt. Maj.) [B, 38 Bn.], 442
Flesher, Andrew (2nd Sgt.) [C, 8], 262
Fletcher, George W. [K, 14], 377
  Henry Y. [K, 14], 377
  James [C, 56], 330
  Stephen G. [F, 9], 353

Flinn, George W. [I, 8], 269
Flippen, Lucian M. [B, 18], 275
Flippin, James A. [C, 53], 403
Flora, Samuel B. [H, 53], 411
Flournoy, Jacob M. (3rd Cpl.) [E, 56], 333
Flowerree, Charles Conway (Lt. Col.) [7], 207
Flowers, David [H, 1], 189
  James R. [A, 8], 261
Floyd, Alexander [H, 11], 233
  Americus (2nd Cpl.) [H, 53], 411
  Edward A. [B, 56], 328
  Nathan D. (1st Sgt.) [H, 11], 233
Fluke, Abraham W. [D, 11], 227
Flynt, James T. [E, 19], 298
  William D. [E, 19], 298
Flythe, Thomas J. [D, 3], 197
Foiles, Henry P. (Mus.) [H, 3], 201
Follin, William R. (4th Sgt.) [H, 8], 268
Fonkhowitzer, John M. [I, 19], 305
Fontaine, Clement R. (Maj.) [57], 418
  Samuel C. (2nd Lt.) [H, 24], 251
Ford, Frederick W. [B, 38 Bn.], 443
  James [A, 38 Bn.], 440
  John A. [B, 53], 401
  John P. [C, 19], 295
  Layton N. [I, 18], 287
  P. Fletcher (Jr. 2nd Lt.) [A, 57], 419
  Peyton R. [K, 18], 289
  Robert M. [C, 38 Bn.], 445
  Simon Peter [C, 38 Bn.], 445
  William J. [A, 57], 344
  William N. [A, 7], 210
Fore, Joel P. [H, 18], 285
  John A. [H, 57], 432
  John J. [H, 18], 285
  John L.L. [H, 18], 285
  Julius L. [H, 18], 285
  Leonidas P. [H, 18], 285
Forloine, Thomas G. [C, 9], 349
Fortner, James H. [D, 7], 213
  William C. [D, 7], 213
Fortune, Absalom M. (3rd Cpl.) [D, 19], 296
  Joel M. (3rd Lt.) [D, 19], 296
  Meridith Winston [G, 19], 301
  William [E, 11], 228

Forward, John W. [A, 3], 193
Foster, Benjamin F. [F, 18], 281
    Edward B. [D, 38 Bn.], 448

    Farris [F, 28], 318
    George A. [K, 19], 306
    Horace H. [G, 18], 283
    James A. [C, 14], 364
    James M. (3rd Cpl.) [A, 14], 360
    John H. [A, 53], 400
    John W. [F, 18], 281
    Samuel B. (Cpl.) [C, 18], 276
Fouch, John H. (6th Cpl.) [A, 38 Bn.], 439
Foushee, David M. (Cpl.) [C, 7], 212
Foust, Bolling G. [B, 38], 383
    Fountain J. [B, 38], 383
Fout, Robert D. [A, 28], 310
Fowler, Thomas H. [G, 57], 430
    William A. [K, 53], 415
Fowlkes, Anderson J. (Bvt. 2nd Lt.) [F, 18], 281
    Andrew J. [C, 18], 276
    Hiram O. [C, 18], 276
    James T. [C, 18], 276
    Patrick H. (Mus.) [C, 53], 403
    Richard H. [B, 38 Bn.], 443
Fox, Edward M. [H, 11], 233
    Newton T. [C, 8], 263
    Samuel A. [D, 56], 332
    Thomas [C, 7], 212
Fraetas, Canazio (2nd Lt.) [E, 3], 198
Frailing, William J. [G, 28], 320
France, James P. [H, 24], 251
Francis, Nathaniel T. (1st Lt.) [G, 3], 200
    Thomas J. [D, 8], 264
Franklin, Abner M. (2nd Cpl.) [I, 19], 304
    Arthur W. [I, 19], 305
    Benjamin E. [C, 3], 196
    Fendall [B, 1], 182
    Henry T. [A, 38 Bn.], 440
    James, Jr. (3rd Lt., AQM) [11], 221
    Joel M. [D, 28], 315
    John J. [K, 18], 289
    Joseph D. [D, 28], 315
    Philip H. (2nd Cpl.) [G, 11], 231

    Robert H. [B, 11], 224
    Samuel T. [C, 11], 225
Franks, C.F. [E, 8], 265
Frashure, Albert R. (2nd Cpl.) [I, 24], 253
Fray, William H. [A, 7], 210
Frayser, William R. (3rd Cpl.) [E, 18], 279
Frazer, Joseph A. (Capt.) [E, 56], 333
Frazier, William M. [I, 57], 434
Freeman, Allen [I, 11], 235
    Charles [C, 19], 295
    J.W. [D, 1], 186
    James G. [A, 38 Bn.], 440
    Samuel [I, 11], 235
    William T. [A, 38 Bn.], 440
Freidlin, John [A, 3], 194
French, Hugh H. (1st Cpl.) [E, 18], 279
Fretwell, Samuel L. [E, 53], 406
Friend, Thomas R. [C, 9], 177
Fridley, John H. [K, 28], 324
Frier, Jacob B. (3rd Lt.) [D, 11], 227
Frith, William M. (2nd Lt.) [C, 14], 363
Fritz, Peter [B, 38 Bn.], 443
Fry, Allen L. (Sgt.) [D, 7], 213
    Joseph [C, 8], 263
    Thomas V. (1st Lt.) [A, 7], 209
    William O. (Capt.) [A, 7], 209
    William T. (Capt., AAG) [Kemper], 178
Fryer, James P. [K, 57], 436
Fulcher, Thomas J. (3rd Sgt.) [I, 7], 217
Fulford, John C. (1st Sgt.) [H, 3], 201
Fulgham, Mills L. [I, 3], 203
Fulkes, James W. [A, 11], 223
Fulks, James M. [G, 19], 301
    Robert [H, 11], 233
Fuller, Berryman [B, 38], 383
    Brittain [B, 38], 383
    Henry B. [B, 38], 383
    James R. [G, 1], 187
    John J.W. (4th Cpl.) [G, 3], 200
    Josiah E. (4th Sgt.) [B, 38], 382
    Waddy Thompson [B, 38], 383
Fulsher, Paul C. (4th Sgt.) [I, 19], 304
Funkhouser, James D. (Mus.) [F, 38], 390
Fuqua, Charles D. [E, 28], 317
    George H. [E, 3], 198

James W. [E, 3], 198
Peter P. [D, 1], 186
William R. [D, 14], 367
Furcron, Henry W. [D, 1], 186
Furgason, James [K, 11], 236
Furgusson, Eldridge [K, 11], 236
Furr, Henry C. (3rd Cpl.) [F, 8], 266
    Thompson (3rd Sgt.) [F, 8], 266
Furry, Andrew J. [A, 8], 261

-G-

Gaar, William H. (Mus.) [7], 208
Gaines, E.W. [B, 38 Bn.], 443
    Henry F. (2nd Cpl.) [K, 18], 288
    John C. [I, 56], 340
    John L. [C, 7], 212
    John M. (Surg.) [18], 272
    R. Brawner [D, 8], 264
    Richard T. (4th Sgt.) [G, 28], 319
    Robert R. [E, 38], 388
Gale, William H. [I, 3], 203
Gallaher, James T. [D, 18], 278
Gallehugh, George W. [A, 7], 210
Gallop, John, Jr. [A, 3], 194
Galt, James D. (Surg.) [19], 291
Gammon, James A. [K, 38], 394
    John C. [I, 57], 434
    Levi J. (3rd Cpl.) [I, 57], 433
Gannon, Daniel [C, 9], 349
Gant, Richard H. [D, 8], 264
Gantt, Henry (Col.) [19], 291
Gardner, Charles S. [D, 3], 197
    Ezra J. [D, 3], 197
    Ira T. [H, 56], 338
    James R. [F, 57], 429
    Joseph C. (Sgt.) [A, 38], 380
    William J. [D, 3], 197
Garland, David S. (2nd Lt.) [H, 19], 303
Garman, George W. [D, 11], 227
Garner, Alfred H. (3rd Sgt.) [A, 56], 327
    Calvin (3rd Sgt.) [H, 14], 374
    David [E, 9], 351
    James A. (2nd Lt.) [A, 56], 327
Garnett, Richard Brooke (Brig. Gen.), 255
    Thomas M. (2nd Sgt.) [F, 56], 335
Garrett, Albert D. [H, 14], 374

James W. [G, 14], 372
John R. [B, 1], 183
Joseph W. [H, 18], 285
Garrison, Albert [E, 9], 351
    H. White [H, 56], 338
    Ira P. [B, 19], 506
    James R. (2nd Cpl.) [E, 9], 351
    James T. [I, 7], 506
    John [E, 9], 351
    John R. [I, 56], 340
    Joseph W. [I, 56], 340
Garth, James C. [B, 19], 294
Garthright, John E. [K, 56], 341
    Philip T. [K, 56], 341
Garton, James H. [H, 38], 392
    W.A. [F, 7], 215
Gary, Hezekiah B. [G, 1], 187
    Samuel W. (Sr. 2nd Lt.) [A, 3], 194
    William J. (3rd Cpl.) [H, 53], 411
Gaskins, Thomas J. [G, 9], 354
    William H. (1st Sgt.) [K, 8], 269
Gaulden, Jabez S. [B, 38], 383
Gauldin, John J. (Cpl.) [K, 38], 394
    William [K, 38], 394
Gaulding, James H. [D, 38], 386
    John R. [I, 57], 434
Gay, Littleton A. (1st Lt.) [D, 3], 196
    William C. [B, 38 Bn.], 443
Gayle, Levin C. (Sgt.) [G, 9], 353
    Nathaniel G. (2nd Lt.) [G, 9], 353
Gearhart, William R. [B, 24], 242
Gee, Benjamin C. [B, 56], 328
    Leonidas J. (1st Sgt.) [B, 56], 328
    Walter A. [B, 56], 329
Geer, Alexander [C, 57], 424
Geiger, George E. (1st Lt., ADC) [Kemper], 179
Gentle, David L. [A, 38 Bn.], 440
Gentry, Charles W. [G, 1], 187
Geoghegan, Joel W. [E, 14], 368
George, John (4th Cpl.) [D, 8], 264
    Lewis W. [B, 56], 329
    Robert A. [G, 24], 250
    Robert W. [H, 53], 411
    Thomas (Cpl.) [G, 9], 353
    William [E, 57], 427
    William H. (5th Sgt.) [D, 53], 404
Gheen, George [G, 8], 267

Hagerman, John T. [K, 18], 289
Hagood, John H. [H, 53], 411
Hailey, James T. [K, 38], 394
Haines, Henry G. [K, 18], 506
Haizlip, Jefferson [D, 57], 425
Hale, Charles A. [D, 7], 214
    Ellis (2nd 2nd Lt.) [C, 24], 243
    John L. (5th Sgt.) [D, 28], 315
    Robert (1st Cpl.) [C, 57], 424
Haley, Charles W. [F, 11], 230
    James M. [C, 14], 364
    Malcolm L. [K, 24], 254
    McMurry [E, 57], 427
    Peter [I, 18], 287
    Samuel H. [I, 24], 253
    Samuel M. [K, 18], 289
    Thomas J. [A, 38], 381
Hall, Anderson A. [B, 56], 329
    Beverly B. [E, 38], 388
    Edmund N. [F, 56], 335
    George W. (4th Sgt.) [E, 9], 351
    George W. [F, 56], 335
    Henry J. [C, 7], 212
    Henry J. [E, 19], 298
    Howson M. [K, 3], 205
    James D. [F, 38], 390
    James F. [H, 56], 338
    James P. [B, 24], 242
    John (3rd Cpl.) [I, 3], 202
    John O. [E, 38], 388
    Mathew (1st Sgt.) [E, 9], 351
    Robert W. [H, 53], 411
    Stephen C. [C, 11], 225
    Timothy T. [F, 56], 336
    William F. [H, 57], 432
    William S. [E, 19], 298
    William T. [D, 14], 367
    William T. [C, 24], 244
Hallinan, James (Capt.) [C, 1], 183
Halsey, Charles A. [C, 38 Bn.], 446
Hamblett, Edward W. [I, 56], 340
    Jesse W. [I, 56], 340
    Thomas P. [I, 56], 340
Hambrick, Joseph A. (Maj.) [24], 239
Hamersley, William R. [I, 56], 340
Hamilton, Alonzo [H, 18], 285
    George W. [D, 11], 227
    Jacob (3rd Cpl.) [G, 19], 301
    James H. (5th Cpl.) [K, 28], 310

James M. [G, 19], 301
James P. [I, 19], 506
John T. [H, 18], 285
Varland [G, 19], 301
William M. (2nd Sgt.) [G, 18], 282
Hamlet, James M. (4th Sgt.) [H, 18], 284
Hammonds, Alonzo W. [H, 53], 411
    James T. [H, 53], 411
    William E. [H, 53], 411
Hamner, Edward Bruce [C, 19], 295
    Robert M. (2nd Lt.) [B, 56], 328
    William P. (2nd Lt.) [B, 19], 293
Hampton, Augustus F. [D, 9], 350
Hancock, Charles [I, 14], 376
    John H. (Cpl) [D, 57], 425
    Lafayette [F, 38], 390
    Samuel [F, 38], 390
    Simon [D, 28], 315
Hanes, James C. (5th Sgt.) [F, 11], 230
Haney, Bazel (Cpl.) [F, 7], 215
    R.A. [F, 7], 215
Hankins, Henry C. [B, 38], 383
    William D. (1st Cpl.) [F, 38], 389
Hann, William H. [E, 8], 265
Hanrahan, George T. [H, 3], 202
Hansbrough, Elijah T. [I, 11], 235
Hansford, Calvin P. (5th Sgt.) [H, 1], 188
    James [D, 9], 350
Harcum, George C. [D, 3], 197
Hardaway, Junius W. [G, 18], 283
    Robert N. [G, 18], 283
Harden, Hopkins (2nd Lt.) [C, 19], 295
Hardiman, John Edward (3rd Cpl.) [I, 56], 339
Harding, John B. [D, 19], 297
    Junius [F, 53], 408
    Milton [G, 9], 354
    William H. [A, 38 Bn.], 440
Hardy, Henry C. [E, 57], 427
    James H. [E, 38], 389
    James T. (2nd Lt.) [K, 11], 236
    John R. [I, 28], 323
    John T. [G, 18], 283
    Lewis E. [G, 18], 283
    Obadiah [H, 38], 392
    Presley [H, 38], 393

Richard G. (3rd Sgt.) [C, 9], 348
Richard J. (2nd Sgt.) [K, 38], 394
Thomas A. [F, 8], 257
Thomas A. (2nd Lt.) [A, 14], 360
Hatchett, Augustus F. [I, 53], 413
Logan A. [I, 53], 413
Hatter, Morgan A. [G, 19], 301
Powhatan B. [G, 19], 301
Havener, Joseph F. [H, 8], 268
Hawker, Thomas S. [A, 38], 381
Hawkins, Augustus [G, 7], 217
Charles H.C. [B, 38 Bn.], 443
Charles W. (4th Cpl.) [G, 7], 216
John W. [A, 7], 210
Lucus P. [I, 19], 305
R.A., Sr. [K, 19], 307
Samuel A. [K, 19], 307
Thomas H. [B, 53], 401
William S. (Cpl.) [K, 57], 435
Hawks, J.H. [G, 53], 409
Hawley, James O. [F, 19], 299
Newton A.E. [I, 28], 323
William R. [H, 57], 506
Haws, William [E, 8], 506
Hawthorn, Peter W. [G, 56], 337
Hawthorne, Benjamin J. (Capt.)
[Armistead], 344
Hay, James R. [B, 11], 222
Thomas W. [G, 1], 187
Hayes, Richard H. [K, 53], 415
Haymaker, Philip [F, 11], 230
Robert D. (1st Cpl.) [K, 24], 254
Haynes, Robert L. [E, 11], 229
William B. [K, 53], 415
Hays, Thomas J. [K, 19], 307
Hazlewood, Charles T. [D, 11], 227
Newton H. (1st Sgt.) [D, 38 Bn.],
447
Payton A. [B, 53], 399
Robert R.R. [F, 14], 370
Headen, John W. (1st Lt.) [A, 24], 240
William D. [I, 24], 253
Headrick, Columbus [E, 57], 427
Jacob, Jr. [E, 57], 427
Heath, George R. [B, 1], 183
J. Brent (10th Cpl.) [A, 38 Bn.],
439
James E. [F, 14], 370
Logan W. [K, 56], 341

W.L. [B, 38 Bn.], 443
Heaton, John M. (Mus.) [7], 208
Heck, Martin Van [A, 28], 310
Heckman, Creed T. [B, 24], 506
David P. (Capt.) [C, 57], 423
James A. [C, 57], 424
Joseph W. (4th Cpl.) [C, 57], 423
Heffernon, John [C, 19], 295
Heffran, Stephen [A, 38 Bn.], 440
Heflin, J. Thomas [A, 38 Bn.], 440
Heiffling, John R. [B, 7], 211
Helms, George T. (2nd Sgt.) [B, 57],
421
John W. (3rd Sgt.) [A, 24], 240
Hempston, Robert T. [H, 8], 177
Henderson, J.J. [H, 19], 303
John E. [F, 53], 408
John L. [G, 19], 301
John S. [K, 28], 324
Robert (4th Cpl.) [F, 56], 335
Hendrick, James D. [E, 11], 229
Lucius J. [G, 14], 372
Murray [G, 38], 391
William D. [B, 11], 224
William L. [G, 38], 391
William T. [G, 38], 391
Hendrickson, Elisha D. (3rd Cpl.) [C,
28], 313
Henkle, John [H, 56], 338
Henley, George W. (Capt.) [I, 19], 304
Henshaw A.L. [G, 7], 217
Robert S. (4th Sgt.) [G, 7], 216
Hensley, Charles C. [B, 24], 242
Heptinstall, Leslie H. (2nd Lt.) [G, 24],
250
Herbert, William E. [B, 3], 195
William W. [Maj., CS)
[Armistead], 343
Hereford, Hardin H. [H, 24], 251
Herndon, Edward J. [F, 19], 299
G.A. [B, 38 Bn.], 443
John A. (Capt.) [D, 38], 386
L.T. [C, 38 Bn.], 446
Nicholas W. [F, 19], 300
William G. [I, 7], 218
Herring, B. Franklin [H, 56], 338
Gideon L. (1st Cpl.) [A, 3], 194
Henry A. [E, 19], 506
John H. [E, 19], 298

N.B. [I, 7], 218
Robert H. [I, 9], 356
Herrington, Elias M. (2nd Lt.) [K, 8],
269
Hewitt, William L. [D, 38 Bn.], 448
Hickman, Josiah T. [H, 3], 202
Hickok, John F. [D, 11], 227
Martin V.B. (5th Sgt.) [D, 11],
222
Hicks, Andrew S. (3rd Cpl.) [B, 53],
401
Herndon F. [K, 7], 219
Jeremiah [C, 24], 244
Martin [C, 24], 244
William R. [C, 24], 244
William R. [E, 53], 506
Higgason, William B. [F, 56], 336
Higginbotham, Aaron L. [I, 19], 305
Alexander (1st Cpl.) [F, 3], 199
Clifton V. [H, 19], 303
James L. [G, 19], 301
Joseph A. [I, 19], 305
Paul M. [I, 19], 305
Hight, John W. [D, 7], 214
Hiler, Peter S. [I, 57], 434
Hill, Alvin T. (Capt.) [G, 7], 216
Charles T. (3rd Lt.) [I, 19], 304
James B. (3rd Lt.) [D, 53], 404
James O. [H, 38], 393
James R. (5th Sgt.) [C, 57], 423
James W. [K, 57], 436
John R. [A, 38], 381
John Wesley (3rd Lt.) [A, 19], 292
Joseph R. (3rd Sgt.) [A, 8], 260
Joseph W. [A, 38], 381
Sion [G, 3], 200
William [K, 57], 436
William H. (Cpl.) [C, 7], 212
William H. [E, 19], 298
Hillsman, John C. [B, 11], 224
William H. [B, 11], 222
Hines, Brainard W. (Capt.) [F, 24], 248
John H. [E, 57], 427
Thomas H. [D, 57], 425
Hinson, George [K, 8], 270
Hite, Edward S. [K, 14], 377
George W. [A, 56], 328
H.C. [H, 1], 189
Isaac W. (2nd Cpl.) [H, 19], 303

John T. [F, 11], 230
Hitt, Martin L. [G, 7], 217
Paskill A. [G, 7], 217
Hix, A.L. [B, 38 Bn.], 443
George F. [B, 38 Bn.], 443
John W. [I, 28], 323
Hixon, Abner H. [D, 8], 260
Hobbs, Eldbridge L. [C, 14], 364
N.R. [G, 53], 409
Richard M. [C, 9], 349
William E. [C, 53], 403
Hobson, Eppie M. (Ord. Sgt.) [11], 221
Hockaday, James H. (3rd Sgt.) [B, 53],
401
John R. (1st Sgt.) [B, 53], 400
Hodges, Edward P. [B, 38], 383
George R. (1st Cpl.) [D, 24], 246
Habron [G, 57], 177
James Gregory (Col.) [14], 359
Joseph H. [C, 38], 385
Josiah [A, 3], 194
Josiah [D, 24], 246
Landon [G, 57], 431
Nathan H. (1st Sgt.) [A, 3], 194
Patrick H. (2nd Cpl.) [A, 3], 194
Richard S. (4th Sgt.) [F, 57], 428
Thomas M. (Capt.) [A, 3], 194
William A. [A, 57], 420
William H. [A, 57], 420
William R. [G, 57], 431
Willis T. [I, 57], 434
Hodnett, James D. [I, 18], 287
Phillip [H, 24], 251
Thomas B. [E, 53], 406
William [I, 18], 287
Hodsden, Wilfred J. [F, 9], 353
Hoffman, Francis W. [A, 38 Bn.], 440
J.W. [K, 7], 219
Moses A. [K, 7], 219
Hofler, Elias [H, 3], 202
Hogan, James A. [G, 28], 320
James E. [B, 14], 362
Joseph [B, 38 Bn.], 443
William H. [B, 14], 362
Hoge, Edward T. (3rd Sgt.) [E, 24], 247
Hogwood, John [B, 53], 401
Joseph T. [B, 53], 401
Holcombe, Ellis H. [C, 11], 225
Holden, Thomas W. (Sgt.) [G, 8], 267

Holdron, Henry H. [D, 28], 315
Holfoot, Robert [E, 9], 351
 Robert [E, 53], 406
Holladay, Joseph H. [F, 9], 353
Holland, Abram F. (2nd Lt.) [G, 57], 430
 Constantine [K, 38], 395
 Exum [F, 9], 353
 George W. [G, 3], 200
 James A. (Capt.) [A, 18], 273
 John [K, 38], 395
 Malory M. [I, 3], 203
 Matthew [F, 3], 199
 Richard Thomas [F, 3], 199
 Robert C. (2nd Sgt.) [I, 28], 322
 Samuel H. [E, 9], 351
 Thomas C. (1st Lt.) [G, 28], 319
 William P. [G, 11], 179
 Zachary T. [A, 14], 360
Holley, William H. [I, 53], 413
Holliday, William L. (4th Cpl.) [C, 8], 263
Hollins, George T. [F, 56], 336
 James E. [A, 11], 223
 William C. [F, 56], 336
Holloway, Robert G. [C, 18], 276
Holman, Samuel D. [A, 57], 418
Holmes, George W. [K, 53], 416
 John W. (5th Sgt.) [D, 3], 197
 Julius C. [B, 38 Bn.], 443
 Robert [G, 38], 391
Holstine, Andrew J. [G, 24], 250
Holt, Burwell N.M. [I, 56], 340
 James P. [I, 56], 340
 John Lea [I, 56], 340
 John R. [E, 11], 229
 Joseph H. (Capt., AQM) [28], 309
 Richard M. [I, 56], 340
 Robert A. (2nd Sgt.) [I, 56], 339
 William D. [K, 18], 289
 William J. [C, 18], 276
Honts, George D. [A, 28], 310
Hood, John T. [B, 38 Bn.], 443
Hoofman, Moses [H, 38], 393
Hooton, Samuel C. (3rd Sgt.) [F, 18], 281
Hopgood, Albert [G, 14], 372
Hopkins, John D. [C, 38 Bn.], 506
 John O. [F, 53], 408

John W. (2nd Sgt.) [G, 53], 409
Hopper, George W. [K, 38], 395
 John H. [K, 38], 395
Hord, Benjamin H. [G, 1], 187
 William F. [G, 1], 187
Horner, Charles A. [C, 9], 507
 Joseph B. [C, 9], 507
Horsely, George W. [F, 57], 429
Horseman, Samuel E. [G, 8], 267
Horsley, Thomas [G, 57], 431
Horton, Edwin R. [B, 11], 224
 Thomas B. (Capt.) [B, 11], 223
Host, Andrew C. [K, 9], 357
 George [B, 3], 195
Hotelen, Henry [G, 38], 391
Houchens, John W. [A, 19], 293
 Joseph W. [C, 14], 364
 Thomas M. [A, 19], 293
Hough, Harry [H, 17], 177
Houpt, George A. [G, 28], 321
House, James [E, 56], 334
 Richard J. [F, 14], 370
Houseman, Joseph C. [D, 38 Bn.], 448
Housman, George C. [K, 57], 436
Houston, Andrew M. (Capt.) [K, 11], 236
 David Gardiner, Jr. (Capt.) [D, 11], 227
 Edward M. [K, 11], 236
 Thomas D. (1st Lt.) [K, 11], 236
Howard, Benjamin F. (Capt.) [I, 1], 190
 James T.B. [H, 3], 202
 John A. [F, 28], 318
 John W. (3rd Sgt.) [K, 14], 376
 Samuel J. [F, 28], 318
 Thomas R. (Asst. Surg.) [9], 346
Howell, Alexander F. [B, 14], 362
 Dillard C. [A, 24], 240
 John H. [D, 53], 405
 Nicodemus L. [B, 14], 362
 Thomas [A, 24], 240
Howerton, Joseph T. (5th Sgt.) [E, 38], 388
 W.W. [G, 53], 409
 William H. (4th Sgt.) [E, 38], 388
Howle, Isaac H. [B, 53], 401
Howlett, Thomas A. (2nd Sgt.) [C, 9], 348
 Thomas T. [D, 14], 367

561

Howser, William C. (Sgt.) [A, 38 Bn.], 439
Hoy, James M. [B, 24], 242
Hubbard, Alexander (1st Cpl.) [C, 28], 313
    J.S. [K, 53], 416
    James M. [A, 18], 274
    M.R. [G, 28], 321
    Samuel R. (5th Sgt.) [H, 18], 284
    Talifero G. [G, 28], 321
    William A. [D, 18], 278
    William J. [H, 18], 285
Huckstep, Benjamin J. [F, 7], 215
    J.P. [F, 7], 215
    Jacob E. [B, 19], 294
Huddleston, William T. [A, 57], 420
Hudgins, B.P. [G, 53], 409
    Elias P. (Ord. Sgt.) [1], 181
    Henry C. (1st Lt.) [K, 9], 357
    R.R. [G, 53], 410
    Ransom [C, 18], 276
Hudson, George R. [E, 24], 248
    James R. [E, 24], 248
    John R. (1st Cpl.) [E, 24], 248
    John W. (3rd Cpl.) [G, 7], 216
    Joseph D. [D, 38 Bn.], 448
    Mastin [A, 56], 328
    Samuel [G, 7], 217
    Thomas J. [B, 56], 329
    William T. [B, 53], 401
Huff, Ferdinand A. [A, 24], 241
Huffman, Anderson [B, 28], 312
    Andrew, Jr. [C, 28], 313
    Andrew J. [C, 28], 314
    Joseph [C, 28], 314
    Ransom P. [C, 28], 314
    Thomas [I, 11], 235
    Thomas [B, 28], 312
Hughes, Anthony T. [D, 14], 367
    Barnet W. [B, 11], 224
    Henry C. (Cpl.) [A, 18], 273
    Henry H. [D, 19], 297
    John [B, 19], 294
    John W. [K, 53], 507
    Joseph H. [A, 28], 311
    Moses P. [G, 19], 302
    Richard (Chief Mus.) [7], 208
    Samuel P. [G, 19], 302
    Walter B. [E, 38], 389

William H. [C, 38 Bn.], 446
Hughey, A.T. [K, 38], 395
Hughs, Aaron [F, 11], 230
Hughson, Aubrey (3rd Cpl.) [F, 56], 335
Hull, John E. [C, 7], 212
Hume, Francis [C, 7], 212
    Thomas, Jr. (Chap.) [3], 193
    William S. [A, 7], 210
Hummer, George W.F. [H, 8], 259
Humphlet, John T. (1st Cpl.) [I, 9], 356
Humphrey, Joseph R. [H, 38], 393
Humphreys, John H. [B, 19], 294
    Nathaniel [C, 56], 330
Hundley, Benjamin F. [D, 3], 197
    Charles W. [D, 38], 387
    James M. [K, 38], 395
    Jason B. [A, 38], 381
    Joshua W. [G, 19], 302
Hunt, B.B. [K, 11], 236
    Booker F. (4th Sgt.) [D, 18], 277
    Elisha B. [F, 18], 281
    James L. [A, 38 Bn.], 440
    John C. [K, 57], 436
    John W. (2nd Cpl.) [F, 38], 390
    Michael [B, 38 Bn.], 443
    William N. [D, 18], 278
    William R. (2nd Cpl.) [A, 11], 222
Hunter, George F. [C, 14], 364
    Joseph A. [F, 28], 318
    William H. [B, 56], 329
Hunton, Eppa (Col.) [8], 259
    George H. (1st Cpl.) [K, 7], 219
    John (Mus.) [7], 208
Hurst, Benjamin F. (4th Sgt.) [C, 8], 262
Hurt, George T. [C, 9], 349
    H.W. [K, 7], 220
    James J. [D, 7], 214
    John H. (3rd Sgt.) [H, 11], 233
    William S. [E, 11], 229
Huse, Jesse H. [K, 57], 436
    Samuel B. [K, 57], 436
Huston, John H. (2nd Cpl.) [B, 28], 311
    William M. [D, 24], 246
Hutcherson, James F. (Cpl.) [G, 38], 391
    John D. (1st Sgt.) [G, 57], 430
    William H. (Sgt.) [D, 38], 386

Hutcheson, John F. (3rd Sgt.) [F, 24], 248
Hutchins, George W. (Capt.) [B, 3], 195
    Robert A. (2nd Sgt.) [B, 3], 195
Hutchison, Benjamin H. (2nd Lt.) [D, 8], 264
    J.L. [G, 8], 267
    John (3rd Cpl.) [D, 8], 507
    John R. (1st Lt., ACS) [8], 259
    Thomas Benton (1st Lt., Adjt.) [8], 259
Hutter, James Risque (Capt.) [H, 11], 233
Hutts, John W.T. [G, 57], 431
Hyden, Joseph L. (2nd Cpl.) [F, 24], 249
Hylton, John H. [A, 24], 241
    Mathias F. [A, 24], 241
    Sparrel L. [A, 24], 241
Hyman, William P. [D, 38 Bn.], 448

-I-

Iden, Abner [A, 38 Bn.], 440
    John N. [A, 38 Bn.], 440
    John R. [B, 8], 262
Inge, Caswell F. [F, 38], 507
    Lawson E. [B, 24], 242
Ingraham, S.H. [B, 38 Bn.], 443
Ingram, Thomas E. [I, 18], 287
    William [K, 56], 341
Inman, Memory A. [D, 38], 387
Insco, Isaac [F, 14], 370
    Robert O. [F, 14], 370
Irby, Edmund [G, 18], 283
    Morgan G. [B, 38 Bn.], 443
    Samuel T. [H, 14], 374
Irola, Emanuel [C, 24], 244
Irvine, Robert H. [I, 19], 256
Irving, Charles Scott (Capt.) [C, 19], 295
    Robert R. [C, 19], 295
Isaacs, George W. [K, 28], 324
    John R. [K, 11], 237
Ish, Milton A. [I, 1], 191
Ives, Richard W. (1st Cpl.) [H, 14], 374
Ivey, Benjamin B. [G, 3], 200
    O.L. [G, 11], 232

-J-

Jacheri, Pompeo [B, 19], 175
Jackson, Andrew (Mus.) [D, 14], 366
    Benjamin E. [D, 8], 264
    David W. [F, 38], 507
    E.M. [K, 18], 507
    George H. (Cpl.) [G, 18], 282
    George T. [C, 3], 196
    Green M. [A, 38], 381
    John D. [G, 1], 187
    John H. [A, 7], 210
    Joseph A. [D, 14], 367
    Lewis [A, 38], 381
    Thomas [K, 56], 341
    Thomas B. (Jr. 2nd Lt.) [C, 3], 196
    William [A, 14], 360
    William H. [K, 7], 220
    William M. [C, 9], 349
Jacobs, David P. [B, 57], 422
    John, Jr. [B, 1], 183
    John D. [H, 38], 393
    Thomas A. [B, 14], 362
    Welford C. [I, 11], 235
Jamerson, George W. [H, 24], 251
    Thomas [H, 24], 251
James, Benjamin D. [I, 11], 235
    Charles H. [I, 11], 235
    Cornelius E. [F, 3], 199
    Isaac L. (3rd Cpl.) [B, 24], 242
    John B. [I, 11], 235
    John T. (4th Sgt.) [F, 8], 266
    John Thomas (1st Lt.) [D, 11], 227
    Randolph B. (4th Cpl.) [K, 9], 357
    Richard [G, 14], 372
    Robert R. [K, 3], 205
    Thomas B. (1st Cpl.) [A, 8], 261
    Townsend A. [A, 8], 261
Janney, Isaac [A, 57], 420
Jarman, William D. [I, 7], 218
Jarratt, Tazwell T. [D, 24], 246
    Theophilus (4th Sgt.) [F, 53], 407
Jarrell, J.E., Jr. [F, 7], 215
Jarvis, David A. [D, 1], 186
    Ottaway [B, 38 Bn.], 443
Jefferson, Haily R. [K, 38], 395
    James T. (3rd Cpl.) [E, 57], 426
    Willaim Taze [E, 57], 427
    William Thomas [E, 57], 427
Jelks, James K. [D, 3], 197

William F. [G, 19], 302
Joseph, Wilson B. [H, 1], 189
Joy, George [I, 1], 191
Joyce, Richard J. (1st Lt.) [A, 38], 380
Joyner, John H. [D, 3], 197
    Matthew [D, 3], 197
    Robert T. (4th Cpl.) [D, 3], 197
Julius, John [E, 57], 427

-K-

Kabler, Frederick [C, 11], 226
    William S. [C, 11], 226
Kane, John [B, 38 Bn.], 443
    William A. [A, 38 Bn.], 441
Kean, Charles (4th Sgt.) [C, 1], 184
    Christopher C. [A, 18], 274
Kearns, John W. [A, 38 Bn.], 507
Keaster, L.B. [H, 56], 338
Keaton, James P. [E, 11], 229
Keatts, John R. [C, 38 Bn.], 507
    Lawson S. [B, 38], 383
Keblinger, Wilber J. (3rd Cpl.) [B, 19], 294
Keefauver, Edward [D, 11], 227
Keeling, William H. [H, 3], 202
Keen, Daniel F. (2nd Sgt.) [I, 57], 433
    David S. [I, 53], 398
Keene, James H. [B, 38 Bn.], 443
Keesee, Robert H. (4th Sgt.) [B, 18], 275
Keeter, James [G, 14], 372
Keeton, James P. [C, 56], 330
Kegan, Martin [H, 57], 432
Keiningham, John C. [D, 1], 186
    William H. (Sr. 2nd Lt.) [D, 1] , 185
Keirson, Archer L. [A, 56], 328
Keister, Andrew M. [I, 24], 253
Keith, Asa [A, 24], 241
Kelley, Bryant [D, 38 Bn.], 448
Kelley, Edward [K, 28], 324
    Edward W. [K, 56], 341
    George J. [A, 28], 311
    Henry P. [K, 56], 341
    William H. (Capt.) [K, 28], 324
    William H. [C, 38 Bn.], 446
    William J. (4th Cpl.) [K, 28], 324
Kello, James R. [B, 9], 347
Kelly, George F. [D, 8], 265

Henry C. [H, 53], 411
John [D, 11], 227
John (1st Cpl.) [E, 11], 228
Julius C. [E, 24], 248
Kelsic, John R. [G, 9], 354
Kemper, James G. [I, 11], 235
    James Lawson (Brig. Gen.), 178
    John J. (Cpl.) [A, 38 Bn.], 439
    Joshua [A, 38 Bn.], 441
Kendal, George [A, 38 Bn.], 441
Kendall, Henry C. [F, 8], 266
    Richard A. (4th Cpl.) [B, 7], 210
    William B. [B, 7], 211
Kendrick, William F. [G, 1], 187
Kennedy, James F. [K, 7], 220
    Joseph A. (1st Lt.) [A, 11], 222
    Philip [F, 19], 300
Kennett, James F. [E, 57], 427
Kenney, George H. [C, 24], 244
    Nicholas J. (2nd Cpl.) [C, 24], 243
    William H. [C, 24], 244
Kennon, James H. (2nd Sgt.) [K, 19], 306
    Joseph [C, 56], 330
    Robert W. [F, 56], 336
    William M. (2nd Cpl.) [C, 56], 330
Kent, James R. (4th Cpl.) [G, 11], 231
    James W. (1st Cpl.) [C, 19], 295
    Robert A. [G, 11], 232
    William H. [G, 11], 176
Keplar, John Hanson (1st Sgt.) [D, 1], 185
Kercheval, John W. [F, 8], 266
Kerfoot, William F. [B, 8], 262
Kermick, Benjamin F. [A, 38 Bn.], 507
    Francis M. [A, 38 Bn.], 507
Kern, Henry L. [A, 28], 311
Kerns, John N. [E, 28], 317
Kerrick, J.T. [A, 38 Bn.], 441
    W.T. [A, 38 Bn.], 441
Kersey, Thomas F. [F, 56], 336
Kesler, John [H, 53], 411
    Peter [E, 57], 427
Kessler, James G. [K, 28], 324
    James H. [D, 11], 227
Keys, Alexander [C, 3], 196
    Edmond T. (2nd Cpl.) [C, 3], 196
Keyseear, John [A, 7], 210

Keyton, S.F. [H, 56], 338
   Washington J. [K, 11], 237
   William L. (1st Cpl.) [I, 7], 218
Kidd, Alexander B. [G, 19], 302
   Alexander R. [G, 19], 302
   Allen B. [B, 56], 329
   Edward R. [B, 56], 329
   J. Luther [I, 7], 218
   Landon R. [G, 19], 302
   Lorenzo D. [G, 19], 302
   William F. [B, 56], 329
Kidwell, James W. [G, 8], 267
   Newton J. [B, 8], 262
   Thompson (4th Cpl.) [F, 8], 266
Kilby, Andrew J. [G, 7], 217
   Henry Clay [B, 7], 211
   Joseph M. [G, 7], 217
   Thomas M. [G, 7], 217
   Walter R. (2nd Cpl.) [H, 1], 188
   William A. [C, 7], 212
Kilgore, Mallory (4th Cpl.) [A, 3], 194
Kimbrough, Cary A. [D, 53], 405
Kindrick, Linwood [H, 38], 393
Kines, Daniel [A, 38 Bn.], 441
King, Charles H. (4th Sgt.) [E, 24], 247
   Elias W. [C, 14], 360
   Emanuel [K, 3], 205
   George N. (2nd Sgt.) [B, 53], 400
   William H. [E, 24], 248
Kinney, James [G, 24], 250
Kinzie, William C. [B, 28], 312
Kirby, John P. [D, 9], 350
   Johnson [H, 3], 202
Kirk, James M. [K, 24], 254
Kirkbride, John [C, 24], 244
Kirkland, James M. [H, 53], 411
   Joseph J. [G, 3], 201
Kirkpatrick, Joseph [K, 8], 270
Kirks, William A. [G, 57], 431
Kirtley, Bushrod C. [C, 14], 364
   John A. (3rd Cpl.) [K, 7], 219
   Samuel C. [C, 14], 364
   W.B. [K, 7], 220
Kissee, John H. [D, 57], 425
Kissinger, Henry H. [F, 24], 249
Kitterman, George W. (3rd Lt.) [A, 24], 240
   J.A. [I, 8], 269
Kivet, Alexander L. (3rd Sgt.) [B, 9],

347
Knewstep, Miles [B, 53], 401
Knight, Benjamin F. [B, 9], 347
   Charles [G, 3], 201
   Daniel C. (3rd Cpl.) [H, 19], 303
   H.D. (1st Cpl.) [G, 53], 409
   Henry C. (2nd Lt.) [E, 38], 387
   Osson P. [F, 28], 318
   William [B, 8], 507
Knighton, Albert [C, 56], 331
Kyle, Robert G. (1st Cpl.) [F, 11], 230

-L-

Lacey, Robert M. [I, 53], 413
Lackey, George [B, 57], 422
   Josiah [B, 57], 422
   Samuel L. [E, 14], 369
Lacy, David W. (Mus.) [7], 208
Ladd, Henry L. [K, 53], 416
   Robert T. [K, 14], 377
Lafargue, Henry [A, 18], 274
Laffoon, Jesse G. [D, 18], 278
   John G. [D, 18], 278
Laine, James C. [D, 3], 197
Lake, John L. (1st Lt.) [K, 8], 269
Lamb, Theoderick L . [E, 3], 198
Lambert, George D. (4th Sgt.) [B, 56], 328
   John S. [G, 8], 267
Lamkin, Joseph (3rd Cpl.) [H, 24], 251
   Oliver P. [K, 53], 416
Lampkin, J.W. [B, 38 Bn.], 443
Lancaster, Joseph O. [F, 3], 200
   William Thomas (2nd Cpl.) [F, 3], 199
Land, Henry M. [K, 38], 395
   James W.T. [G, 9], 354
Landrum, James E. (Bvt. 2nd Lt.) [H, 19], 303
Lane, James B. [K, 19], 307
   John H. [D, 38 Bn.], 448
   John H. [H, 56], 338
   Lorenzo [A, 19], 293
   William A. (Cpl.) [A, 38 Bn.], 439
   William G. [C, 14], 364
Langford, James [F, 19], 300
   William [F, 19], 300
Langhon, Isham [B, 14], 362
Langley, Francis H. (Maj.) [1], 181

John, Jr. [F, 14], 370
Lanham, Thomas L. [B, 8], 262
Lanier, Adolphus M. (1st Lt.) [D, 38], 386
    Charles H. [E, 56], 334
    Legrand H. (3rd Sgt.) [E, 56], 333
    Virginius W. [C, 53], 403
    Wesley [E, 56], 334
Lantz, Lang R. [D, 11], 227
Laprade, Cornelius B. [I, 14], 376
    Everett G. [I, 14], 376
LaPraid, William W. [G, 57], 431
Larkins, John [F, 9], 507
Lash, James K.P. [H, 3], 202
Lassiter, Richard [I, 9], 356
Latane, John L. (Capt.) [H, 53], 410
Latham, Albert [D, 38 Bn.], 448
Lattimer, John W. [G, 9], 354
Lavender, Joseph G. [A, 57], 419
    Robert R. [G, 57], 431
    Tazwell C. [A, 57], 420
Law, Amos B. [G, 57], 431
    George W.C. [K, 38], 395
    John B. [D, 24], 246
    John C. (1st Sgt.) [D, 24], 246
    Joseph [G, 57], 431
    Milton B. [D, 24], 247
    Nathaniel C. [D, 24], 247
    Peter C. [G, 57], 431
    Samuel S. [E, 53], 407
    William D. [D, 24], 247
Lawhorne, Edward P. [I, 19], 305
    Isham [I, 19], 305
Lawless, George W. [I, 24], 253
    McNealey A. [I,. 24], 253
    Thomas J. [I, 24], 253
    William L. [D, 38 Bn.], 448
Lawrence, Albert [F, 3], 200
    George W. (4th Sgt.) [A, 9], 344
    George W. [E, 57], 427
    Gideon L. [A, 24], 241
    James H. (2nd Lt.) [E, 57], 426
    Lewis M. (1st Cpl.) [K, 8], 270
    William R. [H, 24], 252
Lawson, Henry H. [I, 24], 253
    John O. [H, 38], 393
    Thomas G. [I, 56], 340
    William M. (4th Sgt.) [H, 1], 182
    Wilson T. (1st Cpl.) [A, 24], 240

Layard, William Samuel [G, 1], 187
Laycock, John F. [H, 8], 268
Layne, Nehemiah [H, 56], 338
    Robert C. [H, 56], 338
Layton, John L. [A, 7], 210
Lazenby, George W. (2nd Lt.) [B, 11], 223
LeGrand, Peter A. (3rd Cpl.) [C, 11], 225
LeTellier, John Henry (Capt.) [K, 24], 254
    Joseph C. [E, 19], 298
    William B. (2nd Lt.) [E, 19], 297
Leach, Peter T. [K, 8], 270
League, William S. [H, 18], 285
Leak, Thomas J. [I, 24], 253
Leake, William J. [E, 19], 298
Leary, John H. (5th Cpl.) [B, 38 Bn.], 442
Leath, Branch O. [C, 18], 276
    James R. [C, 18], 276
    John W. [D, 53], 344
    Joseph E. [C, 18], 276
Leathers, James A. [K, 19], 307
Lee, Charles D. (QM Sgt.) [57], 418
    Henderson L. (Capt.) [G, 38], 391
    James G. [A, 57], 420
    John A.J. (Bvt. 2nd Lt.) [C, 28], 313
    John T. [H, 18], 285
    Richard H. [I, 57], 434
    William A. [A, 57], 420
    William E. [K, 53], 416
Leek, Presley [G, 7], 217
Lefever, Samuel C. [A, 38 Bn.], 441
Leffel, John M. (2nd Sgt.) [C, 28], 313
Leftwich, James B. (3rd Lt.) [F, 28], 317
    James P. (2nd Sgt.) [G, 28], 319
    John S. (Sgt. Maj.) [14], 359
    Lynch A. [B, 14], 362
    Preston L. [G, 28], 321
Legg, Alexander F. [E, 7], 215
    John T. [E, 7], 215
    William [K, 8], 270
Leggett, Walter M. (5th Sgt.) [B, 3], 195
Legwin, Charles H. [G, 57], 177
    William A. [G, 57], 419

Leitch, Samuel G. (1st Lt., ACOO) [Pickett], 175
Lemmon, John McL. [D, 11], 227
    Nathan E. [D, 11], 227
    Robert N. [D, 11], 227
Lemon, Barnett E. (2nd Cpl.) [K, 28], 324
    Joseph P. [I, 28], 323
    William [K, 57], 436
Leneve, Samuel A. [C, 18], 276
Leslie, Samuel [C, 24], 244
    Samuel D. (1st Lt.) [A, 8], 260
    William A. [A, 8], 261
Lester, George W. [A, 24], 241
    Giles W. (1st Sgt.) [A, 14], 360
    Hartwell F. [I, 56], 340
    John C. [F, 57], 429
    Thomas P. [I, 1], 191
    William T. [I, 56], 340
Levell, Joseph W. (3rd Sgt.) [K, 7], 219
Lewellyn, Charles M. (Hosp. Stew.) [19], 291
    John A. (1st Lt., Adjt.) [19], 291
Lewey, Joseph [D, 7], 214
Lewis, Benjamin G. [I, 18], 287
    Benjamin W. [A, 57], 420
    George W. [G, 9], 354
    J.D. [H, 18], 285
    James W. [E, 56], 334
    John E. [G, 28], 321
    John H. (Jr. 2nd Lt.) [G, 9], 353
    John J. [I, 18], 287
    John R. [C, 14], 364
    John R. [D, 53], 405
    John T. (Jr. 2nd Lt.) [E, 14], 368
    Joseph S. [I, 57], 434
    Magnus M. (Ch. Surg.) [Pickett], 175
    McKemmy (1st Sgt.) [I, 9], 355
    Philip J. [E, 56], 334
    Richard B. (1st Sgt.) [E, 14], 368
    Richard S. [H, 53], 411
    Robert M. [A, 18], 274
    Samuel M. (4th Cpl.) [A, 57], 420
    Thomas (1st Lt., Adjt.) [38 Bn.], 438
    William [I, 9], 507
    William L. [B, 38], 383
    William W. [C, 7], 212

Light, Charles M. [F, 38], 390
    George W. [H, 14], 374
    John R. [H, 14], 374
    William S. [H, 14], 374
Lightfoot, John (Capt., ACS) [7], 207
Ligon, John T. (2nd Lt.) [C, 53], 402
Lindsay, Asberry D. (1st Cpl.) [K, 19], 306
    Joshua Mc. [B, 11], 179
    William Daniel [D, 38 Bn.], 448
Lindsey, Cincinnatus D. [K, 18], 289
    Jeter J. [C, 38 Bn.], 446
    John S. (Sgt.) [A, 38], 380
Link, Christian H. [F, 24], 249
Linkenhoger, Mathew [K, 28], 324
Linkinhoker, Abraham Thomas [K, 57], 436
    Cary B. [K, 57], 436
    Phillip S. [K, 57], 436
Linthicum, Charles F. (Capt., AAG) [Garnett], 256
Lipes, Harvey D. [K, 57], 436
    John M. [K, 57], 436
    John W. (3rd Cpl.) [B, 28], 311
    William L. [K, 57], 436
Lippitt, Charles E. (Surg.) [57], 418
Lipscomb, Charles P. [E, 11], 229
    Edward T. [G, 56], 337
    James H. (Capt.) [K, 53], 414
    Junius L. [C, 18], 277
    Thomas A. (2nd Sgt.) [D, 53], 404
Litchfield, Jacob [I, 9], 507
Litchford, Edward L. [G, 11], 232
Little, Adoniram J. [I, 3], 203
    James T. [B, 11], 224
Littlepage, John L. (1st Sgt.) [B, 1], 182
    Lewis L. [D, 53], 405
Litton, James E.P. [G, 11], 232
Liverman, Hardy A. [A, 3], 194
Livesay, Turner T. (1st Sgt.) [E, 3], 198
Lloyd, Benjamin S. [D, 38 Bn.], 448
    Robert H. [C, 56], 331
Loafman, Allen C. [E, 14], 369
    James H. [G, 56], 337
Locke, James W. [G, 56], 337
Lockett, John T. [K, 57], 436
    Philip [G, 14], 372
Lockhart, Ashburn [F, 56], 336

Lockridge, Calvin [D, 53], 507
Loehr, Charles T. (4th Cpl.) [D, 1], 185
Loftis, James M. [K, 14], 377
Logan, David T. [I, 19], 305
    John A. (1st Lt.) [H, 14], 373
    John K. (Sgt.) [A, 38], 380
    Richard, Jr. (Capt.) [H, 14], 373
    Samuel P. [I, 19], 305
Lollis, George A. [E, 28], 317
    Richard P. (1st Cpl.) [E, 28], 316
Londeree, William P. (4th Cpl.) [D, 19], 296
Long, Edward J. [K, 7], 220
    Green B. (Jr. 2nd Lt.) [F, 11], 229
    Henry C. [K, 3], 205
    James T. [F, 7], 216
    Reuben [B, 38 Bn.], 443
    W.F. [F, 11], 230
Loomis, James M. [H, 3], 202
Looney, James M. [C, 28], 314
Lord, John R. [G, 1], 187
Lorton, George [E, 24], 248
Lovelace, Charles H. [G, 53], 410
    John [I, 18], 287
    John T. [H, 14], 374
    William A. [C, 38], 385
Loveless, George T. [H, 8], 268
Loving, Benjamin V. [C, 38 Bn.], 446
    Cleophas A. [C, 8], 263
    Edwin B. [I, 1], 191
    James E. [G, 19], 302
    John J., Jr. (1st Cpl.) [G, 19], 301
    John J.W. [G, 19], 302
    Michael [D, 38 Bn.], 449
    Richard J. [C, 14], 364
    William H. (4th Sgt.) [G, 19], 301
Lovins, Arthur J. [I, 24], 253
Lowe, James J. [B, 9], 347
Lowman, Cyrus W. [D, 11], 227
Lowry, Granville N. [D, 38 Bn.], 449
    John W. [K, 14], 377
    Marshall M. (1st Sgt.) [F, 28], 317
    Wyatt [F, 56], 336
Loyd, Calvin L. [A, 18], 274
    Pleasant W. (1st Cpl.) [I, 28], 322
Lucado, Leo F. (Capt., ACS) [11], 221
Lucas, George P. [F, 11], 230
    John B. [F, 11], 230
    Josephus [F, 24], 249

Rice M. [F, 11], 230
    Samuel M. [F, 24], 249
    William D. [B, 38 Bn.], 507
Luck, John H. [C, 38 Bn.], 446
Lugar, James H. [C, 28], 314
Lumber, William H. (4th Sgt.) [B, 3], 195
Lumpkin, William J., Jr. [B, 1], 183
Lumsden, Richard W. (4th Cpl.) [B, 19], 294
Lunceford, Benjamin R. (1st Cpl.) [C, 8], 262
    Evans O. [C, 8], 263
    James D. [F, 8], 266
Lupton, Jacob C. [H, 57], 432
Lutze, Theodore E. [E, 53], 407
Lydick, James H. (Mus.) [G, 11], 231
Lynch, Christopher [B, 24], 242
    James H. [G, 57], 431
    John L. [B, 24], 242
    Thomas J. [B, 56], 329
Lynn, Joseph F. (Sgt.) [G, 8], 267
    Robert [C, 8], 263
Lynsky, Martin C. (4th Sgt.) [I, 57], 433
    Patrick H. [I, 57], 434
Lyon, John P. [B, 24], 242
    Stephen B. [C, 24], 244

-M-

Mabrey, Joseph J., Jr. [A, 24], 241
Mackasey, Robert F. (4th Cpl.) [G, 38], 391
    Thomas S. [G, 38], 391
Mackey, John H. [C, 9], 349
Maclin, Thomas B. [H, 53], 411
Macon, Miles C. (Capt.) [B, 38 Bn.], 442
Madison, George D. [F, 19], 300
    James [F, 19], 300
    James A. [E, 19], 298
Magruder, John B. (Col.) [57], 418
Mahan, Abner A. [E, 57], 427
    Joseph C. (3rd Sgt.) [E, 57], 426
Mahane, W.P. [D, 1], 186
Mahanes, Tavener O. (4th Cpl.) [E, 19], 298
Mahon, Gideon [I, 57], 434
    Pleasant [K, 38], 395

Plyant [K, 38], 395
Mahone, Daniel H. (Cpl.) [H, 3], 201
    Edward [K, 57], 436
    James H. [C, 38 Bn.], 446
    Willmore W. (Cpl.) [H, 3], 201
Mahoney, William H. [H, 3], 202
Maiden, E.R. [C, 1], 184
Maier, John [E, 11], 229
Maitland, Hartwell J. [E, 56], 334
    James M. [E, 56], 334
    William H. [E, 56], 334
Maitlin, John [D, 28], 315
Maiton, William R. [E, 56], 334
Major, George C. [A, 38 Bn.], 441
    John E. (Jr. 2nd Lt.) [K, 53], 414
Mallett, Beverly [G, 38], 391
    Horace L. [G, 38], 391
    Silas C. [G, 38], 391
Mallory, William J. [B, 1], 183
Maloney, Clem H. [K, 18], 289
Mangas, William J. [K, 28], 324
Mann, John T. [H, 38], 393
Manning, Armstead R. [B, 53], 401
    William T. [B, 38 Bn.], 443
Mansfield, James D. (4th Sgt.) [B, 24], 241
Mantle, Henry [C, 38 Bn.], 446
Manuel, John [D, 57], 425
    Robert W. [D, 57], 425
    Willis A. (3rd Cpl.) [B, 7], 210
Marable, Albert W. [K, 53], 416
    Edward W. (3rd Sgt.) [K, 53], 414
    James E. [K, 53], 507
    Richard H. [K, 53], 416
Marion, John L. (3rd Sgt.) [E, 11], 228
Marker, Thomas J. [C, 53], 403
Markham, William T. [K, 11], 237
Marks, Lewis (3rd Cpl.) [G, 3], 200
    Samuel C. [C, 53], 403
    Thomas V. [D, 38 Bn.], 449
Marron, Bernard [C, 53], 403
Marsh, John C. [H, 56], 338
    William F. [H, 56], 338
Marshal, Charles H. [E, 11], 229
Marshall, Ballard [C, 24], 245
    Benjamin F. [K, 56], 341
    Clement C. (4th Sgt.) [K, 38], 394
    Edward C. (Ord. Sgt.) [38 Bn.], 438

Francis Q. [G, 18], 283
George M. [A, 38], 381
Humphrey [K, 38], 395
J.S. [F, 7], 216
Jacquelin A. (Sgt.) [A, 38 Bn.], 439
James M. (Sgt.) [A, 38], 380
Martin P. (Cpl.) [A, 38 Bn.], 439
Quintin A. [C, 53], 403
Thomas H. [A, 18], 274
William [A, 38 Bn.], 441
William C. (1st Lt.) [A, 38 Bn.], 439
Martin, A.J. [F, 28], 318
    Andrew S. [F, 24], 249
    Brice E. [F, 57], 429
    Ellison W. (1st Lt.) [H, 1], 188
    George D. [C, 38 Bn.], 446
    George S. [F, 24], 249
    Henry [K, 19], 307
    Isaac N. [A, 24], 241
    James B. (3rd Cpl.) [C, 14], 364
    James P. [C, 28], 314
    James S. [C, 11], 226
    James W. [D, 24], 247
    John A. [K, 19], 307
    John C. [H, 18], 285
    John C. (Sgt.) [G, 57], 430
    John H. [F, 11], 230
    John S. [D, 24], 507
    Johnson B. (5th Sgt.) [B, 7], 210
    Joseph H. (1st Sgt.) [C, 14], 363
    Joseph W. [A, 53], 507
    Mallory [H, 38], 393
    Mathew [C, 57], 424
    Michael C. [F, 24], 249
    Patrick K. [B, 38 Bn.], 443
    Peter H. [D, 18], 278
    Preston H. (4th Cpl.) [A, 24], 240
    Rawley White (Lt. Col.) [53], 398
    Richard [E, 56], 334
    Richard S. (1st Sgt.) [I, 57], 433
    Robert [C, 57], 424
    Robert J. [K, 53], 416
    Robert W. [F, 38], 390
    Samuel H. [K, 19], 307
    Sylvester G. (3rd Lt.) [K, 19], 306
    Theodore R. [H, 1], 182
    Thomas B. [H, 24], 252

Washington O. [B, 38 Bn.], 443
William G. [E, 14], 369
William H. [G, 1], 188
William J. [K, 53], 416
William T. [K, 56], 341
William T. (1st Cpl.) [B, 38 Bn.], 442
Woodson A. [D, 18], 278
Mason, Daniel M. (Sgt.) [A, 38 Bn.], 439
George B. (4th Sgt.) [H, 19], 303
John J. [F, 28], 318
John K. [G, 57], 431
John L. (2nd Sgt.) [H, 24], 251
John R. (1st Sgt.) [I, 56], 339
John W. [D, 38 Bn.], 449
Joseph W. [B, 57], 422
Morris W. [C, 11], 226
Samuel E. [H, 19], 304
W.A. (QM Sgt.) [19], 291
Massey, William B. [B, 57], 422
Massie, John W. [I, 19], 305
Mastern, James [C, 38 Bn.], 446
Masters, Edward N. (Mus.) [E, 53], 406
Matherly, Madison [K, 38], 395
Mathers, George W. [A, 38 Bn.], 441
T.J. [A, 38 Bn.], 441
Mathews, Andrew W. (2nd Cpl.) [E, 24], 248
George T. [D, 24], 247
John H. [C, 56], 331
John J. [C, 14], 364
Spencer G. [G, 28], 321
Matthews, Albert E. (Capt.) [H, 8], 268
Andrew J. [C, 28], 314
Barnaba B. [F, 9], 353
David [F, 9], 353
J. Kemp [G, 14], 372
John T. [G, 57], 431
Joseph O. [C, 7], 212
Thomas [C, 38 Bn.], 446
Wiley J. [G, 57], 419
Mattocks, Richard T. [C, 8], 263
Maupin, C.B. [H, 56], 339
David G. (3rd Cpl.) [H, 56], 337
Gabriel O. [H, 57], 432
James R. [H, 56], 339
Maury, William Wirt (3rd Sgt.) [A, 19], 292

Maxey, Bruce E. [B, 57], 422
Charles R. [D, 56], 332
Claiborne H. (3rd Cpl.) [A, 56], 327
Edward L. [D, 56], 333
Frederick C. (3rd Cpl.) [A, 57], 420
Levi P. [B, 57], 422
William W. [B, 57], 422
Maxwell, James W. [D, 19], 297
May, Charles E. (4th Sgt.) [F, 14], 370
George P. [G, 19], 302
George W. (Ord. Sgt.) [56], 326
James M. [G, 19], 302
John S. [C, 56], 331
William H. [I, 57], 434
Mayham, John W. [B, 38], 383
Mayhue, William H. [D, 57], 425
Mayo, James M. [H, 57], 433
Joseph, Jr. (Col.) [3], 193
Thomas P. (Surg.) [3], 193
Mays, Anderson [I, 19], 305
George W. (2nd Cpl.) [K, 24], 254
George W., Jr. [H, 19], 304
George W., Sr. [H, 19], 304
Joseph R. [D, 38 Bn.], 449
Marcellus H. [H, 19], 304
Nathaniel A. (5th Sgt.) [H, 19], 303
Robert D. [G, 19], 302
Thomas L. (1st Sgt.) [K, 57], 435
William C. [D, 38 Bn.], 449
McAlister, Jehu H. [K, 57], 436
McAllister, John B. [B, 11], 224
McAlpine, James N. (Surg.) [Armistead], 344
McArtor, John R. (3rd Sgt.) [B, 8], 261
McBride, Robert [I, 57], 434
William T. [G, 57], 431
McCann, Daniel C. (2nd Cpl.) [B, 38 Bn.], 442
Isham [K, 14], 377
Joseph J. [K, 3], 205
McCarthy, Daniel [D, 38], 387
Florence (Chap.) [7], 207
McCartney, Thomas Benton (Capt.) [B, 28], 311
McCarty, James M. [E, 38], 389
William F. [E, 8], 265

McCary, Benjamin J. [C, 1], 184
McCauley, John O. [F, 8], 266
   Riland [K, 19], 307
   Robert W. [H, 56], 339
McClanahan, James T. (4th Cpl.) [K, 8], 270
McClarin, James W. (Mus.) [E, 56], 333
McClary, James G. [A, 7], 210
   William [G, 28], 321
McClelland, Joseph E. [K, 11], 237
McClenny, James M. [B, 9], 348
McClure, Andrew J. [A, 28], 311
McComac, Edward P.W. [F, 53], 408
   John W. [F, 53], 408
McCommac, James M. [K, 57], 437
McConchie, John [I, 11], 235
   William [I, 11], 235
   William A. [I, 11], 235
McConkey, Samuel A. (Sr. Surg.) [Garnett], 256
McCook, William H. (4th Cpl.) [C, 38 Bn.], 445
McCormick, John [H, 38], 393
   John B. [C, 38], 385
   William L. [C, 38], 385
McCory, Craven P. [D, 38 Bn.], 507
   James C. [D, 38 Bn.], 449
   Thomas D. [D, 38 Bn.], 449
McCoy, Rufus K. [D, 9], 350
   William H. [I, 3], 507
McCrary, John H. (2nd Lt.) [G, 19], 301
McCrea, William H. [B, 38 Bn.], 443
McCroskey, John Miles [F, 24], 249
McCrossen, James [C, 1], 184
McCulloch, Robert (Capt.) [B, 18], 274
McCune, Robert H. [D, 18], 278
McCurdey, John H. [C, 38 Bn.], 446
   Peter [B, 38 Bn.], 443
McDaniel, Alexander [D, 38 Bn.], 449
   Charles T. [D, 28], 315
   David E. [K, 24], 254
   Major W. [I, 57], 434
   William [E, 24], 248
   William H. [I, 57], 434
McDonald, Charles [F, 19], 300
   George C. [K, 38], 395
McDowell, Joseph M. [K, 38], 395

   Joseph T. (5th Sgt.) [E, 57], 426
   Robert A. [A, 38], 381
   Robert B. [K, 38], 395
McFalls, John [I, 28], 323
McFarland, William P. [H, 3], 202
McFarlin, William H. [E, 14], 369
McGee, Richard H. [D, 14], 367
McGehee, George V. [C, 56], 331
   James E. (5th Sgt.) [F, 56], 335
McGhee, Elkanah T. [G, 57], 431
   John B. [D, 38 Bn.], 449
   John L. [K, 56], 341
   Peter C. [K, 56], 342
   Richard [C, 38 Bn.], 446
   William A. (4th Cpl.) [K, 56], 341
   William H. [E, 57], 427
McGinness, Phillip B. [C, 38 Bn.], 446
McGinnis, Thomas W. (1st Sgt.) [H, 19], 303
McGregor, William H. [F, 38], 390
McGruley, James B. [D, 38 Bn.], 449
McGuffin, John T. [D, 24], 247
McGuire, James E. [B, 53], 401
McHaney, William R. [F, 38], 390
McHone, James [C, 24], 245
   Micajah [C, 24], 245
McIntire, James Davis (2nd Lt.) [F, 19], 299
McIntosh, George [G, 8], 260
   John [G, 8], 260
   Robert W. [F, 8], 260
McKennon, William [B, 38 Bn.], 443
McKinney, George W. [K, 3], 205
McLain, Abram S. (3rd Sgt.) [F, 19], 299
   James E. [C, 14], 364
McLaughlan, Hugh [I, 1], 191
McLaughlin, John D. (Art.) [C, 38 Bn.], 445
   William (1st Cpl.) [B, 9], 347
McLear, James M. [I, 1], 191
McLees, John (1st Sgt.) [K, 53], 414
McLemore, Benjamin F. (1st Sgt.) [G, 3], 200
   Junius [K, 53], 416
McMellon, John W. [B, 57], 422
   William H. [B, 57], 422
McMillan, James W. (3rd Cpl.) [A, 53], 399

James E. (2nd Lt.) [C, 57], 423
John H. [C, 57], 424
Thomas W. [G, 1], 188
Thomas W. [F, 11], 230
William S. (Sgt.) [G, 57], 430
Miley, Caldwell G. [F, 8], 266
Milhollen, E.A. (Bvt. 2nd Lt.) [E, 8], 265
Millam, James E. (1st Sgt.) [G, 53], 409
Miller, David [C, 38 Bn.], 446
Erastus T. [B, 28], 312
Ira A. (2nd Lt.) [H, 56], 337
James B. (1st Lt., Prov. Mar.) [Garnett], 256
John J. (4th Cpl.) [C, 28], 313
John R. [C, 38 Bn.], 446
Joseph T. (3rd Lt.) [E, 38], 387
Patrick H. (2nd Sgt.) [A, 3], 194
Robert D. [F, 18], 281
William A. (2nd Lt.) [F, 18], 281
William T. (1st Cpl.) [G, 1], 187
Millner, Cornelius W. (Jr. 2nd Lt.) [I, 57], 177
James W. [K, 38], 395
Mills, Caleb W. [D, 38], 387
John J. [F, 56], 336
Major G. [B, 24], 243
Nathaniel H. [C, 56], 331
Thomas M. [C, 56], 331
Walter C. [I, 53], 413
William H. [C, 56], 331
Miltier, Daniel [D, 9], 350
Milton, Charles A. [B, 8], 262
William L. [K, 8], 270
Minetree, William D. [E, 3], 198
Minnich, William E. (4th Sgt.) [K, 28], 324
Minor, Andrew T. [I, 1], 191
Peter H. [E, 19], 298
Minter, Jesse L. [D, 28], 315
Mitchel, William L. [D, 1], 182
Mitchell, Albert T. [F, 28], 318
Benjamin R. [H, 18], 286
Charles L. [F, 28], 318
Daniel B. [C, 3], 196
David W. [H, 38], 393
George W. [D, 1], 186
George W. [G, 38], 391

George William (1st Lt.) [H, 3], 201
Henry C. [D, 38], 387
John Rice [A, 11], 223
John S. [I, 53], 413
John W. [F, 28], 318
Lindith R. [G, 28], 321
R.O. [F, 7], 216
Robert D. (1st Cpl.) [G, 28], 319
Robert F. [C, 3], ,196
Robert M., Jr. (Capt.) [A, 11], 222
Thomas H. [A, 11], 223
Thomas J. [G, 7], 217
William H. [B, 56], 329
William H. (4th Cpl.) [F, 28], 317
William R. [E, 38], 389
William W. [B, 14], 362
Modena, Benjamin J. [C, 56], 331
Moffitt, Robert F. [K, 8], 508
Money, E. Frank (Sgt.) [G, 8], 267
Monroe, Charles [G, 19], 302
John T. [C, 11], 226
Nelson (3rd Sgt.) [G, 19], 301
William J. [C, 11], 226
Monserrate, Michael D. [H, 3], 202
Montague, Charles P. [H, 53], 411
Monte, William G. [G, 9], 354
Montgomery, John B. [C, 57], 424
Moody, Joseph D. [E, 53], 407
Thomas D. [F, 9], 353
Moon, Daniel P. [I, 53], 413
Jacob N. [C, 19], 295
Julian K. [C, 14], 365
Ransom B. (Capt., AQM) [53], 398
Samuel W. [C, 19], 295
William W. [I, 18], 287
Mooney, David G. [D, 56], 333
E. [F, 7], 216
Madison [E, 19], 298
Sidney C. [C, 24], 241
Thomas J. [A, 19], 293
Moore, Alexander B. (2nd Sgt.) [D, 8], 256
Benjamin [K, 24], 254
Charles W. (1st Lt.) [C, 7], 211
Daniel J. [C, 7], 212
George H. [E, 14], 508
George T. (4th Cpl.) [D, 14], 366

Hartwell S. [D, 56], 333
Henry H. (2nd Sgt.) [G, 38], 391
Henry M. (1st Cpl.) [G, 14], 371
Henry P. [B, 18], 275
Hiram [D, 38 Bn.], 449
J.P. [D, 56], 333
James G. [I, 3], 203
James H. (2nd Lt.) [B, 56], 328
James M. [G, 11], 232
Jerry [D, 38 Bn.], 449
John [A, 38 Bn.], 441
John B. [G, 14], 372
Joseph E. [B, 56], 329
M.J. [E, 18], 280
P.S. [D, 56], 333
R.S. [A, 38 Bn.], 441
Samuel T. (Cpl.) [A, 18], 273
Thomas [A, 38 Bn.], 441
Tilford J. (3rd Sgt.) [K, 57], 435
William J. [B, 18], 275
William R. [E, 56], 334
William S. [D, 38 Bn.], 449
Moorefield, John W. (2nd Cpl.) [H, 14], 374
William A. (Com. Sgt.) [14], 359
Moorman, Samuel E. [B, 11], 224
William H. [F, 28], 318
Moran, A.F. [A, 38 Bn.], 441
William [C, 57], 424
Morecock, Albert M. [K, 53], 416
Morefield, P.H. [B, 38 Bn.], 508
Moreland, James B. [G, 9], 354
Morgan, Austin F. (Cpl.) [G, 18], 282
George T. [G, 38], 391
James W. [C, 53], 403
John J. [G, 38], 391
John J. (1st Cpl.) [A, 57], 419
Lafayette [E, 38], 389
Robert W. [C, 11], 226
Thomas C. [G, 28], 321
William [D, 9], 350
William H. [G, 28], 321
Moriarty, John (5th Sgt.) [C, 1], 184
Moring, Floyd C. [C, 53], 403
Morris, Albert J. [D, 8], 265
Charles S. [K, 9], 508
Eldridge (Capt.) [G, 1], 187
George H. [C, 14], 365
George P. [B, 38 Bn.], 443

James A. [B, 11], 224
James E. [B, 19], 294
James E. [D, 53], 405
James W. [K, 14], 377
John Henry [C, 14], 365
John Hillary [C, 14], 365
John R. [H, 57], 433
John W. [C, 14], 365
Joseph B. [C, 38 Bn.], 446
Nathaniel W. [C, 19], 296
Robert B. [C, 14], 365
Robert J. [H, 57], 433
Silas M. [G, 28], 321
Thomas [C, 7], 212
Thomas C. (1st Lt.) [C, 14], 363
Uriah C. [C, 9], 349
William E. [E, 56], 334
William L. (2nd Cpl.) [C, 19], 295
Morrisett, John T. [C, 9], 349
William [B, 3], 195
Morrison, John R. [K, 38], 395
William A. [K, 18], 289
Morriss, Zachariah T. [K, 3], 205
Morrissett, Peter B. (Cpl.) [B, 3], 195
Morton, Charles B. (Surg.) [7], 207
Jacob T. [A, 53], 400
Jacob W. [I, 56], 340
James W. [E, 18], 280
Jeremiah, Jr. [C, 7], 208
Nathaniel S. (1st Cpl.) [F, 18], 281
Samuel H. (Sgt.) [C, 18], 276
Tazewell S. [D, 1], 186
William A. [K, 11], 237
Mosby, William B. [H, 1], 189
Moseley, James E. [A, 57], 344
Thomas F. [B, 38 Bn.], 443
Moser, Charles (Mus.) [H, 53], 411
Moses, Charles T. [H, 18], 286
John T. (5th Sgt.) [G, 53], 409
Joseph M. (Jr. 2nd Lt.) [G, 53], 409
Moss, Alexander C. [D, 1], 186
Motley, Daniel J. [B, 38], 383
George M. [H, 14], 374
Joseph [H, 14], 374
Richard W. [H, 38], 393
Robert D. [H, 14], 374
William D. [A, 38], 381
Mottley, John T. [C, 18], 273

Mountcastle, John L. [K, 53], 416
    William D. [B, 24], 243
Mouring, Thomas [H, 1], 189
    William H. (Cpl.) [B, 3], 195
Moyer, Jacob [K, 19], 307
Moyers, J.M. [F, 57], 179
Muck, Daniel H. [K, 38], 395
    Samuel H. [K, 38], 395
Mullen, Henry W. (Cpl.) [K, 57], 435
Mullins, Andrew J. [B, 57], 422
    Booker [B, 57], 422
    George C. (Cpl.) [D, 7], 213
    Henry M. [B, 57], 422
    John W. (1st Lt.) [D, 7], 213
    William [I, 57], 434
Muncey, Wiley Winton [D, 7], 214
Munda, James E. [B, 38 Bn.], 443
Mundy, Isaac L. [E, 19], 298
    Jonathan B. [E, 19], 298
    Thomas W. (2nd Sgt.) [E, 19], 297
Murden, Joshua [B, 3], 194
Murphy, Enos [G, 9], 355
    John W. [D, 57], 425
    Pleasant [F, 57], 429
    Robert B. [D, 57], 425
    Wyatt B. [D, 57], 425
Murray, Elisha [F, 3], 200
    Lafayette [C, 14], 365
    R.A. [G, 14], 372
    William H. (5th Sgt.) [K, 3], 204
Murrell, Charles H. (1st Cpl.) [C, 11], 225
    Charles P. [D, 18], 278
    James W. [A, 38], 381
    Robert A. [C, 11], 226
Murrie, James M. (1st Lt.) [B, 18], 274
Murry, Barney [D, 11], 227
    Jacob P. [D, 11], 227
    John A. [D, 11], 228
    Oliver H. (4th Sgt.) [D, 11], 227
Muse, Edwin H. (2nd Lt.) [G, 18], 282
    John C. [D, 24], 247
Musgrove, Christopher A. [B, 14], 362
Mustain, Creed G. [D, 57], 425
    J.C. [G, 53], 410
    R.A. (Capt.) [G, 53], 409
    Thomas N. [D, 57], 425
Myers, Alfred [B, 28], 312
    C.A. [B, 38 Bn.], 444

    Charlton E. [B, 28], 312
    Jacob W. [B, 28], 312
    John W. (1st Sgt.) [I, 19], 304
    Joseph S. [F, 11], 230
    Peter C. [H, 8], 508
    Robert [A, 38], 381
    Samuel W. (4th Sgt.) [H, 11], 233
    Stephen A. [G, 9], 355
    Stephen R. [D, 38], 387
    Thomas H. (Sgt.) [D, 9], 350
    Wilson P. [A, 38], 381
Myrick, Henry L. [G, 3], 201
    Nathaniel T. [G, 3], 201
    Walter [F, 53], 408

-N-

Naff, Abram I. (5th Sgt.) [F, 57], 428
    Isaac M. [F, 57], 429
Nance, Paschal J. [G, 38], 321
Napier, James M. [C, 19], 296
    John R. [C, 19], 296
Nash, Richard James [G, 9], 355
    William H. [A, 3], 195
Naylor, John T. [H, 57], 433
Neal, Abraham Thomas [G, 53], 410
    James H. [H, 14], 374
    James H. [E, 14], 369
    John W. [I, 18], 287
    S.S. [I, 1], 191
Neathawk, Edward S. [A, 53], 400
Neathery, Joseph H. (2nd Cpl.) [A, 53], 399
Neese, W.H. [D, 56], 333
Neighbours, Green L. [D, 28], 315
    Jonathan T. [D, 28], 315
Nelms, Elijah [E, 9], 352
Nelson, Frank W. (1st Lt.) [A, 56], 327
    Hugh (Capt.) [F, 28], 317
    Kinloch (1st Lt. Ord. Off.)
    [Kemper], 179
    William G. (2nd Cpl.) [G, 14], 371
    William H. (4th Sgt.) [A, 56], 327
    William S. [G, 11], 232
Nethery, Alexander [G, 38], 392
    George D. [G, 14], 372
    Richard E. [K, 14], 377
Neville, Louis C. [E, 11], 229
    William S. [G, 9], 355
New, James W. [K, 53], 416

Thomas W. [K, 53], 416
Newcomb, Henry J. [G, 56], 337
James H. [G, 56], 337
James R. [C, 18], 277
William T. [G, 38], 392
Winfield T. [C, 53], 403
Newlon, James M. (4th Cpl.) [B, 8], 261
Newman, Alexander [B, 38 Bn.], 444
Callohill M. [B, 14], 363
Mills N. [F, 53], 408
Robert [D, 53], 508
William R. [D, 8], 265
Newton, George A. (1st Sgt.) [B, 38 Bn.], 442
George W. [D, 38], 387
Henry J. [G, 14], 372
John [G, 14], 372
Joseph [E, 14], 369
Patrick J. [G, 14], 373
William J. [D, 56], 333
William T. [G, 14], 373
William W. [D, 56], 333
Nichol, Thaddeus W. (Mus.) [7], 209
Nicholas, Lorenzo D. [D, 56], 333
Robert C. (Capt., ACS) [56], 326
William H. [D, 56], 333
Nichols, Charles [C, 57], 424
George H. (Bugler) [C, 38 Bn.], 445
James W. [C, 57], 419
John G. [I, 28], 323
Nicholson, Richard H. [F, 14], 371
Niday, David P. [C, 28], 314
Niemeyer, John C. (1st Lt.) [I, 9], 355
Nimmo, Hiram [E, 19], 298
Noakes, James N. [B, 7], 211
Nobles, Benjamin R. [C, 1], 184
Noblin, Alexander [K, 14], 377
John H. [G, 14], 373
Noel, James H. [E, 11], 229
Thomas F. [C, 14], 365
Noell, James D. (2nd Sgt.) [A, 53], 399
William T. [D, 38 Bn.], 449
Nofsinger, Lewis (1st Sgt.) [D, 11], 227
Nolting, George A. [H, 1], 189
Norfleet, Jesse [I, 9], 356
Norman, Henry J. [K, 38], 395
James M. (Sgt.) [C, 38], 384

Norris, James B. [H, 57], 432
James H. [H, 56], 339
James L. (Sgt.) [A, 38 Bn.], 439
James R. [H, 57], 433
William H. [H, 57], 433
Norsworthy, John S. [G, 3], 201
Northcross, Richard W.M. [F, 53], 408
Norton, George F. (Capt.) [D, 1], 185
Hugh [D, 38], 387
Norvell, George P. (2nd Lt.) [E, 11], 228
Joseph B. [E, 19], 298
Ryland H. (3rd Sgt.) [H, 1], 188
Nowlan, Thomas B. (3rd Sgt.) [E, 3], 198
Nowlin, William S. (Asst. Surg.) [38], 379
Nuchols, James A. [B, 38], 383
Nuckolds, David R. [B, 38], 383
Nuckols, Edward G. [H, 1], 189
Nunn, Edmund [I, 24], 253
Josiah W. [H, 24], 252
Nunnally, Edward D. [C, 38 Bn.], 446
Samuel E. [C, 53], 404
William T. [C, 9], 349

-O-
O'Brian, Hugh [I, 14], 376
O'Brien, Timothy (4th Sgt.) [B, 19], 294
Bat [K, 8], 270
O'Bryant, Thomas H. [A, 57], 420
O'Conner, M. [B, 19], 294
O'Donnell, Patrick C. (Cpl.) [H, 3], 201
O'Keeffe, James (Mus.) [G, 1], 187
O'Kennon, Peter [A, 14], 361
O'Neill, John [D, 19], 297
Oakes, Charles H. [E, 57], 428
Edward B. [D, 38], 387
James A. [B, 38], 384
James L. [B, 38], 384
John K. (3rd Cpl.) [B, 38], 382
Thomas C. (3rd Sgt.) [B, 38], 382
Thomas H. [E, 14], 369
Oakley, James K. [C, 38 Bn.], 446
Thomas [C, 38 Bn.], 508
Oaks, Robert J. [E, 38], 389
Obenshain, James P. (4th Sgt.) [A, 28],

310
Joel B. [A, 28], 311
Samuel S. [A, 28], 311
William R. [A, 28], 311
Odell, Thomas M. (2nd Sgt.) [E, 53], 406
Oden, Alexander [C, 7], 213
James C. [B, 7], 211
Ogden, Lewis W. (3rd Sgt.) [B, 1], 182
Old, John J. [G, 11], 232
William B. [F, 53], 408
Oliver, Elisha D. (Capt.) [I, 18], 286
James W. (Asst. Surg.) [7], 207
John J. [F, 38], 390
Samuel A. [G, 19], 302
William H. [D, 38 Bn.], 449
Omohundro, Robert L. (4th Cpl.) [C, 19], 295
Thomas W. (3rd Sgt.) [C, 19], 295
Ooles, Uriah [I, 57], 434
Ore, James P. [A, 28], 311
Organ, Marcellus [H, 53], 411
William A. [H, 53], 412
Orndorff, Mason D. [D, 38 Bn.], 449
Orrender, Mathew T. [E, 38], 389
Osborn, John H. [E, 57], 428
Osborne, John E. (5th Sgt.) [D, 18], 277
Osburn, Decatur (1st Sgt.) [A, 8], 260
Otey, Edward T. [B, 1], 183
George [C, 38 Bn.], 446
John M. [B, 57], 422
Kirkwood (Maj.) [11], 221
William Thomas [K, 28], 324
Ousley, Thomas [H, 14], 374
Overbey, P.H. (5th Sgt.) [G, 14], 371
Warren [K, 14], 377
Overby, Henry [G, 18], 283
L.W. (QM Sgt.) [56], 326
Thomas [I, 57], 434
Overfelt, Merit [F, 57], 429
Robert [F, 57], 429
Overstreet, Alexander [G, 11], 232
Benjamin F. [G, 28], 321
James V. [G, 28], 321
Jesse W. (3rd Cpl.) [B, 14], 362
Jesse W. [G, 28], 321
John P. [B, 1], 183
Samuel W. [B, 14], 363

Overton, John W. [C, 53], 404
Owen, Albert H. [A, 53], 400
Beverly B. [A, 38], 381
Coleman B. [E, 57], 428
David L. [B, 38], 384
Drury [D, 57], 508
George R. [C, 38], 385
Henry Thweat (Capt.) [C, 18], 275
James J. [E, 38], 389
James W. [H, 14], 374
James W. [D, 57], 426
John D. [D, 57], 176
Joseph T. [K, 38], 395
Pleasant D. (5th Sgt.) [I, 18], 286
Thomas W. [A, 38], 381
William J. [G, 14], 373
William O. (2nd Sgt.) [B, 14], 361
William R. [A, 38], 381
William T. [G, 38], 392
William T. [E, 57], 428
Wilson [H, 38], 393
Owens, Albert B. [G, 9], 344
Charles [K, 9], 508
John B. [I, 28], 323
John Crowder (Maj.) [9], 346
Thomas C. [G, 9], 355
Thomas E. [F, 8], 266

-P-
Pace, Archibald B. [C, 14], 365
Benjamin H. [H, 57], 433
Edmund M. (Cpl.) [B, 18], 275
William J. [C, 14], 365
Padgett, Charles [F, 28], 318
John F. [D, 53], 405
John J. [E, 11], 229
Joseph [F, 28], 318
Page, Andrew L. [K, 57], 437
D.D. [I, 19], 305
John J.A. [K, 57], 437
Royal M. [I, 19], 305
Zebulon K. [F, 7], 216
Painter, James B. (1st Cpl.) [K, 28], 324
Paitsel, Daniel E. [B, 28], 312
Palmer, Henry (4th Sgt.) [K, 14], 376
Isaac, [A, 24], 241
Samuel [A, 24], 241
William [G, 38], 392

Palmore, John T. [G, 56], 337
Pamplin, David L.A. [A, 8], 261
Parish, Samuel [E, 28], 317
    William D. [E, 56], 334
Park, Charles T. [E, 14], 369
    Thomas A. [E, 14], 369
Parker, Calvin L. (3rd Cpl.) [I, 1], 190
    George W. [G, 24], 508
    Lewis C. [D, 38 Bn.], 449
    William J. [I, 9], 356
Parkerson, George W. [I, 3], 203
    Mills D. [I, 3], 203
    William J. [E, 9], 352
Parks, Charles P. (1st Cpl.) [K, 11], 236
Parr, John H. (Adjt.) [7], 207
Parris, Thomas H. [E, 11], 229
Parrish, Booker S. [A, 11], 223
    William G. [C, 14], 365
Parrott, George W. (1st Sgt.) [D, 19], 296
    James [K, 14], 377
    Lewis [G, 14], 373
    William N. (2nd Sgt.) [I, 7], 217
Parry, Richard L. (4th Cpl.) [D, 53], 405
Parsel, Benjamin F. [G, 57], 431
    Isaiah (Cpl.) [G, 57], 430
    William [A, 57], 420
Parsons, Cornelius [E, 56], 334
    Joseph [I, 53], 413
    Spencer [B, 38], 384
    William H. [E, 3], 198
    Zorobald (Com. Sgt.) [53], 398
Partin, Daniel W. [D, 14], 367
    Samuel B. [F, 18], 281
Partlow, Elisha S. [B, 7], 211
Pate, John B. [C, 57], 424
Pates, John A. [C, 38 Bn.], 446
Patram, Edward F. (3rd Sgt.) [I, 14], 375
Patterson, Cornelius [E, 53], 407
    George W. [G, 28], 321
    George W. (3rd Sgt.) [D, 19], 296
    John M. [D, 19], 297
    John T. [E, 28], 317
    Robert H. [D, 19], 297
    Thomas W. [E, 28], 317
    William [G, 1], 188
    William H. (5th Sgt.) [D, 38 Bn.], 447

Pattillo, John H. (2nd Sgt.) [A, 56], 327
Patton, Waller Tazewell (Col.) [7], 207
Paul, James E. [F, 57], 419
    William L. [F, 57], 429
Paulett, Andrew J. [H, 18], 286
    John T. [F, 18], 281
    Samuel W. [F, 18], 282
Paxton, Cyrus H. (2nd Lt.) [A, 18], 273
    Samuel B. [B, 28], 312
Payne, Arthur [A, 38 Bn.], 441
    Benjamin H. (2nd Sgt.) [C, 14], 363
    Bernard [A, 38 Bn.], 441
    Fielding F. (2nd Lt.) [B, 8], 261
    Francis M. (4th Sgt.) [A, 24], 240
    George A. [C, 14], 365
    James William [H, 1], 189
    Jefferson (3rd Cpl.) [C, 57], 423
    Jesse Armistead (2nd Lt.) [B, 1], 182
    Jesse F. [A, 38 Bn.], 441
    John F. [A, 18], 274
    John R. [C, 38], 385
    John T. [D, 28], 315
    Joseph H. (1st Cpl.) [D, 28], 315
    Joseph T. [C, 38], 385
    Leroy [D, 38], 387
    Pleasant H. [G, 1], 188
    Remus M. (3rd Sgt.) [I, 57], 433
    Richard J. [D, 57], 426
    Tucker W. (4th Sgt.) [C, 14], 363
    William A. (3rd Sgt.) [C, 57], 176
    William E. [A, 38 Bn.], 441
    William F. [B, 18], 275
    William H. [A, 38 Bn.], 441
    William M. (QM) [11], 221
    William T. (3rd Sgt.) [D, 57], 177
Peace, Edwin M. [K, 56], 342
Peake, Luke R. [F, 38], 390
    Mark L. [F, 38], 380
    Thomas L. [F, 38], 390
Pearcy, William [D, 28], 315
Pearson, James [A, 38 Bn.], 441
    James W. (Cpl.) [A, 38 Bn.], 439
    John T. [B, 19], 294
    Richard E. [A, 38 Bn.], 441
Peay, Robert P. [H, 24], 252
Peck, Benjamin W. (3rd Sgt.) [G, 24],

580

Pillow, Daniel A. [C, 11], 226
    Samuel B. [I, 53], 413
Pinckman, Thomas [G, 14], 373
Pinson, Allen [G, 14], 373
Piper, R.R. (Sgt.) [F, 7], 215
Pippin, Elijah [B, 38 Bn.], 444
Pitman, John D. [E, 9], 352
Pitt, Julian V. (Mus.) [G, 38], 391
Pittman, William H. [D, 3], 197
Pitts, Benjamin F. (Cpl.) [E, 7], 214
Planck, A. [E, 18], 280
Plaster, Mark [I, 24], 253
    William Conrad (1st Sgt.) [I, 24], 252
Pleasants, Christopher S. [B, 56], 329
    John (Drummer) [I, 1], 190
Poff, William B. [C, 57], 424
Poindexter, Edward W. [C, 56], 331
    James E. (Capt.) [H, 38], 392
    William D. [G, 11], 232
    William R. (3rd Sgt.) [H, 38], 392
    William Thomas [C, 56], 331
Pointer, William B. [D, 53], 405
Points, Joseph D. [A, 19], 293
    Polk [A, 19], 293
Polak, Jacob [I, 1], 191
Polend, Charles J. [C, 8], 263
Pollard, Eugene M. [I, 14], 376
    George M. (2nd Sgt.) [H, 18], 284
    James E. [A, 14], 361
    Joseph R. [A, 14], 361
    Robert C. [D, 53], 405
    Sheppard [E, 28], 317
Pollock, Thomas Gordon (Capt., AA&IG) [Kemper], 179
Pond, Everett M. (2nd Sgt.) [G, 3], 200
    Robert T. [K, 53], 416
Ponton, Henry E. [G, 19], 302
    N.B. [G, 19], 302
    Richard Hartwell [G, 19], 302
    William H. [G, 19], 302
Pool, John E.P. (4th Sgt.) [E, 14], 368
    John H. [C, 24], 245
    William A. [K, 3], 205
Poore, Robert Henry (Maj.) [14], 359
Pope, Charles W. (4th Cpl.) [B, 38 Bn.], 442
    Herod [G, 3], 201
    Joseph W. (2nd Cpl.) [G, 3], 200

Popham, Thomas G. (Capt.) [B, 7], 210
Porter, Henry T. (Jr. 2nd Lt.) [B, 7], 210
    Pulaski P. (1st Lt.) [B, 19], 293
    William S. (5th Sgt.) [I, 11], 234
Porterfield, Albert G. [F, 24], 249
    David H. (1st Sgt.) [F, 24], 248
    George W. [F, 24], 249
Posey, Benjamin [A, 38], 381
    George W. [A, 38], 381
Poulton, William F. (Cpl.) [H, 8], 268
Powell, Alex E. [C, 1], 184
    Algernon W. [E, 53], 407
    Benjamin F. [B, 3], 195
    Benjamin F. (1st Sgt.) [H, 24], 251
    Charles W. [E, 9], 352
    Cornelius (3rd Cpl.) [E, 9], 351
    Edward [H, 57], 433
    F.W. (3rd Sgt.) [A, 38 Bn.], 439
    Gilbert W. [B, 56], 329
    Henry J. [E, 9], 352
    Henry M. [G, 28], 321
    James A. [E, 38], 389
    James E. [C, 38 Bn.], 446
    John T. (1st Lt.) [G, 19], 300
    Joseph W. [D, 38], 387
    L.E. [F, 28], 318
    Matthew W. [F, 9], 353
    Richard M. [K, 14], 377
    Robert H. [D, 38], 387
    Thomas [D, 53], 405
    Thomas A. [K, 19], 307
    Thomas J. [H, 38], 393
    Willard L. (3rd Lt.) [F, 19], 299
    William B. [E, 53], 177
    William H. [I, 19], 305
    William H. [D, 53], 405
Power, William H. [I, 18], 287
Powers, John (2nd Cpl.) [K, 11], 236
Poyner, William H. [H, 53], 412
Prease, Charles W. [G, 1], 188
Presgraves, George W. [I, 8], 269
    James R. (3rd Cpl.) [I, 8], 269
    John R. (2nd Lt.) [I, 8], 268
    William T. [I, 8], 269
Preston, Edward T. [K, 18], 289
Prewett, David D. [D, 38], 387
    Ephraim [D, 38], 387
    Joseph [D, 53], 405

Prewitt, Abel [D, 38], 387
Price, George H. (4th Cpl.) [F, 24], 249
    Henry C. (3rd Cpl.) [F, 11], 230
    James A. [F, 24], 249
    Samuel C. (Capt., AQM) [18], 272
    William H. (2nd Lt.) [I, 56], 339
Prichard, William B. (Capt.) [B, 38], 382
Priddy, E. [D, 1], 186
    William B. [H, 57], 433
Prillaman, Christian S. (2nd Lt.) [B, 57], 421
    Fleming M. (5th Sgt.) [B, 57], 421
    Isaac C. (2nd Lt.) [B, 57], 421
Pritchard, Henry J. [A, 38 Bn.], 441
    James I. [D, 11], 228
Pritchett, Belfield [E, 19], 299
    James D. [E, 19], 299
    Peter [H, 56], 339
Proffit, Henry J. [H, 19], 304
    William N. [H, 19], 304
Pruden, Joseph H. [F, 9], 508
    Keeney [F, 9], 353
Pruitt, Elijah [I, 53], 413
Pryor, William Hamlen (Maj.) [3], 193
Puckett, James A. [I, 14], 376
    John H. [I, 14], 376
    John T. [C, 9], 349
    John W. [I, 14], 376
Puggh, Joseph A. [D, 56], 333
Pugh, Charles E. [A, 11], 223
    Clark W. [A, 24], 241
    Columbus C. [D, 57], 426
    John J. [C, 11], 226
    Presley A. [I, 56], 340
Pulley, Benjamin [G, 3], 201
Purcell, John P. (3rd Sgt.) [G, 56], 336
    Thomas [F, 9], 353
Purduy, William S. [B, 56], 329
Purdy, George E. [H, 24], 252
Purvis, Albert A. [G, 19], 302
    Clifford C. [G, 19], 302
    Joseph E. (2nd Sgt.) [G, 19], 301
    William H. [G, 19], 302
Puryear, Isaiah [E, 14], 369
    Mathew J. [C, 3], 196
Pyron, John H. [I, 57], 434

-Q-
Quinn, Archibald S. [I, 19], 305
    James F. (4th Sgt.) [C, 19], 295

-R-
Raber, Henry L. [A, 8], 261
Rabey, Thomas [I, 9], 356
Racer, Charles [I, 7], 218
    George H. [K, 7], 220
    James O.B. (1st Sgt.) [K, 7], 219
Rader, George W. [F, 11], 230
    Oliver Perry [D, 11], 228
    William [F, 11], 230
Radford, Greenville R. [C, 57], 424
Ragan, James H. (1st Lt.) [F, 11], 229
    John J. [I, 57], 434
Ragland, Evan J. (2nd Lt.) [A, 53], 399
    Joseph H. [C, 38 Bn.], 446
Ragsdale, James J. [I, 57], 434
Rainey, Charles W. (2nd Lt.) [A, 11], 222
    Mathew J. [G, 38], 392
    P.L. [F, 14], 371
    Robert W. [B, 56], 329
Rakes, Sparrel [C, 57], 424
Ramsay, Warren [G, 14], 373
Ramsey, Henry C. [B, 57], 422
    James Y. [E, 14], 369
    Jesse H. [D, 24], 247
    William B. [E, 14], 369
    William B. [B, 57], 422
    William H. [B, 57], 177
    William Henry (Capt.) [E, 57], 426
    William S. [I, 53], 413
Ramy, T.G. [B, 38 Bn.], 444
Randolph, Peyton (Capt., AIG) [Armistead], 343
    William L. (1st Lt., Ord. Off.) [Armistead], 344
Ransom, Henry C. [K, 18], 289
    Robert Smith (Capt.) [I, 57], 433
Ranson, John [F, 18], 282
Rash, James S. [I, 56], 340
    William H. [B, 53], 401
Rawlings, James W. [B, 8], 262
Rawls, Francis H. [A, 14], 361
    George T. [D, 3], 197
Ray, Abner [B, 57], 422

Eusibeous [B, 57], 419
George F. [A, 38], 381
John [B, 57], 422
William R. [B, 57], 422
Rayford, A.C. [B, 38 Bn.], 444
Albert N. [B, 9], 348
Rea, R.B. [I, 7], 218
William T. (3rd Sgt.) [K, 19], 306
Read, James W. [D, 38], 387
John Postell Williamson (Maj.)
[38 Bn.], 438
Stephen P. (1st Lt.) [F, 14], 369
Reames, Edward H. [K, 18], 289
Isham D. [C, 9], 349
Peter S. (1st Cpl.) [B, 53], 401
William H. [G, 18], 283
Reaney, John P. [E, 3], 198
Reaves, Thomas L. [K, 14], 377
Reay, Jerman F. [H, 24], 252
Joseph O. [H, 24], 252
Rector, Albin [A, 38 Bn.], 441
Charles H. [A, 38 Bn.], 441
Marion [A, 38 Bn.], 441
Thomas S. (1st Cpl.) [A, 11], 222
Redd, Richard L. [G, 56], 337
Thomas (1st Cpl.) [D, 53], 404
William S. (2nd 2nd Lt.) [H, 24],
251
Redford, Cornelius A. [G, 1], 188
Redman, Stephen [K, 57], 437
Reed, Charles W. (1st Sgt.) [G, 8], 267
David C. (3rd Sgt.) [G, 3], 200
Richard S. [C, 7], 213
Reese, Abner R. [F, 53], 408
Joseph M. [G, 38], 392
Richard [B, 38 Bn.], 444
William [F, 53], 408
William S. [E, 24], 248
Reeve, Edward P. (1st Lt.) [D, 1], 185
Reeves, Daniel D. [B, 38 Bn.], 444
John F. [H, 8], 268
Reid, James H. [K, 11], 237
Robert E. [D, 9], 350
William H.A. [K, 11], 237
William P. (1st Sgt.) [B, 8], 261
Reinhart, William W. [H, 57], 433
Repass, Stephen A. (2nd Lt.) [I, 28],
322
Revell, George A. [G, 9], 355

Randall [G, 9], 355
Rey, William T. [C, 38 Bn.], 446
Reynolds, Benjamin L. [D, 38 Bn.],
449
Coleman [B, 38], 384
George W. [H, 53], 412
James R. [K, 19], 307
John L. [B, 28], 312
Joseph D. [B, 38], 384
Ralph C. (3rd Sgt.) [B, 28], 311
Samuel T. [E, 14], 369
Terrill [I, 28], 323
Rhoades, Richard B. (Sgt.) [C, 7], 212
Rhodes, Aaron E. [I, 28], 323
Andrew J. [F, 19], 300
Franklin [H, 56], 339
Hezekiah [H, 56], 339
Robert P. [F, 19], 300
Rice, James J. [H, 38], 393
James P. (2nd Sgt.) [E, 38], 388
William A. [H, 53], 412
William A. [C, 11], 226
Richards, Jesse H. [A, 38], 381
John R. (Asst. Surg.) [56], 326
King D. [A, 57], 420
Richardson, Benjamin E. [F, 57], 429
Edward G. (2nd Sgt.) [A, 28], 310
John (Capt.) [F, 56], 335
John S. [C, 14], 365
John S. [C, 38], 385
John T. [E, 14], 369
John W. (Mus.) [F, 3], 199
Peter [D, 28], 316
Richard B. (2nd Cpl.) [A, 28], 310
Richard J. (3rd Sgt.) [C, 14], 363
Robert H. [G, 14], 373
Robert S. [C, 14], 365
Sylvester H. (2nd Lt.) [B, 53], 400
William [F, 56], 336
William D.H. [A, 38], 381
William James (Capt.) [D, 9], 350
William T. [K, 56], 342
Richerson, Peter [C, 57], 424
Richeson, Jesse V. (1st Lt.) [H, 19],
303
Ricketts, Reuben [E, 38], 389
Rickman, Ethelbert T. [K, 3], 205
Jennings [K, 14], 377
Riddick, Amos [I, 9], 356

Robert E. [F, 3], 200
Riddle, George W. [I, 53], 413
    John A. [B, 38], 384
    Thomas C. [I, 53], 413
Ridout, David T. [B, 56], 329
Riggins, Charles A. [E, 14], 177
    John J. [F, 18], 282
    Robert D. [G, 38], 392
Rigna, Henry [E, 57], 428
Rigney, Jehu H. [C, 24], 245
Riley, A. [I, 7], 218
    William [A, 38 Bn.], 508
    William H. [A, 38 Bn.], 441
Ripley, Marvin V.B. (5th Sgt.) [K, 57], 435
Ritchie, Francis H. (Mus.) [C, 53], 403
Ritenour, Ambrose B. [B, 7], 211
Rivercomb, Richard H. (1st Lt.) [G, 7], 216
Rives, Abram [C, 38], 385
    Edward (Surg.) [28], 309
    Ephraim [C, 38], 385
Roach, Elijah T. [K, 18], 289
    George W. [C, 8], 263
    John A. [G, 28], 321
Roane, Alonzo B. [G, 9], 508
Roark, Booker [F, 38], 390
    William P. [F, 38], 390
Robbins, Daniel [B, 53], 401
    James P. [B, 53], 402
Roberson, Benjamin S. [C, 57], 424
    Hezekiah [G, 57], 431
Roberts, Benjamin D. [K, 7], 220
    John [G, 28], 321
    John C. [A, 14], 361
    John Lynch [E, 8], 317
    Patrick H. [H, 18], 286
    Pleasant A. [C, 11], 226
    Richard F. [C, 38 Bn.], 446
    William H. [A, 14], 361
Robertson, Abner [C, 18], 277
    Daniel C. [K, 38], 395
    Edward S. (2nd Lt.) [D, 57], 425
    Elisha Z. [D, 56], 333
    George W. [H, 53], 412
    Granville W. [F, 57], 429
    Henry H. [K, 38], 395
    Joel T. [D, 57], 426
    John J. [F, 57], 429

John S. [D, 38], 387
John T. [D, 57], 426
Joseph R. [C, 38 Bn.], 446
Robert A. (Cpl.) [C, 18], 276
Samuel A. [I, 57], 435
Thomas D. [C, 19], 296
William B. (2nd Sgt.) [I, 14], 375
William E.F. (1st Cpl.) [B, 38], 382
William H.K. [A, 18], 274
William J. (3rd Cpl.) [D, 56], 331
William T. [K, 38], 395
Robey, Austin [F, 38], 390
    C. Ozias (Cpl.) [G, 8], 267
    George W. [F, 38], 390
    Lewis H. [G, 8], 267
    William J. [G, 8], 267
Robins, Logan S. (1st Lt.) [B, 1], 182
Robinson, Albert [D, 53], 405
    Benjamin H. (Sr. 2nd Lt.) [B, 38 Bn.], 442
    E.H. [F, 28], 318
    Eugene D. (1st Lt.) [D, 53], 404
    Jacob T. [G, 53], 410
    James C. [B, 38 Bn.], 444
    James E. [I, 1], 191
    James H. (2nd Lt.) [K, 9], 357
    Jesse A. [F, 18], 282
    John [A, 38 Bn.], 441
    John E.W. [A, 28], 311
    John H. [E, 38], 389
    Lorimer B. [D, 53], 405
    Rufus W. (2nd Sgt.) [B, 19], 293
    William A. [C, 56], 331
    William H. [B, 38 Bn.], 444
Rodenhizer, John W. [H, 14], 375
Roffe, Lewis J. (1st Cpl.) [G, 38], 391
Rogers, Cuthbert B. [D, 8], 265
    George W. [H, 11], 233
    James B. [A, 11], 223
    Jesse W. [D, 14], 367
    John [C, 38 Bn.], 446
    M.M. (1st Lt.) [A, 38 Bn.], 439
    Robert W. [E, 8], 265
    S. Aden [D, 8], 265
    Thomas S. [G, 1], 188
    William H. [B, 38 Bn.], 444
Roller, Albert H. (1st Sgt.) [I, 28], 322
Rollins, Alfred F. [A, 8], 261

Romine, Joseph B. (2nd Cpl.) [G, 7], 216
Ronk, Samuel [E, 28], 317
Rooke, Martin V. [F, 53], 408
Roop, Fleming S. [F, 11], 231
    H.R. [F, 11], 231
Roper, Edwin [B, 38 Bn.], 444
Rorer, Charles H. [D, 57], 176
Ross, James E. [C, 14], 365
    Lewis T. [I, 24], 253
    Robert Budds [D, 38 Bn.], 449
    Thomas H. (3rd Sgt.) [D, 38 Bn.], 447
    William D. [C, 14], 365
Rosser, Jabez R. (Jr. 2nd Lt.) [C, 11], 225
    James M. (Jr. 2nd Lt.) [K, 7], 219
    Walter C. [C, 11], 226
Rosson, Emanuel Barnette [K, 7], 220
    George W. [G, 7], 217
Rountree, Daniel R. [C, 38 Bn.], 446
Rourke, John [B, 38 Bn.], 444
Rover, Armistead D. (5th Sgt.) [B, 14], 361
Rowe, Jason E. [D, 3], 197
Rowland, Rufus F. (4th Sgt.) [G, 24], 250
    William P. (4th Sgt.) [K, 57], 435
Rowles, Wilford G. (1st Lt.) [D, 57], 424
    William [E, 57], 428
Rowlett, James T. [C, 9], 349
    John F. [D, 14], 367
    Peter A. [C, 9], 349
Royster, James A. [G, 1], 188
    Norborne L. [G, 1], 188
Royston, Zachariah V. [B, 8], 262
Rucker, A. McD. [F, 28], 318
    Alfred R. [A, 14], 361
    Andrew J. [D, 28], 316
    John C. (3rd Cpl.) [F, 28], 317
    William T. [D, 24], 247
Rudasill, Andrew C. (3rd Sgt.) [B, 7], 210
Rudd, George W. [F, 14], 371
Ruddell, George W. [I, 28], 323
    James H. [I, 28], 323
    Michael [I, 28], 323
Rudisill, Jacob R. (2nd Lt.) [D, 56], 331

Runyon, Alexander C. [E, 24], 248
    William B. [E, 24], 248
Russell, Jacob P. (3rd Sgt.) [E, 9], 351
    James W. [A, 8], 261
    Samuel C. [C, 9], 349
    William T. [A, 14], 361
Rutledge, Granville H. [F, 24], 249
Ryals, James D. [E, 18], 177
Ryan, Obediah [D, 28], 316
    Patrick P. (Mus.) [K, 14], 376

-S-

Sadler, John F. [E, 56], 334
    Samuel C. [E, 56], 334
Sale, George W. (5th Sgt.) [K, 11], 236
    James Irving (2nd Lt.) [H, 53], 410
    James P. [G, 11], 232
    John E. [G, 9], 355
Salmon, James (3rd Lt.) [E, 19], 297
Sandbower, John D. [B, 7], 211
Sanders, Thomas L. [E, 56], 334
Sandifer, Robert T. [B, 11], 224
    William A. (5th Sgt.) [B, 11], 223
Sandridge, G.W. (4th Cpl.) [H, 56], 337
    James J. (2nd Cpl.) [E, 19], 298
    W.O. [I, 7], 218
    William R. [I, 7], 218
    Zachariah [I, 7], 218
Sarver, Adam A. [C, 28], 314
    Demarcus [D, 7], 214
    Michael A. [C, 28], 314
Satterfield, Onslow J. [K, 14], 377
Saunders, Armistead W. [H, 8], 268
    Benjamin F. [H, 8], 268
    Fleming (Capt.) [D, 24], 245
    Frederick C. (2nd Lt.) [E, 24], 247
    George [C, 8], 263
    George F. [A, 38 Bn.], 441
    Gustavus [F, 24], 249
    Hector A. [H, 8], 268
    James B. [F, 38], 390
    James D. [D, 57], 426
    James H. [F, 24], 249
    John T. [E, 56], 334
    Robert A. [D, 38 Bn.], 449
    Robert W. [D, 53], 405
    Samuel T. [D, 18], 278

Josiah W. [B, 57], 422
Ralph S. [B, 38], 384
Robert M. [E, 38], 389
Samuel C. [F, 11], 231
Samuel C. [H, 24], 252
Tavenor S. [K, 38], 395
Thomas [D, 57], 426
William B. [C, 24], 245
William T. [C, 38], 385
William T. [D, 57], 426
Shepard, Samuel M. (5th Sgt.) [A, 57], 419
Shepherd, Abraham, Jr. [C, 14], 365
Sheppard, Josiah (4th Cpl.) [D, 18], 277
William A. (1st Cpl.) [E, 3], 198
Shickel, Theophilus J.H. (2nd Sgt.) [K, 57], 435
Shields, David T. [A, 18], 274
John H. [A, 18], 274
William A. [I, 18], 287
Shifflett, Octavius M. (3rd Sgt.) [H, 57], 432
Shiflett, James [F, 19], 300
Thomas [C, 14], 365
Shipman, John M. [I, 8], 269
Shively, William [C, 57], 424
Shockley, Martin V.B. (Capt.) [C, 24], 243
Richard [C, 24], 245
William [C, 24], 245
William H. (1st Cpl.) [I, 24], 253
Shoemaker, George W. [I, 1], 191
Shook, James B. [B, 38 Bn.], 444
Shope, John [F, 19], 300
Short, Andrew J. [I, 28], 323
George W. [K, 24], 254
Gideon A. [H, 53], 412
William B. [E, 56], 334
Shorter, Tazewell C. [G, 57], 431
William H. [K, 11], 237
Woodson H. [D, 18], 279
Shotwell, Randolph A. [H, 8], 268
William J. [C, 7], 207
Shrigley, Jacob R. [A, 8], 261
Shumate, James L. (5th Sgt.) [K, 38], 394
Samuel H. [K, 38], 395
Silcott, James B. [E, 8], 265

Sillman, Charles L. [A, 38 Bn.], 441
Silvey, Alfred [K, 11], 237
Simmons, Benjamin O. [D, 3], 197
Benjamin W. [F, 14], 371
George H. [G, 3], 201
Peter [G, 3], 201
Samuel [B, 56], 329
Thomas H. (5th Sgt.) [A, 24], 240
William [D, 11], 228
William [B, 56], 329
William S. [B, 11], 224
Simms, Alexander [G, 28], 321
Edmund B. [C, 7], 213
William H. [H, 18], 286
Simpkins, Richard L. [A, 24], 241
Simpson, Andrew J. (3rd Sgt.) [D, 1], 185
Archer M. [C, 38], 385
Charles W. (5th Cpl.) [E, 11], 222
John C. [D, 11], 228
Ulum B. [D, 57], 426
William J. (2nd Cpl.) [E, 28], 316
William R. [I, 53], 414
Sims, William B. [B, 14], 363
Sinclair, Wallace W. [C, 8], 260
Singleton, Abram [F, 38], 390
James [G, 38], 392
James F. [H, 14], 508
Joseph [F, 38], 379
Sink, Jesse [B, 24], 243
John H. (4th Cpl.) [B, 24], 242
William [B, 24], 243
Sinnott, John J. [H, 1], 189
Sisson, Newton H. [C, 7], 213
Sizemore, John B. [K, 14], 377
Thomas L. [G, 14], 373
Skeeter, William J. [I, 9], 356
Skelton, Alexander [A, 53], 400
Skillman, John W. [I, 8], 260
Skinnell, Joseph [D, 38 Bn.], 449
Skinner, Abraham [D, 9], 350
Charles E. [B, 8], 262
James H. [F, 28], 318
Robert [K, 7], 220
Slagle, David H. [A, 11], 223
Slate, William P. [E, 56], 334
Slater, John R. [I, 7], 218
Slaughter, John B. (1st Sgt.) [D, 53], 404

James [G, 24], 250
James L. (2nd Lt.) [I, 14], 375
John H. (3rd Lt.) [I, 14], 375
Pleasant A. [C, 19], 296
Sneed, Henry H. (3rd Sgt.) [G, 38], 176
John [I, 7], 508
John J. [G, 38], 392
Richard E. [I, 7], 508
Robert L. [C, 38], 385
Thomas W. [B, 38 Bn.], 444
Snellings, George T. [C, 38 Bn.], 447
Snidow, George L. (1st Cpl.) [F, 24], 248
James P. (1st Lt.) [F, 24], 248
William H.H. (Sgt.) [D, 7], 213
Snoddy, Lorenzo L. [A, 57], 421
Snodgrass, Tilghman E. (3rd Lt.) [B, 28], 311
Snow, Pulaski P. [H, 57], 433
William J. [B, 14], 363
Somerville, Robert B. [C, 7], 208
Souter, James R. [E, 7], 215
Southall, Delbert T. [A, 57], 421
Henry M. (1st Cpl.) [K, 53], 414
Southard, Richard [B, 38 Bn.], 444
William R. [I, 57], 435
Southards, James [F, 7], 216
Southern, Leander [E, 24], 248
Sowers, Caleb [A, 24], 241
Edward L. [I, 53], 414
Spangler, Clifton H. (1st Lt.) [A, 28], 310
Sparks, Champ C. (1st Cpl.) [G, 7], 216
Spence, James [G, 8], 260
Spencer, Albert G. [D, 38 Bn.], 449
Andrew J. [B, 57], 422
James A. (1st Cpl.) [K, 14], 376
James W. (2nd Cpl.) [D, 56], 331
Samuel T. [K, 18], 289
Samuel T. [C, 19], 296
Silas [D, 38 Bn.], 449
Sion D. (5th Sgt.) [K, 18], 288
William A. [D, 38 Bn.], 449
William B. (Art.) [B, 38 Bn.], 442
William G. [A, 18], 274
William H. [K, 18], 289
Sperry, John T. (1st Sgt.) [K, 28], 324
Spessard, Hezekiah C. [C, 28], 314
Michael Peters (Capt.) [C, 28],
313
Spickard, H.L. [B, 1], 183
John G. [D, 11], 228
Spinks, E.F. [E, 8], 265
Spivey, James F. [D, 3], 197
Jeremiah J. [D, 3], 197
Spraggins, William S. (2nd Cpl.) [G, 1], 187
Sprouse, Henry [F, 19], 300
St. Clair, B.S. [H, 1], 189
W.P. [F, 11], 231
William H. (2nd Sgt.) [D, 11], 227
St. John, Alexander A. [I, 56], 341
Stagg, James [B, 1], 183
Stainback, George W. [E, 56], 335
George W. (4th Cpl.) [E, 56], 333
Stallings, Archibald A. [K, 38], 395
Javan [I, 9], 356
Stanley, Burwell, [B, 57], 419
Charles T. [K, 57], 437
Crockett J. [H, 24], 252
Dennis P. [B, 57], 422
Ferdinand [B, 57], 419
George W. (4th Cpl.) [D, 38 Bn.], 447
William H. [F, 24], 249
Starkey, Nathaniel [B, 24], 243
Robert M. (2nd Cpl.) [B, 57], 421
Starks, William E. [C, 28], 314
Steber, John [C, 28], 314
Steel, Adison P. [I, 56], 340
O. Frank [G, 8], 267
Steele, Charles T. [B, 28], 312
Steger, A.G., Jr. [D, 1], 186
Charles E. [D, 56], 333
Stell, Clark E. [H, 3], 202
Stephens, Benjamin F. [K, 38], 395
Elias R. [A, 11], 223
Jesse [E, 9], 352
Jesse C. [G, 28], 321
Robert W. (2nd Sgt.) [F, 53], 407
William A. [I, 11], 235
William O. [C, 24], 245
Stephenson, James A. (Com. Sgt.) [8], 259
John B. (3rd Cpl.) [D, 3], 197
Sternberger, Moses (2nd Lt.) [K, 14], 376
Stevens, Albert L. [G, 19], 302

Isaac D. [E, 57], 428
James W. [F, 38], 390
Richard P. [G, 19], 302
Stewart, Charles [C, 38 Bn.], 447
George W. [D, 3], 198
James R.F. [D, 28], 316
James T. [G, 9], 355
John R. (1st Lt., Adjt.) [3], 193
John S. (1st Lt.) [D, 28], 314
John W. [G, 19], 302
Philip H. [A, 11], 223
William H. [E, 11], 229
Stinnett, C.P. [H, 19], 304
J.J. [H, 19], 304
Paulus P. [H, 19], 304
William T. [D, 19], 297
Stinson, George M. [A, 57], 421
Stith, Benjamin A. (5th Sgt.) [H, 53], 411
Cincinnatus [G, 18], 283
William E. [H, 53], 412
William W. (2nd Lt.) [K, 18], 288
Stoaber, William A. (3rd Cpl.) [B, 1], 182
Stockton, John N.C. (1st Lt., Adjt.) [1], 181
Thomas K. [F, 57], 429
Stokes, Allen W. [B, 38], 384
Benton H. (1st Sgt.) [F, 57], 428
Collins [K, 38], 395
Edward S. [H, 3], 202
William C. [D, 38], 387
Stone, Elisha M. (2nd Lt.) [D, 7], 213
George W. [K, 57], 176
John M. [F, 38], 380
Moses H. [B, 57], 422
Samuel M. [D, 38 Bn.], 508
Stephen B. [B, 57], 422
Thomas A. [D, 28], 316
William B. (1st Sgt.) [C, 19], 295
William R. [A, 57], 421
Story, Columbus (Jr. 2nd Lt.) [G, 7], 216
James R. (5th Sgt.) [G, 7], 216
Stoughton, Francisco P. [D, 38 Bn.], 449
Stovall, Joseph G. [G, 24], 250
Strange, Jacob [D, 19], 297
James A. [F, 19], 300

Stratton, Henry F. (2nd Cpl.) [G, 19], 301
Straughan, Stafford H. [D, 19], 297
Street, Richard H. [B, 1], 183
Streets, William M. [G, 7], 217
Stribling, Henry C. (Sgt.) [A, 38 Bn.], 439
Robert H. [I, 11], 235
Robert Mackey (Capt.) [A, 38 Bn.], 439
Strickland, James L. [C, 38], 385
Stringfellow, Bruce W. (1st Lt.) [I, 11], 234
Stringfield, Chapman J. (4th Sgt.) [I, 3], 202
Strong, Nathaniel H. [F, 56], 336
Stuart, Ralph H. (5th Sgt.) [C, 9], 348
William Dabney (Col.) [56], 326
Stultz, George W. [H, 24], 178
Peyton W. [F, 57], 508
Stump, Elijah [C, 57], 176
Green B. [I, 28], 323
Stunz, Charles W. [H, 24], 252
Sturdivant, George W. [G, 3], 201
Styne, Andrew J. (2nd Lt.) [K, 57], 435
James M. (1st Lt.) [K, 57], 435
Sublett, Chasteen M. [D, 1], 186
John P. [D, 7], 214
Suddith, Benjamin B. [E, 7], 215
Martin [A, 38 Bn.], 441
Oscar F. [C, 8], 263
Sullens, James W. [D, 53], 405
Sullings, G.L. [B, 1], 183
Richard [C, 38 Bn.], 447
Sullivan, J.E. (1st Lt.) [C, 38 Bn.], 445
John H. [E, 53], 407
Michael [E, 11], 229
Woodson J. [C, 38 Bn.], 447
Summerson, J.E. [H, 56], 339
Surber, Levi [B, 28], 312
Sutherland, William H. (1st Lt.) [C, 24], 243
Sutler, John T. [B, 19], 294
Sutphin, Floyd [C, 24], 245
James S. (Capt.) [K, 14], 376
Sutton, John C. [B, 38 Bn.], 444
William (5th Cpl.) [C, 38 Bn.], 445
Swain, James T. [C, 8], 263

Rowlan B. [A, 28], 311
Thomas H. [A, 38 Bn.], 441
William E. [K, 8], 508
Swan, Hugh B. (3rd Sgt.) [H, 18], 284
Swann, James M. (3rd Sgt.) [E, 14], 368
Swartz, John B. [C, 8], 263
Sweeney, James T. (3rd Cpl.) [G, 53], 409
Stephen B. [B, 53], 402
Sweet, Patrick H. [D, 53], 405
Swink, George W. (2nd Lt.) [G, 8], 266
Joseph C. [G, 8], 267
Switzer, George M. [A, 24], 241
Sydnor, Eppa (3rd Cpl.) [H, 14], 374
Sykes, Joseph H.M. (Asst. Surg.) [3], 193
William H. [E, 9], 352
Symington, W. Stuart (1st Lt., ADC) [Pickett], 175

-T-

Tabb, Thomas (Capt., AQM) [3], 193
Taliaferro, Edwin [I, 1], 191
William C., Jr. [I, 1], 191
William T. (1st Lt., Adjt.) [24], 239
Talley, George F. [F, 56], 336
Henry M. (1st Sgt.) [G, 14], 371
Robert B. [F, 56], 336
William H. (1st Lt.) [F, 56], 335
Tankersley, Alexander [C, 38], 385
Tanner, Robert K. [E, 7], 215
Willis R. [F, 28], 318
Tansill, George S. (Sgt. Maj.) [7], 207
James G. (1st Lt.) [E, 7], 214
Tapscott, Vincent A. (1st Sgt.) [D, 56], 331
Tate, Calvin O. [F, 56], 336
Fleming D. [F, 56], 336
John S. [F, 56], 336
Nathan G. [F, 56], 336
Tatum, John T. [B, 38], 384
Tavenner, A.O. (3rd Cpl.) [E, 8], 265
Joseph A. (1st Lt.) [E, 8], 265
Thomas E. [F, 8], 266
Taylor, Benjamin [D, 14], 367
Bennett (Capt.) [F, 19], 299
Charles A. [D, 38 Bn.], 449

David M. [H, 56], 339
Eben [A, 8], 261
Enos [E, 9], 352
Eugene G. (1st Sgt.) [B, 19], 293
George W. [B, 56], 329
Henry [A, 24], 240
Jacob S. [C, 28], 314
James [F, 19], 300
James D. (1st Sgt.) [F, 3], 199
James L. [I, 24], 253
James R. [G, 11], 232
Joel F. [D, 19], 297
John [A, 3], 195
John B. (Capt.) [K, 57], 435
John M. [C, 24], 245
John R. [D, 3], 198
John R. [E, 19], 299
John S. (1st Lt.) [D, 14], 366
John W. (5th Sgt.) [C, 14], 364
John Wade [F, 11], 231
Joseph [F, 19], 300
Kirkbride (1st Sgt.) [H, 8], 268
Newton [I, 57], 435
Peterson G. [G, 8], 267
Robert H. (1st Cpl.) [E, 14], 368
Robert J. [B, 56], 329
Thomas J. [K, 7], 220
Thomas S.L. (1st Sgt.) [D, 7], 213
Thomas W. [F, 53], 408
William Benjamin [I, 9], 356
William H. (Asst. Surg.) [19], 291
William H. [I, 53], 414
William R. [D, 18], 279
Williamson B. [I, 9], 356
Tee, John C. (Cpl.) [H, 3], 201
Teel, Josiah W. [B, 24], 243
Temple, Elverton E. [C, 53], 404
Thomas P. (Surg.) [53], 398
William P. (Sgt.) [C, 18], 276
Tench, Edwin J. [D, 24], 247
Tennent, Charles B. [C, 38 Bn.], 447
Julian R. [C, 38 Bn.], 447
Terrell, Berry [C, 38 Bn.], 447
John E. [F, 56], 336
Richmond Q. (3rd Sgt.) [F, 56], 335
Terry, John D. [K, 14], 377
John W. (1st Cpl.) [B, 14], 361
Peter [C, 57], 424

Tillett, Samuel R. [H, 8], 268
Timberlake, Albert [B, 53], 402
    Benjamin N. (2nd Cpl.) [E, 53], 406
    George A. (3rd Lt.) [E, 53], 406
    James W. [B, 53], 402
    John Corbett (Maj.) [53], 398
Tindall, John (1st Cpl.) [D, 19], 296
    Louis C. [D, 56], 333
Tinsley, H.B. [F, 28], 319
    Homer [B, 14], 363
    James W. [C, 7], 213
    Jerome [B, 14], 363
    Peter (Chap.) [28], 309
    Samuel H. [D, 57], 426
    Thomas H. (3rd Sgt.) [B, 14], 361
Tinsman, Francis M. (2nd Sgt.) [F, 8], 266
    John M. [F, 8], 266
Tipton, William R. [E, 24], 248
Tolbert, John N. [B, 7], 211
Toler, H.H. [H, 1], 189
    John D. [H, 38], 393
    John J. [E, 57], 428
Tomlinson, William J. [I, 57], 435
Tompkins, James E. [B, 11], 508
    John [C, 1], 185
    Thomas G. [G, 9], 355
Tonkin, William F. (1st Lt.) [G, 9], 353
Toombs, R.A. [I, 7], 219
Toomey, Jerry [B, 1], 183
Toot, William A. (Sgt. Maj.) [11], 221
Torgee, George W. [D, 38 Bn.], 449
Tosh, Daniel (Cpl.) [D, 57], 425
    Josiah [B, 53], 402
    Samuel H. [I, 18], 287
Totty, George W. [C, 9], 349
    John [C, 9], 349
Towler, Joseph L. [B, 38], 384
Townes, Daniel C. (Capt.) [A, 38], 380
Townsend, James C. [D, 57], 426
    John T. [B, 18], 275
Trail, Creed V. [C, 57], 424
    Daniel M. [D, 24], 247
    William V. [C, 57], 424
Trainham, Christopher C. (Hosp. Stew.) [56], 326
    David C. [C, 56], 331
Trammel, Andrew J. [I, 57], 435

Traylor, James A. [H, 53], 412
    Thomas [I, 14], 376
    Thomas E. (5th Cpl.) [I, 1], 190
Tredway, Thomas B. (3rd Sgt.) [I, 53], 412
    William Marshall, Jr. (Capt.) [I, 53], 412
Trenor, George W. [B, 28], 312
Trent, John [B, 24], 243
    John E. [F, 11], 231
    William [B, 24], 243
    William J. [F, 11], 231
    William J. [K, 38], 395
Trevey, William B. [A, 28], 311
Trevillian, E.C. [D, 19], 297
    James G. (Surg.) [38], 379
Trewolla, Alfred P. [C, 38 Bn.], 447
    Samuel P. (3rd Cpl.) [C, 38 Bn.], 445
Trotter, George I. [A, 18], 274
    Isham E. (1st Cpl.) [E, 56], 333
Trout, Henry S. (2nd 2nd Lt.) [I, 28], 322
True, John M. [B, 19], 294
    Levi [E, 38], 389
    Lewis J. [E, 38], 389
Trueman, Jackson [C, 1], 185
Truman, Thomas J. [K, 56], 342
Trussell, Howard (1st Cpl.) [F, 8], 508
Tuck, Anderson (2nd Cpl.) [D, 53], 404
    Davis [B, 14], 363
    Detrien P. (3rd Cpl.) [K, 3], 204
    Edward A. (1st Lt.) [K, 14], 376
    George [B, 14], 363
    George P. [H, 53], 412
    Joseph [G, 53], 410
    Joseph D. [B, 14], 363
    Joseph P. (4th Cpl.) [K, 14], 376
    Paul P. (1st Sgt.) [K, 3], 204
    Phaltile R.T. [K, 3], 205
    Phaltile W.S. (2nd Sgt.) [K, 3], 204
    Richard H. (Capt.) [K, 3], 204
    Stephen H. [B, 14], 363
    Thomas [B, 14], 363
    William M. (2nd Lt.) [K, 3], 204
Tucker, Andrew [B, 28], 313
    Archer B. [A, 53], 400
    Bentley H. (4th Sgt.) [K, 56], 341

Charles J. [I, 19], 305
Eli B. [D, 53], 405
Hillery [C, 53], 404
James E. [K, 56], 342
James G. (1st Sgt.) [F, 53], 407
James W. [F, 38], 390
John T. [K, 56], 342
Owen H. (2nd Lt.) [B, 28], 311
Richard [C, 38], 386
Samuel E. [A, 53], 400
Theophilus I. (Cpl.) [G, 18], 282
Thomas [C, 38 Bn.], 447
William [C, 38 Bn.], 447
William H. [A, 18], 274
William R. [F, 14], 371
William S. [C, 53], 404
Tulloss, William H. [I, 11], 235
Tunstill, James D. [G, 18], 283
John W. [G, 18], 283
Josephus M. [G, 18], 283
Turner, Albert C. [A, 53], 400
Alexander W. (1st Lt.) [B, 14], 361
Benjamin F. [I, 3], 203
Benjamin F. [C, 7], 213
Charles H. [H, 11], 233
Chester B. [F, 11], 231
G.M. [G, 11], 232
George K. [G, 28], 321
George W. [G, 3], 201
Henry [E, 9], 352
James G. [G, 28], 321
John [I, 28], 323
John F. [G, 3], 201
John H. [A, 11], 223
John R. (4th Sgt.) [F, 11], 230
John W. [D, 3], 198
Joseph [G, 3], 201
Joseph H. [C, 38], 386
Josiah [H, 24], 252
Robert G. [G, 28], 321
Thomas A. [K, 24], 254
Thomas J. (2nd Lt.) [A, 38], 380
Velerius [C, 9], 349
William B. (1st Cpl.) [B, 24], 241
William J. (Capt.) [D, 53], 404
William J. [F, 57], 429
William W. [D, 1], 186
William W. (1st Sgt.) [C, 38], 384

Willis W. [K, 38], 396
Turpin, Alfred S. (Mus.) [I, 57], 433
Peter [F, 28], 319
Sanford [D, 38 Bn.], 449
William A. [D, 38 Bn.], 450
Turski, Francis [E, 11], 229
Tutor, Samuel A. (3rd Cpl.) [B, 56], 328
Tuttle, Ezra B. (ACS) [14], 359
Tweedy, Edmund A. [C, 11], 226
Fayette B. [C, 11], 226
George Dabney [C, 11], 226
Smith P., Jr. [C, 11], 226
Twisdale, George W. [E, 14], 369
Twyford, Revel T. [B, 38 Bn.], 508
Tyler, Edmund A. [D, 8], 265
George Bailey (QM Sgt.) [8], 259
Joseph W. (2nd Cpl.) [H, 57], 432
Samuel G. [C, 38 Bn.], 447
Thomas R. [H, 57], 433
William A. [K, 28], 324
Tynan, Francis T. (3rd Sgt.) [H, 3], 201
Tyree, Charles D. [A, 11], 223
J.S. [I, 19], 305
James H. [B, 38 Bn.], 444
John [B, 53], 402
Lucas P. [H, 19], 304
Thomas M. (Capt.) [E, 38], 387
Tyson, John W. [A, 7], 210

-U-
Udurley, Moses [B, 38 Bn.], 444
Uhles, David (4th Cpl.) [B, 38], 382
Underwood, Bushrod [A, 38 Bn.], 441
John T. [A, 24], 241
William A. [A, 24], 241
William B, [I, 28], 323
William L. [A, 24], 241
Unrue, Henry [K, 11], 237
Updike, William A. [B, 14], 363
Upton, Thomas W. [F, 38], 344
Urquhart, William J. [D, 9], 350
Utt, William L. [C, 24], 245

-V-
Vaiden, Algernon S. (1st Sgt.) [E, 53], 406
Page H. [B, 53], 402
Valentine, Edward W. [G, 11], 232

Samuel W. (1st Lt.) [D, 9], 350
Thomas [F, 18], 282
William S. (4th Sgt.) [C, 53], 402
Webb, Ferdinand H. [D, 28], 316
George S. (Mus.) [19], 292
George W. (4th Sgt.) [C, 28], 313
John A. [G, 18], 283
John W. [C, 7], 213
John W. [C, 57], 424
Jordan C. (Cpl.) [G, 18], 282
Lagiah E. [G, 18], 283
Moses G. [B, 24], 243
Richard O. [C, 7], 213
Theodore S. (2nd 2nd Lt.) [B, 24], 241
William C. [A, 19], 293
William F. [F, 24], 249
William W. [A, 19], 293
Webber, Marcus D.L. [B, 11], 224
Webster, Henry L. [E, 28], 317
Richard H. [I, 8], 269
Weddle, Ahab [A, 24], 241
Weeks, Charles C. [A, 24], 241
Joseph [A, 38 Bn.], 441
Welch, Elias W. [A, 38 Bn.], 441
Wells, Berry C. [F, 18], 282
Charles E. [E, 3], 198
Edward T. [E, 3], 198
Franklin M. [H, 24], 252
George M. (Com. Sgt.) [24], 239
James M. [D, 38 Bn.], 450
Jesse W. [D, 38 Bn.], 450
John C.C. [B, 24], 243
John T. [B, 11], 257
Robert J. [H, 24], 252
Roland B. [H, 24], 252
Thomas R. [D, 3], 198
William H.L. [D, 38 Bn.], 450
William J. [C, 3], 196
William T. [H, 24], 252
William W. (2nd Cpl.) [D, 14], 366
Welsh, Willis W. [E, 7], 215
Wescoat, James R. [C, 14], 365
West, Henry G. [G, 3], 201
James T. [C, 38 Bn.], 447
John A. [B, 14], 363
Napoleon B. (1st Cpl.) [K, 3], 204
Robert G. [B, 14], 363

William [B, 14], 509
William E. [H, 3], 202
William H. [B, 38 Bn.], 444
Westbrooks, James S. [E, 38], 389
Westmoreland, D.H. [G, 53], 410
David P. [C, 3], 196
Jesse H. [G, 53], 410
William A. [D, 1], 186
Weymouth, John E. (1st Lt.) [E, 18], 279
Wharton, Richard G. (1st Lt., Adjt.) [56], 326
Wheat, N.F. [D, 1], 186
Wheeler, John H. [C, 38 Bn.], 447
Solomon [D, 28], 316
Thomas [D, 28], 316
Wheeley, John F. [D, 1], 186
White, Abram [C, 38], 386
Charles [B, 3], 195
Charles R.T. [F, 24], 249
Edward P. [A, 3], 195
George D. [G, 9], 355
George W. [H, 14], 375
George W. [A, 38 Bn.], 441
George W. [G, 53], 410
George W. [I, 53], 414
Harvey G. (1st Sgt.) [G, 24], 250
Henry M. [G, 24], 250
Henry P. [G, 57], 431
Ira [C, 24], 245
James L. [H, 14], 375
James O. [D, 24], 247
James P. (Artificer) [B, 38 Bn.], 442
James T. [D, 3], 198
Jerrie M. (2nd Cpl.) [C, 38], 384
John L. (2nd Lt.) [H, 14], 373
John R. (Capt., ACS) [3], 193
John W. [G, 57], 431
Osceola T. (Jr. 2nd Lt.) [A, 3], 194
Samuel H. (1st Lt.) [C, 19], 295
William (Lt. Col.) [14], 359
William [K, 56], 342
William M. [C, 14], 365
William T. (3rd Sgt.) [I, 1], 190
William W. (Sr. 2nd Lt.) [D, 3], 196
Whitehead, James Wyatt (Jr. 2nd Lt.) [I, 53], 412

John Dudley (Capt.) [H, 3], 201
Joseph H. [D, 18], 279
Kincaid [G, 19], 302
N. [E, 18], 280
Whitehurst, Marshall P. [G, 9], 347
Whitesel, John W. (5th Sgt.) [B, 19], 294
Whitlock, John (Mus.) [A, 7], 209
John H. [C, 56], 331
Whitlow, James H. [A, 57], 421
John R. [G, 53], 410
William P. (2nd Cpl.) [E, 11], 228
Whitmore, John [K, 57], 437
Whitt, Burgess [E, 24], 248
John A. [K, 14], 377
John T. (3rd Cpl.) [K, 14], 376
Joseph B. (1st Lt.) [K, 24], 254
Whittaker, William B. [G, 24], 250
Whittemore, Henry E. [B, 56], 329
Whitten, James C. [F, 28], 319
James W. [H, 11], 233
Thomas L. (1st Sgt.) [E, 28], 316
Whittle, Powhatan Bolling (Lt. Col.) [38], 379
Whitworth, Isaac [F, 11], 231
Whorley, James W. [G, 28], 321
L. Tazwell [G, 28], 322
William [F, 28], 319
Wicker, Elisha [C, 38 Bn.], 447
Robert Tate [D, 38 Bn.], 450
William E. [D, 38 Bn.], 450
Widdifield, Martin V. [B, 56], 329
Wier, John A. [K, 3], 205
Wigginton, Andrew Jackson [I, 24], 253
C.M. [I, 24], 253
Thomas S.H. (4th Sgt.) [I, 24], 253
William J. [I, 24], 254
Wilbourn, John P. [K, 3], 205
Wilcher, William J. [K, 57], 437
Wildman, Elisha S. (2nd Lt.) [G, 28], 319
Wildt, Lewis (Drummer) [I, 1], 191
Wiles, James T. (Cpl.) [A, 38], 380
Wiley, John W. [I, 3], 204
Wilkerson, David A. [C, 38], 386
George P. [G, 9], 509
James T. [D, 18], 279

John W. [D, 18], 279
Richard A. (3rd Cpl.) [E, 53], 406
Richard F. [K, 3], 205
Robert C. [K, 3], 205
Robert N. (2nd Cpl.) [D, 18], 277
Robert W. [C, 38], 386
Thomas C. [G, 14], 373
Walter S. [C, 38], 386
William A.J. [C, 11], 226
William P. [G, 14], 373
Wilkes, Benjamin H. [I, 56], 341
Joseph W. [K, 18], 289
Richard F. [G, 57], 431
Wilkins, George [I, 9], 356
Henry [I, 9], 356
James F. [G, 14], 373
Richard B. (2nd Cpl.) [K, 14], 376
William [B, 3], 195
Wilkinson, George C. (4th Sgt.) [D, 14], 366
Henry C. [D, 14], 367
Henry S. (Jr. 2nd Lt.) [B, 9], 348
John H. [G, 14], 373
John K. [G, 1], 188
John T. [C, 9], 349
Joseph H. [D, 14], 367
Thomas C. [K, 18], 289
William L. (3rd Sgt.) [D, 14], 366
Willard, Benjamin B. (4th Sgt.) [G, 38], 391
Williams, Absalom B. [C, 24], 245
Alexander L.P. (4th Cpl.) [I, 56], 339
Andrew W. (Capt., Paymstr.) [Pickett], 175
Archibald W. [G, 28], 322
Benjamin H. [E, 56], 335
Beverly W. [B, 53], 402
Charles H. [C, 8], 263
Clement W. [I, 56], 341
David L. [C, 38], 386
David M. [B, 53], 402
David P. [B, 56], 329
David R. [F, 53], 408
Early L. (1st Sgt.) [C, 24], 243
Edward B. [K, 9], 357
Embren E. (5th Sgt.) [E, 56], 333
Erasmus [H, 14], 375
Floyd S. [F, 24], 249

Francis M. [I, 24], 254
George W. [D, 3], 198
Granderson B. [C, 9], 509
Green W. [E, 56], 335
Henry B. (3rd Sgt.) [C, 28], 313
Henry K. [D, 3], 198
J.M. [G, 11], 232
James A. [E, 56], 335
James E. [A, 57], 421
James H. [E, 56], 335
James M. [F, 24], 249
Jesse [E, 56], 335
John D. [I, 24], 254
John D. [G, 28], 322
John L. [D, 3], 198
John P. [H, 18], 286
Joseph B. [B, 53], 402
Joseph S. [B, 53], 402
Lemuel H. (Cpl.) [G, 9], 354
Leonidas F. [H, 53], 412
Lewis Burwell, Jr. (Col.) [1], 181
Ludwell [D, 8], 265
Millard C. [G, 9], 355
Milton G. (3rd Cpl.) [B, 38 Bn.], 442
Nathan T. [F, 53], 408
Richard [E, 56], 335
Richard H. [C, 3], 196
Robert H. [I, 57], 435
Robert N. [D, 3], 198
Samuel L. [D, 9], 347
Samuel T. [H, 18], 286
Starling J. [E, 56], 335
Thomas P. [G, 28], 322
William [A, 57], 421
William C.G. [A, 38], 382
William Ovid [G, 18], 283
William Wallace (4th Sgt.) [K, 9], 357
Williamson, Absalom [G, 14], 373
James [F, 11], 231
Joshua [H, 38], 393
Robert [G, 14], 373
Robert W. [D, 28], 316
Slaughter D. [A, 28], 311
Tinsley R. [G, 28], 322
W.J. [G, 7], 217
William F. (2nd Cpl.) [D, 24], 246
William H. [B, 11], 224

William S. [C, 3], 196
Williard, Humbleton C. [K, 3], 205
Williford, Richard H. [I, 3], 204
Samuel [I, 3], 204
Willingham, Andrew B. (4th Sgt.) [A, 53], 399
Willis, Count D.A. [E, 57], 428
George C. [G, 57], 431
James E. [E, 57], 428
Joseph G. (Sgt.) [C, 7], 212
Rust W. [F, 19], 300
Wills, Charles A. [I, 1], 191
E.A. [G, 53], 410
John R. (ACS) [28], 309
Willis C. [G, 19], 302
Wilmer, T.P. [A, 11], 223
Wilmoth, John A. [G, 38], 392
Pleasant [H, 24], 252
Richard H. [E, 56], 335
Wilsher, Charles T. [I, 19], 306
Stafford K. (2nd Sgt.) [I, 19], 304
Wilshire, Robert A. [F, 56], 336
Wilson, Alexander J. [B, 38 Bn.], 444
Alpheus S. (2nd Cpl.) [B, 14], 362
Andrew J. [B, 38 Bn.], 444
Edward G. [F, 28], 319
George W. [F, 9], 353
George W. [A, 57], 421
George W.E. [F, 28], 319
James [G, 14], 373
James E. [F, 28], 319
James F. [D, 53], 405
John R. [F, 28], 319
Lee [G, 14], 373
Nathaniel Claiborne (Maj.) [28], 309
R.H. [F, 28], 319
Richard [G, 14], 373
Robert M. [A, 57], 421
Thomas J. [F, 28], 319
William, Jr. [I, 57], 435
William C. [K, 38], 396
William W. [K, 3], 205
Wines, Elias [A, 38 Bn.], 441
Winfree, George [D, 14], 367
George A. [E, 3], 198
Isaac H. [K, 24], 254
Joseph [D, 14], 367
Winger, Christopher C. [K, 57], 437

Martin V.B. [K, 57], 437
Wingfield, Albert B. [D, 56], 333
    Charles H. (1st Sgt.) [A, 19], 292
    L.R. [D, 1], 186
    Lewis F. [D, 24], 247
    M.J. [D, 1], 186
    Mathew W. [A, 19], 293
    Nimrod T. [B, 56], 330
    S.L. [D, 1], 186
    Thomas F., Jr. [A, 19], 176
    William [F, 28], 319
    William H. [C, 11], 226
    William Lewis (Capt.) [D, 28], 314
Wingo, Benjamin M. (3rd Sgt.) [A, 14], 360
    John K. [F, 24], 249
    Lawrence H. [C, 53], 404
    William W. [I, 1], 191
Winn, George W. [G, 18], 509
    William H. [G, 18], 283
Winston, Arthur W. [C, 7], 213
    Charles J. [G, 11], 222
    William H.H. [G, 11], 232
Wirtz, Noah [A, 53], 400
    Samuel [A, 53], 400
Wiseman, Henry [D, 53], 509
Wiserman, John F. (1st Sgt.) [I, 7], 217
Withers, Walter L. (Hosp. Stew.) [11], 222
Witt, E.J. (4th Sgt.) [G, 53], 409
    James A. [G, 28], 322
    James R. [A, 53], 400
Wolf, Thomas B. [I, 7], 509
Wolfe, Ezra M. [I, 7], 219
    Luther T. (Sgt. Maj.) [19], 291
Wolfrey, Jerry [C, 7], 213
Woltz, Thomas H. [E, 14], 369
Womack, Benjamin L. [C, 11], 226
    Benjamin T. [C, 53], 404
    Charles [G, 53], 410
    Charles H. [H, 14], 375
    Edmond L. [D, 18], 279
    James H. [I, 28], 323
    James K. [H, 14], 375
    John W. [I, 18], 288
    Polk Dallas (4th Sgt.) [I, 18], 286
    R.E [H, 1], 190
Wood, Aelick F. [I, 7], 219

Alfred T. [E, 19], 299
C.C [H, 56], 339
Christopher C. (1st Sgt.) [H, 57], 431
Elias [C, 24], 245
George [C, 24], 245
George A. (Hosp. Stew.) [57], 418
George W. [D, 19], 297
Henry William [D, 53], 406
James F. [E, 19], 299
John M. [K, 19], 307
John W. (Sgt.) [G, 9], 353
Richard B. (Jr. 2nd Lt.) [B, 19], 293
Robert W. [C, 53], 404
Solomon [E, 24], 248
Teleman [I, 19], 306
Washington M: [E, 19], 299
William A. [G, 1], 188
William D. (5th Sgt.) [G, 19], 301
William D. (2nd Cpl.) [K, 19], 306
William H. [D, 19], 297
William H. [H, 56], 339
William H. (1st Cpl.) [K, 56], 341
William J. [I, 18], 288
William Nathaniel (2nd Lt.) [A, 19], 292
William R. (2nd Sgt.) [H, 56], 337
William T. [I, 7], 219
William Walter (Capt.) [G, 14], 373
Woodall, James S. [B, 38], 384
Woodard, James G. [B, 7], 211
Woodcock, William E. [K, 53], 416
Woodford, William S. [B, 14], 363
Woodhouse, Thomas C. [G, 9], 355
Woods, John J. (5th Sgt.) [K, 19], 306
    Patrick (3rd Sgt.) [C, 1], 182
    Robert C. (Capt., AQM) [24], 239
    Robert H. [K, 19], 307
Woodson, Aylett R. [C, 38 Bn.], 447
    Frederick W. [D, 18], 279
    James Garland (Capt.) [K, 19], 306
Woodward, James H. [I, 28], 323
    Robert A. [B, 38 Bn.], 444
    Roland H. (5th Sgt.) [B, 53], 401
    William A. (3rd Cpl.) [C, 19], 295
    William H. (3rd Lt.) [B, 53], 400

William J. (2nd Cpl.) [B, 53], 401
William W. [G, 7], 217
Woody, Austin [D, 19], 297
James H. [B, 53], 402
Pleasant J. [K, 56], 342
Ralph S. (1st Lt.) [E, 57], 426
William T. (1st Lt.) [G, 1], 187
Woolfert, Henry [K, 19], 307
Woolridge, Joel L. [H, 18], 286
Wootten, Henry E. [B, 18], 275
Wootton, Anderson [A, 57], 421
Monroe T. [I, 57], 435
Worley, C.R. [G, 53], 410
Worrell, James M. [A, 18], 274
Josiah [C, 24], 245
Seberd W. (3rd Cpl.) [C, 24], 243
Worsham, A.D. [G, 53], 410
Exet D. [G, 53], 398
John B. (4th Sgt.) [D, 24], 246
Thomas [G, 53], 410
William T. (4th Cpl.) [F, 18], 281
Worthington, Robert H. (Asst. Surg.)
[7], 207
Wortman, J.W. [A, 38 Bn.], 509
Wray, Fields J. [B, 24], 243
James W. (2nd Lt.) [E, 11], 228
William A. [E, 56], 335
Wrcn, William O. [C, 14], 365
Wrenn, Fenton Eley (Sr. 2nd Lt.) [I, 3],
202`
Virginius [I, 3], 204
Wright, Andrew J. [K, 38], 396
Archibald R. [F, 28], 319
Carter [C, 38 Bn.], 447
Charles H. [I, 19], 306
Coleman F. [B, 56], 330
Elijah (3rd Sgt.) [G, 1], 187
George H. [K, 56], 342
Gilliam R. (8th Cpl.) [D, 38 Bn.],
448
J.H. [A, 38 Bn.], 441
James L. [B, 56], 330
John W. [B, 56], 330
Paul C. [I, 19], 306
Pleasant [B, 38 Bn.], 444
Robert B. [E, 53], 509
Robert J. [C, 14], 509
Robert K. [C, 19], 296
Samuel L. [D, 38 Bn.], 450

Thomas R. (2nd Sgt.) [E, 57], 428
William [I, 19], 306
William [A, 38 Bn.], 441
William B. [C, 14], 209
Wyant, James C. (Capt.) [H, 56], 337
James D. [K, 19], 307
John E. (1st Lt.) [I, 7], 217
Wyatt, Charles Newton [D, 38 Bn.],
450
Richard S. [F, 57], 429
Wynkoop, James W. (1st Cpl.) [E, 8],
265
P.H. [A, 38 Bn.], 442
S.T. [E, 8], 266
Simeon [A, 38 Bn.], 442
Wynn, Robert S. (Mus.) [E, 38], 388
Wynne, Irwin J. [E, 3], 198
William H. [G, 38], 392
Wyser, Joseph [A, 38 Bn.], 442

-Y-
Yager, Champ C. [A, 7], 210
Edward Z. [D, 7], 214
Yancey, A.C. (3rd Cpl.) [G, 14], 371
Charles D. (3rd Cpl.) [E, 14], 368
Edward H. [G, 14], 373
Jordan L. [E, 14], 369
Joseph S. (1st Lt.) [G, 14], 371
Richard H. [E, 14], 509
William H. (1st Lt.) [E, 14], 368
Yancy, Absalom [A, 56], 328
Francis G. [B, 7], 211
John W. [D, 56], 333
Yates, James W. [G, 56], 337
John T. [I, 18], 288
Josiah D. [D, 9], 350
Samuel E. [I, 18], 288
William T. (2nd Cpl.) [I, 18], 286
William W. (5th Sgt.) [K, 8], 270
Yeaman, William H. [A, 38], 382
Yeatts, Andrew J. [I, 53], 414
Mark A. [I, 53], 414
Youell, Robert [C, 1], 185
Young, Alexander J. [E, 3], 198
Charles P. (2nd Cpl.) [E, 57], 426
George W. [A, 24], 241
George W. [E, 57], 428
Giles H. [B, 24], 243
Henry E. [H, 53], 412

ABOUT THE AUTHORS ...

Kathy Georg Harrison

Kathy Georg Harrison was born in Johnstown, Pa., and attended public schools there. She received degrees in education (B.A.) and history (M.A.) from the University of Pittsburgh. Employed at the Gettysburg National Military Park since 1974, she has served as research historian since 1976 and as chief historian since 1984. Kathy is married to former Gettysburg chief historian Thomas J. Harrison. She spends her office hours trying to preserve the cultural resources of Gettysburg battlefield, and her leisure hours trying to preserve an eighteenth century home south of Hanover. Her hobbies include reading, oil painting, folk art, cross stitching, caring for three dogs and twelve cats, and collecting dust-balls under furniture.

John W. Busey

Born August 31, 1942 in Whitesboro, Grayson County, Texas, John studied at the Oklahoma Military Academy, the University of Oklahoma, and Oklahoma State University before obtaining a Bachelor of Arts degree in history from Central State College in Edmond, Oklahoma. A lifelong student of military history in general, the American Civil War in particular, and the Battle of Gettysburg specifically, his keen interest in the individual soldiers, whose sacrifice on the battlefield is often forgotten or neglected by most historians of the era, resulted in the inspiration and motivation for this study. Co-author of *Regimental Strengths at Gettysburg* in 1982, John's passion for the detailed, accurate presentation of information relating to the armies at Gettysburg has resulted in a study of the Union dead at that battle and efforts to compile a roster of all Confederates present during those terrible three days in July 1863. He works with the U.S. Department of Agriculture's Food Stamp Program in Alexandria, Virginia, and lives in Centreville, Virginia with his wife Sandra, and their family of five girls, one boy, and many animal friends.